W9-DJE-616

Describing Learner Characteristics of Handicapped Children and Youth

Describing Learner Characteristics of Handicapped Children and Youth

Edited by

DAVID A. SABATINO, PH.D.

Professor and Chairperson
Department of Special Education
Southern Illinois University
Carbondale, Illinois

and

TED L. MILLER, PH.D.

Assistant Professor
Department of Special Education
University of Tennessee-Chattanooga
Chattanooga, Tennessee

Grune & Stratton
A Subsidiary of Harcourt Brace Jovanovich, Publishers
NEW YORK SAN FRANCISCO LONDON

Library of Congress Cataloging in Publication Data
Main entry under title:

Describing learner characteristics of handicapped
children and youth.

Includes bibliographies and index.
1. Handicapped children—Education—Addresses, essays, lectures. 2. Handicapped children—Testing—Addresses, essays, lectures. I. Sabatino, David A. II. Miller, Ted L.
LC4015.D385   371.9   78-23700
ISBN 0-8089-1127-9

111 Fifth Avenue, New York, New York 10003. Distributed in the United Kingdom by Academic Press, Inc. (London) Ltd., 24/28 Oval Road, London NW1
Library of Congress Catalog Number 78-23700
International Standard Book Number 0-8089-1127-9
Printed in the United States of America

To M. E. S. and B. L. M.

Contents

Foreword

Educators in the United States have been given the mechanism for a historic breakthrough in providing educational services to all handicapped children. Through PL 94–142, the Congress of the United States has provided an opportunity for educators to rise to new heights of responsibility in the service of children. The failure to respond to the challenges of PL 94–142 could also result in the catastrophe of the century, for educators will never again be given such a carte blanche opportunity to meet the needs of exceptional children and youth who, for two hundred years in American education, have rarely been provided with quality education. Some will challenge this statement, for there are isolated examples of good education for the handicapped, particularly at the elementary levels, and these have been available to limited numbers of children for many years. However, if one visits educational programs in large cities as well as rural areas, in the "center city" and in suburbia, in New England or in Appalachia, in the midwestern or the far-western states, uniform quality education for the handicapped will not be found. While quality education will not come about overnight as a result of the recent legislation, that legislation and its state-level counterparts (PA 198 in Michigan or Chapter 115 in Wisconsin, for example) provide both a challenge and a responsibility which professional educators at all levels cannot ignore. If ignoring the legislation is the policy that they follow, educators will have only themselves to blame in the future when in this area or others the legislative system appears to be unsympathetic to their requests.

Before PL 94–142, the professions were confronted with other significant developments. *Issues in the Classification of Children,* which was generated in multiple volumes by many professional people under the general editorship of Dr. Nicholas Hobbs of Vanderbilt University, brought the total field of child deviance and exceptionality into startling focus. Thoughtfully prepared statements pertaining to each of the traditional areas of disability and exceptionality were prepared. Each area was couched in fine statements pertaining to the issues of classification and to spin-offs consisting of such topics as litigation directed toward the labeling of children, the application of single tests to all children, and the practice of almost fatal and final placement of children into special education programs with little or no due process or recourse to alternate plans.

As a result of these matters, two concepts began to take hold in American special education, neither of which was imposed on general education with thought or sufficient preplanning—that is, *mainstreaming* and *least restrictive placement* of children with special needs. The laudable goal of mainstreaming is to move handicapped children as rapidly as possible into the regular classroom to enjoy the more normalized educational setting of their age peers. If this goal is obtained through a thoughtfully prepared plan* and if selective mainstreaming of exceptional children is undertaken, then positive values are secured for many. If it is not carried out with thought and planning, but as a program resting merely on administrative decision making, then failure and discord are bound to take place. The latter is the state of the concept in too many school systems at this time.

Least restrictive placement, a popular and catchy phrase, is seen by too many educators as synonymous to placement in the regular grades and mainstreaming. I have stated before, and feel even more strongly now, that least restrictive placement as it is usually defined is a fallacious idea and usually results in the most restrictive placement in many school systems. This is true when administrative decisions form the sole basis of policy. The exceptional child mainstreamed into what is presumed to be the least restrictive placement is faced with problems which he or she cannot possibly overcome alone, such as unprepared general educators; historic attitudes toward the handicapped which are still active forces; and lack of readiness for mainstreaming on the part of parents, the student body of the school, and the community as a whole. A national educational program of special education must be predicated on good institutional programs, good special classes, good resource rooms, good home and hospital teaching, good itinerant teaching, as well as ongoing programs of normalization into regular grades. All are needed. In the absence of quality everywhere, a backlash against the concept of

*See Paul, J. S. et al., *Mainstreaming: a practical guide*. Syracuse: Syracuse University Press, 1977.

mainstreaming is bound to arise: one sees it even now becoming a matter of labor contract negotiations and extreme parental concerns.

The authors in this book seek to deal with these significant and historically important problems and developments. The emphasis of this book on *learner characteristics* is important. Too often textbooks in the field of special education have had the handicap per se as their major focus, with chapters written on the anatomy or the eye, the ear, the nervous system, or on a medically oriented taxonomy. The child has been forgotten, along with his characteristics of learning and how these characteristics differentiate him as a learner from all learners in the school. This volume brings children to the forefront and places them against a backdrop of issues in classification, historical development, information regarding specific disabilities, evaluation, and measurement. The ultimate focus throughout, however, is on the learner.

A volume of this nature is particularly important for general educators and administrators who are seeking to understand their roles in the concepts of mainstreaming and least restrictive placement. A general educator cannot possibly accept handicapped children into the regular grades at all times in terms of what they are or what they do, without having a good understanding of those children, their problems, and their place in the historical development of education in the United States. The group of authors who have joined together to produce this book provide general educators with just this understanding.

We return to our original theme. PL 94–142 will either be the greatest thing which has ever happened in the education of exceptional children in this country or it will be an absolute fiasco. The latter will be prevented only by people of good intent in both special and general education who are well founded in the philosophy, literature, and clinical understanding pertaining to special education and essential to fulfilling the intent of the law. This book moves readers in the direction of securing those competencies and understandings.

William M. Cruickshank, Ph.D.
University of Michigan
Ann Arbor, Michigan

Preface

The text you are about to read was written for the *educator* preparing to provide specialized instruction to handicapped children and youth. Historically, the cornerstone of specialized instruction has been diagnostic information about the handicapped. Much of this information has been aligned behind categorical structures. The principal ingredients of traditional assessment of children for placement into handicapping categories, still included in The Education of All Handicapped Children Act of 1975 (Public Law 94–142), present an operational problem for a text such as this one. This problem resides in the fact that the traditional classification structures have a medical, legal, psychological, educational, and social-cultural heritage. Then, too, all of these influences have become enmeshed through a considerably long period of time that has been both tumultuous and possessed of a rich heritage. Thus this book's dual purposes are first, to insure the reader a comprehensive awareness of that heritage, and second, to bridge the information contained in the traditional diagnostic categories by providing recommended best practice procedures for describing the academic and nonacademic behaviors of handicapped children and youth. In order to accomplish these dual purposes the book was written from the assumption that its use will be preceded by at least an introductory course in special education, a course relating rudimentary measurement principles, and, perhaps, one or more "characteristics" courses. Accordingly, the text is intended to pave the way in an instructional series leading to the more advanced and specific instructional and behavioral management courses.

While *Describing Learner Characteristics of Handicapped Children and Youth* was written for special educators as they are currently prepared for professional work, it was also written with an eye toward the many changes that are currently impacting the field. Central among these is the fact that Public Law 94–142 and related legislation will necessitate multidisciplinary communication across an increasingly large body of professional orientations. This will occur as mainstreaming, team management, and individualized programming become ubiquitous realities, not spoken ideals. It is thus hoped that this text will promote a common language of assessment to the many professionals who engage in this complex planning process, and that it will provide useful information for the development of the Individualized Education Plan. Therefore, it is a sincere desire that the book's contents will be useful to *both special and regular educators* in both pre- and in-service professional preparation.

This book is not intended to provide merely a "foundations of measurement" text, a series of test reviews, a behavioral cookbook, or a "user's guide" to tests in print. These materials are widely available in other sources. Instead, those chapters describing learner characteristics relate the current state-of-the-art, an appropriate assessment model, and discussion concerning theoretical assumptions and practical issues that must be explored by the practitioner. The remaining chapters augment this approach by providing technical support, be it statistical, traditional classification structures describing handicapping conditions, or awareness of social issues. Together, the chapters provide an extensive overview of the current state of the art of assessment.

The reader will note that four distinct sections are provided in this volume. Section I is concerned with relating both historical and current considerations in describing learner characteristics for any categorical group of handicapped children. It begins with a history of the measurement of human performance and the development of concern for teaching handicapped learners. Following chapters review learner characteristics of the traditional handicapping condition, statistical assumptions needed to evaluate standardized tests, techniques for describing and tracking targeted behaviors, and legal and ethical issues in assessment.

Section II begins by providing general guidelines to the creation and writing of the Individual Educational Plan. The remainder of the section is devoted to systematic diagnostic procedures for ascertaining the learner characteristics of high-incidence handicapped. It will no doubt interest the reader to note that specific high-incidence groups (generally regarded as the learning disabled, mildly behaviorally disordered, and mildly mentally retarded) are not identified. This conceptual approach was purposefully selected because, diagnostically, far too much has been made of the small differences that are used to differentiate among mildly handicapped children. As a result, categorical references are eschewed in favor of an emphasis upon the measurement of basic learner charcteristics and academic achievement measures.

Section III focuses on the low-incidence handicapped in a manner that is, in some ways, analogous to Section II. Yet here the authors have emphasized and responded to the obvious differences that exist. Low-incidence handicapped children and youth have a great diversity of handicaps, a greater degree of disability, and, as a rule, a constantly recurring proneness to multiple handicaps. In short, these groups present unique sensory, motor, language, and affective learner characteristics that are difficult to measure and that are equally difficult to approach through instructional and behavioral management plans. Traditionally, low-incidence children and youth constitute the categories of trainable and severely and profoundly retarded, and the emotionally disturbed. But more completely, a review must include certain visually, aurally, and physically handicapping conditions that are primary or secondary to mental or emotional disabilities. From an assessment standpoint, the visually, aurally, and physically handicapped may be included in special assessment techniques and management procedures. We have arranged Section III of the text according to this conceptual view.

Finally, Section IV is concerned with the learning and behavioral assessment models which are available for the delivery of instruction to the recently developed specialties of preschool and career education. Both of these age-bounded assessment specialties will surely gain in importance and frequency of appearance as the mandates of PL 94-142 become fully implemented. Consequently, current discussions of assessment are incomplete without reference to the techniques appropriate for these rapidly expanding areas of special education. Chapters 16 and 17 thus respond to the educator's need to know about assessment in these evolving educational responsibilities.

To you, the reader, we dedicate our efforts toward improving the delicate descriptions of learner characteristics. We hope that this effort can contribute to the specialized and effective educational management of the handicapped individuals that you are or will be serving.

We wish you good reading.

Acknowledgments

The editors wish to express their appreciation
to Cheryl Fuller, Marian Manseau, Lynn Reichel,
Jan Romanski, and Sharon Rothman
for their capable and dedicated assistance
in preparing the manuscript for publication.

Contributors

Donald N. Bersoff
UNIVERSITY OF MARYLAND
SCHOOL OF LAW
BALTIMORE, MARYLAND

Edward Earl Gotts
DIRECTOR
DIVISION OF EARLY CHILDHOOD AND PARENTING
APPALACHIA EDUCATIONAL LABORATORY
CHARLESTON, WEST VIRGINIA

Gaylen Kapperman
ASSISTANT PROFESSOR OF SPECIAL EDUCATION
DEPARTMENT OF LEARNING AND DEVELOPMENT
NORTHERN ILLINOIS UNIVERSITY
DeKALB, ILLINOIS

Frances Lamberts, Ph.D.
DEMONSTRATION SPECIALIST FOR EARLY CHILDHOOD AND SEVERELY MENTALLY RETARDED
ILLINOIS REGIONAL RESOURCE CENTER AT NORTHERN ILLINOIS UNIVERSITY
DEPARTMENT OF LEARNING AND DEVELOPMENT
DeKALB, ILLINOIS

John Lloyd, Ph.D.
ASSISTANT PROFESSOR OF SPECIAL EDUCATION
LEARNING DISABILITIES RESEARCH INSTITUTE
DEPARTMENT OF SPECIAL EDUCATION
UNIVERSITY OF VIRGINIA
CHARLOTTESVILLE, VIRGINIA

Sidney R. Miller
SOUTHERN ILLINOIS UNIVERSITY
CARBONDALE, ILLINOIS

Ted L. Miller, Ph.D.
ASSISTANT PROFESSOR
DEPARTMENT OF SPECIAL EDUCATION
UNIVERSITY OF TENNESSEE-CHATTANOOGA
CHATTANOOGA, TENNESSEE

William C. Morse, Ph.D.
PROFESSOR OF EDUCATIONAL PSYCHOLOGY AND OF PSYCHOLOGY
CHAIRMAN, THE COMBINED PROGRAM IN EDUCATION AND PSYCHOLOGY
UNIVERSITY OF MICHIGAN
ANN ARBOR, MICHIGAN

Alan C. Repp, Ph.D.
ASSOCIATE PROFESSOR OF SPECIAL EDUCATION
DEPARTMENT OF LEARNING AND DEVELOPMENT
NORTHERN ILLINOIS UNIVERSITY
DeKALB, ILLINOIS

David A. Sabatino, Ph.D.
PROFESSOR AND CHAIRPERSON
DEPARTMENT OF SPECIAL EDUCATION
SOUTHERN ILLINOIS UNIVERSITY
CARBONDALE, ILLINOIS

Carolyn Scroggs
LEWIS AND CLARK COLLEGE
DEPARTMENT OF SPECIAL EDUCATION
PORTLAND, OREGON

Harvey N. Switzky
ASSOCIATE PROFESSOR OF SPECIAL EDUCATION
DEPARTMENT OF LEARNING AND DEVELOPMENT
NORTHERN ILLINOIS UNIVERSITY
DeKALB, ILLINOIS

James A. Tucker, Ph.D.
DIRECTOR OF PROGRAMS
DIVISION OF PROGRAM DEVELOPMENT AND PROJECT DIRECTOR
LOCAL DIRECTION SERVICE CENTER
DEPARTMENT OF SPECIAL EDUCATION
TEXAS EDUCATION AGENCY
AUSTIN, TEXAS

Describing Learner Characteristics of Handicapped Children and Youth

SECTION I

Historical Review and Current Considerations in Describing Learner Characteristics of Handicapped Populations

The history, even the birth, of special education as an applied field, suggested that man has traits that can be measured and, when once measured, these traits can locate people along a continuum. Although there are ends to that continuum, the early measurement interests were not directed toward those persons falling at the lower end of the distribution. Instructional considerations did *not* begin as a public interest or awareness in habilitation or rehabilitation. Rather, the roots of assessment in special education began as a philosophical argument over the relative contributions of heredity and environment toward determining human capabilities. The nature-nurture argument was more than mere academic rhetoric. It reflected a major social-political position maintained in the divine right of kings and by landed aristocrats. Unjust laws, misconceptions, and attitudinally sponsored nonexistent or poor educational practices—for the majority of persons and, certainly, for nearly all handicapped people—have been a rather predominant human theme.

Until recently many laws remained attuned to the naturistic argument and special education techniques (perhaps especially assessment techniques) were only minimally refined. But, by the 1960s, major changes were set into motion as the result of the demonstrated fact that a handicapped individual's behavior could be changed if appropriate procedures were undertaken. Wound through the changes of this period was a continual refinement and development of assessment techniques and procedures. The section you are about to read is concerned with describing the historical odyssey of assessment, while providing an overview of basic tools and generic approaches used in contemporary practice and, finally, with reporting litigative and legislative impact upon contemporary assessment procedures such as P.L. 94-142.

David A. Sabatino

1

A Review of Diagnostic and Classification Antecedents in Special Education

Educators render frequent judgments about people although these decisions are often poorly defined and frequently questioned. Seemingly, the role of teaching requires: (1) that judgments about other persons be made quickly and accurately, (2) that judgments be made in the best interests of both the person and the learning environment, and (3) that judgments consider the person's opportunity to have learned an academic or nonacademic behavior.

Without doubt, there is an awesome, almost mystic quality given to the judgments that discriminate among learners and the very process by which those judgments were made. To conclude that current judgment processes or the resulting opinions are held in high esteem professionally would be incorrect; for while the value of human judgments regarding the career choice, career development, and even life-style of adults is fairly well accepted among both professionals and laity, the value of human judgments regarding educational decisions of developing children and youth is a highly debated topic. Judgments for instructional purposes have been criticized as undemocratic, unprofessional, unrelated, invalid, unnecessary, and unbeneficial (Szasz, 1961, 1970; Bersoff, 1973; Keough, 1972). This may be paradoxical. Few citizens would have a second thought about discriminating among oranges to cluster and label, and group them by size, color, shape, type, and fitness for designated use. Industry, government, and the military all specify requirements for various human functions on the basis of human traits, a practice that suggests that many people may demonstrate higher performance in certain areas than in others. In fact, our work, pleasure, and lives are predicated on the belief that there is variance in the performance capabilities among people.

It seems unquestionable that we each march to a "different drummer" and that accurate judgments could improve an individual's chances for a healthy, happy, productive life.

The theoretical, speculative, and futuristic concerns for personal development trigger questions related to the wisdom of discriminating human traits for educational purposes. Consequently, boundaries among schools of thought are formed that not only reflect the capability, but the very desirability and advisability of generating educational decisions concerning human differences. Accordingly, the following positions illustrate the diversity of opinion regarding assessment.

Position 1: Inherent in education is a belief that *all* children can be educated to their fullest potential, and that the educational act alters performance. Therefore, assessment of presumed performance is unnecessary. A case in point is that all schools teach mathematics which, in itself, determines the performance of the child. Therefore, the teaching of mathematics establishes the level of mathematical achievement, and assessment is unnecessary.

Position 2: A more recent theme, heralded by humanistic educators is that assessment, tests, labels, and categories have a negative influence and therefore should be avoided. The humanists assume the position that the democratic basis for education is *not* served by assigning learners to educational categories, many of which have been shown irrelevant (Bruininks and Rynders, 1972) and culturally discriminatory (Mercer, 1973).

Position 3: Conservative citizen groups (e.g., The John Birch Society) have gone on record protesting all testing in the schools as undemocratic, communistic, an invasion of personal privacy, and counter to the American ideal that "all men are created equal." An example of the conservative view is contained in Hershey's *"The Child Buyer,"* a book written at the time that the federal government had legislated funding for schools to institute group testing procedures for identifying the academically talented. Hershey's response may be considered reactive to the influx of educational change following Russia's successful Sputnik space program in 1957. However, in this popular novel the school guidance counselor was presented as a secretive government agent on a governmental mission to identify gifted students for isolated study in needed scientific fields. Assessment and identification practices are clearly presented as a surreptitious and invidious attempt to place the state ahead of the individual.

Position 4: Professional educators often express concern over the relevance of educational diagnosis, that is, what value is derived from tests by those who administer them? Often the complaint is heard: "All he does is test," or "IQ scores don't help me with instruction." To the vocal critics of assessment, an inordinate amount of teacher, pupil, and counselor/psychologist time and money goes into testing programs that result in very few instructional benefits (Cohen & DeYoung, 1973). Advocates of this position often maintain that there are no rules available for preparing instructional objectives based on formal test results, hence, they are merely a vestigial artifact.

Position 5: Some professional educators and behavioral scientists believe there are currently few reliable means for determining *how* a child will learn or *what* a child will learn short of teaching him that task. For these professionals, many commonly measured human traits may not exist in nature. Subsequently, measures, rating instruments, and observational techniques designed to diagnostically describe these traits do not supply the necessary information for either concurrent or predictive educational decisions. Even naturalistic observation based on direct perception is questioned as the observer may be describing qualities or traits that are not real, but projected. Once such a trait is identified, a label tends to be attached to and remain with the child throughout the formal educational period (Bartel & Guskin, 1975; Goffman, 1963). The end result of the entire process is that it can become an excuse *not* to teach (Engleman, 1967a).

Position 6: A more moderate view endorsed by many special educators suggests that psychological or educational (commonly referred to as psychoeducational) assessment results in a classification that does not contribute to instructional planning (Lovitt, 1976). But in this view assessment is not entirely removed. Teachers of the handicapped who follow this reasoning are rapidly progressing toward a competency based, informal assessment approach. Many see this criterion approach as replacing formal standardized assessment practices. Advocates claim that the strength of criterion-referenced measures is that they provide the teacher continuous monitoring of the learning process, not the "one shot," perhaps invalid, approach of formal assessment.

Juxtaposed to the above six positions is the view that learner characteristics or traits constituting academic and nonacademic behavior are identifiable and quantifiable to the extent that they are educationally useful. To eliminate all formal standardized assessment may be a greater evil in this era of preparing and implementing an Individualized Education Program for every handicapped child, than the overuse and abuse of "tests" that has resulted in the past. After all, one professional view is that formal assessment is no better or no worse than the professional performing that function. Accordingly, assessment remains at the basis of educational planning at the per child level and, as such, it is essential. Stedman (1976) has recently expressed this need-for-planning theme for one facet of special education, while Skinner (1971) and Toffler (1970) have extended it to the greater society. It appears that planning is with us and measurement of individual characteristics, one aspect of which is assessment, will be included.

In compliance with P.L. 94-142, the Individualized Education Program (IEP) is a reality. Development of an IEP is dependent upon securing information on learner characteristics. A systematic structure for viewing the learner is more important than continuing to classify children in handicapping categories. In fact, a systematic view of the learner may provide the key descriptors for developing, implementing, and evaluating an IEP.

To prepare an IEP, the educator must determine: (1) the academic arena(s) in which a child can perform most satisfactorily, and (2) the type and amount of instructional material that is most appropriate. This text advances the point of view that instructional objectives based on learner characteristics are one educational diagnostic approach deserving careful consideration and dedicated research. For without a theoretical construct to suggest how the learner processes information, learning a specific task will never be understood. The authors are not presenting either a mechanical "cookbook" or hypothetical approach to the description of learner characteristics. Rather it is intended as a means for establishing, implementing, and evaluating the course of an instructional placement and instructional curricula for handicapped learners.

The next section briefly traces the history of assessment of the handicapped from its initial phases in the 19th century to the influential work of Binet.

A HISTORIC REVIEW OF THE ASSESSMENT OF THE HANDICAPPED

Let us suppose that we have discovered with certainty that one of our pupils suffers from a distressing inability to understand what is said in class; he can neither understand well, nor can he judge well, nor can he use his imagination. Even if he is not abnormal, he is still remarkedly retarded academically. What are we to do for him?

If one does nothing, if one does not intervene actively and usefully, the child is going to continue to lose time, and the ineffectiveness of his efforts would lead us to believe that he will end up completely discouraged. This is not an exceptional case; children who have difficulty understanding are legion. One may well say that the matter is a very serious one for all of us. The child who loses the taste for learning in class is not likely to acquire it when he leaves school (Binet & Simon, 1911, p. 140).

Although most contemporaries would agree with the above, this has not always been true. In fact, a number of distinct stages or periods mark the historic progress that has been made in the refinement of interpersonal judgments (hence, remediation) of handicapped persons. It is most difficult to identify the beginning, because there was so little reason for early societies to make more than crude dichotomous judgments about the handicapped. The decision simply related to the handicapped person's ability to perform some task. There were no special educators or commitment to rehabilitation, only the normality of function and dependence; to question "why" a handicap existed was to question God and King. In that framework, education for the masses was unthinkable, and the prevailing theory of social stratum and behavioral determination was that each person's destiny was determined solely by his birthright: to be born noble was a blessing, to be born poor was the tragedy of continued servitude and serfdom. Modification of hereditary status was a very rare event, concepts such as equality of opportunity and growth beyond the station of birth were unknown.

As early as the mid-1500s, an oral approach to communication was attempted with the deaf son of a Spanish nobleman. A few years later in Germany, a manual approach was tried with a hearing-impaired son of a wealthy businessman. When the British government passed its Compulsory Education Act of 1876, one of the results was that a number of students were found of low ability, but not of the idiot or imbecile classification requiring institutionalization. A two-year study resulted in a report submitted to the British Education Ministry which established that 10 percent of the school age population was between the imbecile group and those of dull normal intelligence. The recommendation of the committee was to form special classes for a new classification of children known as *mentally defective*, or those unable to profit from an ordinary school program (Tredgold & Soddy, 1956). Later (1913) a British Royal commissioner relabeled this mentally deficient group of children as feeble-minded, or persons having the most mild degree of mental retardation.

Meanwhile in Germany, the cradle of public education, retarded children were being educated in special classes. In fact, special classes began in Hallen-der-Saale in 1859. By 1905, Saxony alone had some 500 classes, educating nearly 10,000 handicapped children with teaching methods similar to the perceptual-motor curricula found into today's Kindergarten. But nowhere did the spirit of freedom sound as loudly or as vehemently as in France. Louis XIV provided a workshop for blind persons in Paris and, while the purpose of this workshop was to prepare them vocationally in broom making and other suitable arts of earning a living, it also served as a communal hostel. This arrangement was successful; one group even formed an orchestra that performed for the King. But, it should be clear that there remained little need for a differential opinion about handicapped persons. They simply were or were not disabled. To be rich and disabled was to achieve some comfort and little training, to be poor and handicapped was a curse of utter poverty, family scorn, and possibly death.

Yet, as early as the mid-1500s, there were reported incidents of rehabilitation with the prodigy of noblemen in Spain, France, and Germany. Later the wake left by the French Revolution prompted Phillippe Pinel to differentiate between the criminal and the insane and to open the doors of the prisons for the insane. We may presume that Pinel's book on psychiatric diagnosis had a powerful influence on at least one of his students, Jean-Marc Gaspard Itard. Lane (1976) notes that the 26-year-old Itard, having just completed his medical studies, began work with a preadolescent boy who roamed the forests around Aveyron in southern France. The "wild boy," as he was known, had sought human interaction, finally accepting residence with a local farm family.

Itard soon undertook the boy's training in the National Institute for Deaf-Mutes. The importance of the environment became apparent as the boy's behavior changed, contradicting the unanimous medical opinion that the case was hopeless. This furthered Itard's stand against those who contended that the boy was left in the wild because he was an idiot, not an idiot because he was left in the wild. It was these methods of teaching that Itard's student, Edward Sequin, would later use to prove at the Hospital for Incurables that even the most desperate cases can be changed by education. Simultaneously, Esquirol, a leading psychiatrist, defined idiocy and imbecility not as chronic diseases, a position so long been held as the predominate view, but as poorly or underdeveloped "intellectual faculties" (Esquirol, 1838). This work was supported by French neurologist Charcot, who developed sophisticated examination techniques and a systematic classification of central nervous system pathology.

The combined work of these French pioneers resulted in diagnostic procedures, classification systems, and treatment methods based largely on sensory (physiological) stimulation in order to "cure" the mentally retarded. Special education had received its beginning, for it was in the Hospital for Incurables that George Sumner and Maria Montessori witnessed Itard's techniques for judging the degree of educability in a population of low functioning children and youth. The need for ascertaining the "type" and "amount" of "special education" had been born.

Measurement and the Handicapped

The necessity for identification of handicapped children and youth who could profit from education was the beginning of special education assessment. A second group of early scholars were concerned with measuring interpersonal trait differences among people. One of the leaders of the latter school, the Englishman Galton, was interested in identifying and measuring human traits that he could classify. In so doing, he investigated the manner in which people could be classified using anthropometric measures; among them height, weight, and visual and hearing acuity.

By 1889, the famed German psychologist Kraepelin had developed complex measures of perceptual motor function, the lineage of which is evident in the Gestalt School of Intelligence. The appeal and longevity of this work can be appreciated in the realization that the geometric designs originally drawn by Wertheimer have been redeveloped by Bender (1938) as the *Visual-Motor Gestalt Test,* one of the most frequently administered psychological tests.

The Influence of Binet and Early Special Education in the United States

At the turn of the 20th century, the French Minister of Public Instruction was still wrestling with an age-old problem: how to consistently identify the handicapped. Having agreed upon the terminology to be used (idiot, the lowest level; imbecile, the intermediate level; and moron, or mildly mentally retarded), a psychologist, Alfred Binet, and physician, Theodore Simon, were commissioned to develop a consistent means of classifying children. Binet and Simon (1905;1908) produced, through a standardized procedure of observation, a psychological classification of quantifiable differences in children's intellectual characteristics (traits). By 1905, Binet and Simon had developed 29 such tests designed to measure specific traits and by 1908 they had developed a classification of tests beginning at age 3 and continuing up through age 13. Thus, the work preceding 1905 established human intelligence as a comprehensive integration of several traits including memory, attention, comprehension, muscular coordination, spatial relations, judgment, initiative, and ability to adapt. Further, the criteria for measurement of these traits was standardized at various chronological age levels. From this procedure the measurement of human performance took a great leap forward.

The Status of Special Education

Historically, it is difficult to identify a beginning for special education simply because there was little reason for early societies to render anything more than a crude dichotomous judgment about the handicapped. Education for the masses was unthinkable, and the prevailing theory of social stratum was a naturalistic position where each person's destiny was determined solely by his birthright. The dual concepts of equality of opportunity and development of capability for any person beyond the station of their birth was a very rare event. However, over time these philosophies came to dominate education and, with these goals in mind, the earliest institutions in this country were not custodial asylums for the handicapped, but rather training schools for the education and eventual readmittance of students into a structured environment (Rothman, 1971). However, partly due to inadequately trained professional personnel—in great part teachers—and partly due to community and family resistance, only a small number of special students were eventually returned to the communities. As a result, by the last quarter of the 1800s the institutions had become largely custodial in nature (Kauffman, 1971).

While the 1860s and 1870s had marked the initial transition in this country from training to custody in the institutions, a new site for treatment of the mildly handicapped was evolving. By 1875, public school classes for the backward (mildly mentally retarded) were begun in Cleveland; by 1905, Chicago, New York, Providence, Springfield (Mass.), Philadelphia, and Boston had developed special classes. In this expansion of special classes into the public school Wallin (1949) identified two parallel forces: (1) the work in psychology that attempted to determine traits and classify people according to their ability to function (one person in comparison to another); and (2) remedial approaches to the education of handicapped students, employing physiological stimulation, controlled socialization experiences, and other functional skills emphasizing preparation for life. Thus even from the beginning of public special education programs the measurement of human performance had profound impact.

No individual was more aware of these trends than Henry Goddard, Director of Research at the Vineland Training School. Goddard uncovered the Binet tests in 1908 and subsequently published the 1905 scales in the hope that they would assist American educators and psychologists in their struggle to identify and educate the mentally handicapped. Goddard also translated and developed an American standardization for the 1908 scales, and using this standardization (completed in 1910) he prepared a classification of feeblemindedness for the American Association on Mental Deficiency. A student of Goddard, Edgar Doll, added the term "social adequacy" to Goddard's classifications (idiot, imbecile, and moron) and these criteria then became the common terminology for classifying retarded children.

The continued development of the Binet test resided in the hands of Louis Terman. Not content with previous advances, he released a new version of the original scales based upon his definition of intelligence which, for the concise Terman, was simply the ability to "think abstractly." This scale, known as the Stanford-Binet (Doll, 1917), was revised into two separate (L and M) forms (Terman & Merrill, 1937) and subsequently was recombined into a single form in 1960 (Terman, 1960). Almost immediately Terman's version of the Stanford-Binet showed the ability to produce a high positive relationship with reading comprehension, other academic achievement measures, and general school success. To say that the Stanford-Binet tests were widely accepted and highly regarded would be an understatement of considerable degree. In fact, early special class placements for exceptional children, particularly the mentally retarded, were so dependent upon the single Binet criteria that they were called "Binet classes." The impact was so great that by 1927, 11 years following the introduction of Terman's now Stanford-Binet instrument, 15 states had developed special education laws for the mentally retarded. Soon, even more precise measurements were necessary and the Stanford-Binet was rapidly augmented by other measurement devices. The precise assessment of characteristics of handicapped learners had begun in earnest.

CONTEMPORARY STATUS OF DIAGNOSIS IN SPECIAL EDUCATION

The early enthusiasm for the *Stanford-Binet* and similar tests was in no small way related to a professional enthusiasm for diagnostic categories. Paralleling the scientific method it was sometimes vehemently held that diagnosis lead to classification that formed the basis for developing (and implementing) habilitative procedures. But, by the mid-20th century direct linkage had not been found between diagnosis and educational interventions, an event that brought diagnostics into a state of low credibility. Part of the problem lay in a confusion of purpose. Engelmann

(1967b) states that ". . . Diagnosis has become synonymous with testing, and this is part of many contemporary shifts away from substance to technology, in this shift the 'how' defines the 'what' and task defines the questions to be asked of nature, as though the technology of science has pre-existed to science itself and is not really born of it" (p. 231). Engelman's statement reflects precisely the fact that diagnosis *is* often synonymous with testing, a confusion of purpose and technology. This event has resulted in the development of psychoeducational diagnostic tests that are studied for their own sake, whereby the tests themselves often determine *what* is being sought. In short, the irrational purpose of much diagnostic effort was to permit diagnosticians to build a better diagnostic methodology, with or without purpose. Identifying characteristics that inhibit the learning or adjustment process has become secondary in importance to determining how well (reliable or valid) these characteristics are measured or observed.

Considering this conceptual problem it is accurate to characterize the current state of educational diagnosis as confused. Our profession and the supporting professions with which we work use the term differently, and even within the profession there is a general lack of agreement as to what "diagnosis" means. In special education, for example, we can call the analysis of a reading difficulty "diagnosis." We often hear that the administration and reporting of intelligence and other tests is "diagnostic." Diagnosis may even refer to observation, a job analysis profile, or a preschool motor and language test. The absence of a universally agreeable diagnostic procedure in special education is amplified by the fact that practitioners usually fail to concur even on the role of the diagnostician, the importance of the process, or value of the results derived from the child study exercise. The primary reason that diagnosis is so nebulous appears to be that it was viewed for a long period of time as a sacred cow. It existed because it should exist, and it was not to be challenged. Rather, it was to be retained as an art that proceeded all remediation. In this vein, Wolfensberger (1965, p. 64) has summarized what he termed the diagnostic compulsion:

> Among some clinicians, particularly in the medical field, there exists what can almost be described as a diagnosis compulsion. Sometimes diagnosis seems to become more important than anything else, and once diagnosis has been achieved the clinician may behave as if the main task of case management were completed. Even among less diagnosis-oriented professionals, diagnosis is viewed as a sacred cow which has been enshrined in a mystique, and there are many superstitious beliefs associated with its worship.

Diagnosis clearly *can* exist for the sake of diagnosis. Unfortunately special educators, a group that has included individuals who have been the most severe critics of the administration of standardized tests, have yielded to Wolfensberger's diagnostic compulsion. In more than one instance learning disability resource teachers have become more diagnostic and less remedial as they practice their art. One of the favorite roles of the more senior learning disability resource teachers is to enter a "consultative relationship" with regular teachers. In this activity the special education resource teacher assists the regular teacher in establishing a suitable form of instructional and behavioral management procedures. Frequently, however, these special education teacher consultants respond by developing a routine assessment battery for deriving an instructional prescription. The observation of particular interest here is that many of the tests they administer, the manner in which they use them, and the recommendations they make, are similar to those that school psychologists, speech clinicians, and reading specialists have been preparing for years. Only professional affiliation and not the underlying process seems to have changed, to the great consternation of some professional groups.

There is no doubt that rendering judgments about people is difficult. Rendering educational judgments about *how* learning will best proceed is an enormously complex task. Children, especially those who are handicapped, usually fail to follow textbook descriptions and almost never produce textbook behaviors in the classroom. Children constantly violate our expectations and it requires only limited experience in the schools to recognize that the attempt to quickly and accurately appraise a child's performance and provide instructional or management procedures, is an activity filled with hazards. However, if the reader believes that it is necessary to augment judgment of student performance for instructional and behavioral management purposes in the academic arena, then this question must be asked: *How* does the professional special educator make the best possible judgment? Does that judgment require a formal procedure of diagnosis, depending upon tests that generate scores needed to classify and label children? Or, in fact, may it be a description of the behavior observed or measured in interaction with the task, situation, and time variables—as informal assessment which is child, not task, oriented? The remainder of this chapter shall attempt to differentiate between formal and informal diagnosis.

Formal Diagnosis

Most formal assessment instruments have been constructed to measure or describe specific or global behaviors by comparing the performance of one person against the normative function of others of similar age, grade, sex, etc. Most of the personality, perceptual, language, or academic achievement skills measured are assumed to be learner characteristics. However, since we fail to define learning except for operational terms (e.g., intelligence is what an intelligence test measures) we seem to be diagnosing the tip of the iceberg. The variance accounted for when we administer test batteries of perceptual, language, and academic tests is always shockingly low. Major questions remain: How much of a given behavior is sampled by any test? How much of a trait is measured when only one or two aspects are sampled? The problem here is that most tests are designed to measure in both concurrent and predictive fashion, that is, they are designed to tell what is, or what will happen on the basis of the test score. They are *not* designed to predict the result of a specific intervention on the basis of the interaction between the activities required by a task and a given learner characteristic. Thus, standardized tests permit a comparative statement about how one person performs in reference to the group. That type of diagnosis occurs once in a given period of time. The scores may suggest that a student can receive academic or social protection, achieve satisfactorily, or learn to a given level. Formal diagnosis does not reflect how the child learns. It does not say, nor was it designed to indicate, what specific teaching material is most appropriate in achieving an instructional objective.

Hammill (1971, p. 343) notes that,

> . . . formal evaluation is that part of the total diagnostic process (1) that is characterized by the use of standardized tests, (2) that is administered by specially trained persons, and (3) that is of a decidedly quantitative nature and tends to compare a given child's performance with national or regional normative data. The results, therefore, are often reported in terms of quotients, scaled scores, grade equivalents, or percentiles. In general, an attempt is made in formal evaluation to assess many areas of mental functioning, including intelligence, language, academic achievement, speech, perceptual-motor skill, and social-emotional development . . .

What does Hammill (1971, p. 344) have to say about the benefit of this process?

> At worst, the formal evaluation is instructionally useless and will (1) demonstrate the obvious, namely, dwell at length on what is already vividly apparent to the teacher, (2) stress excessively etiological factors, such as brain dysfunction, which are of no value to the teacher, or (3) dwell at length on the interpretation of minimal and dubious evidence.

Thus, in utilizing standardized formal assessment procedures, extreme caution is critical to the educator for three important reasons: (1) test reliability and validity (more on this in Chapter 3); (2) assumptions about what was measured, (e.g., how many human traits are ascertained in a global measure called an IQ score?); and (3) the precise communication of data into an educational management plan. Standardized tests do serve a purpose, but the professional must be judicious in his enthusiasm, carefully noting before entering into the administration of a test what learner characteristics he is attempting to measure, how well his or her instruments can perform the task, and how this information may be of educational value.

Informal Diagnosis

The beginning of this chapter explained the relationship of the early development of special education to that of human assessment. The point was made that psychologists working at the turn of the 20th century were attempting to develop formal appraisal techniques. However, at this same time educators such as Sequin were in the process of developing informal procedures in the teaching relationship with their students. The need for consistent classification procedures to identify the handicapped for placement into special programs led to refinement and dependence on formal (standardized) tests. However, few developers claimed the tests ability to establish appropriate instruction by identifying either effective methods or materials. Standardized tests were designed simply to compare the global score of one person with the normative sample upon which the test was standardized. Unfortunately, in preparing educational prescriptions, it may be far more important to know *how* a child receives and uses information, than *what* he has learned to date. Informal assessment is essential as it permits continuous monitoring of how a child feels towards, interacts with, reacts to, and profits from, a given instructional material. From an educational standpoint, to understand this process is the key to remediation.

Informal assessment may be of many types. For example, Haring and Bateman (1977) organized diagnostic schemes into (1) diagnostic-remedial, the use of formal tests, and (2) task-analytic, the functional analysis of behavioral approaches. The authors carefully differentiated both of these from the diagnostic search for etiologies and both approaches were deemed useful when used educationally. Hammill (1971) and Reese (1976) both suggested that formal and informal assessment should occur simultaneously. For example, Reese (1976, p. 215) outlined seven steps he felt necessary for completing an educational assessment.

1. Review of education history
2. Conferences with previous classroom teachers
3. Review of biographical data and medical history
4. Review of any previous psychological, clinical, or social agency reports

5. Conferences with parents
6. Further evaluation, using both standardized instruments and teacher-prepared inventories, and tests
7. Classroom observations and conferences with the classroom teacher

It may be seen that there are many informal approaches in this outline but that every aspect of this approach is necessary in order to provide a holistic view of the child. Specific academic and information-processing behaviors, an educational objective, and an instructional program can be delineated, focusing on remediating overt nonacademic behaviors that interfere with the instructional process.

In summary, informal assessment procedures make it clear that it is not enough to merely note that a child has an academic skill deficit. Nor is it useful to know that the child's word recognition skills are better or worse than his reading comprehension skills. Rather, it becomes important to recognize that word recognition learning is achieved more efficiently (time to task completion) when the material is presented using one instructional procedure over another. That type of information is only available by teaching the child several word recognition tasks, using different educational approaches across time. This example defines informal assessment; a teacher-made, teacher-delivered task (taught not administered) that permits a close study under observation of the learner in a specified intertask learning process.

SUMMARY

Assessment of the handicapped has been severely criticized in recent years. Criticisms range from humanistic concerns about placement stigma to the central issue concerning the appropriateness, validity, and reliability of testing used to determine educational programs. In an effort to understand the current position of assessment procedures, 19th and 20th century methods have been reviewed and pioneering efforts in the field of special education in the United States have been discussed. A brief history of diagnosis built the foundation for a short discussion of the current procedures of formal and informal diagnosis.

In the next chapter a discussion of the traditional categories used to define handicapping populations is offered. A summary of identifying characteristics and screening procedures will be listed to provide the reader with an awareness of identification and screening techniques, the referral process, and terminology used to relate the etiologies (causes) and diagnostic classifications of handicapping conditions.

REFERENCES

Bartel, N. R. & Guskin, S. The perspective of the labeled child. In N. Hobbs (Ed.), *Issues in the classification of exceptional children*. San Francisco: Jossey-Bass, 1975.

Bender, L. A visual motor Gestalt test and its clinical use. *American Orthopsychiatric Association Research Monthly,* Research Monograph No. 3 (176 pp.).

Bersoff, D. N. Silk purses into sow's ears: The decline of psychological testing and a suggestion for its redemption. *American Psychologist,* 1973, *28,* 892–899.

Binet, A. & Simon, T. Methodes nouvelles pour le diagnostic du niveau intellectual des anormaux. *L'Annee Psychologique,* 1905, *11,* 191–244.

Binet, A. & Simon, T. Le developpement de l'intelligence chez les enfants. *L'Anee Psychologique,* 1908, *14,* 1–94.

Binet, A & Simon, T. *The development of intelligence in children*. Translated by Elizabeth S. Kite. Publications of the Training School at Vineland, Vineland, New Jersey 1916.

Bruininks, R. H. & Rynders, J. E. Alternatives for special class placement for educable mentally retarded children. In E. L. Meyer, G. A. Vergason, & R. J. Whelan (Eds.), *Strategies for teaching exceptional children*. Denver: Love Publishing, 1972.

Cohen, J. S. & DeYoung, H. The role of litigation in the improvement of programming for the handicapped. In L. Mann & D. Sabatino (Eds.), *The first review of special education*. New York: Grune & Stratton, 1973.

Doll, E. A. A brief Binet-Simon scale. *Psychological Clinic,* 1917–1917, *11,* 197–211; 254–261.

Engelmann, S. The relationship between psychological theories and the act of teaching. *Journal of School Psychology,* 1967a, *5,* 92–100.

Engelmann, S. Teaching reading to children with low mental ages. *Education and Training of the Mentally Retarded,* 1967b, *2,* 193–201.

Esquirol, J. E. *Des maladies mentales consideries les rapports medical hygienique, et medico-legal*. Paris: Bailliere, 1838, 2 vols.

Goffman, E. *Stigma: Notes on the management of spoiled identity*. Englewood Cliffs, N.J.: Prentice-Hall, 1963.

Hammill, D. Evaluating children for instructional purposes. *Academic Therapy,* 1971, *4,* 341–353.

Haring, N. G. & Bateman, B. *Teaching the learning disabled child*. Englewood Cliffs, N.J.: Prentice Hall, 1977.

Kauffman, M. Long term retention of a learning set in mentally retarded children. *American Journal of Mental Deficiency,* 1971, *75,* 752–754.

Keough, B. Psychological evaluation of exceptional children: Old hangups and new directions. *Journal of School Psychology,* 1972, *10,* 141–145.

Lane, H. *The wild boy of Aveyron*. Cambridge: Harvard University Press, 1976.

Lovitt, T. C. & Hansen, C. L. Round one: Placing the child in the right reader. *Journal of Learning Disabilities,* 1976, *9*, 347–353.

Mercer, J. R. *Labeling the mentally retarded: Clinical and Social system perspectives on mental retardation*. Berkeley, Calif.: University of California Press, 1973.

Reese, J. H. An instructional system for teachers of learning disabled children. In D. A. Sabatino (Ed.), *Learning disabilities handbook: A technical guide to program development*. DeKalb, Ill.: Northern Illinois University, 1976.

Rothman, D. J. *The discovery of asylum: Social order and disorder in the New Republic*. Boston: Little, Brown, 1971.

Skinner, B. F. *Beyond freedom and dignity*. New York: Alfred A. Knopf, 1971.

Stedman, D. J. State councils on developmental disabilities. *Exceptional Children,* 1976, *42,* 186–192.
Szasz, T. *Myth of mental illness.* New York: Harper & Row, 1961.
Szasz, T. *Ideology and insanity: Essays on the psychiatric dehumanization of man.* New York: Doubleday, 1970.
Terman, L. M. *The measurement of intelligence.* Boston: Houghton Mifflin, 1960.
Terman, L. M. & Merrill, M. *Measuring intelligence.* Boston: Houghton Mifflin, 1937.
Toffler, A. *Future shock.* New York: Bantam Books, 1970.
Tredgold, R. F. & Soddy, K. *A text-book of mental deficiency.* London: Bailliere, Lindall, and Cox, 1956.
Wallin, J. E. Wallace. *Children with mental and physical handicaps.* Englewood Cliffs, N.J.: Prentice-Hall, 1949.
Wolfensberger, W. Diagnosis diagnosed. *Journal of Mental Subnormality,* 1965, *11,* 62–70.

SUGGESTED READINGS

Buros, O. K. (Ed.) Fifty years in testing: Some reminescences, criticisms and suggestions. *Educational Researcher,* 1977, *6,* 3–9.
DuBois, P. H. *A history of psychological testing.* Boston: Allyn and Bacon, 1970.
Hobbs, N. (Ed.) *Issues on classification,* Vol. I and II. San Francisco: Jossey-Bass, 1975.
Levine, M. The academic achievement test: It's historical context and social functions. *American Psychologist,* 1976, *31,* 228–238.
Throndike, R. L. Mr. Binet's test 10 years later. *Educational Researcher,* 1975, *4,* 3–7.

David A. Sabatino

2

Classification for Handicapped Children and Youth

Chapter 1 provided a discussion of the historical significance of diagnosis as it leads to classification. This chapter is a summary of the traditional classification structures and terminologies which are historically and currently applied to handicapped children.

Medical science, dominated by the Hippocratic search for organization, has influenced all human classification. It was obvious to physicians in the 17th century that a scheme to appropriately identify similarities and differences among the 24,000 diseases isolated at that time was important. The carryover is what Zigler (1961) noted as the "confusion in practice"; a major misunderstanding among what is meant by diagnosis, classification, and labeling. Traditionally, diagnosis leading to classification answers four questions. These are:

1. *Is the person different* from the group called normal?
2. What is the *degree of difference* if it does exist?
3. What group of people is he or she *most like in characteristics, etiology, or symptomology?*
4. Can the *origin of the difference* be traced to its ultimate causation?

The current classification structures used to systematically describe etiologies (causes) are based on generalizations about a particular condition, problem, or common characteristics observed in a collective group of handicapped persons. It should be kept in mind that any given individual so classified may have some of the characteristics associated with a given diagnostic category, but may fail to have other characteristics; rarely will he or she display all those described by the original investigator(s) of a particular syndrome.

To assume that all persons with some of the same symptoms possess a particular problem would be erroneous. Nor is this the only difficulty, for there is a series of problems that directly influence the derived diagnostic classification. These include observational errors, the natural variance in people, reporting and communication problems within and among the professions, and the fact that no matter how handicapped persons are, they tend to be more normal than abnormal in development, thereby making differentiations on a normal/abnormal continuum most difficult. On top of all this there is the sociocultural problem that classification structures appear to be etched in stone, and society is not. People en masse change, that is, social conditions reflect how individuals are responded to, and *that,* in turn, influences *how* they respond and therefore appear (Engel, 1969).

These are some of the difficulties facing the special educator. To aid in classification, the Bureau for the Education of the Handicapped has established eight categories of handicapping conditions. Table 2-1 provides a brief set of common characteristics for classifications used to describe handicapped children. It should be recognized that in some cases none of the characteristics accompany a given child. There are few characteristics that provide diagnostic certainty. The ones reported here are therefore generally observable when referencing large populations of a particular group of handicapped children.

MENTAL RETARDATION

The American Association for the Study of the Feebleminded, forerunner of the American Association on Mental Deficiency (AAMD) first published a manual in 1921 presenting statistical information and uniform classification criteria for the mentally retarded. That manual was updated in 1933 and 1941, and by 1957 a fourth manual was released which established clarification on nomenclature. A 1959 revision provided uniform terminology in both the medical and behavioral classification of mentally retarded persons. It was in the 1959 publication that eight subclassifications for identifying the medical pathology related to mental retardation were first described. In that document, intelligence and adaptive behaviors were first ordered into levels (five intellectual levels and four adaptive levels).

Table 2-1
Some Categorized Characteristics Common to Handicapped Children

Mental Retardation	Emotional Disturbance	Hearing Impaired	Visually Handicapped
EMR = Fine and gross motor coordination below average	Distractible	Cupping hands behind ears when attempting to listen	Crusts on eye lids or eyelashes
Delayed oral language development	Daydreams	Turning one side of the head toward speaker to favor better ear listening	Red or swollen eye lids
Motivation difficulties	Impulsive	Unusual behavior in response to oral directions	Watery eyes or discharges
Read below M.A.	Short attention span	a. Inattentive because the strain of listening causes the child to lose interest in what is being said.	Sensitivity to light
Arithmetic skills, fundamentals, and normal reasoning below average	Inability to role-rate frustration	b. Obstinacy or apparent confusion because he does not hear clearly, and since he cannot tell what is expected of him, refraines from making any response.	Reddened conjunctiva
Social and emotional problems of adjustment (rejection from peers)	Destructive	c. Unacceptable responses or inappropriate responses given in eagerness to please others.	Lack of coordination in focusing two eyes
Likely Pathology Birth trauma Biochemical disorders Hydrocephalus Microcephaly Cretinism Down's Syndrome	Inability to accept limits		Frequently rubs eyes
	Rigid		Child may experience headaches or nausea following visual close work.
	Resistant to change		Child complains of itchy, scratchy, or burning eyes.
	Inability or unwillingness to handle responsibility		
	Chronically fearful, apprehensive, depressed		
	Generalized sense of inferiority		

Table 2-1 (continued)

Mental Retardation	Emotional Disturbance	Hearing Impaired
Mildly Retarded Capable of learning academic skills between 3rd and 6th grade levels, literate. *Moderately Retarded* Capable of learning materials between kindergarten and 3rd grade. *Severely Retarded* Capable of rudimentary learning of nonacademic skills, self-care, and elementary speech. *Profoundly Retarded* Capable of some ambulation, many continue permanently bedbound, few learn to speak.	Immature	Inadequate ability to do school work. May hear only part of teacher's instructions and class discussion. Reluctance to participate in class activities. Fear of failure because of not understanding. Discipline problems in class. Defective speech patterns, particularly consonant sounds at beginning and end of words. Delayed language ability
Physically Handicapped	**Communication Disorders**	**Learning Disabilities**
Cerebral Palsy Spasticity (stretch reflex) Athetosia (constant motion) Ataxia (uncoordinated movement) Rigidity (continuous muscle tension) Tremors (rhythmic involuntary motions limited to certain muscle groups) Possible mental retardation Likely to have speech impairments	*Articulation Problems* Omissions substitutions Distortion of consonants or vowels *Voice Problems* Pitch Loudness Voice flexibility Quality and duration	Hyperactivity Perceptual Motor Impairments (difficulty in coordinating a visual or auditory stimulus with a motoric act, such as copying) Emotional outbursts General coordination defects (clumsiness) Distractability

Table 2-1 (continued)

Physically Handicapped	Communication Disorders	Learning Disabilities
Convulsive Disorders Seizures a. generalized b. focal c. psychomotor *Multiple Sclerosis* Muscle weakness Spasticity of extremities Tremors Unsteady gait Visual and sensory communications *Musculoskeletal Conditions* Malformations in upper and lower limbs, spine and joints. Impaired walking, sitting, standing, or use of hands. *Congenital Malformations* Polio Tuberculosis; rheumatic fever; Cystic fibrosis; hemophelia; Asthma; diabetes; nephretes. Hepatitis; mononucleosis.	*Stuttering* Excessive prolongation and repetitions of sounds *Impaired Hearing* Sounds of high frequency and low acoustic power will be misarticulated Nasal, weak, or breathy voice. *Cleft Palate* Hypernasality Nasal emissions Misarticulation *Language Disorder* Developmental aphasia Language differences for the economically disadvantaged and minority group children.	Perseveration Impulsivity Difficulty in recalling learned material (memory) Difficulty understanding abstract concepts Inability to learn or remember reading, writing, arithmetic Difficulty in comprehending or remembering spoken language.

Medical Classification Structure of Mental Retardation

The medical classification of mental retardation uses eight subclassifications. These are:

1. Borderline mental retardation
2. Mild mental retardation
3. Moderate mental retardation
4. Severe mental retardation
5. Profound mental retardation
6. Unspecified mental retardation
7. Mental retardation not otherwise specified
8. Cases under observation, but not yet diagnosed

Each subclassification is based upon a diagnostic set of 10 etiological groupings. These represent the clustering of the disease entities for medical treatment and classification purposes. The eight etiology (cause) clusters (listed below) are supported with two generalized open-ended considerations (environment influences and other conditions).

1. Mental retardation following infection and intoxication
2. Mental retardation following trauma or physical agent
3. Mental retardation due to metabolic or nutritional disorders
4. Mental retardation associated with gross brain disease (postnatal).
5. Mental retardation associated with diseases and conditions due to unknown prenatal influences
6. Mental retardation due to chromosomal abnormality
7. Mental retardation due to gestational disorders
8. Mental retardation due to psychotic disorders

Behavioral Classification Structure of Mental Retardation

The behavioral aspect of mental retardation is divided into intellectual function (measured from performance on intelligence tests) and adaptive behavior (functional independence over a wide range of skills needed to maintain daily life). Five behavioral classification levels will be defined, but it should be kept in mind that the 1973 AAMD manual on classification recommends the use of only four levels (mild, moderate, severe, and profound mental retardation) since borderline intellectual functioning was excluded in that publication. However, the reader should recognize that many states do permit the assignment of borderline children into special classes for the educable or mildly mentally retarded. It should also be understood that the rules and regulations for operating special education programs in many states do not always coincide with the standard classification structures advocated by professional organizations. With this thought in mind we will now examine the intellectual and adaptive behavioral levels of mental retardation.

Intellectual Levels Describing Mental Retardation

BORDERLINE INTELLIGENCE (IQ 70–84)

This classification comprises that group of children in the first standard deviation below the normal group (1 SD). Borderline children frequently master most academic skills and often proceed through school with little or no "special" education. These are the children often termed the six-hour retarded, the six hours corresponding to the school day (Presidents Council on Mental Retardation, 1969). These children also run considerable risk of being misclassified.

MILD MENTAL RETARDATION (IQ 55–69)

This group represents test scores between the second and third standard deviation below the mean. Mildly retarded children are expected to master basic academic skills with special education and to acquire social skills in a nearly normal measurement.

MODERATE MENTAL RETARDATION (IQ 40–54)

This group scores between the third and fourth standard deviation below the mean. The term "trainable mentally retarded" is generally used to describe this group of children because they will master only the rudiments of basic academic skills (e.g., simple number recognition) and must be trained in social and self-help skills. They may reach a level of semi-independent living, perhaps requiring assistance in basic skills (basic banking, preparing income tax returns, completing job applications, etc.). Therefore, some type of cooperative hostel or community dwelling, and protective or sheltered employment is usually necessary.

SEVERE MENTAL RETARDATION (IQ 25–39)

This group scores between the fourth and fifth standard deviation on standardized tests. These children and youth develop concrete communication skills but require general supervision in most daily functions. They can learn to dress themselves, toileting, grooming, and other self-care skills, but some supervision is necessary on a day-to-day basis. They can live in the community in a protected environment and perform routine tasks.

PROFOUND MENTAL RETARDATION (BELOW IQ 24)

This group comprises the fifth standard deviation. Profoundly retarded persons communication skills range from simple language expression and reception to no means of communication. They require custodial care at the upper limit of this range and life sustaining maintenance at the lower levels of mental function.

Table 2-2 provides a review of the IQ ranges which are associated on three commonly administered intelligence tests with the standard deviations or level of deviation associated with the American Association of Mental Deficiency's "intellectual functioning" criterion. Slight variations in the IQ range from test to test are a result of the standardization procedure.

Adaptive Behaviors Describing Mental Retardation

A second series of criteria known as adaptive behaviors, are usually employed in order to classify the mentally retarded. Adaptive behaviors are just what the term implies: the ability to perform those functions needed to maintain life in various environments. These are: self-help skills, dressing, toileting, eating, and drinking. Other behaviors include the social skill development of grooming, social relationships, displaying behavioral responses appropriate to a given situation, communication skills, and physical functioning. The levels of adaptive behavior are shown in Table 2-3.

Adaptive behaviors are frequently ascertained by using measures of social maturity, motor performance, vocational and prevocational skill development on age sensitive formal tests. Age sensitive refers to a score that is derived as an output measure representative of a given individual's performance on a task and which permits him to be compared to others of similar chronological and/or performance age. There is a growing tendency to describe adaptive behavior by sampling through observation what a child actually does in practice. Sample tasks representative of the function to be performed or criterion reference tasks are also often used. Direct observation of actual performance is often used because the question-and-answer format of many social maturity scales rely on an informant who possesses knowledge about the child's function. That task is often given to parents who respond to the questions as they desire the child to perform rather than how the child actually performs. That ex-

Table 2-2
Conversion of IQ Scores According to Standard Deviation Values

Level Deviation Measured Intelligence	Range of Level in Standard Deviation Units	Arthur Point Scale of Performance Tests, Form I	Revised Stanford-Binet Tests of Intelligence Forms L and M	Wechsler-Bellevue Intelligence Scale, Forms I and II, Wechsler Intelligence Scale for Children, Wechsler Adult Intelligence Scale
−1	−1.01 to −2.00	83–67	83–68	84–70
−2	−2.01 to −3.00	66–50	67–52	69–55
−3	−3.01 to −4.00	49–33	51–36	54–40
−4	−4.01 to −5.00	32–16	35–20	
−5	< −5.00	<16	<20	

(Heber, 1961, p. 59.)

Table 2-3
Standard Deviation Ranges Corresponding to Level of Adaptive Behavior

Adaptive Behavior	Range in Standard Deviation Units
No retardation of adaptive behavior	Equal to or greater than −1.00
Level I (Mild but apparent and significant negative deviation from norms and standards of adaptive behavior)	−1.01 to −2.25
Level II (Moderate but definite negative deviation from norms and standards of adaptive behavior)	−2.26 to −3.50
Level III (Severe negative deviation from norms and standards of adaptive behavior)	−3.51 to −4.75
Level IV (Profound negative deviation from norms and standards of adaptive behavior)	< −4.75

(Heber, 1961, p. 62.)

plains why many novice examiners report wide spread scoring differentials between the scores obtained on Intelligence Tests and measures of social maturity (e.g., the *Vineland Social Maturity Scale*).

The output measures derived from adaptive behavior measures are most meaningful in developing treatment plans because adaptive behaviors can be thought of as levels of independent performance on a given task. Simplistically, a person's performance may be fully independent, semi-independent (amount of assistance or supervision needed), or require full support, supervision, or custody. If a person completes a task without assistance, that task does not require further training; if a task cannot be performed at all, an educational question appears as to what type of training must be sought. Adaptive behavior is not at all an either/or response. In fact, a behavior is a complex chain of many events or capacities. An example is learning to provide independent toileting. If the child cannot use the toilet independently, other adaptive behaviors of undressing (a self-help skill) may be the reason. If the child cannot undress using outside and inside pants with elastic waistbands, the reason may not be related to comprehending the task of undressing, but in the motor (hand) performance associated with coordinated finger-thumb opposition. If the thumb cannot be separated from the fingers, and placed in a supine position, and if the hand is not strong enough to expand the elastic, then an adaptation must be made to the task. Perhaps an easy to open nylon press zipper, or an adoption of the normal function in hand use must be taught. It is for that reason that many teachers, particularly those working with the trainable and subtrainable mentally retarded, have placed a great deal more confidence in the direct observation of performance on a real task, than the score from an informant, or the function on development test items.

EMOTIONAL DISTURBANCE/BEHAVIORAL DISORDERS

Of the major categories which purport to classify exceptional children and youth, few appear to have such inconsistency as does the area of study known as emotional disturbance or behavioral disorders (Kanner, 1962). The basic reason for the difficulty of deriving a definition of emotional disturbance is that it requires a definition of normality, a most difficult task (Laing, 1967; Szasz, 1969). Unlike mental retardation, which (by definition) is fixed in the developmental period, emotional development is not only influenced by the development of the nervous system and the opportunity to learn, but it may also be threatened by the events of unpredictable human relationships. To obtain a fixed position in time and space, as is true with mental retardation, is impossible with emotional disturbance: there are those who function normally in all but one situation, where fears of that situation alone, trigger abnormal reactions. Unlike deafness or blindness, it is impossible to determine the degree of deviance in precise psychological or physical measures.

The Diagnostic and Statistical Manual of Mental Disorders (DSM)

The *Diagnostic and Statistical Manual* (American Psychiatric Association, 1968, 2nd ed.) provides nomenclature for mental health based on medical terminology. The first edition (1952) of the DSM listed only four major classifications of childhood emotional disorders: (1) schizophrenic reaction, childhood type; (2) adjustment reaction of infancy; (3) adjustment reaction of childhood, with the subcategories of habit disturbance, conduct disturbance, and neurotic traits; and (4) adjustment reaction of adolescence.

The second edition of the DSM (1968) distinguished more between child and adult disorders than the 1952 edition. It defined 10 distinct categories of childhood emotional disorders (Table 2-4). In this edition the principle *psychoses* was schizophrenia and its subtypes, the principle *neuroses* was the various anxieties, both those felt and expressed, unconsciously and consciously. *Personality disorders* were defined as ". . . characterized by deeply ingrained maladaptive patterns of behavior that

Table 2-4
American Psychiatric Association's Classification of Mental Disorders

I. Mental retardation (degrees and causes listed)

II. Organic brain syndromes (specific causes listed)
   A. Psychoses associated with organic brain syndromes
   B. Nonpsychotic organic brain syndromes

III. Psychoses not attributed to physical conditions listed previously
   A. Schizophrenia
      1. Simple
      2. Hebephrenic
      3. Catatonic
      4. Paranoid
      5. Acute episode
      6. Latent
      7. Residual
      8. Schizo-affective
      9. Childhood
      10. Chronic undifferentiated
      11. Other
   B. Major affective disorders
      1. Involutional melancholia
      2. Manic-depressive illness, manic
      3. Manic-depressive illness, depressed
      4. Manic-depressive illness, circular
      5. Other major affective disorder
   C. Paranoid states
      1. Paranoia
      2. Involutional paranoid state
      3. Other paranoid state
   D. Other psychoses
      1. Psychotic depressive reaction

IV. Neuroses
   A. Anxiety
   B. Hysterical
   C. Phobic
   D. Obsessive-compulsive
   E. Depressive
   F. Neurasthenic
   G. Depersonalization
   H. Hypochondriacal
   I. Other

V. Personality disorders and certain other nonpsychotic disorders
   A. Personality disorders
      1. Paranoid
      2. Cyclothymic

Table 2-4 (continued)

3. Schizoid
4. Exposive
5. Obsessive compulsive
6. Hysterical
7. Asthenic
8. Antisocial
9. Passive-aggressive
10. Inadequate
11. Other

B. Sexual deviations (specific deviations listed)
C. Alcoholism (degrees listed)
D. Drug dependence (drug groups listed)

VI. Psychophysiologic disorders (specific organ systems listed)

VII. Special symptoms (specific symptoms listed)

VIII. Transient situational disturbances (''adjustment reactions'')
A. Infancy
B. Childhood
C. Adolescence
D. Adult Life
E. Late Life

IX. Behavior disorders of childhood and adolescence
A. Hyperkinetic reaction
B. Withdrawing reaction
C. Overanxious reaction
D. Runaway reaction
E. Unsocialized aggressive reaction
F. Group delinquent reaction
G. Other reaction

X. Conditions without manifest psychiatric disorder and non-specific conditions (specific categories listed).

(Achenback, 1975.)

are perceptibly different in quality from psychotic and neurotic symptoms . . . these are life-long patterns, often recognizable by the time of adolescence or earlier'' (p. 41).

Psychophysiologic disorders were seen as physical symptoms that were caused by emotional factors. *Transient situational disturbances* were described as reactions to stress in one or more particular situations, e.g., school phobia, an intense fear reaction to school. *Conditions without manifest psychiatric disorders and nonspecific conditions* were defined as ''conditions of individuals who are psychiatrically normal but who nevertheless have severe enough problems to warrant examination by a psychiatrist'' (p. 51), e.g., delinquency or a compulsive and continuous display or a repetative behavior.

There are several alternatives to the DSM (1968) system. For example, The Committee on Child Psychiatry of the Group for the Advancement of Psychiatry (GAP, 1966) recently developed an alternative (Table 2-5) to the DSM system for the classification of childhood emotional problems. Ackenback (1975) notes:

> . . . that an important innovation is the inclusion of a category entitled 'Healthy Responses.' The committee listed this category first in order to emphasize the need for assessing the strengths of the child and the possibility that what seems to be abnormal may really be a normal reaction. Examples include developmental crises such as the anxiety infants begin to show around six to eight months of age whenever their mothers disappear; phobias among preschool children; compulsive behavior in school-aged children; identity crises in adolescents; and grief reactions to the death of loved ones.

The work of this group represents a core problem with emotional disturbance: it remains an ellusive entity to define. Although the DSM (1968) and the GAP (1966) remain often cited and used, many professionals support modifications of these postures or, depending upon orientation, may totally eschew them.

HEARING HANDICAPPED

It is generally estimated that between 14 and 20 percent of school age children have some difficulty in hearing. The estimates for deafness range from .2 percent to .5 percent of the total school population. These estimates do vary according to geographic region; the major reasons for this variance include the availability of health care, climate, and socioeconomic status. There is also a spurious artifact that lies in the type of hearing screening survey used.

Hearing in schools is generally measured by nurses, speech clinicians, and audiologists, and by tests administered through pure tone audiometers. The resulting graphic display of hearing, indicating the sensitivity of the ear to receive sound, or threshold, is reported in an audiogram. But, as is the case with so many handicapping conditions, it is often the teacher who first detects the problem.

As hearing impairments affect such a large proportion of schoolage children, and because these children will often require special services of one sort or another, a chapter on hearing assessment has been included in this book. Therefore, only the methods of classifying hearing impairments are described in the present chapter.

Table 2-5
Outline of the Classification System Proposed by GAP (1968)

I. Healthy Responses
- A. Developmental crisis
- B. Situational crisis
- C. Other responses

II. Reactive Disorders

III. Developmental Deviations
- A. Deviations in maturational patterns
- B. Deviations in specific dimensions of development (Motor, sensory, speech, cognitive, social psychosexual, affective, or integrative.)

IV. Psychoneurotic Disorders
- A. Anxiety
- B. Phobic
- C. Conversion
- D. Dissociative
- E. Obsessive-compulsive
- F. Depressive
- G. Other

V. Personality Disorders
- A. Compulsive
- B. Hysterical
- C. Anxious
- D. Overly dependent
- E. Oppositional
- F. Overly inhibited
- G. Overly independent
- H. Isolated
- I. Mistrustful

V. Personality Disorders (continued)
- J. Tension-discharge disorders
  - 1. Impulse-ridden
  - 2. Neurotic personality
- K. Sociosyntonic
- L. Sexual Deviation
- M. Other

VI. Psychotic Disorders
- A. Psychoses of infancy and early childhood
  - 1. Early infantile autism
  - 2. Interactional psychotic disorder
  - 3. Other
- B. Psychoses of later childhood
  - 1. Schizophreniform psychotic disorder
  - 2. Other
- C. Psychoses of adolescence
  - 1. Acute confusional state
  - 2. Schizophrenic disorder, adult type
  - 3. Order

VII. Psychophysiologic Disorders (Specific sites are listed)

VIII. Brain Syndromes (Acute, chronic)

IX. Mental Retardation

X. Other Disorders

(Group for the Advancement of Psychiatry)

Classification Variables in Hearing Loss

There are four relevant variables used in classifying types of hearing loss: (1) the site in the ear where the impairment occurs, (2) the age at which the hearing loss originated, (3) the extent to which hearing acuity is impaired, and (4) the type of educational program needed.

Site of Impairment

Impairment in the mechanical transmission of sound waves through the outer ear and middle ear gives rise to *conductive hearing losses*. In most cases, children with conductive hearing impairment of a short-term nature do not require special educational services. If the condition is chronic, special help in speech (lip) reading and speech, and the use of amplification, will usually enable the child to remain in his regular class. Conductive hearing losses should be seen and treated medically.

It is in the inner ear that the sound waves are converted into neural impulses, which are then transmitted via the eighth cranial nerve to the temporal lobes of the brain. Problems of hearing resulting from nerve damage to the inner ear or eighth nerve are referred to as *sensori-neural hearing losses*. Unlike conductive impairments, sensori-neural hearing losses are generally not medically reversible. Because they originate in the neural mechanism, such losses not only reduce the intensity of the signal but may also distort the sounds which are perceived.

Age of Onset

The age at which a hearing loss occurs has extreme psychological and educational significance (Myklebust, 1964). Educationally, *postlingual* losses (occurring after the individual has begun to acquire oral language) are considered less damaging than *prelingual* losses. For postlingually impaired children, there has been considerable aural input, and the natural process of language and speech acquisition has begun. Prelingually deaf children are those who have never had normal hearing or who acquired a hearing loss so early in life that oral language had not developed. These children cannot acquire language by the normal processes, and special educational provisions must be made to enable these children to acquire a communication system.

Extent of Impairment

Hearing impairment may range from very slight to extreme. Impairment may be bilateral or unilateral, and some frequencies may be more affected than others. Most mildly and moderately hearing-impaired children can benefit from the use of amplication and may receive all or part of their education in the educational mainstream, with supplemental help in speech (lip) reading, speech, and language development. Children with severe and profound losses, while also able to benefit from the use of amplification, may need special class placement for the majority of their schooling.

Appropriate Education Program

The range of partial remedial approaches includes auditory training, speech and language therapy, speech (lip) reading, amplification, aural habilitation or rehabilitation, or preferential seating in a regular class. The academic setting may include a supportive resource person in speech, auditory training, or academic remediation, to a self-contained special class in a public school or public/private residential placement.

VISUAL HANDICAPS

Visual performance has traditionally been divided into two diagnostic categories: (1) partially seeing, and (2) legally bind. This dichotomy ignores the unique problems of individuals with low vision. In view of this problem, a Study Group on the Prevention of Blindness convened in 1972 to work on a uniform definition of blindness. The ninth revision of the *International Classification of Diseases* (effective 1978) will divide the total scale of visual performance into three classifications: (1) normal, (2) low vision, and (3) blindness. Each of these classifications overlays with a seven step index that is in common use (Fig. 2-1).

Normal or near-normal vision indicates the ability to perform all visual tasks adequately without special aids; low vision indicates that a person is unable to perform tasks that normally require detailed vision without special visual aids. Moderate low vision indicates that the individual can reach near-normal performance with aids while severe low vision indicates that the performance with aids is at a reduced level. Blindness indicates the inability of a person to perform tasks that normally require gross vision without increased reliance on other senses. Moderate blindness indicates that the individual uses other senses as an adjunct to vision, severe blindness indicates that the individual uses vision as an adjunct to other senses. Total blindness indicates that the individual has no vision.

Since 1934, there has been a growing international tendency to use more functional measures in defining blindness (Graham, 1959). The British legal definition considers a student to be blind when he must be taught by educational methods other than those requiring the use of sight. The American National Assistance Act of 1948 considers financial aid to the "industrial bind" or "economic blind" when they are "unable to perform any work in which eyesight" is essential. The Dutch define social blindness as the inability to negotiate traffic without assistance from special aids, incorporated with a work definition similar to the American National Assistance Act. Fonda (1961) has suggested four classifications for educational purposes with the blind or partially sighted person. It should

(NEAR-) NORMAL		LOW VISION		BLINDNESS		
Normal	Near-normal	Moderate	Severe	Moderate	Severe	Total

Fig. 2-1. Seven step visual classification index.

be noted that attendance in the regular classroom is possible for persons in any of the four categories.

1. Necessity of Braille (1/200 or light perception)
2. Use of one eye; ability to read print of whatever size possible (2/200 to 4/200)
3. Use of low vision aids or large-print materials (5/200 to 20/300)
4. Regular class placement (20/250 to 20/70)

Quantative Aspects of Low Vision and Blindness

LOW VISION

The classification of low vision, traditionally known as partially sighted, is defined as 20/70 or poorer in the better eye with corrective lenses, or requiring the use of other low vision aids. Definitions of visual performance include vision ranging from no light perception to 20/200. Therefore, for practical purposes, the classification of residual vision (low vision) is necessary to aid in the placement of the partially seeing. Even though a child is "blind" according to the legal definition, observation and experience have demonstrated that some children have educationally useful residual vision; that is, a large number of children who fall within the legal definition of blindness are able to operate in schools in various ways through the assisted use of vision.

BLINDNESS

Blindness has historically meant many different degrees of visual loss; in this country it was first defined legally by the House of Delegates of the American Medical Association in 1934. The 1934 definition considered the person to be blind when the visual acuity, in the better eye, did not exceed 20/200 with correction. The current definition sponsored by the United States Office of Education is "central visual acuity not exceeding 20/200 in the better eye with correction or central visual acuity greater than 20/2000 but accompanied by limitation of the field of vision to 20 degrees."

Qualitative Measures of Visual Performance

The terms blindness and low vision describe quantitative levels of performance. To describe qualitatively different dimensions of visual performance, the following terms are used by the International Council of Ophthamology and the American Academy of Ophthamology and Otolaryngology: visual impairment, visual disability, and visual handicap.

Visual impairment indicates a limitation of one or more of the basic functions of the eye and visual system. The most common visual impairments are of visual acuity and visual fields. Other impairments include impairment of color vision, impairment of dark adaptation and night vision, and impairment of ocular motility. The level of impairment can be different for the two eyes of one individual. Frequently the degree of impairment can be reduced by aids that compensate for the disorder.

An impairment in sight that interferes with the ability to perform a visual task causes a visual disability. The most commonly considered visual tasks are reading and writing, orientation and mobility. Visual disability refers to the abilities of an individual but it cannot be applied to the condition of one eye. Since the two eyes can work alone as well as together, loss of one eye will generally not cause a serious disability. Usually the degree of disability can be reduced by aids that enhance the impaired function.

A disability that interferes with a task the individual is expected to perform causes a handicap. It represents a disadvantage that an individual actually experiences due to his visual impairment or visual disability. The disadvantage must be considered in relation to societal and individual expectations and actual environmental demands.

Terminologies Used in Classifying the Visually Handicapped

It is important for the special education teacher to be versed in the terminology pertaining to visual impairment. A brief description of the common visual refractive errors, related diagnostic terms, the anatomical parts of the eye, binocular coordination, and common eye pathologies follow.

REFRACTIVE ERRORS

The three common refractive errors are the most common visual deficits. The term refractive is a descriptive one because it defines the anomally. In the case of *astigmatism,* the light rays are bent causing variation in the wave as it falls on the retina; in *myopia,* the light wave falls short of the retina; in *hyperopia,* it falls beyond the light sensitive area of the retina. Classically, the definitions are:

Astigmatism: Astigmatism is distorted vision caused by a variation in refrac tive power along different meridians of the eye.

Hyperopia (farsightedness): A refractive error in which the focal point of light rays from a distant object is behind the retina.

Myopia (nearsightedness): In myopia, parallel rays of light are brought to focus in front of the retina. Myopia may be caused by largeness of the eyeball or by an increase in the strength of the refractive power of the media. Myopia usually increases during early adolescence and levels off at about 25 years, regardless of external factors such as amount of close work, lighting, rest, vitamins, endocrine balance, etc.

PATHOLOGIES AND DEFECTS OF THE EYE

There are a number of pathologies which commonly affect the eye. The following are the more common.

Nystagmus: An involuntary, rhythmical, repeated oscillation of one or both eyes in any of all fields of gaze.

Stabismus (tropia): The tendency for the eyes to cross, present in about three percent of children. Treatment should begin as soon as the diagnosis is definite in order to insure the development of the best possible visual acuity, a good cosmetic result, and to increase the chance for normal binocular visual function. The idea that "the child may outgrow his crossed eyes" should be discouraged.

Cataract: A cataract is lens opacity.

Glaucoma: A complex of disease entities which have in common an increase in intraocular pressure sufficient to cause degeneration of the optic disk and defects of the visual field. The degree of interference with vision varies from slight blurring to complete blindness.

Retinitis Pigmentosa: A group of dystrophies of the retinal receptors. The rods are slowly destroyed, with secondary atrophy of the remainder of the retina. Night blindness, the first symptom of retinitis pigmentosa, usually occurs in early youth.

Retrolental Fibroplasia: A bilateral retinal disease of premature infants caused by an overly abundant oxygen concentration.

Amblyopia: Uncorrectable blurred vision due to disuse of the eye.

Retinoblastoma: A rare but life-endangering tumor of childhood. The growth usually arises from the posterior retina.

PHYSICAL HANDICAPS

Dorland's medical dictionary (1974) fails to define physical handicaps for an obvious reason: the term is too broad to define in direct reference to a pathogenesis (disease unity). Educators have traditionally used the term physically handicapped to categorize those children and youth who, because of bodily disability, require specialized education. Under such a rubric, physical handicap equates with bodily disability; therefore practically all handicapping conditions are physical (e.g., vision, hearing, forms of mental retardation, and brain injury).

Generally, a physical handicap may contain four characteristics: (1) a neuromuscular disability, resulting from damage to the central nervous system, (2) related to a lower common neural pathway (nerves and muscles outside of the central nervous system), (3) result from an injury or disease that destroys nerves, muscles, or bone peripheral to the central nervous system, and/or (4) be a health impairment which reduces vitality and thereby results in a weakened physical condition.

Diagnostically the two major groups are: (1) *orthopedically handicapped,* and (2) *other health impaired.* The orthopedically handicapped comprise that group of neuromuscular handicapped due to insult or trauma to the central nervous system, and/or a lower common neural-muscular-orthopedic (skeleton system) damage peripheral to the central nervous system. Other health-impaired conditions have very numerous etiologies but have in common a condition that so weakens the individual that he or she must limit or modify the activities they are engaged in.

Orthopedically Handicapped: Cerebral Palsy

Several conditions can result in orthopedic handicaps. A most common etiology is that of cerebral palsy. Since this disease is so common a short discussion of its salient characteristics is provided.

Cerebral (brain) palsy (paralysis) is a nonprogressive disorder of movement or posture beginning in childhood. As one of the most common results of damage to the central nervous system, it affects a large proportion of all live births. Phelps (1950) reported that seven children in 100,000 are born with it; of the seven, one dies in the first year of life, two are institutionalized, one is amendable only to home care, two will respond to treatment, and one will be so mild that treatment is not required. Bleck and Nagel (1975) have clustered cause, type of cerebral palsy, and location of damage into an easy-to-read table. (Table 2-6). These classifications of cerebral palsy all vary in their symptoms. Table 2-7 illustrated the most common terminology and their characteristics. A number of terms may be used to describe the anatomical site of cerebral palsy. Among these are hemaplegic, paraplegic, and quadriplegic. Figure 2-2 illustrates the affected areas.

The type of cerebral palsy may characteristically influence the per-

Table 2-6
Clinical-Pathological Correlation of Cerebral Palsy

Cause	Type	Location of Damage
1. Rh incompatability	Athetosis (deaf)	Basal ganglia (collection of neurons central brain)
2. Prematurity	Spastic diplegia	Periventricular area (on either side of ventricles)
3. Birth trauma	Spasticity	Pyramidal tract
4. Anoxia	Aspastic quadriplegia	Cortical degeneration (surface cells drop out)
5. Cerebral hemorrhage	Spastic hemiplegia	Porencephaly (cavity or hole in brain)
6. Postnatal encephalitis	Quadriplegia	Microgyria and enlarged ventricles (small brain convolutions—enlarge fluid cavity)

Table 2-7
Classifications of Cerebral Palsy

Spasticity—a state of increase over the normal tension of a muscle, resulting in continuous increase of resistance to stretching. The movement is a strong increased stretch reflex causing an exaggerated movement which can be repetitive.

Athetosis—a derangement marked by ceaseless occurrence of slow, sinuous, writhing movements, especially severe in the hands, and performed involuntarily. Unlike the spastic, the extremities have involuntary purposeless movements, purposeful movements are controlled.

Hypertonic—muscles are stiff and movements are awkward.

Ataxia—lack of balance resulting in a loss of coordination especially during movement.

Rigidity—severe form of spasticity.

Tremor—shakiness of an extremity.

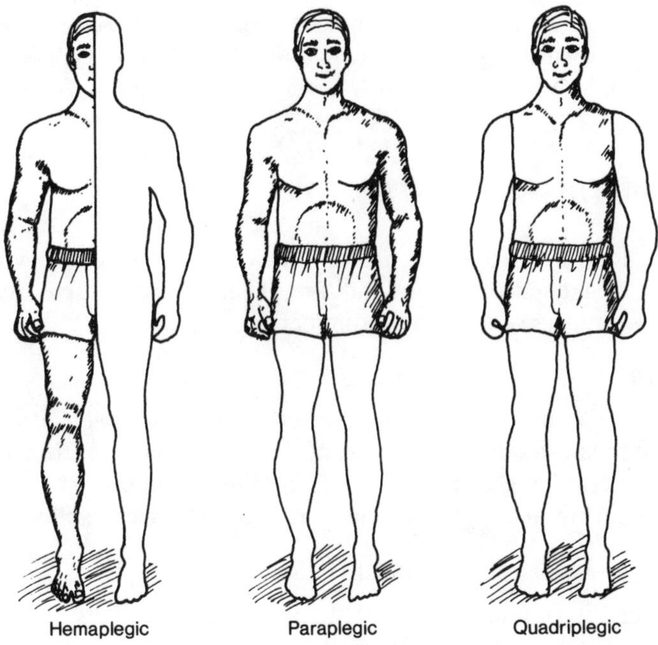

Fig. 2-2. Terms used to describe the anatomical sites of cerebral palsy.

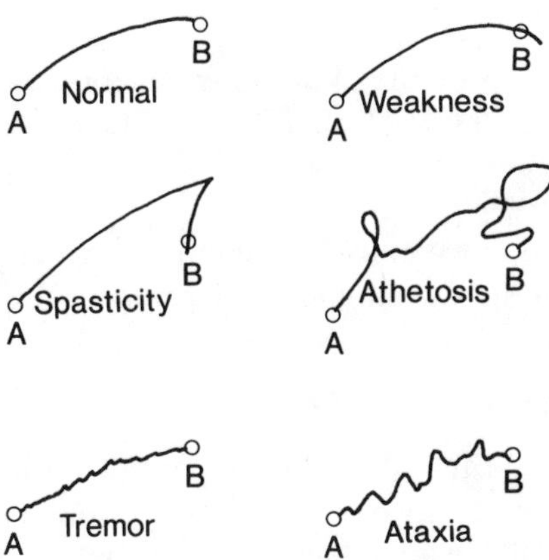

Fig. 2-3. Task graphic drawings for different types of cerebral palsy.

formance of academics. For example, Gesell and Amatruda (1968) (Figure 2-3) have shown the graphic drawings for the different types of cerebral palsy in a task where the child was asked to draw a line from A to B.

OTHER HEALTH IMPAIRMENTS

The following are other health impairments that reduce vitality and result in weakened physical condition. There are of course many other conditions but these are most prominant.

ASTHMA

A disease marked by wheezing, coughing, and a sense of constriction, due to spasmodic contraction of the bronchi lasting from a few minutes to several days. It may result from direct irritation of the bronchial mucuous membrane or from reflex irritation (allergic reaction).

CYSTIC FIBROSIS (MUCOVISCIDOSIS)

A hereditary fetal disease of childhood which affects over 1500 children each year. In this condition the lungs and other organs receive fibrous scarring due to a thick viscuous-mucus that occurs primarily in the lungs and pancreas. It is a recessive genetic disorder, in which there is widespread dysfunction of the endocrine glands, characterized by signs of chronic pulmonary disease, pancreatic deficiency, abnormally high levels of electrolytes in the sweat, and occasionally by billiary circulosis.

DERMATOMYOSITIS

The inflammation of the skin, subcutaneous tissue, and underlying muscle as a result of the occlusion of blood flow.

IDIOPATHIC SCOLIOSIS

Scoliosis of unknown cause is the most common type of scoliosis. In this painless condition, the shoulders or pelvis is often unequal in height, and a hump may develop on the back of the patient.

JUVENILE DIABETES MELLITUS

This is an inherited disorder to carbohydrate, protein, and fat metabolism. The ability to oxidize carbohydrates is more or less completely lost and results in an imbalance of normal insulin mechanism. This produces hyperglycemia with resulting glycosuria and polyuria giving symptoms of thirst, hunger, emaciation, and weakness and also imperfect combustion of fats with resulting acidosis, sometimes leading to dyspnea, lipemia, ketonuria, and finally coma. This condition may also cause other problems by lowering resistance to infections.

LEGG-CALVE-PERTHES DISEASE (OSTEOCHONDROSIS)

This is a disease of one or more of the growth or ossification centers in children. It usually begins as a degeneration or necrosis followed by regeneration or recalcification which effects the head of the affected area.

OSTEOCHONDRITIS DISSECANS

Inflammation of both bone and cartilage resulting in the splitting of pieces of cartilage into the joint, particularly the knee or shoulder joint.

OSTEOGENESIS IMPERFECTA

This is an imperfect bone formation from an inherited condition in which the bones are abnormally brittle and subject to fractures. The basic cause is unknown. Cases appear without any clear-cut hereditary history and seemingly are due from spontaneous change in the genes (mutation).

Communication Disorders

It has been estimated that from 5 to 10 percent (Johnson, 1948) of all school age children have communication (speech, excluding hearing handicaps) disorders. Of the 7.8 percent with speech handicaps (communication disorders), the following breakdown is typical:

Articulation Disorders	= 50.0 percent
Time Disorders—stuttering	= 10.6 percent
Voice	= 6.6 percent
Symbolication—aphasia	= 0.5 percent
Cerebral Palsy	= 1.2 percent
Delayed Speech	= 4.4 percent
Cleft Palate	= 1.2 percent
Deaf	= 4.4 percent
Hard-of-hearing	= 15.4 percent

There are a number of specific articulation disorders including speech sound substitutions, omissions, additions, and distortions. The speech characteristic of children with articulation disorders appears infantile, and it is filled with unintelligible consonants, which should have matured ear-

Table 2-8
Classifications of Speech Pathologies

Apraxia—loss of ability to make voluntary movements or to use tools meaningfully; due to brain injury.
Aphonia—loss of voice.
Aphasia—impairment in the use of meaningful symbols due to brain injury.
Cleft palate—the two halves of the lip, or of the bony upper gum ridge or the two halves of the hard and soft palate fail to grow together and unite.

lier. For this reason, mild articulation disorders are frequently referred to as delayed speech, or infantile perseveration.

The primary disorder of time (or rhythm) is stuttering. Stuttering has several forms, and is not a simple dichotomy. Stuttering may be described as primary, an effortless repetition of young children, which causes no social fears of speaking. When social fears begin, secondary stuttering has occured. The true stutterer is the nervous speaker, or person who talks too fast, omitting words, disorganizing their sentence structure, and filling their speech with repetitions. When slowed down, they do speak normally, however, they usually will not speak slowly for long periods of time.

There are many speech and speech related disorders. Table 2-8 provides a few of these. Perhaps the most interesting speech disorder to the special educator is the problem associated with language symbolization, commonly referred to as dysphasia (disturbed speech) or aphasia (without speech). Associated with damage to the central nervous system, aphasisa requires differential diagnosis because it can be confused with deafness, mental retardation, emotional disturbance (autism), cultural deprivation, or delayed speech. It is difficult to diagnose, but it frequently is associated with brain injury. Aphasia requires a multi-disciplinary team to carefully review the problem from the vantage point of many contributing disciplines.

In addition to these speech problems, some are associated with other handicaps. Such speech problems may bring about a multihandicapping condition. In some cases, more than one speech problem may be observed in a given individual. A common example of the latter occurs in cerebral palsy. About 75 percent of all children with cerebral palsy have articulation problems, about 25 percent have hearing handicaps (many of the hearing handicaps are of a receptive language nature) and an unknown, but significant number have associated aphasia or difficulties of language symbolization. Therefore, a child with cerebral palsy may have multiple speech disorders, and he may also have a multiple handicap due to restriction of physical movement, a speech deficit, and other related deficits.

LEARNING DISABILITIES

Following World War II, it became evident to many educators that a group of children existed in the schools whoe behavior was reminiscent of adults or children with clinical brain damage (Strauss & Lehtinen, 1947). The major difference lay in the fact that the behavior was less pronounced but the perceptual/language or school-related learning characteristics were apparently impaired. These children were defined as *minimally* brain damaged (Clements, 1966) or perceptually impaired, due to their inability to distinguish the distinctive features of graphic form, and organize it (Kephart, 1960; Cruickshank, Benten, Ratzeburg, & Tannhauser, 1961).

Shortly thereafter a joint task force sponsored by the U.S. Department of Health, Education, and Welfare, and the National Society for Crippled Children provided a definition. The Task Force I project (Clements, 1966) was concerned with terminology and definition and recommended the use of the term *minimal brain dysfunction* rather than the term *learning disability*. The latter was chosen because the disturbances in learning behavior, attributable to a dysfunction of the nervous system, extended further than the classroom situation. Subsequently, the task force defined children with minimal brain dysfunction as "near average, average, or above average general intelligence with certain learning or behavioral disabilities ranging from mild to severe which are associated with deviations of function of the central nervous system" (Clements, 1966b, p. 9).

Two years later the National Advisory Committee on Handicapped Children reported to Congress that one of the critical areas of education for the handicapped was that of children with learning disabilities. The confusion over definition seemed to be ended when Congress included in federal legislation (PL 91-230) the definition formulated by the National Advisory Committee on Handicapped Children (1968). This federal definition reads as follows:

> Children with special learning disabilities exhibit a disorder in one or more of the basic psychological processes involved in understanding or using spoken or written language. These may be manifested in disorders of listening, talking, reading, writing, spelling or arithmetic. They include conditions which have been referred to as perceptual handicaps, brain injury, minimal brain dysfunction, dyslexia, developmental aphasia, etc. They do not include learning problems which are due primarily to visual, hearing or motor handicaps, to mental retardation, emotional disturbance, or to environmental disadvantage.

The resulting definition of *learning disabilities* was essentially a definition of exclusion and thus differentiated learning disabled children from those with mental retardation, sensory impairments, social and emotional problems, and cultural differences. It implied a relationship between learning disabilities and conditions referred to in the past as perceptual handicaps, developmental aphasia, dyslexia, brain injury, or minimal brain dysfunction. The major problem in using the federal definition was that it more nearly stated what a learning disability *was not*; whatever the learning disabled child is, he is not disabled due to a hearing, visual, or motor handicap, mental retardation, emotional disturbance, or environmental deprivation.

Today confusion still exists between the concepts of brain injury and learning disabilities (Hammill, 1972). Many authorities stress the commonality between brain dysfunction and learning disabilities to the extent that the terms are used synonymously. However, most educators recognize that this disability category requires instructional assessment and remedial procedures, not medical ones. Thus, learning disability has become a more accepted classification in educational circles. However, controversial arguments continue, as state departments of education grope for psychological and educational assessment procedures.

The Council of Exceptional Children's State Federal Information Clearinghouse devoted their first publication (1970) to the variations among the states in the identification and development of programs for children with learning disabilities. Their conclusion was "The child with learning disabilities is the newest and perhaps the most ill-defined newcomer to the generic category of the handicapped."

Vaughan and Hodges (1973) reported collecting 38 definitions of learning disabilities. Their study indicated that the confusion over definition can be attributed to the fact that learning disabilities have not been the sole responsibility of special education. Several other disciplines such as psychology, medicine, and optometry have vested interests in the field of learning disabilities. As a result, a plethora of definitions has been posed, each attempting to satisfy the needs of the particular discipline it represents.

Mercer, Forgone, and Wolking (1976) studied the definition adopted by 42 states for operationalizing a procedure to determine the type and amount of service and the excess reimbursement cost of identifying a handicapped child. They studied some 75 psychoeducational components of a learning disabled definition, as well as the use of 1968 task force definition itself. They report,

> The analysis of the state definitions reflects the generic nature of the term learning disabilities . . . most states listed descriptive criteria for identifying learning disabled children, but have not operationalized these definitions in terms of

explicit criteria, such as test scores. For the most part, they identify learning disabled children on the basis of the expert opinion of an interdisciplinary team.

They concluded that only two states had made an effort to qualify the criteria for defining a child with learning disabilities. This failure has not been without result. Gillespie, Miller, and Fielder (1975) concluded that poor definitions of learning disabilities have been effective road blocks to meaningful educational services.

With the enactment of PL 94-142 (1975) the United States Office of Education was charged by Congress to:

1. determine which children may be designated as having specific learning disabilities,
2. develop or specify diagnostic procedures to be used in this determination, and
3. monitor procedures to be used in order to determine compliance by state and local education agencies.

The Bureau of Education for the Handicapped (a bureau in the United States Office of Education) responded by listing six academic areas and two basic psychological processes as components upon which a learning disability could be defined. The Bureau then offered an operational criteria to establish a discrepancy between these functions and intellectual ability, age and previous educational experience. Unfortunately, the operational procedure has run into some difficulties (e.g., see Lloyd, Sabatino, Miller, & Miller, 1977) and, once again, the field of special education is without a totally embraced definition of learning disabilities. It would, however, be fair to draw two conclusions: (1) much of the field still relies on the National Advisory Committee on Handicapped Children's 1968 definition, and (2) further attempts to redefine the concept will be forthcoming.

MULTIPLY HANDICAPPED

Any child with more than one disabling condition may be classified as multiply handicapped. Historically, these individuals have been labeled as doubly affected, dual handicapped, doubly defective, multiply disabled, or additionally handicapped. Professionals have also referred to the handicapping conditions themselves in various manners including multiple exceptionality, concomitant disabilities, and manifold disorders.

Although no studies of incidence and prevalence of children with multiple disability have been conducted on a nationwide basis, a number of studies have been executed at the state or local level. While it is recognized that the number of children with multiple disabiities is increasing, studies on incidence and prevalence of such children are characterized by certain inconsistencies. Classification schemes based on disability, confusion in terminology, diverse criteria for defining disability categories, difficulties involved in differential diagnosis, and the unreliability of tests all make it difficult to compile statistics and to estimate the number of children in specific disability groups. However, the following studies present evidence of the extent of multiple disability in a variety of geographic locations in the United States.

Wishik (1964) studied the prevalence, disability, needs, and resources of handicapped children in Georgia, finding that handicapped children had an average of 2.2 disabilities each. Farber (1959) conducted an extensive census of exceptional children in Illinois. He found a total multiple disability prevalence rate of 11 per 1000 children between 7 and 17 years of age. Stifler et al. (1963) found that only 8 percent of a study of 412 handicapped children had one disability, while 70 percent had 3 to 6 additional disabilities.

A clear classification system for the multiply handicapped has not yet been successfully developed. This confusion is most relevant to the field of education because the lack of a good classification system has often resulted in the educational placement of multiply handicapped students according to their one most severe disability. This practice has often failed to meet the students' needs because of inadequate physical facilities or the lack of training and experience of those who work with them.

IDENTIFICATION OF HANDICAPPING CONDITIONS

Table 2-9 presents representative screening devices and their procedural aspects for each of the eight handicapping conditions. The screening devices are only broadly presented here, but carefuly study will be useful for the reading of subsequent chapters.

SUMMARY

This chapter has attempted to briefly convey the essence of the most prevalent handicapping conditions germaine to special education. Eight handicapping conditions were related and pertinent terminology associated with each was given. In addition, a final section dealt with a skeletal outline of assessment procedures commonly employed with each group.

Table 2-9
Representative Screening Devices and their Procedural Aspects for Handicapping Conditions

Handicapping Condition	Screening Device	Procedures
Mentally Retarded	Nationally Standardized Individualized Test of Intelligence and Adaptive Behaviors	Assess intellectual development and adaptive behavior permitting comparison of individuals to the group.
Emotionally Disturbed	Minnesota Multiphasic Personality Inventory	Individual and group administration forms. Yields 14 specific subscores delineating traits reflecting abnormal mental health.
	California Psychological Inventory	Measures character traits that arise directly from interpersonal interaction. Assessment of traits is then hypothesized to allow for the understanding and prediction of social behavior in any situation.
	California Test of Personality	Series of five questionnaires designed to measure personal and social adjustment components in children.
	Lambert-Bower Two-Step Process for Identifying Emotionally Handicapped Pupils	Tap teacher's perception of pupil's behavior, taps peer's perception of pupil's behavior taps child's self-perception.
	Quay-Peterson Checklist	Lists behaviors exhibited by behaviorally disordered children.
	Teacher Observation Teacher's Checklist	Checklist of behaviors teachers observe in classroom, which are considered deviant.

Table 2-9 (continued)

Handicapping Condition	Screening Device	Procedures
Hearing Impaired	Pure Tone Audiometry	Establishes hearing-threshold levels in intensity for a given individual as a function of frequency. May diagnose part of the auditory anatomical system as most likely to be the site of the lesion that results in damage to hearing and etiologic factors or factors that most closely associate with the particular audiometric configuration obtained.
	Air Conduction Audiometry	Administered through headphones to enable charting of hearing thresholds separately for each ear. Sampling is usually done at octave intervals for frequencies from 125 through 8000 Hz.
	Bone Conduction Audiometry	Oscillator attachment (vibrator) is placed firmly against the promontory position of the mastoid process. Sound is induced via bone, bypassing the outer ear and portions of the middle ear.
	Speech Audiometry a. Speech Reception Threshold	Scored in decibels representing a persons ability to hear speech as compared to normal hearing population.
	b. Speech Discrimination Function	Measures intelligibility of speech for the listener wearing amplification equipment which emits a signal comprised of special material.

Table 2-9 (continued)

Handicapping Condition	Screening Device	Procedures
Visually Handicapped	Snellen Chart	Chart is placed 20 ft. from child in order to test visual acuity. A visual acuity of 20/200 indicates that the child reads at 20 ft. the line which should be read by a normally seeing eye at a distance of 200 ft.
	Teacher Observation	Careful observation of the behavior of the child during the measurement of acuity on Snellen Chart.
	Supplements to Snellen a. Convex Lens Distance Vision; test for Farsightedness b. Tests for Vertical and Horizontal Muscle Balance c. Depth Perception test	
Physically Handicapped	Observation of Gross Motor Activities	Gross Motor checklist evaluates coordination/strength, balancing, locomotion, visual motor—upper limbs, visual motor—lower limbs.
	Fine Motor	Checklist evaluates reach/carry/bilateral coordination, grasp/placement/release/eye-hand coordination, prehension/thumb-finger manipulation, visual/visual motor/visual discrimination, spatial relation, graphic/drawing/writing.

Table 2-9 (continued)

Handicapping Condition	Screening Device	Procedures
Other Health Impairments a. Heart Disease	Physical Examination	Observation: Shortness of breath, fatigue, poor growth and development, chest pain, blueness of lips and nail beds, fainting, and chest deformity. Heart rate and rhythm, blood pressure, impulses over the chest, character of heart sound, location and timing of pulse, presence of cyanosis, character of breathing. *Chest x-ray*—reveals size and configuration of the heart and character of blood vessels in the lungs. *Electrocardiogram*—reveals disorders of cardiac rhythm including thickened cardiac walls. *Cardiac catheterization*—measures blood pressures and by measuring oxygen saturation of blood samples obained from heart chambers and related vessels. *Angiocardiography*—x-ray films of the heart shows structural malformations.

Table 2-9 (continued)

Handicapping Condition	Screening Device	Procedures
b. Lungs	Physical Examination	1. Allergy tests (asthma) 2. Test for cystic fibrosis—tube is passed through mouth and stomach into intestines. The juice from the pancreas is aspirated and analyzed for its enzyme content. Low levels of enzymes together with symptoms of lung and intestinal involvement will form the basis for a diagnosis of cystic fibrosis.
c. Absence of Extremities		*Acquired amputation*—child was born normal but limb was removed in part or in total due to accident or surgery. *Congenital amputation*—child was born without limb *Hemimelia*—half of a limb *Amelia*—total absence of limb *Phocomelia*—small appendage that might have been a limb.
	Teacher Observation	Child will use intact limbs and will become very adept with this limb in a compensatory manner.
	Observation of Gross Motor	Balance, gait, extremities
	Observation of Fine Motor	Spastic hand, athetoid hand, motor speech
	Absence of Extremities	
	Other Health Impairments	Heart, lungs

Table 2-9 (continued)

Handicapping Condition	Screening Device	Procedures
c. Absence of Extremities (*continued*)	Physical Examination	*Skull x-ray*—to rule out taxoplasmosis evidenced by calcifications (white spots) on the skull. *EEG*—used to diagnose seizure disorders. *Pneumoencephalogram*—air is injected into brain to detect tumor, or other brain abnormalities. *Brain scan*—radioactive isotopes are injected into blood stream, resulting recording can localize brain tumors. Blood and urine examination pick up chemical abnormalities. *Cerebral artenograms*—radiopaque dye is injected into blood stream. X-ray of skull will show blood vessels and pick up abnormalities of the arteries of the brain, e.g., aneurysm (local dilation of blood vessel).
Communication Disorders	Speech Survey	Brief, personal interview with each child. Speech is screened for deviations of articulation, voice, fluency.
	Teacher Observation and Referral	Teacher makes informal observations—listens to content and sound of child's speech. Speech or language problems then lead to referral to speech clinician.

Table 2-9 (continued)

Handicapping Condition	Screening Device	Procedures
Communication Disorders (*continued*)	Formal Testing Procedures	
	a. Articulation Tests 1. Hejna Developmental Articulation Test 2. Goldman-Fristoe Test of Articulation 3. Templin-Darley Tests of Articulation 4. McDonald Deep Test of Articulation 5. Predictive Screening Test of Articulation (PSTA)	Assesses the spontaneous production of consonant sounds in any or all of the initial, medial and final positions.
	Intelligence Testing	Assesses normal intellectual functioning.
Learning Disabilities	Slosson Intelligence Test	Establishes verbal language learning to-date scales.
	Peabody Picture Vocabulary Test	Establishes non-verbal language learning to-date scales.
	Academic Achievement	Assesses academic achievement.
	Peabody Individual Achievement Test	Untimed wide range screening test with five subtests and total score giving picture of overall level of achievement, no written work required.
	Wide Range Achievement Test	Short wide range screening of spelling, arithmetic achievement, useful as quick estimate of level of scholastic functioning
	Perceptual/Language Functioning	Select tests with high reliability to determine presence or absences of perceptual/ language information processing behaviors.

REFERENCES

Achenback, T. The historical context of treatment for delinquent and maladjusted children: Past, present and future. *Behavioral Disorders,* 1975, *1,* 3–14.

American psychiatric association, diagnostic and statistical manual of mental disorders. Washington, D. C.: American Psychiatric Association (1st ed.), 1952; (2nd ed.), 1968.

Bleck, E. & Nagel, D. *Physically handicapped children: A medical atlas for teachers.* New York: Grune and Stratton, 1975.

Clements, S. D. *Task Force I: Minimal brain dysfunction in children, monograph No. 3.* Washington, D. C. : Government Printing Office, 1966, p. 169.

Council of Exceptional Children's State Federal Information Clearinghouse, 1970.

Cruickshank, W.M., Bentzer, F. A., Rotzeburg, F. H. & Tannhauser, M. G. *A teaching method for brain injured and hyperactive children.* Syracuse: Syracuse University Press, 1961.

Dorland's *Illustrated Medical dictionary* (25th ed.). Philadelphia: W. B. Saunders, 1974.

Engel, M. The tin drum—revisited. *Journal of Special Education,* 1969, *3,* 381–384.

Farber, B. *Illinois census of exceptional children: The prevalence of exceptional children in Illinois in 1958. Report of 1958 Illinois census of exceptional children, circular census 1A.* Springfield: Superintendent of Public Instruction, 1959.

Fonda, G. Definition and classification of blindness with respect to ability to use residual vision. *The New Outlook for the Blind,* 1961, *55,* 6–11.

Gesell, A. L. & Amotruda, C. S. *Developmental diagnosis* (3rd ed.). New York: Harper and Row, 1974.

Gillespie, P., Miller, T. & Fielder, V. D. Legislative definitions of learning disabilities: Roadblocks to effective service. *Journal of Learning Disabilities,* 1975, *8,* 660–666.

Graham, M. D. Toward a functional definition of blindness. *The New Outlook for the Blind,* 1959, *53,* 27–33.

Group for the Advancement of Psychiatry. Psychopathological disorders in childhood: Theoretical considerations and a proposed classification (Vol. VI). Report No. 62, June, 1966.

Hammill, D. Training visual perceptual processes. *Journal of Learning Disabilities,* 1972, *5,* 552–559.

Heber, S. A. Manual on terminology and classification in mental retardation. *Monograph Supplement of the American Journal of Mental Deficiency,* 1961 (2nd ed.).

Johnson, W. *Speech handicapped school children.* New York: Harper, 1948.

Kanner, S. Emotionally disturbed children: A historical review. *Child Development,* 1962, *33,* 97–102

Kephart, N. C. *The slow learner in the classroom.* Columbus, Ohio: Charles E. Merrill, 1960.

Laing, R. D. The study of family and social contexts in relation to the origin of schizophrenis. In J. Romano (Ed.), *Origins of schizophrenia.* Amsterdam: Excerpta Medica, 1967.

Lloyd, J., Sabatino, D. A., Miller, T. L., & Miller, S. R. II. Proposed federal guidelines: some open questions. *Journal of Learning Disabilities,* 1977, *10,* 69–71.

Mercer, C. D., Forgnone, C., & Wolking, W. D. Definition of learning disabilities used in the United States. *Journal of Learning Disabilities,* 1976, *9,* 376–386.

Myklebust, H. R. *The psychology of deafness.* New York: Grune & Stratton, 1964.

National Advisory Committee on Handicapped Children. *First annual report.* Washington, D.C.: U.S. Office of Education, 1968.

Phelps, W. M. The cerebral palsies. In M.Nelson (ed.).

Textbook of pediatrics (5th ed.). New York: W. B. Saunders, 1950.

Presidents Council on Mental Retardation. *The six hour retarded child.* Washington, D.C.: U.S. Government Printing Office, 1969.

State of Illinois Rules and Regulations Governing Special Education, 1973, Article IX Section 29.09.

Stifler, S. R. et al. Follow up of children seen in the diagnostic centers for handicapped children. *American Journal of Public Health,* 1963, *53,* 311–316.

Strauss, A. A. & Lehtinen, L. E. *Psychopathology and education of the brain injured child.* New York: Grune & Stratton, 1947.

Szasz, T. S. Psychiatric classifications as a strategy of social constraint. In T. S. Szasz (ed.). *Ideology and insanity.* Garden City, L.I.: Doubleday, 1969.

Vaughan, R. & Hodges, S. A statistical survey into a definition of learning disabilities: A search for acceptance. *Journal of Learning Disabilities,* 1973, *6,* 658–664.

Wishik, S. M. *Georgia study of handicapped children.* Georgia Department of Public Health, Atlanta, 1964.

Wolf, W. & Anderson, R. *The multiply handicapped child.* Springfield, Ill.: Charles C Thomas, 1969.

Zigler, E. Social deprivation and rigidity in the performance of feebleminded children. *Journal of Abnormal Social Psychology,* 1961, *62,* 413–421.

SUGGESTED READINGS

Mental Retardation

Grossman, H. J. *Manual on terminology and classification in mental retardation* (Special Publication No. 2). Washington, D.C.: American Association on Mental Deficiency, 1973.

Herber, R. *A manual on terminology and classification in mental retardation* (Monograph Supplement, Sec. Ed.). Washington, D.C.: American Association on Mental Deficiency, 1961.

Emotionally Disturbed

Achenbach, T. M. The historical context of treatment for delinquent and maladjusted children: Past, present and future. *Behavioral Disorders,* 1975, 1, 3–14.

Quay, H. C. & Werry, J. S. *Psychopathological disorders of childhood.* New York: John Wiley, 1972.

Zigler, E. & Phillips, L. Psychiatric diagnosis: A critique. *Journal of Abnormal Social Psychology,* 1961, *63,* 413–421.

Hearing Impaired

Myklebust, H. *Auditory disorders in children.* New York: Grune & Stratton, 1954.

Newby, H. A. *Audiology.* New York: Appleton, 1976.

Visually Handicapped

American Academy of Ophthalmology and Otolaryngology and International Council of Ophthalmology. *Classification of visual performance: Tentative definitions.* January 1976.

Fonda, G. Definition and classification of blindness with respect to ability to use residual vision. *The New Outlook for the Blind,* 1961, *55,* 6–11.

Graham, M. Toward a functional definition of blindness. *The New Outlook for the Blind,* 1959, *53,* 27–33.

Sibert, K. The 'legally blind' child with useful residual vision. *International Journal for the Education of the Blind,* 1966, *16,* 17–19.

Physically Handicapped

Bleck, E. & Nagel D. (Eds.). *Physically handicapped children: A medical atlas for teachers.* New York: Grune & Stratton, 1975.

Dorland's illustrated medical dictionary (25th ed.). Philadelphia: W. B. Saunders, 1974.

Communication Disorders

Johnson, W. (Ed.). *Speech problems of children.* New York: Grune & Stratton, 1959.

Pronovost, W. *The teaching of speaking and listening in the elementary school.* New York: McKay, 1961.

Learning Disabilities

Hammill, D. D. & Bartel, N. R. (Eds.). *Educational perspectives in learning disabilities.* New York: John Wiley, 1971.

Mercer, C. D., Forgnone, C., & Walking, W. D. Definitions of learning disabilities used in the United States. *Journal of Learning Disabilities,* 1976, *9,* 376–386.

Salvia, J. & Clark J. Use of deficits to identify the learning disabled. *Exceptional Children,* 1973, *39, 305–308.*

Multiply Handicapped

Wolf, J. & Anderson, R. *The multiply handicapped child.* Springfield, Ill.: Charles C Thomas, 1969.

Ted L. Miller

3
A Review of the Psychometric Approach to Measurement

EDUCATIONAL MEASUREMENT AND THE PSYCHOMETRIC APPROACH

The measurement of student performance is a complex task that can be undertaken in many ways. The variables that characterize a chosen procedure may include single versus multiple domains (focus of measurement), group versus individual administration, systematic versus nonsystematic approaches, teacher-made versus commercially-prepared instruments and norm-referenced versus criterion-referenced procedures. The focus of this chapter will be upon providing teachers the skills with which to understand and evalute the data gained from both individually- and group-administered norm-referenced, commercially-prepared tests. However, throughout the book other approaches will be mentioned and particular attention has been given to the sytematic observation and recording procedures which are characteristic of criterion-referenced measurement (see Chap. 4).

The procedures that are outlined in this chapter have no unique relationship to special populations but simply describe the *psychometric* approach to the measurement of human behavior. Also, this chapter assumes the reader has had some previous experience with the psychometric approach; the chapter makes no pretense about presenting other than the most essential psychometric concepts and procedures in more than the most rudimentary manner. In view of these assumptions, the current presentation must be considered a review rather than an in-depth introduction. Supplemental readings appearing at the end of the chapter can provide the reader with the most elementary or the most elaborate and complete discussion of psychometric procedures. Readings upon the criterion-referenced approach and teacher-made tests are also provided.

In order to assist the understanding of this chapter's contents, the reader may want to review a short and highly simplified glossary.

AN ABBREVIATED GLOSSARY

Norm-referenced test A test that compares an individual's performance to some representative sample of peers. Test interpretation is based on relative comparison to that group.

Criterion-referenced test A test that derives its meaning by comparing an individual's performance to the degree of accomplishment of some set of learner objectives.

Individually-administered test A test that is administered to only one student at a single setting.

Group test A test that is administered to a group of students on one occasion.

Data For the purposes of this chapter, numerical information about a learner; usually test score results.

Descriptive statistics Procedures that allow the collapsing of a collection of test scores obtained from a sample or population in an effort to promote greater interpretability.

Inferential statistics A collection of procedures that allow precision in determining the degree of difference between or among a collection of test scores obtained from a sample.

Population All possible scores from some defined domain, for example, the reading scores of all fourth grade students in the United States, the intelligence scores of all children ages three to six in the United States, etc.

Sample A randomly drawn selection from the domain of some population, samples provide the basis for most tests and assessment devices.

Sampling Any one of several techniques for producing a representative random sample from a population.

Frequency distribution The distribution of specific items by their respective frequency of occurrence. For example, a given classroom test may yield a frequency of 5 "A's," 8 "B's," 16 "C's," etc.

Normal distribution A theoretical distribution of scores that underlies most measures in the behavioral sciences. Assumptions stemming from the normal distribution provide many useful approaches to tests and measurement.

Measure of central tendency The most representative or average score in a normal distribution, or the score that most individuals achieve.

Measure of dispersion Any one of several measures that estimate the variability of scores about central tendency.

Derived score The comparison scores obtained from the norming sample. Derived scores are of two types, developmental scores (usually age and grade equivalent scores) and scores of relative standing (percentiles, deciles, quartiles; standard scores, z scores, stanines).

Correlation A procedure for relating the degree of association or relationship between two or more sets of scores. Correlational procedures (symbolized by r) yield a coefficient between -1.0 and $+1.0$.

Reliability The consistency of measurement of which a test is capable. Expressed as a correlation coefficient, reliability provides a direct index of error in a test.

Content validity Answers the question of how well a test item samples the domain of the population.

Face validity Answers the question of how well a test appears to be able to measure specific types of behavior or traits.

Criterion-related validity Answers the question of how much an individual or group possesses some trait or behavior (concurrent), or how much the individual or group can be expected to possess some trait or behavior (predictive).

Construct validity Answers the question of how well a test measures some hypothetical trait or construct. Typical hypothetical constructs include intelligence, auditory discrimination, attitudes, etc.

Observed score The score that is produced by an individual or group on some test or educational measurement device.

True score The score that could theoretically be achieved by an individual or group under ideal conditions.

Standard error of measurement A procedure that specifies the amount of measurement error in an observed score.

Statistical significance A procedure that allows a probability statement about the similarity or difference between one or more sets of measures.

Standardization The reported results of test samples when adminsitered under rigidly controlled conditions. Scores thus obtained are used as a comparison for an individual's performance.

BASIC STATISTICS

Statistics is a branch of mathematics. Its essential purposes are twofold: (1) to provide organization, hence description of data; and (2) to allow precise, data-based, decision making. A particular statistic is usually referred to as either a descriptive or an inferential statistic. Brown (1970, p. 14) indicates that descriptive statistics are those procedures that "summarize and precisely describe a set of data" while inferential statistics have been termed "the body of methods for arriving at conclusions extending beyond the immediate data" (Hays, 1963, p. 2). Both components are essential to psychometric theory, the "quantitative assessment of an individual's psychological traits or attributes" (English and English, 1968, p. 427). Psychometric measures make extensive use of statistical principles, hence some knowledge of statistics is essential to test users.

The Concept of Sampling

Sampling is one of the more fundamental concepts of statistics that has been applied to psychology. Quite obviously, a test developer cannot standardize a new instrument on everyone in the test's age range in the United States (the population). His/her major option is, then, to derive a sample that is representative of that hypothetical population. In the behavioral sciences, sampling is predicated upon the belief that: (1) adequately drawn proportion of the individual's behavior can be used to estimate his or her future response to all similar circumstances, and/or that (2) a finite sample of individuals is sufficient to infer the population's response to similar circumstances. Thus most tests sample an individual's behavior with the intent of directly comparing the individual's standing with the sample and, indirectly, inferring his or her performance to the characteristics of the population.

Under ideal conditions, samples reflect populations quite well. Unfortunately for educational measurement, samples are sometimes inadequate thus nonrepresentative of the population. Given the test developer's dependence upon samples, great care must be taken to assure that the procedure is properly conducted. Theoretically, the two major tasks in any sampling procedure are assuring adequate randomization and drawing a sufficient number of cases to reflect the population. If either requirement is not properly accomplished *individual* conclusions drawn from test results will certainly be erroneous. Care must be exercised by the test builder to assure representative fairness along such population dimensions as age, sex, grade, socioeconomic background, geographical distribution, ethnic representation, and many other population characteristics. To do otherwise invites the possibility of erroneous conclusions about the population's characteristics and, hence, an unfair appraisal of the individual's performance.

Perhaps a simple example will help illustrate the importance of sample representativeness. Suppose a jar contains 100 marbles, 90 white and 10 red. If the red marbles are not equally spread throughout the white marbles, and as a result, many red marbles are drawn in our sample, we would conclude that the jar contains a ratio of red to white that is higher than 1 in 10. On the other hand, suppose we pulled a single red marble from the jar. Based on this sample, our only logical conclusion would be that the population contained in the jar was identical to this sample of one. Thus we see that if the resulting test is to be useful, considerations of both appropriate randomization and sufficient sample size must be carefully addressed.

Sampling procedures can take place in a number of ways but establishing an appropriate sample for a test instrument is not nearly so simple as the previous illustration might suggest. Many approaches to the task are available. Freund (1967) has described several sampling procedures including systematic sampling, quota sampling, cluster sampling, stratified sampling, and stratified random sampling.

The first possibility, *systematic sampling,* refers to the procedure of drawing a sample at regular intervals (every other, every fifth, etc.) and recording its peformance, as in the case where every 10th light bulb is tested on the assembly line. *Quota sampling* is a procedure in which established quotas (for example, five questionnaires) are simply completed from the first available information. In quota sampling, few, if any, guidelines are offered beyond the requirement of attaining the total quota. Quite understandably, sample accuracy is often weakened. *Cluster sampling* refers to the occasion where some large unit (perhaps a high school) is artificially broken into clusters (such as home rooms), then entire clusters (home rooms) are randomly selected and sampled. In this procedure randomization occurs in the process of drawing clusters, for once drawn, the entire cluster is sampled. *Stratified sampling* occurs when a population—say all children in the state of Arizona—is divided on the basis of some criteria (e.g., ages) and proportions are drawn from the resulting age unit divisions (termed strata). If the total proportion per strata is acquired by a simple random drawing of items for each strata, the entire procedure is termed *stratified random sampling.*

A stratified random sampling technique is most often used in test construction because of its suitability for meeting the requirement of adequate randomization. Most well constructed tests use a stratified procedure to identify subjects in the creation of test norms and most test authors carefully report the criteria for strata selection (e.g., age, sex, income, obvious disabilities, geographical location). In general, the more numerous and specific the strata criterion, and the more cases included, the better the sampling procedure. When examining any test, strong attention must be directed to an examination of the sampling procedure. *No measurement device can be desirable if its sampling procedure is inappropriate.*

Data Scales and Frequency Distributions

It is very important to recognize some differences in the nature of data. Several schemas could be related but all use the concept of discrete data and continuous data. Discrete data refers to the case where a finite number of possibilities exist, as in a college course where only grades pass and fail can be given. Continuous data refers to the case where data can assume many values on a continuous scale, for example, measures of temperature and length.

Data can also be described by the type of scale on which it is placed. *Nominal data* (scale) simply describes categories, as for example, boys–girls or mammals–reptiles. *Ordinal data* provides ranks (first, second, third) with no attempt to judge the relative differences; that is, we have no way of knowing *how* superior first is to second, second is to third, and so on. *Interval data* possesses the quality of equal distance between infinite units, but the data do not possess an absolute measure of zero. *Ratio data* posesses both equal units (1, 2, 3, 4, 5; or 1.1, 1.4, 1.9, etc.) and an absolute zero measure (0.0). Since behavioral data do not ordinarily possess an absolute zero, the interval scale is the most complex utilized in behavioral measurement. Generally, the more complex the data the more sophisticated the measurement and the greater its interpretability. Therefore, test constructors usually strive to attain interval data scales.

The results of an adequate sample will invariably produce a lengthy list of data related to the question of interest. Although these data may be of several types, a common characteristic is always present: data will not be useful for interpretation unless it is logically and orderly arranged. To alleviate this problem individual "raw" scores are often condensed by their frequency of occurrence within bounded categories as, for example, when six children receive "A's," five "B's," eight "C's," etc. Once compiled in this manner, such "collapsed" data are often recorded in a graphical arrangement. A summary of this type is termed a *frequency distribution* because the distribution of scores within category boundaries is indicated by their respective frequency of occurrence. Distributions will vary according to several characteristics, the nature of the data, the procedures used in drawing the sample, and the organizing principles of the distribution. However, all frequency distributions share the common goal of making untreated raw data more interpretable.

Spence, Underwood, Duncan, and Cotton (1968) have reported several types of frequency distributions and their corresponding graphical representations. The simplest distribution is the case in which the scores or data are simply ranked from low to high based on the frequency of events. Table 3-1 demonstrates this distribution. In this illustration, the number of scores equals 100 and these scores are distributed (range) from

Table 3-1
Sample Frequency Distribution for Nongrouped Data

Score	Frequency	Score	Frequency	Score	Frequency
90	2	75	3	60	2
89	3	74	5	59	2
88	0	73	4	58	1
87	0	72	3	57	1
86	2	71	6	56	0
85	1	70	9	55	0
84	2	69	8	54	0
83	2	68	7	53	0
82	2	67	7	52	0
81	3	66	3	51	1
80	2	65	1	50	0
79	3	64	2	49	0
78	2	63	2	48	1
77	1	62	1	47	0
76	2	61	3	46	1
					N = 100

46 to 90. For the sake of continuity, scores which received no frequencies (for example, no one scored 54) receive frequency equal zero.

Suppose these data remained unmanageable, thereby necessitating further condensation to increase their interpretability. The logical procedure would be to simply create bounded ranges of scores, known as class intervals, to which raw score frequencies would be assigned. Figure 3-1 reports such an event using the data of Table 3-1. In this case, an optimally descriptive number of raw scores per interval would be five. Inspection of Table 3-1 reveals that the data demonstrate a high score of 90 and a low score of 46. If we count the number of potential scores (90, 89, 88, etc.), we observe that 45 *potential* data points encompass all raw scores. Since we wish to collapse five raw scores for every new unit (90, 89, 88, 87, 86 = unit one), we may divide 45 (total number of possible raw scores) by five (desired number of raw scores per unit) and we obtain nine as the number of bounded intervals. Upon reexamination of Figure 3-1, note that nine intervals are presented and that each interval's frequency is equivalent to the collection of acquired raw score frequencies in Table 3-1.

Although such a process could be carried to extremes, as in the case where data become discriminated only as high and low, the value of the approach should be obvious. As a result, raw data are invariably collapsed for presentation in test manuals.

Figure 3-2 represents a *cumulative* plot of frequencies from left to right. Note that in such a presentation the column farthest to the right constitutes 100 percent of the observed frequencies. Previous points rep-

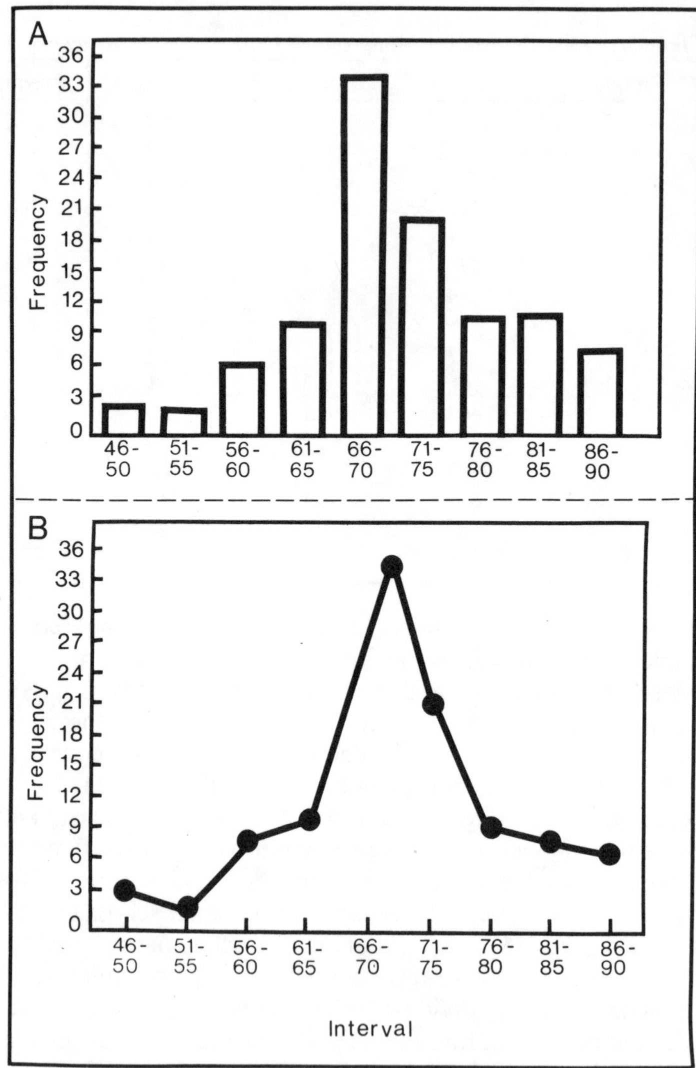

Fig. 3-1. Exemplary graphs of data presented in Table 3-1.

resent the collective percentage of frequencies up to, and including, the class interval. The correct way of interpreting Figure 3-2 (A or B) is, for example, 18 percent of the data fall at, or below the interval 61–65, 73 percent fall at, or below the interval 71–75, and so on, to 100 percent of the data. Such graphs can be very useful for determining an interval's position relative to the distribution of all scores and these presentations are quite common to test manuals and supporting information sources (e.g., teacher's manuals).

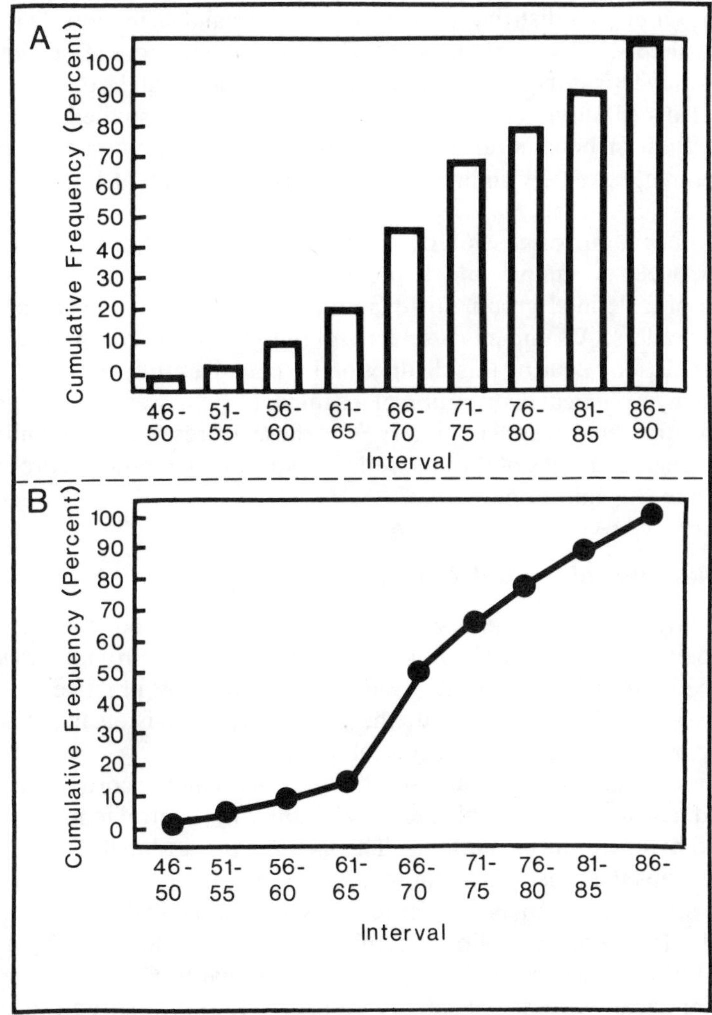

Fig. 3-2. Cumulative graphs of data presented in Figure 3-1.

The Normal Distribution

Many frequency (sampling) distributions are possible. Upon examination of Figure 3-1, it is obvious that there is a tendency for more events (higher frequencies) near the middle and fewer events (lower frequencies) near the high score and low score ends of the distribution. This is a common event in the measurement of human behavior as only a few persons tend to be high or low on a given trait, and more tend to be in the middle range. The general contour of Figure 3-1 is one of the essential characteristics of the distribution that underlies most measures of human behavior. Often this distribution is termed a normal distribution. Described as bell-shaped, it is sometimes called the Gaussian curve after one of its earliest investigators, Carl Gauss (1777–1855). Regardless of its title, the normal distribution represents the most intensively studied theoretical distribution of behavioral events for it contains many assumptions and procedures extremely important to the measurement of human performance.

To begin our discussion of the normal curve, first recall the distinction between a sample and a population. A population comprises all scores of a defined group, for example, the reading achievement of all fourth graders. A sample is a select and representative group, a subset of the population. Bearing this distinction in mind, carefully examine Figure 3-3, the hypothetical distribution of a sample of IQ scores. How might this specific distribution assist in interpeting these scores? Let us examine the salient characteristics of the theoretical distribution in order to provide an answer to this question.

Measures of Central Tendency

First, notice that the distribution is symmetrical and that the tips of the "bell" never touch the horizontal (X) axis. This provides evidence that the distribution is infinite. Although in everyday practice this attribute is seldom fully employed, there is always provision made for the most common and the most atypical scores.

In the normal distribution, the most common score is typically labeled a measure of central tendency. Ordinarily, central tendency is calculated by one of three methods. The *mean* is the arithmetic average and it is perhaps the most prevalent measure of central tendency. Its calculation is straightforward as: Σn scores/n, where Σn is read as "the summation of n (total) scores." For example, if the scores 140, 130, 129, 118, 90 and 70 were observed, the mean would be equal to 677/6 = 112.8. The resulting mean score is considered indicative of the most typical score—about one-half of the observations should fall above, and about one-half should fall below the mean.

Although the *mean* is perhaps the most commonly used measure of central tendency, two alternatives are commonly employed. The first of these is known as the *median,* the middle-occurring score in a distribution of scores ranked low to high in hierarchial fashion. In the above example the median does not directly exist because there is an even number of scores, hence, no middle score. However, the median can be estimated by calculating the average of the two scores equidistant from the high and low ends of the range of sequential scores. In this instance (using the data presented above) median = 129 + 118/2 = 123.5. For cases where an odd

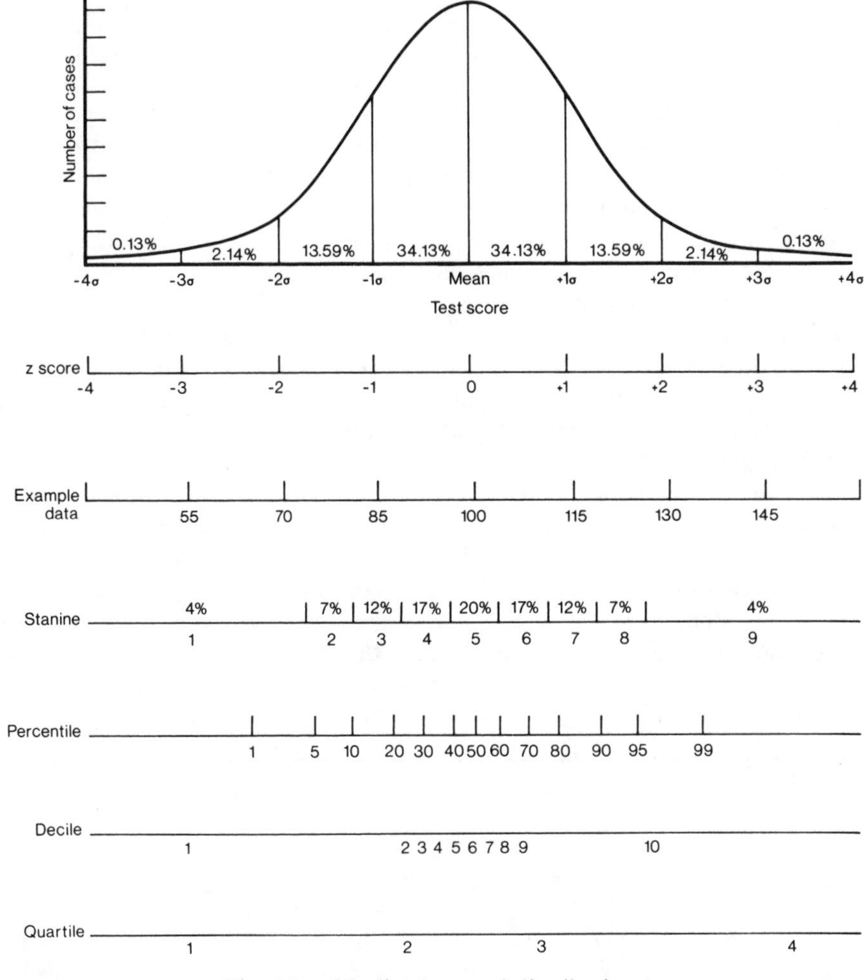

Fig. 3-3. Idealized normal distribution.

number of scores exist, median may be directly identified as (the number of scores + one)/two. Thus, for seven scores, the median score equals eight divided by two, or the fourth score.

The *mode* is the final measure of central tendency to be discussed and simply represents the most frequently occurring score. Like the median, the mode may not exist directly. In the series, 17-18-19-19-21-24, the mode is obviously 19 but in the series 17-18-19-19-21-21 or 17-18-19-20-21-22, the mode does not directly exist. Unlike the median, there is no alternate computation and the distribution is simply stated to be *bimodal* or to be without a modal score, respectively.

Generally, the mode is the least often reported measure of central tendency although most test manuals report the mean and many do report the median. It is always advisable to consider more than one measure of central tendency since under specific conditions one estimate may be more accurate than another. In general, the mean is more stable across samples and certainly more statistical manipulations can be performed with it; but an asymmetrical distribution (one that is not bell-shaped but directed [skewed] toward the positive or the negative end) can highly distort the representativeness of the mean as a measure of central tendency. Consider an example where the median and mode are quite valuable in confirming the estimate of central tendency provided by the mean.

Suppose the incomes of five persons in a college cafeteria are sampled. Three of these persons are undergraduates who are employed at odd jobs and report their annual incomes as \$1000.00 each; a fourth person receives a graduate assistantship at \$4400.00; the fifth person is the head chef employed at a salary of \$15000. If we obtained identical scores on a larger number of persons and plotted these scores we would have a distribution that is not symmetrical about the mean, but somewhat irregular as Figure 3-4 illustrates. Such a distribution is positively skewed, that is, relatively more events (persons' salaries) occurred below the mean, but a small number of events (very high salaries) occurred above the mean, creating an asymmetrical "tail" upon the high end of the curve. An exactly opposite situation would create a curve that would be negatively

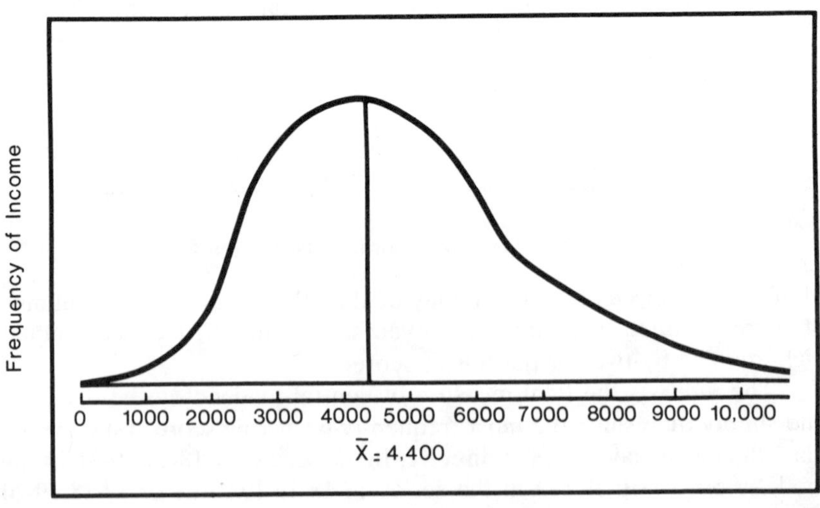

Fig. 3-4. Example of a positively skewed distribution.

skewed. In either case, the mean is not a good indicator of the most commonly occurring score, the curve is likely asymmetrical and alternate approaches are needed if the test's sample is to be satisfactory. Sophisticated techniques exist to describe (or modify) the shape of the distribution and sometimes these are reported in test manuals. However, a comparison of alternate measures of central tendency is one simple preliminary check that can, and should, be made by the test user. A large discrepency in lieu of adequate explanation is cause for concern.

Variance in the Distribution—The Standard Deviation

Measures of central tendency can describe only the most common or frequently occurring score. For many purposes, that is not sufficient information, and it is common practice to describe variance within the distribution in terms of the dispersion from central tendency. Depending upon the characteristics of the data, the distribution of variance about the measure of central tendency can be expected to differ radically. Figure 3-5 illustrates three sets of data with identical mean, but differing distributions of variance about this measure of central tendency. What conclusions can be made about these distributions? First, reaffirm that the mean is 100 in each distribution. Second, since the vertical axis of the figure represents frequency of occurrence, it may be concluded that fewer scores are at, or near the mean, moving from drawing A to B to C. In such an event, it is obvious that more variance in scores exist (A to B to C) because fewer scores are clustered about the mean; that is, relatively more scores tend to be at, or near, the mean in A, and relatively more tend to disperse or "move away" in each successive drawing. This event results in increased variance about the mean.

Perhaps an illustration will assist the reader. Figure 3-5A might represent the case where a class of students received reports of their individual test performance. Few students are very high or very low and most students are within a few points of the mean. Figure 3-5C could represent a similar set of individual scores, but this time scores vary widely, some students are quite high, some are quite low and the mean, by itself, does not provide an altogether accurate picture of the "average" score. Thus the distribution of variance in a sample clearly alters the perception one has of the sample's characteristics.

Although variance in a distribution highly modifies the view one holds of a set of scales, variance (which can be calculated directly) is not a very useful statistic. However, the concept of variance remains viable and forms the basis for one of the more common and useful statistical techniques for describing dispersion in a set of scores. This statistic is

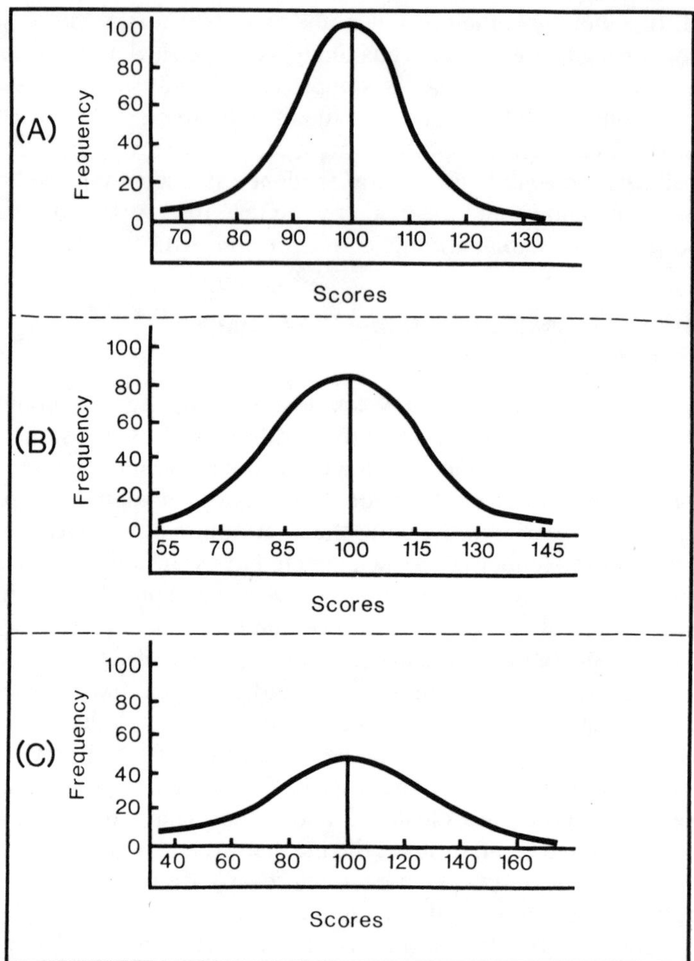

Fig. 3-5. Examples of three groups of data with identical mean but differing variance about the mean.

known as the standard deviation, a procedure reported in almost all test manuals.

The standard deviation can most easily be thought of as a unit of measurement that encompasses a specifiable proportion of data in the normal distribution. Refer again to Figure 3-3 and notice that this figure is based on a hypothetical population of scores with μ (mu) indicating the mean of the population and σ (sigma) indicating the standard deviation of the population. Since entire populations are seldom measured, actual practice will usually witness the symbol $\overline{X}$ to denote sample mean and *SD* to represent sample standard deviation. In this illustration $\overline{X} = 100$ and $SD = 15$, thus, *SD* plotted from left to right corresponds to scores of 55, 70, 85, 115, 130, and 145. (This *particular* example is identical to the mean [100] and standard deviation [15] of the *Wechsler Intelligence Scale for Children—Revised* [1974]. The reader may wish to bear this in mind in order to facilitate comprehension.)

In this illustration, it may be observed that proportions of data (expressed in percentages) are given for each standard deviation away from the mean and that the curve is symmetrical in this proportionality. Thus for any *normal* distribution precise proportions of data are found within specific areas of the curve. Between the $\overline{X}$ and the first *SD* 34.13 percent of all scores appear, between the first and second *SD* 13.59 percent of the data are present and between the second and third *SD* 2.14 percent of the data are present. Beyond the third *SD* .13 percent of the data appear. Since proportions are identified for *either* half of the bell curve, 68.26 percent of the data lies within the bell curve's area encompassed by $\pm$ *SD,* 95.44 percent lies within ± 2 *SD* and 99.52 percent lies within ± 3 *SD.* These estimates are derived from the work of the Russian mathematician P. L. Chebyshev (1894–1921) and provide one of the most useful "psychometric rulers." Later we will see how the normal curve's proportionality allows the special education teacher to collect some very valuable data about the scores observed on a test.

Calculation of the standard deviation is relatively simple, although variations in the procedure exist. For interval scale, ungrouped (noncollapsed), untreated (actual score) data, the data type the teacher would most probably observed on a classroom-teacher-made test, the formula is:

$$SD = \frac{n\,(\Sigma X^2) - (\Sigma X)^2}{n\,(n - 1)}\,.$$

In this formula, Σ (sigma) indicates "the summation of," X^2 indicates "the observation squared," $(\Sigma)^2$ indicates "the quantity squared" and *n* indicates "the number of observations". The symbol $\surd$ (radical) simply means to "take the square root of," for exampe $\sqrt{25} = 5$.

For individuals who have had training in even basic statistics this brief review should allow calculation and use of the *SD* statistic. Readers who do not yet feel comfortable should, at this point, consult an elementary statistics textbook (see *Suggested Readings,* p. 95).

Derived Scores

The measurement of central tendency and variance in a normal distribution is essential to test interpretation for these concepts allow the development of other test quantification procedures; that is, unless precise units of measurement are applied, the very real problem of "large" and "small" raw scores appears. Knowledge that John received a 95 on his spelling test takes on a decidedly different meaning when we become aware that the test consisted of 200 words and that the class average was 150. Similarly, even if we know that gasoline may be purchased at 80¢ per U.S. gallon, 70¢ per liter, and 95¢ per Imperial gallon, direct comparison remains elusive without a great deal of fuss and confusion inherent in the translation to a single measurement scale. The point is simply that interpretable units of measurement must be established if meaningful comparisons are to be achieved.

In order to achieve useful measures, psychometricians make extensive use of *derived scores,* procedures which use the performance of some sample group as the "psychometric ruler" of measurement. Now the reader should fully appreciate the emphasis placed in earlier sections upon the care with which the sample is drawn: derived scores from the basis for test interpretation and, in turn, they are quite dependent upon the sample. *Unless the normative sample is adequate the psychometric ruler represented by derived scores will be inaccurate and the test user will be making faulty conclusions.*

Derived scores are of two basic types: developmental scores (usually age and grade equivalents) and scores of relative standing (e.g., percentiles). *Age equivalent scores* indicate the average (mean or median) number of accurate responses for children of a certain age. *Grade equivalent scores* simply indicate the number of items attained by children of such and such grade placement. Age equivalents are expressed in years and months (sometimes total months) while grade equivalents are usually expressed in grades and tenths of grades. Thus it is common to see a particular child's raw score of 17 expressed as (age equivalent) 8-1 and (grade equivalent) 2.6. This means that a score of 17 is the *average* score of *children in the normative sample* who were eight years and one month of age and in the second year, sixth month of school. Using this approach, the teacher has a measure of this particular child's skill placed on a relative psychometric ruler that is consistent in its measurement. This type of score is quite popular and many common tests, particularly achievement tests, present both forms as an aid for interpreting test results.

Derived scores of relative standing take several different forms. *Percentiles* indicate the percentage of individuals who fall at or below a particular raw score. Referring to our earlier example, assume that this same child's raw score of 17 falls at the 50th percentile. We would interpret this as "50 percent of the individuals in the norming sample fell at or below a raw score of 17." Should his raw score have placed him in the 60th percentile, we would have reached a similar conclusion except that his performance would now have met or exceeded 60 percent of the normative sample. Thus it may be seen that the *higher percentile score one achieves the better his or her relative performance.*

Deciles and *quartiles* may be interpreted in a manner analogous to percentiles. Simply note that each decile contains 10 percentiles and that each quartile contains 25 percentiles; the *relative* values of the scores remained unchanged.

As the reader may have surmised, percentiles are a far more precise measure than either deciles or quartiles. Consequently, percentiles are among the most desirable of the derived scores. A re-examination of Figure 3-5 will assist the reader to fully relate the meaning of percentiles, deciles, and quartiles.

Standard scores represent still another derived score of relative standing in the norming sample. Standard scores transform raw scores (e.g., the above child's score of 17) in such a way that the collection of scores always possess the same mean and the same standard deviation; that is, the scores obtained from this child's class (of which his 17 is a part) are transformed to pre-established norm criteria.

z scores are a particular case of the standard score concept where the mean is operationally set at zero and the standard deviation is set at one. Because the proportion of cases above and below any particular z score is known, the teacher can readily and precisely estimate a student's relative standing. Test raw score to z score conversion tables are quite common to many test manuals, and the areas of the normal distribution represented by specific z scores are presented in most elementary statistics textbooks.

Stanines are another standard score and the final score of relative standing to be discussed. Stanines are simply standard scores which divide the normal distribution into nine parts ("standard nines"). Interpretation of stanines is analogous to other standard scores with allowance made for the fact that nine divisions are made. Stanines are a relatively infrequent statistic on modern tests though many older tests employ this standard score. Again, a review of Figure 3-3 may be of assistance to the reader.

CORRELATION: MEASURING THE ASSOCIATION OF VARIABLES

Thus far we have been primarily concerned with very basic descriptive statistics. It must be recognized that descriptive statistics only illustrate or describe an individual's performance within a sample and, therefore, have essential, though limited value. A number of requirements exceed the capacity of simple descriptive statistics. For example, educators often wish to relate some sample of the individual's behavior to the norm, and it is always essential that the properties of a test are adequately conveyed to the test user. Simpler descriptive statistics cannot accomplish this task.

Correlation is a statistical procedure quite commonly used when the experimenter, or, in this case, the test constructor, cannot directly manipulate the variables under study. For example, several reading achievement tests might be given, the results correlated, and, hopefully, relationships between certain demographic variables and approahces to teaching reading could be established. However, the experimenter or test constructor pays a price for this loss of control: correlations cannot provide measures of cause and effect, but can only describe the strength of the relationship between variables. The reader is cautioned *never* to accept a correlation as a statement of causality.

Correlation measures are usually symbolized by r and the descriptive score or index is known as a *correlation coefficient*. The correlation coefficient represents the strength of association or relationship between two variables, it always possesses a numerical index ranging from -1.00 to $+1.00$. A simplified event leading to a perfect correlation ($+1.00$) is provided in Figure 3-6. In this illustration the plot of two hypothetical test outcomes is given. In the example $r = +1.0$, because identical performance was observed on the two tests, that is, each individual reported an identical score. (To simplify, only intervals were provided in this illustration.) The relationship between the tests in this example is thus inferred to be very high; indeed, it is perfect.

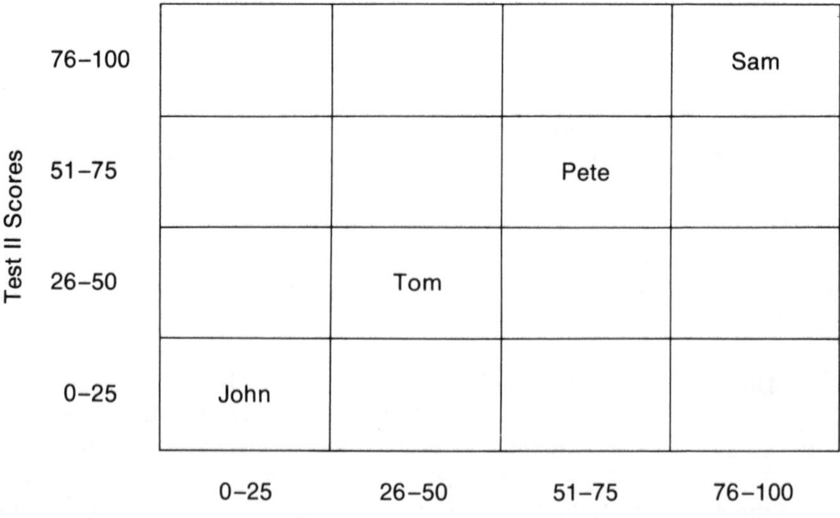

Fig. 3-6. An example of a perfect relationship between two tests.

Figure 3-7 demonstrates the occasion where the two sets produced exactly opposite outcomes. Thus, the relationship *is* perfect (highest to lowest, next highest to next lowest, etc.), but it is inverse and the correlation is expressed not as $r = +1.00$ but as $r = -1.00$. Thus the teacher must always consider not only the magnitude of a correlation, but also the algebraic sign preceding it. Convention dictates that a correlation without a sign (e.g., $r = .80$) expresses a positive relationship.

Often a relationship may not exist between two measures. This event usually occurs when outcomes are random, that is, when there is no systematic relationship between the variables being measured. Clearly, few instances occur where either a perfect positive or perfect inverse relationship exists. However, in educational and psychological measurement reported correlations are usually positive and are apt to be moderately high ($r = .50$ to .80). Extremely low (less than .20) and extremely high (above .90) correlations are relatively rare. Intuitively, this fact should be clear to the experienced teacher: students who score well on one test tend to score well on another, while students who score poorly on one test tend to continue to score poorly on another. But, despite this general tendency, there is always some variation across students due to subject matter, particularly student aptitudes, days of the week the tests were administered and many other possibilities. In the absence of continuous precision many moderately strong relationships are seen among educational test scores.

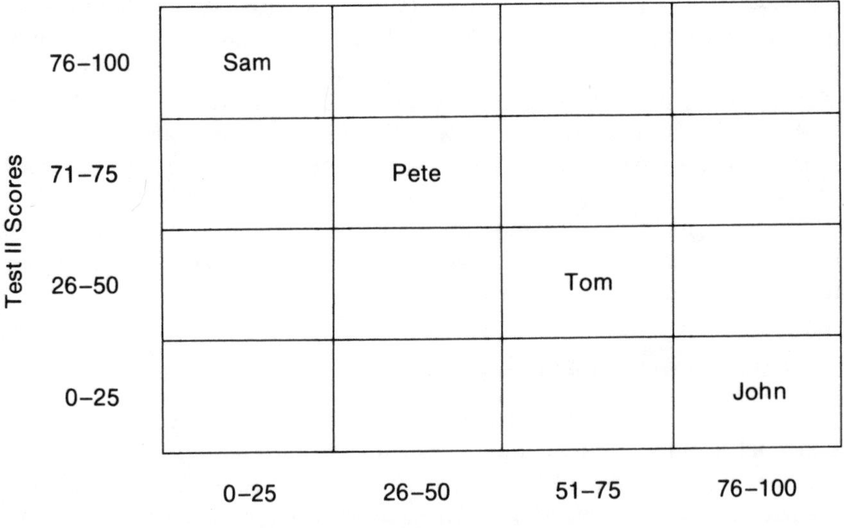

Fig. 3-7. An example of a perfect inverse relationship between two tests.

The Pearson r

The most commonly reported correlational technique is the Pearson Product Moment correlation. The approach is so common that many test manuals report the use of this statistic by simply referring to it as "correlation." There is no doubt that the statistic is extremely useful for measuring the association of test data.

The following calculation procedure can be used with interval scale, ungrouped, untreated data. Data with these characteristics would appear on most teacher-made tests. Therefore, this formula is applicable, for example, in the teacher's calculation of reliability or in measuring the relationship of one teacher-made test to another. Use of the procedure can provide an invaluable guide for the evaluation or modification of classroom tests. The simplified formula is:

$$r = \frac{n\Sigma XY - \Sigma X \Sigma Y}{\sqrt{[n\Sigma X^2 - (\Sigma X)^2]\,[n\Sigma Y^2 - (\Sigma Y)^2]}}$$

Calculation by means of this formula is relatively simple, for the most essential procedures were addressed earlier in the calculation of the standard deviation. Σn, and $\sqrt{}$ retain their precise meaning as does the distinction between X^2 and $(X)^2$. About all that is novel is the fact that we are now dealing with *two* sets of scores X *and* Y. Accordingly, the above formula requires that operations be performed on both sets of scores. The calculated components that are required to "plug into" the above formula are as follows: n (number of observations), ΣXY (the summed cross product of appropriate X and Y scores), ΣX (the total summed value of all X scores), ΣY (the total summed value of all Y scores), ΣX^2 (the total summed value of the square of all X scores), ΣY^2 (the total summed value of the square of all Y scores), $(\Sigma X)^2$ (the total summed value of each X score, squared), and $(\Sigma Y)^2$ (the total summed value of each Y score, squared).

Once again, this computation should be straightforward to many readers. If it is not, the reader is once again encouraged to pursue the topic in a suitable statistics text.

Other Correlational Procedures

There exist several alternative procedures for estimating a correlation coefficient. Although most tests report correlations based on the Pearson Product Moment method, circumstances will occasionally dictate the use of alternate procedures. These alternative procedures and the requirements for their use are reported in many places (see especially Ferguson [1971], Salvia and Ysseldyke [1978], and Siegel [1956]. The reader may find the step-by-step computational procedures described in Bruning and Kintz (1968) to be especially helpful.

Testing the Significance of a Correlation

Correlations may always be placed on a continuum of "high" to "low" values but this does, of course, constitute a subjective appraisal. It is quite possible, however, to objectively test the hypothesis that a given correlation is greater than zero, i.e., the hypothesis that no systematic relationship exists. This section will describe a procedure that allows us to draw a conclusion about the "significance" of a correlation.

Earlier in the chapter, the normal distribution was discussed and some of its salient properties were related. In passing, it was mentioned that other distributions have been identified and their characteristics described. One of these distributions is the *t* distribution, a distribution that allows a test of the value of a correlation.

Usually, the test of a correlation is conducted through a *t* test of the "null hypothesis," a statement established before the test begins. The null hypothesis simply indicates that *no systematic relationship exists,* in this case, that the correlation is equal to zero. In practice, the teacher will likely observe a statement of the *t*-test outcome indicating that the probability is less than 5 in 100 ($p < .05$) of the correlation occurring by chance. More simply, a value may be given with a simple $p < .05$ indicated. In such an event convention dictates that the null hypothesis has been rejected and that a systematic relationship does exist at the *specified* probability level (e.g., $p < .05$). In educational and psychological literature, a "statistically significant" correlation would be in evidence.

Testing the value of a correlation coefficient is a straightforward operation. The general formula is given as:

$$t = r\sqrt{\frac{n-2}{1-r^2}}$$

For the case where $n = 10$ and $r = .90$, we may calculate the value of *t* as:

$$t = .9\sqrt{\frac{8}{1-.81}} = 6.48$$

We then refer to a standard table of *t* values (found in almost all statistics textbooks) and we find that a *t*-score at 8 *df* ("degrees of freedom") must equal or exceed 2.30 to be significant at $p < .05$. Since 6.48 is greater than 2.30, we would reject the null hypothesis and conclude that a systematic relationship does exist. In the above illustration, there is little likelihood (only 5 times in 100) that the correlation occurred by chance. In fact, the above outcome is so great that we may compare it to the values listed for $df = 8$, $p < .001$. Referring again to a statistics text, we find that the obtained t value of 6.48 also exceeds the value listed for $p < .001$ (5.04). Therefore, we can conclude with even greater certainty that the correlation did not occur by chance alone. Although $p < .05$ is the conventionally accepted level of a statistically significant difference, it is common for test manuals to report values of $p < .01$ and $p < .001$. We may be ever more certain of the decision *to reject the null hypothesis as the probability of chance occurrence grows smaller.*

The procedure just described, or highly similar procedures, can be used to test any correlation, and many test manuals report the statistical significance of correlations representing *reliability* and *validity*. However, a caution is warranted: a correlation can be significant yet of insufficient magnitude for many psychometric purposes. Later, we will describe some of the consequences of a perhaps statistically significant yet far too "small" correlation. The reader will then quickly realize that even a moderate correlation can express a relationship far beyond chance yet be too imprecise to be of value in the interpretation and use of a measurement instrument. *Statistical significance should never be the only criteria for judging the adequacy of a correlation coefficient reported in a test manual.*

CONCEPTUAL APPROACHES TO VALIDITY

The validity of a test generally refers to how well the test measures what it purports to measure. Operationally, there are a number of ways of defining and measuring validity, but one immediate caution is in order: Do not judge the validity of a test simply by the numerical indices (correlation coefficients) provided. The behavioral construct measured cannot be inferred from shortened or even erroneous test names. Thus, a test may measure "intelligence" quite accurately in terms of a particular theory of intelligent behavior; yet this accuracy is useless if the examiner does not conclude that the same behaviors are indicative of intelligence. Since the validity of any test is based on its purpose, and the population of specific behaviors that reflect that purpose, the examiner must be sure that the constructs under examination are understood and are not misrepresented. Otherwise, true validity relative to the user's orientation cannot be assumed, despite the validity coefficients observed.

Psychometrically, several *conceptual* aspects of validity have been reported. Numerous authors have reported different concepts, or more frequently, similar concepts with differing labels. Anastasi (1976, p. 134) has presented an exceptionally lucid discussion of validity organized from the guidelines presented in *Standards for Educational and Psychological Tests* (1974). Because the latter publication is a widely available and frequently cited source, and because it represents a cross discipline effort to standardize procedures (the manual was prepared by the American Psychological Association, American Educational Research Associaiton and the National Council on Measurement in Education), the following discussion will parallel the approach given in *Standards*.

Content validity involves the systematic inspection of a test instrument's items in order to determine the representativeness of the behavioral domain that the test purports to sample. Simplistically, content validity can be considered a measure of sample adequacy toward answering the question, "Do the items on this test represent the domain?" One immediately obvious problem for the test constructor is the difficulty of adequately defining the boundaries of the population domain. For example, it is a relatively simple task to sample the content of fourth grade spelling words or to take measure of children's knowledge of addition facts, and in such instances we might expect content validity to be quite high. It is, however, more difficult to adequately determine the content validity of a test of intelligence, for what specific domain constitutes all intelligent behavior?

In general, content validity is most appropriate for achievement and occupational tests but is less applicable for aptitude and personality tests. This should be obvious in that achievement and occupational tests must bear close resemblance to that which they purport to "diagnose" or "predict." Aptitude and personality tests may not have a directly observable and uniquely specifiable content domain, indeed such tests generally attempt to measure "traits"—underlying personological variables that presumably affect the outcomes on specific tasks. Thus, the examiner using such tests may take detailed measures of "traits," such as eye-hand coordination, ability to read small print, general hand dexterity, interest level in mechanics, and ability to comprehend abstract information and to infer future success in a given occupation. For example, the skills listed above do not describe the achievement or occupational behaviors in which a watchmaker must engage, but they appear to be logical traits that summate to form an aptitude for watchmaking. Accordingly, content validity for such trait measures is difficult to achieve.

Face validity is a second major category that deserves our attention. In essence, face validity refers to the test's appearance, answering the question, "Does it appear that the test could measure what it purports to measure?" To be sure, adequate appearance can be an aid in facilitating examiner–examinee rapport, thus it is useful for demonstrating a test's value to the psychometrically unsophisticated. However, face validity is not a direct, objective consideration of the test's ability to "measure what it purports to measure" even though it can provide much support to other validity measures.

Criterion-related validity refers to a test's effectiveness in relating behavior to some specific criteria. Common educational criteria may include grades, teacher reports, successful completion of a program, or on-the-job performance. Within criterion-related validity, two functions emerge, each with separate measures. These two functions are known as concurrent validity and predictive validity. *Concurrent validity* is essentially concerned with the analysis (or diagnosis) of current status; *predictive validity* is directed toward the estimation of future performance. Questions such as "Is this child developmentally disabled?" and "Is this child likely to become developmentally disabled?" serve to illustrate the respective emphases of concurrent and predictive validity. Both of these issues are essential to educational measurement, though one may be much more emphasized in any given circumstance. Unfortunately, criterion validity is one of the most criticized measures of validity; it is at the core of some major conflicts concerning testing. Additional comments will be made about this in Chapter 5 within the general topic of test bias.

Construct validity is the extent to which a test measures a theoretical construct or trait that is presumed to be an underlying determinant of behavior. In education and psychology, hypothetical constructs are legion; examples include intelligence, verbal fluency, perceptual-motor integration, anxiety, and many others. Obviously, this form of validity is of major importance, so important in fact, that in many instances other measures of validity are useless without it.

Construct validity is complex to measure. Anastasi (1976, pp. 152–158) denotes six major approaches to ascertaining construct validity. It is important to describe the salient aspects of the six approahces, because each has different underlying assumptions and uses.

The first approach to construct validity, *developmental changes*, simply refers to the measurement of a construct as the individual develops over time. Many theoretical constructs are presumed to follow some hierarchical arrangement; hence, behavioral change ought to be evident as the child matures. However, developmental change is not by itself a sufficient criteria because it does not define the domain. After all, many behaviors could change over time, but still not reflect an adequately sampled construct.

Correlations with other tests are frequently cited as evidence of construct validity and this must be the case if tests measure the same construct, e.g., intelligence tests. However, excessively high correlations in lieu of some additional information being provided is inappropriate since this event would essentially represent a replication of previous tests.

Factor analysis is a statistical procedure by which underlying constructs may be identified. Essentially, the technique provides correlational relationships between and within clusters of items. Clusters with high intraitem correlations are taken to be highly similar, and the total number of items then becomes reduced to manageable clusters with each presumably related to the construct under measure. Factor analysis is a useful tool, but it should be stated that the clusters, or factors (principle components) as they are known, are named in an after-the-fact basis. Thus, the name attached to the factor is, at best, an educated guess and does not automatically infer the properties of the inferred construct.

A fourth method for estimating construct validity is really quite similar to one method of calculating reliability. *Internal consistency* simply suggests that high internal consistency can only be achieved if a similar construct is captured by the test; hence, a homogeneous domain must produce measures of a single construct. While it is true that heterogeneous influence is reduced, internal consistency does not provide a direct measure of the construct. Homogeneity does not automatically assure that the domain is the one of interest, though it may be sampled consistently. To use a single example, perfect consistency in stringing beads may be observed, but this perfect correlation does not, by itself, indicate that stringing beads is valid as a judgment for a construct labeled "intelligence."

A fifth procedure for determining construct validity is the *experimental method*. In this procedure a test that is designed, for example, to measure verbal reasoning, should evidence gains across persons of differing sensitivity to, or training in, verbal reasoning. In this manner an experimental outcome is used to infer the validity with which the test measures the construct.

Finally, *convergent and discriminant* validation (Campbell & Fiske, 1959) specifies that, for a test to be valid, it must significantly correlate with variables appropriate to the construct (convergent validation) and nonsignificantly correlate with variables unrelated to the construct (discriminant validation). Simply stated, convergent and discriminant validation demands that a valid instrument correlate only with variables appropriate to the construct measured by the test. A systematic procedure for determining convergent and discriminant validity (the multitrait-multimethod procedure) has been proposed (Campbell & Fiske, 1959) and is discussed in some detail by Anastasi (1976, pp. 156–158). The interested reader is referred to that source.

In summary, validity is an essential component of any psychological or educational test. Indeed, Ahmann and Glock (1971, p. 277) describe "validity" as the most important component of any measuring instrument. But validity is only one characteristic of a good test and, even so, must be detailed and measured in many ways. More often than not, each of the approaches to establishing validity can be severely criticized. Thus, careful inspection of the test manual is *always* warranted. Judgments made about specific tests must be at least partially determined as a result of the adequacy of the approach taken to determine validity.

CONCEPTUAL APPROACHES TO RELIABILITY

Reliability is a construct so central to the development and use of psychoeducational measurement that it is impossible to discuss assessment without understanding its meaning. In the simpest sense, reliability refers to the consistency of a measure. It should be obvious that even under optimal conditions test scores will vary because of extraneous factors. For example, errors in marking selected responses, misreading of questions, errors in grading, personalogical or situational variables, all contribute to the discrepancy seen across tests. Reliability provides an index to judge the freedom of an assessment device from such unwanted influence, for in measurment a controlled score is essential. As Anastasi (1976, p. 28) indicates, little confidence can be placed in an instrument that records an IQ of 120 on Monday and 70 on Friday. Therefore, a test's consistency or stability is essential if either the instrument's diagnostic or predictive information is to be of any value.

An instrument's reliability is always expressed as a correlation coefficient, the larger the coefficient the greater the consistency of the test. Thus a test with a reported reliability of .90 is much more consistent and free from error than one with a relaibility of .55.

Several different approaches can be used to estimate an instrument's reliability. At least four methodological procedures are in common use, each somewhat different in approach and outcome. Since test reliability is so important, it is worthwhile to investigate these procedures in detail.

Test-retrest reliability (sometimes, simply "retest" reliability) is one common proceudre for determining a test's stability. Essentially, the procedure is the dual adminsitration of a test to a common sample of persons separated only by time. As its name implies, the scores resulting from the two administrations are correlated and the outcome is taken as a measure of the test's reliability. Unfortuantely, test-retest reliability is affected by a number of conditions including the fact that it is very difficult to create identical testing situations. Change in the examinee's mood, new knowledge gained during the test-retest period, examiner procedure, and a seemingly endless array of other factors may produce effects reflected in the score outcomes. Further, as a test-retest is obviously conducted on two occasions, time between administrations is a major factor. Thus, a test has not one, but as many test-retest reliabilities as there are possible test-retest time periods (Anastasi, 1976). Because of this conceptual problem and the difficulties expressed above, test-retest reliability may well produce inappropriate conclusions. In summary, a test-retest approach must surmount many difficulties and as a result reliabilities achieved in this manner must be carefully viewed. Two cautions are consistently warranted: (1) always check the length of time between administrations; and (2) compare test-retest reliabilities with those obtained by any other methods reported in the test manual. Test-retrest reliability can be a major consideration for judging the suitability of a test but, by itself, it is probably an insufficient criterion.

Alternate form reliability is simply the correlation of at least two forms of the same test and is heavily based on the concept of content sampling, a procedure that estimates the proportion of the test sample that was drawn from the domain (population) of all potential items. If the sampling procedure is an unbiased estimate of the domain, we may assume that the reliability will be correspondingly high, hence the tests then presumably cover the same material. If the sampling procedure was biased or insufficient, reliability must necessarily be low, since two separate tests have been created. Unfortunately, there is a potential flaw in this approach: even under the best sampling procedures, the happenstance of subject's past experiences will probably lower reliability. That is, if several items should appear only on Form A that were not learned in recent study, but on the basis of other past experiences, reliability will be lowered by this event. In addition, alternate form reliability has a time component effect that must always be considered for the reasons described earlier.

Split-half reliability referst o the case where items on a single test are dichotomized in some manner (first-second half or more usually odd-even) and correlated to provide an index of reliability. It is hypothesized that such a procedure provides an index of homegeneity, since items are drawn from the same domain and, therefore, must yield high consistency. However, three cautions are necessary. First, an equal number of items must reflect a single problem in the domain. Second, items must require a similar response; it is absurd to correlate dissimilar questions. Finally, questions to be correlated must have approximately equal levels of difficulty since a large discrepancy in item difficulty could erroneously reduce the reliability estimate. In summary, individual items should not be correlated if they do not reflect similar domains or if they do not have similar levels of difficulty. In spite of these cautions, a properly developed split-half procedure is an excellent measure of reliability.

The fourth and final method of calculating reliability *is to obtain a measure of the consistency of each item on the test to the total text.* This procedure is usually accomplished by means of the *coefficient alpha* technique or the older and more limited *Kuder-Richardson 20* formula (often abbreviated as KR-20). Both methods proceed on the assumption that a homogeneous test will necessarily be more internally consistent, hence more reliable than a heterogeneous measure. For assessment instruments that presume to sample a single domain of skills (e.g., aptitude), internal consistency procedures are excellent. However, in measuring domains of potentially heterogeneous composition (e.g., multi-trait models of intelligence), the approach is not a wise choice and will result in drastically reduced estimates of reliability.

The four approaches described above are nearly synonymous with procedures for calculating reliability in psychoeducational assessment devices. Each has characteristic strengths and each is more or less suitable for any given occasion. However it is always wise to examine the method(s) chosen for any given test to determine the adequacy of the actual procedure (e.g., sufficient numbers, sufficient time between test-retest, etc.) and finally to compare the agreement of the results of two or more procedures. In addition, reliability will usually vary across the subtests within a total test and invariably will be different across age ranges. The test user must always select the reliabilities most appropriate to the particular characteristics of any single administration (age, subscales, etc.) before passing judgment.

THE USE OF PSYCHOMETRIC CONSTRUCTS IN THE INTERPRETATION OF TESTS

Preliminary Cautions

At the outset of this section, it must be reemphasized that the value of the normed test lies most completely in two criteria: (1) the adequacy of the test's standardization procedure, and (2) the faithful adherence of the examiner to the procedures specified for administration and use. Most of the events that undermine the effectiveness of normed tests can be traced to violations in one of these areas. Poorly developed standardization procedures produce an inherently useless instrument. Similarly, poor administration produces a faulty record, perhaps compounded by extrapolation ("guestimation") beyond the test's stated capability. The reader should keep in mind that a test's outcome is the comparison of *a student's performance with a select sample of other similar students*. If the test was poorly standardized, or if the individual examiner did not follow the administrative rules accurately, the test score *must* be inaccurate. Even under the best of circumstances all tests contain some components of measurement error. An examiner must always be aware of this fact and constantly follow the procedures necessary to keep error at an estimatable minimum. This section will assist the educator to evaluate the merits of any particular test.

The Interrelatedness of the Constructs of a Normed Test

The reader will recall that all normed tests contain a most common score and provisions for extreme scores at either end of the distribution of the normed sample. We have previously described procedures for estimating the most common score (mean, median, mode). Also mentioned were the most common measures of dispersion away from this central score. In addition, we have discussed the properties of the normal distribution, the concept of correlation, and the essential aspects of reliability and validity. Our task now is to relate and make use of these constructs.

We will start with the standard deviation. Recall that Figure 3-5 presented three examples of a normal distribution with the means set at 100 and the standard deviation set at 10 (Figure 3-5A), 15 (Figure 3-5B), and 20 (Figure 3-5C). These distributions vary considerably in their peakedness, or kurtosis as it is known. Figure 3-5A is decidedly *leptokurdic* or pointed, while Figure 5-C is *platykurdic* or flattened out. Since we know that over 99 percent of the observations of a population (or sample) of scores can be found within three standard deviations of the mean (remember Chebyshev's theorem) what can we say about the scores of Figure 3-5A-C? First, we can note that the consistency of the measures becomes increasingly small as we move from A to B to C. Figure 3-5A represents the case where relatively few scores are greatly different from the mean; Figure 3-5C represents the case where many scores are much above or much below the mean. Using Chebyshev's theorem, we can see that the respective range of scores (Figure 3-5ABC) that encompass 99.74 percent of the data are 70 through 120, 55 through 145, and 40 through 160. Thus, we must necessarily be more generous of the range of scores in the distribution as the standard deviation increases in magnitude. This fact leads us to our first major use of a test's constructs.

The Standard Error of Measurement

The above situation has many implications for test interpretation, because sample distributions form the norm by which an individual score is always compared. Remember that no score observed on any single test administration is more than an approximation of an ideal (true) score obtained under theoretically perfect conditions. By making use of several constructs, we can estimate the amount of error associated with true score. The procedure used to accomplish this is referred to as *standard error of measurement (Sem)* and, since an observed score is only a sample in a range of scores that likely contain true score, the test administrator must always calculate and make use of the standard error of measurement.

The *Sem* is defined as:

$$Sem = SD\sqrt{1-r^2}.$$

In this formula, SD = standard deviation, r = the correlation coefficient for reliability, and one (1) is a constant always present in the calculation. Using the data of Figure 3-5 calculation of the range of scores that is required to encircle true score is provided (Table 3-2). Notice that data in Table 3-2 are organized in rows (data varying by standard deviation) and columns (data varying by the reliability of the test). For this example, reliability was hypothetically placed at $r = .80$ and $r = .90$.

Inspection of the six estimates of standard error indicate that the resulting values vary systematically. Holding r constant, *Sem* always increases as the *SD* increases; holding *SD* constant, higher reliability al-

Table 3-2
The Hypothetical Sem for Three Sets of Data with Identical Mean and SD's of 10, 15, and 20

$$\text{Sem} = \text{SD}\sqrt{1 - r}$$

Figure A Data	
r = .80	r = .90
Sem = $10\sqrt{1 - .8^2}$ = 6.0	Sem = $10\sqrt{1 - .9^2}$ = 4.36
95% Sem = 1.96Z × 6.0 = 11.76	95% Sem = 1.96Z × 4.36 = 8.55
99% Sem = 2.58Z × 6.0 = 15.48	99% Sem = 2.58Z × 4.36 = 11.25
Figure B Data	
r = .80	r = .90
Sem = $20\sqrt{1 - .8^2}$ = 12.0	Sem = $20\sqrt{1 - 9^2}$ = 8.72
95% Sem = 1.96Z × 12.0 = 23.52	95% Sem = 1.96Z × 8.72 = 17.09
99% Sem = 2.58Z × 12.0 = 30.96	99% Sem = 2.58Z × 8.72 = 22.50
Figure C Data	
r = .80	r = .90
Sem = $30\sqrt{1 - .8^2}$ = 18.0	Sem = $30\sqrt{1 - .9^2}$ = 13.08
95% Sem = 1.96Z × 18.0 = 35.28	95% Sem = 1.96Z × 13.08 = 25.64
99% Sem = 2.58Z × 18.0 = 46.44	99% Sem = 2.58Z × 13.08 = 33.75

ways produces a lower *Sem*. The largest *Sem* is associated with the case with the largest *SD* and the lowest *r* (*Sem* = 18.0); the lowest *Sem* is associated with the smallest *SD* and highest *r* (*Sem* = 4.36). Throughout this table, *Sem* varies from 4.36 to 18.0, a considerable range of values. Thus we see that two components, the test's reliability and the magnitude of the *SD* greatly influence the amount of error associated with any observed score.

Most test manuals report the *Sem* directly although caution should be taken to select an appropriate value for an individual case because the *Sem* will vary across age ranges. However, not all test manuals do report *Sem* directly and, on those occasions, the examiner should calculate the statistic. Adequate interpretation of test performance cannot proceed without knowledge of the *Sem*.

Estimating a True Score

The standard error of measurement is an estimate of the magnitude of error in an observed score but often it is advisable to further increase the precision of our estimate of true score. Nunnally (1967, p. 220) has provided a simple procedure for estimating the actual value of true score. This can be accomplished through the use of the formula:

$$X' = \bar{X} + (r)(X - \bar{X})$$

where X' = the estimated true score, (r) = the test's validity coefficient, X = the actual (observed) test score, and $\bar{X}$ = the test's mean. By way of illustration, let us consider a child who receives a score of 80 on a test with a reported reliability of .90 and a mean of 100. Substituting these values, we obtain an estimated true score of 82 (82 = 100 + [.90] [80] − 100). In this case, the estimated true score—what the child should obtain under ideal conditions—is two points greater than the observed score.

Establishing a Confidence Interval about Estimated True Score

Although estimating a true score may be more accurate than accepting an observed score the result remains only an estimate: we can never be sure of the precise true score. Since accuracy is vital for many decisions and since we cannot be certain about the value of true score, it is often advisable to establish a *confidence interval* about the estimated true score. That is, using the skills we now have, we may specify a *range of scores* within which the true score will lie a prespecified percent of the time.

In order to establish the confidence interval, first recall that

Chebyshev's theorum allows us to know the proportion of observations that fall within specified areas of the normal curve. That is, we note that 68.26 percent of all observations fall within +1 *SD*, 95.44 percent fall within +2.00 *SD*, and 99.52 percent fall within +3.00 *SD*. We may use this knowledge to establish a confidence interval that will contain true score at the desired level of probability. To accomplish this, one need only do the following: (1) obtain an estimate of true score, (2) multiply the *Sem* by the appropriate probability level (e.g., 1.96 = 95 percent), (3) add the value of step two to step one, and (4) subtract the value of step two from step one. The values of steps three and four define the upper and lower limits of a range of scores within which true score must fall at the probability assigned. Let us consider an example.

Previously, we found an estimated true score to be 82. We will assume that the standard error of measurement of this test is three and that we wish to be 95 percent "sure" of capturing true score. Accordingly, we would multiply 1.96 (a *Z* score of +1.96 = 95 percent of the normal distribution) times 3.0 (5.88) and add and subtract the product from the true score (87.88 and 72.12). In this case, the child's true score would lie between 72.12 and 87.88 95 percent of the time. A similar procedure could be calculated for 99 percent or any other desired level of accuracy.

It is interesting to note that the use of this procedure forces us to make allowance for the relative accuracy of our measuring devices. The reader who demands the use of this procedure—and the procedure should almost always be used—will quickly come to appreciate the limitations of existing psychoeducational measures. He or she will also soon appreciate the differing accuracy of specific tests common to special education and the many difficulties inherent in some procedures (e.g., diagnostic-prescriptive teaching—see Ysseldyke, 1973; Ysseldyke and Salvia, 1974). In summary, it is fair to suggest that many inaccurate program and placement decisions can be avoided by the teacher's careful consideration of the amount of error present in any educational measure.

GUIDELINES FOR THE PRACTITIONER

As has been stated previously, flaws in procedure that adversely affect test data can almost always be traced to one of two factors: (1) a poorly developed test, or (2) a poorly administered test.

The first concern is largely that of the test constructor and is very much aligned to concerns of validity and reliability. There is little that the test user can do except select good tests and avoid improperly developed ones. That, of course, is really quite a lot; tests that are not used are soon discontinued from the market place.

The second concern is a direct result of the examiner's skills and subsequent test administration behaviors. Here the examiner has nearly total influence because few, if any, regulating agencies evaluate an examiner's skill on a regular basis. The caution here is simply be certain you know how to properly administer and score the test.

Both of the concerns are interlocking and essential, attention to only one will likely produce inaccurate results. So, in concluding this chapter, two very fundamental issues will be addressed: (1) What can the examiner do to be assured that his or her personal responsibilities are met?, and (2) What are some appropriate psychometric guidelines by which a test can be judged for its adequacy?

Looking at the Examiner's Test Administration Behavior

Most persons would probably agree that a test should be relatively simple to administer, score, and interpret if it is to be useful. Indeed, exceedingly complex tests are usually administered by professionals with special training beyond that of most educators. Persons who are considering the administration of a particularly difficult test must always be certain that their skills are commensurate with the standardized demands of administration, scoring and interpretation.

Other concerns of the examiner are simple, but are often overlooked. For example, the examiner must assure the comfort of the examinee and the elimination of distractions, he or she must be certain that all materials are available and in readily usable condition, and the examiner must assure that no obvious procedures or circumstances that could invalidate the test appear. These responsibilities are part of a continuous self-monitoring procedure whereby the conscientious examiner systematically examines the details of administration. A good policy involves periodic observation of the examiner's test administration procedure by another professional. Otherwise, it is quite possible that faulty administration can continue unchecked through innumerable examinations. Adhering to even these simple rules could deter many inappropriate test results and educational decisions.

Looking at the Test

Standards for Educational and Psychological Tests (1974) provides a series of general considerations for evaluating a specific test. Among the more pertinent considerations are the following:

1. A manual must be provided that reports the essential aspects of the test and includes information to evaluate a test's claims.

2. A test's development should be fully explained, revision dates must be given.
3. Manuals should caution agaisnt frequent examiner errors.
4. The purposes and applications of the specific test must be given.
5. Examiner qualifications should be stated in the manual.
6. Directions for administration must be sufficiently detailed so as to allow for examination under standardized conditions.
7. Scoring directions must be of sufficient detail to reduce the possibility of scoring error to a minimum.
8. Normative data (sample characteristics, procedural characteristics, reliability and validity) must be clearly indicated.

Referring to validity, *Standards* (pp. 25–48) offers a number of suggestions. Included among these are the following:

1. The manual must report the validity for each purpose the test authors purport the test to be useful.
2. Validity must be differentiated as to its conceptual type. Blanket statements—"validity is" or "fair validity" are not useful since undifferentiated validity does not provide adequate informaiton for the test user.
3. Validity profiles must be reported for each subtest as well as the test taken as a whole.
4. Item-test correlations should not be presented as evidence of criterion related validity.
5. The population from which the sample was drawn must be specified and the means by which the sample was identified should also be provided. Sample size should be stated.
6. All measures of criteria (academic or nonacademic behaviors) must be described (criterion-related validity).
7. Measures of central tendency (mean, median, mode) and dispersion from the mean (range, standard deviations) must be given.
8. Data must be given that allows the user to determine the confidence that can be placed in an observed score.
9. Evidence of bias against subsamples (e.g., minority groups) should be reported.
10. Theoretical constructs (e.g., intelligence, perceptual motor integration) must be fully described (construct validity).

Referring to reliability, *Standards* (1974, pp. 48–55) emphasizes numerous points, the most salient of which are:

1. The test manual must report sufficient evidence to allow the user to judge the adequacy of the test for its stated purpose.
2. Examples of reliability and standard error of measurement should be

given in order to allow the user to judge the extent of the evidence supporting the test constructor's claims.
3. The reliability of a test, relative to the characteristics of its sample, must be given.
4. Specifying the characteristics of the sample is essential, e.g., by age, grade, geographical location, racial composition, income level, etc.
5. Conventional statistics should be used whenever possible. Unusual statistical procedures should be avoided or explained in sufficient detail to allow the examiner insight into the procedure.
6. Parallel forms must cite evidence of comparability.
7. The time between test-retest administration must be provided.
8. If a test manual suggests that a score represents a psychological or educational trait, evidence of internal consistency must be provided either by the split-half, the coefficient alpha or the KR-20 formula.
9. The consistency of the test's score should be reported across time.

These recommendations are essential in judging the validity and reliability of any test and will be useful to the special educator. While the absolute magnitude of correlation coefficients is difficult to specify, generally the specific type of validity and the most important measure(s) of reliability for any test ought to yield a coefficient of at least .85 with higher coefficients being even more desirable. Correlations significantly below .85 are of doubtful value in describing what is measured and how consistently this measurement is being accomplished.

A FINAL NOTE

Remember that a solidly-constructed, well-reported test is often judicious in inferring the data that can be drawn from the procedure. Excessive claims (e.g., testimonials) are often an indication that the measurement device is touted as being more than is statistically possible. The reader is encouraged to review the guidelines provided throughout this chapter, the entire contents of *Standards of Educational and Psychological Tests* (1974), and specific test reviews published elsewhere (Buros, 1968, 1972, 1974). These sources can provide a critical scale for weighing a specific test's educational merit.

SUMMARY

Throughout this chapter, an attempt has been made to synthesize and simplify a number of complex topics. The reader has been provided a brief discussion of basic statistical procedures, including sampling, descriptive statistics, and correlational procedures. Following this introduction, the reader was offered a review of concepts of validity and reliability and some essential procedures for evaluating a test score. Finally, some criteria for evaluating the merits of a specific test and some guidelines for examining one's own skills completed the chapter.

It should be noted that many, many volumes have been written on psychometric procedures and this chapter has reviewed only the most basic and common content. Far more complex presentations await the reader who wishes to pursue the topic and, for convenience, some of the better offerings are referenced in the *Suggested Readings* section. Despite this, the reader who thoroughly understands this chapter need not be alarmed. He or she likely possesses the psychometric knowledge to allow very effective use of test and measurement procedures. *Application is the key,* however, and it is hoped that the reader will truly reflect upon the chapter's contents as he or she develops educational plans for handicapped students.

REFERENCES

Ahmann, J. S. & Glock, M. D. *Evaluating pupil growth: Principles of tests and measurements.* (4th ed.) Boston: Allyn & Bacon, 1971.

Anastasi, A. *Psychological testing.* (4th ed.) New York: Macmillan, 1976.

Brown, F. G. *Principles of educational and psychological testing.* Hinsdale, Ill.: The Dryden Press, 1970.

Bruning, J. L. & Kintz, B. L. *Computational handbook of statistics.* Glenview, Ill.: Scott-Foresman, 1968.

Buros, O. K. (Ed.) *Reading test and reviews.* Highland Park, N.J.: Gryphon Press, 1968.

Buros, O. K. (Ed.) *Seventh mental measurements yearbook.* Highland Park, N.J.: Gryphon Press, 1972.

Buros, O. K. (Ed.) *Tests in print II.* Highland Park, N.J.: Gryphon Press, 1974.

Campbell, D. T. & Fiske, D. W. Convergent and discriminant validation by the multitrait-multimethod metrix. *Psychological Bulletin,* 1959, *56,* 81–105.

English, H. B. & English, A. C. *A comprehensive dictionary of psychological and psychoanalytical terms: A guide to usage.* New York: David McKay, 1968.

Ferguson, G. A. *Statistical analysis in psychology and education.* (3rd ed.) New York: McGraw-Hill, 1971.

Freund, J. E. *Modern elementary statistics.* (3rd ed.) Englewood Cliffs, N.J.: Prentice-Hall, 1967.

Hays, W. L. *Statistics.* New York: Holt, Rinehart & Winston, 1963.

Nunnally, J. *Psychometric theory.* New York: McGraw-Hill, 1967.

Salvia, J. & Ysseldyke, J. E. *Assessment in special and remedial education.* Boston: Houghton-Mifflin, 1978.

Siegel, S. *Nonparametric statistics: For the behavioral sciences.* New York: McGraw-Hill, 1956.

Spence, J. T., Underwood, B. J., Duncan, C. P., & Cotton, J. W. *Elementary statistics.* (2nd ed.) New York: Appleton, 1968.

Standards for educational and psychological tests. Washington, D.C.: The American Psychological Association, 1974.

Wechsler, D. *Manual for the Wechsler Intelligence Scale for Children—Revised.* New York: Psychological Corporation, 1974.

Ysseldyke, J. E. Diagnostic-prescriptive teaching: The search for aptitude-treatment interactions. In L. Mann & D. A. Sabatino (Eds.), *The first review of special education.* Philadelphia: JSE Press, 1973.

Ysseldyke, J. E. & Salvia, J. Diagnostic-prescriptive teaching: Two models. *Exceptional Children,* 1974, *41,* 181–185.

SUGGESTED READINGS

The reader is advised that the following suggested readings cover the topics of this chapter in some detail. In order to provide materials sufficiently comprehensive to meet the requirements of most students, the selected readings vary in complexity and, therefore, exhibit considerable overlap. It should *not* be necessary for an individual to read all the listed references, rather the reader can select sources that match his or her technical sophistication and task requirements. Readings preceded by an asterisk (*) are considered to be particularly useful for the reader who has had little previous experience with measurement.

General Readings

*Bruning, J. L. & Kintz, B. L. *Computational handbook of statistics.* Glenview, Ill.: Scott-Foresman, 1968.

Ferguson, G. A. *Statistical analysis in psychology and education.* (3rd ed.) New York: McGraw-Hill, 1971.

Kerlinger, F. N. *Foundations of behavioral research: Educational and psychological inquiry.* New York: Holt, Rinehart & Winston, 1964.

Standards for educational and psychological tests. Washington, D.C.: The American Psychological Association, 1974.

Readings Concerning Norm-Referenced Tests.

Anastasi, A. *Psychological testing.* (4th ed.) New York: Macmillan, 1976.

*Becker, W. C. & Englemann, S. *Teaching 3: Evaluation of instruction.* Chicago, Ill.: Science Research Associates, 1976.

Brown, F. G. *Principles of educational and psychological testing.* Hinsdale, Ill.: The Dryden Press, 1970.

Cronbach, L. J. *Essentials of psychological testing.* (3rd ed.) New York: Harper & Row, 1970.

Gearheart, B. R. & Willenberg, E. P. *Application of pupil assessment information: For the special education teacher.* Denver: Love Publishing, 1974.

*Noll, V. H. & Scannel, D. P. *Introduction to educational measurement.* (3rd ed.) Boston: Houghton-Mifflin, 1972.

*Salvia, J. & Ysseldyke, J. E. *Assessment in special and remedial education.* Boston: Houghton-Mifflin, 1978.

Readings Concerning Criterion Referenced Tests.

Gronlund, N. E. *Preparing criterion-referenced tests for classroom instruction.* New York: Macmillan, 1973.

Pophan, W. J. (Ed.) *Criterion referenced measurement: An introduction.* Englewood Cliffs, N.J.: Educational Technology Publications, 1971.

Readings Concerning Teacher-made Tests.

Gronlund, N. E. *Measurement and evaluation in teaching.* New York: Macmillan, 1965.

Gronlund, N. E. *Constructing achievement tests.* Englewood Cliffs, N.J.: Prentice-Hall, 1968.

Kryspin, W. J. & Feldhusen, J. F. *Developing classroom tests: A guide for writing and evaluating test items.* Minneapolis: Burgess Publishers, 1974.

Alan C. Repp

4 Describing and Monitoring Behavior

Behavior analysis is a system for studying human behavior that has grown from the laboratory and philosophical writings of B. F. Skinner and his associates (e.g., Ferster & Skinner, 1957; Skinner, 1938, 1948, 1953, 1959, 1968, 1969, 1971, 1974). Central to the laboratory work was an insistence on numerical descriptions of behavior that would allow one to predict with some degree of success what would happen next; and central to the applied work in this field is a similar insistence that will allow the teacher, the therapist, the social worker, etc., to predict how well their clients will function in various environments. The purpose of this chapter is to discuss some of these numerical descriptions as they are presently being used in education.

Although thousands of different kinds of behaviors are the bases of our educational programs, each of those can generally be described as being in one of two classes: (1) behavior that is free to occur within the educational setting, or (2) behavior that occurs within discrete trials. The former includes behaviors like "talking out," something one can do anytime within the classroom period. The latter includes behaviors like "two," said by a student after the teacher says, "Jack, what is one plus one?" At first, the distinction may seem arbitrary, for surely the student could say "two" at any time during the class. The point, however, is that when a child frequently says "two" throughout the day, not in response to appropriate antecedent events, the behavior is classified in the first category and is said to be a free operant.

Consider the situation in which a teacher works with a student for 10 minutes, presents flashcards with numbers on them, and asks the student to write in cursive the numbers being presented. This behavior falls into the *discrete trial* category. The child's writing behavior does not depend just on behaviors of the child; it also depends on the behavior of the teacher. If the teacher stops to talk with another child for a minute, then the student cannot respond for that period because the teacher has not presented the next trial. Now consider the situation in which the teacher allows the child 10 minutes to work by himself, gives him 100 cards with numbers on them, and asks him to write in cursive as many of the numbers on the cards as he can within the 10 minutes. This behavior falls into the *free operant* category. The child's individual responses do not depend on the teacher's continued presentations; rather, he is free to respond as rapidly as he can present cards to himself and write answers.

The importance of the distinction between free operant behavior and behavior that occurs only as a result of a trial is that there are fewer restrictions on the way the former should be measured than there are on the latter.

DEFINING BEHAVIOR

Both types of behaviors share the same type of definitional criteria that are quite similar to those put forth by Mager (1975) in his discussion of instructional objectives. A behavioral definition should: (1) describe the behavior in objective terms; (2) include the conditions under which it will be recorded; (3) be complete, providing appropriate information on what should and should not be included; and (4) describe the behavior so that it can be measured. An example of a definition meeting these conditions would be:

> Verbal Initiation: verbalization, in the classroom during study period, by a student to another student or to the teacher after at least 30 seconds of noninteraction between the child and others. The response is scored as an initiation regardless of whether the person to whom the initiation is directed responds. Exclude: laughing, crying, talking to oneself, singing or making any other musical sounds, making imitative animal, automobile sounds, etc. To measure the behaviors, one would count one verbal initiation as a response that occurs after a period of at least 30 seconds of no responding, regardless of the length (e.g., 15 seconds or 45 seconds; 5 words or 100 words).

Consider the definition for a moment to determine whether it meets the four criteria for a behavior definition. Is the behavior described in objective terms? Yes, it describes behavior that is observable and is not subjective. One does not need to "guess" whether the response occurred; one can easily measure whether it has occurred. Are the conditions under which the behavior should be counted clearly specified? Yes, one should record responding during study period in the classroom. Responding should not be recorded during free time, or an arithmetic period, or a physical education period. Does the definition indicate whether certain related behaviors should be excluded? Yes, one should not record laughing, crying, talking to oneself, singing, making musical sounds, or making certain imitative sounds. These exclusions remove some ambiguity from the definition and should promote consistency of recording throughout the period that the behavior is under study. Does the behavioral definition allow measurement?—Yes, the definition instructs one to measure behavioral occurrences by counting the number of responses meeting the definition.

Now consider the following definition:

Spontaneous Verbalization: verbalization that is not elicited by a teacher's question, command, or instruction, and that is not part of an ongoing teaching situation (e.g., reading aloud).

Are the conditions under which the behavior should be recorded specified? Not explicitly; we can only presume that the behavior should be recorded throughout the day whenever the student is in any classroom. Is the behavior described in objective terms? Yes, the behavior is defined in a manner that does not force one to guess whether the behavior occurred. Does the definition specify whether any related behaviors that should be excluded? No, although there are no exclusions. Is the behavior measurable? Yes, although the rules by which it will be measured have not been specified.

MEASURING BEHAVIOR

Principal Methods of Data Collection

Behavioral measurement is, above all else, numerical. Once one describes what behavior to measure and how to define that behavior, one needs to decide how to measure it. Within the field of applied behavior analysis, there are four major methods of collecting data that involve the measurement of behavior. These four are frequency recording, interval recording, duration recording, and time sampling. To these, a fifth (task sampling) will be added, and, for each, this section will provide: (1) a definition, (2) examples, and (3) suggestions for appropriate use.

FREQUENCY RECORDING*

In this procedure, one merely writes the times at which the observation period begins and ends, and then counts the number of items the behavior occurs during that period. Such a procedure could be used to determine how many times a self-abusive child hits himself on his head with his hand, or how many questions a child asks in her arithmetic class, or how many times a teacher praises her students' correct responding during each class period of the day.

While frequency recording can be used for any behavior, there are some precautions: (1) One must ensure that the recording period is noted, for data cannot be compared on a day-to-day basis if recording occurs for a different and unnoted time base from day to day. For example, if we found that a child hit himself 50, 42, 40, 18, and 12 times, we might say the behavior is improving. But, given the additional information that the recording periods were 120, 120, 60, 30, and 20 minutes, we would certainly not believe that the behavior improved. (2) One must ensure that if the behavior is within the discrete trial paradigm there are notations of both the numbers of correct and incorrect responses, of the length of the teaching period, and of the total number of trials. The first notation allows one to determine the ratio of correct responses to possible correct responses. The second allows one to determine whether this ratio changes when the length of time to respond changes; it also allows a uniform expression of that ratio (per time) when the period does change (e.g., 75 percent correct per minute). The third notation allows one to check the data by determining whether the sum of the correct and incorrect responses equals the total number of trials. (3) One must determine whether the responses are relatively uniform in length and other relevant characteristics. For example, if one counted 3, 4, 3, 2, and 4 occurrences of "out-of-seat" behavior in a spelling class, one might correctly presume the behavior was occurring at a stable frequency. However, if the behaviors occurred for a sum total of 3, 8, 5, 20, and 30 minutes in the spelling class, then one's assumption that the frequency report was a complete description of what was occurring in the classroom would be incorrect. In this case, one would need more information than that provided just by frequency recording. (4) One must mark on the recording sheet periods of time during which responding occurred. For example, if one counted the frequency of responding for 6 hours of school each day and reported that 50, 62, 81, 37, and 68 responses occurred each day of this week, one would not have so much information as if one simply divided the session into a number of recording subperiods (e.g., 12 subperiods of 30 minutes each). Doing this,

*Frequency recording is often termed event sampling, but the former term will be used as it better describes what one does when collecting data by this procedure.

Time	Responses	Number	Total
0-30 minutes	𝍸 𝍸 𝍸 𝍸 𝍸 𝍸 𝍸 /	36	36
30-60	𝍸 𝍸	10	46
60-90	/	1	47
90-120		0	47
120-150		0	47
150-180		0	47
180-210	//	2	49
210-240	/	1	50
240-280		0	50
280-320		0	50
320-360		0	50

Fig. 4-1. The number of responses per 30 minutes as collected by frequency recording.

it is possible that 36, 52, 79, 20, and 48 of the responses occurred the first 60 minutes of each day. A portion of the recording sheet for day one could be like that shown in Figure 4-1 in which the session is divided into a number of subperiods and the recorder marks the number of occurrences of responding.

INTERVAL RECORDING

In this procedure, a session is divided into a number of intervals, the observer is cued by a timing device at the end of each interval, and then marks the presence or absence of a response in the preceeding interval. At the end of the session, the number of intervals with responding are divided by the total number of intervals to provide a ratio of the total intervals in which responding occurred. Although there can be variations of the basic procedure, most are trivial (e.g., Powell, Martindale, & Kulp,

1975) and the basic method of recording simply whether or not responding occurs in an interval, regardless of the length of its occurrence, prevails. Figure 4-2 is an example of interval recording and indicates the correct recording behavior of the data collector. Let the upper line represent responding during 60 seconds, and let the lower pair represent the data collector's form. In the first 60 seconds, two responses occurred, with the first occurring during both the 0 to 10 second and the 10 to 20 second intervals and with the second occurring during the 30 to 40 seconds interval. The data recorder indicated that responding occurred during the first, second, and fourth intervals, and that no responding occurred during the third, fifth, and sixth intervals. In the second 60 seconds, no responses occurred in the 0 to 10 second interval, four responses began in the second interval, one continued throughout the second and ended in the fourth, three occurred in the fifth, and none occurred in the sixth. For this minute, although there was a total of seven responses, the data sheet indicates that responding occurred during four of the six intervals.

Unlike frequency recording, interval recording can be appropriate both for behaviors with a consistent length of responding and for behaviors with an inconsistent length of responding. For example, one could measure out-of-seat behavior that occurred for varying lengths of time and still obtain valid assessments of responding in the classroom if one used interval recording. The major problem with interval recording actually concerns behavior that occurs for consistently short intervals, and the relationship of interval size to the rate of responding is crucial. For example, an examination of data gathered through interval recording with responding at a high rate (10 per minute), of a short duration (less than a second), and described through 10 second periods of recording, showed that interval recording grossly underestimates responding by failing to provide information on 60 percent of the responses (Repp, Roberts, Slack, Repp, & Berkler, 1976). This loss of information occurs simply because many responses occur within a single recording interval, and scoring these intervals as ones with responding suggests that there was only one occurrence in each of these intervals. The second and the eleventh scoring intervals in Figure 4-2 are examples of this problem, with four and three responses occurring in each, respectively. While the issue is complicated when examined technically, a practical resolution is simple. Before one begins using interval recording, the behavior should be sampled in order to determine the shortest interval *between* responses that occurs more than a few times per hour. With this information, an interval can be selected that is small enough to prevent the occurrence of more than a few intervals with more than one response. For example, if we observed 100 occurrences of a behavior, noted the time *between* each response, arranged those inter-response times in ascending order, and

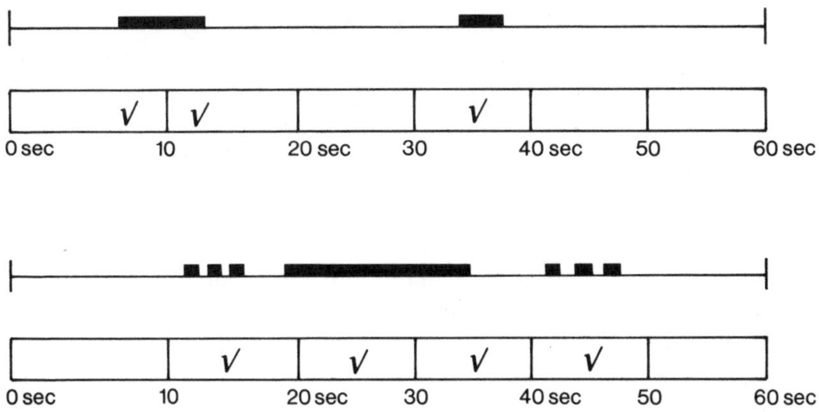

10-second Intervals = 12

Response Intervals = 7

No Response Intervals = 5

$R/(R+N) = \frac{7}{(7+5)} = .58$

▬ = Response

Fig. 4-2. The number of 10-second intervals in which responding occurred, as collected by interval recording.

found those times to be 7, 8, 11, 12, 12, 12, 15, 16 . . . 310 seconds, we could choose 10 seconds as a recording interval and predict from this sample that only 2 of the 98 intervals with responding actually contained more than one reponse. The loss of information* would be small, and 10 seconds would be an appropriate and convenient size for the recording interval.

DURATION RECORDING

In interval recording, one is actually making an (admittedly) inaccurate estimate of the percent of the total time in which responding occurred—the ratio of intervals to which responding occurred/total

---

*To provide an index of the information lost, one can (1) count the number of intervals in which *at least* one response occurred and represent this number by x, (2) count the number of intervals in which *only* one response occurred and represent this number by y, and (3) determine an index of information lost (l) by the formula $l = (x-y)/x$. In our example, two intervals contained two responses, and 96 intervals contained only one response, so the index of information lost would be $l = (98-96)/98$ or .02. This figure means that we did not account for two percent of the number of responses that occurred, an error that seems reasonable to accept.

number of intervals is that estimate. To be more precise, one could simply count the number of seconds in each episode of responding, sum this count over the session, and divide the cumulative time responding by the total observation period. This ratio is a more precise estimate of the percent of the total time in which recording occurred than the ratio provided by interval recording. The preference shown for the latter usually results from its being easier to use when recording a number of responses. For example, to record six behaviors by interval recording, one would only need a single timing device to signal the end of each interval, and a recording sheet with six areas corresponding to the six behaviors. To gather data on the same six behaviors through duration recording, one would need six timing devices and operate each relative to its related behavior. While relating each device to a single behavior is simple after a few minutes practice, purchasing six timing devices is often not so simple.

In duration recording, the observer should simply note the starting and ending time of each recording session and then note the duration of each response. Figure 4-3 is an example of a portion of such a recording sheet. In order to record data, the duration in seconds of each response is timed by using a stopwatch. In this example, recording began at 9:04 and ended at 9:51, and 5 responses were recorded (with the duration of the first 38 seconds, the duration of the second 46 seconds, etc.). The total duration of the 5 responses was 816 seconds, while the total duration of the recording period was 2820 seconds, so the ratio of time responding to total time was .29 (from $\frac{816}{2820}$).

Duration recording is really appropriate for gathering information on any type of ongoing responding, but of course seems burdensome for responses that are of short duration (e.g., a few seconds), and, in this case, should be rejected in favor of frequency recording. Its value is in providing accurate information on responding that varies in duration or that occurs for some appreciable duration which is inaccurately represented by frequency recording (e.g., 3 episodes of self-injurious behavior that occur for 312, 810, and 760 seconds) or by interval recording. In situations where information is needed on both the duration and the rate of responding, one could, of course, record both the duration and the occurrence of each response.

TIME SAMPLING

In time sampling, the observer *ignores* the behavior for a relatively long period (e.g., 20 minutes), and then, after a signal, quickly scans the situation and records the behavior(s) observed. For example, recording self-injurious behavior on a 10-minute time sample would not be done by observing for 10 minutes and then for one second, then record whether or not the behavior was occurring, and then repeat the ignore-observe-

Date 9/7/77 Observer 1 P.M. Activity free time
Subject D.J. Observer 2 R.C. Response rocking

Recording began 9:04
Recording ended 9:51

Response Duration in Seconds

Began	Duration	Cumulative Time
9:10	38	38
9:16	46	84
9:17	612	696
9:40	108	804
9:50	12	816

Total Responses 5
Total time responding 816
Total time recording 2820
% time responding .29

Fig. 4-3. The duration of reading responses as collected by duration recording.

record cycle again. At the end of the session, the number of observations are totaled, then the number of observations in which responding was recorded, and the former is divided into the latter to provide a ratio of responding to the opportunities for responding to be recorded. As shown in Figure 4-4, the observer looked at the subject at 9:10, 9:20, 9:30, 9:40, and 9:50 and found that on three of those occasions, the subject was not in her seat and did not have permission to be out of her seat. The total observations are summed, the total number of observations in which responding occurred is summed, and the former is divided into the latter to provide a ratio of responding to possible responding during recording.

Time sampling has some distinct advantages and some distinct disadvantages for describing ongoing responding. The advantages are: (1) for a teaching environment like a classroom, it is by far the easiest method for the instructor to use because it requires only a few seconds of observing and recording time, unlike the other methods which require continuous observation by the teacher which, of course, can interfere with teaching;

Date 6/1/78 Observer 1 T.M. Activity spelling
Subject T.R. Observer 2 S.U. Response out-of-seat
Time-sample ____________

Time	Response		Time	Response	
	Yes	No		Yes	No
9:10	✓				
9:20		✓			
9:30	✓				
9:40	✓				
9:50		✓			

Responding Observations 3
Total Observations 5
% Responding 60

Fig. 4-4. The occurrences of out-of-seat behavior as collected through 10-minute time samples.

(2) being the easiest, it is much more likely to be maintained in a program for behavioral change when a single person must be the data collector and the teacher; and (3) it can be flexible in terms of recording time. Although the example in Figure 4-4 described a constant interval (10 minutes) between observation intervals, such constancy is not necessary. Observation could be on a variable pattern such as every 10, 15, 30, 15, and 10 minutes, or 10 minutes after class begins, the middle of the class period, and 10 minutes before class ends. The important consideration is that the observation periods be predetermined and not left to "whenever I remember." The latter alternative provides very biased descriptions of behavior as the occurrence of behavior will usually serve as a cue to record it. While such a cueing property is necessary for frequency recording, it is totally inappropriate for time sampling and violates the datum provided by this procedure (i.e., the percent of observations in which responding occurred).

The major disadvantage of time sampling is that the data it produces to describe behavioral occurrences are greatly affected by the frequency of behavior and by the duration of responding. Quite simply, the more frequently responding occurs, the longer its duration of responding, and the more frequent the time sample, the more accurately time sampling will describe what is continuously occurring in the environment (Repp, Roberts, Slack, Repp, & Berkler, 1976).

TASK SAMPLING

Much of the current work with seriously handicapped populations (e.g., profoundly or severely retarded persons) involves breaking a task into its subcomponents or steps, and teaching these subcomponents in a forward or backward order (usually termed shaping or backward chaining, respectively). To assess the effectiveness of the teaching program and of the task analysis, most programmers record the frequency of correct and incorrect responses of each step of the task analysis. Data are often then cast as the number of sessions to criterion for each step, with an ensuing comparison across all steps of the program. This procedure is followed to determine whether each step of the task requires roughly the same number of responses to reach criterion.

While this method of recording is in actuality frequency recording, the data are treated differently as the response is not usually a free operant, but rather is in the discrete trial paradigm where the instructor signals the student to begin the response necessary to complete that step. An example of this approach is given by Horner (1971) who sought to teach a mentally retarded child with spina bifida to use crutches. The task was divided into two major components: use of parallel bars and use of crutches—with each of these divided into 6 and 10 subcomponents, respectively. The child was given 25 trials per session and was moved from one step to the next after 23 or more successful trials for 3 consecutive sessions. Horner recorded both the number of successful trials per session and the number of sessions per step for each subcomponent of the task. Results showed that, for teaching use of parallel bars, 5 sessions were necessary to reach criterion for the first step, 5 for the second, 6 for the third, 3 for the fourth, and 10 for the fifth, and 23 for the sixth. Such data can be very valuable as it describes difficulties with the child's behavior and/or with the task analysis for the last two steps. With this information, one can determine variables affecting the success of the program (e.g., steps five and six might have been too complicated and should have been broken into a number of simpler components).

Collecting Data on More Than One Behavior at a Time

Although examples given in the preceeding section were for recording only one behavior at a time, with the exception of task sampling, each is commonly used to record more than one behavior at a time. For frequency recording, duration recording, and time sampling, the major problem is coordinating the observer's recording behaviors so that they accurately represent what occurred in the environment. To assist in this task,

Page ______ Activity (a) ______ O1 ______ Interval ______
Day ______ (b) ______ O2 ______ Started ______
Date ______ (c) ______ IOA ______ Ended ______
Session ______ Location ______ Staff ______ Staff ______

Int. ______

Subject 0	0	1	2	3	4	5	6	7	8	9
	Instructions	Verbal App.	Vrbl. Disapp.	Guidance	Nonvrbl App.	No. Intracton	Conversation	Materls. Prep.	Recording	Spl. Procedure
TS #1 ( )										
1.0		0	0	0	0	0	0	0	0	0
2.0		0	0	0	0	0	0	0	0	0
3.0		0	0	0	0	0	0	0	0	0
4.0		0	0	0	0	0	0	0	0	0
5.0		0	0	0	0	0	0	0	0	0
6.0		0	0	0	0	0	0	0	0	0
7.0		0	0	0	0	0	0	0	0	0
8.0		0	0	0	0	0	0	0	0	0
9.0		0	0	0	0	0	0	0	0	0
10.0		0	0	0	0	0	0	0	0	0
	I	V A	V D	G	N A	N I	C	M	R	Sp
TS #2 ( )										
11.0		0	0	0	0	0	0	0	0	0
12.0		0	0	0	0	0	0	0	0	0

Int. ______

Subject 0	0	1	2	3	4	5	6	7	8	9
	Instructions	Verbal App.	Vrbl. Disapp.	Guidance	Nonvrbl App.	No. Intracton	Conversation	Materls. Prep.	Recording	Spl. Procedure
TS #1 ( )										
1.0		0	0	0	0	0	0	0	0	0
2.0		0	0	0	0	0	0	0	0	0
3.0		0	0	0	0	0	0	0	0	0
4.0		0	0	0	0	0	0	0	0	0
5.0		0	0	0	0	0	0	0	0	0
6.0		0	0	0	0	0	0	0	0	0
7.0		0	0	0	0	0	0	0	0	0
8.0		0	0	0	0	0	0	0	0	0
9.0		0	0	0	0	0	0	0	0	0
10.0		0	0	0	0	0	0	0	0	0
	I	V A	V D	G	N A	N I	C	M	R	Sp
TS #2 ( )										
11.0		0	0	0	0	0	0	0	0	0
12.0		0	0	0	0	0	0	0	0	0

Int. ______

Subject 0	0	1	2	3	4	5	6	7	8	9
	Instructions	Verbal App.	Vrbl. Disapp.	Guidance	Nonvrbl App.	No. Intracton	Conversation	Materls. Prep.	Recording	Spl. Procedure
TS #1 ( )										
1.0		0	0	0	0	0	0	0	0	0
2.0		0	0	0	0	0	0	0	0	0
3.0		0	0	0	0	0	0	0	0	0
4.0		0	0	0	0	0	0	0	0	0
5.0		0	0	0	0	0	0	0	0	0
6.0		0	0	0	0	0	0	0	0	0
7.0		0	0	0	0	0	0	0	0	0
8.0		0	0	0	0	0	0	0	0	0
9.0		0	0	0	0	0	0	0	0	0
10.0		0	0	0	0	0	0	0	0	0
	I	V A	V D	G	N A	N I	C	M	R	Sp
TS #2 ( )										
11.0		0	0	0	0	0	0	0	0	0
12.0		0	0	0	0	0	0	0	0	0

I	V A	V D	G	N A	N I	C	M	R	Sp
13.0	0	0	0	0	0	0	0	0	0
14.0	0	0	0	0	0	0	0	0	0
15.0	0	0	0	0	0	0	0	0	0
16.0	0	0	0	0	0	0	0	0	0
17.0	0	0	0	0	0	0	0	0	0
18.0	0	0	0	0	0	0	0	0	0
19.0	0	0	0	0	0	0	0	0	0
20.0	0	0	0	0	0	0	0	0	0
TS #3 ( )									
21.0	0	0	0	0	0	0	0	0	0
22.0	0	0	0	0	0	0	0	0	0
23.0	0	0	0	0	0	0	0	0	0
24.0	0	0	0	0	0	0	0	0	0
25.0	0	0	0	0	0	0	0	0	0
26.0	0	0	0	0	0	0	0	0	0
27.0	0	0	0	0	0	0	0	0	0
28.0	0	0	0	0	0	0	0	0	0
29.0	0	0	0	0	0	0	0	0	0
30.0	0	0	0	0	0	0	0	0	0

ΣR = __________

ΣI = __________

% = __________

I	V A	V D	G	N A	N I	C	M	R	Sp
13.0	0	0	0	0	0	0	0	0	0
14.0	0	0	0	0	0	0	0	0	0
15.0	0	0	0	0	0	0	0	0	0
16.0	0	0	0	0	0	0	0	0	0
17.0	0	0	0	0	0	0	0	0	0
18.0	0	0	0	0	0	0	0	0	0
19.0	0	0	0	0	0	0	0	0	0
20.0	0	0	0	0	0	0	0	0	0
TS #3 ( )									
21.0	0	0	0	0	0	0	0	0	0
22.0	0	0	0	0	0	0	0	0	0
23.0	0	0	0	0	0	0	0	0	0
24.0	0	0	0	0	0	0	0	0	0
25.0	0	0	0	0	0	0	0	0	0
26.0	0	0	0	0	0	0	0	0	0
27.0	0	0	0	0	0	0	0	0	0
28.0	0	0	0	0	0	0	0	0	0
29.0	0	0	0	0	0	0	0	0	0
30.0	0	0	0	0	0	0	0	0	0

ΣR = __________

ΣI = __________

% = __________

I	V A	V D	G	N A	N I	C	M	R	Sp
13.0	0	0	0	0	0	0	0	0	0
14.0	0	0	0	0	0	0	0	0	0
15.0	0	0	0	0	0	0	0	0	0
16.0	0	0	0	0	0	0	0	0	0
17.0	0	0	0	0	0	0	0	0	0
18.0	0	0	0	0	0	0	0	0	0
19.0	0	0	0	0	0	0	0	0	0
20.0	0	0	0	0	0	0	0	0	0
TS #3 ( )									
21.0	0	0	0	0	0	0	0	0	0
22.0	0	0	0	0	0	0	0	0	0
23.0	0	0	0	0	0	0	0	0	0
24.0	0	0	0	0	0	0	0	0	0
25.0	0	0	0	0	0	0	0	0	0
26.0	0	0	0	0	0	0	0	0	0
27.0	0	0	0	0	0	0	0	0	0
28.0	0	0	0	0	0	0	0	0	0
29.0	0	0	0	0	0	0	0	0	0
30.0	0	0	0	0	0	0	0	0	0

ΣR = __________

ΣI = __________

% = __________

Fig. 4-5 (top and bottom). A form for recording by the time-sampling procedure in which, at each instance of observation, the observer records which of the 10 behaviors the subject was exhibiting.

one usually makes recording sheets similar to those for single behaviors except that there are a number of columns per recording sheet, with this number equal to a multiple of the number of behaviors recorded (e.g., two pairs of columns for recording two behaviors; one set of four columns for recording four behaviors).

In interval recording, the problem, although still simple, is slightly more complex. As such, an example for collecting data on twelve responses through interval recording will be used. There are several steps to this procedure, and these are: (1) defining the behaviors, (2) designing behavior codes or abbreviations that will fit conveniently on the recording sheet, (3) deciding on the identifying information to be included, (4) deciding rules for recording, and (5) deciding on an interval size. Figure 4-5 presents a sample form that has been in use for recording a variety of behaviors in a wide variety of situations. The identifying information includes (1) the day, date, and session; (2) the times at which the observation period began and ended; (3) the activity in which the subjects were engaged while being observed; (4) the location of the observation; (5) the session number; (6) the name of the primary observer; (7) the name of the secondary observer whose data are used to compute interobserver agreement scores; (8) the size of the observation interval; (9) the page number of this sheet for the day's recording; and (10) the staff present.

The next set of information includes the recording interval size (Int), which in this example was 6 seconds, and the identification numbers (ID#) of the persons being observed, which in this case are 36, 21, and 87. Following this set, there are 9 sections for data, formed by 3 major columns and 3 major rows. Within each of the 3 major columns are 10 minor columns into which one enters the responses being recorded. In this example, 9 responses are being recorded and these include staff: giving "instructions," providing "verbal approval," providing "verbal disapproval," etc. While these statements are abbreviated and coded in each major column, they are expanded on an accompanying sheet of definitions that the observers must memorize and provide some functional definition of knowledge through interobserver agreement scores meeting a prestated criterion (explained in next section).

Within each of the 3 major columns are also 30 rows, each corresponding to one interval of observation, providing in this example 180 seconds of observation time for each subject for each page used. Because the manner in which one distributes observations across subjects within a session can affect the data (Deitz, Roberts, & Slack, 1976; Thompson, Holmberg, & Baer, 1974), one should go across columns and complete each row across 3 subjects before returning to the next row and to the first subject.

A second type of data can also be recorded on the form and may provide interesting information. We know that some persons may drastically change their behavior when they know they are being observed (Deitz, Roberts, & Slack, 1976), and even though most researchers ignore this issue, some assessment of this problem can be made. In this plan, the initial observation is made by a time-sampling procedure in which the observer records what was occurring the moment he entered the area in which recording is to occur. The behavior(s) that was occurring is entered into the TS#1 section and this procedure is repeated after every 10 observations with interval recording. The information from these two time samples is entered into TS#2 and TS#3. Because both time sampling and interval recording use the same datum, i.e., the percent of observations in which responding occurred, two comparisons can be made. The first is a comparison of TS#1 with the other time-sampling data in this session. When many observation sessions occur, perhaps 50 or 100, enough data are available to determine whether the subject's behavior changes from the moment the observer enters (perhaps initially unnoticed) the recording area. The second comparison is of all the TS data with all the interval data to provide a statement of the validity of the time-sampling data (since the interval data are produced by continuous recording, the TS data are samples of it, and some such assessment needs to be made).

The length of time to make the calculations is obviously a function of the amount of data recorded, but in this example which has 900 bits of data per page, less than one minute is required for the calculations on each page. When a computer is available, the form can be read by an optical scanner, and the time required is obviously very small. When scoring "by hand," one merely counts the number of slashes in each of the columns and enters in the bottom row the fraction of intervals of observations in which responding occurred. These are then summed across the pages to provide a total for each day.

Inter-observer Agreement

Although applied behavior analysis has transferred to applied settings many of the principles and procedures that were developed in the laboratories of experimental psychologists, it has not transferred the use of the sophisticated and reliable instruments that have been developed in laboratories for recording those behaviors. As a result, behaviorists have, of course, used human beings to measure the behavior of other human beings. Many problems occur with this approach the most basic of which has been well summarized by Baer, Wolf, and Risley (1968, p. 93):

A useful tactic in evaluating . . . a study is to ask not merely, was *behavior* changed? but also *whose* behavior? Ordinarily, it would be assumed that it was the subject's behavior which was altered; yet careful reflection may suggest that this was not necessarily the case. If humans are observing and recording the behavior under study, then any change may represent a change only in *their observing and recording responses, rather than in the subject's behavior* (italics added). Explicit measurement of the reliability of human observers thus becomes not merely good technique, but a prime criterion of whether the study was appropriately behavioral.

To address the problem of whose behavior indeed has changed—the subject's or just the observer's—behaviorists have become increasingly interested in factors affecting the extent to which two independent observers agree that responding has occurred. While some report this comparison as one of the product-moment correlations (see Chap. 3), most (Kelly, 1977) report it as a simple percentage score that describes the degree to which two independent observers agreed that responding occurred. While there are considerable problems in the observer's behaviors that can cause unreliable data (e.g., observer drift, observer reactivity—see Johnson & Bolstad, 1973; Kent, Kanowitz, O'Leary, & Cheiken, 1977; O'Leary, Kent, & Kanowitz, 1975; Romanczyk, Kent, Diament, & O'Leary, 1973), the present section will be concerned with how the data collection system should be designed to prevent errors of assessment that occur arithmetically and simply because of inappropriate collection design.

FREQUENCY RECORDING

Inter-observer agreement scores in frequency recording can be calculated in four ways. The first occurs when there is a permanent record of responding (e.g., written responses to arithmetic problems) and results in little ambiguity. In this procedure, two observers independently score each response or a sample of the responses, and the number of agreements on each response is multiplied by 100 and then divided by the sum of agreements and disagreements to provide the percentage of observer agreement. The second method involves ongoing responding in which observers count the occurrences of each behavior within the session. Inter-observer agreement is then calculated by dividing the larger number of responses counted into the smaller and multiplying by 100 to provide a percentage score. For example, if one observer recorded 112 responses in a session, and another observer recorded 106, the percentage score would be calculated according to the formula $(\frac{106}{112}) \times (100)$, or 95 percent. While this method, which has been labeled the *Whole Session* method (Repp, Deitz, Boles, Deitz, & Repp, 1976) is very popular, it has been criticized because there is no designation of the time at which the observers recorded responding, and high agreement scores could be produced even though the observers did not record behavior occurring at the same time. For example, Observer A could record 20 responses, all in the first half of the session, while Observer B could record 20 responses, all in the second half. Although the observers in this example clearly did not agree on when responding was occurring, the index of inter-observer agreement would be reported as 100 percent ($\frac{20}{20} \times 100$).

In an effort to lessen the probability that such errors could be occurring, some investigators have employed variations of the Whole Session method, one of which is called the *Response × Response* method (Repp, Deitz, & Roberts, 1976). An example of the method was provided by Van Houten & Sullivan (1975) who marked instances of teacher praise on recording sheets having a space provided for each second of each minute of the sessions. The number of responses was counted in each session, and the data were plotted as responses per minute, a very typical procedure. Their recording procedure, however, allowed for a very atypical assessment of observer agreement by defining agreement as responses marked by two observers, which did not differ by more than two seconds. Percentage of inter-observer agreement was calculated by multiplying 100 times the number of agreements and dividing by the sum of the agreements and disagreements. A similar attempt at reducing the probability of this type of error was made by Bailey & Meyerson (1970) and by Gladstone & Sherman (1975) whose observers recorded responding on event recorders and who defined agreement as an instance in which the two observers engaged the event recorder relays within *n* seconds (one second for the former study and five seconds for the latter), with this determination being made by inspection of the event recorder tapes.

There is a fourth method that is also a variation of the Whole Session method. It is called the *Partial Session* method (Repp, Deitz, & Roberts, 1976) and involves dividing a session into several large intervals, arranging fractions for each interval by the Whole Session method, and combining all numerators and all denominators for the entire session. For example, if a 60-minute session were divided into six 10-minute intervals, and data were recorded by two observers, as depicted in Figure 4-6, one would find the overall agreement score by summing the smaller numbers in each interval, by summing the larger numbers in each interval, and by dividing the former by the latter. For this example, the percent of inter-observer agreement would be 83, from ($\frac{14}{19} \times 100$). By contrast, the Whole Session score would have been 94 percent, from ($\frac{16}{17} \times 100$). That these methods can provide very large differences on the same data (Repp, Deitz, & Roberts, 1976) is an important factor when using inter-observer

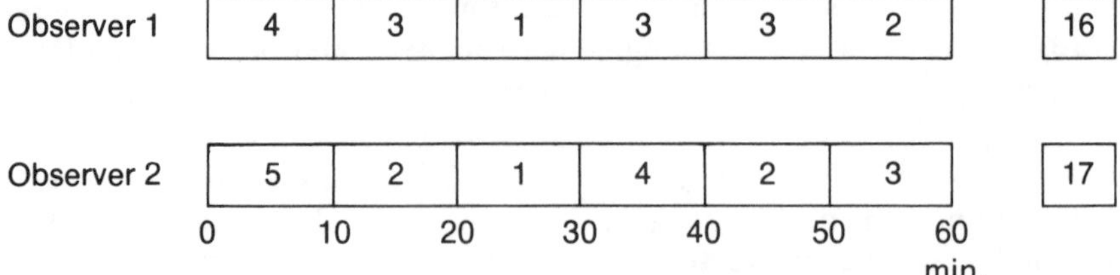

$$\text{Overall agreement} = \frac{4+2+1+3+2+2}{5+3+1+4+3+3} = \frac{14}{19} = .74$$

Fig. 4-6. Inter-observers agreement calculated by the partial session method.

scores to test the validity of the data collection system. When possible, one should use the Response × Response method. If it does produce too complicated a system, one should use the Partial Session method as it will provide more valid results than will the Whole Session method.

INTERVAL RECORDING

Inter-observer agreement scores calculated on data collected through interval recording reflect the agreement between observers that responding did or did not occur. The basic procedure is to compare the intervals on which both observers agreed with the total number of intervals of agreement and disagreement according to the formula

$$\text{inter-observer agreement} = \frac{\text{intervals of agreement}}{\text{intervals of agreement} + \text{intervals of disagreement}}$$

For example, if the data in Figure 4-7 represent two observers' record of responding, the percent of inter-observer agreement could be calculated by adding the number of intervals in which the two observers agreed either that responding did or did not occur (16 intervals), by adding the intervals in which the two observers did not agree that responding did occur (4 intervals), and by dividing the former by the sum of the former and the latter (16 + 4). The percent of inter-observer agreement in this case equals 80 $[(\frac{16}{16+4})]$ and suggests a moderate agreement score that could probably be improved by better response definitions or by training observers more carefully. Some, however, might say that the degree of observer agreement shown here is totally unacceptable, and that considerable work still needs to be done before the data collected could be used for assessment. The basis for this argument is the stand that agreement scores sould reflect agreement *only* on intervals in which responding *occurred* and should not reflect agreement on intervals in which responding did not

Interval	Observer 1	Observer 2	Agree Using All Intervals	Agree Using Response Intervals Only
1			A	—
2			A	—
3			A	—
4			A	—
5	✓	✓	A	A
6			A	—
7	✓	✓	A	A
8	✓	✓	A	A
9			A	—
10	✓		D	D
11			A	—
12	✓	✓	A	A
13		✓	D	D
14		✓	D	D
15			A	—
16	✓	✓	A	A
17			A	—
18			A	—
19	✓		D	D
20			A	—
			A = 16 D = 4	A = 5 D = 4

Fig. 4-7. Inter-observer's record of responding calculated through interval recording.

occur. With this approach, the formula for calculating inter-observer agreement ratios is:

$$\text{Inter-observer agreement} = \frac{\text{intervals of agreement on responding}}{\text{intervals of agreement on responding} + \text{intervals of disagreement}}$$

With this formula, the number of intervals in which both observers agreed that responding occurred (5 intervals) is added, the number of intervals in which the observers disagreed that responding did occur is added (4 intervals), and then the former is divided by the sum of the former and the latter (5 + 4). The percent of agreement *on response occurrence* is only 56 $[(\frac{5}{5+4})]$ and supports the position that considerably more work needs to be done before one can use the data collected in this system. The differences in these two approaches to calculating inter-observer agreement reflects a considerable difference in the care exacted by the supervisors of data systems, with the former and less precise method actually being the more prevalent of the two. It should, however, never be used as it promotes weaknesses in collecting data and can lead to incorrect decisions on the progress of clients.

Factors other than the method of calculating agreement can also cause spuriously high scores. One such factor is the rate of the response being recorded. As the rate increases, the probability increases that both, not just one of the observers, will have recorded responding. In addition, there is an assured decrease in the number of intervals in which only one observer recorded responding, and, hence, an assured increase in the observer agreement scores. A similar problem results when responding is not occurring with equal probability across the session, but occurs predominantly in a few portions. The latter pattern of responding causes an effect like that of high rates of responding, because, for those few segments in which most responding occurs, the rate is relatively high. Again, the number of intervals in which the two observers disagree that responding occurred will decrease, and the inter-observer agreement scores will increase. The *only* solution to this problem is, of course, to make the size of the recording interval small enough to minimize the number of intervals during which more than one response occurs.

DURATION RECORDING

Agreement scores for duration recording can be calculated like agreement scores for frequency recording. As in the Whole Session method, one can sum the durations recorded by each observer, multiply the smaller by 100 and divide by the larger, and report the result as the percent of observer agreement. For example, if one observer recorded 836 seconds of stereotypic responding in 30 minutes and another recorded 912, the percent of inter-observer agreement would be 92 ($\frac{836}{912} \times 100$). Another means of calculating agreement scores would be to compare the record of each response, a procedure analagous to the Response × Response method in frequency recording. Using the method, both observers would record the length of each response, the smaller duration recorded for each response by either observer would be added across the session, the larger number recorded in each instance would be added across the session, the former sum could be multiplied by 100 and divided by the latter sum, and the result would be reported as the percent of interobserver agreement on that response during that session. For example, if one observer recorded 110, 86, 212, 119, 36, 18, and 255 seconds as the duration of responding, and a second observer recorded 120, 76, 240, 141, 26, 31, and 278 seconds, the percent of inter-observer agreement would be:

$$A = (100) \times \left(\frac{110 + 76 + 212 + 119 + 26 + 18 + 255}{120 + 86 + 240 + 141 + 36 + 31 + 278}\right) = \frac{816}{932} = 88.$$

While the difference between 88 and 92 percent is small, and can probably be dismissed, the difference between the latter, more rigorous method and the former could be greater in other examples and could signal problems in response definition, observer training, or other factors.

TIME SAMPLING

In time sampling for behavioral data (as opposed to some ecological data collection systems in which one writes a description of events occurring at the moment of observation), one in essence is noting simply whether a particular response occurred. As such, the data are reported in the same manner in which data collected by interval recording are reported: the percent of observations in which a response occurred. With this similarity, one might expect inter-observer agreement to be calculated in the same manner, and that assumption is correct. One can either report agreement on all the observations, or one can report agreement calculated only on those observations in which one or both observers recorded responding. The same relationship between these two methods holds for data collected through time sampling, i.e., the latter will produce lower scores—so the latter method should be used.

MONITORING EVENTS

The interest in developing both exacting methods of recording behavioral occurrences and continuing evaluations of the data collection system through inter-observer agreement reports is the prelude to the real interest: descriptions of that which is occurring in the environment. Once methods for data collection have been explored and the appropriate method selected, one can begin collecting data that reflect environmental events and then make decisions based upon those events.

There are an enormous number of events which behaviorists record. Some in the educational field involve large systems for assessing the progress of clients (e.g., Bumpass, 1977; Repp & Lazarus, 1977). Others describe attempts to assess teaching environments that include client behaviors, staff behaviors, and the physical environment (e.g., Boles & Bible, 1978; Favell, 1977; Repp, in press).

An example is an observation system that was developed in 1976 by the Behavior Modification Committee at the Georgia Retardation Center to provide information on all programs at the Center. Figure 4-8 describes

OBSERVER CHECKLIST

STUDENT ______________________________ LOCATION ____________
DATE ______________________ TIME ______________________
ACTIVITY IN PROGRESS: ____
____
STAFF RESPONSIBLE ____
____
____
____
____
____

DATA COLLECTOR ____
SCORE ______________
INTER-OBSERVER AGREEMENT SCORE ______________

COMMENTS:

Fig. 4-8. An observation system for recording and communicating programs.

this system and provides an example of four components necessary for such a system: (1) an identification sheet, (2) the data collection form, (3) definitions of items on the data collection form, and (4) examples for some of those items.

The identification sheet provides information on the student, staff, location, and data collector, as well as a summary score of the data. The observer checklist provides short descriptions of the conditions to be observed and requires a short entry [yes (+), no (−), or not observed (0)] to 26 descriptions in 5 categories. The checklist combines methods of recording rather than being comprised only of one method. For example, in the first section, items 1, 2, 5, 6, and 7 are based on a time-sampling procedure in which the sample is taken once during the session, with that sample occurring when the individual enters the teaching room. Items 3, 4, 8, 9, 10, and 11 are based on a frequency recording procedure in which the observer notes whether the response was appropriate or inappropriate, and then summarizes those occurrences on this form (e.g., the observer collects data for item 3 for 10 minutes and finds 7 commands with and 3 without the student's name, 9 of 10 trials with the student given time to respond, 10 trials with appropriate gestures, and 5 of 10 trials conducted calmly and politely. The observer would then sum the appropriate situations (31), the inappropriate (9), and divide the former by the sum of the former and latter ($\frac{31}{31+9}$). The rsulting ratio (0.78) does not meet the criterion for entry of "yes" on the collection form (90 percent of staff–

target student interactions are appropriate), so the observer enters a "–" for "no").

Since complete descriptions of each of the 26 items would make the checklist forms much too long, these descriptions are separated and presented in the definition section. The latter contains definitions complete enough to ensure that two observers, familiar with the setting, could agree on events occurring in the environment. The final section contains examples of items contained in the checklist and serves to supplement the definition section. With it, we have a complete data collection system that can be useful to supervisors needing to know the effects of their programs designed to train staff to teach the clients for whom they are responsible.

SUMMARY

This chapter has provided some descriptions and examples of behavioral systems for describing and monitoring environmental events. Regardless of the system employed or the behaviors to be studied, all behavioral systems have a total interest in summarizing events numerically, and in order to do so, they need (1) objective and measurable definitions of those events, (2) a recording system, and (3) a means of continually monitoring the validity of the data collection system, a means provided by interobserver agreement procedures.

REFERENCES

Baer, D. M., Wolf, M. M., & Risley, T. R. Some current dimensions of applied behavior analysis. *Journal of Applied Behavior Analysis,* 1968, *1,* 91–97.

Bailey, J. & Meyerson, L. Effect of vibratory stimulation on a retardate's self-injurious behavior. *Psychological Aspects of Disability,* 1970, *17,* 133–137.

Boles, S. M. & Bible, G. H. The student service index: A method for the assessment, repair, and maintenance of existing residential service environments. In M. S. Berkler, G. H. Bible, S. M. Boles, D. E. D. Deitz, and A. C. Repp (Eds.), *Current and future behavioral trends for the developmentally disabled.* Baltimore: University Park Press, 1978.

Bumpass, J. The outline of the POR system modified for the institution. Paper presented at the 101st Annual Meeting of the American Association on Mental Deficiency, 1977.

Deitz, D. E. D., Roberts, D. M., & Slack, D. J. An analysis of the effects of various strategies and conditions for observing staff behavior in an institutional instructional setting. Paper presented at the Annual Meeting of the Southeastern Psychological Association, 1976.

Favell, J. E. An institution-wide evaluation and feedback system. In R. E. Crow (Ed.), *Staff training and motivation in treatment services for the developmentally disabled.* South Bend, Indiana: Northern Indiana State Hospital, 1977.

Ferster, C. B. & Skinner, B. F. *Schedules of reinforcement.* New York: Appleton, 1957.

Gladstone, B. W. & Sherman, J. A. Developing generalized behavior-modification skills in high-school students working with retarded children. *Journal of Applied Behavior Analysis,* 1975, *8,* 169–180.

Horner, R. D. Establishing use of crutches by a mentally retarded spina bifida child. *Journal of Applied Behavior Analysis,* 1971, *4,* 183–189.

Johnson, S. M. & Bolstad, O. D. Methodological issues in naturalistic observation: Some problems and solutions for field research. In L. A. Hamerlynck, L. C. Handy, & E. J. Mash (Eds.), *Behavior change: Methodology, concepts, and practice.* Champaign, Ill.: Research Press, 1973.

Kelly, M. B. A review of the observational data-collection and reliability procedures reported in The Journal of Applied Behavior Analysis. *Journal of Applied Behavior Analysis,* 1977, *10*(1), 97–101.

Kent, R. N., Kanowitz, J., O'Leary, K. D., & Cheiken, M. Observer reliability as a function of circumstances of assessment. *Journal of Applied Behavior Analysis,* 1977, *10,* 317–324.

Mager, R. F. *Preparing instructional objectives* (2nd ed.). Belmont, Ca.: Fearon Publishers, 1975.

O'Leary, K. D., Kent, R. N., & Kanowitz, J. Shaping data collection congruent with experimental hypotheses. *Journal of Applied Behavior Analysis,* 1975, *8,* 43–51.

Powell, J., Martindale, A., & Kulp, S. An evaluation of time-sample measures of behavior. *Journal of Applied Behavior Analysis,* 1975, *8,* 463–467.

Repp, A. C. *Mental retardation: A behavioral approach.* Philadelphia: W. B. Saunders, in press.

Repp, A. C., Deitz, D. E. D., Boles, S. M., Deitz, S. M., & Repp, C. F. Differences among common methods for calculating interobserver agreement. *Journal of Applied Behavior Analysis,* 1976, *9*(1), 109–113.

Repp, A. C., Deitz, D. E. D., & Roberts, D. M. A comparison of methods for assessing interobserver agreement in frequency recording. In A. C. Repp (chair.), Methodological considerations in data collection. Paper presented at the 10th Annual Meeting of the Association for Advancement of Behavior Therapy, 1976.

Repp, A. C. & Lazarus, S. G. A system for accountability of service delivery for the mentally retarded. Paper presented at the 101st Annual Meeting of the American Association on Mental Deficiency, 1977.

Repp, A. C., Roberts, D. M., Slack, D. J., Repp, C. F., & Berkler, M. S. A comparison of frequency, interval, and time-sampling methods of data collection. *Journal of Applied Behavior Analysis,* 1976, *9,* 501–508.

Romanczyk, R. G., Kent, R. N., Diament, C., & O'Leary, K. D. Measuring the reliability of observational data: A reactive process. *Journal of Applied Behavior Analysis,* 1973, *6,* 175–184.

Skinner, B. F. *The behavior of organisms: An experimental analysis.* New York: Appleton, 1938.

Skinner, B. F. *Walden two.* New York: Macmillan, 1948.

Skinner, B. F. *Science and human behavior.* New York: Macmillan, 1953.

Skinner. B. F. *Cumulative record.* New York: Appleton, 1959.

Skinner, B. F. *The technology of teaching.* New York: Appleton, 1968.

Skinner, B. F. *Contingencies of reinforcement: A theoretical analysis.* New York: Appleton, 1969.

Skinner, B. F. *Beyond freedom and dignity*. New York: Knopf, 1971.
Skinner, B. F. *About behaviorism*. New York: Knopf, 1974.
Thompson, C., Holmberg, M., & Baer, D. M. A brief report on a comparison of time-sampling procedures. *Journal of Applied Behavior Analysis,* 1974, *7,* 623–626.
Van Houten, R. & Sullivan, K. Effects of an audio cueing system of the rate of teacher praise. *Journal of Applied Behavior Analysis,* 1975, *8,* 197–201.

SUGGESTED READINGS

Brandt, R. M. *Studying behavior in natural settings*. New York: Holt, 1972.
Hutt, S. J., & Hutt, C. *Direct observation and measurement of behavior*. Springfield, Ill.: Charles C Thomas, 1970.
Kazdin, A. E. *Behavior modification in applied settings*. Homewood, Ill.: Dorsey Press, 1975.
Morris, R. J. *Behavior modification with children: A systematic guide*. Cambridge, Mass.: Winthrop, 1976.
Repp, A. C. *Mental retardation: A behavioral approach*. Philadelphia: Saunders, in press.
Sulzer-Azaroff, B., & Mayer, G. R. *Applying behavior analysis procedures with children and youth*. New York: Holt, 1977.
Tharp, R. G., & Wetzel, R. J. *Behavior modification in the natural envrionment*. New York: Academic Press, 1969.

Appendix I. Behavior Modification Proposal Review Committee Observer Checklist

+ = Yes
− = No
0 = Not observed

ENVIRONMENT CONDUCIVE TO APPROPRIATE BEHAVIOR

___ 1. Appropriate activity is occurring for target student at beginning of observation
___ 2. Appropriate activities are occurring for 90 percent of students at beginning of observation
___ 3. 90 percent of staff–target student interactions are appropriate
___ 4. 90 percent of staff–student interactions are appropriate
___ 5. Can the person who is in charge of the section be easily identified?
___ 6. Students are appropriately dressed and groomed
___ 7. The environment is clean and neat
___ 8. Student is reinforced consistently for appropriate behavior
___ 9. Student is reinforced immediately for appropriate behavior
___10. Student is reinforced appropriately for appropriate behavior
___11. Tasks trained were appropriate to student

PROCEDURES ADHERED TO AS SPECIFIED IN PROGRAM

___1. Student's inappropriate behavior as defined by program is consequated as defined by program.
___2. Consequation is consistent
___3. Consequation is immediate
___4. Consequation is appropriate
___5. Student is not reinforced for inappropriate behavior

DATA COLLECTION

___1. Data recorded as specified by program
___2. Data recorded consistently
___3. Data recorded accurately
___4. Data is reviewed daily by QMRP
___5. Data is graphed and displayed for feedback purposes
___6. Program is in student's record with all signatures

STUDENT TRAINING

___1. Staff showed adequate patience during training
___2. Staff handled student respectfully

STAFF TRAINING

___1. Sufficient number of staff trained as specified by program
___2. Staff, when asked by observer, can explain procedures being used and rationale for procedures.

Appendix II. Definitions

ENVIRONMENT CONDUCIVE TO APPROPRIATE BEHAVIOR

1. Observe whether target student is involved in ongoing activity when observer enters the room.
2. Count number of students inovlved in ongoing activity as soon as observer enters the room; 90 percent involved = +; less than 90 percent = −.
3. Observer counts number of appropriate staff-target student interactions for minimum of five minutes; 90 percent appropriate = +; less than 90 percent appropriate = −. Appropriate interactions defined as: (1) gives command with student's name; (2) gives student time to respond before intervening; (3) uses gestures, demonstration, and/or graduated guidance where necessary; (4) all interactions are calm and polite.
4. Observer counts number of appropriate staff–student interactions for a minimum of five minutes (May be done at the same time as #3); 90 percent appropriate = +; less than 90 percent appropriate = −. Appropriate interactions are defined in #3.
5. The person in charge is available to staff and can be easily determined by the observer.
6. Students have on all articles of clothing, have shoe laces in shoes, have socks on both feet, have on matched clothes and matched socks, have hair combed, etc.
7. The activity room or classroom, etc. is clean, i.e., no clothing on floor, no towels, paper towels, etc., on floor or cabinets.
8. Student is reinforced following each appropriate response or according to a specific schedule as specified in program. Appropriate behavior as defined in student's approved behavior modification program—90 percent criterion.
9. Student is reinforced as quickly as possible following appropriate behavior. There appears to be no doubt as to which behavior is being consequated. No observable lag occurs between emitted response and consequation—90 percent criterion.
10. Verbal praise is delivered enthusiastically. Reinforcement prefer-

ence has been determined. Reinforcer appears to be age-appropriate, and appropriate to setting so that setting appears to be likely to perpetuate behavior as defined by program—100 percent criterion.

11. Tasks trained appear to be age-appropriate and taught under circumstances approximating as nearly as possible those under which the behavior is ultimately to occur. (Not to be included in total score; minus will not result in lowered score.)

PROCEDURES ADHERED TO AS SPECIFIED IN PROGRAM

1. Consequation as defined by program follows at least 90 percent of the responses requiring consequation as defined by program.
2. No observable lag occurs between response and consequation as defined by program—90 percent criterion.
3. Consequation is delivered as defined by program only following response requiring consequation as defined by program—100 percent criterion.
4. Reinforcement is delivered contingent upon appropriate behavior. Appropriate behavior is defined as absence of target behavior, and in addition student is not exhibiting any behavior that would be classed as maladaptive by the observer—100 percent criterion.

DATA COLLECTION

1. Data recorded each time response defined by program as requiring consequation occurs—90 percent criterion.
2. Data recorded reflects observable responses—100 percent criterion.
3. Data sheet is initiated daily by QMRP—100 percent criterion.
4. Data is graphed and available to staff participating in the program—100 percent criterion.
5. Program is in student's record with all required signatures.

STUDENT TRAINING

1. Trainer consequated appropriately as defined by program, provided and faded prompts as required according to program, determined op-

timal length of training session, determined optimal performance of student, and remained calm throughout session.
2. Trainer's voice tone, physical contact with student, and content of verbalizations were not derogatory to student.

STAFF TRAINING

1. Sufficient number of trained staff available at all times to implement approved program.
2. Staff member can describe the approved program adequately, define the procedures being used and give examples of situations in which those procedures would be appropriate.

Appendix III. Examples

ENVIRONMENT CONDUCIVE TO APPROPRIATE BEHAVIOR

	(−)	(+)
1.	Target student is not involved in any activity when observer enters the room.	Target student is involved in appropriate activity when observer enters the room.
2.	————	————
3.	Staff member tells student to "sit down" and immediately guides student to the chiar.	Staff member tells student to "sit down" and gives student an opportunity to comply prior to additional help, i.e., gesture, graduated guidance.
4.	————	————
5.	Staff does not know who is in charge, or person in charge is seldom on the section and cannot be reached.	Staff does know who is in charge, and person in charge is available to staff.
6.	Students are not dressed, i.e., are without shoes or shirts, etc.	All students are appropriately dressed and groomed.
7.	————	————
8.	Student places circle in form board in response to command. Staff member is talking to another staff member and does not notice or reinforce all correct responses.	Student places circle in form board in response to command. Staff praises student enthusiastically and delivers reinforcement.
9.	Student puts on pants in response to command. Staff fumbles and reaches for reinforcer only after response is emitted, taking several seconds to deliver it.	Students puts on pants in response to command. Staff immediately praises student enthusiastically and delivers reinforcement.

10.	Adult student completes classroom task. Staff says, "Good boy," hugs and pets student lavishly and places Fruit Loop in student's mouth.	Adult student completes classroom task. Staff says, "Good job," and and delivers token.
11.	————	————

PROCEDURES ADHERED TO AS SPECIFIED IN PROGRAM

Student's program requires that he be removed to T.O. room for hitting. Student hits another student several times:

	(−)	(+)
1.	Staff is engaged and does not notice student behavior.	Staff immediately removes student to T.O.
2.	Staff A removes student every time he raises his hand. Staff B removes student only after contact is made with another person.	*All* staff remove student for hitting only.
3.	Staff notices students fighting only after several seconds and removes student to T.O.	Staff immediately removes student to T.O.
4.	Staff removes student and reprimands him sternly on their way to T.O.	Staff removes student to T.O. with no conversation.
5.	Student, although not hitting, is screaming at other students; staff reinforce.	Student, although not hitting, is screaming at other students; staff attempt to engage student in competing response.

DATA COLLECTION

	(−)	(+)
1.	Heading of data sheet blank with all columns filled in.	Heading and all columns filled in.
2.	Data recorded only when incident occurred in area where clipboard is placed.	Data recorded everytime specified behavior occurs.
3.	Inappropriate behavior occurred for 5 seconds; was recorded to have occurred for 20 seconds.	Data recorded reflects actual behavior of students and staff.

4.	____________	____________
5.	____________	____________
6.	____________	____________

STUDENT TRAINING

	(−)	(+)
1.	Staff is training student to put on coat, student is making no progress. Staff becomes irritable and begins to make commands gruffly; student cries.	Staff is training student to put on coat. Student is making no progress; staff feels himself becoming frustrated and decides to end session.
2.	Staff makes sarcastic remarks about student to other staff throughout session.	Staff attends only to student and task throughout session, speaking only to provide student with feedback.

Donald N. Bersoff and
Ted L. Miller

5

Ethical and Legal Issues of Behavioral Assessment

Many aspects of public education are being criticized. Thsi criticism is so ubiquitous and far-reaching that some authors (Illich, 1971; Silberman, 1970) suggest a radical reconstruction or even elimination of this institution as it currently exists. Reflecting the turmoil of the larger society, public education has experienced a myriad of problems. Special education, as an aspect of public education, has not been immune from castigation. One arena of controversy that particularly involves the special educator is assessment. Although the assessment of individual differences is a multi-faceted practice (see Chap. 1), its most frequent medium is standardized tests. In fact, there is no doubt that testing is a pervasive activity in the public schools. Yearly, in excess of 250 million standardized tests are administered in the public schools (Brim, Glass, Neulinger, Firestone, & Lerner, 1969)—a number sufficiently large to assure that few children will remain outside the scope of assessment programs. Almost no child identified for potential special education placement avoids becoming a test taker, a phenomenon which has evoked severe repercussions. This chapter will briefly review many of the more important legal and ethical issues which have arisen in the context of evaluating the exceptional child.

---

*Substantial portions of this chapter. in somewhat different form, have or will appear elsewhere. The reader is referred to Bersoff, D. and Oakland, T. Law and ethics in psychoeducational assessment. In J. Ysseldyke and T. Oakland (Eds.). *Psychological Assessment*. Wash., D.C., APA. Div. 16 (in press).

EDUCATION AND THE HANDICAPPED CHILD

While contemporary readers may find it difficult to consider an absence of special programs in public schools, public education programs for the handicapped are only slightly over 75 years old (Abraham, 1976; Aiello, 1976). It is true that an elaborate institutional system existed from colonial days (Rothman, 1971; Wolfensberger, 1972) through which treatment to a largely undifferentiated population of handicapped individuals was dispensed. In these institutional arrangements at least one factor was unique: nonhandicapped persons invariably imposed roles on handicapped individuals that greatly reduced their status in comparison to "normal" peers (Wolfensberger, 1972). A common consequence of this practice was exclusion or separation, if not through outright institutionalization, then often by exclusion from the public schools (Carlson, 1975; Katz, 1971). This isolation was frequently based on what Mercer (1977) has termed the "Anglicization" process, the insistence that individuals conform to the language and behavioral patterns of the predominant Anglo culture. As a result, "handicapped" individuals frequently endured limitations on their civil rights. For example, in *Watson v. City of Cambridge* (1893), a Massachusetts court ruled that a student could be expelled for disorderly conduct or imbecility. Some years later the Wisconsin Supreme Court (*Beattie v. State Board of Education* (1919) upheld the school's right to exclude a physically handicapped child because his presence was determined to have a "depressing and nauseating" effect upon other students or teachers. Thus, at the turn of the century, educators were relatively free to exclude individuals who did not conform to subjective standards or arbitrarily developed behavioral codes.

As the century progressed, "special" education began to appear as a part of public school services. For many reasons (including the prevalent notion of exclusion), the services that evolved were commonly offered through self-contained isolated classes. As the number of students frequently outnumbered available classrooms, a process for determining eligibility became necessary. Binet's work (see Chap. 1) has shown promise in this area and, as a result, psychometric testing quickly became the primary benchwork for certifying eligibility. It was this need to assess for placement purposes that closely linked special education, testing, and, eventually, the law.

EDUCATION AND THE LAW

It is beyond the scope of this section to delineate the myriad relationships between law and public education. However, we include a synopsis (following Mandel's [1975] outline) to provide a framework for understanding the information in subsequent sections. As Mandel notes, the purpose of law is to provide a uniform and equitable series of criteria by which to control human behavior. From this perspective the activities of persons may be evaluated and, if necessary, altered. The potential sources of law are legion but a basic dichotomy is that between public and private law. Private law is devoted to the control of behavior independent of public authority. In contrast, public law is enacted by a recognzied governmental authority and, as such, generally has greater and farther ranging influence. Depending on which governmental body promulgates it, public law is enforceable for all persons within its jurisdiction be it county, state, or nation.

The scope of specific public laws exists in a hierarchical arrangement based on the governing body responsible for its creation. Larger governmental units, like Congress, issue laws of greater influence while smaller bodies, like state legislatures or town councils, pass laws that affect fewer people. Specific laws affecting a smaller segment of the population are pemissible only insofar as they do not conflict with the statements contained in more general or global public laws. More encompassing laws often only state broad principles and then delegate authority to smaller governmental units to develop more precise procedures for implementing those principles. For example, a state may pass a general rule of conduct allowing a city to tax its citizens to support public education, while the voters of the city and their representatives determine the details of the structure through the passage of municipal ordinances. As long as the latter does not conflict with the general guidelines appearing in state law, the municipal law governs and controls. However, should the state law be in conflict with federal law, the municipal law would also be defective despite the fact that it derived its authority from state law. Because the U.S. Constitution does not mention education directly, the control of the public schools is generally considered to be a state function although, as we shall see, there is increasing federal involvement in education. In any event, the state's control of education may take place only in a manner that is congruent with the U.S. Constitution.

Judicial decisions begin as disputes. In education, disputes usually start as a result of a private citizen challenging the conduct of a public official. For example, a parent may argue that a state public school law with regard to special education placement unconstitutionally restricts his or her child's opportunity for a free, appropriate education equal in quality to that of nonhandicapped children. In such cases, a formal petition for a court decision may be requested. This official request is termed a complaint; the individual (or party) filing the request is the plaintiff; the party whose actions are complained about is the defendant.

Not all complaints reach the courts. Typically, a preliminary hearing will determine the legitimacy of the plaintiff's claim and the court's ultimate ability to provide suitable redress. Should this pretrial hearing determine that genuine issues exist that can be remedied through judicial action, the case can go to court. In a jury trial the judge determines the legal appropriateness of proceedings and instructs the jury on applicable law while the jury makes a decision based on factual evidence. Sometimes a non-jury trial is held, the judge serving as decider of both fact and law.

The outcome in a lower court may not satisfy one or both parties involved in the suit. In such instances, an appeal to a higher (jurisdictionally more encompassing) court may take place. The number of appeals to such courts is limited depending upon whether an appeal may be taken as a right, the importance of the issue, the persistence of the persons bringing the appeal, and the arguments marshalled to persuade the court to entertain their appeal. In each case, the appealing party attempts to indicate an error in the lower court's decision and seeks to reverse the verdict below. Whatever the outcome, like a trial court, the decision of an appellate court provides behavioral control only over the extent of its domain. A suit that has succeeded in obtaining a favorable decision within a state may have no precedential value in neighboring states. Despite its governmental sanction for that domain, the court's decision is not law in circumstances external to it. However, even though these decisions may not carry the impact of enforceable law, they often provide the basis for persuasive argument in other jurisdictions. The weight of the argument is greatly influenced by the level of the court that made the ruling. In very few instances, cases may travel to the final arbiter, the United States Supreme Court, whose decisions are binding on all of us.

THE DEVELOPMENT OF A RIGHT TO EDUCATION

The practices prevalent in the early 1900s that led to the exclusion of handicapped children did not begin to abate until after midcentury. Although the Supreme Court had declared in 1954 *(Brown v. Board of Education)* that an educational opportunity "be made available to all on equal terms," many children, particularly those with special needs, were being systematically excluded from the classroom and denied state-mandated, free public education. Two basic arguments were used by school districts to deny these children education. The first was the proposition that some children were uneducable or untrainable and therefore did not belong in the public schools. The second was that even if such children could be accommodated, the financial costs would be so great that it would be an unwarranted burden on the schools. These arguments were undercut by judicial action in two now famous cases, *Pennsylvania Association for*

Retarded Children (PARC) v. Commonwealth (1972) and *Mills v. D.C. Board of Education* (1972).

The federal district court in Pennsylvania, relying heavily on the expert opinions of special and general educators and psychologists, ruled that all mentally retarded children were capable of benefitting from training and ordered the state to provide them a free educational program. In addition, Pennsylvania voluntarily agreed it would no longer classify any child as uneducable or untrainable. The rights won by retarded children in *PARC* were soon extended to all children regardless of handicap in *Mills*. The District of Columbia Board of Education had contended that insufficient funds made it impossible to provide a publicly supported education for every kind of exceptional child. The court did not agree. Even if money were a relevant consideration, it said, the interest of the government in conserving financial resources was outweighed by its responsibility to educate excluded children. Furthermore, to provide free public education to some children and to deny it to others (those labeled exceptional) was a violation of both due process and the right to equal protection of the laws under the Constitution.

In fighting for the proposition that no child is uneducable, advocates for the handicapped have contributed to a significant redefinition of education. No longer can it be defined solely in terms of academic instruction or the capability of a child to master a normal scholastic program. The meaning has now been broadened to include any kind of training that a child might need. As a Maryland judge in one "right to education" suit defined it, education is "any plan or structured program administered by competent persons that is designed to help individuals achieve their full potential. . . . Every type of training is at least a subcategory of education" (*MARC v. Maryland,* 1974). Suits such as *Wyatt v. Stickney* (1971), *Ricci v. Greenblatt* (1972), and *New York Association of Retarded Children, Inc. v. Rockefeller* (1972) have extended these guarantees to handicapped individuals institutionalized in public facilities. The current thrust is now to insure that the education that is provided is done only after an appropriate assessment and delivered in accordance with an individually developed intervention program (*Frederick L. v. Thomas,* 1976).

Accordingly, right to education suits are particularly germane to the topic of litigation in testing and special education. They emphasize that individual differences are recognizable, and in order to be appropriate, educational responses must match observable needs. As a result, we might anticipate that measurement of characteristics and needs is considered a pivotal factor in determining the appropriateness of any educational intervention; that is, measurement is necessary for identification purposes and for determining the effectiveness of intervention. Simply stated, a "special" educational response requires a series of procedures to determine the legitimacy and nature of that special response. In practice, these decisions have frequently been based on tests with resulting problems that have involved legal intervention. We now turn to some of these problems.

AREAS OF CONCERN

Ross, DeYoung, & Cohen (1971) have identified five general areas arising in special education that can lead to litigation. All, in one way or another, involve the use of tests or testing practice.

Inappropriate Tests

In this regard, one argument maintains that many tests in current use do not measure skills, traits, or aptitudes that are of educational relevance; that is, current tests may not be measuring important learner characteristics (Salvia & Ysseldyke, 1978).

A second argument refers to the technical procedures by which tests are constructed. Most tests rely on a standardization procedure; that is, a sample of individuals is drawn from a population and this sample then becomes the basis for judging an individual (see Chap. 3). A claim often made is that many tests do not adequately represent the experiences and background of an individual in their sampling procedure. Hence, an individual's performance is judged in reference to experiences and conditions he or she cannot possibly have had. The result is obvious: nonrepresentative performance on the test.

The third argument concerns the reliability and validity of tests. Many tests in common educational practice may not possess sufficient reliability to be useful over time and many may not possess convincing evidence of adequate validity. (See Chap. 3 and various test reviews throughout the text for an elaboration of this argument.)

Incompetent Administration

"Incompetent" administration can be alleged in at least two ways. First, the individual examiner may not have had sufficient training or experience to properly conduct and interpret psychometric measures. Perhaps an equally frequent indictment is the claim that even a thoroughly trained examiner may be incompetent to assess a child due to differences in social, cultural, or personal variables between them. For example, the argument has been presented that white, middle-class examiners ought not to assess lower class or minority children because the examiners' backgrounds have not prepared them to elicit or understand the responses of such children. The theoretical concept of "competence," then, can be extended beyond the mastery of purely technical skills to a more diverse collection of personal attributes.

Lack of Parental Involvement

A major issue in the assessment and placing of a child in a special program has been a general lack of information gleaned from parents. Often special education assessment practices proceed with very little attention given to the individual's behavior as it occurs and as it is perceived by others in locations outside of the school. Bronfenbrenner (1977), among others, has made clear the necessity of these data if we are to understand human development. For example, behaviors that are adaptive to the child in his 18-hour day away from school may not be so productive when demonstrated in school. Without knowledge of the child's adaptive behaviors in the nonschool bound environment, professionals have often labeled the child for the seeming inability or reluctance to conform to certain behavioral standards in the school. Often the labeled phenomenon is justified only within the context of the school—it ceases to exist as a child centered trait once knowledge of the child's background is available.

What we see demonstrated here is the fact that the failure to attend to the total child through the involvement of parents and significant others in the *community beyond the school* has been a major flaw in special education assessment and intervention practices. In the past, parents frequently were not notified, let alone made fully knowledgeable of the assessment of their child. Thus the necessity of parental involvement is not only a theoretical necessity but a concept closely tied to the right to privacy and the doctrine of informed consent. Since guaranteeing privacy and assuring informal consent is fundamental to current ethical and legal guidelines for assessment, we will soon describe it in some detail.

Special Education is Inadequate

The fourth general contention that has precipitated much discussion is the adequacy of special education services. Although closely tied to the right to education issue, allied concern emerges involving tests and testing practices; if the "treatment" or intervention of special education is inadequate, it cannot support testing and identification for such services. Thus, without evidence of benefit, testing could lose any support it might enjoy as a "necessary" preliminary action in a treatment paradigm.

Placement Stigma

Since the time of Binet (circa 1906), tests have served as "scientific" evidence to determine eligibility for special service or to justify exclusionary practices. Almost from the beginning of the widespread use of tests, the practice was attacked (Lippman, 1922). Since tests served to place children in special educational arrangements and as these arrangements have generally been ineffective (Dunn, 1968; MacMillan, 1971; see especially Bruininks & Rynders, 1972), the use of tests for this purpose has been questioned. Indeed Cohen & DeYoung (1973) have stated that special classes cause "irreparable harm" due to the stigma of separation and since placement stigma is doubly erroneous if the accuracy of the selection procedure is not perfect, a central issue concerns the technical accuracy and the fair use of tests in selection procedures.

By and large these five issues encompass the major points concerning special education that have been challenged in the courts. In many instances, a single suit has addressed more than one of these issues and, within each of these issues, several points of contention often exist. But as a rule, at least three constitutional guarantees dominate the suits. These are: (1) the right to equal protection, (2) the right of privacy, and (3) freedom from unwarranted stigmatization or damage to reputation by the government. The right to equal protection is interpreted as the right to an educational opportunity; that is, schools cannot discriminate among groups of people unless there is some substantial and legitimate rationale for doing so. The right to privacy, in part, prevents the government from unrestrictedly gathering or disseminating personal information or curtailing individual choice or freedom with regard to procreation, marriage, and family life. Finally, the individual's right to be free of unwarranted stigmatization is interpreted as the right, among others, to contest the means by which one is labeled as handicapped for placement in special education classes. But, it should be pointed out that these guarantees emanate from the U.S. Constitution and hence are continually defined and refined.

In the remaining portion of this section the three constitutional guarantees enumerated earlier will be pursued through an expanded review of the five issues identified by Cohen and DeYoung (1973). The discussion of each issue will illustrate the major impetus for the legal challenges, provide representative court cases and, in so far as is possible, relate the current interpretation of each adjudicated action. The final section of the chapter will use these outcomes as a springboard for a discussion of the most pertinent aspects of current legislation.

INAPPROPRIATE TESTS

Although several factors have led to the widespread use of inappropriate tests, Bersoff (1973) suggests that two professional failures have been the primary contributors. First, psychologists and educators have allowed themselves to believe that underlying traits guide and direct behavior to such an extent that behavioral responses are largely independent of the surrounding environment. As a result, efforts have concentrated on measuring traits which are believed to be consistent across settings. Much evidence and speculation (Altman, 1975; Apter, 1977; Barker, 1963, 1968; Feagans, 1972; Mischel, 1968; Moos, 1974; Phillips, Draguns, & Martlett, 1975; Proshansky, Ittelson, & Rivlin, 1970; Rhodes, 1967, 1974; Sattler, 1973; Sommer, 1969) suggest that the trait orientation has been overestimated in its capacity to predict behavior and for its utility in evaluating and intervening with handicapped persons (Brooks & Baumeister, 1977a, 1977b).

The second major error committed by test developers is that in their rush to make tests efficient, they may have lost sight of their original purpose—to gather samples of behavior that can be used to differentiate among individuals. Instead, tests have been subjected to increasingly sophisticated statistical manipulation yielding measures that are easy to administer and score but which may not provide accurate or important information. As Wesman (1968, p. 272) has stated, "Efficiency is certainly desirable—but *validity* is *crucial.* How tests were constructed is interesting and even germane; how they work is the critical issue." Thus, psychometrists have focused their attention on the intricacies of test refinement rather than on the objectives of testing. Since the major goal of assessment ought to be a contribution to decisions regarding intervention (Bijou & Peterson, 1971; Peterson, 1968; Wittrock, 1970), it may be conjectured that many tests simply do not fulfill this purpose (Carver, 1974).

Another difficulty lies in the development of a culturally fair measure—one that does not discriminate unfairly on the basis of race or social experiences. Anastasi (1972) has argued that it is impossible to construct a test free of cultural influence. However, she also believes that the development of a test that draws only from experiences common across cultures—a "culturally fair" test—is possible. Accordingly, a number of approaches might be attempted including "non-language" tests, or tests that involve the manipulation of materials presumably common to all cultures. However, it can be argued that most tests are influenced by cultural difference and that this difference may alter the relative performance achieved by the individuals under examination. Thus, tests identifying a significantly higher proportion of handicapped individuals with certain cultural or racial characteristics, might be considered inappropriate to assign individuals to specific curricula. In fact, the overrepresentation of minority students, assigned primarily on the basis of standardized intelligence tests, has been an extremely potent and abrasive vocal issue (Flaugher, 1974; Frazer, Miller, & Epstein, 1975; Linn, 1972; McClelland, 1973; McNemar, 1975; Schmidt & Hunter, 1974; Thorndike, 1971).

Given these commonly recognized concerns, it is surprising that the widespread use of standardized tests was not seriously challenged until the past decade. The first significant challenge to the practice of using formal tests to label and place school children in tracks is considered to be *Hobson v. Hansen* (1967). In this suit, the tracking system in the Washington, D.C. public schools was attacked. The decision ordered the cessation of tracking but did not eliminate ability grouping as such. The suit resulted from the disproportionately high number of black children placed in the lower tracks and the significantly fewer number placed in the upper tracks. The court maintained that only if the disparity of treatment could be justified would such practice be maintained, otherwise the tracks were "wholly irrational and . . . unconstitutionally discriminating" (fn. 211):

> The evidence shows that the method by which track assignments were made depends essentially on standardized aptitude tests which, although given on a system-wide basis, are completely inappropriate for use with a large segment of the student body. Because these tests are standardized primarily on and are relevant to a white middle class group of students, they produce inaccurate and misleading test scores when given to lower class and Negro students (p. 514).

Hobson v. Hansen involved the use of group achievement tests but soon other tests were challenged. In *Diana v. State Board of Education* (1970), a suit was brought on behalf of nine Mexican-American children who were placed in special education classes for the mildly retarded primarily on the basis of scores obtained on the *Stanford-Binet* and *Wechsler Intelligence Scale for Children.* One of the plaintiffs in *Diana* received an IQ score of 30 when the test was administered by an English-speaking examiner. Subsequent administration in Spanish yielded a score 49 points higher, several points above the California criteria for placement in EMR classes. Other children were also found to have been erroneously placed. *Diana,* settled out of court, resulted in major changes in the California school code with regard to assessment and placement practices.

EMR placement and IQ testing were soon back in the courts in California in a case known as *P. v. Riles* (1972). This time the plaintiffs were black children in the San Francisco elementary schools who were placed in EMR classes after scoring below 75 on one of several tests authorized by the State Department of Education. The plaintiffs produced evidence that racial imbalance existed in these classes. For example, black children constituted about 29 percent of all students in the San Francisco school system, but 66 percent of the students in the EMR program. In California as a whole, while black children comprised 9 percent of the school population, they comprised 28 percent of all children in EMR classes. Having presented these data, the plaintiffs argued that the burden had been shifted to the school system to explain this racial imbalance. If the San Francisco school system could not explain this disparity, it was argued by the plaintiffs that it should then be enjoined (order to refrain) from using the IQ tests to place black children in EMR classes.

This strategy concerning shifting the burden of proof to the defendants was borrowed from *Griggs v. Duke Power Co.* (1971), a case decided by the Supreme Court the previous year. There, in an action brought under Title VII of the 1964 Civil Rights Act (which prohibits discrimination in employment because of race, color, religion, sex, or national origin), black employees challenged the use of intelligence tests as a condition of employment or transfer to certain positions for which they were otherwise qualified. The employers claimed that, while the test criterion may have had a discriminatory effect in that fewer blacks were hired or promoted, there was no intent to discriminate. The Court, however, interpreted Title VII as proscribing "not only overt discrimination but also practices that are fair in form, but discriminatory in operation" (p. 431). Thus, the court viewed *the consequences* of the practice in question, not simply the motivation. Once the discriminatory effect was shown, the burden was then on the employer to show "that any given requirement . . . have a manifest relationship to the employment in question" (p. 432).

This reasoning was persuasive in *P. v. Riles*.* The school system offered the explanation that black children were more frequently found in EMR classes, not because of inherited differences in intelligence, but rather because of the poor nutrition of their mothers. In addition, the school system had followed California's education code in using a number of measures besides IQ scores to place children. Nevertheless, the court agreed to enjoin the administration of IQ tests for purposes of placing black children in classes for the educably retarded. The court found that

*It probably would not be so in suits brought today, given the Supreme Court decision in *Washington v. Davis* (1976). In cases brought under the Constitution, as was *Riles*, not under Title VII, plaintiff must show discriminatory *intent*, not merely effect.

substantial emphasis was placed on the IQ test score resulting in such disproportionality as to constitute a denial of equal protection.*

In the two years followng the Court's issurance of the injunction in *Riles,* there were more court maneuvers. In early 1975 the State of California issued a memorandum and accompanying resolution stating that until further notice none of the IQ tests on its approved list (the *WISC* and *Stanford-Binet,* among others) could be used in placing any child, *of any race,* in EMR classes.

Issues regarding educational opportunities and the use of tests with minority group children reappeared in a second major court case eventually decided by the U.S. Supreme Court (*Lau v. Nichols,* 1974) involving the San Francisco school district. Plaintiffs, Chinese students, charged that the school district failed to provide bilingual language instruction to all children in need of these programs. Ruling in favor of the plaintiffs the Supreme Court recommended that a task force be created to set forth procedures which insured the proper use of educational programs and assessment techniques with bilingual or non-English-speaking students. Their report, issued by the Office for Civil Rights (OCR) in the summer of 1975, recommended that: (1) schools use information from home interviews, observations of children in school, and/or a test of language dominance in programming for bilingual children; (2) information acquired from other diagnostic and prescriptive measures that identify the nature of each student's educational needs be used to implement an educational program meeting the diagnosed needs of each child; and (3) the assessment and instructional personnel be linguistically and culturally familiar with the students' backgrounds and the programs be free from discrimination in terms of course content. In short, *Lau v. Nichols* not only reaffirmed earlier decisions but extended the rights and remedies of culturally different children. The import of the case in fostering bilingual education has recently been analyzed by Teitelbaum & Hiller (1977) but the true impact may not be directly felt for some time.

To date, the issue of inappropriate tests has not been resolved. Many authorities believe that a culturally free assessment device is not truly feasible and that considerable error will continue to exist in measurement. However, safeguards have been established based on legal precedent, including requirements that a number of tests be used to estimate intelligence or achievement, that minority students be tested by minority

*These rulings were made in the context of a request for a preliminary injunction, not a final ruling. Five years after this preliminary injunction was granted, the case finally came to trial and as of this writing (July 1978) was not yet resolved. Since the case may well have major and long-term effects on measurement practices in special education, the reader is advised to follow case developments as they occur.

examiners, that multiple sources of data (e.g., interviews) be taken into consideration, and that no single measure be used to justify placement.

These techniques provide some assurance that tests are not used inappropriately, but they do not guarantee that appropriate tests will be used. Mercer (1977) has recently developed a test purported to assess minority children validly (see Chap. 7). Even so, it is safe to say that the current state-of-the-art seeks fairness as much in review procedures (due process) as in improved assessment technology.

INCOMPETENT ADMINISTRATION

Rosenfeld and Blanco (1974) have reported evidence of a high degree of incompetence of some ''trained'' examiners working in public school settings. The authors suggest that incompetence probably is not as rare as one might expect and, in fact, may be relatively prevalent. School psychologists, among those involved in special education, have come under especially vigorous attack. For example, in a suit challenging assessment practices in Boston (*Stewart v. Phillips,* 1970), the complaint alleged that:

> So-called Boston ''school psychologists'' are unqualified to interpret the limited classification devices that the Boston School system currently employs—Boston ''school psychologists'' have been minimally trained, and thus their testing results in an incompetent, discriminating, and unprofessional classification (p. 12).

Suits that arise from professional incompetence are termed malpractice suits. Malpractice itself is a nebulous term. McDermott (1972) notes one commonly cited definition (*Bd. of Exam. of Veterinary Med. v. Mohr,* 1971):

> Malpractice . . . is . . . any professional misconduct or any unreasonable lack of skill or fidelity in the performance of professional or fiduciary duties; illegal or immoral conduct; improper or immoral conduct; misbehavior; wrongdoing; evil, bad, objectionable, or wrong practice; evil practice, acts or doings; illegal or unethical practice; practice contrary to established rules; practice contrary to rules.

The key aspect in malpractice is conduct outside the conventional or established rules of the profession. Turnbull (1977, p. 51) sees such suits as an increasing effort to assure accountability. Moreover, he notes that suits against institutions have been most frequently entertained by the courts in order to assure ''accountability on a grand scale.'' Institutional suits rarely carry personal liability, but suits against individuals almost always do. Further, there is reason to believe that the trend toward an increasing number of suits for individual malpractice will continue and that physicians will no longer be the primary target. For example, in 1975 the Supreme Court in *Wood v. Strickland* specifically held that school officials are not immune under certain circumstances from personal liability for money damages. It thus appears that malpractice suits in special education could proliferate and could involve individuals professionally.

LACK OF PARENTAL INVOLVEMENT

A constant criticism of special education in general and testing practices in particular has been the tendency of schools to assume excessive decisional power over students. The Supreme Court has continually held that the denial of constitutional rights under the defense of programmatic benefit for a minor is not defensible; that is, an educational agency cannot deny constitutional prerogatives in the "best interest" of the child simply because he or she has not achieved adult status. In 1969, in *Tinker v. Des Moines Independent Community School District,* the Court clearly stated that students are persons under the Constitution and that they are protected by its guarantees even after they enter the schoolhouse door. Thus, in schools, as in other public agencies, the Constitution prevents arbitrary and irrational control of the behavior of an individual.

One of the constitutional rights, developed over the last dozen years by the Supreme Court, is the concept of privacy. Defining the right of privacy has been difficult for the ocurts, the legislature and legal scholars (see, e.g., Beaney, 1966; Parker, 1974; Westin, 1967). There are, however, two somewhat overlapping aspects identified as constituting the right. One is the right not to suffer governmental prohibition or penalties as the result of engaging in private activity; the other is to be free from governmental gathering, storage, and dissemination of private information (see Dorsen, Bender, & Neuborne, 1976). However, it is probably true that "the right of privacy is largely a subjective, incorporeal right, difficult to identify and incapable of measurement" (Reubhausen & Brim, 1965, p. 1186). Whatever else it might mean, there is agreement that one component of privacy is the right to determine when and in what manner personal information is communicated to others:

> The essence of privacy is . . . the freedom of the individual to pick and choose for himself the time and circumstances under which, and most importantly, the extent to which, his attitudes, beliefs, behavior and opinions are to be shared with or withheld from others. The right of privacy is, therefore, a positive claim to a status of personal dignity—a claim for freedom . . . of a very special kind (Reubhausen & Brim, 1965, pp. 1189–1190).

Alternatively,

The decisive element . . . that defines [a breach of privacy] . . . is the acquisition or transmission of information without the voluntary consent or initiative of those whose actions and words generate the information (Shils, 1966, pp. 282–283).

The judiciary has never attempted to define privacy but has been content to indicate the activities within its scope. In *Roe v. Wade* (1973), the case establishing a woman's right to abortion, the Supreme Court acknowledged the guarantee of personal privacy extended to conduct related to marriage, procreation, contraception, family relationships, child rearing, and education. It is unclear to what extent the constitutional right of privacy reaches other areas.

Somewhat aligned with privacy in that it enhances the respect for persons is the informed consent doctrine, a concept that emerged in the context of the physician–patient malpractice suits. Generally, it is now held that physicians violate their obligations to patients and subject themselves to liability for malpractice if they fail to reveal potential dangers and other important facts concerning suggested treatment or withhold information concerning available forms of treatment. The underlying legal and philosophical premise of the informed consent doctrine is the notion of "thoroughgoing self-determination" (*Natanson v. Kline,* 1960, pp. 406; 1104). As a result, the patient is entitled to all the facts necessary to make an informed, intelligent choice before consenting to medical intervention.

Typically, the duty to disclose is not absolute. It is tempered by what may be called the materiality rule. Physicians need not disclose risks that are likely to be known to the average patient or are in fact known to the particular patient involved due to past experience. Rather, the extent of disclosure is determined by the materiality of the risk. As defined in a leading case: "Materiality may be said to be the significance of a reasonable person, in what the physician knows or should know is his patient's position, would attach to the disclosed risk or risks in deciding whether to submit or not to submit to surgery or treatment" (*Wilkinson v. Vesey,* 1972, p. 689). Thus, at trial the jury must decide whether the physician disclosed enough information for the reasonable patient to make an intelligent decision to accept or reject the proposed treatment. If the prudent juror would have forgone the treatment if advised of an undisclosed fact or risk, then that fact or risk would be material. Some of the information falling within the materiality rule and thus necessitating disclosure are: (1) inherent and potential hazards of the proposed treatment; (2) alternatives to that treatment; and (3) the likely result if the patient choses to remain untreated.

There is no reason for the informed consent doctrine to be limited to physician–patient relationships. In many ways the insensitivity of behavioral practitioners to the interests of those they treated matched that of the medical profession and by the mid-1960s it was clear that special educators were not to be immune from legal constraints. For example, in *Diana v. Board of Education* (1970) the state agreed that (1) the parent must be fully notified of any pschological tests prior to the activity taking place; (2) written agreement to place a child in special education must be secured prior to placement; and (3) a parental conference informing the parents of all data outcomes and planned actions must take place (Cohen & DeYoung, 1973). Thus, we see in informed consent the requirement of a complete explanation of all activities as well as potential outcomes. Partially as a result of *Diana* and similar cases parental input at all stages of assessment, data sharing and program development are now incorporated into the most prominant legislation affecting school age handicapped children (PL 94-142). Some details of that law and related legislation will be offered in a later section.

SPECIAL EDUCATION IS INADEQUATE

There are a number of arguments that can be presented that question the value or adequacy of special education. One long-standing criticism has been that special education functions as a "burial ground" (Cohen & DeYoung, 1973, p. 267); that once assigned, students are infrequently released. Perhaps this argument is now mostly historical since the concepts of the least restrictive setting (Deno, 1970; Reynolds, 1962), mainstreaming and periodic review of placement and programming distinctions are mandated by the Education for All Handicapped Children's Act (1975) and the regulations implementing Section 504 of the Rehabilitation Act of 1973. In these laws parents are assured the right to challenge identification, evaluation, and placement of their children by special education professionals.

Howevever, even though special education may no longer function as an unmonitored burial ground, there may be some cause to doubt the effectiveness of many special education practices. A number of practices might be outlined but two are particularly germane: (1) educational placement strategies, and (2) diagnostic prescriptive teaching. Dunn's (1968) article initiated a tremendous flow of criticism of special education instructional grouping practices. Although alternatives to "self contained" classrooms are now widespread, there is little evidence yet to support their actual instructional effectiveness.

A second major aspect of education that has received extensive criticism is diagostic-prescriptive teaching. For example, Ysseldyke (1973) has challenged the current effectiveness of the aptitude by treatment interaction evaluation model. Since this model is central to effective diagnostic prescriptive intervention and individualized instruction, both common tenets of many special education programs, the result is obvious: programs based entirely on such methods run a risk of being inadequate. Although several authors (Cronbach & Snow, 1977; Hunt, 1975; Tobias, 1976) see ultimate promise in the aptitude by treatment interaction paradigm, this approach currently lacks demonstrated validity.

Dunn (1973, pp. 7–8) suggests that there are at least four components that make "special education special." These include: (1) specially trained professional educators; (2) special curricular content; (3) special methodology; and (4) special instructional materials. While Dunn did not review the effectiveness of each of these components (and indeed that would require a book length manuscript by itself) he does indicate that opinion varies as to how many of these elements are required to constitute special education. Assuming that each of the four contributes some effect in successful remediation, it can be seen that many programs are more or less adequate depending upon the number of components that are in operation at any one time. Without even addressing the issue of "quality" in these areas, it is quite easy to surmise that many programs have been unsatisfactory. This is not so much of an indictment as it may seem for most special education programs are recent additions to schools and, hence, suffer from problems typical to new programs. But, it is probably fair to say that in many cases special education has been unable to provide the services that were promised simply because many special components were not in place. Coupled with the furor over common practices outlined previously, it is not unusual that a charge of inadequacy has often been leveled at special education.

PLACEMENT STIGMA

Perhaps few issues are as controversial in special education as diagnostic labeling. Diagnostic labels can be defined as the categorical designation of a handicapping condition to which a person is assigned based on measures of specific behaviors or trait characteristics. The historical evolution of this approach has been detailed in Chapter 1; the emphasis here is on the ethical and legal challenges to the outcomes of appraisal. In a penetrating analysis, Goffman (1963) has shown that a label possessing a social connotation marks the individual for a specific kind of social interaction and tends to segregate the individual from the larger social arena. For certain portions of the society, separated on the basis of specific labels, the consequence is stigmatizing. Stigmatization has been termed "an undesired difference" (Goffman, 1963, p. 5) and is characterized by undesirable social interactions (Bartel & Guskin, 1970; Farber,

1968; Kirp, 1974). Ultimately, the process tends to devalue the person. The individual is then responded to on the basis of a stereotyped image that a label conveys rather than as a human being. A label with its stigmatizing effects may greatly reduce the rights, privileges, and activities of a person (Mercer, 1975). As special education has maintained a practice of labeling individuals (Mercer, 1975) and, as tests are pivotal in this schema, the outcomes of labeling have often been laid on the doorstep of testing.

There can be little doubt that the effects of stigmatizing labels are debilitating to the individual student. Kirp (1974, p. 22) has stated it well:

> For many children, adverse school classification is particularly painful because it is novel. It represents the first formal revelation of differences between them and other children. . . . Children perceive all too well what the school's label means.

The general awareness of the problem of stigma in educational labels became so acute by the late 1960s that Eliot Richardson, then Secretary of HEW, commissioned a special investigation of labeling practices and outcomes (Hobbs, 1975). In general, the resulting document indicates two avenues which converge in the discussion of testing, labeling, and the stigma of special classification. First, one can call the educational practice per se into question. In this view, testing serves only as an intervening medium, pernicious to the extent that it supports an unwarranted practice. Second, and of more importance in this discussion, is the consequence of using what many believe to be inappropriate tests. As one court has warned:

> When a program talks about labeling someone as a particular type and such a label could remain with him for the remainder of his life, the margin of error must be almost nil (*Merriken v. Cressman,* 1973, p. 920).

As may be suspected, few, if any, current measurement practices are so technically precise (Ysseldyke, 1973; Ysseldyke & Salvia, 1974; Salvia & Clark, 1973). Thus, if labeling practices continue within public education and if tests are used as the primary data collector, erroneous decisions will continue. The danger of stigma resulting from such practice has led to the requirement of what are commonly called due process hearings. Such hearings permit parents to challenge the labels or handicapping conditions the schools propose to use as a basis for special education placement. Two landmark cases contesting long-term exclusion practices (*PARC v. Commonwealth,* 1971; *Mills v. Board of Education,* 1972) provided the precedent for the protections that must be guaranteed before placement can occur (Buss, 1975, p. 302):

1. Notice in advance of the hearing of the factual and theoretical basis of the proposed reclassification

2. The right to submit evidence
3. The right to cross-examine any witness supporting the school's position
4. The right to be represented by a lawyer
5. The right to have the case decided by an independent hearing officer
6. The right to learn the details of the school's position, including examination of the student's school records
7. The right to state-provided independent psychological examination

As Buss (1975, p. 302) has indicated:

> . . . the essence of what these various benchmarks suggest is that a person who is about to be adversely affected by government action is entitled to notice of the basis of government's action and an opportunity to respond to the government position by way of proving contrary facts or additional facts that tend to be a different conclusion or to reinterpret the total set of facts submitted by the government and/or the affected person so that a different conclusion seems appropriate.

Due process is intended to balance the interests of all parties in decisions that affect them. Kirp (1974, p. 52) has noted that:

> Due process hearings, if handled with sensitivity to the real interests of both the school and the child, encourage better individual placements as well as reconsideration of the school's assumptions concerning which classification decisions are useful and necessary.

Due process is, then, a major safeguard that can substantially improve special education services by assuring that any decisions that are made are fair to all parties.

SUMMARY OF LITIGATION

The information presented above represents only a small portion of the cases concerning special education practice. These suits have emphasized the right to education and reaffirmed that special education practices must not jeopardize constitutional guarantees. But, if we have just passed through the era of litigation, the mid-1970s is clearly the era of legislation. Assessment practices of school personnel are very much affected by this legislation. Within the federal sphere, the three most influential statutes are the Education Amendments of 1974 (PL 93-380, 88 Stat. 484), The Education for All Handicapped Children Act of 1975 (PL 94-142, 89 Stat. 773), and the Rehabilitation Act of 1973 (PL 93-112, 87 Stat. 355, as amended by PL 93-516, 88 Stat. 1617).

EDUCATION AMENDMENTS OF 1974 (PL 93-380)

PL 93-380 is in large measure only of historical interest as it was amended significantly by PL 94-142. However, it deserves comment for placing school systems on notice that federal financial assistance for special education was contingent on the development of state plans establishing "a goal of . . . full educational opportunities to all handicapped children" and means "for insuring that handicapped children and their parents or guardians are guaranteed procedural safeguards in decisions regarding identification, evaluation and educational placement. . . ." As one small part of the protective devices, parents were to be given the right to "examine all relevant records with respect to . . . classification or educational placement, and obtain an independent educational evaluation of the child." To prevent misclassification of minority children, school systems were ordered to develop methods for insuring that any assessment devices used "for the purposes of classification and placement of handicapped children will be selected and administered so as not to be racially or culturally discriminatory."

What is of current interest in PL 93-380 is section 513, better known as the "Buckley Amendment." Sometimes labeled the Family Education Rights and Privacy Act, the Buckley Amendment established many rights with regard to access to school records. Basically, the law provides that all educational institutions receiving funds under any federal program administered by the U.S. Office of Education must allow all parents access to relevant records directly related to their children and an opportunity for a hearing to challenge those records on the grounds that they are inaccurate, misleading, or otherwise inappropriate. In addition, the law requires that institutions obtain written consent of parents before releasing to third parties personally identifiable data about students from records. Parents also have the right to receive a list of those persons who have been permitted to see their children's records, have the right to be notified each time their children's records are transmitted to the courts under judicial order or subpoena, and the right to be notified by the school of these provisions. All these rights transfer to public school students when they become 18 years of age and to all students, regardless of age, if they attend post-secondary educational institutions.* The ultimate penalty for failure to comply with the Act is termination of federal funds administered by the Office of Education.

The Buckley Amendment created immediate confusion, concern, and

---

*Some of these rights are held concurrently by parents and their children if the children remain dependents for income tax purposes.

chaos. In an attempt to clarify and calm, as well as implement the intent of the Act, the Department of HEW, after much delay, published a detailed set of regulations (Federal Register, June 17, 1976; 45 C.F.R. §99). Of pertinence to special educators are the definitions of educational records and specification of those records which may be excluded from access. The regulations define an educational record as that which is "directly related to a student, and . . . maintained by an educational agency or institution or by a party acting for the agency or institution." Thus, accessible records are *any* records in the possession of the school system related to a student even if they are created by independent sources or contractors for service. However, they do not include that material which is kept solely by the person who created the information. Thus, anecdotal notes written by a special educator during the course of assessment and shown to *no one else* (temporary substitutes are excepted, but not supervisors) need not be shown to parents even if they so request (although the special educator certainly may do so if he or she wishes). However, when these regulations are read in accordance with the demands of other federal regulations with regard to the right of parental access to all relevant records concerning special education classification, the test protocols shared at a case conference committee responsible for deciding appropriate placement will almost certainly be accessible to parents and/or eligible students. This means that in many instances both the test blank and the responses of the test-taker can no longer be hidden. (The ethical dilemma in which this places some service personnel has been discussed by Bersoff, 1975.)

EDUCATION FOR ALL HANDICAPPED CHILDREN ACT OF 1975 (PL 94-142)

The broad mandates outlined under PL 93-380 were carefully delineated the following year in PL 94-142. The express purpose of the Act is to "assure that all handicapped children have available to them . . . a free appropriate public education which emphasizes special education and related services designed to meet their unique needs, to assure that the rights of handicapped children and their parents or guardians are protected, to assist States and localities [in these endeavors], and to assess and assure the effectiveness of efforts to educate handicapped children" regardless of the severity of their handicap.

The assistance promised in the statement of purpose is primarily financial. Like its predecessor, PL 94-142 makes federal reimbursement (up to 40 percent of the excess cost of the education of handicapped children by 1982) contingent on the explicit performance of a number of requirements. The goal of full educational opportunity is reiterated, with the specification that free, specially designed schooling be provided for all handicapped children (mentally retarded, hearing impaired, speech impaired, visually handicapped, seriously emotionally disturbed, orthopedically or otherwise health impaired, specific learning disabilities) within ages 3 to 18 by September 1, 1978 and within ages 3 to 21 by September 1, 1980.

An inherent feature of the definition of a free appropriate education is the development for every handicapped child of an individual education program (IEP). This program, written in conjunction with an administrator, a teacher, the parent, and where appropriate the child, must contain the following:

1. A statement of present levels of educational performance
2. A statement of annual goals, including short-term instructional objectives
3. A statement of specific educational services to be provided, including the extent to which the child will be educated in a regular classroom
4. The projected date for initiating the program and its anticipated duration
5. Appropriate objective criteria and evalaution procedures for determining, at least once a year, whether the instructional objectives are being met

PL 94-142 not only reaffirms the principles of nondiscriminatory assessment and parental access to records relevant to identification, evaluation, and placement but further specifies minimal due process protections that parents must be afforded with regard to assessment and placement. Of importance to special educators who conduct assessments are those requirements concerning parental permission for evaluation and the right to call school employees as witnesses. As written, the Act mandates that parents must receive prior *notice* before the school performs a psychological evaluation. Notice is not equivalent to consent. Notice is merely the provision of information to parents that the school will examine their child. Consent is permission. Thus, on the surface, under PL 94-142, schools need not secure approval for testing or other evaluation. However, in a set of regulations implementing the Act, published on August 23, 1977 (*Federal Register,* 1977), parental *consent* is required until the school system, in a formal hearing, successfully challenges the parental refusal to consent (Pryzwansky & Bersoff, 1978).

Further, parents have the right to trigger a full dress impartial hearing any time they have a complaint with regard to identification, evaluation, or placement. As part of this hearing parents have the right to representation by counsel or any persons of their choosing and have the right to compel the attendance of, and to cross-examine witnesses, including special education personnel involved in assessment and placement decisions. This means that school psychologists and others involved in assessment are vulnerable to intense scrutiny of their credentials and performance, whether it be the reliability and validity of the evaluation measures they employ, the interpretations they make from the information gathered, or the recommendations they offer as a result of their evaluation.

Kabler (1977) has suggested that the impact of PL 94-142 will take place in five major areas: (1) expansion of services to underserved populations, (2) protection in evaluation procedures and the development of individualized educational plans, (3) assurance of a least restrictive placement, (4) easier parental access to records, and (5) the right to present complaints. From these five major provisions he sees several outcomes. Among these are the following:

There will be an increased need for a large number of well-trained school psychologists. It is not stretching this point of view to suggest that an increasing number of special educators, thoroughly trained in psychoeducational procedures, will also be needed. Second, a multi-disciplinary approach to assessment will become more commonplace. The development of individual educational plans will require new assessment procedures and considerable parental involvement. Third, specialty areas of assessment may become more commonplace, i.e., specialists trained in early childhood assessment, assessment of the multiply handicapped, and so on. Fourth, in-service training will become more prevalent as the skills required for implementing PL 94-142 are disseminated to a larger professional audience. Finally, a much broader consideration of placement alternatives and a more formally involved series of proceedings will be necessary to identify the appropriate educational milieu.

One of the amendments that PL 94-142 made to prior legislation was the addition of children with specific learning disabilities to the definition of handicapped persons. For purposes of the Act, Congress defined learning disability in the traditional words of the exclusionary description found in many standard texts (e.g., Myers & Hammill, 1969) and quoted in Chapter 2 (page 22). However, Congress also mandated that the Commissioner of Education publish both regulations and specific criteria for determining when a child was to be considered learning disabled and diagnostic procedures for arriving at this judgment. It also provided that the definition could be changed if necessary. All this was in an apparent attempt to limit the number of children labeled as learning disabled and to provide some uniformity in their identification and assessment. The Office of Education called in a number of experts from education, psychology, and medicine to help. After a year, in a report and proposed set of regulations (Federal Register, November 29, 1976), the Office concluded:

1. It is not possible to specify all the components of each specific learning disability, except to say that in each there is a major discrepancy between expected achievement and ability.
2. Several theories exist as to the cause of learning disabilities.
3. There is no universally accepted explanation as to how and why such children learn or do not learn.
4. It is not possible to list specific standardized diagnostic instruments appropriate for these chidlren nor are there any generally accepted instruments helpful in this regard.

Further, the Office of Education reminded practitioners that when standardized tests are applied to populations not included in the standardization sample, discrimination against certain (unnamed) groups is likely. Finally, it decided that federal regulation of the diagnostic process would be "extremely expensive and impractical," requiring extraordinary costs in time and money as well as reassignment of those involved in diagnosis and evaluation. Thus, it left the Congressional definition intact and contented itself with requiring a severe discrepancy between academic achievement and intellectual ability (derived through a statistical formula), specifying those members who must be part of the team evaluating potential learning disabled children, and only vaguely delineating the devices to be used in the evaluation process. In sum, the proposed regulations and the formula proposed to measure severe learning discrepancy (SLD) did little to advance the theory, assessment, or diagnosis of learning disabilities. The diagnosis was clearly tied to measured intelligence as the criterion for ability, with all the pitfalls and problems that entails. The proposed regulations and the SLD formula particularly raised strong concern from almost every quarter.

Because of this criticism, and to fulfill its obligation to Congress, HEW revised the proposed learning disabilities regulations and published final rules in the Federal Register on December 29, 1977. The exclusionary definition of learning disabilities was kept almost entirely intact. The universally abhorred formula was deleted but the requirement for a severe discrepancy between achievement and intellectual ability in one of seven areas (e.g., basic reading skill, written expression, mathematics calculations) was retained. In addition to the evaluation procedures required for all handicapped children delineated in § 121a.532 of the August 23, 1977 regulations, the learning disabilities regulations require evaluation by a multidisciplinary team consisting of the child's teacher and at least one person qualified to conduct individual diagnostic tests such as a school psychologist, speech-language pathologist, or remedial reading teacher. Further, each child was required to be observed in the regular classroom setting.

REHABILITATION ACT OF 1973 (PL 93-112 AS AMENDED BY PL 93-516)

In a multipurpose law to promote the education and training of handicapped persons, Congress declared in the final provision of the Rehabilitation Act of 1973, section 504, that "No otherwise qualified handicapped individual in the United States . . . shall, solely by reason of his handicap, be excluded from participation in, be denied the benefits of, or be subjected to discrimination under any program or activity receiving Federal financial assistance." In mid-1976 after much delay and many drafts, the Office for Civil Rights, HEW published a lengthy set of regulations implementing this broad right-granting section (Federal Register, May 4, 1977). Subpart D of six subparts pertains to preschool, elementary, and secondary education. In addition to reiterating already established principles with regard to the education of handicapped children, OCR requires that any education program for such children be based on evaluations meeting the following requirements, all of which have direct impact on the assessment practices of special educators:

1. No placement or denial of placement can occur without a full and individual evaluation of each child's special educational needs.
2. All evaluation devices must be validated for the specific purpose for which the school proposes to use them.
3. Any assessment must contain more than tests designed to provide a single general intelligence quotient.
4. No one test or means of evaluation can be used as the sole criterion for placement.
5. Evaluation, other than tests, of such attributes as adaptive behavior, physical condition, and cultural backgrounds must be administered.

Finally, the regulations require periodic re-evaluation of each child's progress and needs. The careful reader should note that if the restrictions of these regulations, especially #2 are seriously followed, few, if any standardized tests in existence would be appropriate for the evaluation of handicapped children or those proposed for special education placement.

SUMMARY

There was a time when the behavior of school officials went virtually unexamined by the legal system. Courts, pleading lack of expert knowledge, were wary of interfering in the discretion of administration or teachers to educate their students. As late as 1968 the Supreme Court was reaffirming the understanding:

> Judicial intervention in the operation of the public school system of the Nation raises problems requiring care and restraint. . . . Courts do not and cannot intervene in the resolution of conflicts which arise in the daily operation of school systems and which do not directly and sharply implicate basic constitutional values (*Epperson v. Arkansas,* 1968, p. 104).

As should be evident from this chapter, the era has ended. Public education for the handicapped—special education—has by no means been tranquil. Indeed, the decade of 1965–1975 found a steady flow of decisions incriminating special education practices. Courts have become vocal in matters regarding testing and several landmark definitions have irrevocably altered assessment procedures and policies in schools. The outcomes of litigation have been incorporated in a series of umbrella laws, particularly PL 94-142, which prescribes minimum standards for acceptable practice. Thus, many past concerns are now tied to the threat of termination of federal financial assistance and the issues of the past decade which prompted a torrent of litigation seem to have been addressed by the legislative process.

However, confrontation will continue on a local basis. PL 94-142 is open to broad interpretation. Key phrases—"the least restrictive environment," "nondiscriminatory assessment," "complete and appropriate assessment" are by their nature quite vague. Since this is the case, implementation at local levels is certain to create conflicts, thereby prompting hearings and renewed litigation. In short, practitioners would do well to remain aware of the outcomes of these imminent events, for the current authors are moved to believe as were Cohen & DeYoung (1973), that the actions discussed in this chapter represent only the beginning of an increasingly close relationship between special education, testing, and the law.

REFERENCES

Abraham, W. The early years: Prologue to tomorrow. *Exceptional Children,* 1976, *42,* 330–335.

Aiello, B. Especially for special educators: A sense of our own history. *Exceptional Children,* 1976, *42,* 244–252.

Altman, I. *The environment and social behavior: Privacy, personal space, territory, crowding.* Monterey, Ca: Brooks/Cole, 1975.

Anastasi, A. Culture fair testing. In G. H. Bracht, K. D. Hopkins, & J. C. Stanley (Eds.), *Perspectives in educational and psychological measurement.* Englewood Cliffs, N.J.: Prentice-Hall, 1972.

Apter, S. J. Applications of ecological theory: Toward a community special education model. *Exceptional Children,* 1977, *43,* 366–373.

Barker, R. G. (Ed.) *The stream of behavior.* New York, Appleton, 1963.

Barker, R. G. *Ecological psychology: Concepts and methods for studying the environment of human behavior.* Stanford, Ca: Stanford University Press, 1968.

Bartel, N. R. & Guskin, S. L. A handicap as a social phenomenon. In W. Cruickshank (Ed.), *Psychology of exceptional children* (3rd ed.). Englewood Cliffs, N.J.: Prentice-Hall, 1970.

Beaney, W. M. The right to privacy and American law. *Law and Contemporary Problems,* 1966, *31,* 253–271.

Bersoff, D. N. Silk purses into sow's ears: The decline of psychological testing and a suggestion for its redemption. *American Psychologist, 1973, 28,* 892–899.

Bersoff, D. N. Professional ethics and legal responsibilities: On the horns of a dilemma. *Journal of School Psychology,* 1975, *13,* 359–376.

Bijou, S. W. & Paterson, R. F. The psychological assessment of children: A functional analysis. In P. McReynolds (Ed.), *Advances in psychological assessment.* Palo Alto, Ca: Science and Behavior Books, 1971.

Brim, O., Glass, D., Neulinger, J., Firestone, I., & Lerner, S. *American beliefs and attitudes about intelligence.* New York: Russell Sage Foundation, 1969.

Bronfenbrenner, U. Toward an experimental ecology of human development. *American Psychologist,* 1977, *32,* 513–531.

Brooks, P. H. & Baumeister, A. A. A plea for consideration of ecological validity in the experimental psychology of mental retardation: A guest editorial. *American Journal of Mental Deficiency,* 1977a, *81,* 407–416.

Brooks, P. H. & Baumesiter, A. A. Are we making a science of missing the point? *American Journal of Mental Deficiency,* 1977b, *81,* 543–546.

Bruininks, R. H. & Rynders, J. E. Alternatives for special class placement for educable mentally retarded children. In E. L. Meyer, G. A. Vergason, & R. J. Whelan (Eds.), *Strategies for teaching exceptional children: Essays from Focus on Exceptional Children.* Denver: Love Publishing, 1972.

Buss, W. What procedural due process means to a school psychologist: A dialogue. *Journal of School Psychology,* 1975, *13,* 298–310.

Carlson, R. A. *The quest for conformity: Americanization through education.* New York: John Wiley, 1975.

Carver, R. P. Two dimensions of tests: Psychometric and edumetric. *American Psychologist,* 1974, *29,* 512–518.

Cohen, J. S. & DeYoung, H. The role of litigation in the improvement of programming for the handicapped. In L. Mann & D. Sabatino (Eds.), *The first review of special education* (Vol. 2). Philadelphia: JSE Press, 1973.

Cronbach, L. J. & Snow, R. E. *Aptitudes and instructional methods: A handbook for research interactions*. New York: Irvington, 1977.

Deno, E. Special education as developmental capital. *Exceptional Children*, 1970, *37*, 229–237.

Dorsen, N., Bender, P., & Neuborne, B. *Emerson, Haber, & Dorsen's political and civil rights in the United States* (Vol. 1). Boston: Little, Brown, 1976.

Dunn, L. M. Special education for the mildly retarded—Is much of it justified? *Exceptional Children*, 1968, *35*, 5–22.

Dunn, L. M. (Ed.) *Exceptional children in the schools: Special education in transition*. New York: Holt, 1973.

Farber, B. *Mental retardation: Its social context and social consequences*. Boston: Houghton Mifflin, 1968.

Feagans, L. Ecological therapy as a model for constructing a theory of emotional disturbance. In W. C. Rhodes and M. L. Tracy (Eds.), *A study of child variance* (Vol. 1). Ann Arbor: University of Michigan Press, 1972.

Flaugher, R. L. The new definition of test fairness in selection: Developments and implications. *Educational Researcher*, 1974, a23, 13–16.

Frazer, W. G., Miller, T. L., & Epstein, L. Bias in prediction: A test of three models with elementary school children. *Journal of Educational Psychology*, 1975, *67*, 490–494.

Goffman, E. *Stigma: Notes on the management of spoiled identity*. Englewood Cliffs, N.J.: Prentice-Hall, 1963.

Hobbs, N. (Ed.) *Issues in the classification of children* (Vols. 1 and 2). San Francisco: Jossey-Bass, 1975.

Hunt, D. E. Person-environment interaction: A challenge found wanting before it was tried. *Review of Educational Research*, 1975, *45*, 209–230.

Illich, I. *Deschooling society*. New York: Harper & Row, 1971.

Kabler, M. L. Public Law 94-142 and school psychology: Challenges and opportunity. *The School Psychologist Digest*, 1977, *6*, 19–30.

Katz, M. B. *Class bureaucracy and schools*. New York: Praeger, 1971.

Kirp, D. L. Student classification, public policy, and the courts. *Harvard Educational Review*, 1974, *44*, 7–55.

Linn, R. L. Fair test use in selection. *Review of Educational Research*, 1972, *43*, 139–160.

Lippman. W. The abuse of tests. *New Republic*, 1922, *32*, 297–298.

MacMillan, D. L. Special education for the mildly retarded: Servant or savant? *Focus on Exceptional Children*, 1971, *2*, 1–11.

Mandel, R. L. The law and education: A brief overview. *Journal of School Psychology*, 1975, *13*, 287–297.

McClelland, D. C. Testing for competence rather than for intelligence. *American Psychologist*, 1973, *28*, 1–14.

McDermott, P. A. Law, liability, and the school psychologist: Malpractice and liability. *Journal of School Psychology*, 1972, *10*, 397–407.

McNemar, Q. On so-called test bias. *American Psychologist*, 1975, *30*, 848–851.

Mercer, J. R. Psychological assessment and the rights of children. In N. Hobbs (Ed.), *Issues in the classification of children* (Vol. 1). San Francisco: Jossey-Bass, 1975.

Mercer, J. R. The struggle for children's rights: Critical juncture for school psychology. *The School Psychology Digest*, 1977, *6*, 4–19.

Myers, P. & Hammill, D. *Methods for learning disorders*. New York: John Wiley, 1969.

Mischel, W. *Personality and assessment*. New York: John Wiley, 1968.

Moos, R. H. *Evaluating treatment environments: A social ecological approach*. New York: John Wiley, 1974.

Parker, R. B. A definition of privacy. *Rutger's Law Review*, 1974, *27*, 275–296.

Peterson, D. R. *The clinical study of social behavior*. New York: Appleton, 1968.

Phillips, L., Draguns, J. G. & Bartlett, D. P. Classification of behavior disorders. In N. Hobbs (Ed.), *Issues in the classification of children* (Vol. 1). San Francisco: Jossey-Bass, 1975.

Proshansky, H. M., Ittelson, W. H., & Rivlin, L. G. (Eds.), *Environmental psychology: Man and his physical setting*. New York: Holt, 1970.

Pryzwansky, W. & Bersoff, D. N. Parental consent for psychological evaluations: Legal, ethical and practical considerations. *Journal of School Psychology*, 1978 (in press).

Reynolds, M. A framework for considering some issues in special education. *Exceptional Children*, 1962, *28*, 367–370.

Reubhausen, D. M. & Brim, D. G Privacy and behavioral research. *Columbia Law Review*, 1965, *65*, 1184–1215.

Rhodes, W. C. The disturbing child: A problem of ecological management. *Exceptional Children*, 1967, *33*, 449–455.

Rhodes, W. C. Human ecology and human care. In K. F. Kramer & R. Rosonke (Eds.), *State of the art: Diagnosis and treatment*. Monograph of the proceedings of the National Regional Resource Center Conference, Reston, Virginia, September, 1974.

Rosenfeld, J. G. & Blanco, R. F. Incompetence in school psychology: The case of Dr. Gestalt. *Psychology in the Schools*, 1974, *11*, 263–269.

Ross, S., DeYoung, H., & Cohen, J. S. Confrontation: Special education and the law. *Exceptional Children*, 1971, *4*, 5–12.

Rothman, D. J. *The discovery of the asylum: Social order and disorder in the new republic*. Boston: Little, Brown, 1971.

Salvia, J. & Clark, J. Use of deficits to identify the learning disabled. *Exceptional Children*, 1973, *39*, 305–308.

Salvia, J. & Ysseldyke, J. *Assessment in special and remedial education*. Boston: Houghton Mifflin, 1978.

Sattler, J. M. Intelligence testing of ethnic minority-group and culturally disadvantaged children. In L. Mann & D. Sabatino (Eds.), *The first review of special education* (Vol. 2). Philadelphia: JSE Press, 1973.

Schmidt, F. L. & Hunter, J. E. Racial and ethnic bias in psychological tests: Divergent implications of two definitions of test bias. *American Psychologist*, 1974, *29*, 1–8.

Shils, E. Privacy: Its constitution and vicissitudes. *Law and Contemporary Problems*, 1966, *31*, 281–306.

Silberman, C. E. *Crisis in the classroom: The remaking of American education*. New York: Vintage Books, 1970.

Sommer, R. *Personal space: The behavioral basis of design*. Englewood Cliffs, N.J.: Prentice-Hall, 1969.

Teitelbaum, H. & Hiller, R. J. Bilingual education: The legal mandate. *Harvard Educational Review*, 1977, *47*, 138–170.

Thorndike, R. L. Concepts of culture-fairness. *Journal of Educational Measurement*, 1971, *8*, 63–70.

Tobias, S. Achievement treatment interactions. *Review of Educational Research*, 1976, *46*, 61–74.

Turnbull, R. H. III. Accountability: an overview of the impact of litigation on professionals. *The School Psychology Digest*, 1977, *6*, 46–52.

Wesman, A. G. Intelligent testing. *American Psychologist,* 1968, *23,* 267–274.

Westin, A. F. *Privacy and freedom.* New York: Atheneum, 1967.

Wittrock, M. C. The evaluation of instruction: Cause-and-effect relations in naturalistic data. In M. C. Wittrock & D. E. Wiley (Eds.), *The evaluation of instruction.* New York: Holt, 1970.

Wolfensberger, W. *Normalization: The principle of normalization in human services.* Toronto: National Institute on Mental Retardation, 1972.

Ysseldyke, J. E. Diagnostic-prescriptive teaching: The search for aptitude-treatment interactions. In L. Mann & Sabatino (Eds.), *The First Review of Special Education.* New York: Grune & Stratton, 1973.

Ysseldyke, J. E. & Salvia, J. Diagnostic-prescriptive teaching: Two models. *Exceptional Children,* 1974, *41,* 181–186.

SUGGESTED READINGS

Cardon, B. W., Kuriloff, P. J., & Phillips, B. N. *Law and the school psychologist: challenge and opportunity.* New York: Human Sciences Press, 1975.

Hobbs, N. (Ed.) *Issues in the classification of children* (Vols. 1 and 2). San Francisco: Jossey-Bass, 1975.

Koocher, G. P. (Ed.) *Children's rights and the mental health professions.* New York: John Wiley, 1976.

LIST OF CASES

State *ex rel* Beattie v. Board of Education, 169 Wis. 231, 172 N.W. 153 (1919).

Bd. of Examiners of Veterinary Med. v. Mohr, 485 P.2d 235 (Oklahoma, 1971).

Brown v. Board of Education, 347 U.S. 483 (1954).

Diana v. Board of Education, Civil Action No. C-70-37 (N.D. Cal. 1970).

Epperson V. Arkansas, 3 3 U..S. 97 (1968).

Frederick L. v. Thomas, 419 F. Supp. 960 (E.D. Pa. 1976).

Griggs, v. Duke Power Co., 401 U.S. 424 (1971).

Hobson v. Hansen, 269 F. Supp. 401 (D.D.C. 1967), *aff'd en banc. sub. nom.,* Smuck v. Hobson, 408 F.2d 175 (D.C. Cir. 1967).

P. v. Riles, 343 F. Supp. 1306 (N.D. Cal. 1971).

Lau v. Nichols, 414 U.S. 563 (1974).

Maryland Ass'n. for Retard. Child. v. Maryland, No. 77676 (Md. Cir. Ct., Balto., City, April 9, 1974).

Merriken v. Cressman, 364 F. Supp. 913 (E.D. Pa. 1973).

Mills. v. D. C. Board of Education, 348 F. Supp. 866 (D.D.C. 1972).

Natanson v. Kline, 186 Kan. 393, 350 P.2d 1093 (1960).

New York Ass'n. for Retard. Child., Inc. v. Rockefeller, 357 F. Supp. 752 (E.D.N.Y. 1972).

Pennsylvania Association for Retarded Children v. Commonwealth, 334 F. Supp. 1257; 343 F. Supp. 279 (E.D. Pa. 1971).

Ricci v. Greenblatt, Civil Action No. 72-496-F (D. Mass. 1972).
Roe v. Wade, 410 U.S. 113 (1973).
Stewart v. Phillips, Civil Action No. 70-1199 F (D. Mass. 1970).
Tinker v. Des Moines Independent Community School District, 393 U.S. 503, (1969).
Washington v. Davis, 426 U.S. 229 (1976).
Watson v. City of Cambridge, 157 Mass. 561, 32 N.E. 864 (1893).
Wilkinson v. Vesey, 110 R.I. 606, 295 A.2d 676 (1972).
Wood v. Strickland, 420 U.S. 308 (1975).
Wyatt v. Stickney, 325 F. Supp. 781 (M.D. Ala. 1971).

STATUTORY MATERIALS

PL 93-112 as amended by PL 93-516 (Rehabilitation Act of 1973).
PL 93-380 (Educational Amendments of 1974).
PL 94-142 (Education for All Handicapped Children Act of 1975).
Federal Register, June 17, 1976, j*41*, 24670-24675.
Federal Register, November 29, 1976, *41*, 52406-52407.
Federal Register, May 4, 1977, *42*, 22676-22702.
Federal Register, August 23, 1977, *42*, 42474-42518.
Federal Register, December 29, 1977, *42*, 65082-65085.

SECTION II

Ascertaining and Describing Learner Characteristics in Educationally Handicapped Populations

Many problems confront the practicing special educator. Two of the major ones are (1) operationalizing definitions of high incidence handicapping conditions (e.g., learning disabilities) and (2) extracting information about the learner and the learning environment which may be used in decisions on the most appropriate placement in the least restrictive alternative, and the preparation and implementation of the individual education program.

The chapters contained in Section II of this volume address these two issues by requesting that the reader invest in a systematic view of learner characteristics of the handicapped. Utilization of a systematic view of learner characteristics demands that the special educator use a consistent set of observations and report traits in a consistent language. Thus, dependence on specific tests—or presumptive categorized biases—can give way to the systematic search for answers when academic and nonacademic behaviors draw the attention of the observer.

Model assessment strategies for perceptual-cognitive, language, and the most prevalent academic assessment procedures are provided, based upon the systematic organization of assessment information ascertained from specification-selected learner characteristics. It is felt that these topics are far more descriptive and accurate and, consequently, avoid the increasingly duplicate discussions of highly similar categorical groupings. Taken together, the contents of this section form a nucleus of information for the construction of individual educational programs for high incidence handicapped children and youth.

David A. Sabatino

6

Systematic Procedure for Ascertaining Learner Characteristics

Public Law 94-142, the Education of the Handicapped Act of 1975, requires that an individual education program (IEP) be prepared as the first step in educating all handicapped children. The importance of an IEP cannot be overemphasized as it delineates the specific educational objectives and strategies for each handicapped child. It represents the beginning of instructional accountability in special education.

To initiate an IEP, all information concerning the student must be examined against the backdrop of (1) what opportunity the child has had to learn, and (2) how that material was taught. Beyond this, the IEP reflects the type and amount of learning experience necessary to achieve some specified learning goals. The National Association of State Directors of Special Education (NASDSE) (1976) has prepared a very concise statement explaining the IEP:

> *Individual Education Program (IEP).* A written statement describing the educational objectives for and the services to be provided to each handicapped child. Educational objectives and services include both instruction and those related services required to meet the unique needs of the handicapped child and are derived from a careful evaluation of the child and his environment. The elements included in the plan are statements of present educational performance, annual goals, short-term instructional objectives and services to be provided to meet these objectives, conditions under which services will be delivered (where, when, and by whom) and evaluation criteria.

In addition, the NASDE (1976) work suggests that the plan must proceed on at least two levels. These levels are:

The total service plan—that plan which describes long term goals and strategies for both instructional and related services (and) the *individual implementation plan* which states short term objectives and specific strategies for intervention.

In effect then, the IEP is the structure through which educational technology of the 1980s will flow in order to describe (and maintain accountability for) the description of learner characteristics for special education instruction.

The measurement of children's performance is an integral part of the IEP. But, since most education takes place in the public schools, which are organizations contained within the hierarchy of community, county, state, and federal structures, there are constraints on *what* can be measured, *how* that measurement can be conducted, and *what* treatment may be evoked. And, although the IEP is a requirement of PL 94-142, few teachers yet have sufficient professional preparation to describe learner characteristics with ease, accuracy, comfort, and in an organized manner. Formal and informal assessment provides most of the information for the instructional outcomes of the IEP. For conceptual purposes, at least, the IEP may be divided into: (1) instructionally related management, and (2) behaviorally related management. The teaching procedures or strategies for instituting instructional management are numerous. Likewise, there are several designs for delivering instructional services in special education, the more common of which will be addressed in the last section of the chapter.

To summarize, educators work within a social organization with expectations and restraints guiding professional behavior. The school is a setting where children are expected to learn; teachers are there to help them and an IEP may be considered a tool in that effort. The rest of this chapter describes systematic procedures useful in structuring educational objectives and strategies for the handicapped.

MODELS OF SYSTEMATIC DIAGNOSIS

In Chapter 1 it was established that educational diagnosis should consider three areas of input: (1) the person, (2) the person's ability to form relationships, and (3) the learning enviornment. Rarely do we obtain too little diagnostic data pertaining to these three areas. Frequently we obtain too much data and the task becomes one of filtering and organizing that information into an educationally meaningful recommendation. Unless the information collected is systematically organized around a useful framework, three problems will result: (1) the observer will be *viewing only the apparent,* failing to examine less conspicuous behaviors; (2) the observer will not have a consistent basis for observing different people, under varying conditions, or in different relationships; and (3) there will not be a common format for viewing inter- or intraindividual behaviors against various classroom environments. Let us emphasize that it is *not* being suggested that the same tests, or the same observational procedures be administered to every person being described. Rather, it is stressed here that a diagnostic format that systematically identifies and isolates cultural, academic, and nonacademic behaviors will overlook fewer essentials than a haphazard respond to a problem. Moreover, such a systematic study of learner characteristics leads to a step-by-step procedure for ascertaining and describing behaviors. In view of this need a number of prominent special educators have approached this problem. A few of these models will be discussed.

Dunn's Model

Dunn (1968, pp. 12–13) includes several step-by-step diagnostic procedures in developing a sound diagnostic procedure.

> The first step would be to make a study of the child to find what behaviors he has acquired along the dimension being considered. Next, samples of a sequential program would be designed to move him forward from that point. In presenting the program, the utility of different reinforcers, administered under various conditions, would be investigated. Also, the method by which he can best be taught the material should be determined. Different modalities for reaching the child would also be tried. Thus, since the instructional program itself becomes the diagnostic device, this procedure can be called diagnostic teaching. Failures are program and instructor failures, not pupil failures. . . . This diagnostic procedure is viewed as the best available since it enables us to assess continuously the problem points of the instructional program against the assets of the child. After a successful and appropriate prescription has been devised, it would be communicated to the teachers in the pupil's home school and they would continue the procedure as long as it is necessary and brings results. From time to time, the child may need to return to the center for reappraisal and redirection.

In essence then, Dunn suggested a paradigm or pattern for assessment that provides a continuous use of data suited to a particular child. In addition, Dunn made clear that failures should not be attributed to the child but rather a failure in the educational system surrounding the child.

Dunn, in this statement, essentially set a pattern of accountability which seems destined for continuation through the IEP procedures of P.L. 94-142.

Quay's Model

Quay (1968) suggested a conceptual framework that permits the assessment of exceptional children on educationally relevant variables. In his information processing model Quay indicates that the composition of an educationally relevant variable is one which can be manipulated as a learning process in the classroom. He then defines an input, response, and reinforcement model that provides those things that must be considered as important dignostic variables. For example, he notes that the acuity in all senses might be a point of initial observation or measurement of input considerations. Then the diagnostician would be concerned with the response counterpart which might be dexterity, or the ability to respond accurately and appropriately. The third component, reinforcement, would be orientation toward the stimulus so that the child may respond. Orientation is a reinforcer but it also assists the child with future stimulus inputs. Following acuity as an input is perception, which is the ability to differentiate relevant dimensions of a stimulus. Organization is the required response to incoming perceptual information, and storage refers to the ability to retail stimulus data. Effect is the capacity of a reinforcer to actually reinforce; delay of reinforcement and the amount of a reinforcer are terms that denote when and how much reinforcement was applied. Ratio is the frequency with which the correct response is reinforced. The graphic representation portraying the input, response, and reinforcement model is reproduced in Figure 6-1. It may be seen that the above categories are further enhanced by the inclusion of modalities on the ordinate of the figure. The result is, at the least, an organizational schema for the collection of measurement data. At the most, it may assist in identifying areas of strength or weakness in the individual child. This, of course, is a primary concern for measurement in the IEP.

Information-processing models such as Quay's, which describe learning procedures, are not new. Neisser (1967, Simon (1967), and Broadbent (1958), are only a few of the scientists who have directed their life's work toward the belief that information is processed in a systematic manner. Unfortunately, while most scientists will agree that information flows into and from the central nervous system, there is no agreement on how it is processed. Thus, although such models have great appeal, there is generally only tentative evidence that supports their premises. The value of any

	PARAMETERS													
	Input				Response				Reinforcement					
	FUNCTIONS				FUNCTIONS				FUNCTIONS					
MODALITIES	Acuity	Orien-tation	Percep-tion	Failure to Store	Dexter-ity	Orien-tation	Organi-zation	Delay	Acuity	Orien-tation	Effect	Delay	Amt.	Ratio
Visual														
Auditory														
Tactile														
Motor														
Verbal														
Primary														
Social														
Information														

Fig. 6-1. The parameters, modalities, and functions of classroom learning. From Quay, *Exceptional Child,* 1968 *35,* p. 28.

information processing may lie more in its organizational, hypothesis formulation-testing abilities, than its capability to actually represent the learning event.

Iscoe's Model

There are simple models to establish systematic diagnosis which avoid the arguments posed by the disagreement on the nature of the specific information processes that make up learner characteristics. Iscoe (1972) has developed a simplified scale for the functional classification of exceptional children. He specifies three domains, each having three functional and/or performance-based considerations within them. The three domains in this classification process are:

1. Physical Domain
   A. Visibility—the child's appearance.
   B. Locomotion—the ability to move around.
   C. Communication—oral language or other communication skill.

II. Perceived Adjustment Domain
   A. Peer acceptance—how well does (s)he get along with peers.
   B. Family interaction—consistent dynamics of relationships among family members.
   C. Self-esteem—self-concept, feeling toward self.

III. Educational Domain
   A. Motivation—to work at the suggestion of the teacher.
   B. Academic level—actual school performance.
   C. Educational Potential—projected school performance based on intelligence tests or other measures.

Iscoe has developed a rating form that the reader may wish to examine in some detail (Table 6-1). The output of the rating scale is a communication facilitating profile that may be used in planning and evaluating programs of treatment. The profile provides a multirater input; various members of the same or different disciplines may learn to use the language of the rating form in a consistent manner. Thus, an advantage of the scale lies in providing mutually intelligible responses. But, the key to this systematic rating device is that all users are trained to use the same language. Therefore, the terminology of the instrument must mean the same thing to the examiner and all who will use the information. For example, in the case where a resource teacher would provide service at a building level with this device, interrater reliability should be ascertained. This would also be true of other similar circumstances. The reader is referred to Chapter 4 for a discussion of interrater agreement calculation procedures.

Table 6-1
Proposed Rating Form

Date ____________

Name ________________________ Age _____ Sex _____ Problem ____________
Rater Clinic, Agency,
and Speciality ____________________ or School ____________________________

Supplemental Information ____

Circle the number most appropriate to the child. Ratings are always made comparative to normal children of same sex and age.

VISIBILITY

1. The physical appearance gives no indication of the condition. Note—for gifted children, use this rating unless there is another condition along with being gifted.
2. There are some very slight indications of the condition, apparent to the trained specialist but not to the layman.
3. There are some fairly obvious signs of the disability or condition. It would be apparent to the layman.
4. There are moderately severe indications of the condition. The child stands out more than in #3 but less than in #5.
5. The condition is severe, it stands out clearly to all concerned.

LOCOMOTION

1. No apparent or reported difficulty in this area.
2. A little restriction but not enough to warrant special help.
3. Moderate restriction. Can keep up with his peers in some ways; in others, needs help or direction of others.
4. Moderately severe restriction. Needs help or direction most of the time; more than in #3, less than #5.
5. Severe restriction of locomotion. Needs constant help and direction.

COMMUNICATION

1. No difficulty at all, observed or reported.
2. Slight difficulty apparent to the trained worker, not to the layman.
3. Moderate difficulty, observable to the layman.
4. Moderately severe difficulty, easily noticeable to the layman. Not as severe as #5, but more severe than #3.
5. Severe difficulty manifested in this area.

PSYCHOLOGICAL ACCEPTANCE

1. No problem exists in this area. Well accepted and sought after by peers. This is mutual.
2. Slight problem, possibly transient in nature. Not evident to any but experienced professionals. Acceted by great majority of peers.

Table 6-1 (continued)

3. Some evidence of difficulty. Noticeable to the layman after a while. Evident to the professional even though problem may be transient in nature. Still has some peer acceptance but general relationship to his group is brittle.
4. Moderately severe. Rejected by most of peers. Problem is not likely to be transient. Little effort to seek out friends. Social skills poorly developed.
5. Severe rejection by peers. Not accepted, little effort expended in making friends. Socialization at a minimum and the problem most likely one of long standing.

From Iscoe and Payne in Trapp & Hamelstein, *Readings on the exceptional child,* 1972, pp. 16–20.

Hickey and Hoffman's Model

Hickey & Hoffman (1973) contend that most educational diagnoses merely relate to achievement levels. They believe that the following four aspects should also be assessed:

(A) Cognitive style (concrete/abstract)
(B) Learning style (visual/auditory/kinesthetic)
(C) Need for teaching structure (remedial, speech class)
(D) Preferred mode of instruction (independent study, one-to-one, small and large group)

Once these data are obtained then prescriptive learning packages or activities may be developed that take into consideration the various combinations of learner characteristics. Both formal and informal procedures can be identified throughout this book that will provide measurement data in each of the four aspects of Hickey and Hoffman (1973) model.

Caterall's Model

Caterall (1970) has described a model of service delivery which has diagnostic implications. The major aspects of this model are the directness of approach (direct or indirect intervention) and the focus of approach (the environmental or personal interaction plane). The taxonomy described by Caterall assists the diagnostician consider the many influential factors of learning. Among them are the role of the teacher, the role of support personnel, the classroom environment, the directness or indirectness of the intervention.

Caterall (1970, p. 5) provides the following definitions that have relevance both in measurement and instruction:

(A) Things that can be done around the student—Environmental Interventions.
(B) Things that can be done to the student—Installed Interventions.

(C) Things that can be accomplished by the student—Assigned Interventions.
(D) Things that can be done with the student—Transactional Interventions.

An example of environmental interventions would be special class placement; installed intervention would be changing or adding reinforcers to increase or stabilize a behavioral response; indirect assigned intervention would be the completion of social role playing designed to assist the student handle "real" social situations; while, transactional intervention is direct student-interviewer relationships such as contact-schedule product of assigned lessons, or desired behavioral response.

In general, Caterall's (1970) taxonomy is straight forward and easy to understand. Its use seems quite practical in formulating student IEPs.

	WHAT	WHO	HOW
STAGE I	Identifying skills for group instruction based on the following: A. Demands of core program B. Analysis of "Hard Data"	TEACHERS AND READING SPECIALIST	Core program material
STAGE II	Individualized implementation of in-class program based on the following: A. Pupil response B. Teacher observation of pupils in group C. Reading Specialist observations of pupils in group D. Analysis of appropriate instructional sequence	Classroom teacher individualizes according to pupils needs within classroom Consultation with the reading specialist may be necessary	Selected supplementary materials according to mode and need of pupil. Techniques: Utilize a variety of materials —manipulative, paper-pencil, observational, combination.
STAGE III	Specific Prescription using supplemental services based on the following: A. Pass-fail test data B. Classroom response C. Prerequisite skills	READING SPECIALIST	Implementation of specific skills by reading aide or tutors using selected materials chosen by Reading Specialist

Fig. 6-2. Three-stage diagnostic teaching plan format.

Louisville Public School Model

A three-stage diagnostic format for implementing educational prescriptions in response to the what, which, and how a method or materials are to be taught was developed by a special project in the Louisville Public Schools. The stages and what, which, and how dimensions are described in the following prescriptive teaching plan (Fig. 6-2). An interesting feature of the Louisville plan lies in its use of the resource concept; i.e., the model specifies how much of each service will be required to meet some identified pragmatic goal. By so aligning personnel and curriculum materials the instructor has a much improved opportunity to arrange educational resources for maximum effectiveness.

MODELS OF LEARNING PROCESSES

Educational management models are needed to explain how human learning takes place. This includes a study of how environmental information is received by the sensory organs, perceptually interpreted as meaningful symbols, and converted to language concepts for cognitive awareness and control of the environment. The following models which attempt to explain how learning takes place are themselves outlines for subsequent assessment program models. There are differences in these models, but for the most part, they are very similar. This suggests that the disagreement between most of these models is not one addressed to the behavior to be assessed, but how it is to be measured or described.

Sabatino's Model

Sabatino (1968) developed a descriptive model which shows that environmental stimulation begins as sensory input in the receptors, where it is coded neurally for transmission to the perceptual centers. Perception is the interpretation of sensory information into meaningful units for further relay to the language reception centers. In these centers, language is formed into symbolic conceptual units. The higher centers must be able to receive, express, associate, and mediate symbolic conceptual units in a systematic manner if language is to be used normally. The model implies that the integration, sequencing, and storage (memory) of perceptual information is from both visual and auditory input. Perception follows, and arousal occurs as the interconnection between a meaningful perceptual input is relayed to the appropriate units within the language centers of the central nervous system. This last point has important educational implications: a lack of arousal may be the reason that certain information cannot maintain a child's attention and therefore is not directed into the symbolic

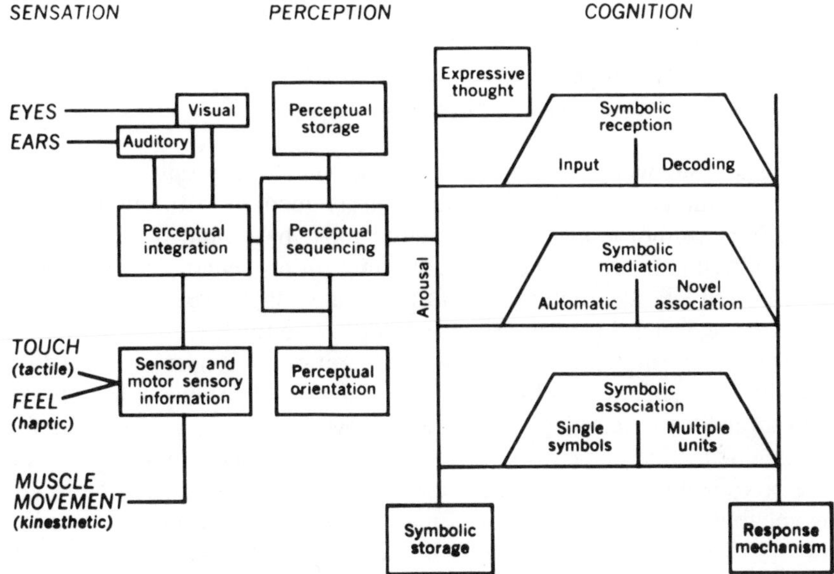

Fig. 6-3. The model used to describe the information-processing behaviors. From Wendell, K. Diagnosing hearing difficulties: A sequential strategy. *DLD,* 1970, *6,* pp. 15–21.

conceptual centers where it can be "learned." Figure 6-3 is a graphic display of the information-processing model.

From a practical standpoint, the information-processing model developed by Sabatino results in a systematic assessment procedure using a descriptor system. The purpose of the descriptor system is to insure that most academic and nonacademic behaviors which can be described, are described. The basic description may suggest that the behavior is within a normal range for that particular child's age, or it is indeed inhibiting the child's function in that and related areas of performance.

The psychoeducational diagnostician using similar systems should view it as a pilot does a preflight check-off of his aircraft. The research to date (Sabatino, 1968; Ryckman & Wiegerink, 1969; Sabatino & Hayden, 1970a, 1970b) suggests there are at least four areas that must be described in this check-off: visual perception, auditory perception, perceptual integration, and receptive-expressive language. Since these four information-processing behavioral complexities can only be studied through selective stimulus input, and while the exact nature of the component traits of each complex behavior is not clear, a stimulus response descriptor system has been developed to assist the diagnostician classify learner characteristics. The system has four major classifications:

1. Sensory-motor
2. Perceptual-motor
3. Language-cognitive
4. Academic-social/environmental relationship.

These four were selected because they make it possible to classify learner characteristics for study and for assignment to instructional materials. Sensory-motor disabilities are the most basic and frequently the most difficult to remediate in obtaining improvement in academic achievement. Perceptual-motor training may show some transfer to academic learning, but it is primarily to provide for the classification of perceptual information, storage, and integration of sensory information received by visual and auditory senses. Language learning is directly related to academic learning, for without language, there is little basis for learning academic subject matter. However, language training as in the case of vocabulary development, does not automatically mean that reading vocabulary will also increase. Finally, while direct academic remediation of achievement skills provides the most efficient time to successfully accomplish objective increase in academic skill growth, it will not improve coordination or balance, perception, and possibly new language learning. In short, educational prescriptions can provide the training of a specific academic or nonacademic behavior. The professional judgment of the educator is required to determine the behavior or academic skill that needs the most attention. To facilitate the judgment process, a system identifying many of the more important specific human learning characteristics is provided in Table 6-2. Needless to say, repeated academic failure has a profound effect on the social and classroom development of handicapped children and youth. Therefore, any assessment of academic skills should include how the child feels about academic learning and the school environment.

Wendell's Model

Wendell's (1970) outline of sequential strategy, a systematic diagnostic procedure, is more comprehensive in scope than the one proposed by Sabatino. In the model Wendell proposes four stages and multiple substages. These are:

- Stage 1. Screening Assessment
  - A. Observation and Conversation
  - B. Testing
- Stage 2. Evaluation of Screening/Assessment
- Stage 3. Hypothesis Testing
  - A. Testing

Table 6-2
Descriptor System for Classifying Learner Characteristics

1.0	MOTOR
1.1	Gross
1.11	Coordination-Balance
1.12	Strength-Endurance
1.2	Perceptual-Motor
1.21	Eye-Hand Coordination
1.22	Directionality
1.3	Body Awareness
2.0	PERCEPTION
2.1	Visual
2.11	Discrimination
2.12	Memory
2.13	Integration/primary visual input
2.2	Auditory
2.21	Discrimination
2.22	Memory
2.23	Integration/primary auditory input
2.3	Tactile
3.0	LANGUAGE
3.1	Conceptual
3.11	Concrete
3.12	Functional
3.13	Abstract
3.2	Expressive
3.21	Vocabulary
3.22	Syntax
3.3	Receptive
4.0	ACADEMICS
4.1	Reading
4.11	Letter Recognition
4.12	Word Attack
4.121	Phonics
4.122	Structural Analysis
4.13	Word Recognition
4.14	Vocabulary
4.15	Comprehension
4.2	Spelling
4.3	Writing
4.31	Manuscript
4.32	Cursive
4.4	Arithmetic
4.41	Numeration
4.42	Computation
4.43	Measurement

B. Consultation
C. Experimental Investigation
Stage 4. Diagnostic Formulation
A. Provisional Diagnosis
B. Full Diagnostic Formulation

Table 6-3 provides the sequential strategies and performances which should be examined in a systematic manner. The sequential strategy for further investigation is indicated by number arrangement (the extreme right-hand column in Table 6-3). By examining the sequence the diagnostician can obtain some clinical feel for related behaviors that must be assessed or at least considered.

Wendell's diagnostic teaching model not only asks if a material or method works, but it also requests the diagnostician to specify a hypothesis on *why* and *how* the learner will react to a given instructional or behavioral management strategy. The diagnostic teaching system proposed by Wendell demands that the diagnostician know the following information:

1. Adequacy of physical conditions
2. Development of basic cognitive skills

Table 6-3
Wendell's Outline of Sequential Strategy

Stage 1. Screening Assessment	
A. Observation & Conversation	
Rapport, motivation and attention	44
Social adequacy and interests	37–39
Adjustment	35–38, 41, 42
History: personal	40
medical	42
educational	41
Sensori-motor state	24–27, 29–31
health	42
Speech	28
B. Testing	
General abilities (abbreviated individual intelligence test)	
verbal	10–13, 22, 23
nonverbal	18–23
Educational achievement	
Reading (word recognition)	(+) 1; 4–6
Spelling (word spelling)	(+) 2, 4, 6, 7
Math (oral problem with explanation of method)	(+) 3; 8, 9

Table 6-3 (continued)

Stage 2. Evaluation of Screening Assessment	
A. Possible outcomes	
1. Rapport too poor for reliable evaluation	
a. discontinue testing and observe	44
b. build rapport for subsequent testing	
2. Formulate hypotheses	
a. no problem: discontinue assessment	
b. problem not psycho-educational; re-refer	
c. screening indicates areas for further investigation (stage 3)	
3. No hypothesis possible	
Stage 3. Hypothesis Testing	
A. Testing	
Educational skills (assessment leading to 44, 45 where required)	
1. Adaptive skills: Reading (comprehension)	10–13
2. Spelling (comprehension)	10–13
3. Math (problems)	12–14, 1
4. Basic skills: Reading: knowledge of letter sounds	14–16, 18, 19
5. blending	14, 18, 28
6. knowledge of spelling patterns	14–17 and rules 22
Spelling: knowledge of letter sounds	14–16, 18, 19
spelling patterns	14–17 and rules 22
7. handwriting	19, 29, 33
8. Math: written sums	20
basic operations	22, 31
Cognitive skills (assessment leading to 44, 45 where required)	
10. Language: expressive: vocabulary	14, 18, 26, 28
11. syntax	14, 15, 18
12. receptive: vocabulary	14, 15, 18
13. syntax	14, 15, 18
14. Memory: auditory: verbal	18
15. non-verbal, rhythm	18
16. visual: simple	19
17. sequential	19
18. Perception: auditory	26, 27
19. visual	24, 25, 31
20. Perceptuo-motor: pencil copying	19, 29, 31, 21
21. e-dimensional copying	19, 29, 31
Concept development & reasoning	
22. e.g., Piagetian analysis (seriation, conservation & levels of reasoning)	12, 13, 19, 44
23. e.g., cognitive style (e.g., Kagan's reflexivity—impulsivity)	44

Table 6-3 (continued)

Sensory screening		
24. Vision:	acuity	42
25.	eye-movement	42
26. Hearing:	speech sounds	42
27.	pure tone	42
Motor function screening		
28. Articulation		43
29. Fine motor skills		39, 40–42
30. Gross motor skills		39, 40–42
31. Awareness of body co-ordinates		41
Lateral preference		
32. Eye		40–42
33. Hand		40–42
34. Foot		40–42
Adjustment		
35. Personality		40–42
36. Attitudes		40–42
37. Family relations		40
38. Peer group relations		40, 41
39. Social adequacy		40, 41
B. Consultation		
40. Family and personal history (psychiatric social worker, local authority health and welfare workers)		
41. School behavior: peer and teacher–pupil relations; study habits. (School headmaster, class teacher, counsellor.)		
42. Medical information (e.g., pediatric, psychiatric, E.N.T.)		
43. Speech (speech pathologist)		
C. Experimental investigation (cognitive and behavioral)		
44. e.g., response to graded clues, brief instruction and rewards in free-field or structured		45
Stage 4. Diagnostic Formulation		
A. Provisional diagnosis		
45. 1. recommend (a) experimental action (e.g., in classroom), (b) retesting, (c) serial testing		
2. problem not primarily psychoeducational: transfer case as appropriate		
B. Full diagnostic formulation and recommendation for action, including provision for report back on adequacy of diagnosis.		

From Wendell, *Journal of Learning Disabilities,* 1970, p. 18.

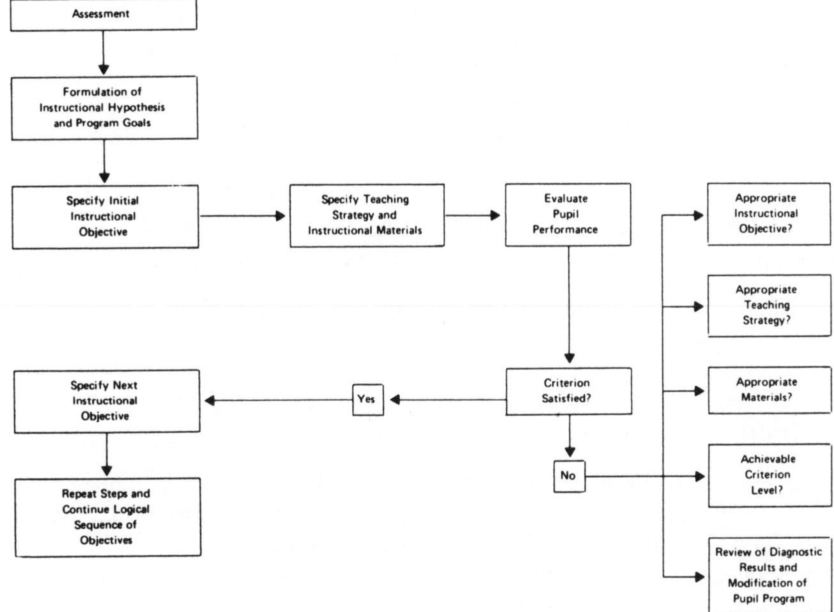

Fig. 6-4. System used to develop an instructional program. From Sabatino, D. A. *Learning Disabilities Handbook*. DeKalb, Ill.: Northern Illinois University Press, 1976, p. 224.

3. Acquisition of relevant concepts
4. Hypothesis of how the learner will possibly respond to a specified task
5. Motivational level
6. History of previous learning and response to formal instruction.

DIAGNOSTIC PRESCRIPTIVE TEACHING METHODS

Reese's Model

Reese (1976) has created an instructional system useful for developing an instructional program (Fig. 6-4). In the model, program goals are established; instructional objectives are presented; and instructional strategies are developed.

The key components of Reese's (1976) system are:

1. Instructional Hypothesis and Program Goals
   The program goals are aimed at remediating:
   a. a specific academic problem
   b. a specific information processing behavior
   c. an overt behavior that interferes with the instructional process
2. Instructional Objectives

Following the establishment of a program goal, the teacher needs to develop specific instructional objectives including three parts:

   a. the skill or behavior the teacher wants to develop
   b. the amount of time the teacher thinks it will take to develop that skill or behavior, and
   c. the degree of success or accuracy the child should demonstrate.
3. Instructional Strategies.

The instructional strategy is the teaching method and material, the behavior management procedure, used to achieve instructional objectives. The two most important considerations in developing the teaching strategy involve the evaluation of the methodologies and materials and the determination of an instructional sequence.

Peter's Model

Peter (1965) was one of the first to articulate a diagnostic system of fucntional analysis or intraindividual assessment known as "prescriptive teaching" or "diagnostic prescriptive teaching." Although this model is most closely associated with the field of learning disabilities (see, for example, the discussion in Kauffman & Hallahan, 1974), it is equally applicable for all exceptional children.

Peter notes that diagnosis must consider the "problem," "situational" and "school" variables. The 12 cells around the tope of the model viewed in Figure 6-5 present the diagnostic variables. The problem variables are handicap, disability, and injury. An injury indicates actual physical damage, disability describes a functional problem, and a handicap hinder performance of a task. A list of variables (nature of pathology, therapeutic procedures, time factors and social conditions) interact with the problem variables to define, rather precisely, the nature of the child's problem. The prescription itself focuses on those variables which can be changed through teacher/system intervention. These events (A–J in Fig. 6-5) are teaching methods, specific objectives, ancillary services, placement personnel, subject matter, instructional materials, special equip-

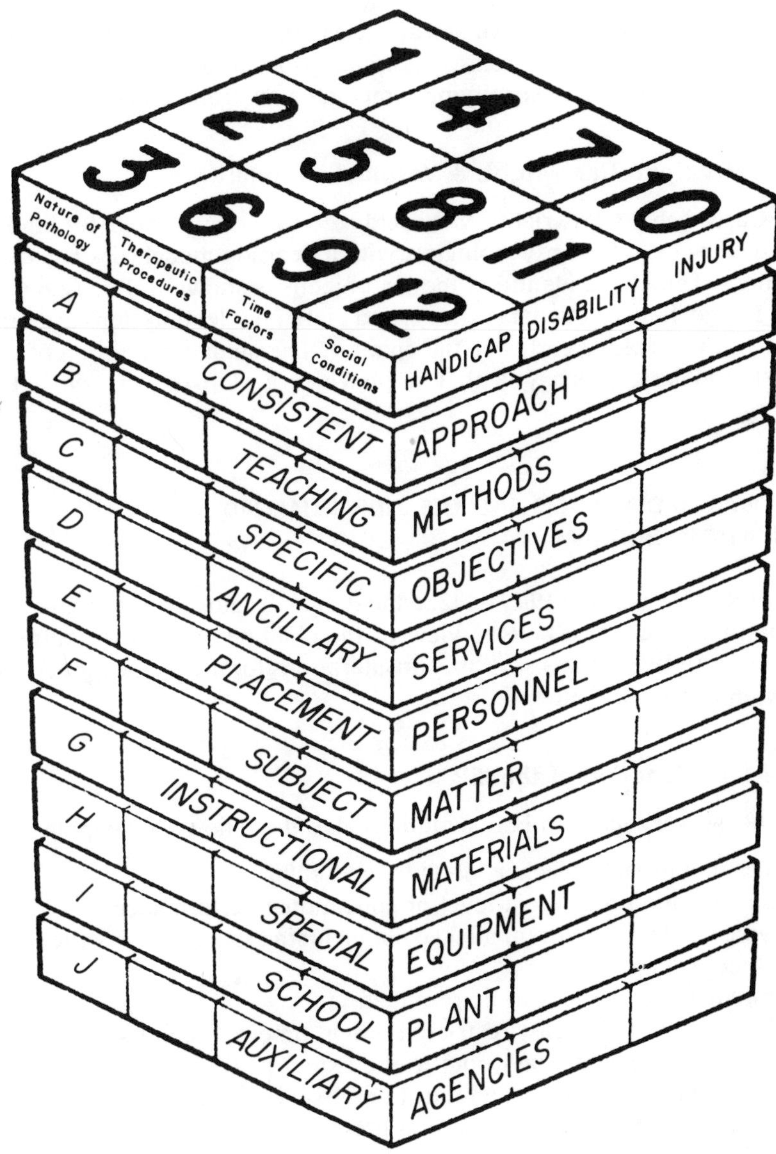

Fig. 6-5. A model for translating findings into a prescription for teaching. From Peter, L. J. *Prescriptive teaching*. New York: McGraw Hill, 1965, p. 63.

ment, school plant, and auxiliary agencies. It may be seen that the outcome of this model is a precisely defined problem and, at the least, an objectified approach to specifying remediable environmental events.

Cartwright, Cartwright, & Ysseldyke Model

Cartwright, Cartwright, & Ysseldyke (1973) contrasted traditional approaches by school psychologists with a decision model for diagnostic teaching. They have identified the six objectives shown in Figure 6-6.

The goal, instructional strategy, and material selection steps are similar to ones discussed earlier in the chapter. The unique dimension of this decision-making process is that it provides a step to "try out" the material.

SYSTEMATIC DIAGNOSIS AND THE INDIVIDUALIZED EDUCATION PROGRAM

Under the aegis of PL 94-142, educational diagnosis has expanded its scope to assure that a holistic view of the child be used to structure an appropriatre IEP. In this section, considerations for the IEP are given and a potential model is offered.

An Explanation of the IEP

At the very least an IEP should involve the following components

1. Team approach (teacher, parents, and child)
2. Specification of present level of educational performance
3. Goals and objectives (annual goals, including short-term instructional objectives)
4. Educational services to be provided
5. Placement in the least restrictive environment (a child shall participate in the regular classroom to the extent possible)
6. Statement of initiation and duration of services
7. Objective criteria and evalaution procedures
8. Schedule and procedure for review (must be at least annually
9. Adequate procedural safeguards

The complete educational program for each handicapped child consists of a series of plans contained in the IEP: the total service plan, the individual implementation plan, and the daily objectives contained in daily lesson plans. The most general is the total service plan, which is

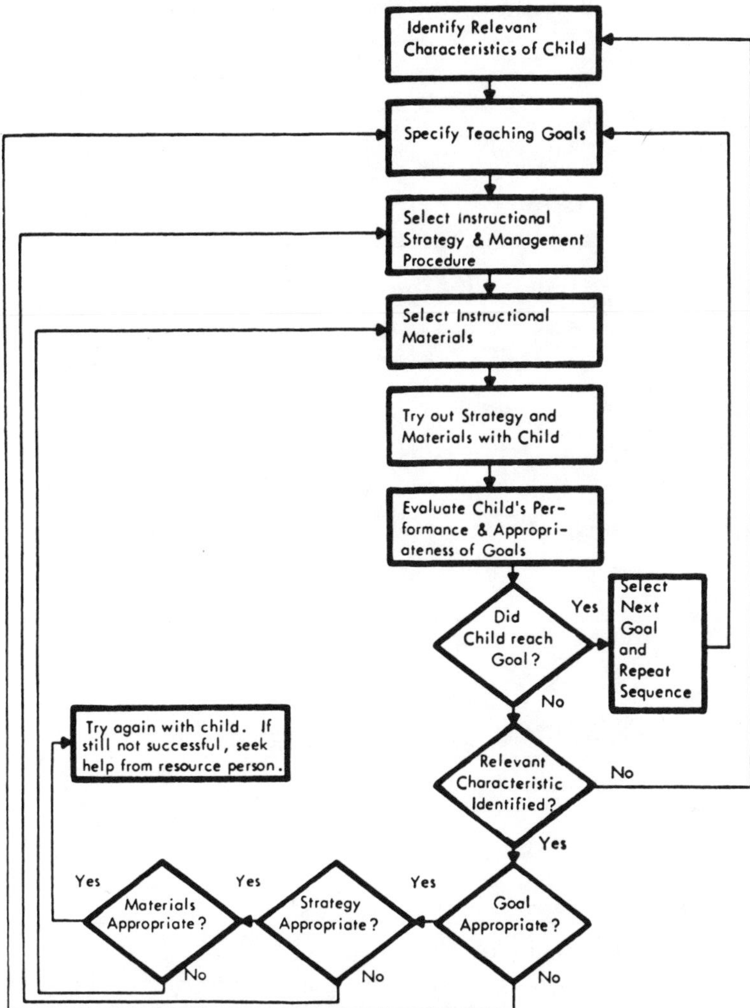

Fig. 6-6. Decision model for diagnostic teaching. From Cartwright, Cartwright, Ysseldyke, *Psychology in the Schools,* 1973, *10, p. 7.*

developed by a committee of professionals, parents, and ancillary personnel familiar with the child. From the general goals formulated by this committee, specific teachers develop the individual implementation plan, which is a specific breakdown of the general goals into instructional objectives. Daily objectives are then derived from the individual implementation plan. Persons may be involved in planning at all three of the levels

Individual Education Program: Total Service Plan

Child's Name ____________

School ____________

Date of Program Entry ____________

Prioritized Long-term Goals:

Summary of Present Levels of Performance:

Short-Term Objectives	Specific Educational and/or Support Services	Person(s) Responsible	Percent of Time	Beginning and Ending Date	Review Date

Percent of Time in Regular Classroom

Committee Members Present ____________

Placement Recommendation

Dates of Meeting ____________

Committee Recommendations for
Specific Procedures/Techniques, Materials, Etc. (include information about learning style)

Objective Evaluation Criteria for each Annual Goal Statement

Fig. 6-7. A model plan for the IEP. From National Association of State Directors of Special Education. *Functions of the placement committee in special education*. Washington, D.C.: NASDSE, 1976, p. 29.

indicated, but it is the committee that has ultimate responsibility for developing and implementing the program. An example of the total service plan derived from the IEP is shown in Figure 6-7.

RECOMMENDED PROCEDURE FOR ESTABLISHING AN IEP

In a systematic procedure to derive the diagnostic information necessary to provide an IEP, several steps are important. All of these steps require two primary ingredients: continuous inservice and good faith communication among members. The major steps are:

1. referral procedure
2. diagnostic procedure
3. reporting procedure
4. program monitory procedure.

Since each of these steps is vital to the total IEP, a review and example of each is now provided.

The Referral Procedure

The referral process is the first step in assuring the proper identification of handicapped children. It includes several distinct components, such as preparing the entire school staff to identify and communicate their questions and observations accurately. Most referral forms contain common information, including *identifying information* about the child: name, birthdate, address, parent's name, grade, number of siblings, parent or family information. A second section frequently includes *school achievment data,* test scores from previously administered instruments, class rank or rating. A third section often relates the *reason for referral,* i.e., why the child has been identified. Other sections include observations regarding: *school behavior, health or medical data,* and *family attitude.*

Every school system or administrative district within a school system has established referral procedures. However, there are several important points that should appear on referrals:

1. Complete identification material
2. Procedures tried with the student
3. Length of the intervention program
4. Student's response to the program
5. Teacher recommendation on future programs

Also, reference should be made to behavioral expectations and performance of the student.

Referrals are intermediary between identification and screening, but more typically referrals are preparatory to in-depth assessment. In either case, referrals are critical because they serve as an initial point of professional concern and are instrumental in educating professional attention.

The following referral model is predicated on the availability of resource staff (counselors, psychologists, reading or resource teachers): (1) It promotes precise use of behavioral descriptors, enhancing the communication process; (2) it prompts the referring teacher to be precise in his or her judgment about a given level of performance; and (3) it permits other observers to quickly note patterns of strengths and weaknesses by studying the profile.

Many of the subtle handicapping conditions in children and youth are difficult to detect. Indeed, some of the not so subtle handicaps, such as sensory problems, may be well camouflaged by the child even at moderate levels of impairment. Children who have mild or moderate developmental difficulties are frequently not detected until they reach the classroom. This finding is particularly true in the upper ranges of the mildly mentally retarded, learning disabled child, and the mildly sensory handicapped. The child may not recognize that what he sees, hears, thinks, or perceives is unlike that which is heard, seen, perceived, or thought by his peers. It is frequently not until entrance to the classroom where specific academic skills are taught and failure becomes obvious, that the handicapped child begins to view himself as different, and/or becomes viewed as different by others. In a class of kindergarten or first-grade children, the more mildly handicapped may not even be differentiated by initial academic achievement tasks.

It has been standard practice to use open-ended essay response referral forms. The primary difficulty with the open-ended essay form is that it does not relate precise data on any given set of academic or nonacademic behaviors. Thus, it may not convey useful information.

A more precise referral form has been developed. As seen in Figure 6-8, it requires the teacher to judge several academic and nonacademic behaviors denoting the age or grade level of performance on which he or she would estimate the child functions.

Proper referral is only as likely as the procedures established for identification can make it. Identification of the mild to moderate handicapped child with sensory difficulties, the mildly mentally retarded, and learning disabled child without concomitant behavioral disability requires skilled observation. At still another, more sophisticated level of identification, the difficulty of discerning *within* the range of acceptable or unacceptable behaviors becomes an immense undertaking. A primary reason that behavioral problems pose major difficulties to the observer is the fact that the observer is dealing with social, cultural, and school-related conditions and few, if any, absolutes. In the case of the sensory impaired, there is an absolute: observations can be made on how well the person interacts with his environment through the senses. Thus, the above case seems to have been a near oversight. The three relative conditions which make the observation of behavior disorders so difficult are: (1) the range of acceptable behaviors, as opposed to unacceptable behaviors, varies with the observer (teacher variance); (2) the student reacts to situations differently (student variance); and (3) there exists a difference in the ability levels, achievement levels, and expectancies for both academic and nonacademic behavior among school buildings (variance among schools).

ID NUMBER ______________

MODEL LEARNING DISABILITIES SYSTEMS
TEACHER REPORT OF PUPIL TRAITS

PUPIL NAME ______________________________ AGE _____ GRADE ____ ____

TEACHER ______________________ SCHOOL ______________ DATE __________

Please evaluate the child on each item in comparison to other children in the same grade by circling the appropriate grade level at which the child is functioning.

1. Word Recognition
   Pre-K K 1.0 1.5 2.0 2.5 3.0 3.5 4.0 4.5 5.0 5.5 6.0 6.5
2. Word Analysis Skills
   Pre-K K 1.0 1.5 2.0 2.5 3.0 3.5 4.0 4.5 5.0 5.5 6.0 6.5
3. Reading Vocabulary
   Pre-K K 1.0 1.5 2.0 2.5 3.0 3.5 4.0 4.5 5.0 5.5 6.0 6.5
4. Reading Comprehension
   Pre-K K 1.0 1.5 2.0 2.5 3.0 3.5 4.0 4.5 5.0 5.5 6.0 6.5
5. Arithmetic Computation
   Pre-K K 1.0 1.5 2.0 2.5 3.0 3.5 4.0 4.5 5.0 5.5 6.0 6.5

Fig. 6-8. Model learning disabilities systems teacher report of pupil traits. From Sabatino, D. A. *Learning Disabilities Handbook.* DeKalb, Ill.: Northern Illinois University Press, 1976, p. 143.

These three possible sources of variance tend to escalate the difficulty in detecting with precision the specific behaviors in children or youth displaying behavioral disorders.

Definition of criteria which determine if a given behavior is essentially normal or troublesome has usually been based on (1) the type of behavior displayed; (2) the frequency of occurrence and interaction or social dimensions, number of persons involved, as well as whom it involves; and (3) ramifications or consequences. Seldom is just one of these dimensions examined. The frequency of the behavior is paramount, to the extent that some of the more popular behavioral problem checklists (such as the Quay & Peterson, 1967) ask the respondent to determine if the child or youth displays the behavior at all, or if seldom, or frequently. The frequency with which a behavior occurs may denote its degree of aberrance. If it is difficult to observe masturbation in the classroom, affects no other student, and if performed only once, the activity would only constitute an "alert" for the experienced teacher. Should, however, masturbation become an overt, frequent, attention-getting occurrence, the identification of that behavior would require planned management as a target behavior, and/or referral for assistance to a support team.

Skilled regular teachers do identify handicapping conditions, and skilled special educators, school psychologists, and speech and language clinicians do have corrective responses following a diagnosis. The principle factor, however, is professional preparation and staff development through in-service of regular education. In a classical study (Wickham, 1928) teachers were asked to identify emotionally disturbed children. They responded by distinguishing primarily those children who displayed annoying, aggressive characteristics. Children who were even intensely withdrawn were not referred. Ten years later, Wickham's (1928) Cleveland, Ohio study was replicated by Rogers (1939) in Columbus, Ohio. But, as a part of the replication, the teachers who were asked to identify the children were provided in-service training. As a result of the in-service preparation, the teachers identified both withdrawn and aggressive children with emotionally based problems. They did not identify those who merely misbehaved aggressively. Therefore, the one conclusion that must be drawn central to the identification process (and subsequent referral process) of handicapped children, is the importance of in-service staff development with regular teachers. The identification of handicapped children may hinge more on a complete program of staff development than any other factor.

Many procedures can lead to a referral for special services. More recently, educators have begun to develop a process termed screening. The commonality between screening and identification is that both are processes for selecting children for referral to a more thorough diagnostic process. However, identification generally means selection through a review of achievement test data, and actual observation of classroom and corridor behavior. Screening generally refers to a formalized procedure of testing, or examination, utilizing a predetermined criteria to select children with handicaps. In effect the screening process attempts to identify those children with mild handicaps who have eluded the teacher's observation.

Again, the importance of in-service should be emphasized. Staff should be acquainted with the coordination of the screening program and their particular role. The population to be screened should be defined and the precise testing instruments and procedures involving their use should be thoroughly explained. The expected outcome of screening should also be discussed.

A screening procedure is completed within a given time period and, therefore, is not an open ended identification procedure. If a child moves into the district, or if a child undergoes emotional trauma, a screening procedure will not suffice because the problem did not exist at the time of screening. Thus, it is vital that identification and screening work hand-in-hand as precursors of diagnosis.

In any case, whether identification proceeds formally, informally, or optimally through both procedures, the referral should proceed through a format similar to Figure 6-8. In this way the conditions are set for the second component of the IEP, individual diagnosis.

Diagnostic Procedure

For the purposes of this chapter, *an educational diagnosis may constitute any procedure or process of ascertaining academic or nonacademic behavioral information which will contribute to the IEP. That includes data necessary for classification, resulting from the study of sensory, neurological, physical, mental, or social and emotional function. The data may be collected by contributing disciplines (e.g., medicine, social work, etc.). The purpose of an educational diagnosis is to describe how a handicapping condition(s) interferes with performance on specified educational tasks or results in behaviors which include social or vocationally-related human functions. A prognostic statement based on recommended interventions is the expected outcome and must be included.* There is little question that an educational diagnosis is of much value in the absence of (1) [personological] data, (2) data related to the interaction of a person in relationship with others, and (3) data related to the learning environment, i.e., the environment describing what has been taught and how.

The desired result of an educational diagnosis is to provide (1) recommended instructional-behavioral management, (2) recommended educational placement, and (3) expected academic and nonacademic behavioral change as a result of various specified interventions, or the outcome in the absence of any intervention strategies.

Information used for diagnosis must be as comprehensive as possible. Physical and cognitive functioning should be evaluated; classroom behavior should be observed; family and peer interactions should be analyzed. The NASDE (1976) guidelines for development of an IEP recommend consideration of the seven areas shown in Table 6-4.

There are many sources of information available for use in evaluating the above areas. The NASDE (1976) publication suggests possible sources that provide useful information (Table 6-5).

When the available data are collected, a conference should be held involving the teacher, parents, and child (where appropriate) in order to determine the need for further assessment.

Reporting Procedure

There are two techniques for reporting information derived from diagnostic entries. The traditional approach is one of preparing a written narrative including the following headings:

1. Identifying Information
   a. Student's name
   b. Chronological age

Table 6-4
NASDE Recommended Guidelines for Development of an IEP

1. Educational functioning
   a. achievement in subject area
   b. learning style
   c. strengths and weaknesses
2. Social-emotional functioning
   a. social/psychological development
      attending/receiving
      responding
      valuing
      organizing
      characterizing
   b. self-help skills
3. Physical functioning
   a. visual
   b. hearing
   c. speech
   d. motor/psychomotor
      gross motor
      fine motor
      medical health
4. Cognitive functioning
   a. intelligence
   b. adaptive behavior
   c. thinking processes
      knowledge
      comprehension
      application
      analysis
      synthesis
      evaluation
5. Language functioning
   a. receptive
   b. expressive—to what kind of input
   c. nonverbal
   d. speech
6. Family
   a. dominant language
   b. parent-child interactions
   c. social service needs
5. Environment
   a. home
   b. school
   c. interpersonal
   d. material

Table 6-5
NASDE Suggested Sources of Information

1. School Records	Inspection of cumulative and other available records can be helpful in determining whether or not there are factors that might help to account for the reason for referral, whether or not there seem to be any trends in problem growth, and whether other areas seem to be in need of closer evaluation.
2. Standardized Tests	Standardized tests may be used to obtain information on how one child compares with other children. In many cases, standardized tests are required for determination of eligibility. This type of test covers such areas as intelligence, achievement, and personality.
3. Developmental Scales	These scales compare areas of child development within the child and as compared with other children. They are especially useful with younger or more severely handicapped children, pinpointing both strengths and weaknesses.
4. Criterion-Referenced Tests	This type of test places the child at a certain level in some area of skill development. It is especially helpful for planning purposes because criterion statements can be used as goals for instruction.
5. Observation	Observational data can focus on a very specific child characteristic, such as a child's interaction with other children, and can point out areas in need of further evaluation and confirm or disconfirm other information. Observations may be formal or informal and include such things as anecdotal records, interaction analysis, checklists, and rating scales. These observations may take place in any setting, including the home. Observational data is best obtained by those who are close to the child in his/her normal environment.
6. Interviews	Interviews with the parent, the child, and/or the teacher yield information which lends perspective to other kinds of information. They also pinpoint areas that may be priority needs or strengths.

Table 6-5 (continued)

7. Work Samples	Work samples are similar to criterion-referenced testing; they provide information concerning the level of the child in some areas of skill development. They are useful in planning intervention in academic areas.
8. Consultants	Consultants may provide information which is not usually available to an educational planner. This may include medical, therapeutic, and family information and may be used to plan services in related areas, define limitations on other planning, or identify areas of major need.

   c. Parents
   d. Address
   e. School
   f. Grade
   g. Teacher
2. Reason for Referral
   A restatement as to why the child was intiially referred.
3. Developmental History
   a. Statement of developmental milestones
   b. Any deviation in normal development
4. Educational History
   a. Previous school experience
   b. Relationship with peers/teachers
   c. School-related behaviors
5. Test Results
   a. The results from previously administered tests
   b. The result from currently administered tests
6. Recommendations

A number of studies have been completed on the impact of the narrative report written by school psychologists (Lucas & Jones, 1970). The conclusion from these studies generally reflect the finding that narrative reports are: (1) difficult to read, (2) ambiguous, (3) time consuming to read, and (4) troublesome to convert into instructional and behavioral management terminology which is meaningful to all readers, including a parent's legal council, or regular educators. It is the author's contention that an individualized education profile, that uses the same learner characteristics that were used in the referral and attempts to report those same characteristics observed or measured during assessment, enhances communication.

The individualized education profile replaces the narrative report with a graphic description of the assessment results indicating general academic and learning aptitude strengths and weaknesses. From this profile, the teacher can plan management strategies. He or she may also use this information for directing any instructional assessment; e.g., if reading comprehension is low and word analysis high on academic screening, she/he might first look diagnostically at reading comprehension. If this work-up provides the teacher with sufficient information for instructional planning, then instruction could begin. Or, if this work-up indicates a need for further diagnostic information, the learning disabilities teacher would continue instructional assessment.

The profile serves as a guide to the teacher for planning the instructional assessment and for setting instructional objectives. A sample of an individualized education profile is provided in Figure 6-9. The following instructions should make operation of the profile possible.

1. Fill out pupil information section
   a. pupil name
   b. I.D. number—should be assigned before any testing is done
   c. sex
   d. birthdate—month and year
2. Raw scores should be converted to grade equivalents. Language scores should be converted to mental age (MA), then subtract five to obtain grade equivalent.
3. Blocks should be filled in (from left to right) up to appropriate grade equivalent score level for each individual category as indicated by converted screening test results.
4. Locate highest grade equivalent score (verbal conceptualization or non-verbal conceptualization). Draw a line from the top of the screening profile to the bottom along the grade equivalent line corresponding to highest language score. This line represents the highest level of expectancy for the student's overall performance.

It should be noted that the profile is simpler and quicker to complete, more objective, and more readily interpretable. For those who so desire, additional information categories could be added with little trouble or effort. In sum these advantages seemingly make the profile attractive as a component of the IEP process.

MODEL LEARNING DISABILITY SYSTEMS
INDIVIDUAL PROFILE RECORD

PUPIL NAME ______________________
I.D. NUMBER __________ SEX _____ BIRTHDATE __________

I. SCREENING PROFILE: DATE ______________

	K	1.0	1.5	2.0	2.5	3.0	3.5	4.0	4.5	5.0	5.5	6.0
ACADEMIC ACHIEVEMENT												
Spelling												
Arithmetic												
Word Recognition												
Reading Comprehension												
LANGUAGE												
Verbal Conceptualization												
Non-Verbal Conceptualization												
VISUAL PERCEPTION												
Discrimination												
Retention												
Sequencing												
AUDITORY PERCEPTION												
Discrimination												
Retention												
Sequencing												

II. HANDICAPPING CONDITIONS:

A. Physical —Upper Involvement: ________
—Lower Involvement: ________
B. Vision —Corrected: ________
—Uncorrected: ________
C. Hearing —Corrected: ________
—Uncorrected: ________

III. SCHOOL AND HOME INFORMATION:

A. ____________ Present Grade
B. ____________ Classroom Teacher
C. ____________ If child has ever been retained, list grades.
D. ____________ What special services is the child presently receiving?

Fig. 6-9. Model learning disability systems individual profile record. From Sabatino, D. A. & Boeck, D. G. (Eds.) *A systems approach to provide educational services to children with learning disabilities*. University Park, Pa.: Model Learning Disabilities Systems of Pennsylvania, 1973, p. 56.

E. ______________ Parent Name and Address

____

____

F. ______________ Home Telephone Number

IV. ADDITIONAL INFORMATION

____

____

____

____

____

V. ASSIGNMENT:

	Date Enrolled	Date Withdrawn
A. Assessment Class	________	________
B. Resource Room	________	________
C. Strategist	________	________
D. Other	________	________

VI. PROGRAM OBJECTIVES:

Objective 1: ______________________________________

____

Objective 2: ______________________________________

____

Objective 3: ______________________________________

____

Objective 4: ______________________________________

____

Objective 5: ______________________________________

____

Objective 6: ______________________________________

____

Objective 7: ______________________________________

____

Objective 7: ______________________________________

____

Objective 8: ______________________________________

____

Objective 9: ______________________________________

____

Objective 9: ______________________________________

____

Objective 10: ______________________________________

____

Fig. 6-9 (continued)

Program Monitoring

The major points in a continuous educational plan are (1) the *instructional objective,* which delineates what will be accomplished; (2) the *instructional strategy,* which delineates how it will be accomplished. There is an interdependency between these two aspects. If an instructional objective is too demanding, it is unlikely that a workable strategy will result. On the other hand, if it is too easy, any strategy may accomplish the goal. A sequence of strategies could fail to address the objective through selection of the wrong instructional method or material or could be improperly sequenced, with too large a step between each strategy.

There are two commonly used procedures for the monitoring of instructional objectives: (1) a pre- and post- norm-referenced measure which generally means using a commercially available standardized test; and (2) a criterion-referenced measure, which generally means using part of the material to be taught, or the observation of the behavior to be modified as the criteria to task output response measure. Most authorities in the field (e.g., Gorth & Hambleton, 1972) now advance the belief that in the absence of norm-referenced tests designed to ascertain the specific skills designated in instructional objectives, criterion-referenced measures should be used. The reader will recall that a criterion-referenced measure is simply an individual score expressed as a percentage of accomplishment of some task. It is not necessarily a pre- and posttest device and often is used to provide a continuous measure of the instruction being delivered. Criterion-referenced measures are "deliberately constructed to yield measurements that are directly interpretable in terms of specific performance standards" (Glaser & Nitko, 1971, p. 653). Shoemaker (1972, p. 215) considers the important output measure of a criterion-referenced evaluation to be "the raw difference score obtained by subtracting an examinee's test score from the criterion test score, defining the minimally acceptable level of achievement."

Reese notes that, "A criterion-referenced measure is a daily test of the child's progress toward an objective, the results of which are plotted or profiled. . . . The performance standard is achieved when the child reaches the desired level of accuracy or success (usually 80 to 90 percent) within the specified time period as stated in the objective" (Reese, 1976, p. 223). Thus, if a teacher selects 10 words from a paragraph that the child missed in oral reading, writes an objective stating that: "The student will learn the following 10 words in one week to an 80 percent criteria, using a picture-word, word vocabulary sight approach," then he or she has developed an instructional objective, word recognition, under the instructional goal of reading, and has stated the words and teaching method, thus the instructional strategy. A criterion-referenced evaluation will provide a

Model Learning Disabilities System

Instructional Data Record

Pupil Name ____________ I.D. Number ____________

Instructional Objective: ____________

______

Prescription: ____________

Evaluation: Norm Reference — Pre: ______ Post: ______ (______)

Criterion Reference — % of Achievement: ______

Criterion Achieved — Yes: ______ No: ______

Why: ____________

Time: Minutes/Day______ Minutes/Week 1:______ Total Minutes:______

Task		1	2	3	4	5		1	2	3	4	5
	Dates											

Fig. 6-10. Model learning disabilities system instructional data record. From Sabatino, D. A. & Boeck, D. G. (Eds.) *A systems approach to provide educational services to children with learning disabilities*. University Park, Pa.: Model Learning Disabilities Systems of Pennsylvania, 1973, p. 63.

daily performance log; the standard to be achieved has been established (80 percent accuracy); the teacher will know if the strategy is achieving the objective, and if the objective is realistic. In short, to paraphrase Gorth & Hambleton (1972), continued assessment will determine what the child has learned, what is to be taught, how much is remembered, and what remains to follow the next instructional objective. Figure 6-10 provides an example of an instructional objective (including strategy)

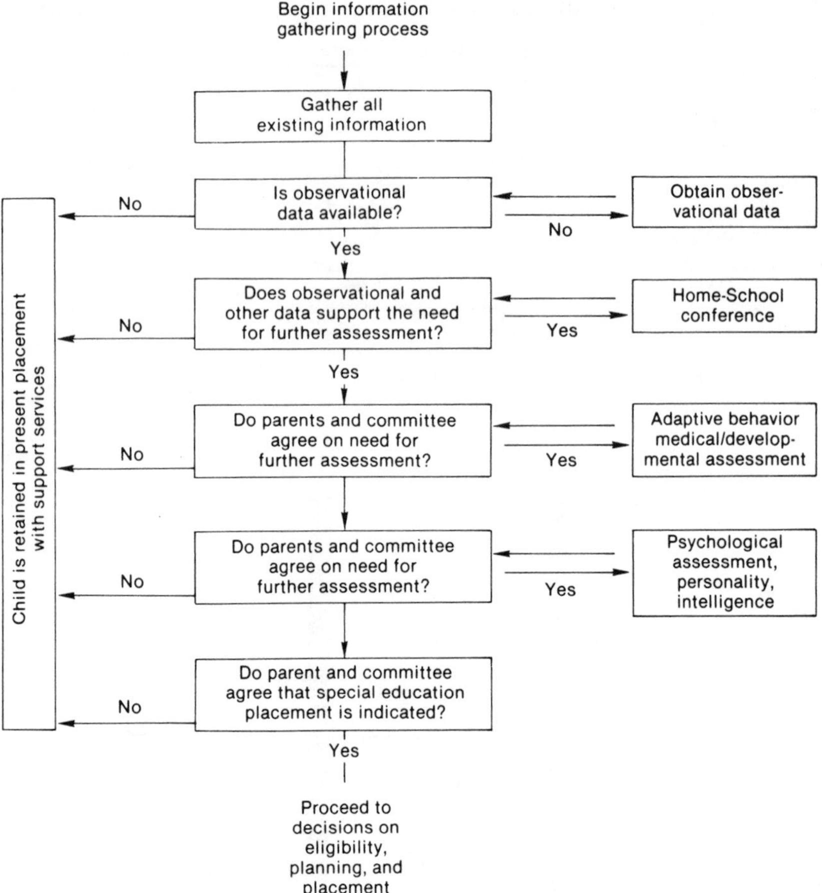

Fig. 6-11. Initial procedures for child evaluation. From National Association of State Directors of Special Education. *Functions of the placement committee in special education*. Washington, D.C.: NASDSE, 1976, p. 23.

criterion-referenced evaluation system. Its use will, according to Reese (1976), answer the following four questions:

1. Is the initial instructional objective appropriate?
2. Is the instructional strategy appropriate?
3. Is the criterion level of success within the child's limits?
4. Is there a need for reviewing the assessment information and modifying the instructional hypothesis?

Figure 6-11 provides an example of a continuous monitoring system, providing the teacher(s) valuable data on the instructional objective, instructional strategies, time spent, criteria level achieved, and entries for any pre- and posttest results. It should be added that frequent (5 to 10 weeks) pre- and posttest evaluation of a sequence set of instructional objectives provides information on how the child relates to others his age or grade. Continuous monitoring through the use of a criterion-referenced system permits an evaluation of a child's performance against the task. In some combinations, especially with academic achievement, a norm-referenced pre- and posttest structure (instructional objectives) and a criterion-referenced system may be used together. Monitoring of a target behavior, by counting individual trials to task, on-task, off-task behaviors is actually a criterion-referenced continuous monitoring system. The specific issues related to describing an initial target behavior and monitoring the intervention process have been discussed in Chapter 4.

SUMMARY

This chapter has presented systematic procedures for ascertaining learner characteristics. Six models of systematic diagnosis were presented that illustrate methods in current use. The two models of ascertaining learning processes discussed emphasized the manner in which a student learns is of particular value in establishing an educationally useful diagnosis. Three models of diagnostic prescriptive teaching revealed the value of pretest instruction, posttest sequence for teaching deficiencies in a specific area.

The second half of the chapter discussed four aspects involved with developing an IEP. Referral is the first step followed by diagnosis. The outcome of diagnosis is specific instructional objectives and strategies. These are delineated in the third step and fourth steps—reports of child progress and continuous program monitoring. The overall purpose of the chapter was to assist the teacher of handicapped children in preparing IEPs.

REFERENCES

Broadbent, D. E. *Perceptions and communications.* Oxford: Pergamon Press, 1958.

Cartwright. G. P., Cartwright, C. A., & Ysseldyke, J. E. Two decision models: Identification and diagnostic teaching of handicpaped children in the regular classroom. *Psychology in the Schools,* 1973, *10,* 4–11.

Caterall, C. D. Taxonomy of prescriptive intervention. *Journal of School Psychology,* 1970, *8,* 5–12.

Dunn, L. M. Minimal brain dysfunction: A dilemma for educators. In H. C. Haywood (Ed.), *Brain damage in school aged children.* Arlington, Va.: Council for Exceptional Children, 1968.

Glasaer, R. & Nitko, A. Measurement in learning and instruction. In R. Thorndike (Ed.), *Educational measurement*. Washington, D.C.: American Council on Education, 1971.

Gorth, W. & Hambleton R. Measurement considerations for criterion-referenced testing and special education. *Journal of Special Education,* 1972, *6,* 303–314.

Hickey, M. E. & Hoffman, D. Diagnosis and prescription in education. *Educational Technology,* 1973, *6,* 35–37.

Iscoe, I. & Payne, S. Development of a revised scale for the functional classification of exceptional children. In E. P. Trapp & P. Himelstein (Eds.), *Readings on the exceptional child,* second edition. New York: Appleton, 1972.

Kauffman, S. M. & Hallahan, D. P. The medical model and the science of special education. *Exceptional Children,* 1974, *41,* 97–102.

Lucas, M. & Jones, R. Attitudes of teacher of mentally retarded children toward psychological reports and services. *Journal of School Psychology,* 1970, *8,* 122–130.

National Association of State Directors of Special Education. *Implementing PL 94-142.* Washington, D.C.: NASDSE, 1976.

Neisser, U. *Cognitive psychology.* New York: Appleton, 1967.

Peter, L. J. *Prescriptive teaching.* New York: McGraw-Hill, 1965.

Quay, H. C. The facets of educational exceptionality: A conceptual framework for assessment, grouping instruction. *Exceptional Child,* 1968, *35,* 25–32.

Quay, H. C. & Peterson, D. R. *Behavior problem checklist.* Champaign, Ill.: Children's Research Center, 1967.

Reese, J. H. An instructional sytem for teachers of learning-disabled children. In D. Sabatino (Ed.), *Learning Disabilities Handbook: A technical guide to program development.* DeKalb, Ill.: Northern Illinois University Press, 1976.

Rogers, C. R. The clinical treatment of the problem child. New York: Houghton Mifflin, 1939.

Ryckman, D. B. & Wiegerink, R. Factors of the Illinois Test of Psycholinguistic Abilities: A comparison of 18 factor analyses. *Exceptional Children,* 1969, *36,* 107–113.

Sabatino, D. A. Information processing behaviors associated with learning disabilities. *Journal of Learning Disabilities,* 1968, *1,* 440–450.

Sabatino, D. A. & Hayden, D. L. Psychoeducational study of selected behavioral variables with children failing the elementary grades, Part I. *The Journal of Experimental Education,* 1970, *38,* 49–57; 48–57.

Shoemaker, D. Improving criterion-referenced measurement. *Journal of Special Education,* 1972, *6,* 315–323.

Simon, H. A. An information-processing explanation of some perceptual phenomena. *British Journal of Psychology,* 1967, *58,* 1–12.

Wendell, K. Diagnosing learning difficulties: A sequential strategy. *Journal of Learning Disabilities,* 1970, *6,* 15–21.

Wickman, E. K. *Children's behavior and teacher's attitudes.* New York: Commonwealth Fund, 1928.

SUGGESTED READINGS

Sabatino, D. A. *Learning disabilities handbook: A technical guide to program development.* DeKalb, Ill.: Northern Illinois University Press, 1976.

National Association of State Directors of Special Education. Implementing PL 94-142. Washington, D.C.: NASDSE, 1976.

David A. Sabatino and Ted L. Miller

7
The Measurement of Perceptual-Cognitive Behaviors

The chapter to follow has as its theme the assessment of learner characteristics that are usually associated with cognition. Two major sections are included: (1) the measurement of visual and auditory perception, and (2) the measurement of intelligence. In the style of this text we have attempted to take the reader beyond the mechanical procedures of administering and scoring tests that appear frequently and, accordingly, a considerable amount of energy is devoted to describing the many conceptualizations of perceptual processes and intelligence. These views are then woven into the various assessment procedures that are most commonly used. Since perception and intelligence have been voluminously studied, no attempt could be made to provide an exhaustive review of the topics in the space available here. Because of this fact the reader is particularly encouraged to consult the suggested readings section at the end of the chapter.

ASCERTAINING PERCEPTUAL FUNCTIONING: WHAT IS PERCEPTION?

Unfortunately, at the time of this writing, the special educator appears to hold a disagreeable view toward perception. The reason, as the test review sections in this chapter will reveal, has been a widely-held criticism about the reliability and validity, therefore usability, of perceptual tests. There are, however, a few facts which the special educator should keep in mind before literally tossing all perceptual tests, and therefore intervention materials, to the winds. Primary among these is the fact that all new learning is dependent upon the awareness of novel environmental stimuli. Therefore, perception is critical to all theories of learning and, subsequently the formation of intelligence and cognitive style. As a result, it is vital that the reader retain a distinction between criticism of the concept of perception and criticism of the measurement of the concept.

It is generally held that perception begins in arousal of the nervous system. We might observe this in the maintenance of a child's attention in the classroom or the startled gaze that accompanies the unanticipated sound of a book dropping to the floor. Yet, perception is more than a switchboard function for incoming information for it involves acting, reacting, thinking, organizing, and emotionality. Carr has defined perception as: ". . . a form of mental activity in which the meaning of present situations, objects, and events is determined, in part, by past learning" (Chaplin & Krawiec, 1960).

In order to understand what Carr was saying, think for a moment about the difference in "old or previous learning" and "new or novel learning." The shape, size, color, or use of a word, thing, or place may provide the perceiver all the information he needs to form a complete concept about that which he has perceived in the past. For example, the word "snow" may trigger a complete mental picture of winter, or the letters *c t,* although not a word, places little demand on the experienced reader to visualize cat, or the sleek, black and white animal sleeping in front of a warm, gentle fire. But, to that same experienced reader, the word *Kwashiorkor* has little or no meaning. If the reader were informed that Kwashiorkor is a neurological developmental deficiency due to amino acid deficiency, then the word or even abbreviation *Kwash,* would suddenly provide meaningful information. In short, perception acts as the multidimensional filter for information into the nervous system and from the nervous system.

Perception covers so many interactions between man and the environment that it is difficult to define and measure. In a general sense, perception may be considered as the ability to rapidly and accurately order incoming environmental information into meaningful symbols by filtering unwanted information from the nervous system. Thus, perception deals with the discriminate features of environmental objects. The importance of this function is obvious since the student must select, classify, and code environmental events into meaningful neural information before learning can occur.

Assessment of Perceptual Function

There are several problems in the clinical description of perceptual function. First, there is the definition of the trait being measured. Second, there are questions about the validity of the measures used to operationally define perceptual function. The third problem is the question of the existence of the trait and therefore the question of what is ascertained by assessment. Is there such a trait as visual perception distinct from other cognitive processes? The answer is not a resounding "yes," but rather that "it would appear so." Has the state of our descriptive power to elicit measures of that trait proceeded to a fine science? The answer would be a resounding "no."

Let us begin our discussion of perceptual assessment by noting that the environment impinges upon the sensory receiving mechanisms. These mechanisms are peripheral to the central nervous system and are represented by the end organs of sensory perception, primarily the eye and ear. Exactly *how* the perceptual processes receive and interpret sensory data is a question of explanation provided only by model, paradign, and theory. Therefore, the measures used to extract perceptual function (or the absence of it) are necessarily based on models, paradigms, and theoretical constructs of how that process works. Needless to say, perception is a process of the central nervous system, and therefore is not directly observable. We only assume the measurement of its dimensions by the response obtained from an individual. Therefore, a pure measure of what the person perceives has rarely been possible. In fact, generally we measure only a vocal or manual motor response. Therefore, a faulty response or, for that matter a correct one, may deny the examiner a true picture of "perpectual" performance.

Perception is difficult to distinguish from other cognitive processes. Frequently, perception is measured as an aspect of intelligence. For example, Binet used the concept of perception to define intelligence as "that which is called intelligence in the strict sense of the word, consists of two principle things: first, perceiving the exterior world and secondly, reconsidering these perceptions as memories altering them" (Binet & Simon, 1905, p. 93). Pronko (1966, p. 74) points up the confusion in the vagueness and looseness of perceptual semantics: "The term perception refers to (a) the thing perceived, (b) the perceiving of the thing, (c) the perception projected back out from the organisms inside to the place where the thing really is, and (d) the mysterious goings-on within the organism."

Perception, as a function, seems to reside between sensation, or the reception of sensory information, and the formation of language structures which promote a cognitive grasp on the world. Perception must surely include the recognition and differentiation of sensory stimuli received by the central nervous system, interacting with the initial sensory information, incorporating it in the higher cognitive structures. Perception must not be confused with the sensory function in the peripheral (to the central nervous system) end organs of sight, hearing, touch, taste, or smell. However, the real problem is not the differentiation of sensation from perception, but the differentiation of perception from cognition (Sabatino, 1969).

According to Piaget (Flavell, 1963), perception in young children is composed of two phases. The initial or primary perception is concerned with a simple fixation of a point in space. Perceptual activity at the advanced phase reflects sensori-motor intelligence. Bruner (1957, 1964), too, distinguishes perceptual and conceptual inferences. He sees perceptual influences as less docile or reversible than higher level inferences. In addition, Bruner suggests that certain forms of primitive organization are inherent in the perceptual field, irrespective of learning, and these make possible the differential use of cues in identity categorizing. Nevertheless, Bruner (1957) argues that it is "foolish and unnecessary to assume that the sensory 'stuff' on which higher order categorizations are based is . . . of a different sensory order than more evolved identities with which our perceptual world is normally peopled" (p. 35).

The phenomena which has created the most controversy about the measurement of perception have been the operational definitions applied to those traits reasoned to represent that process. There is little disagreement that at least two distinct perceptual processes exist, one visual and one auditory (Sabatino, 1973). However, the height of the disagreement is directed at the component skills which may be attributed to the behavioral complexity known as perception. Theorists, experimentalists, educators, and test developers from several of the behavioral sciences have developed tests designed to measure those ccmponent skills they felt comprise this process. We now turn to an examination of some of those attempts.

THE MEASUREMENT OF VISUAL PERCEPTION

A number of reading tests, many intelligence tests (especially those which assess nonverbal or performance behaviors) and most certainly the bulk of the visual-motor, or visual-motor integration perceptual tests seemingly ascertain the capability of the examinee to differentiate or distinguish a critical feature of a geometric shape, a picture symbol, or letter

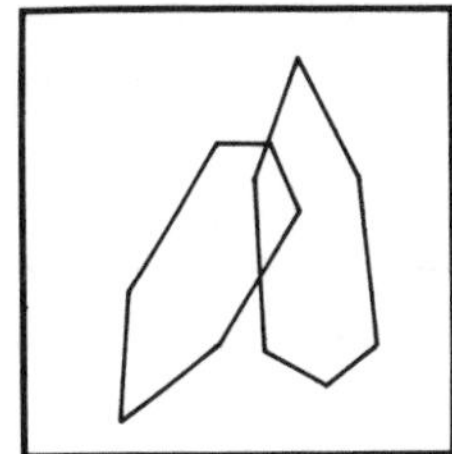
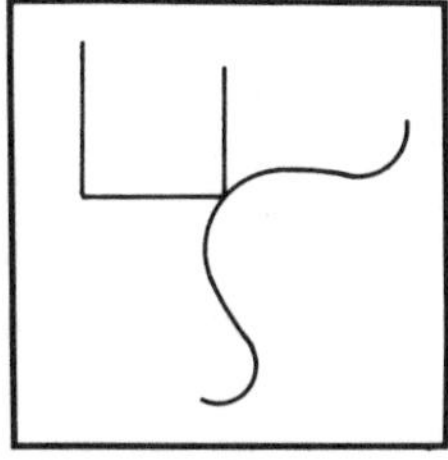

Fig. 7-1. Examples of geometric shapes administered in the *Bender Visual Motor Gestalt Test*. (Bender, 1938.)

and word symbol. In part, this is a result of the fact that the assessment of visual perceptual function had its origin in the experimental work, in the works of the Gestalt psychologists. The results of these efforts have been a collection of tests that were developed in the 1920s and 1930s for experimental purposes. Among the most commonly administered tests for clinical purposes is the *Bender Visual-Motor Gestalt Test,* which began as a laboratory measure of Gestalt function (Wertheimer, 1923). In the current time frame, the reason that visual perception, or, more aptly visual-motor perception, is assessed so frequently is that the tests are easy to administer, psychology has a rich history of concern with visual perception, and there does seem to be a correlational relationship between visual perception and academic achievement.

Visual perceptual tests such as the *Bender Visual-Motor Gestalt Test* have been used to ascertain intelligence (Armstrong & Hauck, 1960), diagnose brain damage (Shaw & Cruikshank, 1956), adademic achievement (Koppitz, 1958), emotional difficulties (Clawson, 1959), and perceptual process (Koppitz, 1962). A problem appears to exist in the fact that visual perception may relate to intelligence, but is not a criterion for ascertaining it. The global dynamics of what may be measured by nine geometric designs is probably somewhat less than an individual's total perception of the world. It may be accurate to state that what is measured is the perception of geometric figures, and that many reading achievement and other developmental processes are probably related in fact to the development of visual perception. Typical figures from the *Bender-Gestalt Test* are shown in Figure 7-1.

No better example of a commonly used visual motor perceptual test as used by educators is available than that of the *Frostig Developmental Test of Visual Perception* (DTVP) (Frostig, 1964). The DTVP purports to measure five essential processes of the visual perceptual behavioral complex (Maslow et al., 1964). These processes have been designated as: (1) eye-motor coordination, (2) figure-ground perception, (3) form constancy,

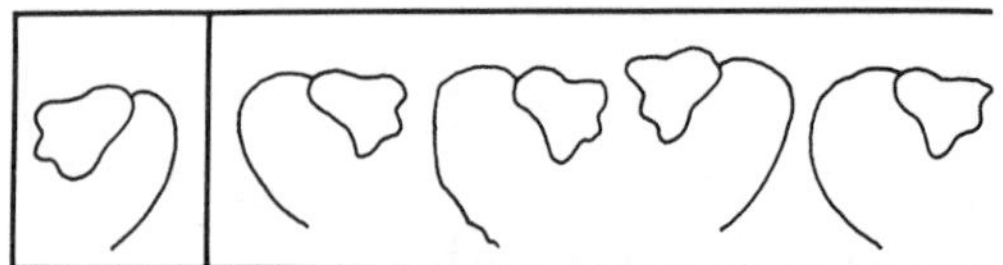

Fig. 7-2. A common example taken from the Frostig DTVP.

(4) position in space, and (5) spatial relations. Although Frostig did not assume that these five visual perceptual abilities were the only ones involved in the total process of visual perception, she did cite them as having particular relevance to school performance. Examples of a task from the DTVP appear in Figure 7-2.

Several researchers have attempted to determine the capability of the Frostig DTVP to ascertain five perceptual traits by applying a data analysis procedure known as factor analysis. The principle of factor analysis may be considered here as a statistical technique used to determine the degree to which measures are independent. Using this technique, Olson (1968) and Boyd & Randle (1970) report that the five subtests of the Frostig DTVP generate only one factor; this suggests that all five tests measure only one trait. Corah & Powell (1963), Cawley, Burrow, & Goodstein (1968), and Becker & Sabatino (1971) have found that the subtests of the Frostig DTVP essentially measure only two traits. Becker and Sabatino (1971) provided the five subtests a maximum opportunity to cluster into factually independent traits and found that the Frostig DTVP measured three specific traits with kindergarten age children. These were: visual-motor skills, figure-ground perception, and visual discrimination skills. It is not important that the five presumed independent measures of visual perceptual behavior measure one, two, or three traits as independent measures. What is important is that they do not measure the five perceptual traits named by the test authors as being described in the subtests of the Frostig DTVP. This fact perhaps best illustrates the sources of the poor respect that many professionals held for such tests. Indeed the DTVP is not an exception to the rule for many test developers name traits according to what their instrument is supposed to measure. Most certainly, one of the best examples has been the *Illinois Test of Psycholinguistic Abilities* (ITPA), (Kirk, McCarthy, & Kirk, 1968).

The ITPA has been responsible for generating as much research since its introduction in 1961 as the Binet and Wechsler Scales combined in an equal period. The experimental edition of the ITPA (1961) contained nine subtests, the revised (1968) edition has 10 regular subtests and two supplemental subtests (Table 7-1). The ITPA is one of the few tests based on a model used to explain human function. In this case, the model is Osgood's (1957) two-dimensional scheme of communication. Two channels are described: the sensory input (perceptual) channels of (1) auditory and, (2) visual reception. The authors proposed that, in addition to the two channels of perception, two other dimensions be considered: levels of organization and psycholinguistic processes. Two levels of organization were proposed. The representation level requires the mediating use of symbols to inject meaning: that is, the perceptual experience relies on the presence of the stimulus. The automatic level, in contrast, relies on previously learned perceptual experiences. The psycholinguistic process included the processes of receiving visual and auditory perceptual information, the experience process (communicating by some means) and the formation of language, which seems to occur between receiving and expressing information.

There are several excellent reviews of the literature covering all aspects of this text. Certainly, the reviews by Sedlak & Weener (1973) are detailed and complete. Their work tends to show that the reliability of the ITPA subtests range from the mid-30s to the low 80s. This is significant because, as they point out, a reliability of .70 is not suitable for individual diagnosis.

In keeping with our previous discussion on factorial analytic treatment and the fact that ITPA is a widely used diagnostic test employed with handicapped children, we must ask "what does it measure?" According to its authors, it was constructed to ascertain the perceptual avenues and central language formation processes. There is cause to doubt that it can accomplish this objective. Sedlak & Weener (1973) reviewed 20 factorial studies, 16 of these previously reviewed by Meyers (1969) upon the experimental addition. Although many of the factorial studies had design flaws, most did show that two factors existed, one communication channel did cluster the subtests on the nature of the sensory input, be it visual or auditory. In a later study by Wisland & Many (1969), nine of the subtests loaded on one factor. Thus, while the results reported are inconsistent, there is evidence to suggest that the ITPA does not measure 10 distinct traits. Therefore, when a diagnostician notes that a child possesses visual closure as opposed to visual sequential memory problem, and that remediation should be initiated to correct the visual closure deficient, the diagnostician may not be describing a real deficit. In fact, the trait described may be real in nature only to the extent that the authors created a test to measure them.

In this section we have briefly examined the learner characteristics which comprise the human trait known as visual perception. A great deal of work has been reported in this area and many diverse assessment models exist. Table 7-2 provides the reader a quick review of selected tests or subtests of visual perception.

To summarize, it would appear that there is a trait which relates to

Table 7-1
Contrast of the Experimental and Revised Editions of the ITPA

Subtest		Change from E to R[a]	Description
		Representational level	
E	R		
Auditory Decoding	Auditory Reception	Items increased from 36 to 50	Vocabulary test requiring Yes-No response (e.g., Do chairs eat?)
Visual Decoding	Visual Reception	Items increased from 24 to 40	Matching a picture stimulus with a picture from the same category (e.g., waste-baskets and garbage cans)
Auditory-Vocal Association	Auditory Association	Items increased from 26 to 42	Verbal-analogies test (e.g., Grass is green. Sugar is ________.)
Visual-Motor Association	Visual Association	Items increased from 28 to 42	Relating a pictorial stimulus with its conceptual counterpart (e.g., bone goes with dog)
Vocal Encoding	Verbal Expression	Additional scoring criteria	Describing common objects verbally (e.g., block)
Motor Encoding	Manual Expression	Maximum point total increased from 27 to 41	Expressing an idea with gestures (e.g., Show me what you should do with this [hammer].)

Table 7-1 (continued)

Subtest		Change from E to R[a]	Description
		Automatic level	
E	R		
Auditory-Vocal Automatic	Grammtic Closure	Items increased from 22 to 33	Supplying correct grammatical form to complete a sentence (e.g., Here is a dog. Here are two ________.)
	Visual Closure	New subtest	Locating specific objects in a scene filled with distracting visual stimuli (e.g., bottles in a kitchen scene)
Auditory-Vocal Sequencing	Auditory Sequential Memory	Items increased from 20 to 28; maximum number of digits increased from 7 to 8	Repeating digits as in the Binet
Visual-Motor Sequencing	Visual Sequential Memory	Items increased from 15 to 25; stimuli changed	Placing geometric shapes in proper sequence from memory
	Auditory Closure	Supplementary test	Completing a word vocally that has one or more phonemas missing
	Sound Blending	Supplementary test	Identifying a word from hearing individual phonemes

[a]E = experimental edition; R = revised edition.
From Sedlak & Weiner. In L. Mann & D. Sabatino (Eds.), *The first review of special education.*

Table 7-2
Selected Visual Perception Tests or Subtests

Name of Test	Author	Age Range (yrs.)	Traits Measured	Publisher	Cost	Reliability
Developmental Test of Visual Motor Integrative	Keith E. Beery, Norman A. Buktenica	2–15	Perceptual-motor closure, Recognition of similarities, Recognition of differences	Follett Pub. Co.	$8.25 per 15 tests $4.56 per manual	Split-half 0.93 Test-retest 0.83–0.87
Visual Retention Test	Arthur L. Benton	8 and over	Immediate visual retention	The Psychological Corporation	$5.00 per set of cards $2.30 per manual	Test-retest 0.76
Dennis Visual Perception Scale	Royce Dennis Margaret Dennis	1–6	Visual perception	Western Psychological Services	$9.50 set of 25 test booklets, key and manual	NA
Developmental Test of Visual Perception 3rd ed.	Marianne Frostig, Phyllis Maslow	3–8	Eye motor coordination, figure-ground disc, form constancy, position in space spatial relations	Consulting Psychologists Press, Inc.	$10.00 per examiners kits of tests, scoring keys, cards & manual	Test-retest (total) 0.84

Table 7-2 (continued)

Name of Test	Author	Age Range (yrs.)	Traits Measured	Publisher	Cost	Reliability
Southern California Figure-Ground Visual Perception Test	A. Jean Ayers	4–10	Figure-ground visual perception	Western Psychological Services	$15.00 per kit of cards, booklets, manual	Test-retest 0.37–0.52
Motor Free Visual Perception Test	Ronald Colarusso Donald Hammill	4–8	Spatial relationships, visual discrimination, figure-ground visual closure visual memory	Academic Therapy Publ.	NA	0.88 Test-retest 0.81
Minnesota Perception-Diagnostic Test	G. B. Fuller J. T. Laird	8–15	Visual perception, visual motor abilities	Journal of Clinical Psychology	$5.00 for manual and 50 profiles	Test-retest 0.37–0.60
Bender Motor Gestalt Test	Lauretta Bender	5–10	Visual motor perceptual discrimination	Western Psychological Corp.		Kippetz norms Test-retest 0.55–0.69

the ability to discriminate visual information received by the central nervous system. That information is then selectively filtered and retained in a short-term retention cycle, or lost. Therefore, a short-term visual-perceptual memory component seems to exist. To go beyond these two traits and describe other component behaviors of the visual learning characteristics is not well founded by supportive research. The reader will have the opportunity to review a well documented performance model in the section on auditory perception.

THE ASSESSMENT OF AUDITORY PERCEPTION

Auditory perception, which should appear to be the sensory-perceptual correlary of visual perception, is relatively unexplored. The reason is that the auditory process seems more complex, since sound is a more complete multidimensional stimuli than light. Consequently, physiologically the auditory receiving system appears to be more complex than the visual in the sense that it is more difficult to know where the sensory function of hearing begins and where it ends, and it is more difficult to know where auditory perception stops and language learning begins. What then, is the auditory perceptual process?

Usually auditory-perceptual development is viewed as a process of change in the ability to differentiate characteristics of, and impose structure on, auditory stimuli. The development of these parallel processes of differentiation and structuring, along with the development of memory processes, makes up the three major components of the process of auditory perception. Figure 7-3 summarizes one such model. Its components refer to behavioral constructs rather than anatomical units, since the recent trend in the field has been to provide a psychological rather than physiological interpretation of auditory perception.

The model indicates that incoming sensory stimuli are received from the external auditory receptors in a short-term storage unit labeled *echoic memory,* after Neisser (1967). The echoic-memory unit is similar to the mechanism which was described by Hull (1952) and Peterson (1963) as the "stimulus trace" mechanism. Auditory stimuli are stored here for very brief periods of time in an undifferentiated form. If the contents of this unit are not attended to shortly after stimulation, they are lost through a process of rapid decay. The storage unit is, in a sense, passive, because no structuring or organizing influences act on it. The duration of echoic memory most likely increases with maturation in early childhood.

The *discriminative filter* abstracts the distinctive features of the incoming auditory stimuli, and "attends" or "tunes"; this process results in an active focusing on a limited amount of the available stimuli. The selec-

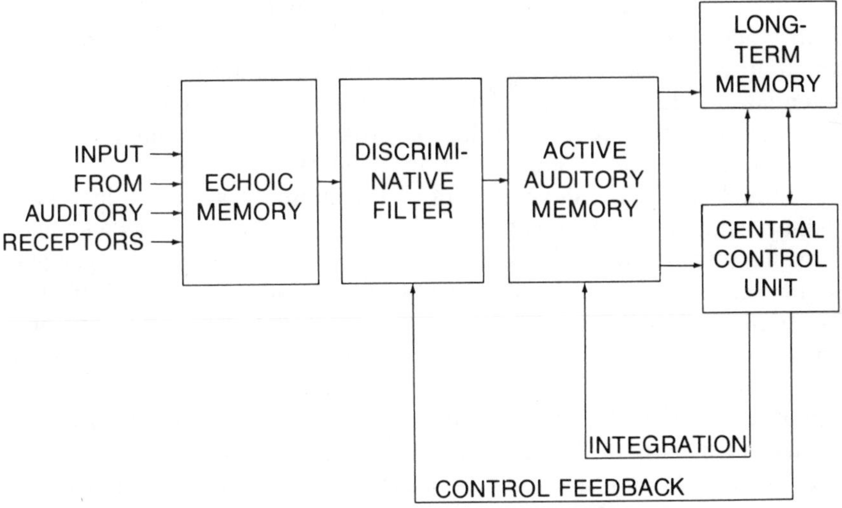

Fig. 7-3. Model of auditory perception.

tive filter is the mechanism which accepts some incoming stimuli and rejects or strongly attenuates all other stimuli, thus preventing an overloading of the subsequent perceptual mechanisms. The filter is set, or tuned, by a central control unit which is influenced by events stored in active auditory memory and by other knowledge in long-term storage. Developmentally, the child learns to discriminate among the various characteristics that define auditory stimuli—pitch, intensity, phonemic distinctions, spatial direction, voice quality, and so forth—and to focus on only that part of the available auditory stimuli which is relevant. Auditory-perceptual learning may be defined at this stage, as a process of abstracting from auditory stimuli, its many different dimensions and making increasingly finer differentiations within each of the abstracted dimensions. The developing ability to abstract this information is paralleled by an increase in the capacity to focus on a subset of the total auditory stimuli and to ignore the remainder.

The *active auditory memory* is a unit in which active organization occurs. Through a process of integration, the incoming stimuli are grouped and recoded into larger units. Research has indicated that these larger units are based on the acoustic and linguistic properties of the stimuli. Acoustic properties such as rhythm and pitch patterns serve as a basis for the construction of larger units. Word composition, phrase structures, and sentence structures are derived from linguistic knowledge—

also an important basis for integration. The amount of material that can be held in active auditory memory is a function of the integrative process which draws on the perceiver's past experiences and relates them to the potential structural characteristics of the incoming stimuli. As a child learns the structural features of language-based auditory stimuli, the unit size that can be held in active auditory memory increases.

In addition to the development of the ability to structure incoming auditory stimuli, the sheer size of the storage unit also increases with age. As Miller (1956) pointed out in his classic paper, the amount which can be held in active auditory memory depends on the number of units as well as the "richness" or "compactness" of the units. Previous studies of memory span, immediate memory, or short-term memory were measures of active auditory memory. However, most previous research fails to take into account the integrative and structuring activities of short-term perceptual memory unit. The definition of the unit as "active and integrative" implies that its functioning can best be studied using stimuli which vary in acoustic and linguistic structure.

In comparison with active auditory memory, the *long-term memory* unit is passive rather than active, has almost infinite (rather than limited) capacity, and permanent (rather than transient) storage. Although the processes involved in storage and retrieval in long-term memory are experimentally intriguing, their study would go beyond the scope of a project on auditory perception. Long-term memory is important because of the influence of stored information on attention, discrimination, and integration; but a report on the assumed contents of structure of long-term memory is not considered relevant for this study.

The model implies that the integration, sequencing, and storage of perceptual information operates on both visual- and auditory-perceptual intakes. Arousal occurs as the interconnection between a unit of meaningful perceptual information and the appropriate conceptual units within the cortex. A lack of arousal may be the reason that certain information never receives attention and, therefore, is not directed into the symbolic-conceptual centers.

Lowry (1970) used the term "auditory-perceptual function" to describe the ability to differentiate each sound of the language from every other. As a child develops skill in discriminating sounds, he must also be able to recognize them in all possible phonetic contexts, and later to gain the same meaning from the spoken and written word. The child who has difficulty hearing differences in speech sound also has difficulty repeating sequences involving those sounds.

Some children have difficulty in sound recognition, or the selection of relevant from irrelevant auditory stimuli. Such children suffer from an auditory figure-ground disability. It is assumed that they experience difficulty listening in the classroom. Their behavior is often marked by distractibility, short attention span, and lack of response to the auditory stimuli.

Some of the commonly used tests of auditory perception are sound-recognition tests, such as the *Wepman Auditory Discrimination Test* (Wepman, 1958), the PERC test (Drake, 1965) and the *Boston University Speech Sound Discrimination Picture Test;* these tests pose speech-sound-discrimination tasks which require the child to respond to a pair of words by indicating whether they sound the same or different (see also Chap. 8 and 11). In their research review of central-processing dysfunctions in children, Chalfant & Scheffelin (1969, p. 13) commented:

> Norms are available for the Wepman and are being secured for the PERC. The chief difference between the two tests is that the child is required to say "same" or "different" to each pair of words on the Wepman, whereas he is required to say "same" or "not the same" on the PERC.

Several researchers have commented on the difficulty posed by having only two response alternatives (Coltheart & Curthoys, 1968), since a subject has a 50 percent chance of getting the correct response by random guessing. Furthermore, inconsistency in examiners' speech patterns, children's phonetic competence and vocabulary familiarity, the test conditions (extraneous environmental noise), and cultural biases can easily influence the test results. Snyder & Pope (1970) could not confirm the norms published by Wepman. The investigators found, for example, that 67 percent of their subjects exceeded the cutoff score for auditory discrimination problems, as given in the test manual. The authors believed, however, that with refinements at the age levels with which they were working (6-year-old subjects, N = 204), the Wepman test could be a useful device for the assessment of auditory discrimination; "but the test user should consider discrepancies with norms in arriving at a realistic understanding of his test data" (p. 1010).

Possibly criterion cutoff scores, or any scores that differentiate one group from another or categorize a child as being deviant, are not necessary. Flower (1968) suggested focusing on individual differences and believed that certain educational strategies might be more effective than others when the particular subskills, strengths, or weaknesses of a child are known. A number of workers are trying to specify the type of speech-sound-discrimination difficulty a child may have, rather than hypothesizing an organic impairment or merely noting that there is a failure to perform at a level equal to that of others his age.

Rudegeair & Kamil (1970) reviewed the literature on the following speech-sound-discrimination tests: the *Travis and Rasmus Test* (1931), *Templin* (1957), and *Wepman* (1958); they also reported a study by Skeel,

Calfee, & Venesky (1969), who tested the efficacy of discrimination of fricatives in preschool children. They concluded that the correlation between poor articulation ability and poor discrimination was significant, but an item analysis found that the articulation error patterns differed from the discrimination error patterns. Rudegeair & Kamil (1970) believed that such results were related to a third factor, i.e., general language-processing ability. To test this hypothesis, they conducted two experiments. In the first, nonsense syllables were used with 12 first-grade and 12 kindergarten children. Mixed lists of repeated-contrast pairs, initial-contrast pairs, and final-contrast pairs were presented (by tape recorder); each list was presented for six days. In the second experiment, the real-word items from the Wepman were used. The results showed that repeated-contrast pairs were easier to discriminate than either initial- or final-contrast pairs, and that there was no difference between initial- and final-contrast pairs. Performance on the first day was significantly poorer than on all other days; there was no difference among the other five days. According to the researchers, the results have two major implications: that repeated testing is necessary with young children; and that with repeated-contrast pairs, one may obtain a more complete assessment of phonological discrimination ability in children.

Tests of auditory discrimination such as the Templin and Wepman are useful in determining whether a child can distinguish similarities between syllables or words, but they do not identify children whose primary disability is with sound perception within words. Since so many different kinds of auditory disturbances interfere with reading, it is necessary to explore a child's ability in many areas: in hearing similarities and differences in words; in distinguishing similar parts of words; in following an auditory sequence; in blending sounds into words and, conversely, in dissecting word wholes into syllables or individual sounds. Although there seems to be agreement among authorities that all these auditory discrimination skills are essential to reading, especially beginning reading, there has been relatively little pertinent research other than correlational studies (Evans, 1969).

LEARNING PREDICTIONS BASED ON PERCEPTUAL TESTS

In the past few years, considerable attention has been paid to the relationship between perceptual development and reading, both in regards to success in beginning reading and in reading disability. Most authors agree that visual discrimination is a prerequisite skill for reading success (Muehl & Kremenak, 1966; Taylor, 1961) although not all agree on the value of this concept as a predictor of reading success. Researchers have, however, noted relationships between success on visual perception tests and success in reading. Goins (1958) indicates that reading retardation stems from ineffective visual perception while Bryan (1964) found that visual perception was a better predictor of reading success for kindergarteners and first-graders than IQ or reading readiness scores. Gibson (1967), in her review of the literature on the prediction of reading via visual perceptual measures, was able to draw the following conclusions: (1) visual discrimination and knowledge of letters are better predictions than matching letters directly from memory, and (2) pictures and geometric designs are valid content for reading readiness tests although verbal visual discriminations are better predictors.

Other studies support conclusions similar to Barritt's (1968) view. Koppitz (1958) has indicated that visual discrimination has a predictive relationship to beginning reading. Pupils who are better able to discriminate letters and words generally were found to score higher on tests that measure later reading achievement. Keogh and Smith (1967) found that *Bender Visual Motor Gestalt Test* results were an adequate predictor of educational attainment in the upper elementary grades when administered in kingergarten. This test is primarily a measure of visual perception of form, with no assessment of memory for form or sequence. Olson (1966) concluded that the *Frostig Developmental Test of Visual Perception* predicted reading achievement in the second grade in seeking the variables that would predict future reading disabled students, noted that poor readers tended to achieve poorer *Bender Visual Motor Gestalt Test* scores than did control group readers.

Recent views of correlational research (Hammill & Larsen, 1974) have explored the relationship of measured auditory and visual perceptual skill to school achievement in general and particularly to reading. In these studies, approximately 1,000 coefficients drawn from more than 100 different investigations were analyzed. In the first of these, studies that used correlational statistical procedures to explore the relationship of reading to measures of auditory discrimination, memory, blending, and auditory-visual integration, spatial relations, memory and visual discrimination to academic learning were examined. It was concluded that there was little support in the available literature for the widespread belief that visual perception skills are essential for academic achievement. Apparently, a large percentage of children who do adequately on tests on audition and vision experience difficulty in academic learning. An equally sizeable percentage who do poorly on the same tests exhibit no difficulty in mastering academic subjects.

The consensus of the correlational research reviewed suggests that measured auditory and visual skills are not sufficiently related to reading to be particularly useful in educational practices.* These findings, however, are in apparent contradiction to those investigations which have found significant differences between the performance of good and poor readers on various measures of auditory and visual perceptual abilities (e.g., eye-hand coordination, form constancy, auditory memory, auditory discrimination). Although there are several possible explanations for this disparity between the correlational and perceptual-performance difference studies, it remains for researchers to resolve this basic issue in order to more fully understand the relationship of perceptual abilities to reading.

PERCEPTION AND HANDICAPPED LEARNERS

Perception may be defined as the selection of specific stimuli from those in the environment; the integration and structuring of those newly received stimuli in the nervous system against process learning; and the naming of the perceptually received stimuli. As a result of central nervous system disturbances, the perceptual modalities may be impaired. This requires the educator and diagnostician to be aware and persistently understand the child's *readiness* to perceive as well as his or her *capacity* to perceive in a given situation.

Sabatino (1968) found that children referred to as having learning disability problems had good use of language, but were depressed in perceptual functions. Keogh (1965) has stated that the child's representation of his or her world is dependent on the level of cognitive development at which he or she is currently functioning. Her study of the *Bender Visual Motor Gestalt Test,* as a test of reading predictor has supported the proposition that perception is an integral part of the development of intelligence. Normal subjects were found to be superior to retarded children in perceptual development.

Many of the tests used by diagnosticians utilize an individual's production of geometric design after seeing the design. These tests can be properly regarded as visual-motor tasks. In order to copy the design, the

*An interesting dialogue concerning the effectiveness of psycholinguistic training is developing as this book goes to press. The Hammill & Larsen (1974) article was critiqued by Minskoff (1976) yet subsequent articles (e.g. Arter & Jenkins, 1977) have largely been critical of perceptual assessment and (visual-auditory) modality training and supported Hammill & Larsen's conclusions. The issue is hardly resolved, however. Recently Lund, Foster & McCall-Perez (1978) reanalyzed the Hammill & Larsen data and cast doubt upon the validity of that study's conclusion. A rejoinder has been promised, thus it appears that the central issue of perceptual assessment and its related remedial implications will be debated for some time to come.

child must first formulate a correct mental image of the figure and then have the motor ability to transfer the design to paper. It is quite possible for the individual to have formulated a correct design and yet be unable to translate this visual image to paper properly. For handicapped individuals, it might be desirable to separate the motor functions from the visual task.

Rosenblith (1965), in a series of visual perceptual studies, obtained paired-comparison judgments of simple geometric figures from, among others, brain-damaged children. He found only minimal differences between the performance of the brain-damaged and normal children. Similarly, Sabatino (1969) investigated the auditory perceptual function of brain-damaged children. He found they performed consistently lower (poorer) on an experimental test of auditory perception, suggesting a lower level of organizational and integrational ability of meaningful auditory information from other sounds. To test the saliency of that aspect of handicapped children to perform auditorily in controlled noise, the test stimuli were mixed with a noise easily distinguished by normal listeners, but producing a most difficult task for the learning disabled children.

Thus, perception appears to be an important factor in the learning ability and learning style of handicapped learners, but explains only a small part of the total learning process for most learners, especially those who do not have severe handicaps resulting in serious learning problems. A review of auditory perceptual tests indicates that the large majority are either reading subtests or speech screening subtests, the majority of which have low reliability. Table 7-3 provides the reader with a list of selected tests, the author, age level, or ability measured, and reliabilities where that information exists.

Perceptual Integration

In the chapter on reading assessment (Chap. 9), Lloyd discusses the complex nature of the reading task. In normal learning, reading seems to require the conversion of graphic symbols into meaningful phonological units. The reading process is more than merely cracking the graphic code to visualize a meaningful symbol and then perform perceptual tasks. The visual symbol must be converted to a meaningful language concept.

In short, an integration of information from the visual and auditory perceptual channel seems to be occurring. How else, in fact, could a person read graphics, or listen to others read, and write the graphic symbol being received aurally? Reading is a dual process that, except for the handicapped learner who may be missing one of the sensory channels or have perceptual deficits, is an integrated function.

Table 7-3
Selected Auditory Perception Tests or Subtests

Name of Test	Author	Age Range (yrs)	Traits Measured	Publisher	Cost	Reliability
Auditory Discrimination Test	Wepman, J. N. (1958)	5–8	Discrimination of English phonemes	Language Research Associates	$5.00: 50 tests and manual; $0.50: specimen set	Test-retest 0.91
Detroit Test of Learning Aptitude	Baker, H. J. & Leland, B. (1968)	3 and over	Auditory attention span for related syllables, auditory attention span for unrelated words	Bobbs-Merrill	$14.85: completed set of testing materials	Test-retest 0.96
Diagnostic Reading Tests (Stanford)	Committee on Diagnostic Reading Tests (1968)	5–18	Auditory discrimination, oral word attach	Committee on Diagnostic Reading Tests (1968)	$2.50: specimen set kindergarten through 4th grade battery; $1.75: specimen set lower-level battery; $4.50: specimen set upper-level battery	NA
Durrell Analysis of Reading Difficulty	Durrell, D. D. (1955)	6–12	Hearing sounds in words, learning to hear sounds in words, auditory discrimination	Harcourt Brace Jovanovich	$3.00: complete kit	NA

Table 7-3 (continued)

Name of Test	Author	Age Range (yrs)	Traits Measured	Publisher	Cost	Reliability
Gates-McGinitie Reading Tests: Readiness Skills	Gates, A. J. & MacGinitie W. H. (1969)	5–6	Auditory discrimination, auditory blending	Teachers College Press, Columbia University	$0.75: specimen	Split-half 0.88–0.94
Goldman-Fristoe-Woodcock Test of Auditory Discrimination	Goldman, R., Fristoe, N., & Woodcock, R. W. (1970)	4 and over	Quiet background and noise, discrimination of English phonemes under these two conditions	American Guidance Service, Inc.	$18.50	Test-retest quiet 0.87 noise 0.81
Harrison-Stroud Reading Readiness Test	Harrison, M. L. & Stroud, J. B. (1950)	5–6	Auditory discrimination, context and auditory clues	Houghton Mifflin	$2.10; $0.50: specimen set	NA
Illinois Test of Psycholinguistic Abilities (ITPA)	Kirk, S. A., McCarthy, J. J., & Kirk, W. D. (1968)	2–10	Auditory association, auditory sequential memory, auditory closure, sound blending, auditory decoding	University of Illinois Press	$43..50	Test-retest subtest range 0.21–0.90
Kindergarten Auditory Screening Test	Katz, J. (1971)	4–6	Environmental noise, phonemic distinctive features, speech sound discrimination	Follett Educational Corp.	$5.00	NA

Table 7-3 (continued)

Name of Test	Author	Age Range (yrs)	Traits Measured	Publisher	Cost	Reliability
Roswell-Chall Auditory Blending Test	Roswell, F. G., & Ghall, J. S. (1963)	6–9	Synthesizing sounds and sound clusters into words	Essay Press	\$2.50; \$0.50: specimen set	Test-retest 0.86–0.93
Screening Test for Auditory Perception (STAP)	Kimmel, G. M. & Wahl, J. (1969)	7–12	Vowels, consonants, rhyming words, sound patterns, word differences	Academic Therapy Publ.	\$9.25	Test-retest 0.80
Tests of Auditory Perception	Susan J. Visco	5–14	Group = 1. sound versus no sound 2. sound discrimination 3. sound pattern disc. Individual = 1. attention to auditory stimuli 2. sound versus no sound 3. sound localization 4. sound discrimination 5. sound pattern disc. 6. figure ground 7. associating sound sources	Educational Activities, Inc.	NA	NA

Of all the perceptual functions, perceptual integration is the poorest understood. The result is that applied tests just literally do not exist for the practitioner. A number of studies are, however, illustrative here of research in the area. We will review one of these briefly.

Birch & Belmont (1965) administered a series of cards with three patterns of dots. The examiner first tapped out a pattern. The subject was to listen to the tapped pattern and then look at three sets of dot patterns. One set represented the tapped pattern, the others did not. The examiner then required the subject to point to the appropriate pattern, i.e., the pattern representing the previously tapped sound. Those children who had the greatest difficulty on this task were the most difficult to teach under remedial conditions of reading instruction. These subjects were found to be unable to deal effectively with tasks requiring judgments of auditory-visual equivalence. Thus, the ability to treat visual and auditory patterned information as equivalent, differentiated the good reader from the poor reader. A copy of the original test patterns is shown in Figure 7-4.

In summary, perceptual integration would appear to be the internal stimulation of the opposite modality, i.e., visual perceptual information is received and a signal system translates the meaning to the auditory per-

AUDITORY TAP PATTERNS	VISUAL STIMULI		
	EXAMPLES		
• •	••	• •	•••
• ••	•••	• ••	•• •
•• •	•••	• ••	•• •
	TEST ITEMS		
•• ••	• •••	• •• •	•• ••
• •••	••••	• •••	••• •
••• ••	•••••	•• •••	••• ••
• •• •	• •• •	•••••	•• ••
••• •• •	••• •• •	•• ••• •	• ••• ••
•• •••	••• ••	•• •••	•••• •
•• •• ••	•• •• ••	•••• ••	••• • ••
•• •• ••	•• ••• ••	••• •• ••	••• ••• •
•• • •••	•• •• ••	•• • •••	•• ••• •
• ••• ••	• •• •••	• ••• ••	•• • •••

Fig. 7-4. Original test pattern used by Birch and Belmont (1965).

ceptual modality. Research information on the assumed trait is very limited, and awaits much dedicated work. It does seem likely that this function holds promise as a predictor of what modality may be used as a unisensory or multisensory receiving mechanism.

We will now turn to a review of intelligence, a concept intimately related to perception.

THE MEASUREMENT OF INTELLIGENCE

Few topics in the psychological and educational literature have received the extensive and prolonged efforts devoted to the topic of intelligence. Arguments have long ranged over definitions of the concept of intelligence and resulting measurement practices and these arguments have been an inextricable part of special education. Indeed, as has been emphasized in Chapter 1, special education literally grew up in response to the development of the standardized intelligence test. Recently, however, this synergism has been shaken, for intelligence is no longer seen as *the* single important global descriptor of learning characteristics in handicapped children. Indeed, most special educators now view the assessment of intelligence as only one component in the description of learner characteristics, albeit an important and necessary one.* Current legislation has done little to reverse this trend and, in fact, may have promoted it. Therefore, the special education teacher may anticipate continued reference to the measure through reports, staffings, and placement decisions although he or she will probably not be called upon to administer intelligence tests. In view of these statements, we include the following overview of the complex area of the measurement of intelligence.

Of necessity, this chapter will address only a fraction of the material that has arisen over the past 100 year history. The first topic of this section will address the historical development and current views of the concept of intelligence. The second will briefly focus on some very contem-

*An example of special education's continued reliance on the concept of intelligence was recently emphasized in a proposed model for the identification of learning disabled children. The November 29, 1976 issue of the *Federal Register* proposed that a "severe discrepancy level" between intelligence (IQ) and achievement be established by means of the "SDL Formula." The formula essentially made identification of LD children highly dependent upon the measurement of intelligence. Despite the fact that the formula has since been widely criticized (largely for its failure to recognize standard error of measurement) it remains obvious, at least for this population of children, that the measurement of intelligence is still viewed as essential. Doubtless this belief prevails in the identification of most if not all handicapping conditions. Thus, IQ, if not essential to programming, remains essential to identification and placement.

porary issues affecting the continued practice of intellectual assessment. The third and final section will relate instruments and techniques that are commonly associated with the assessment of intelligence.

THE EVOLUTION OF A CONCEPT

Historical Development

Intelligence, as a construct, is uniquely entwined with the measurement of individual differences. Anastasi (1965, p. 2) indicates that one of the earliest instances of the study of individual differences took place in 1796 in the Greenwich Astronomical Observatory. Here Maskelyne discharged his assistant Kinnebrook, for failure to record data that approximated his own by less than one second. Since rather short durations seriously affected the progress of ongoing study, it soon became essential to astronomers that individuals record data with a high rate of (interrater) agreement. As a result, by the second half of the nineteenth century, astronomers had build rather complex devices for measuring and allowing for variations in individual differences.

Unlike astronomers, the earliest experimental psychologists tended to ignore individual differences and, instead, attempted to identify commonalities across persons. Wundt's famous psychophysical laboratory, established in Leipzig, Germany in 1879, could be characterized in the previous manner. However, individuals were entering the mainstream of psychology who would soon exert an opposite orientation. E. H. Weber (1795-1878) and G. T. Fechner (1801–1887) have been cited by Sattler (1974, p. 7) as among the more prominent of the early investigators of individual differences. These investigators of "psychophysical methods" (Marx & Hillix, 1963) were soon to be complemented by the enormous contributions of Sir Francis Galton (1882–1911) to the study of individual measurements.

James Cattell (1860–1944) studied under Wundt and visited with Galton before his return to the United States and subsequent appointment at the University of Pennsylvania. Cattell was among the first to use the phrase "mental test" (1890) and perhaps following his lead, Lightner Witner (1896) soon established a "laboratory clinic" at the University of Pennsylvania (Bardon & Bennett, 1974, p. 15).

Until the early part of the 20th century the assessment of individual difference was not heavily involved with the assessment of intelligence. During the early years of the new century a variety of contributions laid down the roots of what would be the assessment of intelligence. For example, Kraepelin was measuring perception, motor function, and memory while Ebbinghaus was involved in studies of computation, memory and sentence completion. But of all these contributors, none would have more effect than Alfred Binet and Theodore Simon, for these Frenchmen were developing the first practical instruments for the measurement of intelligence.

Subsequent development of the Binet Scales are well known and need not be dwelt on here. It is sufficient to merely note that following the introduction of the Binet-Simon test to the United States, the assessment of intelligence for special educational purpose began in earnest.

Current Views of the Concept of Intelligence

While many tests designed to measure intelligence have appeared over the years, it would remain fair to say that there has never been a unanimous opinion about the definition of intelligence. Part of this confusion lies in the fact that intelligence is not a hard and fast entity. Instead, it is a hypothetical construct intended to convey some precision to a collection of human behaviors that are judged as more or less intelligent. This seemingly subtle distinction has led to confusion in the professional world and a great deal of misunderstanding with the laity.

Wechsler (1975, p. 135) has stated that the diversity of opinion concerning intelligence "has continued unabated" although minor efforts to resolve the issue have been attempted for over 50 years. In the course of that 50-year trek a number of conceptualizations have been offered. Vernon (1969) suggested that three meanings are commonly associated with the term intelligence. In the first case intelligence has largely meant genetic inheritance or an innate intrinsic capacity. In the second case intelligence has been viewed as an observed behavior which is the result of genotype (genetic) and phenotype (environmental) interaction. In this instance intelligence is the result of the mental constructs created by continuous interaction. Finally, intelligence has been labeled to be whatever an intelligence test measures. While at first the latter seems to be a flippant comment, it should be noted that a construct such as intelligence might still function effectively within this definition.

Although Vernon's (1969) approach offers a glimpse at the range of positions that have been offered, it may be well to examine a few of the more influential explanations that have been offered. There have been many. For example, as early as 1921 the editorial staff of the *Journal of Educational Psychology* was concerned with the multidimensional views of intelligence then being offered. According to Wechsler (1975, p. 135) this particular article was a landmark for two reasons. First, it enumerated the issues that would confront psychologists and educators. Second, it clearly delineated the multiple views that were being held even at that time. Over the years this second trend has accelerated to the point that several views emerge rather clearly.

Summarizing these views, Sattler (1974, pp. 9–15) suggests that theories of intelligence can be dichotomized between those that are and those that are not derived from the statistical approach known as factor analysis (see Chap. 3). Nonfactor approaches include those of Binet & Simon (1905), Wechsler (1958) and Piaget (1963, 1966), factor views are perhaps most complete in the work of Guilford (1967). We will briefly review these positions.

Binet & Simon (1905) held intelligence to be composed of a number of separate capabilities; among them were judgment, practical sense, initiative, and adaptability to new circumstance. However, in actuality, Binet & Simon's criterion was the ability to identify children who would (or would not) profit from existing educational circumstance. The components that Binet & Simon suggested as a part of intelligence were, in the final analysis, only carefully considered speculation.

Wechsler (1958, p. 7) described intelligence as "the aggregate or global capacity of the individual to act purposefully, to think rationally and to deal effectively with his environment." According to Sattler (1974, p. 9), Wechsler herein seems to imply "that intelligence is composed of qualitative different elements or abilities." But, it is not only the absolute qualities of these abilities but the way in which they are combined (interact) that define intelligence. Clearly, Wechsler's (1958) definition is pragmatic and has appeal but there has been a failure to properly support many of the key points of the definition, for example, what behaviors might constitute acting "purposefully"?

For Piaget (1963, 1966), intelligence is developed through the dual processes of accommodation and assimilation. In accommodation the learner alters internal patterns to conform to environmental demands while assimilating an internal schema receptive to and subsequently integrating novel environmental events. Sattler (1974, p. 9) has expressed the synergism of the activity well: "Assimilative processes permit intelligence to go beyond a passive coping with reality, while accommodative processes operate to prevent intelligence from constructing representations of reality which have no correspondence with the real world."

The definitions offered by Binet & Simon, Wechsler, and Piaget have had heavy impact on the practice of measurment of intelligence. Indeed, these definitions underlie the most prevalent approaches to current measurement practices. However, a number of theorists have proposed factor analytic derived theories of intelligence. These proponents have heavily influenced research efforts but their contributions have had substantially less influence in practice. Among the more prominent of the factor theorists are Charles Spearman, E. L. Thorndike, L. L. Thornton, R. B. Cattell, and J. P. Guilford. All of these theorists held a common belief that intelligence is not a unitary skill or characteristic, but rather a conglomeration of many separate characteristics. Variation among these individuals' positions lies in two sources: (1) the methods or procedures used to support the multiple factors, and (2) the number of identified "factors" that are presumed to summate to intelligence.

From time to time the factor approach to defining intelligence has been more or less influential. However, Cattell's (1940) *Primary Mental Abilities Test* has been one of the few attempts to implement the theory. This test has enjoyed some success and has been used rather extensively. Yet of the factor theorists, Guilford has been perhaps the most influential in recent years. This theorist's structure of Intellect Model (Guilford, 1967) is represented as a three-dimensional cube. The three dimensions represented in the model are operational categories, content categories, and product categories. Operations can be seen as the processes executed on the content or substantive information processed by the individual. These two dimensions, operations and content interact to produce products, the resulting outcome of the cognitive process. Each of the three dimensions is divided into specific subcategories. This results in five level (operations) by four level (contents) by six level (product) model of 120 distinct factors. Guilford's (1967) model has promoted a considerable amount of speculation but it has not promoted commercials available for the assessment of intelligence, at least in wide scale use. Moreover, it has been criticized (e.g., Eysenck, 1967) and can best be considered as most useful for research and theory building.

Before turning to some contemporary issues affecting the measurement of intelligence it would be well to note that concepts of intelligence have not ceased at the factor theories just presented. New models are continuously forthcoming and we have made no attempt here to either elaborate upon existing models or to describe the most recent additions. For accomplishing either of these purposes the reader is particularly encouraged to consult the suggested readings at the end of this chapter.

CONTEMPORARY ISSUES IN THE MEASUREMENT OF INTELLIGENCE

A number of issues have appeared that have made the meausrement of intelligence controversial. Not the least of these is the fact that intelligence is poorly (or at least not agreeably) defined. Still, as Lambert (1973) has noted, despite all criticisms intelligence tests remain among the better of our assessment tools for understanding behavior. And, as noted earlier, their inclusion in categorical definitions is certainly a factor promoting their continued use. But, despite these points, a number of issues tend to substantially alter or even terminate the use of intelligence tests. These issues are of extreme importance to anyone who either administers or otherwise uses these tests, which, of course, includes special education teachers. Although the following is not an exhaustive list, the issues mentioned here have been instrumental in altering or limiting the contemporary use of measures of intelligence.

The Examinee's Rights

The first set of issues might be subsumed under the topic of failure to provide adequate personal rights to examinees. This topic is actually a collection of omissions and failures many of which have been described in Chapter 5. Although intelligence measures have not been the only measure used erroneously, their relative status and their long historical involvement with classification structures have rendered them extremely culpable. Measures of intelligence have, then, borne the brunt of the criticism directed at many test practices.

Heritability

A second issue that has surfaced again and again has been the issue of heritability in the acquisition of intelligence. In recent years the issue has been most forcefully discussed following the publication of Jensen's (1969) article. Although originally intended as a question directed at the efficacy of early intervention programs, Jensen's comments soon touched off a long series of debates concerning the differential heritability of types of intelligence (Bereiter, 1969; Cronbach, 1969; Brazziel, 1969; Elkind, 1969; Kagan, 1969; Hunt, 1969; Crow, 1969; Scarr-Sulapetak, 1971; Shockley, 1971; Herrstein, 1971). Though strong arguments have been made for both ends of the continuum of determinism, it would be relatively safe to say that a satisfactory explanation remains elusive for researchers. However, the long public debates have provided many instances of misinformation on emotionally charged issues. Partly as a result of this, measuring intelligence has become even more controversial than it was prior to the late 1960s.

Test Bias

Test and examiner "bias" has emerged as a significant issue in the testing of children. Test bias usually refers to the case where some subgroup of individuals are systematically over or under predicted or identified.

Statistical models of test bias are numerous (Flaughner, 1974) and some authors (Anastasi, 1967; Kagan, 1969) contend that many current tests are truly biased. A number of contributing factors have been suggested, including cultural differences in motivation (Zigler & Butterfield, 1968), speed and practice conditions (Dubin & Osburn, 1969), examiner differences (Cohen, 1965), anxiety level (Chambers, Hopkins & Hopkins, 1972; Cox, 1964; Egeland, 1967; Marso, 1970; Smith, 1965), and language (Labov, 1970; Palmer & Gaffney, 1972). Although there have been many attempts to explore and ameliorate these problems, progress, regrettably, has been slow.

Educational Use

A fourth issue of considerable importance has been the general argument that intelligence tests provide little information that is educationally useful. It is not too far fetched to imagine professionals lined up behind each position ready to duel for their particular orientation. A few points may assist the reader to prepare for this confrontation. First it probably is true that many intelligence tests are inappropriately administered, scored, and interpreted. Individually administered intelligence tests tend to be complex and their real worth may well lie in the clinical skill of the examiner, scorer, and interpreter. Second, alternatives range from the total rejection of tests and testing to individuals interested in further test development. It would seem that the *Learning Potential Assessment Devices* of Budoff and his associates (Babad & Budoff, 1974; Budoff, 1967; Budoff & Friedman, 1964; Budoff & Gottlief, 1976; Budoff, Meskin, & Harrison, 1971; Hamilton & Budoff, 1974), the work of Fuerstein (Fuerstein, 1970, Narrol & Bachor, 1975) and Haywood (Haywood, 1967; Haywood & Switzky, 1974) may well prove valuable in the future. These devices are unique in that they measure the ability of individuals to learn under specified conditions. The result is a measure unique in its ability to predict the conditions under which an individual will best acquire the desired information.

A somewhat analogous approach to modification of the traditional approach to the measurement of intelligence has been termed the assessment of cognitive styles. During the past 20 to 30 years considerable effort has been devoted to the measurement of cognitive style, or, as Witkin (1976, p. 39) describes it "characteristic modes of functioning that we reveal throughout our perceptual and intellectual activities in a highly consistent and pervasive way." These "characteristic modes" are not unlike many aspects of intelligence and, as such, deserve attention as an incipient stage for reshaping approaches to the measurement of intelligence. Both the learning potential and the cognitive style concepts allow nuances of perceptual and language function to be included in the measurement of intelligence. Both seek to identify the *processes* that the individual employs in acting intelligently on environmental stimuli. Thus, the value of these approaches is linked to their ability to describe the manner of learning in addition to the outcomes of learning. As research progresses, the educational impact of these approaches to the measurement of "intelligence" will almost certainly be felt. An excellent review of some prominant contemporary alternatives to the assessment of intelligence can be found in Kratochwill (1977).

Examiner Qualifications

This issue has been substantially dealt with in Chapter 6. It is only reaffirmed here because of the complexity of most intelligence batteries and the high degree of examiner sophistication required to appropriately administer, score, and interpret the devices.

Labeling

Intelligence tests are often seen as the pernicious villain in labeling, but, in actuality this probably is not fair: tests are tools, intelligence tests are one type of tool. Technically, many of the better intelligence tests are among the most sound of our psychometric instruments and labeling as a social phenomenon could (and does) exist independent of intelligence tests. If labels are to be used in special education, accuracy probably would not be improved by the cessation of use of the tests.

Summary of Issues

Despite the effects of these issues, many of which will be far-reaching, it is doubtful that the measurement of intelligence will soon disappear from the educational scene. It is, however, probable that changes in measurement technique and permissible practices will occur. The remainder of this section reviews some of the currently more prevalent approaches to the measurement of intelligence.

A REVIEW OF MAJOR INSTRUMENTS INVOLVED IN THE MEASUREMENT OF INTELLIGENCE

A review of assessment measures of intelligence could be quite extensive; literally hundreds of measures have been developed. However, only a few instruments have predominated test use in the field. Most intelligence tests used in special education are now individually administered (often by a school psychologist), although group tests are sometimes still administered. As a result, considerably more emphasis will be placed on individually administered tests.

INDIVIDUAL MEASURES OF INTELLIGENCE

The Stanford-Binet

The Binet-Simon scales, which first appeared in 1905, consisted of 30 separate scales arranged in ascending order of difficulty. Subsequent alterations adopted to the 1908 and 1911 scales introduced several changes and revisions and covered the age ranges of 3 to adult level. Over the years the Binet-Simon test has undergone many translations. The most successful in the United States was that conducted by Terman (1916) which resulted in the Stanford-Binet. In this revision many new items were included and a complete restandardization was carried out on a United States population. In 1937 a revision of the Stanford-Binet was undertaken (Terman & Merrill, 1937) which resulted in a considerable expansion of the test, including a downward extension to ages one and one half years. This revision was developed in parallel form (L & M) and remained in widespread use until 1960. The third revision of the Stanford-Binet took place in that year (Terman & Merrill, 1960) and was essentially a combination of the best items to be found on Form L & M of the 1937 revision. According to Anastasi (1976) a major purpose of this revision was to assure continuity of well-studied items while at the same time including new materials which were temporarily and culturally appropriate for examinees of the 1960s.

The most recent revision of the Stanford-Binet appeared in 1972. Although the items remained unchanged from the 1960 revision, an entirely new sample of individuals was selected for standardization. In this process great care was exercised to assure representativeness in the sample. The only cases that were excluded were children for whom their primary language was not English.

The Stanford-Binet (all forms) is a rather complex and difficult test to administer. The test is organized by years from age two to superior adult. Between ages 2 and 5 the test proceeds in half-year intervals, between 5 and 14 age levels are based on yearly intervals. Beyond age fourteen the test levels include Average Adult and Superior Adult, I, II, and III. All age levels contain six subtests except Average Adult which has eight. All subtests within an age range are presumed to be of equivalent difficulty; an alternate test is provided at each level and may be substituted for any of the subtests contained within the level.

In the administration of the Stanford-Binet each subject is exposed only to items within the necessary age range; no subject takes all items. Specific procedures are provided to estimate basal ages (the starting point) and ceiling (the stopping point). All items are scored for passing or failing, there are no "in-between" measures. As might be expected considerable diversity of items exist in order to provide challenging tasks for each age range. For example, the earliest stages include tasks such as item identification and block building while more advanced levels increase reliance on language and abstract problem solving.

Reliability and validity consideration of the Stanford-Binet are particularly good. Most of the reliability coefficients reported for IQ at different age levels meet or exceed .90. Since the standard deviation for the test is set at 16, the standard error of measurement is about 5 points at most age levels. Content validity for the Binet is best considered by its wide range of seemingly age appropriate tasks. In so far that these items seem to represent what many persons term intelligence the test possesses reasonable content validity. Criterion-related validity is best ascertained for the Binet in terms of its ability to suggest the degree of academic success. The Binet correlates highly with most academic content, but it is exceptionally well related to coursework which emphasizes verbal content. Reported criterion-related validity coefficients tend to range from the high 0.40s to the low 0.70s. Somewhat less is known about the construct validity of the Stanford-Binet. A number of factor studies have revealed consistent cluster across all ages with certain skills needed at specific age ranges. In all, evidence for construct validity is not overwhelming but is satisfactory.

One of the major advantages of the Stanford-Binet is the wealth of data that provides an interpretive clinical framework for specific results. For many professionals the Stanford Binet is *the* standard measurement of intelligence and it is widely used for educational and clinical diagnosis.

The Wechsler Scales

Wechsler has prepared three scales for the measurement of intelligence at various age ranges. The tests [*Wechsler Adult Intelligence Scale—WAIS* (1955), *Wechsler Intelligence Scale for Children—WISC* (1974), and *Wechsler Preschool and Primary Scale of Intelligence—WPPSI*] have many features in common. For example, all items are grouped into subtests of increasing difficulty and each test yields a Verbal IQ, a Performance IQ and a Full Scale IQ. However, because the tests are arranged for limited age ranges (WPPSI, 4 to 6½ years; WISC, 6½ to 16½; and WAIS, 16 through adult) some divergence in form is inevitable. Therefore, each test will be reviewed independently.

The WAIS first appeared in 1955 as a development of the earlie *Wechsler Bellevue Intelligence Scale* (1939). Eleven subtests were clustered under The Verbal scale (six) and the Performance Scale (five). Th Verbal Scale subtests are Information, Comprehension, Arithmetic Similarities, Digit Span, and Vocabulary. The Performance Scale contain Digit Symbol, Picture Completion, Block Design, Picture Arrangement and Object Assembly. Generally all scales are administered though it i possible to achieve satisfactory screening data through omitting som of the scales and prorating scores to summate to a Verbal or Performance IQ.

Each of the eleven subtests requires a different task of the examine which, presumably, is somewhat independent (nonduplicative) of th tasks. The following six tasks make up the Verbal Scale. *Information* requires the subject to respond to a series of questions illustrative of common adult knowledge in our culture. In *Comprehension* the examinee describes actions that ought to be done on specific occasions, why certai practices ought to be done, the meaning of proverbs, and so on. Seemingly the scale measures practical sense and judgment. *Arithmetic* requires the subject to solve problems *without* aid of pencil and paper *Similarities* requires the examinee to relate two items by components tha they hold in common. In *Digit Span* the examiner requires the examine to repeat (forward and backward) number sequences given orally. *Vocabulary* requires a definition of up to 40 increasingly difficult words.

The Performance Scale contains five subtests. In *Digit Symbol* th examinee is required to code symbols to digits as rapidly as possible. I *Picture Completion* the examinee must report what part of a picture i missing. *Block Design* requires the examinee to arrange a number of multicolored blocks to conform to a stimulus. *Picture Arrangement* demand that a number of pictures be arranged to relate a logical story. Finally *Object Assembly* is much like a puzzle, in that items are arranged to produce a meaningful picture.

The reliability of the WAIS was developed on three age ranges: 18 t 19, 24 to 34, and 45 to 54. Full Scale IQ's reliabilities were given as 0.97 Verbal Scale IQ reliabilities were given as 0.96, and Performance Scal IQ's ranged from 193 to 0.94. Subscale reliabilities are often lower, ranging from 0.60 (Digit Span, Picture Arrangement, and Object Assembly) t 0.96 (Vocabulary). Since much is often made of profile analysis of WAI (and WISC) scores, it is always advisable to keep these reliability estimates in mind (Ysseldyke, 1973).

The WAIS manual does not report validity data and only scattere information has appeared in the literature. Of these reports perhaps th most important has been the repeatedly high correlation observed between the Stanford-Binet and the WAIS (usually around 0.80). Facto analysis has demonstrated that the subtests of the two scales as well as the two scales are not independent. In fact, Cohen (1957) reported that three factors (verbal comprehension, perceptual organization, and memory) represent the components tapped by the WAIS.

The WISC, an extension of the very successful WAIS, was developed for use with children. The test has recently been revised (*Wechsler Intelligence Scale for Children—Revised,* 1974) and this version will be discussed here. The WISC-R consists of twelve subtests organized in the familiar Verbal IQ, Performance IQ, Full Scale IQ format. Usually, however, only ten of these subtests are used. The subtests for the Verbal Scale are Information, Similarities, Arithmetic, Vocabulary, Comprehension, and Digit Span (alternate); Picture Completion, Picture Arrangement, Block Design, Object Assembly, Coding and Mazes (alternate) complete the Performance Scale. Although the WAIS and the original WISC presented all Verbal then all Performance items, WISC-R administration alternates subtests from each scale. With the exception of mazes the subtest content parallels that of the WAIS, although every effort was made to utilize child-appropriate pictures and materials.

The score format of the WISC-R nearly parallels the WAIS. The mean IQ for the Verbal, Performance, and Full Scale are set at mean = 100 with a standard deviation of 15. Twenty-two hundred children ages 6½ to 16½ made up the standardization sample, 100 boys and 100 girls at each year level. Slight variations in ages were allowed within each range. The sample was very carefully selected and was stratified on geographic region, urban-rural residence, race (white and nonwhite) and occupation of head of household. All told, children were selected from 32 states and Washington, D.C.

Reliability estimates for the WISC-R are of the split-half and test-retest variety; they are provided for all subtests and scales. The average split-half reliabilities for Verbal, Performance, and Full Scale IQ are respectively, 0.94, 0.90, and 0.96. Test-retest reliability is given as 0.93, 0.90, and 0.95. Subtest reliabilities are an improvement upon the WISC and range from 0.70 to 0.86 (split-half) and 0.65 to 0.88 (test-retest). The standard error of measurement for the Full Scale IQ is about 3 points. *Sem* is somewhat larger for the Verbal and Performance sections and for all subtests.

References to validity are omitted from the test manual. The reader is referred to Zimmerman & Woo-Sam (1970) for a discussion of the topic.

The final and perhaps most infrequently used test in the Wechsler series is the *Wechsler Pre-School and Primary Scale of Intelligence* (WPPSI). This test nearly parallels that of the WISC and WISC-R and represents an attempt to measure the intelligence of young children (4 to 6½ years). Of the eleven subtests, eight are downward extensions of the original WISC, the remaining three are unique to the WPPSI. The familiar Verbal, Performance, and Full Scales IQ's are provided by the test. The mean IQ is again set at 100 with standard deviation equal to 15.

The WPPSI was standardized on a national sample of 1,200 children, 100 boys and 100 girls at each half-year interval (4, 4½, 5, and so on). Stratification of the sample was carried through on the basis of urban-rural residence, proportionately of white-nonwhite, geographical region, and father's occupation level. From this sample, reliability estimates (split-half) were: Full Scale between 0.92 and 0.94, Verbal IQ 0.87 and 0.90 and Performance IQ between 0.84 and 0.91. Eleven-week test-retest reliabilities were Full Scales 0.92; Verbal, 0.86; and Performance, 0.89. Validity estimates with this test are particularly meager. The reader is referred to Anastasi (1976) and Sattler (1974) for a review of the available data.

ADAPTATIONS OF INTELLIGENCE TESTS FOR SPECIAL AUDIENCES

While the Stanford-Binet and the Wechsler Scales have become synonymous with the individually administered measures of intelligence, a number of other tests have appeared which are either (1) adaptations or modifications for special populations or, (2) provide scores that bear considerable resemblance to the more typical measures of intelligence. Since many of these instruments will be discussed in other chapters we will only mention these tests under the broad topics "Measures of Infant Intelligence," "Adapations for Sensory Impaired," and "Cross Cultural Testing."

Measures of Infant Intelligence

These tests are largely reviewed in Chapter 16. However, to provide continuity, the following tests are representative of this group: *The Gesell Developmental Schedule* (Gesell & Armatruda, 1947), *The Bayley Scales of Infant Development* (Bayley, 1969), *The Ordinal Scales of Psychological Development* (Uzgiris & Hunt, 1975), *The McCarthy Scales of Children Abilities* (McCarthy, 1972), and numerous screening instruments, (e.g., *The Denver Developmental Screening Test,* Frankenburg, Dodds, & Fandal, 1972). Of these tests only *The McCarthy Scales of Children's Abilities* (McCarthy, 1972) will be discussed here.

The McCarthy Scales of Children's Abilities (MSCA) (1972) is suitable for children 2½ to 8½ years of age. Six scales are provided in the test: (1) Verbal, (2) Perceptual-Performance, (3) Quantative, (4) General Cognitive, (5) Memory, and (6) Motor. The General Cognitive Scales approximate the traditional notion of a general intelligence score. It is composed of a combination of information from the first 3 scales. The 6 scales that are represented on the test are derived from 18 subtests. Some of the subtests overlap across scales and the General Cognitive Scale is composed of the results of 15 subtests. The mean General Cognitive Score is 100, the standard deviation is given as 16. The General Cognition Score is stated to be a measure of the child's functioning at the time of the test, it is not intended to reflect etiology.

The MCSA was standardized on 1,032 children with about 100 children at each of the ten half-year ranges between 2½ and 5½, and one year ranges between 5½ and 8½. The sample was stratified on boys-girls, white-nonwhite, geographic region, father's occupational level, and urban-rural residence. Children with obvious physical defects and children who could not understand English were excluded.

Estimates of the reliability for the General Cognitive Index were obtained by the split-half method and, across ages, this figure is given as 0.93; the remaining five scales range from 0.79 to 0.88. Test-retest reliabilities for a one-month interval drawn for a sample of 125 children in three age ranges yielded 0.90 for the General Cognitive Index and from 0.69 to 0.89 for separate scales. Validity data is quite meager.

The McCarthy Scales of Children's Abilities is a relatively complicated and lengthy test to administer. However, many of the scales are attractive to and elicit attention from difficult to test children. A skilled examiner may find the test useful.

Adaptations for the Sensory Impaired

Measures of intelligence in this category are most intimately associated with the measurement of hearing or visually impaired individuals (see the discussions in Chaps. 11 and 12). A few tests in this category are, however, devoted to the testing of orthopedically handicapped chidlren. One of these tests, the *Columbia Mental Maturity Scale* (CMMS) (Burgemeister, Bloom, & Lorge, 1972) is particularly germane and will be briefly discussed.

The *Columbia Mental Maturity Scale* first appeared in 1954 and was most recently revised in 1972; it was developed specifically for use with cerebral palsied children. The format of the test consists of 92 rectangular cards with three, four, or five drawings per card. In each case the examiner's task is to identify the item (which may vary by shape, color or other conceptual groupings) that does not belong with the others.

The CMMS was standardized on 2,600 children between the ages of 3 to 6 and 9 to 11. The sample was stratified on most of the usual variables.

Split-half reliabilities range from 0.85 to 0.91, short term test-retest (7 to 10 days) coefficients are reported to be in the mid-0.80s. Correlations with achievement tests have fallen between the high 0.40s and the low 0.60s, while a correlation with the *Stanford-Binet* has been reported at 0.67. In general, the CMMS may be helpful in screening and for use with orthopedically handicapped children. It should not be used as a substitute for more conventional scales.

Cross-Cultural Testing

A number of attempts have been made to develop tests to measure intelligence in a way that is not influenced by cultural background. A number of tests have emerged in response to this challenge. These include: The *Progressive Matrices* (Raven, 1965), the *Leiter International Performance Scale* (Leiter, 1969), the *Goodenough Draw-a-Man Test* (Goodenough, 1965), the *System of Multicultural Pluralistic Assessment* (Mercer & Lewis, 1977), and many others. Three of these will be reviewed here.

The *Progressive Matrices* (Raven, 1965) was developed in Britain and was designed to reflect Spearman's g factor of intelligence. The test essentially taps the relationships among abstract items in each of the 60 items within the test. Each item consists of a plate from which a part is missing. The examinee's task is to identify the part (from six or eight alternatives) that will complete the plate. This general task also appears in the *Coloured Progressive Matrices* (for children ages 5 to 11 years and the mentally retarded), a puzzle (wood block) form of the *Coloured Progressive Matrices,* and in a form for superior adults. The last test is restricted in use and is generally difficult to obtain.

The *Progressive Matrices* (all forms) suffer several faults. First, the samples may not be appropriate in the United States because the standardization was completed in England. Second, reliabilities are only moderate, ranging from the 0.40s to the mid-0.70s. Third, the manuals are generally inadequate and do not correspond to acceptable standards (see Chap. 3). In many ways the Raven Tests may best be suited for screening and research purposes. In that capacity the test(s) is usually rated as excellent.

The *Leiter International Performance Scale* has a long history of use in cross-cultural circumstances. The basic test format consists of inserting blocks into a wooden form in logical correspondence with the variable keys placed over the form. Presumably a wide range of functions are captured by the many varied tasks included in this continuous block-into-frame procedure. Among the tasks are picture completion, number estimation, analogies, spatial relations, similarity, memory, and others.

The test is arranged in age levels for 2 to 18, although the IQ obtained at different age ranges probably has different meanings due to the nature of the tasks. Split-half reliabilities range from 0.91 to 0.94, but the characteristics of the population from which these data were derived may have been less than optimal. Validity estimates are weak, though correlation with the Stanford-Binet and the WISC range from 0.56 to 0.92.

The *Leiter International Performance Scale,* like the *Progressive Matrices,* suffers from an incomplete manual and a general lack of rigor in standardization. Both tests demonstrate a great amount of potential merit that could be more fully developed given time and effort.

The final test to be reviewed here is the *System of Multicultural Pluralistic Assessment* (SOMPA) (Mercer & Lewis, 1977). SOMPA is designed to test children in the cognitive, perceptual motor, and adaptive behavior areas. The test is, according to its authors, useful for ascertaining learning potential without the masking effects of health or sociocultural factors. SOMPA is built from a multidimensional approach, some components (perceptual motor development, health) conform to the "medical model," while others (adaptive behavior in family and community, student role in the school system) conform to the social system model. Still others (learning potential) are based on Mercer's (1973) pluralistic model. The reader is referred to Mercer (1973), (1977), and Mercer & Richardson (1975) for a comprehensive review of their multi-dimensional approach to assessment.

The process of collecting information in the SOMPA model consists of two basic phases: (1) *the Parent Interview* and (2) *Student Assessment.* The Parent Interview is composed of three units: (1) Adaptive Behavior Inventory for Children, (2) Sociocultural Scales, and (3) Health History Inventories. The Adaptive Behavior Inventory measures behavior in the family and neighborhood, skill in interpersonal relations with adults and peers, ability to take care of physical and health needs and behavior in nonacademic school roles. The Sociocultural Scales attempt to describe the salient aspects of the child's family. These are measures of social, cultural, and economic characteristics of the family setting. The Health History Inventories explores the child's health history and involves a record of diseases, accidents, and operations as well as questions concerning the mother's pregnancy.

The Student Assessment section more closely approximates the traditional psychoeducational examination. Six tests contribute to the Student Assessment. These are: (1) the *Wechsler Intelligence Scale for Children—Revised,* (2) the *Bender Visual Motor Gestalt Test,* (3) Physical Dexterity Tests, (4) Visual Acuity, (5) Auditory Acuity, and (6) Weight by Height chart. Discussions of the *WISC-R* and *Bender Visual Motor Gestalt Test* may be found earlier in this chapter; auditory and visual acuity measures are most thoroughly discussed in Chapters 11 and 12, respectively. The Physical Dexterity Tasks are described as a series of gross and fine motor tasks which help to identify neurological improvement. The Weight by Height Scale is simply a medical index that reports appropriate W/H ratios that are indicative of good health.

The Parent Interview section of the SOMPA may be administered and scored by a paraprofessional who has been trained and who is thoroughly familiar with the test use. Scoring is completed after the paraprofessional leaves the home. The student assessment section of the test is administered by highly trained professionals, psychologists typically administering the WISC-R and the *Bender Visual Motor Gestalt* while school nurses or others appropriately trained personnel administer the remaining scales (visual-auditory acuity, physical dexterity, weight by height).

The profile of the SOMPA is arranged according to the Medical, Social System, and Pluralistic Model components. Most subtests are reported in scaled scores plotted on horizontal displays which represent percentile scores. Each display is marked with an "at risk" section or, more specifically, the percentile range within which scores may exhibit concern. A considerable amount of data is provided by which interpretation of the profiles is possible.

In all, SOMPA appears to be a well thought through approach to many of the problems of cross-cultural measurement. While not a panacea, it is at least as appropriate as other techniques and, because of its rich empirical heritage, represents a valuable step in the goal of cultural fair testing.

GROUP MEASURES OF INTELLIGENCE

Over the years a rather extensive list of group intelligence tests have appeared. As has been suggested previously, group testing of intelligence is of comparatively small influence in special education at this time. However in the not too distant past, as in some specific contemporary efforts (e.g., screening activities), group tests have had a role because of their ease of administration and scoring, low cost and because sophisticated examiners were not required. These advantages are, perhaps, offset by diminished rapport, difficulty in detecting attenuating situational variables (illness, fatigue, or anxiety, for example), and lack of test format flexibility.

Of all the group tests that have appeared, a relative few have been influential for special education. Often these tests have had different, but seemingly synonymous designation (e.g., "intelligence test," "general ability," "learning potential," "mental maturity"), although the general construct seems to be intelligence. Among tests representative of the description are the *California Test of Mental Maturity* (Sullivan, Clark, &

Tiegs, 1965), *The Kuhlman-Anderson Tests: A Measure of Academic Potential* (Kuhlman & Anderson, 1961), *The Otis-Lennon Mental Ability Test* (Otis & Lennon, 1970), *The Boehm Test of Basic Concepts* (Boehm, 1969), *Analysis of Learning Potential* (Durost et al., 1970), *Lorge-Thorndike Intelligence Tests: Multiple Level Edition* (Lorge & Thorndike, 1957), the *Quick Test* (Ammons & Ammons, 1962), the *Slosson Intelligence Test* (Slosson, 1963), and the *SRA Short Test of Educational Ability* (SRA, 1970). As representative tests of this group, the *Otis-Lennon Mental Ability Test* and the *Slosson Intelligence Test* will briefly be described.

The *Otis-Lennon Mental Ability Test* first appeared in 1936, the latest edition appeared in 1967–1969, and is available in two forms. The Primary Level consists of two levels: Primary I (kindergarten) and Primary II (the first half of first grade). This distinction has been criticized as meaningless (Smith, 1972) since only the scoring procedure is altered. Elementary I and Elementary II levels are useful for grades 1.6 to 3.9 and 4 to 6, respectively. Intermediate and Advanced levels are designed for use in grades 7 to 9 and 10 to 12. As might be expected, all materials are paper and pencil, that is, the examinee selects the appropriate response and indicates it directly.

According to Milholland (1972), the Otis-Lennon series is technically one of the best of the group measures of intelligence, although reservations about the value of any such measure must be considered. Alternate form reliability ranges from 0.83 to 0.89 below grade 4, above grade 4, reliabilities are invariably in the 0.90s. Abundant data are provided concerning validity. The well-organized manual provides data concerning content criterion and construct validity as drawn from the guidelines of *Standards for Educational and Psychological Tests and Manuals* (1966).

In general, the Otis-Lennon test can be considered exemplary of this type of measurement procedure, and may be considered a good predictor of academic achievement.

The *Slosson Intelligence Test for Children and Adults* (SIT) (Slosson, 1963) is described by its developer as a quick screening device useful for children and adults. It has been used in both individual and group test situations but, owing to its overwhelming appearance as a screening measure, it is here discussed under group devices. A major advantage of the SIT lies in the fact that it can be administered and scored within 10 to 30 minutes. The test consists of questions organized for one-half month credit (up to 2 years), 1 month credit (up to 4 years, 11 months), 2 months credit (up to 15 years, 10 months), and 3 month credit (up to 27 years). Most of the questions are verbally administered, a few at the very low end require only the infant's attention, grasping reflex, and other similar motor activities.

The IQ from the SIT is derived by the now largely supplanted ratio method (MA/CA X 100). The manual is barely adequate. It provides easy to follow directions for administering and scoring and hints about difficult to test situations (infants) and interpretation (e.g., scatter analysis). Details concerning the standardization population are very sketchy. It is reported that all persons were residents of New York State and many had vaguely described handicaps ("disturbed, negativism, withdrawn, and as having reading difficulties"). Reliability estimates (test-retest at two months) yielded a coefficient of 0.97 for 139 individuals ages 4 to 50. The mean IQs hovered about 100 and the standard error of measurement is given as 4.3 points. Validity estimates are poorly presented and those that are available may be spuriously high since the items represent adaptations of the Stanford-Binet and therefore, must surely evidence high correlations (Himelstein, 1972).

The SIT suffers from several problems. First, the data regarding its construction are nebulous; the population is undefined and less than rigorous procedures were applied in its identification. The ratio IQ method makes the test highly suspect with older subjects and, because part of it is drawn from frequently used tests at the infant end of the scale (e.g., the Gesell Developmental Schedule), the test represents more of a duplication than a new approach. The manual is sketchy and tributes from unspecified personnel make the test appear even less able to stand on its own merit. In short, the SIT is representative of many group tests in that the few advantages gained are often mitigated by the increased suspicion with which the prudent examiner must view the scores.

SUMMARY

This chapter has provided a brief overview of the assessment of two overlapping and exceedingly complex areas: (1) visual-auditory perception and, (2) intelligence. No effort was made to provide an exhaustive review since the material available under these topics is voluminous. It should be noted that perception and intelligence are among the most heavily assessed constructs in special education and, taken together, underly many theories of the nature of handicapping conditions and remedial strategies. Future work in this area will almost certainly lead to (1) a greater integration of perceptual and cognitive theories, (2) a more definitive battery of tests for determining cognitive style as opposed to crude measures of general intelligence, (3) a better understanding of how these attributes interact with educational contributions to influence students' learning, and (4) better developed remedial activities.

REFERENCES

Ammons, R. B. & Ammons, C. H. *The Quick Test*. Missoula, Mont.: Psychological Test Specialists, 1969.

Anastasi, A. (Ed.) *Individual differences*. New York: John Wiley, 1965.

Anastasi, A. Psychology, psychologists and psychological testing. *American Psychologist, 1967, 22,* 297–306.

Anastasi, A. *Psychological testing* (4th ed.). New York: Macmillan, 1976.

Armstrong, R. G. & Hauck, P. A. Correlates of the Bender-Gestalt scores in children. *Journal of Psychological Studies,* 1960, *11,* 153–158.

Arter, J. A. & Jenkins, J. R. Examining the benefits and prevalence of modality considerations in special education. *Journal of Special Education,* 1977, *11,* 281–298.

Babad, E. Y. & Budoff, M. Sensitivity and validity of learning potential measurement in three levels of ability. *Journal of Educational Psychology,* 1974, *66,* 439–447.

Bardon, J. I. & Bennett, V. L. *School psychology*. Englewood Cliffs, N.J.: Prentice-Hall, 1974.

Barritt, L. S. The auditory memory of children from different socioeconomic backgrounds: A partial replication. Paper presented at the American Educational Research Association Meeting, Chicago, February 1968.

Bayley, N. *Bayley Scales of Infant Development*. New York: The Psychological Corp., 1969.

Becker, J. T. & Sabatino, D. A. Reliability of individual tests of perception administered utilizing group techniques. *Journal of Clinical Psychology,* 1971, *27,* 86–88.

Bereiter, C. The future of individual differences. *Environment, heredity and intelligence* (Reprint Series of the *Harvard Educational Review),* 1969.

Binet, A. & Simon, T. Methodes nouvelles pour le diagnostic du niveau intellectual des anormaux. *L'Annee Psychologigue,* 1905, *11,* 93, 191–244.

Birch, A. G. & Belmont, S. Auditory-visual integration, intelligence and reading ability in school children. *Perceptual and Motor Skills,* 1965, *20,* 295–305.

Boehm, A. *Boehm Test of Basic Concepts*. New York: The Psychological Corp., 1969.

Boyd, L. & Randle, K. Factor analysis of the Frostig Developmental Test of Visual Perception. *Journal of Learning Disabilities,* 1970, *3,* 253–255.

Brazziel, W. F. A letter from the south. *Environment, heredity and intelligence* (Reprint Series of the *Harvard Educational Review*), 1969.

Bruner, J. S. On perceptual readiness. *Psychological Review,* 1957, *64,* 123–152.

Bruner, J. S. The course of cognitive growth. *American Psychology,* 1964, *19,* 1–15.

Bryan, Q. R. Relative importance of intelligence and visual perception in predicting reading achievement. *California Journal of Educational Research,* 1964, *15,* 44–48.

Budoff, M. Learning potential among institutionalized young adult retardates. *American Journal of Mental Deficiency,* 1967, *72,* 404–411.

Budoff, M. & Friedman, M. Learner's potential as an assessment approach to the adolescent mentally retarded. *Journal of Consulting Psychology,* 1964, *28,* 434–439.

Budoff, M., Meskin, J., & Harrison, R. H. Educational test of the learning potential hypothesis. *American Journal of Mental Deficiency,* 1971, *76,* 159–169.

Budoff, M. & Gottlieb, J. Special-class EMR children mainstreamed: A study of an aptitude (learning potential) x treatment interaction. *American Journal of Mental Deficiency,* 1976, *81,* 1–11.

Burgemeister, B., Blum, L., & Lorge, I. *Columbia Mental Maturity Scale*. New York: Harcourt, Brace & World, 1972.

Cawley, J. F., Burrow, W. H., & Goodstein, H. A. An appraisal of Head Start participants and non-participants. Research report, University of Connecticut, Contract OEO4177, Office of Economic Opportunity, 1968.

Cattell, P. *Cattell's Infant Intelligence Scale.* New York: The Psychological Corp., 1940.

Chalfant, J. C. & Scheffelin, M. A. Central processing dysfunctions in children: A review of research. *NINDS Monograph,* 1969, No. 9.

Chambers, A. C., Hopkins, K. D. & Hopkins, B. R. Anxiety, physiologically and psychologically measured: Its effects on mental test performance. *Psychology in the Schools,* 1972, *9,* 198-206.

Chaplin, S. P. & Krawiec, T. S. *Systems and theories of psychology.* New York: Holt, 1960.

Clawson, A. The Bender-Gestalt Visual Motor Gestalt Test as an index of emotional disturbance in children. *Journal of Project Technology,* 1959, *23,* 198–206.

Cohen, E. Examiner differences with individual intelligence tests. *Perceptual and Motor Skills,* 1965, *20,* 13–24.

Cohen, J. A factor-analytically based rationale for the *Wechsler Adult Intelligence Scale. Journal of Consulting Psychology,* 1957, *21,* 451–457.

Coltheart, M. & Curthoys, I. Short-term recognition memory for pitch: Effect of a priori probability on response times and error rates. *Perception and Psychophysics,* 1968, *4,* 85–89.

Corah, N. L. & Powell, B. J. A factor analytic study of the Frostig Development Test of Visual Perception. *Perceptual and Motor Skills,* 1963, *16,* 59–63.

Cox, F. R. Text anxiety and achievement behavior systems related to examination performance in children. *Child Development,* 1964, *35,* 909–915.

Cronbach, L. J. Heredity, environment and educational policy. Environment, heredity and intelligence (reprint series of the Harvard Educational Review), 1969.

Crow, J. F. Genetic theories and influences: comments on the value of diversity. Environment, heredity and intelligence (reprint series of the Harvard Educational Review), 1969.

Dubin, J. A. & Osburn, H. Speed and practice: Effects on Negro and white test performances. *Journal of Applied Psychology,* 1969, *53,* 19–23.

Durost, W., Gardner, E., Madden, R. & Prescott, G. *Analysis of learning potential.* New York: Harcourt, Brace, Jovanovich, 1970.

Egeland, B. Influence of examiner and examinee anxiety on WISC performance. *Psychological Reports,* 1967, *21,* 409–414.

Elkind, D. Piagetian and psychometric conceptions of intelligence. Environment, heredity, and intelligence (reprint series of the Harvard Educational Review), 1969.

Evans, J. R. Auditory and auditory-visual integration skills as they relate to reading. *The Reading Teacher,* 1969, *22,* 625–629.

Eysenck, H. J. Intelligence assessment: A theoretical and experimental approach. *British Journal of Educational Psychology,* 1967, *37,* 81–98.

Flaughner, R. H. The new definitions of test fairness in selection: Developments and implications. *Educational Research,* 1974, *3,* 3–16.

Flavell, J. H. The developmental psychology of Jean Piaget. Princeton, N.J.: Van Nostrand, 1963.

Frankenburg, W., Dodds, J., & Fandal, A. *The Denver Developmental Screening Test.* Denver, Colorado: National Institute of Health General Research Support Grant, 1970.

Frostig, M. *Frostig Developmental Test of Visual Perception.* Palo Alto, Ca.: Consulting Psychologists Press, 1964.

Fuerstein, R. A dynamic approach to the causation, prevention, and alleviation of retarded performance. In H. C. Haywood (Ed.), *Social-cultural aspects of mental retardation.* New York: Appleton, 1970.

Gesell, A. & Armatruda, C. S. *Developmental diagnosis* (2nd ed.). New York: Hoevar-Harper, 1947.

Gibson, E. J. *Principles of perceptual learning and development.* New York: Appleton, 1967.

Goins, J. T. Visual perceptual abilities and early reading progress. *Supplementary Educational Monographs,* 1958 (87 pp.).

Goodenough, F. & Harris, D. B. *Goodenough-Harris Drawing Test.* New York: Harcourt Brace Jovanovich, 1965.

Guilford, J. P. *The nature of human intelligence.* New York: McGraw-Hill, 1967.

Hamilton, J. V. & Budoff, M. Learning potential among the moderately and severely mentally retarded. *Mental Retardation,* 1974, *12,* 33–36.

Hammill, D. D. & Larsen, S. C. The effectiveness of psycholinguistic training. *Exceptional Children,* 1974, *41,* 5–15.

Hamelstein, P. Slosson Intelligence Test for Children and Adults. In O. K. Buros (Ed.), *The seventh mental measurements yearbook.* Highland Park, N.J.: The Gryphon Press, 1972.

Haywood, H. C. Experimental factors in intellectual developments: The concept of dynamic intelligence. In J. Zubin & G. Jervis (Eds.), *Psychopathology of mental development.* New York: Grune & Stratton, 1967.

Haywood, H. C. & Switzky, H. N. Children's verbal abstractions: Effects of enriched input, age, and IQ. *American Journal of Mental Deficiency,* 1974, *78*, 556–565.

Herrnstein, R. J. *IQ in the meritocracy.* Boston: Little, Brown, 1971.

Hull, C. L. *A behavior system: An introduction to behavior theory concerning the individual organism.* New Haven: Yale University Press, 1952.

Hunt, J. M. Has compensatory education failed? Has it been attempted? Environment, heredity and intelligence (reprint series of the Harvard Educational Review), 1969.

Jensen, A. R. How much can we boost I.Q. and scholastic achievement? *Harvard Educational Review,* 1969, *39,* 1–123.

Kagan, J. M. Inadequate evidence and illogical conclusions. Environment, heredity, and intelligence (reprint series of the Harvard Educational Review), 1969.

Keogh, B. K. The Bender-Gestalt as a predictive and diagnostic test of reading performance. *Journal of Consulting Psychology,* 1965, *29,* 83–84.

Keogh, B. & Smith, C. Visuo-Motor ability for school prediction. *Perceptual and Motor Skills,* 1967, *25,* 101–110.

Kirk, S. A., McCarthy, J., & Kirk, W. *Illinois Test of Psycholinguistic Abilities.* Urbana, Ill.: University of Illinois Press, 1968.

Koppitz, E. M. The Bender Gestalt Test and learning disturbances in young children. *Journal of Clinical Psychology,* 1958, *14,* 292–295.

Koppitz, E. M. Diagnosing brain damage in young children with the Bender Gestalt Test. *Journal of Consultative Psychology,* 1962, *26,* 541–546.

Kratochwill, T. R. The movement of psychological extras into ability assessment. *Journal of Special Education,* 1977, *11,* 299–311.

Kuhlman, F. & Anderson, R. *Kuhlman-Anderson Test.* Princeton, N.J.: Personnel Press, Inc., 1961.

Labov, W. The language of nonstandard English. In F. Williams (Ed.), *Language and poverty.* Chicago: Markham, 1970.

Lambert, N. M. The school psychologist as a source of power and influence. *Journal of School Psychology,* 1973, *11,* 245–250.

Leiter, R. G. *The Leiter International Performance Scale.* Los Angeles, Ca.: Western Psychological Services, 1969.

Lorge, I. & Thorndike, R. *Lorge-Thorndike Intelligence Tests.* Boston: Houghton Mifflin, 1957.

Lowry, L. M. Differences in visual perception and auditory discrimination between American Indian and white kindergarten children. *Journal of Learning Disabilities,* 1970, *3,* 359–363.

Lund, K. A., Foster, G. E., & McCall-Perez, F. C. The effectiveness of psycholinguistic training: A reevaluation. *Exceptional Children,* 1978, *44,* 310–319.

McCarthy, D. *McCarthy Scales of Children's Abilities.* New York: The Psychological Corp., 1972.

Marso, R. N. Classroom testing procedures, test anxiety and achievement. *Journal of Experimental Education,* 1970, *38,* 54–58.

Marx, M. H. & Hillix, W. A. *Systems and theories in psychology.* New York: McGraw-Hill, 1963.

Maslow, P., Frostig, M., Lefever, D. W., & Whittlesey, J. R. B. The Marianne Frostig Developmental Test of Visual Perception: 1963 standardization. *Perceptual and Motor Skills,* 1964, *19,* 463–499.

Mercer, J. R. & Lewis, J. F. *System of multicultural pluralistic assessment.* New York: The Psychological Corp., 1977.

Mercer, J. R. *Labeling the mentally retarded.* Berkeley, Ca.: University of California Press, 1973.

Mercer, J. R. The struggle for children's rights: Critical juncture for school psychology. *The School Psychology Digest,* 1977, *6,* 4–19.

Mercer, J. R. & Richardson, J. G. Mental retardation as a social problem. In N. Hobbs (Ed.), *Issues in the classification of children.* San Francisco: Jossey-Bass, 1975.

Meyers, C. E. What the *ITPA* measures: A synthesis of factor studies of the 1961 edition. *Education and Psychological Measurement,* 1969, *29,* 867–876.

Miller, G. A. The magical number seven, plus or minus two: Some limits on our capacity for processing information. *Psychological Review,* 1956, *63,* 81–97.

Millholland, J. E. Otis-Lennon Mental Ability Test. In O. K. Buros (Ed.), *The seventh mental measurements yearbook.* Highland Park, N.J.: The Gryphon Press, 1972, pp. 370–371.

Minskoff, E. H. Research on the efficacy of remediating psycholinguistic disabilities: Critique and recommendations. In P. L. Newcomer & D. D. Hammill (Eds.), *Psycholinguistics in the schools.* Columbus, Oh.: Charles E. Merrill, 1976.

Muehl, S. & Kremenak, S. Ability to match information within and between auditory and visual sense modalities and subsequent reading achievement. *Journal of Educational Psychology,* 1966, *57,* 230–239.

Narrol, H. & Bachor, D. G. An introduction to Fuerstein's approach to assessing and developing cognitive potential. *Interchange,* 1975, *6,* 1–16.

Neisser, U. *Cognitive psychology.* New York: Meredith, 1967.

Olson, A. V. The Frostig Developmental Test of Visual Perception as a predictor of specific reading abilities with second grade children. Elementary English, 1966, *43,* 869–872.

Olson, A. V. Factor analytic studies of the Frostig Developmental Test of Visual Perception. *Journal of Special Education,* 1968, *2,* 429–433.

Osgood, C. E. Motivational dynamics of language behavior. In M. R. Jones (Ed.), *Nebraska symposium on motivation.* Lincoln: University of Nebraska Press, 1957.

Otis, A. S. & Lennon, R. T. *Otis-Lennon Mental Ability Test.* New York: Harcourt Brace Jovanovich, 1970.

Palmer, M. & Gaffney, P. D. Effects of administration of the WISC in Spanish and English and relationship of social class to performance. *Psychology in the Schools,* 1972, *9,* 61–64.

Peterson, L. R. Immediate memory: Data and theory. In C. N. Cofer & B. S. Musgrave (Eds.), *Verbal behavior and learning.* New York: McGraw-Hill, 1963.

Piaget, J. *The origins of intelligence in children.* New York: International Universities Press, 1952.

Piaget, J. *The psychology of intelligence.* Paterson, N.J.: Littlefield, Adams, 1963.

Pronko, N. H. A critical review of the theories of perception In A. Kidd & J. Rivoire (Eds.), *Perceptual development in children.* New York: International Universities Press, 1966.

Raven, J. C. *Progressive matrices.* New York: The Psychological Corp., 1965.

Rosenblith, J. F. Judgments of simple geometric figures by children. *Perceptual and Motor Skills,* 1965, *21,* 947–990 (Monograph Suppl. 2-V21).

Rudegeair, R. E. & Kamil, M. L. Assessment of phonological discrimination in children. Technical Report No. 118, March 1970, Wisconsin Research and Development Center for Cognitive Learning, The University of Wisconsin, Contract OE 5-10-15-4, U.S. Office of Education, Department of Health, Education, and Welfare, 1970.

SRA Short Test of Educational Ability. Chicago: Science Research Associates, 1970.

Sabatino, D. A. Information processing behaviors associated with learning disabilities. *Journal of Learning Disabilities,* 1968, *1,* 440–450.

Sabatino, D. A. The construction and assessment of an experimental test of auditory perception. *Exceptional Children,* 1969, *36,* 729–737.

Sabatino, D. A. Auditory perception: Development, assessment and intervention. In L. Mann & D. Sabatino (Eds.), *First review of special education* (Vol. 1). Philadelphia: JSE Press, 1973.

Sattler, J. M. *Assessment of children's intelligence.* Philadelphia: W. B. Saunders, 1974.

Scarr-Salapetak, S. Race, social class and IQ. *Science,* 1971, *174,* 1285–1295.

Sedlak, R. A. & Weener, P. Review of research on the Illinois Test of Psycholinguistic Abilities. In L. Mann & D. Sabatino (Eds.), *The first review of special education* (Vol. 1). Philadelphia: JSE Press, 1973.

Shaw, M. C. & Cruickshank, W. M. The use of the Bender-Gestalt Test with epileptic children. *Journal of Clinical Psychology,* 1956, *12,* 192–193.

Shockley, W. Models, mathematics, and the moral obligation to diagnose the origin of Negro IQ deficits. *Review of Educational Research,* 1971, *41,* 369–377.

Skeel, M., Calfee, R. C., & Venezky, R. L. Perceptual confusions among fricatives in preschool children. Technical Report No. 73, 1969, Research and Development Center for Cognitive Learning, The University of Wisconsin.

Slosson, R. *Slosson Intelligence Test (SIT).* East Aurora, N.Y.: Slosson Educational Publications, 1963.

Smith, C. P. The influences of text anxiety scores of stressful versus neutral conditions of test administration. *Educational and Psychological Measurement,* 1965, *25,* 135–141.

Smith, A. E. Otis-Lennon Mental Ability Test. In O. K. Buros (Ed.), *The seventh mental measurements yearbook.* Highland Park, N.J.: The Gryphon Press, 1972. pp. 370–371.

Snyder, R. J. & Pope, P. New norms for and an item analysis of the Wepman test at the first grade, six-year-level. *Perceptual and Motor Skills.* 1970, *31,* 1007–1010.

Sullivan, E., Clark, W., & Tiegs, E. *California Test of Mental Maturity.* New York: McGraw-Hill, 1965.

Taylor, E. M. *Psychological appraisal of children with cerebral defects.* Cambridge, Ma.: Harvard University Press, 1961.

Templin, M. C. *Templin auditory discrimination test: Certain language skills in children.* Minneapolis, Minn.: University of Minnesota Press, 1957.

Terman, L. M. *The measurement of intelligence.* Boston: Houghton Mifflin, 1916.

Terman, L. M. & Merrill, M. A. *Measuring intelligence.* Boston: Houghton Mifflin, 1937.

Terman, L. M. & Merrill, M. A. *Stanford-Binet Intelligence Scale*. Boston: Houghton Mifflin, 1960.

Travis, L. E. & Rasmus, B. The speech sound discrimination ability of cases with functional disorders of articulation. *Quarterly Journal of Speech,* 1931, *17,* 217–226.

Uzgiris, I. C. & Hunt, J. M. V. *Assessment in infancy: Ordinal scales of psychological development*. Urbana, Ill.: University of Illinois Press, 1975.

Vernon, P. E. *Intelligence and cultural environment*. London: Methuene, 1969.

Wechsler, D. *Manual for the Wechsler preschool and primary scale of intelligence*. New York: Psychological Corporation, 1967.

Wechsler, D. *Manual for the Wechsler Intelligence Scale for Children—Revised*. New York: Psychological Corp., 1974

Wechsler, D. *Manual for the Wechsler Adult Intelligence Scale*. New York: Psychological Association, 1955.

Wechsler, D. *The measurement and appraisal of adult intelligence* (4th ed.). Baltimore: Williams & Wilkins, 1958.

Wechsler, D. Intelligence defined and undefined: A relativistic appraisal. *American Psychologist,* 1975, *30,* 135–139.

Wepman, J. M. *Auditory discrimination test*. Chicago: Language Research Associates, 1958.

Wertheimer, W. Studies in the theory of Gestalt psychology. *Psychology in the Schools,* 1923, *4,* 32–36.

Wisland, M. V. & Many, W. A. Factorial study of the Illinois Test of Psycholinguistic Abilities with children having above average intelligence. *Educational and Psychological Measurement,* 1969, *29,* 367–376.

Ysseldyke, J. E. Diagnostic-prescriptive teaching: The search for aptitude-treatment interactions. In L. Mann & D. A. Sabatino (Eds.), *The first review of special education* (Vol. 1). Philadelphia: JSE Press, 1973.

Zigler, E. & Butterfield, E. G. Motivational aspects of changes in IQ test performance of culturally deprived nursery school children. *Child Development,* 1968, *39,* 1–14.

Zimmerman, I. L. & Woo-Sam, J. Research with the Wechsler Intelligence Scale for Children: 1960–1970. *Psychology in the Schools,* 1972, *9,* 232–271 (Special Monograph Supplement.)

SUGGESTED READINGS

Anastasi, A. (Ed.) *Individual differences*. New York: John Wiley, 1965.

Boring, E. G. *A history of experimental psychology* (2nd ed.). New York: Appleton, 1950.

Broadbent, D. E. *Perception and communication*. Oxford: Pergamon Press, 1958.

Bush, W. J. & Waugh, K. W. *Diagnosing learning disabilities* (2nd ed.). Columbus, Ohio: Charles E. Merrill, 1976.

Chalfant, T. C. & Scheffelin, M. A. *Central processing dysfunctions in children: A review of research*. NINDS Monograph (#9). Bethesda, Md.: U.S.O.E., 1969.

Cronbach, L. J. Five decades of public controversy over mental testing. *American Psychologist,* 1975, *30,* 1–14.

Estes, W. K. Learning theory and intelligence. *American Psychologist,* 1974, *29,* 740–750.

Gibson, E. J. *Principles of perceptual learning and development*. New York: Meredith, 1967.

Gibson, J. & Gibson, E. Perceptual learning: Differentiation or enrichment? *Psychological Review,* 1955, *62,* 32–41.

Gulliksen, H. Looking back and ahead in psychometrics. *American Psychologist,* 1974, *29,* 251–261.

Hammill, D. & Wiederholt, J. Review of the Frostig Visual Perception Test and the related training program. In L. Mann & D. Sabatino (Eds.), *The first review of special education* (Vol. 1). Philadelphia: JSE, 1973.

McClelland, D. C. Testing for competence rather than for intelligence. *American Psychologist,* 1973, *28,* 1–14.

McNemar, Q. On so-called test bias. *American Psychologist,* 1975, *30,* 848–851.

Meyers, C. E. & Sundstrom, P. E., & Yoshida, R. K. The school psychologist and assessment in special education. *School Psychology Monograph,* 1974, *2,* 3–57.

Neisser, U. *Cognitive psychology.* New York: Meredith, 1967.

Sabatino, D. A. Auditory perception: Development, assessment and intervention. In L. Brown & D. Sabatino (Eds.), *First review of special education* (Vol. 1). Philadelphia: JSE, 1973.

Sattler, J. M. Intelligence testing of ethnic minority-group and culture-disadvantaged children. In L. Mann & D. Sabatino (Eds.), *The first review of special education* (Vol. 2). Philadelphia: JSE Press, 1973.

Sattler, J. M. *Assessment of children's intelligence.* Philadelphia: W. B. Saunders, 1974.

Schmidt, F. H. & Hunter, J. E. Racial and ethnic bias in psychological tests: Divergent implications of two definitions of test bias. *American Psychologist,* 1974, *29,* 1–8.

Wechsler, D. Intelligence defined and undefined: A relativistic appraisal. *American Psychologist,* 1975, *30,* 135–139.

Witkin, H. A. Cognitive styles in learning and teaching. In S. Messick (Ed.), *Individuality in learning.* San Francisco: Jossey Bass, 1976.

Witkin, H. A. Some implications of research on cognitive style for problems of education. In M. Gottsegan & G. Gottsegan (Eds.), *Professional school psychology* (Vol. III). New York: Grune & Stratton, 1969.

Zimmerman, I. L. & Woo-Sam, J. Research with the Wechsler Scale of Intelligence for Children: 1960–1970. *Psychology in the Schools,* 1972, *9,* 232–271 (Special Monograph Supplement.)

Frances Lamberts

8
Describing Children's Language Behavior

> *The fundamental quality of one's voice, the phonetic patterns of speech, the speed and relative smoothness of articulation, the length and build of the sentences, the character and range of the vocabulary, the scholastic consistency of the words used, the readiness with which words respond to the requirements of the social environment, in particular the suitability of one's language to the language habits of the persons addressed. . . .*
>
> (Edward Sapir, 1970, p. 19)

Sapir's eloquent characterization points to two fundamental dimensions of language behavior. One is structural and relates to sounds, words, and the "build" of sentences; the other is social-perceptual and relates to appropriateness of its use in communicative settings. This chapter will elaborate on the above characterization. It cannot lay down a simple set of "instructions for assembly of language profile," for there are no simple guidelines. Rather, it treats the task of assessing language behavior within the broader context of knowledge of the structural system and its acquisition. Accordingly, it is discussed under five headings: major theoretical orientations to language; definition of language as framework for assessment; dimensions of language—structure and function; language acquisition; and language assessment.

MAJOR THEORETICAL ORIENTATIONS

Numerous theories have been proposed to explain children's learning of language. The major theoretical conceptualizations can be said to fall into two broad categories: theories with a behavioral orientation, and theories with a cognitive orientation (Menyuk, 1971; Staats, 1974). Behavioral theorists maintain that language behavior and development can be accounted for by strict stimulus-response and reinforcement principles. In this view, the infant acquires language because his initially random vocalizations are rewarded through adult attention. When the infant learns that vocal behavior fulfills a communication function, i.e., someone reacts as a result of it, the behavior becomes autonomous. Thereafter, linguistic behavior is differentiated; that is, specific behavioral classes are established. For example, the contrastive verbal marking of multiple versus single objects, *dogs,* and *shoes* versus *dog* and *shoe*. The differentiation and resultant linguistic growth are now mediated by the fact that reinforcement becomes contingent upon appropriate responding. Responses illustrating different grammatic categories or concepts are shaped by environmental manipulation, and generalization accounts for the child's eventual learning of the grammatic concepts involved. Behavioristic formulations of language underlie a widely used test (Kirk, McCarthy, & Kirk, 1968) and much recent work in remediation of language impairment (Guess, Sailor, & Baer, 1974; Sloane & MacAulay, 1968).

Cognitively oriented theories find the basis for language development in the child's ability to observe and search for regularities in the occurrences around him, to symbolize and, from his integrated perceptions, derive a symbolic knowledge of the environment. The capacity to search for regularities and patterns is held to be innate and to apply both at a general-cognitive and the linguistic level. The human infant has a special facility for observing and abstracting the constancies in the extralinguistic environment (cognitive knowledge of the world), as well as the constancies in the linguistic environment (abstraction of patterns and structure of language) from the complex impressions that impinge incessantly upon his nervous system. Cognitively oriented theories dominate the psycholinguistic studies of child language learning (Bloom, 1970; Clark, 1973; Ervin-Tripp, 1973; Slobin, 1971, 1973). In this chapter, language learning will be presented from the cognitivist point of view. Behavioral views may be found in Mowrer (1954, 1960), Osgood (1953, 1957), Skinner (1957), and Staats (1968).

DEFINITION OF LANGUAGE AS A FRAMEWORK FOR ASSESSMENT

Any rational approach to the assessment and teaching of language must be based on a theory and definition of what it is that is to be assessed and taught. *Theory* is here used to refer to how children come to have language, the mechanisms by which they acquire it, factors that influence the acquisition process, and the meaning of language for the child's social and mental growth. *Definition* refers to the substance of what it is that children acquire when they learn language. Below are a few definitions of language.

> Languages are composed of speech sounds, syllables, morphemes, and sentences, and meaning is largely conveyed by the properties and particular use of these units (Menyuk, 1971, p. 15).
>
> Language may be functionally defined as an arbitrary system comprised of sets of vocal symbols which represent a conceptual system used by man to communicate (Carrow, 1972, p. 54).
>
> Language is essentially a system of symbols, a symbol being defined as something that stands for something else by convention or code rather than just by familiarity or resemblance. The symbols in language must be systematically related to one another and must be capable of generating novel utterances, so that knowledge of a language implies that the user can both understand and produce utterances which have never previously been understood or produced (Mittler, 1976, p. 8).
>
> (Language is) a system of signs and the possible relations among them which, together, allow for the representation of an individual's experience of the world of objects, events, and relations (Bloom, 1975, p. 249).

It is evident that some of these definitions emphasize the *communication* aspect of language, others its *representational nature,* and others its *structure*. However, there are notions central to most. We will identify these commonalities as a conceptual framework for our discussion of language assessment.

1. Language involves *symbols* which represent experiences; we must, therefore, obtain an estimate of the size of children's symbol sets (vocabulary).

2. Symbol combinations convey meaning; therefore, we must judge the child's knowledge of the *rules* for symbol combination (grammar).
3. Language is not necessarily oral. Human beings can use a number of signals or artifacts symbolically and communicate successfully in different media—through writing, morse code, drum beats, and rhythms or gestures, for example. There is little inherently better about any one medium. However, in the case of oral language, the symbols are made up of *vocal sounds;* we must, therefore, also assess the child's knowledge of the set of phonemes (speech sounds).
4. Communication has interpersonal dimensions that are not strictly related to knowledge of the linguistic code. A person must know how, when, and when not to speak to a given addressee. These required competencies are of a social-personal nature and, since language use requires communicative skills in addition to linguistic ability, we must also assess the child's competence with regard to interpersonal *uses* of language.

Language is often described as having certain other universal characteristics (Chapman, 1972; Hockett, 1963), and we would expect to find these fundamental characteristics reflected in children's language, as well. Brown (1973) holds three as the most important of the universal properties of language: meaningfulness or semanticity, displacement, and productivity. In many discussions of the nature of the language, the notion of duality of patterning is also cited.

We normally think *meaningfulness* to be so basic to language as to take it for granted. But there are children whose irrelevant and noncommunicative chatter reminds us that learning the connection between language symbols and things in the real world is not always automatic (Jones & Wepman, 1965). *Displacement* refers to the possibility to transmit information by means of language across time and place about events to which one is not, or never has been, a participant. Children do not start out using language in this manner (Bronowski & Bellugi, 1973). At first, their speech is a running commentary on events of the here and now. When references to things and events not present become more frequent, they are regarded as a sign of cognitive and linguistic growth. *Productivity* refers to the ability to use language in novel ways and/or novel situations and to understand it when most every sentence we hear or see in print is new to us. Yet there are children, particularly among the more severely retarded, whose language is predominantly, if not solely, restricted to stereotypic expressions. *Duality of patterning* refers to the fact that the limited set of basic elements in language (sounds and words) can be combined and recombined in many different ways to build new messages.

These characteristics make language a vehicle for cultural transmission of knowledge, and thus a powerful tool for learning. Without it, knowledge would be limited to a person's own experiences.

DIMENSIONS OF LANGUAGE: STRUCTURE AND FUNCTIONS

If we are to plan and implement corrective strategies for atypical language behavior, we must have detailed descriptive knowledge of the dimensions of language. To be successful in diagnosis and training of children with language impairments, teachers and other persons in relevant professions are urged to become a "discipline . . . which concentrates on phonology, morphology, syntax, semantics, rhythm, and phonation" (McLean, 1972, p. 3), be the child with the linguistic impairment mentally, behaviorally, or otherwise handicapped or not.

The quotation from McLean contains some of the terms used by linguists to describe the structural dimensions of language. Only a very brief explanation will be presented here; the reader is referred to Brown (1965), Buchanan (1963), and Langacker (1973) for comprehensive discussions.

Phonology

The first level of language structure is its sound system or phonology. As Sapir (1921) remarks, the average lay person assumes languages to be built from a small number of sounds that coincide roughly with the letters of the alphabet. In fact, the speech sounds of most languages form a considerably larger set than the sets of alphabet letters—English having about 45 phonemes as against an alphabet set of 26. Phonemes or speech sounds are not unique sounds but ranges of sound which the native speaker perceives as being functionally equivalent. A great many different variants of a sound, e.g., of "b" as in the word boat, if pronounced by different speakers, by the same speaker on different occasions, in different moods, at varying speeds, or in words with other sounds adjoining—would all be heard as "b" even though their actual (acoustic) value might be markedly different; that is, the sound "b" may vary over a considerable range of the acoustic continuum or of speech muscle configurations, and these variations will go unnoticed by the speaker or listener. If, however, the quality of the sound changes so much that the change is significant to the native speaker, then a phonemic change has occurred as, for example, in the change from "boat" to "goat." These words are perceived as different, and the difference is of one speech sound or phoneme. Phonemes are, therefore, often defined as the smallest range of sound whose substitution for another sound produces a meaning change. Even though phoneme substitution results in meaning change, the phonemes or speech sounds are themselves devoid of meaning. This characteristic of sounds is important to remember, for sometimes teachers and clinicians do not appreciate that material which cannot be related to some external, meaningful referent, is not easily discriminated or learned (Ervin-Tripp, 1973). Fry (1966) cites the availability of such minimally contrasting words as, for example, pen-Ben, comb-dome, or hand-hound in any language as one of the main factors which facilitate speech sound learning in infancy. If the child has an external criterion, i.e., if he or she is certain that the things designated by these words are different, he will much more readily notice and learn the respective differences in the sounds.

Phonemes can be classified in one of several ways. One categorization derives from a description of where and how within the articulatory pathway the current of air is modified to produce a given speech sound. The classification is said to be by place and manner of articulation. The sound "m" is a nasal sound (manner of articulation) because the airstream is allowed to resonate in the nasal cavity, and the lips are in contact (place of articulation). For the sound "f," on the other hand, the breath is conducted through a narrow passage in the mouth (manner of production) and the articulators which make contact are the upper teeth and lower lip (place of production). The consonant sounds can be located in a grid (Table 8-1) in which the axes are defined by the different places and manner of sound articulation. The vowel sounds are described with reference to relative height of the tongue and degree of rounding of the lips during production. (For a detailed discussion of the English sound system see Buchanan [1963] and Brown [1965]).

Phonemes may also be described as consisting of "features." Features are binary distinctions, such as whether a sound is voiced or not, nasal or not. A small pool of features is thought to make up the sounds of all the languages of the world. The speech sounds in any language can be compared as being different or similar in degree according to the number of such features they share. The more features they share, the more similar they are, and the more easily misidentified. Their feature composition is also thought to be one reason why children learn speech sounds earlier than others (Menyuk, 1972). Jakobson (1971) has proposed that in speech sound learning children follow the principle of maximum contrast, i.e., they first learn to distinguish sounds which have the fewest features in common. Features can be used as a scale for measuring the perceptual distance between phonemes (Brown, 1965), and feature analysis approaches are being attempted for remediation of childrens' articulation errors (Costello, 1975).

Table 8-1
Place and Manner of Articulation in English Consonant Phonemes

	Bilabial	Labio-Dental	Dental	Alveolar	Palatal	Velar	Glottal
Stop	p b			† d		k g	
Fricative		f v	θ = θ	s z	ʃ = ʃ 3		h
Affricate				†ʃ = †ʃ d d3			
Glide	w				y		
Liquid				l r			
Nasal	m			n			

Familiarity with some basic principles of speech-sound production and classification, combined with knowledge of the normal course of speech-sound development (Dale, 1972; Ervin-Tripp, 1966) is not excess luggage for the teacher. McLean (1976) advances a strong case for basing remedial speech training on both place-manner and phonemic-feature categorizations. He suggests that the initial goal for speech-sound training in children with severe limitations be the development of at least one phoneme in each of the sound categories described by *manner* of articulation. Then another phoneme within the same class but having a different *place* of articulation should be taught. Then, as phonemes in the different classes become available, the *feature* of voicing should be the criterion for remedial sound selection. Such a sample sequence for remedial speech-sound training (using sounds in only one manner of articulation class) is illustrated in Figure 8-1.

A set of sounds is not all the child needs to learn of the phonology of his native language, for languages differ in the ways in which sounds can combine to form words. In some languages, sound sequences such as *mpshtiell* may be quite acceptable (Hamp, 1967), whereas such a combination of beginning sounds would not be permissible in English. By about three years of age, children have learned which sound combinations are typical of their language and which are not (Menyuk, 1972).

Correct sounds and permissible sequences do not yet exhaust what the child has to learn of the phonetic habits of language. Superimposed on the sounds is a dynamic system of emphasis and intonation by means of

Type of Sound:	Manner	+	Place	+	Feature
Stop:	/b/		/d/		/p/

Fig. 8-1. Progression in speech-sound teaching following systematic categorization criterion.

which subtle intentions and meanings are communicated. This can easily be exemplified in two sentences:

1. She uses teaching aids effectively.
2. Teaching aids learning, effectively?

The adult listener's interpretation of these sentences is that the first is an informative statement, and the second a doubting question. This knowledge about the basic intent of the messages is conveyed by intonation. In the first case, the pitch of the voice falls on the last word but it rises sharply, with some additional stress and prolongation, in the second. The listener also knows that the first statement is about devices that help teachers teach children, while the question in the second regards the aid children may or may not receive from the activity of teaching. This knowledge about content of the messages is conveyed by the shift in emphasis and voice pitch from *teaching* aids in sentence one to teaching *aids* in sentence two. The devices of intonation—variations in loudness and pitch of the voice and duration of stressed syllables—add a level of acoustic dynamics that inform the listener not only where the sentence ends but what its overall intention is and to which part of it the speaker wishes to draw attention. It seems evident that learning the sound system of language—the phonemes and their possible combinations, and the intonation superimposed on them—is no small feat and places high demands on the perceptual abilities of the young child.

Morphology

The units at the next level of organization, words in ordinary usage, are the linguist's *morphemes*. Morphemes may be defined as the smallest elements in language which *have* meaning. Thus "picture," "weave," and "small" are words and, synonymously, morphemes. So are "pictures," "weaver," and "smallest." These are combinations, each, of their respective *free* morpheme or root word, and a *bound* morpheme. The free morpheme can stand alone in a sentence, the latter has to be affixed to another morpheme. The bound morphemes above, *-s* (pictures), *-er* (weaver), and *-est* (smallest) are morphemes denoting plurality, agent, and superlative comparison.

Morphemes are defined by their consistency in meaning, which we implicitly recognize even if they are not words per se. For example, when we encounter past tense *-d* (or one of its variants), or *-en, -less,* or *-ize,* we recognize their role in many contexts, e.g., *glowed, soundless, penalize, revived, enlighten, penniless, commercialize.* At the morphological level of language, then, the linguistic elements are meaningful by definition. But regarding the child's task in learning these units, particularly vocabulary, it must be appreciated that the relationship between words and the things they stand for is quite arbitrary. There is no inherent reason why things have the designations by which they are named. For the learner, the consequence of the arbitrary nature of words is that knowing the meaning of one is generally of little help in determining the meaning of another. Knowing, for example, what "cup" represents does not facilitate learning "pup" or "cut," despite their phonetic similarities. In the final analysis, words must for the most part be learned by rote. The young child's task in regard to word acquisition is not unlike that of an adult learner of a second language who is determined to study its vocabulary, though the child has the advantage of much greater facility in associating words and their referents. Although the analogy may seem far fetched, Cooper (1970) has argued that first and second language learning should be considered analogous processes.

All words are either single morphemes or combinations of morphemes. Vocabulary learning, as discussed above, could therefore be considered part of the child's task in learning morphology. In linguistic descriptions, however, vocabulary is often regarded as an aspect of semantic ability. Discussions of children's acquisition of the morphological system are usually limited to the more common bound morphemes (Brown, 1973; Johnston & Schery, 1976). The separation of vocabulary from morphology is also reflected in many standardized language tests.

Syntax

The term syntax is derived from a Greek word meaning to order or arrange. As applied to language, it generally refers to the entire network of rules which underlie the structural organization of language. We have already seen the operation of ordering rules—phonemes can be combined only in the order that is characteristic of a given language; free and bound morphemes can be combined only in specific sequences to make allowable words, e.g., *cumbersome* but not *some-cumber.* At the semantic level, different positions or contexts of the same word may alter its meaning, e.g., "The paints are fading," "He paints for a living."

In the narrower and more conventional sense, the meaning of syntax is restricted to those organizational rules which define the relationships of words in sentences. Syntax can be said to deal with *the structure of sentences.* Sometimes syntax is used interchangeably with "grammar," but the latter term includes, in linguistic descriptions, both morphology—the rules for combining morphemes into words, and syntax proper—the rules for combining words into sentences.

That human languages have syntax is one of the most important characteristics which distinguish them from the limited communication codes of animals. The crucial point here is, of course, that the combinations and recombinations of words produce messages which are consistent in word order, and that the child learning language uses word order consistently almost from the very beginning of multi-word speech. In the rapid stabilization of word order, and in the high degree to which the child shows word order consistency from the beginning, children offer a marked constrast to even the now famous linguistic chimpanzee, Washoe. Washoe's Simian language used all possible combinations of learned signs, e.g., "you tickle me," "you me tickle," "me you tickle," but much of the time the combinations did not correspond with the meaning Washoe apparently intended. Yet, Washoe received intensive and carefully programmed language training lasting up to eight hours a day for many years. The child's capacity for independent learning of syntax clearly stands out in contrast.

We may get a "feel" for the power of syntax to express many nuances of meanings from these sentence variants quoted from Bloom (1975, p. 250).

"The man threw the ball."
"The ball was thrown by the man."
"Did the man throw the ball?"
"Who threw the ball?"
"What did the man throw?"
"It was the ball that the man threw."

Syntax gives language an enormous scope of expression, and it has awed philosophers, psychologists, and linguists for centuries that children the world over seem to abstract and learn its main principles in a few short years. What, then, can we briefly say about syntax that can help us observe what children say and understand? How can we judge their syntactic competence?

First, if the essence of syntax lies in the ability to produce new combinations of the same words in different situations, then it is clear that sentences form two classes. Conventionalized expressions like "How are you?" and "Good morning" and the like are a nonproductive class since they usually do not change. Neither do many idiosyncratic expressions, for exmaple, "I'll tell my mom," "Sit down," "What's your name?", etc. In the evaluation of a child's language, such nonproductive sentences would be listed but not analyzed.

The second class of sentences, which comprise all others, are termed productive utterances. We shall describe a few major structural features of the type upon which any judgment of children's syntactic ability must focus. (For a full description of sentence structure, and a method of analyzing children's spontaneous oral language, the reader is referred to Crystal, Fletcher, & Garman [1976]).

In a traditional classification reflecting the overall progression in children's language acquisition, sentences are often described as being simple, elaborated or expanded, conjoint, or complex. A *simple sentence* is a sentence with a basic subject-verb, or subject-verb-object pattern, such as in: "John sleeps," "Daddy watched the game," "I gave him the coat," and sentences in which the verb has a complement, as in "Mr. Smith is a doctor," "He doesn't look healthy," "John wasn't ready." An *expanded sentence* is one in which the meaning of the basic proposition of the simple sentence is modified through addition of adjectives, pronouns, determiners, or adverbial phrases of various kinds, such as in: "My favorite toy is the truck," "This truck is mine," "These knives are sharp," "John slept on the couch last night." Expansion is also seen in more elaborate form of the verb, e.g., instead of the simple "he comes," "John didn't come," "He'll be coming in the morning." The important point about this type of sentence is that, even though it may be considerably longer and contain more information than the simple sentence, it expresses only *one* proposition. In terms of the linguist's description (cf. Crystal et al., 1976; Dever, 1972), it contains only one clause. The *conjoint sentence* contains two propositions (clauses), both of which have equal grammatic status. The propositions are simply strung alongside each other and connected by a coordinating conjunction such as *and, but;* for example, in: "John walked home, but Francis took a bus."

In the *complex sentence,* the clauses do not have an equal-status relationship but one is part of the structure of the other, it is "embedded" in the other. In complex sentences, the statements are connected by subordinating conjunctions such as *because, when, since;* for example, in: "John walked home, because he didn't have money for the bus"; or "He waited, until his father arrived."

We are familiar with complex sentences as having dependent and independent clauses. The dependent clause cannot stand alone but is part of the structure of the other, e.g., "until his father arrived" cannot stand as a sentence by itself, but "He waited" can.

The child's language learning progresses from establishment of the basic elements of simple, one-proposition sentences, through gradual "filling in" of grammatic elements in these sentences, to juxtaposition of two or more propositions, and to eventual complex embeddings. The gross progression in sentence mastery can be schematized, showing only one

	Proposition I			Proposition 2	
	Subject	Verb (Adverbial)		S	V
Simple Sentence	John	comes			
	John	is coming (home)			
Expanded Sentence	John	came (home just now)			
	My brother John	will come (home tomorrow)			
Conjoint Sentence	John	came (home)	and	(he)	ate
Complex Sentence	My brother	came (home)	just when	my sister	was leavinc

Fig. 8-2. Typical progression of sentence mastery.

sentence type as example, as in Figure 8-2. Later in this chapter, we will present a simplified time scale over which this aspect of children's linguistic development takes place, and in the assessment section some procedures for its quantification will be described. It should be emphasized that the structural elements of a sentence can be analyzed further, and the reader is referred to Crystal et al., for a very comprehensive description.

Semantics

Sapir (1970, p. 6) describes language as "a perfect symbolic system . . . for the handling of all references and meanings that a given culture is capable of." Whatever objects or qualities of its environment and experiences a culture wishes to distinguish, language allows it to assign a name to them. Languages reflect the life space and experiences of different societies, and often quoted facts such as the Burmese having six different words for rice result from the salience of such commodities or experiences in the particular culture.

The words in any language have a meaning that relates them to the world outside but also grammatically to other words. For example, the word "mug" relates differently to the outside world, i.e., has a different meaning in this sentence: "I am not going to drink from a mug" than in "I n not going to mug you." The meaning change results from alteration of rammatic context. Semantics is the study of *meaning relations* in lanuage; semantic competence is the ability to derive the meaning of a sennce, and of connected sets of sentences.

It seems obvious that a person must know the words of which a sennce is composed if he is to understand it. However, vocabulary alone is ot sufficient. Rosenberg (1970) lists the following as exemplifying seantic competencies which a language user must develop: vocabulary, cluding synonymous words, and different meanings for the same word; nowing when sentences are ambiguous; knowing when sentences are nomalous; ability to verify the truth value of sentences; definitional abily; and ability to paraphrase.

English *vocabulary* is estimated to be "in the region of at least half a illion words" (Quirk, et al., 1972) of which the average literate adult ctively commands about 100,000 and can recognize and understand any more (Joos, 1964). Knowing that a container we often drink from is alled "cup" illustrates knowledge of one vocabulary item. On other ocasions, the same concept might call for words like mug, glass, tumbler, a cup, and the same word may call for an interpretation different from container for drinking," as, for example, in "He won the cup." A peron who knew only "cup" or only the first-named meaning of that word ight be limited in the vocabulary aspect of semantic ability.

Sentence *ambiguity* can result from at least two reaons. In "They are umblers," it results from the possibility of assignment of different meangs to "tumblers" (clown, gymnast, or drinking vessel). As it stands, the entence does not provide enough information to allow unambiguous inerpretation. In "They are shooting companions," ambiguity results from he possibility of different grammatic functions of "shooting," (adjective, r transitive verb). In either case, semantic competence implies that the nguage user is aware that ambiguity exists and must be resolved.

Sentence *anomaly* is illustrated in sentences such as Chomsky's ften quoted "Colorless green ideas sleep furiously," in which perfectly ood lexical (vocabulary) items add up to nonsense because of the way hey are juxtaposed. Anomalous sentences violate so-called rules of coccurrence, i.e., words co-occur which for semantic reasons normally do ot. Greenness is not a meaningful characteristic of abstract entities like leas, and "green" and "colorless" are logically antagonistic. Again, emantic competence implies awareness of such violations.

Verification of the *truth value* of sentences is the ability to judge the orrectness of a stated proposition. The task can be very simple. For xample, in "Missy is brushing her teeth," the sentence might refer (in imple sentence structure) to an event in which the listener is a particiant. The same proposition stated in more complex language, e.g., "The girl brushing her teeth right now, is Missy," might be much harder t evaluate for a child. And for a proposition about a distant event, fo example: "Graham Greene wrote *'Proof absolute',"* the ability to judg truthfulness would obviously depend on the information available to th listener.

Definitional ability is involved in the so-called vocabulary tests c standard mental ability measures. When the child is asked "What is x?" and expected to give a verbal restatement containing critical characteris tics of the concept referred to as x, he is asked to *define* word x. This, lik other abilities in language, develops in stages. Children first simply give repetition of the word—"Apple is an apple," then a description of physi cal characteristics—"Apple is something we eat," and eventually superordinate concept—"Apple is a fruit."

Paraphrasing involves restating a sentence, or the meaning of group of sentences, in one's own words. For example: "John did not g out tonight," is a paraphrase of "John stayed at home tonight," and re stating the main idea or ideas of a paragraph is to paraphrase it.

Pragmatics

Since communication is the primary function of language, ability i the different skill areas we have thus far described is not sufficient for th communicator. These competencies (phonology, syntax, etc.), refer t knowledge of the language code itself. Pragmatics refers to the ability t use the code appropriately in social situations. Appropriateness of lan guage must consider its diverse communicative purposes. A communica tion may be (1) trying to persuade, (2) exchange or ask for information, (3 make demands, (4) express, or endeavor to induce, emotion, (5) mak reference to things or events, or (6) simply establish contact. These func tions can be seen to be different from the "private" ones in thinking problem solving, scheduling, or reminiscing about the day's events, fo example.

There are both linguistic and extralinguistic aspects to consider i determination of appropriateness of a communication. The linguistic as pect refers to productive and receptive mastery of language. In a give communicative context, it particularly includes understanding of the pre ceding verbal message. If the listener misunderstood the speaker's mes sage, his own subsequent response will likely not be fitting. But othe factors will influence his response behavior as well. Among these are suc things as the status of the persons present, their role relationships wit respect to each other, the particular topic being discussed and the interes it holds for the listener, and the physical environment in which the com nunication takes place. Children as young as three can be observed to use horter sentences when speaking to infants than when talking to older hildren and adults. Even at that age, that is, they display indirectly their erception of a purely social aspect of communication—namely of the ddressee's communicative ability. Clark, Hutcheson, & Van Buren 1974) document many revealing observations on children's reactions to erbal requests, which may not always correspond with the intentions of he adults. The child appears to act upon his own perceptions and hypoth-ses as to what is likely being said in a particular context and by particular peakers. It is clearly important that the child develop sensitivity for the xtralinguistic and social cues which are present in the communication ituation.

ANGUAGE ACQUISITION

When we are faced with severely defective or even absence of lan-uage in a child, we may have to go beyond language, per se, to search for easons. Before *vocal language* can emerge and grow, the child must how *behaviors* which are appropriate to language. In the most general erms, these behaviors are of three types. First, they show that the child as functional *knowledge* of things and events in his environment, i.e., he ecognizes objects and persons and their characteristic functions or ac-ivities. Such knowledge is said to be imperative for language learning—'the learner must know the referent for learning of language to occur'' Ervin-Tripp. 1973, p. 261). Second, the child should also show *symbolic lay behavior* which indicates his awareness that a thing can be made to tand for another, like words ''stand for'' experiences. Finally, the child nust also show nonvocal acts which indicate a *desire to communicate,* as vhen he ''shows off'' to gain a person's attention, or when he points to omething as a form of request or ''explanation.'' The teacher would want o establish availability of these three types of behaviors prior to the mergence of vocal language and serving alongside the latter for some ime once vocal language has begun.

We may expect the unfolding of language to follow certain grossly lelimitable stages, and language assessment should locate the child with egard to these. The developments during the first year of life, the period f *prelinguistic vocalizations,* have been described by Fry (1966) and enneberg (1967). They may be said to involve primarily the child's learn-ng to control and coordinate the speech organs and make sounds and ound segments at will. This is followed by a roughly six-month period luring which the child produces primarily *one-word sentences* which appear to be intended as "whole" statements, requests, commands, o questions. However, they consist of only single words which are (1 idiosyncratic, (2) not necessarily permanent, and (3) have an exceedingl simple and characteristic sound structure to which the description "phonology of the first 50 words," has been applied (Ingram, 1976). Dur ing the stage of primarily *two-element sentences,* which typically begin between 18 and 24 months of age, the child produces words with a distinc tive intonation which indicates that these words are not merely jux taposed but "go together." These new, two-word sentences are though to reflect the child's perception of significant *relationships* among thing (Brown, 1973; Miller & Yoder, 1974) as, for example, the relationship o location between a ball and a table when he says "ball table." This perio also marks the beginning of rapid vocabulary expansion corollary t which is the need for mastery of the speech sounds. The most activ period for speech-sound development is from 1½ to 4 years, by whic time all the vowel sounds and a number of the consonant sounds hav been mastered. Acquisition of the vowel sounds is normally completed b age 3, that of the consonant sounds is usually accomplished by age 8 an is represented in Figure 8-3. During the period of mostly *three-elemen sentences,* the child combines the patterns of previous stages into ne units and begins to use the grammatic morphemes like plural ("boots") past tense ("moved"), and the past participle ("broken") whose order o acquisition has been documented by Brown (1973). The process of gram matic expansion, and of combination of earlier structures, continue through the next stage of *sentences of four or more elements.* During thi stage, the grammatical morphemes become fully established, and th basic structures of simple (one-proposition) sentences are firmly set. Th stage ends around age four when "most sentences become close to well formed, simple sentences" (Ingram, 1976, p. 11). For the most part further language growth may be said to involve sentence conjunction an ability to embed propositions in complex sentence forms, vocabulary ex pansion, learning of complicated words, and mastering of infrequently oc curring and irregular verb forms; and, in general, the area of stylistic use of language.

It would be naive to think that language grows in a vacuum. In norma development, a strong relationship of language with mental growth an with stages in physical maturation has been found to exist. An ab breviated characterization of major milestones in cognitive, motor, an language learning, as described by Ingram (1976), Lenneberg (1967), an Piaget (1962), is given below to alert the teacher to that interrelationshi of many skills in the total evaluation of the child (Table 8-2).

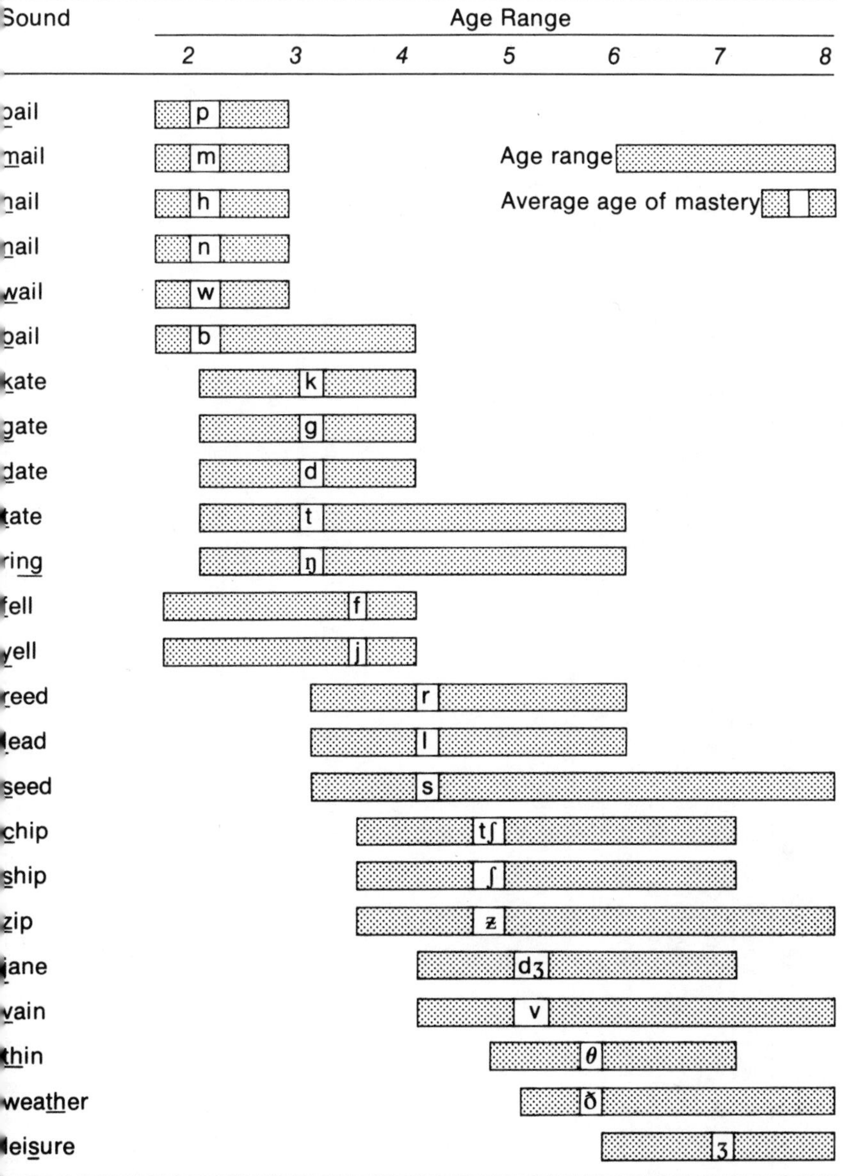

Fig. 8-3. Development of the Consonant Sounds. (Adapted from Sander, *JSHD*, 1972.)

Table 8-2
Stages in Cognitive, Motor, Language, and Speech-Sound Development*

Piaget's Stages	Motor Stages	Language Stages	Phonological Stages
Sensori-motor period (0–1.6): Develops systems of movement and perception; achieves notion of object permanence.	Supports his head in prone position at 3 mos.; sits with props at 5 mos.; can sit alone and bear his weight but not yet stand at 6 mos.; creeps and takes sidesteps at 10 mos.; walks when held by one hand at 12 mos.	Prelinguistic communication thru crying, gestures, smile; around 12 mos. use of one-word utterances; follows simple commands and responds to "no."	Prelinguistic vocalization; coos for 15–20 sec. at 3 mos.; vowel-like cooing sounds are interspersed with consonant sounds at 5 mos.; cooing changes to babbling resembling one-syllable utterances at 6 mos.; continuous repetition of syllables becomes frequent and intonation patterns distinct. Phonology of the first 50 words.
Preoperational period (1.6–7.0): Preconcept period (1.6–4.0). Symbolic representation. Child can refer to past and future though most of his talk is concerned with his own activity in the here and now; symbolic play predominates.	Has stiff and propulsive gait, and creeps downstairs backwards at 18 mos.; runs but falls often at 24 mos.; walks stairs up and down with one foot forward, jumps into air with both feet, at 30 mos.; and builds tower of six cubes at 30 mos.	Telegraphic stage. Child makes two-, three-, and four-element sentences which are telegraphic. Sentences express basic meaning relationships in the environment, e.g., possession or location. Sentences increase in length and grammatic completeness to around age 4 when most are close to well-formed, simple sentences.	Phonology of single morphemes. With rapid development of vocabulary, speech-sound expansion begins. Words are simple, consisting of root morphemes only. Sound production errors prevail until around 4 when most simple words are correctly articulated.

Table 8-2 (continued)

Piaget's Stages	Motor Stages	Language Stages	Phonological Stages
Intuitive period (4.0–7.0) Child relies on immediate perception to solve problems; begins to be involved in social games; develops concept of reversibility.	Jumps over rope, catches ball in arms, walks in line at 4 yrs.; bounces and catches ball, kicks stationary ball 10 to 15 feet at 6 yrs.	Child strings sentences together with coordinating conjunctions, begins to use relative clauses (e.g., "I know what he wants").	Completes the speech-sound inventory; learns the last troublesome sounds around age 7; has good production of simple words; begins to use longer words.
Concrete operations period (7–12 yr.). Has thought process of reversibility and can solve conservation problems.	Runs without colliding and changes directions quickly, throws objects both over- and underhand (age 8); walks balance beam, hits moving objects (9); walks straight line, endurance and strength are increasing muscular development is evident (10+).	Juxtaposition of sentences through coordination decreases, sentence embedding increases. Child makes and understands complex sentences.	Child learns rules relating speech-sound changes and word-structure elaboration (e.g., moral—morality); learns derivational-structural rules of word formation.
Formal operations period (12–16 yrs.). Child learns ability to use abstract thought, can hypothesize and solve problems by reflection.	Plays organized games.	Child can reflect on grammaticality of speech and solve linguistic problems by analogy and intuition.	Child can decide upon possible sound changes in words and masters ability to spell.

*Adapted from Ingram, Phonslogical disability in children (1976); Lenneberg, Biological foundations of language (1967).

LANGUAGE ASSESSMENT

General Considerations

As we approach the task of evaluating a set of skills and processes as multifaceted as that involved in language, we may restore an important point which applies to the general evaluation of behavior. The measurements we make can never capture all the complexity, nuances, and diverse manifestations of (language) behavior. We can only selectively sample some subset of that behavior in certain situations, and from the sample infer availability of the full range of the behavior in all the situations which call for it. For example, we might test a child's understanding of only three, four, or half a dozen of the more than 50 simple prepositions (e.g., *in, under, with, behind, above*). This would be a sampling of the total set of prepositions. Likewise, we might ask the child to place an object behind another object but not to place it behind himself or to point to an object in a picture partially hidden by another object. This would be a sampling of the situations in which "behind" appropriately applies. In either case, we infer from the child's performance of limited behaviors, that the type of behavior is more widely established in the behavioral repertoire, i.e., that the child knows more prepositions than we have tested. Thus, at the least, we hope to establish, through testing the child on a few prepositions, that the basic concepts are understood.

COMPREHENSION AND EXPRESSION

Language comprises the ability to both emit vocal messages and to understand messages produced by others. Thus dual use of language is variously referred to as comprehension-production, reception-expression, or decoding and encoding. The decoding task in listening begins with sensory analysis of the air waves which arrive at the ear and ends with a representation in the listener's mind of his interpretation of the speaker's message. The encoding task in speaking begins with some communicative intent followed by selection of words to represent the message, and ends with the articulation of an orderly, sequenced string of phonemes.

Contrary to the widely held notion that children can understand "everything" long before they can express themselves, some linguists argue that comprehension tests best reveal a child's linguistic ability (Bellugi-Klima, 1968). They see comprehension tasks as placing a greater burden on knowledge of language per se and to be more revealing of linguistic competence. The latter applies particularly to the child's spontaneous and self-initiated talk. Clark et al. (1974) have raised a serious argument that talking (expression) may be *easier* for the young child than understanding others' talk (comprehension). The reason is that when the child is talking, he is doing so on the force of his own motivation, and "he will be remarking on those aspects of the situation which for him are prominent (p. 49)." But when another person is speaking, the child "must redirect his attention to attain their view of the situation (p. 49)." Such attentional adjustments are often difficult for children to make.

However, the issue of whether or not, or to what degree, children's receptive understanding of language structure is more advanced than their ability for expressive use, is being much debated in the psycholinguistic literature (Ingram, 1974). On whichever side of this theoretical issue one's leanings may be, a number of points with fundamental relevance to assessment have been highlighted through the debate.

Point one. Assessment of a child's competence in language must involve both the receptive and the expressive mode. We cannot judge his language ability to be adequate merely because he is talkative and his communications are not obviously defective; neither can we judge it on appraisal only of what he understands.

Point two. Tasks in which the child is required to perform a specified action (e.g., select a designated object or picture, or verify an examiner statement or picture choice through a yes/no indication), exemplify evaluation of comprehension. Tasks in which the child describes an object, action, or picture, or repeats a model statement given by the examiner exemplify evaluation of production, or expression.

Point three. Many standardized language tests assess only receptive or only expressive ability, but a number have separate scales or subtests in both modes. The teacher must be aware of the need to select tests or use informal test procedures which sample both.

Point four. Teachers must become more careful not to overestimate the child's linguistic ability on the basis of correct responses to instructions and other verbalizations which arise in the context of daily activities. Children learn to respond to the whole context of messages addressed to them in more or less routine contexts. On the basis of their memory of past experiences, they form expectancies as to the most likely verbal message given them in such contexts and thus may be able to respond appropriately even if they do not fully understand the message itself (Clark et al., 1974). Adults typically accompany their instructions with many nonverbal cues in the form of bodily or facial gestures which will aid the child's interpretation. Therefore, in order to accurately judge the child's ability to respond to *language* rather than the total communicative context, the teacher is urged to "peel off" from the verbal message all the extralinguistic cues which the child may be using in interpretation (Chapman, 1972; Mittler, 1976).

Gestures. One important area of the teacher's observation concerns a child's use of gestures. In many cases, with young or verbally immature children, the school regards gesturing as an inappropriate means of expression which must be substituted by oral expression as speedily as possible. The positive value of gestural communication is often overlooked. Such communication, after all, allows the child the experience of a rewarding exchange with an adult or other child. His subsequent desire for further communicative opportunities may then slowly be shaped in the direction of oral communication.

LANGUAGE, COMMUNICATION, AND SPEECH

It should be clear from our discussion of "gesture language" that the three terms in the heading, though related, are not synonymous. It is important to see the distinction between them clearly. There are persons with language pathologies such as in aphasia or autism who may produce a great flow of words without communicating meaning, and without having recognition of their failure at communication. There may be nonverbal persons who communicate eloquently through gestures, writing, painting, or other means.

Language serves as a *means* to the end of communication; communication being the *process* of sending, receiving, and interpreting messages. Language may be the particular symbolic code we have described in this chapter, but it may also utilize other conventionalized symbols. Speech, in turn, refers to the motoric expression of language, i.e., the particular (vocal-motoric) medium through which language is actualized for communication.

Assessment Procedures

In order that a child's relative strengths and weaknesses can be seen and in order to serve the teacher's primary interest of program development, language assessment should cover all the major skill areas. A word of caution is appropriate, however. Since no one test is available that adequately measures all these areas, intra-child comparisons of strengths and weaknesses will usually be based on data from different tests. One may not be able to make a simple, normative interpretation of the obtained data since tests differ in the care devoted to standardization, and in exhaustiveness of coverage (see guidelines, Chap. 3). However, the basic question for the teacher remains: "In what area is the child most limited?" The following discussion is intended to provide an overview and guide of suitable procedures to measure the different communication skill areas.

To assess crucial *language-related behaviors* in a preverbal child or when vocalization is yet barely emerging, the teacher may rely on informal testing and observation for which the following list may suggest suitable situations.

1. Does the child show recognition of objects he has seen a number of times before, i.e., does he show *identification* behavior which can lead to naming?
2. Does the child show awareness of *existence* of familiar objects when they are not in his presence or are taken away from him, i.e,, does he show the awareness and search behaviors which can later develop into questioning?
3. Does he have awareness of *recurrence* of objects/events? For example, if he is engaged in a "pat-a-cake" or "hand-me-the-ball" game, does he know the game can be continued and the ball brought back over and over again, i.e., does he show behavior of expectancy which can later lead to verbal demands or requests?
4. Does he show awareness of spatial and temporal ordering of things/events? For example, does he go to the coat rack upon coming to school and at dismissal time, i.e, does he have the behaviors which can lead to expression of *location* and *time* concepts?
5. Does he show awareness of the concept of *possession,* for example, does he choose/defend *his* toy, seat, garment, etc., and know which belong to other children, i.e., does he have the behaviors which later are verbalized in statements with possessive pronouns or the possessive morpheme?
6. Does he show awareness of qualities or *attributes* of objects, for example, does he show preference for color, size, or shape when given objects to choose from, or does he sort them into groupings on the basis of such characteristics, i.e., does he show the behaviors which can later lead to descriptive statements or information requests relative to identification?
7. Does he show awareness of who or what the appropriate *agents* and *recipients* of objects and actions are? For example, when requesting a lace to be tied or when "delivering" a piece of soap does he know where to go (to person or sink), i.e., does he have the behaviors which can lead to expression in simple agent, action, object statements?

VOCABULARY

One of the most widely used tests of comprehension vocabulary is the *Peabody Picture Vocabulary Test* (Dunn, 1965). It requires the child to respond by pointing to one of four pictures for which a test word is given by the examiner. The 150 test words (nouns, verbs, and adjectives) are arranged in increasing order of difficulty, and the test is discontinued when a ceiling response level is reached. Test administration takes 15 minutes on the average, and no special preparation is required for administration or scoring. Duplicate forms allow for readministration of the test at suitable intervals. A percentile score and a mental-age score can be derived from the raw score. The mental-age score is most appropriate for a broad comparison of vocabulary versus other language skills. It should be understood as mental age for receptive vocabulary, or vocabulary age, rather than as mental age in the sense in which this term is used in mental-ability assessment. The age span covered is 2.6 to 18 years. It should be pointed out that, while the test allows for determination of an IQ, Carr, Brown, & Rice (1967) have not found this to have a high correlation with IQs derived from standardized tests such as the *Wechsler Intelligence Scale for Children* (1958). Therefore, the teacher is enjoined not to make use of a PPVT IQ which, in any event, does not contribute to the goal of remedial language programming. An expressive version of the Peabody (70 items from Form B of the original test) was constructed by Nation (1972) to allow explicit comparison of a child's usage and comprehension of the same lexical items.

In addition to, or perhaps instead of, a broad appraisal of a child's general vocabulary knowledge, the teacher may want to assess familiarity with more limited and specific vocabulary sets. This would be desirable when a child's language is severely restricted. In the case of retarded or autistic children, for example, it may be most useful to measure understanding of vocabulary directly related to their environments—e.g., of food, furniture, or clothing items, actions persons can perform, etc. Such an evaluation can sample the respective word sets more exhaustively; moreover, it can lead directly to intervention and thence to observation of the child's capability in learning new words.

For informal assessment of specific vocabularies, the teacher must procure suitable test materials. Picture dictionaries organized by conceptual categories (e.g., animals we know) can be a starting point. For seriously handicapped children, photographs or slides representing their own home and school environments may be profitable. *The Boehm Test of Basic Concepts* (Boehm, 1971) is an example of a standardized test which explores comprehension of a specific vocabulary set. It tests 50 spatial, quantity, temporal-order, and directional terms (e.g., "corner," "every," "after," "left") often used in instructions to kindergarten and first-grade children. The test requires the child to mark appropriate pictures in a test booklet. It has duplicate forms, and administration takes 30 to 40 minutes. Class average can be obtained from the raw scores, and a given child's score can be converted to a percent. Recognition that children who have not mastered concepts such as tested in the Boehm test may experience failure in the early school years was among the primary motives behind language intervention efforts such as *Distar* (Engelmann & Osborn, 1976; Osborn, 1975). The test also provides good coverage of the verbal concepts requisite for counting and higher-level number skills. Mentally retarded children's inefficiency in quantitative learning is thought to reflect lack of these verbal concepts (Hargis & Ahlersmeyer, 1970).

THE SOUND SYSTEM

Among the defects that cause intelligibility to be impaired, *articulation* errors are by far the most common. They refer to omission of sounds in many or all word contexts, to substitution of sounds, or to production of sounds in a distorted manner. Less frequent but generally more serious defects are those involving *voicing* and respiratory *coordination*. Children showing the latter problems, e.g., speaking consistently in a voice which is too high- or low-pitched or of unnatural volume, or with frequent hesitations or stammering, require referral to a language clinician. Generally speaking, administration of articulation tests, too, presupposes considerable training in speech analysis and use of a phonemic alphabet. Several of the formal articulation tests have screening-test versions which may be usable by teachers after careful familiarization with the materials, e.g., Templin-Darley's (1968) and McDonald's (1968) screening tests.

Templin-Darley's screening test consists of 50 pictures. For each picture, the teacher may either say a specified sentence and have the child imitate, or she may attempt to elicit the test word from him. In either case, she observes the child's production of the test word and, particularly, a specific sound within that word. For example, for the sound "θ" as in *thumb,* the picture shows a raised thumb, and the test sentence is "This finger is called a_______." To score the test, the teacher determines how many test words the child correctly articulated. The manual provides cut-off scores for eight age levels (three to eight years). If a child obtained fewer correct responses than the cut-off score, the manual suggests that he be referred to a speech therapist for full diagnosis. McDonald's screening test is intended as a tool for quick assessment of a child's ability with sounds which 5-year-old children often misarticulate. Nine consonant sounds are tested in 31 words. The test procedure is to have the child make a "big word" from two "little words" for which he sees pictures.

For example, he says "cupcake" for pictures of a cup and a cake, and "housekey" for pictures of a house and a key. From the number of times he pronounces each sound correctly a phonemic profile is obtained for comparison with the profile of 700 kindergarten children in the standardization sample. Determination of whether to refer a child for further clinical evalaution depends not only on the number of contexts in which his articulation of a sound is correct but also on the shape of his profile relative to the curve of the norm sample.

It will often be desirable for the teacher to make informal estimates of a child's speech-sound ability, either as a form of preliminary assessment or to verify the findings from a screening test. This can be done by simply asking the child to repeat sets of words that elicit a given sound in a few different contexts as, for example, with the following words for the vowel sound "ae" and the consonant sound "s":

"ae"	hat	cap	apple	man
"s"	so	see	hiss	whistle

Here the teacher focuses on the child's ability to make the indicated sound several times and ignores the other sounds. After testing the child on all the common English sounds, the teacher uses developmental guides on speech-sound acquisition (see Table 8-2) to determine how seriously limited the child might be, if further evaluation is warranted, and for which specific sounds remediation should first be sought. The teacher would keep in mind that all vowel sounds are normally mastered by children at age three (Ingram, 1976), whereas consonant-sound mastery takes much more time, up to approximately eight years for some children.

The teacher will also use observation to supplement this informal assessment. As a crude but useful criterion, the teacher may note if a child at age four can usually be understood by unfamiliar persons. To establish the degree of intelligibility, one can simply have the child name pictures aloud while an unfamiliar person (hidden behind a screen) records what he or she thinks the child is saying. Actual agreement scores should be calculated. (General procedures for calculating agreement can be found in Chapter 4 of this volume.)

An informal assessment checklist for the most common English speech sounds is presented in Table 8-3. In an appropriate procedure, the child is asked to repeat several words for a given speech sound. His ability to produce the given *sound,* not necessarily the whole word, is the criterion. Meaningfulness of words to the child need not be a consideration in this informal evaluation since the objective is that he be able to produce a given *sound* in English sound combinations (words).

Table 8-3
Informal Assessment of Availability of Major English Speech-Sounds

/a/	car far	bah bar	balm mar	ma	tar
/u/	boot root	mood booty	moody	goose	goosy
/ʊ/	cook rule	foot full	soot would	hook	book
/ɔ/	lawn taut	dawn caught	fall saw	ball	bought
/ʌ/	fun cut	bun dumb	ton hum	none	but
/ei/	take Dane	bake cake	name rain	lame	make
/i/	eat tea	meat Dean	wheat keep	feet	bee
/ai/	ride Mike	kite like	dime fine	rhyme	nine
/ou/	boat toe	coat hoe	moan load	no oval	dough
/e/	bed heed	red when	Betty men	net	get
/au/	now bow	cow loud	how redoubt	doubt	bout
/æ/	can hat	man mat	cat bat	dad	daddy
/I/	hit knit	kick tick	Dick Ricky	tickle	Micky
/ɔi/	boy	annoy	toy	enjoy	Leroy
/ə/	about	eaten	above	ago	waken
/p/	pea cup	pie ape	paw pat	pit pony	penny happy
/m/	moat moon	my home	me dumb	mop mommy	man comb
/h/	hat hip	ham beehive	hop head	hum hello	hug howl
/n/	knee main	nod many	penny nut	nap dinner	rain no
/w/	we what	wade woe	wham wit	wet witty	witch wiener

Table 8-3 (continued)

/b/	bee	bake	by	bed	bite
	bus	tub	knob	obey	table
/k/	key	coat	cat	cow	come
	cake	cook	cooky	neck	Ricky
/g/	go	gun	game	goose	gay
	gate	muggy	gummy	wig	mug
/d/	do	day	dog	Dan	lady
	die	down	doe	mud	hide
/t/	two	toe	tie	take	tide
	kitten	time	kite	top	Tommy
/ŋ/	ding	dong	wing	king	gang
	finger	gong	eating	bang	hang
/f/	phone	food	fade	huff	puff
	puffy	knife	foot	fan	fake
/j/	yew	yellow	yes	yell	yawn
	yummy	yam	loyal	yolk	yet
/r/	ray	rye	raw	rain	row
	ready	race	rib	ride	rope
/l/	look	lie	look	lay	lake
	light	lick	tell	follow	Lee
/s/	say	Sam	sun	sunny	sock
	seek	sissy	bus	ice	house
/tʃ/	cheap	chime	chew	chain	chummy
	watch	couch	which	cheese	catch
/ʃ/	show	shut	shiny	shake	shine
	shade	fish	dish	wash	shoot
/z/	dozen	zoom	easy	weasel	zoo
	daisy	buzzing	dozing	zip	erase
/dʒ/	jam	Jack	Jason	jeep	edge
	joy	juice	joke	page	jig
/v/	vow	moving	give	van	dive
	dove	vote	heavy	seven	movie
/θ/	thigh	thing	thief	thin	with
	bath	mouth	thank	tooth	teeth
/ð/	this	bathe	then	they	those
	mother	father	either	weather	gather
/ʒ/	measure	vision	rouge	azure	leisure

MORPHOLOGY AND SYNTAX

A number of standardized tests and research based procedures are available to appraise children's understanding of the working of grammatic rules. Berko (1958) developed an ingenious research technique which has been replicated many times with both normal and retarded children and can readily be adapted by the teacher. The procedure consists of presenting to the child a simple drawing representing an imaginary figure called, for example, a *wug*. The child is shown two such figures and asked to give their name (i.e., wugs). Berko's test contains 27 items for the common morphemes such as plural, possession, comparative/superlative forms of adjectives, and past tense. While Berko's test requires children to say the desired grammatic form, Carrow's (1973) *Test for Auditory Comprehension of Language* is a receptive test. It contains 101 items testing children's recognition of words (nouns, verbs, adjectives, prepositions, and adverbs) and their comprehension of phrases and sentences utilizing these words. The phrases and sentences contrast specific grammatic forms like active-passive, singular-plural, or progressive tense. In each case, the child points to one of three pictures. The items passed can be converted to a total age-score equivalent, and for given test items the scoring form indicates at what approximate age 75 percent and 90 percent of the children in the standardization sample passed it. For example, the item "The girl is serving" (present progressive tense) was passed by most children at age three, whereas "The donkey is carried by the man" (passive voice) was not passed by most children until age 6. Unfortunately, Carrow's normative sample was small (200 children in 4 age groups from 3 to 6 years) and acceptance of the age data for individual test items must be made with caution. Nevertheless, the information is valuable in allowing a teacher to evaluate a child's response *profile*. Responses on specific subclasses of test items (e.g., morphology, syntax, vocabulary) can also be analyzed separately. Bartel, Bryen, & Keehn (1973) have reported on the use of this test with trainable mentally handicapped children.

A shorter grammar-comprehension test is Lee's (1969) *Northwestern Syntax Screening Test,* which measures 20 concepts through picture choice. The child is asked both to point to the picture described by the examiner, and in a separate subtest to describe the picture himself after cueing. This subtest measures imitative rather than spontaneous production. Items passed can be converted to an age score. Miller & Yoder's (1975) test also assesses comprehension of grammatic contrasts (e.g., possessive, reflexivization, singular/plural) in sentences. Forty-two sentence pairs are given, for example: "The little dog is sleeping," "The big dog is sleeping." The total of 84 sentences is divided into two sets, with one member of the sentence pair in each set. For each sentence, the child chooses a picture from four. An advantage of the Miller & Yoder test is that all the test sentences are short and controlled for length (all contain four or five words), are in a tense form children learn early (present progressive) unless tense is being assessed, and contain only one proposition. That is, they assess the child's mastery of the grammar of the *simple sentence.*

Bellugi-Klima (1968) describes a series of object manipulation tasks to test grammatic contrasts. For example, the child may be given two dolls and asked to play-act: "The boy is washed by the girl" and "The girl is washed by the boy." The constructions being tested are arranged in four levels of difficulty following the order in which they normally evolve in children's speech. This test is suitable for young children who can be engaged in pretend play, but it may not be useful for emotionally maladjusted children, or for children with motor problems which would preclude successful manipulation of the objects.

Yet another technique is illustrated in the *Michigan Picture Inventory* (Lerea, 1958; 1962). The *Michigan* examines many grammatical concepts (e.g., possessive, prepositions, and pronouns) in 69 test items illustrated in pictures. This test uses the "cloze" missing-word technique in which the child is required to supply the missing test word in the examiner's statement. The test measures both expression and comprehension.

Menyuk (1963, 1964) and others (e.g., Anastasiow & Hanes, 1974) have used *sentence imitation* as a simple technique to measure children's grammatical development. Menyuk, having first studied and documented the occurrence of grammatic forms in normally developing and language-impaired children, utilized some of these forms in 56 test sentences in children of varying ages. The test's criterion is whether or not the child's reproduction of sentences contains the critical feature which is being tested. The procedure specifies which construction is being tested in each sentence, as in the following example:

Feature tested	Test sentence
Conjunction	Peter is over here, and you are over there.

If a child imitated this sentence as two disjoint statements, for example, "Peter is here. You are over there," he would be scored as not having attained the feature, sentence conjunction. The items in Menyuk's test range from simple, expanded, and conjoint to complex-level sentences. Lamberts & Ysseldyke (in press) and Lovell, Hersee, & Preston (1969) have described the use of Menyuk's test sentences in exploration of retarded children's language ability, and have provided more detailed scoring examples.

While Menyuk's test is not standardized, Carrow (1974) developed a standardized sentence-imitation test, the *Elicited Language Inventory*. The Inventory contains 51 sentences ranging in length from 2 to 10 words and testing different sentence types (e.g., questions, declarative statements) and the following grammatic categories: adjectives, articles, adverbs, singular and plural nouns, pronouns, verbs, prepositions, demonstratives, conjunctions, and contractions. The Inventory items illustrate all levels of sentence complexity. Usually the administration and scoring of the Inventory requires about 45 minutes. The administration is tape recorded and the child's imitation, transcribed and scored from the tape. Specific scoring instructions are provided, and percentile ranks and age-equivalence scores can be derived.

The *Stephens Oral Language Screening Test* (SOLST, 1977) is a short test which provides efficient screening for prekindergarten, kindergarten, and first-grade children. The test procedure consists of elicited imitation. The child's version of model sentences is scored for degree of similarity to the models. For each of 15 sentences, a numerical score from 0 (exact repetition) to 7 (unintelligible response or no response) is given. The sentences are constructed with vocabulary items containing crucial, late-developing consonant sounds such as /ʃ/. /θ/, or /s/. From the same set of 15 sentences, both a syntax and an articulation score can be derived with relative ease. For the sum total of the scores, cut-off points are indicated. For children above or below given cut-off points it is suggested that they may be considered to 1) fall well within the normal developmental range, 2) be borderline and possibly require further observation or evaluation, and 3) be well outside the normal range of developmental syntax or speech-sound command.

Though the SOLST was designed for language and speech personnel, it may be considered an instrument that is feasible for teachers and of considerable practical use for them.

Although the literature reveals some controversy regarding the role of imitation in language training and assessment (Ruder & Smith, 1974), most students of child language see the child's imitation as a valid reflection of what he knows about the grammatic workings of his language. Imitation in language evaluation is particularly appropriate for teacher use since it is adaptable to any level of language ability reached by children and since the teacher can usually engage the children in "pretend imitation" without any concern or test anxiety on their part. Tape recording is desirable for accurate scoring, and since the tape can serve as a valuable reference in future evaluations.

SEMANTIC ABILITIES

For evaluation of semantic abilities other than vocabulary, few guidelines are yet available. However, isolated subtests from standardized tests may be used as models for teacher made informal procedures to assess semantic competencies. Both the *Basic Concepts Inventory* (Engelmann, 1967) and the *Durell-Sullivan Reading Capacity Test* (1937) can be used to test children's comprehension of single sentences and short paragraphs, respectively. In the *Durell,* the child is read a paragraph-length story describing an event. He is then asked a series of recall questions that he answers by choosing one picture from a set of four. The Engelmann test has three parts, two of which are particularly appropriate for semantic competencies assessment. The 10 items in Part 1 require picture choice in response to examiner statements. The tasks consist of identification of objects, their properties, characteristics, or functions, for example, as in "Find the one that does not talk and does not bark." The eight items in Part 2 require imitation of sentences and verbal or gestural responding to questions. For example, the child is given a sentence to repeat: "A girl looked at the book" and then asked "Who looked at the book?" The test provides no age norms but gives guidelines for interpretation of errors.

Test procedures like these can guide the child toward paraphrasing ability since the questioning focuses his attention on important ideas he should retain from a given story or sentence. Informally, paraphrasing ability may be measured with reading-comprehension materials such as exemplified in the Boning series (Boning, 1973). Sentences or paragraphs can be read aloud to the child and his retelling checked for retention of the main ideas. Again, tape recording and transcribing of the child's retelling is necessary for accurate scoring and will be very valuable for observation of the child's progress on such tasks. Such other semantic skills as recognition of sentence anomaly and word defining are illustrated in the Auditory Decoding subtest of the ITPA and the vocabulary subtests of the *Stanford-Binet Intelligence Test.*

PRAGMATIC COMPETENCE

Unfortunately, little guidance can be found concerning assessment of pragmatic competence since research into the sociolinguistic aspects of developing communication ability has only recently begun. In procedures outlined in the experimental literature (Beveridge & Tatham, 1976; Rosenberg, 1972) children are put into a contrived communication situation in which one child must describe an indicated one from an array of stimuli. The description must be in sufficient detail to allow his partner to identify the stimulus. The speaker's efforts at completeness, accuracy, and specificity of description provide an indication of his ability to switch speaker/listener roles and judge the listener's need for information. The judged egocentricity of their spontaneous or semispontaneous speech is also used as an indication of children's ability to gear their language to the information needs or points of view of other persons. Lovell et al. (1969) used this characterization, which is based on Piaget's (1955) theoretical description of child language development, as a point for comparison of normal and educable mentally handicapped children's speech. Unfortunately, implementation and scoring of such procedures have not been sufficiently standardized to make them useful to teachers or even, generally, to language clinicians. However, as Mittler (1970) points out, though adequately standardized tests that can be administered with relative ease and on a wide basis are still in need of development for some of the relevant skill dimensions, language testing is an active area of research that

Table 8-4
A Checklist for Potential Areas of Language Problems

Yes	No	Category
____	____	Is there evidence of hearing, visual, emotional, or mental impairment which would impede normal language development?
____	____	Is there evidence of structural abnormality in the articulator organs?
____	____	Does the child evidence communicative intention, and can he use and understand gestures?
____	____	In oral language, are expressive and receptive ability documented?
____	____	Does the child initiate speech on his own, or does he use language only reactively?
____	____	Are the majority of his utterances at a level (one-word utterance, two- or three-element phrase, etc.) appropriate for his age and development (see Table 8-3)?
____	____	Is he intelligible in oral communication?
____	____	Does he use many of the common English speech sounds inaccurately, imperfectly, or not at all?
____	____	Are voice or rhythm problems (respiratory coordination) present?
____	____	Is his general vocabulary adequate in relation to age and to achievement in other language-skill areas?
____	____	If language is severely restricted, does he require much time or many trials to learn a new, common vocabulary item?
____	____	Does he have adequate command of grammar in relation to age and to achievement in other language skill areas?
____	____	Does he use language to express different communicative functions?
____	____	Is the child's talk usually appropriate to the situation, and does he show ability at utilizing situational, nonverbal cues?

reflects deep current concern with analysis and remediation of children's communication impairment.

In summary, the teacher will want to seek answers to many questions using documented observation, assessment procedures, and data from tests as described above. With information on the child's relative performance in different areas of language growth and use, goals for individualized language education can be formulated from a sounder basis. To assist the teacher, the checklist presented in Table 8-4 may help establish a systematic approach to assessment.

SUMMARY

This chapter has discussed some formal and informal assessment procedures through which one may ascertain children's linguistic functioning. It is the central theme of this chapter that language cannot be separated from children's ability to organize information and construct a cognitive foundation of knowledge about the environment. This knowledge, in turn, depends on ability to receive and process environmental sensory stimulation, and derive precepts of objects/events reflecting past experiences. Language is seen as part of, and deriving from, a child's general cognitive processing ability.

Language is by nature a structured system of symbols used for communication. To function successfully as a communicator, the child must acquire mastery of several sets of skills and rules relating to both the structure of language and its use in social settings. He must acquire the elements, and learn the phonological, grammatic, and semantic rules, which make his own speech utterances understood by others and allow his interpretation of novel utterances by others. And he must learn the paralinguistic rules that relate speech to particular environmental settings, persons, and events. The learning of both the linguistic code and the rules governing its interpersonal use occurs over a developmental growth period of at least seven years and is normally implicit and largely determined by maturation. However, recent studies (Bernstein, 1964; Horton, 1974; Labov, 1966) have shown the impact of social-environmental factors on language development and use, and in teaching language impaired children, deliberate environmental manipulations clearly can have large beneficial effects (Drash, 1972; Eisenson, 1972; Guess et al., 1974; Sloane & MacAuley, 1968). The chapter has presented some brief background in and guide to further reading on the structure, components, and stages in development of the multidimensional cognitive-perceptual ability we label "language."

The teacher is the person principally responsible for preparing, implementing, and monitoring the educational program activities that are to facilitate children's growth, or ameliorate disabilities. The discussion of language assessment was, therefore, purposely biased toward tests that have minimal absolute requirements for psychological or clinical training. A range of formal and informal procedures was discussed within a framework which points out the need for establishment of a child's functioning in the many skill areas encompassed by language.

Lastly, while emphasis was placed on teacher awareness and assessment of what have come to be called cognitive *prerequisites* for language, the reverse intimate relation of linguistic ability to mental growth must be kept in mind. It is hard to conceive how a person can reflect on and thus enrich his knowledge from experience unless the latter is coded and processed in a symbolic, verbal form. Itard, the pioneer 19th-century educator who wrestled with the problem of teaching a nonverbal child aptly stated his painful awareness of the crucial need for language in mental processing and learning, as follows: "All the simple and complex ideas we receive from education (can) combine in our mind solely by means of our knowledge of signs (language)." Without language to "fix" ideas and knowledge gained, these are "fugitive" and too easily forgotten (Itard, 1962, p. 60).

REFERENCES

Anastasiow, N. J., & Hanes, M. L. *Sentence repetition task.* Bloomington, Ind.: Institute for Child Study, 1974.

Bartel, N. R., Bryen, D., & Keehn, S. Language comprehension in the moderately retarded child. *Exceptional Children,* 1973, *39,* 927–934.

The Basic Concepts Inventory. Engelmann, S. Chicago: Follett Educational Corp., 1967.

Bellugi-Klima, U. *Evaluating the child's language competence.* ERIC: ED 019141, 1968.

Berko, J. The child's learning of English morphology. *Word,* 1958, *14,* 150–177.

Bernstein, B. Elaborated and restricted codes: Their social origins and some consequences. In J. J. Gumperz & D. Hymes (Eds.), *The ethnography of communication.* Special publication of *American Anthropologist,* 1964, *66,* Part 2.

Beveridge, M. C., & Tatham, A. Communication in retarded adolescents: Utilization of known language skills. *American Journal of Mental Deficiency,* 1976, *81,* 93–96.

Bloom, L. *Language development. Form and function in emergent grammars.* Cambridge, Mass.: MIT Press, 1970.

Bloom, L. Language development. In F. D. Horowitz (Ed.), *Review of Child Development Research.* Vol. 4. Chicago: University of Chicago Press, 1975.

Boehm Test of Basic Concepts. Boehm, A. New York: The Psychological Corporation, 1971.

Boning, R. A. *Specific skills series.* New York: Barnell Loft, 1973.

Bronowski, J., & Bellugi, U. Language, name, and concept. *Science,* May 1973, *168,* 669–673.

Brown, R. Language: The system and its acquisition. Chaps. 6 and 7 in *Social psychology.* New York: Free Press, 1965.

Brown, R. *A first language.* Cambridge: Harvard University Press, 1973.

Buchanan, C. D. *A programmed introduction to linguistics: Phonetics and phonemics.* Lexington, Mass.: D. C. Heath, 1963.

Carr, D. L., Brown, L. F., & Rice, J. A. The *PPVT* in the assessment of language deficits. *American Journal of Mental Deficiency,* 1967, *71,* 937–939.

Carrow, E. Assessment of speech and language in children. In J. E. McLean, D. E. Yoder, & R. L. Schiefelbusch (Eds.), *Language intervention with the retarded: Developing strategies.* Baltimore: University Park Press, 1972.

Carrow, E. *Test for Auditory Comprehension of Language.* Austin, Texas: Learning Concepts, 1973.

Carrow, E. *Elicited Language Inventory.* Austin, Texas: Learning Concepts, 1974.

Chapman, R. S. Some simple ways of talking about normal language and communication. In J. E. McLean, D. E. Yoder, & R. L. Schiefelbusch (Eds.), *Language intervention with the retarded: Developing strategies.* Baltimore: University Park Press, 1972.

Clark, E. V. What's in a word? On the child's acquisition of semantics in his first language. In T. E. Moore (Ed.), *Cognitive development and the acquisition of language.* New York: Academic Press, 1973.

Clark, R., Hutcheson, S., & Van Buren, P. Comprehension and production in language acquisition. *Journal of Linguistics,* 1974, *10,* 39–54.

Cooper, R. L. What do we learn when we learn a language? *TESOL Quarterly,* 1970, *4,* 303–314.

Costello, J. Articulation instruction based on distinctive features theory. *Language, Speech, and Hearing Services in the Schools,* 1975, *6,* 61–71.

Crystal, D., Fletcher, P., & Garman, M. *The grammatical analysis of language disability.* New York: American Elsevier, 1976.

Dale, P. S. *Language development: Structure and function.* Hinsdale, Ill.: Dryden Press, 1972.

Dever, R. B. *T.A.L.K. Teaching the American language to kids.* Experimental Materials. Final Report 27.3. Bloomington, Ind.: Center for Innovation in Teaching the Handicapped, 1972.

Drash, P. W. Rehabilitation of the retarded child: A remedial program. *Journal of Special Education,* 1972, *6,* 149–159.

Dunn, L. M. *Peabody Picture Vocabulary Test.* Circle Pines, Minn.: American Guidance Service, 1965

Durrell-Sullivan Reading Capacity and Achievement Tests: Reading Capacity Test. Durrell, D. D. & Sullivan, H. B. New York: Harcourt, Brace and World, 1937.

Eisenson, J. *Aphasia in children.* New York: Harper & Row, 1972.

Engelmann, S. & Osborn, J. *Distar language.* Chicago: Science Research Associates, 1976.

Ervin-Tripp, S. Language development. In L. W. Hoffman & M. L. Hoffman (Eds.), *Review of child development research.* Vol. 2. New York: Russell Sage Foundation, 1966.

Ervin-Tripp, S. Some strategies for the first two years. In T. E. Moore (Ed.), *Cognitive development and the acquisition of language.* New York: Academic Press, 1973.

Fry, D. B. The development of the phonological system in the normal and the deaf child. In F. Smith & G. A. Miller (Eds.), *The genesis of language: A psycholinguistic approach.* Cambridge, Mass.: MIT Press, 1966.

Guess, D., Sailor, W., & Baer, D. M. To teach language to retarded children. In R. L. Schiefelbusch & L. L. Lloyd (Eds.), *Language perspectives—acquisition, retardation, and intervention.* Baltimore: University Park Press, 1974.

Hamp, E. P. Language in a few words: With notes on a rereading, 1966. In J. P. DeCecco (Ed.), *The psychology of language, thought, and instruction.* New York: Holt, Rinehart and Winston, 1967.

Hargis, C. H. & Ahlersmeyer, D. E. The significance of grammar in teaching arithmetic to educable retarded children. *Education and Training of the Mentally Retarded,* 1970, *5,* 104–108.

Hockett, C. F. The problem of universals in language. In J. H. Greenberg (Ed.), *Universals in language.* Cambridge, Mass.: MIT Press, 1963.

Horton, K. B. Infant intervention and language learning. In R. L. Schiefelbusch & L. L. Lloyd (Eds.), *Language perspectives—acquisition, retardation, and intervention.* Baltimore: University Park Press, 1974.

Ingram, D. The relationship between comprehension and production. In R. L. Schiefelbusch & L. L. Lloyd (Eds.), *Language perspectives—acquisition, retardation, and intervention.* Baltimore: University Park Press, 1974.

Ingram, D. *Phonological disability in children.* New York: Elsevier, 1976.

Itard, J. M. G. *The wild boy of Aveyron.* Translated by G. M. Humphrey. Englewood Cliffs, N.J.: Prentice-Hall, 1962.

Jakobson, R. Why "Mama" and "Papa"? In A. Bar-Adon & W. F. Leopold (Eds.), *Child language: A book of readings.* Englewood Cliffs, N.J.: Prentice-Hall, 1971.

Johnston, J. R. & Schery, T. K. The use of grammatical morphemes by children with communication disorders. In D. M. Morehead & A. E. Morehead (Eds.), *Normal and deficient child language.* Baltimore: University Park Press, 1976.

Jones, L. V. & Wepman, J. M. Language: A perspective from the study of aphasia. In S. Rosenberg (Ed.), *Directions in psycholinguistics.* New York: Macmillan, 1965.

Joos, M. Language and the school child. *Harvard Educational Review,* 1964, *34,* 203–210.

Kirk, S. A., McCarthy, J. J., & Kirk, W. D. *Illinois Test of Pyscholinguistic Abilities.* Urbana, Ill.: University of Illinois Press, 1968.

Labov, W. *The social stratification of English in New York City.* Washington, D.C.: Center for Applied Linguistics, 1966.

Lamberts, F. & Ysseldyke, J. E. Group oral language training with TMH children based on 'Learning to Think' material. *Education and Training of the Mentally Retarded,* 1978 (in press).

Langacker, R. W. *Language and its structure: Some fundamental linguistic concepts* (2nd ed.). New York: Harcourt, 1973.

Lee, L. *Northwestern Syntax Screening Test.* Evanston, Ill.: Northwestern University, 1969.

Lenneberg, E. H. *Biological foundations of language.* New York: John Wiley, 1967.

Lerea, L. Assessing language development. *Journal of Speech and Hearing Research,* 1958, *1,* 75–85.

Lerea, L. *Michigan Picture Language Inventory,* 1962.

Lovell, K., Hersee, D. E., & Preston, B. M. A. A study of some aspects of language development in educationally subnormal pupils. *Journal of Special Education,* 1969, *3,* 275–284.

McDonald, E. T. *A Screening Deep Test of Articulation.* Pittsburgh: Stanwix House, 1968.

McLean, J. E. Introduction: Developing clinical strategies for language intervention with mentally retarded children. In J. E. McLean, D. E. Yoder & R. L. Schiefelbusch (Eds.), *Language intervention with the retarded: Developing strategies.* Baltimore: University Park Press, 1972.

McLean, J. E. Articulation. In L. L. Lloyd (Ed.), *Communication assessment and intervention strategies.* Baltimore: University Park Press, 1976.

Menyuk, P. A preliminary evaluation of grammatical capacity in children. *Journal of Verbal Learning and Verbal Behavior,* 1963, *2,* 429–439.

Menyuk, P. Comparison of grammar of children with functionally deviant and normal speech. *Journal of Speech and Hearing Research,* 1964, *7,* 109–121.

Menyuk, P. *The acquisition and development of language.* Englewood Cliffs, N.J.: Prentice-Hall, 1971.

Menyuk, P. *The development of speech.* Indianapolis, Ind.: Bobbs-Merrill, 1972.

Miller, J. F. & Yoder, D. E. An ontogenetic language teaching strategy for retarded children. In R. L. Schiefelbusch & L. L. Lloyd (Eds.), *Language perspectives—acquisition, retardation, and intervention.* Baltimore: University Park Press, 1974.

Miller, J. & Yoder, D. E. *The Miller-Yoder Test of Grammatical Comprehesion* (Experimental edition), Madison, Wisc.: University of Wisconsin, 1975.

Mittler, P. J. Language disorders. In P. J. Mittler (Ed.), *The psychological assessment of mental and physical handicaps.* London: Tavistock, 1970.

Mittler, P. Assessment for language learning. In P. Berry (Ed.), *Language and communication in the mentally handicapped.* Baltimore: University Park Press, 1976.

Mowrer, D. H. The psychologist looks at language. *American Psychologist,* 1954, *9,* 660–694.

Mowrer, D. H. Hearing and speaking: An analysis of language learning. *Journal of Speech and Hearing Disorders,* 1960, *23,* 143–153.

Nation, J. E. A vocabulary usage test. *Journal of Psycholinguistic Research,* 1972, *1,* 221–231.

Osborn, J. *Language programs.* Presentation at National Convention of the Council for Exceptional Children, Los Angeles, Ca., 1975.

Osgood, C. E. *Method and theory in experimental psychology.* New York: Oxford University Press, 1953.

Osgood, C. E. A behaviorist analysis of perception and language as cognitive phenomena. In *Contemporary approaches to cognition.* Cambridge: Harvard University Press, 1957.

Piaget, J. *The language and thought of the child.* Cleveland: World Publications, 1955.

Piaget, J. *Play, dreams, and imitation in childhood.* New York: Norton, 1962.

Quirk, R., Greenbaum, S., Leech, G., & Svartvik, J. *A grammar of contemporary English.* New York: Seminar Press, 1972.

Rosenberg, S. Problems of language development in the retarded. In H. C. Haywood (Ed.), *Social-cultural aspects of mental retardation.* New York: Appleton, 1970.

Rosenberg, S. The development of referential skills in children. In R. L. Schiefelbusch (Ed.), *Language of the mentally retarded.* Baltimore: University Park Press, 1972.

Ruder, K. F. & Smith, M. D. Issues in language training. In R. L. Schiefelbusch & L. L. Lloyd (Eds.), *Language perspectives—acquisition, retardation, and intervention.* Baltimore: University Park Press, 1974.

Sander, E. K. When are speech sounds learned? *Journal of Speech and Hearing Disorders,* 1972, *37,* 55–63.

Sapir, E. *Language: An introduction to the study of speech.* New York: Harcourt, Brace & World, 1921.

Sapir, E. *Culture, language, and personality.* In D. G. Mandelbaum (Ed.), *Selected essays.* Berkeley, Ca.: University of California Press, 1970.

Skinner, B. F. *Verbal behavior.* New York: Appleton, 1957.

Sloane, H. N., & MacAuley, B. D. *Operant procedures in remedial speech and language training.* Boston: Houghton Mifflin, 1968.

Slobin, D. I. Developmental psycholinguistics. In W. O. Dingwall (Ed.), *A survey of linguistic science.* College Park, Ma.: University of Maryland Linguistics Program, 1971.

Slobin, D. I. Cognitive prerequisites for the development of grammar. In C. A. Ferguson & D. I. Slobin (Eds.), *Studies in child language development.* New York: Holt, Rinehart and Winston, 1973.

Staats, A. W. *Learning, language and cognition.* New York: Holt, Rinehart and Winston, 1968.

Staats, A. W. Behaviorism and cognitive theory in the study of language: A neo-psycholinguistics. In R. L. Schiefelbusch & L. L. Lloyd (Eds.), *Language perspectives—acquisition, retardation and intervention.* Baltimore: University Park Press, 1974.

Stephens Oral Language Screening Test. Irene Stephens, 1977. (Available from Interim Publishers, 3900 Scobie Road, Peninsula, Ohio, 44264.)

Templin, M. & Darley, F. L. *The Templin-Darley Tests of Articulation.* Iowa City: University of Iowa, 1968.

Wechsler Intelligence Scale for Chidlren. New York: The Psychological Corporation, 1958.

SUGGESTED READINGS

Billings, V. Development of language in the normal child. In J. E. McLean, D. E. Yoder, & R. L. Schiefelbusch (Eds.), *Language intervention with the retarded: Developing strategies.* Baltimore: University Park Press, 1972.

Brown, R. Language, the system and its acquisition. Chaps. 6 and 7. In R. Brown, *Social psychology.* New York: Free Press, 1965.

Bricker, D. D. & Bricker, W. A. Psychological issues in language development in the mentally retarded child. In I. Bialer & M. Sternlicht (Eds.), *The psychology of mental retardation: Issues and approaches.* New York: Psychological Dimensions, 1977.

Carroll, J. B. Words, meanings and concepts: Part I. Their nature; Part II. Concept teaching and learning. In J. P. DeCecco (Ed.), *Readings in the psychology of language, thought and instruction.* New York: Holt, Rinehart and Winston, 1967.

Eisenson, J. *Aphasia in children.* New York: Harper & Row, 1972.

Fry, D. B. The development of the phonological system in the normal and the deaf child. In F. Smith & G. A. Miller (Eds.), *The genesis of language: A psycholinguistic approach.* Cambridge, Mass.: MIT Press, 1966.

Kastein, S. & Trace, B. *The birth of language. Case history of a non-verbal child.* Springfield, Ill.: Charles C Thomas, 1966.

Lenneberg, E. H. Language disorders in childhood. *Harvard Educational Review,* 1964, *34,* 152–177.

McCarthy, D. Language development. In A. Bar-Adon & W. F. Leopold (Eds.), *Child language: A book of readings.* Englewood Cliffs, N.J.: Prentice-Hall, 1971.

Menyuk, P. *The acquisition and development of language.* Englewood Cliffs, N.J.: Prentice-Hall, 1971.

Mittler, P. Assessment for language learning. In P. Berry (Ed.), *Language and communication in the mentally handicapped.* Baltimore: University Park Press, 1976.

Yoder, D. E. & Miller, J. F. What we may know and what we can do: Input toward a system. In J. E. McLean, D. E. Yoder, & R. L. Schiefelbusch (Eds.), *Language intervention with the retarded: Developing strategies.* Baltimore: University Park Press, 1972.

John Lloyd

9 Ascertaining the Reading Skills of Atypical Learners

Many atypical learners have inadequate reading skills. If their reading skills are not improved, these learners have greater chances of failure in other school-related areas as well as in reading (Cawley, Goodstein, & Burrow, 1972; Gillespie & Johnson, 1974). In order to provide appropriate remedial services, it is necessary to ascertain what skills they have and do not have. An assessment that produces this information provides a starting place for remediation. Many approaches to the assessment of reading skills have been presented in both the special education and reading literature. This chapter includes discussions of these approaches under four general headings: (1) informal reading inventories, (2) applied behavior analysis, (3) an essential skills hierarchy, and (4) traditional reading tests.

Before discussing these approaches to ascertaining reading skills, it is necessary to develop a definition of reading. A definition serves the purpose of providing a common starting place for discussion. Without it the author and reader might entertain entirely different ideas with regard to ascertaining the reading skills of atypical learners.

A DEFINITION OF READING

Reading has been defined in many ways (see Chall, 1967, for examples). For the purposes of the present chapter reading is considered to be a two-stage process (after Bateman, 1973; Glass, 1971). In the first stage

The author appreciatively acknowledges the valuable assistance of Lynne Hendershott in the preparation of this chapter.

the reader is simply decoding the printed squiggles, converting them from a visual-spatial form into an auditory-temporal form. It is this stage of reading that makes it possible for a person to read both sense and nonsense material. It is also this stage that makes it possible for the reader to perform the second stage. In the second stage the reader is simply understanding what is meant by the auditory-temporal information. The second stage of reading is usually called comprehension and is as easy (and as hard) as understanding what one hears.

When the two stages are combined, a working definition of reading English emerges: *Reading is the conversion of print into auditory equivalents and the subsequent interpretation of these equivalents' meanings based on previously learned oral language skills.*

To be sure, this definition probably does not satisfy all of the experts in reading. For instance, it might be argued that there are occasions when reading is not performed orally. Consequently, it would seem that this definition, with its reliance upon oral language skills, may be inappropriate for describing silent reading. However, the definition does not require decoding into oral equivalents, but rather, decoding into auditory equivalents. It is entirely possible to ''hear'' a sound, word, or sentence in one's head. Another objection stems from situations in which recoding into auditory equivalents may be unnecessary or may even disrupt comprehending. The argument might be based on Baron's (1973) study showing that some words—particularly homophones such as *knot* and *not*—can be confused if they are only heard. Obtaining the meaning for *knot* when the word was *not* might be impossible with purely auditory analysis. However, the proposed definition does not actually rule out visual or contextual analysis, and such analysis would allow the reader to resolve the *knot* and *not* dilemma. Also, for competent readers the decoding stage may be partially by-passed under certain conditions (Kolers, 1970; Rosinski, Golinkoff, & Kukish, 1975) which have not yet been firmly established. It seems reasonable that it may occur when material is highly familiar and, hence, the decoding process is virtually automatic (LaBerge & Samuels, 1974). In general, the by-passing evidence is not sufficiently strong to adopt the view that the meaning of printed material is derived without any acoustic recoding (Rozin & Gleitman, 1977), particularly during children's acquisition of reading skills.

Although it has been argued (e.g., Goodman, 1967; Smith, 1971) that decoding is not an essential skill in reading, there are several reasons that the definition used in this chapter does not incorporate that position. First, the theoretical position of direct access of meaning from print has not been specified in sufficient detail to allow its verification (Gibson & Levin, 1975). Therefore, its adoption would seem premature. Second, and from a practical point of view perhaps most important, the direct access position would require that the reader have a very large memory for words. If readers worked with the parts of words—either individual letters or letter clusters—then there would have to be some means of retaining these parts and putting them together into words; it is difficult to explain this process without recourse to an auditory or phonological step. Without the auditory step readers would be treating English as a virtually pictographic language. Treating English as a logographic or picturelike language would require readers to remember a tremendous number of words as separate entities (Gough, 1972; Rozin & Gleitman, 1977; Wallach & Wallach, 1976). In fact, the number of whole word units that readers would have to remember would stagger Chinese scholars who constantly work with a logographic written language (Rozin & Gleitman, 1977). The English language is an alphabetic language, not a logographic language (Gibson & Levin, 1975; Gleitman & Rozin, 1973). An attempt to teach the reading of English as a direct access language skill would deny the great advantage of alphabetic languages: The limited number of symbols (letters) can be recombined into the virtually unlimited number of words in the spoken language. When readers can fluently convert the printed word into phonological equivalents, then they have their entire speaking vocabulary available for comprehension. Since this chapter is concerned with ascertaining the reading skills of atypical readers, assessment of their skills must be comprehensive, including analysis of decoding competence. To adopt a definition consistent with the direct access position would preclude consideration of decoding skills.

The present definition of reading has both practical and theoretical advantages. It is consistent with the alphabetic principle that underlies English. Both stages admit to specification of component skills (see discussion under the heading *Assessing Essential Skills*) which can allow teachers to more precisely identify reading strength and weakness. It suggests the kind of instruction that is in harmony with findings concerning the efficacy of beginning reading programs (see e.g., Bliesmer & Yarborough, 1965; Chall, 1967; Dykstra, 1968; Gurren & Hughes, 1965) and with laboratory studies of initial reading instruction methods (see, e.g., Bishop, 1964; Carnine, 1977; Jeffery & Samuels, 1967).

APPROACHES TO ASCERTAINING READING SKILLS

In this section several general approaches to the problem of ascertaining reading skills will be discussed. These approaches all attempt to measure reading or reading-related performance. However, they attack the task from different positions. Consequently, the means employed to measure reading performance differ to some degree. Two approaches—

assessment based on essential skills and traditional testing—are not covered here; they are dealt with under separate headings in the following section.

The history of reading (Matthews, 1966) is varied and the influences of many disciplines are revealed in it. For the purpose of this chapter, however, only assessment approaches that provide educational direction will be considered. For this reason it is unnecessary to review the contributions of medical diagnoses which primarily focus on organic causes (see, however, Money, 1962). The topic of the present discussion is determining the reading skills of school-age learners.

One early attempt was made by Monroe (1932a) to describe the performance of disabled readers in such a way that remediation would be implied. She developed a system of analyzing learner's reading errors. A test, the *Monroe Diagnostic Reading Test* (1932b), included subscores showing errors in areas such as faulty vowels, faulty consonants, reversals, addition of sounds, omission of sounds, substitution of words, repetitions of sounds, addition of words, omission of words, and reversals and words added. The errors of individual children were compared to average error scores and were profiled on a graph in order to get a picture of the types of errors made by the learners. The instrument is important not only because it was designed to provide remedial direction, but also, because it influenced the development of later tests which have been used in relation to reading (Kirk, 1976).

Differential Abilities Assessment

In the last 15 years a different approach to assessing the performance of children has been employed. Several tests have been developed that were designed to measure learner's skills in areas presumably related to reading skill. These instruments were based on the ideas that (1) children with reading problems—and children with other problems as well—have correlated disabilities that can be identified, and that (2) remediation of the deficits in these areas, or teaching that takes advantage of strengths in correlated areas, will result in improved reading skills (Bateman, 1967; Ysseldyke & Salvia, 1974).

THE FROSTIG

One major activity in this area resulted in the publication of the *Developmental Test of Visual Perception* (Frostig, Lefever, & Wittlesey, 1964). The test is designed to reveal skill in the overall area of visual perception and skill in specific areas including (1) visual-motor coordination, (2) figure-ground perception, (3) form constancy, (4) perception of position in space, and (5) perception of spatial relations. Presumably, if a learner's performance in one of these areas was inadequate it might disrupt performance in higher cognitive areas such as reading. The argument would state: If a learner has difficulties in the area of perception of position in space, then the child might perceive *b* as *d* and vice-versa. Consequently, the child would have difficulty discriminating between these letters and, hence, reading words in which they appear.

The Frostig, as it is often called, is probably one of the most widely used tests in the area of learning disabilities (Hallahan & Kauffman, 1976). However, as a test it has come under considerable critical scrutiny (Hammill & Wiederholt, 1973; Ysseldyke, 1973). Moreover, there is little empirical evidence to suggest that remediation of visual-perceptual deficits leads to improvement in reading performance (Hammill, 1972; Hammill & Wiederholt, 1973).

THE ILLINOIS TEST OF PSYCHOLINGUISTIC ABILITIES (ITPA)

Another approach to assessing learner performance in areas related to reading was pioneered by Kirk and his associates. Kirk (1976) wrote that his attempts to develop means for diagnosing correlated disabilities (i.e., problems in related areas) was influenced by the work of Monroe (1932ab). It is apparent in the profile of the ITPA (Kirk, McCarthy, & Kirk, 1968). A child's scores on the various subtests of the ITPA (auditory reception, visual reception, auditory association, visual association, verbal expression, manual expression, grammatic closure, visual closure, auditory sequential memory, visual sequential memory, auditory closure, and sound blending) are converted into standardized scores and plotted graphically to reveal strengths and weaknesses. Like the Frostig, the ITPA has been the subject of numerous studies of its psychometric characteristics (Proger, Cross, & Burger, 1973; Sedlak & Weener, 1973) and also, has been questioned on grounds of its usefulness (Waugh, 1975). Remedial programs designed to ameliorate problems revealed by the ITPA (Bush & Giles, 1969; Karnes, 1972; Kirk & Kirk, 1971; Minskoff, Wiseman & Minskoff, 1972) have also been challenged on grounds of theoretical premises (Mann, 1971; Mann & Phillips, 1967) and effectiveness (Hammill & Larsen, 1974a, 1974b; Newcomer & Hammill, 1975).

UNEVEN WISC PROFILE

Still another approach to examining the performance of children which has been applied to problems in reading has been diagnosis through an analysis of subtest scores on the *Wechsler Intelligence Scale for Children* (WISC) (Wechsler, 1974). Bannatyne (1968) and Rugel (1974) have attempted to isolate different types of learners on the basis of patterns of subtest scores. Presumably, the educational value of such categorization would lie in providing direction or remediation. Objections to the theoretical underpinnings of this approach have also been raised (Mann, 1971; Mann & Phillips, 1967; Ysseldyke, 1973).

The controversy over these issues in the field of learning disabilities need not be of concern here, however. The purpose of this chapter is to examine means for assessing reading skills. Differential abilities tests, regardless of whether they are psychometrically sound, and correlated disability remediation programs, regardless of whether they are effective, do not provide direct information about reading performance. They do not reveal what reading skills learners do or do not have.

Informal Reading Inventories

An informal reading inventory (IRI) is an individual (i.e., one teacher, one learner) assessment in which the teacher attempts to identify the learner's skill level by observing reading performance on material of increasing difficulty. Work with IRIs was pioneered by Betts (1946). According to the proponents of IRIs (Johnson & Kress, 1965; Zintz, 1975), they have several advantages: (1) they are easily constructed; (2) they reveal several levels of reading skill; (3) they show types of reading errors; (4) they may provide clues about a learner's word attack strategies; and (5) they provide an opportunity to observe the learner's other behaviors during reading. Perhaps the most frequently cited advantage of IRIs is that they reveal several levels of reading skill (Betts, 1946; Kaluger & Kolson, 1969; Learner, 1976; Robeck & Wilson, 1974; Zintz, 1975). Standardized reading tests such as those discussed later in this chapter are seen as providing only an indication of "frustration" level performance; that is, the grade level score of most reading tests indicates what the learner can do under restricted (e.g., short duration) conditions. At the frustration level on an IRI, "The child is able to recognize less than 90% of the words with a comprehension score of 50% or less. This reading level is too difficult for the child, who does not understand the material. It should not be used for instruction" (Learner, 1976, p. 82). Table 9-1 shows all the various levels of performance for IRIs.

The more common form of an IRI—passage reading—is constructed by selecting passages from a set of materials which increase in difficulty. Usually this is accomplished by drawing passages from each level of a common basal reading series. Smith (1959) has published a book with selections for the early grades. Zintz (1975) recommended drawing two passages from each level, one to be read orally and one to be read silently. He also suggested that the passages be drawn from the end of the first third of each book in order to avoid excessive review of vocabulary from the previous book, a feature common to most spiralling basal readers.

Table 9-1
Levels of Skill Revealed by Informal Reading Inventories

Level	Decoding Accuracy (%)	Comprehension Accuracy (%)	Implication
Independent	98	100	Student may work on own, without help at his level
Instructional	95	75	Student will profit from instruction at this level
Frustration	90 or less	50 or less	Too difficult for student
Capacity	Not assessed	75	Student's probable level of potential

Since the grade levels assigned to books vary from publisher to publisher, it is probably appropriate to adopt Learner's (1976) recommendation that each passage be checked for readability. Bormuth (1968), Dale & Chall (1948), Flesch (1949), Fry (1968), and Spache (1953) all provide methods for determining the readability of passages; Fry's method is probably the most accessible and easily used.

ADMINISTRATION

IRIs are usually administered one-to-one, although silent versions may be given in groups (Johnson, 1960). It is usually easier to tape record sessions so that more exact error coding is possible. The teacher selects a passage which should be below the student's independent level. The student is instructed to read it. During the reading the teacher marks another copy of the passage, noting the types of errors* the student makes (Table 9-2). When the student has completed the passage, the teacher notes the amount of time required and proceeds to ask comprehension questions based on the passage. The teacher records whether the answers were accurate. Presenting the next higher passage, the teacher repeats the steps just specified. This continues until the learner's behavior indicates frustration and the teacher is fairly certain that decoding accuracy is lower than 90 percent. At that time, in order to gain an estimate of the learner's potential to understand material, the teacher may read passages aloud and ask the comprehension questions.

To determine the learner's levels of performance the teacher ascertains the percentage of correct decoding and question answering. The

*There is some disagreement about whether regressions or repetitions should be counted as errors. Ekwall (1974) presented discussion and data bearing on this question.

Table 9-2
Some Conventions for Marking Errors in Oral Reading

Type of Error	Description	Marking
Assistance	Teacher had to supply word after 5 seconds	Underline words aided.
Hesitations	Learner hesitated at word but teach did not have to supply assistance	✓ check above hesitated word.
Insertions	Learner inserts word not on page	Put in word or word parts with caret (∧).
Mispronunciation	Learner does not accurately pronounce word	Write in learner's "pro-noun-shun" (pronunciation) above the missed word.
Omissions	Learner leaves out a word or words and reads on	Circle the omitted word(s) or punctuation.
Order reversals	Learner inverts word order	Mark reversals with this symbol: ⌐⌙
Regressions	Learner reads word(s) and then rereads them	Put a wavy line under word(s) repeated.
Self corrections	Learner makes a mistake but corrects it spontaneously	When the learner sc errors errs note the mistake and write sc above it.
Substitutions	Learner reads one word as another	Then When the learner substitutes a word underline the omitted word and write in the given one.

Passage example:
These people They had been
The person had been waiting all afternoon for a call. She was anxious to know whether her poem would win the contest and the fifty dollars prize. If it did then.she could take her friend, Jack, out to a fine dinner. But little did she know that the phone.

passages that fit the criteria stated in Table 9-1 correspond to the levels listed there. For example, if a learner reads a passage of grade level 3.2 difficulty with 95 percent accuracy in decoding and 80 percent accuracy in answering comprehension questions, then the teacher assumes that grade level 3.2 material is at the learner's instructional level. An estimate of decoding rate can be derived by dividing the time required to read a passage into the total number of words contained.

Another type of IRI that is used in ascertaining reading skills requires neither passages nor elaborate marking systems. Instead, graded word lists are presented to a learner and only word reading accuracy is measured. Examples of this type of IRI may be found in LaPray & Ross (1969), Learner (1976), Zintz (1975), and in other sources. Some studies (Clay, 1967; Libermann, Shankweiler, & Orlando, 1971) have reported high correlations between performance on graded word lists and performance on contextual materials; that is, the grade level scores derived from word list IRIs and from some standardized reading tests are very similar. The principle advantage to using word lists is their ease and speed in administration.

RESTRICTIONS ON IRIs

Like any means of measurement, IRIs are only estimates of skill. Unlike standardized tests, however, IRIs are not rigorously constructed. As a consequence, they are likely to be subject to even greater measurement error (see Chap. 3) than standardized instruments. Therefore, the results of an IRI must be interpreted with caution.

The point made earlier about the variability among publishers' texts with supposedly identical grade levels is another source of limitation on IRIs. Using readability formula to control for this variability will help but probably will not cover other interpublisher differences. For example, consider the differences in vocabulary between series. Basal reading programs use some idiosyncratic vocabulary items to make their stories work. Learners who have not been exposed to the particular series from which IRI passages are drawn or who have not been taught code-cracking skills may be at a loss when confronted with the idiosyncratic vocabulary in an IRI. As a consequence, teachers using IRIs should not be surprised by wide discrepancies between "capacity" and other performance levels.

Finally, the construction, administration, and evaluation of IRIs requires considerable clinical skill on the teacher's part. Such skills are acquired through extensive practice. During the time the teacher practices with IRIs in order to acquire clinical skill, the teacher may make inappropriate decisions. In terms of students' learning, this may be costly. For more information about IRIs one may consult some of the references compiled by Johns, Garton, Schoenfelder, & Skriba (1977).

Behaviorally-based Reading Assessment

Behaviorally-based reading assessment is composed of three principle components: (1) direct, continuous measurement; (2) precisely identified conditions; and (3) individual assessment. In this section, these components will be described and an example of assessment based on them will be presented.

DIRECT, CONTINUOUS MEASUREMENT

In behavioral assessment, there must be direct, continuous observation of learners' performance (Hall, 1971; Lovitt, 1967, 1975, 1976; Starlin, 1971; White & Liberty, 1976). The reading behavior of concern must be carefully defined so that different people seeing the learner perform would be able to agree about whether the behavior was occurring. In a general sense, oral reading is such a behavior. However, the behavior "reads orally" is probably too general. Instead, it would be useful to define the behavior in a more finite manner: "reads a word orally." This behavior is likely to occur more frequently than "reads orally"; hence, it provides a more sensitive measure. For a teacher concerned with assessing performance, it is probably more important to know something about accuracy. Therefore, the behavior should be even more discretely defined: (1) "correctly reads a word aloud" and (2) "incorrectly reads a word aloud." To be sure, there are many other reading behaviors that may be of interest; those mentioned above serve illustrative purposes.

When a direct measure of performance is used in assessment, there is a reduction in some of the problems usually associated with measurement. For example, teachers using direct observation techniques do not have to show that their measures are related to the behavior of concern; they are measuring the behavior of concern.

In addition to requiring direct measurement; behaviorally-based assessment also prescribes continuous measurement. The behavior to be assessed is to be observed sufficiently often so that day-to-day variations can be equalized. Usually, this requirement indicates daily measurement. An added advantage of continuous measurement is that it affords teachers the opportunity to see the effects of an instructional program immediately. There is no need to wait for end-of-the-year testing to see how well learners are reading. Consequently, if instruction is not causing the students to acquire reading skills then teachers may make immediate adjustments and judge their effectiveness.

In summary, measurement is at the heart of any assessment scheme. In a behaviorally-based approach, measurement is accomplished by directly and continuously observing carefully defined reading behaviors.

PRECISELY IDENTIFIED CONDITIONS

The second attribute of behaviorally-based assessment requires precise identification of the conditions under which the reading behaviors occur. This requirement is analogous to the standardized testing conditions that are used when giving norm-referenced tests. Instead of using the same test items with many learners, in the behaviorally-based assessment scheme, the conditions may vary for different children.

Precisely identified conditions are required in order for the teacher to be able to know what was occurring when a learner performed the reading behaviors. Some of the classroom conditions which might affect performance are the difficulty of the material, whether the reading was oral or silent, whether the situation was tutorial or group instruction, whether the materials are word lists or paragraphs, what contingencies were in effect, etc. If the teacher knows which conditions were in effect at the time of the assessment, then it is possible to reassess performance under those same conditions at a later date, i.e., the next day, and compare the learner's performance.

INDIVIDUAL ANALYSIS

Lovitt (1975, 1976) considers individual analysis the "heart" of behaviorally-based assessment. In behaviorally-based assessment the learners may perform the reading behaviors in either a group or individual setting. But the analysis of the results is always concerned with individual performance rather than with relating the learner's performance to average group performance. The advantage of individual assessment is that the daily measurements of a learner's performance, whose performance is characteristically uneven, can be analyzed apart from the performance of the group. Such an analysis allows a teacher to make decisions about what instructional techniques may be used with an individual learner.

In general, the behaviorally-based scheme of assessment is not necessarily tied into the use of rewards or other techniques associated with behavior modification. It may be that these are conditions that can cause changes in reading performance. However, the assessment procedure is relatively free of implications about what type of treatments might be used. It is, more precisely, a method of ascertaining the skills of learners under identified conditions. Virtually any teaching technique might be used; the assessment procedures are simply the means for monitoring behaviors.

PRECISION TEACHING ASSESSMENT

In terms of its scheme for monitoring behaviors, precision teaching (Kunzelman, 1970; Starlin, 1971) is very similar to the behaviorally-based assessment discussed above. Precision teaching, however, does not specify teaching procedures; rather, it is concerned with the measurement of learner performance. It is, basically, a system of describing, observing, recording, charting, and analyzing patterns in behavior. Starlin's (1971) presentation of the procedures involved in using precision teaching with reading is excellent. In the following paragraphs, it is used as an example of behaviorally-based assessment.

In precision teaching the behavior to be observed is defined carefully. Starlin presented a number of pinpoints; one of them was the same as the

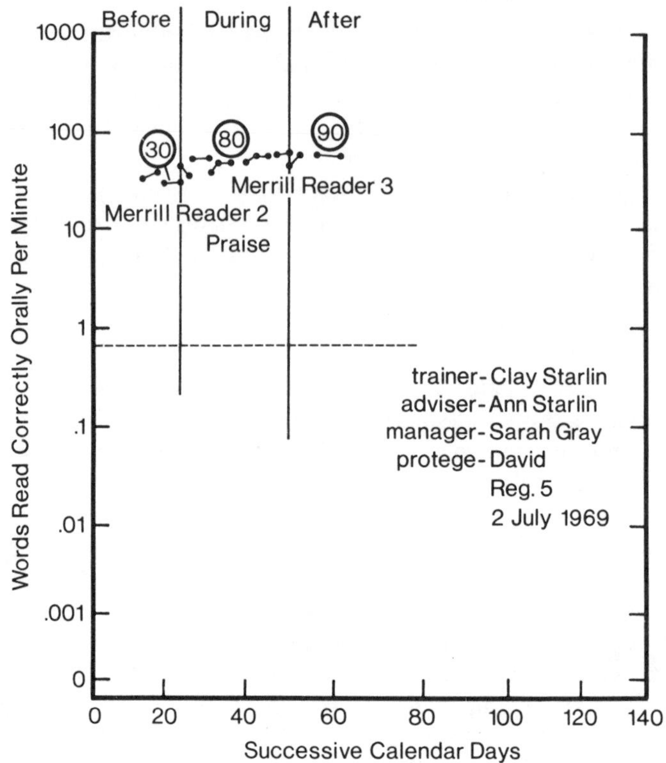

Fig. 9-1. David nears proficiency in Merrill Reader 3.

example used earlier in this section: "words read correctly orally." The learner's performance in oral reading was observed daily under specified conditions; that is, the material to be read was consistent across time and other changes in the situation which affect performance—e.g., teacher praise—were noted. The number of words read correctly was divided by the amount of time in the reading sample. Subsequently, it was charted on semilogarithmic graph paper (see also, White & Liberty, 1976) so that progress could be observed. Figure 9-1 shows this chart.

As can be seen from an examination of the chart, the performance of this learner increased consistently over time. In assessment terms, the value of these data should be apparent: Given the daily measures of performance, the teacher may manipulate parts of the reading situation and examine the effects that these changes have on performance. Thus, one of the purposes of assessment—placing learners in appropriate instructional materials—may be accomplished.

PLACING LEARNERS WITH BEHAVIORALLY-BASED ASSESSMENT PROCEDURES

Lovitt & Hansen (1976a) reported a procedure for placing learners in reading texts by using a combination of behaviorally-based and IRI assessment techniques. They measured three different reading behaviors (correct oral reading rate, incorrect oral reading rate, and correct comprehension percentage) for each of seven students. Initially, reading performance was measured on sample passages selected from the *Lippincott Basic Reading* series (McCracken & Walcutt, 1970). (Hence, there is similarity to an IRI assessment scheme.) Individual performances on the various levels of the series were analyzed and decision rules for placement were developed. "We decided to place a pupil in the highest level reader in which his correct rate was between 45–65 wpm, his average incorrect rate was between 4–8 wpm, and his average comprehension score between 50–75%" (Lovitt & Hansen, 1976a, p. 350). Lovitt & Hansen reported that this method of placing readers was reliable—the learners' performance in the book in which they were placed initially was consistent with their performance during the assessment phase of the study. When combined with a contingent skipping and drilling intervention (Lovitt & Hansen, 1976b), it lead to successful remediation—five students were at expected grade level within six months and all seven within one school year.

SUMMARY

This section has dealt with the rudiments of conducting reading assessment from a behavioral framework. A more complete description of this type of assessment is presented by Repp in Chapter 4. For the purpose of the present chapter, it has been shown that frequent, direct observation, under carefully specified conditions, of precisely identified reading behaviors is one useful means of making individual placement decisions and evaluating individual reading progress.

ASSESSING ESSENTIAL SKILLS

There is considerable evidence to show that early reading instruction that places heavy emphasis on the acquisition of decoding skills results in more accurate decoding and higher comprehension (Bliesmer & Yarborough, 1965; Chall, 1967; Dykstra, 1968; Gurren & Hughes, 1965; Potts & Savino, 1968). There are elements common to successful programs which can be abstracted. As well, a logical analysis of the task of decoding reveals similar elements. When these elements are combined, they then can be reordered into a sequence that provides a logical hierarchy of the component skills involved in decoding. The product of such an analysis is a ladder with each skill represented as a rung leading to the top of the ladder. This approach is similar to the general proposals about learning advanced by Gagné (1970, 1974).

In fact, a number of educators interested in reading have laid out several rungs on the ladder. Jeffery & Samuels (1967) considered mastery of sound-symbol relationships and sound blending skills essential to early decoding. In a laboratory setting they compared the learning and transfer performance of children taught these skills to children taught whole-word recognition skills and to children in a control group. They found the first group markedly superior. These findings were replicated and extended by Carnine (1977). More recently, LaBerge & Samuels (1974) have reiterated the importance of these same components.

Engelmann (1967, p. 196) has presented a similar analysis of early reading skills. He argued that "the first stumbling block . . . is in learning that the letters in a word stand for sounds that are sequenced in time." This sentence obviously suggests the importance of mastering sound-symbol associations and left-right progression. Later in the same article, Engelmann deals with these component skills and blending in greater detail. The Distar-Level 1 reading program (Engelmann & Bruner, 1973) illustrates the teaching of these skills. Basically, the same view has been presented by Bateman (1971, 1973, 1976). She identified the essential early reading skills as including (1) mastery of the left-to-right (→) progression of print, (2) mastery of sound-symbol relationships, and (3) mastery of sound blending skills. Venezky (1975) presented a similar analysis. The skills he identified were (1) attending to letter order (i.e., →), (2) attending to letter orientation, (3) attending to word detail (i.e., letters), (4) sound matching, and (5) sound blending. Many others (e.g., Rozin & Gleitman, 1977; Wallach & Wallach, 1976; Beck & Mitroff, 1972) have argued for inclusion of the same or most of the same components in early reading instruction.

Furthermore, these components have been supported by the effectiveness of beginning reading systems programs, e.g., Lippincott (McCracken & Walcutt, 1976); Distar (Engelmann & Bruner, 1973; Engelmann & Stearns, 1973); and Open Court (Hughes, Carcus, & Trace, 1971), which consistently produce superior reading performance (Bliesmer & Yarborough, 1965; Chall, 1967; Gurren & Hughes, 1965; Stebbins, 1976) and place heavy emphasis on these components.

A Tentative Decoding Hierarchy

On the basis of the preceding discussion, the following hierarchy of early reading skills can be constructed.

SPATIAL DIRECTIONS

The first rung in the ladder is learning that reading proceeds from left to right. The learner need not know the words "left" or "right" nor the directions they indicate. Rather, the learner must know that reading beings at a certain point and proceeds in the direction of this arrow (→). When a learner has not mastered this rung the result may be so-called strephosymbolia (Orton, 1937), or, more commonly, reversals. This subskill can be assessed by observing whether the learner reliably reads words and sentences from left to right.

SOUND-SYMBOL ASSOCIATIONS

The next rung in the initial reading skills ladder of an alphabetic language is learning the sounds associated with the printed symbols. (Note that this does not indicate teaching letter names; Samuels, 1972, has shown that letter naming skill does not cause reading skill.) In learning sound-symbol relationships, the learner also masters the necessary visual discriminations among letters. Some letters, of course, have more than one sound but this problem is easily resolved by using the sound for a letter which is more common or useful [e.g., "one sound this letter (a) makes is aaa like in at"]. Later in instruction the learner is taught that the letter makes a different sound in certain surroundings. Also, some letter combinations make a unique sound—*sh* cannot be produced by making the sounds for the individual letters and blending them. For assessment purposes these sounds may be treated as individual units. Sound-symbol skills can be assessed by having a learner give the sounds for individual symbols, including consonant digraphs.

SOUND BLENDING

The third rung requires that the learner be able to hear a "stretched-out" word and collapse it into the normal speech-rate word: mmmmaaaassss = *mas*. It is important that the learner master this skill so that stops do not interrupt the sounds; it would be difficult, indeed, to blend "muh-aaa-suh" into *mas*. It may be argued that the sound stream cannot be segmented (Gleitman & Rozin, 1973) or that young children have not learned that words are composed of parts (Marchbanks & Levin, 1965) and, therefore, that sound blending is an impossible task. However, there is also reason to assume that competence readers perform this skill at a highly automatic level (LaBerge & Samuels, 1974), that children can learn it (Jeffery & Samuels, 1967), and that without it readers would be stuck with isolated sounds or whole-word, nonalphabetic reading. Sound blending skills can be assessed in a variety of ways. Roswell & Chall (1963) provided a test of blending in which learners listen to slowly pronounced real words and then say them at a normal speech rate. This type of blending is not, however, exactly the same as the blending under discussion here. In reading learners must be able to blend the sounds for the symbols they have seen rather than sounds they've heard. A test of sound blending such as the Roswell-Chall is useful, indeed; but a more exact test would be to have learners whom one can be reasonably certain have directional and sound-symbol skills read simple nonsense words aloud. In this way one is testing a skill more closely related to the decoding stage and can safely assume that the learners are using the competent skills rather than recognizing a word from their oral vocabularies. In fact, as is discussed later, reading simple nonsense words, is a strong test of learners' mastery of component skills.

With mastery of these component skills in combination, a student should be able to read any regular consonant-vowel-consonant (cvc) word and most ccvc, cvcc, and ccvcc words. For example, the word *mad* can be decoded by converting each individual symbol into its sound, converting them in order (→), and blending them into the oral equivalent. Now, by the definition used in this chapter, the reader may determine the word's meaning—comprehend it: "Oh yeah! *Mad.* That's angry or crazy."

With the addition of several more component skills to the ladder it is possible to describe the skills necessary for decoding most of the English language. However, from the available literature the order and number of the remaining components is not apparent. They are presented here in skeletal form only. With the exception of the irregular words and fluency components, all of the following components can be assessed by having learners read nonsense words which conform to the conventions.

LONG VOWEL CONVENTIONS

Several general conventions describe the sound variations associated with vowels. In general, a vowel which occurs in a vowel-consonant-e (-vce) situation usually takes on the long vowel sound. Also, in general, a vowel which is immediately followed by another vowel (-vvc) usually takes on the long sound. Also, if the only vowel in a word or syllable occurs at the end of the cluster, the vowel usually takes on the long sound. Finally, vowels that are immediately followed by the letter *l* or *r* usually take on a sound midway between long and short. Burmeister (1968a,b) called these conventions generalizations. He reviewed several studies of vowel behavior and reported on their usefulness. When learners master these conventions, a tremendous increase in vocabulary is possible.

SILENT LETTER CONVENTIONS

A skill related to long-vowel conventions stipulates that under certain conditions some letters have no sound. For example, the *e* at the end of a -vce string usually is silent; similarly the *gh* cluster following i as in *night* or *high* usually is silent. These and other silent letter conventions help to iron out some of the putative irregularities in the language.

HARD-SOFT CONVENTIONS

Burmeister (1968a,b) also reported on the utility of some consonant generalizations. Some consonants (e.g., *c*) have more than one sound. Initially, it is easiest to treat these as if they had only one sound, but later it is important for learners to distinguish between the conditions where differing values of sound are used. For example, when *c* is followed by *e, i,* or *y* then the sound of the consonant is most likely to be soft as in *city, cede,* or *cycle.*

SYLLABIFICATION

When learners can treat words as clusters of syllables and place accents, then even the usefulness of the first three rungs is greatly expanded. Given mastery of the directional rule (→), sound-symbol relationships, blending, and syllabification, learners should be able to handle cvc/cvc, ccvc/cvc, cvc/cvcc, cvc/ccvc, etc. words. When the component skills just discussed (e.g., long vowel conventions) are added, learners with mastery have the skills to be able to decode the major part of written English.

IRREGULAR WORDS

Some words in the language, however, do not follow these principles entirely. Actually there are not many irregular words (Deverell, 1971; Hanna, Hanna, Hodges & Rudorf, 1966). For the purposes of assessment is is probably necessary to ascertain skills in reading irregular words separately from skills in reading words that conform to spelling-to-sound conventions.

FLUENCY

In order for learners to be able to convert a printed word into its speech equivalent, they must be able to blend the sounds into a normal speech rate form. Similarly, for learners to be able to convert printed passages into narrative, they must be able to fluently decode strings of words. Decoding must become virtually automatic; LaBerge & Samuels (1974) have presented data and arguments showing why this is important and how it happens. Without automatized decoding, learners' performance might sound like labored, word-by-word reading. Fluency, of course, cannot be attained without mastery of the prior rungs on the ladder; without the prior skills learners would be reduced to guessing, picture reading, and general inaccuracy. Also, fluency that includes responding to punctuation, cannot be assessed in reading isolated words; it requires performance on a written passage. To some extent, fluent passage decoding indicates mastery of the prior rungs. However, this is not an absolute statement. Passages of written material provide clues other than those useful in decoding; context, for example, may suggest that some words appear in certain places. Hence, passage reading includes decoding and other skills. Passage reading is not a clean test, therefore, when one wishes to assess decoding skills alone.

Given skill in these areas, readers should be able to handle most written English. These are especially important for atypical learners since they are not the masters of incidental learning that typical learners are and, therefore, are more likely to need very firm mastery of basic reading competencies (Haring & Bateman, 1977).

It might be argued that given these skills a reader could adequately decode but fail to comprehend. However, it is difficult to conceive of a learner in such a situation unless the material was incomprehensible when presented orally. As stated previously, a reader who can fluently decode should be able to perform the same comprehension activities with printed language as he or she could with equally difficult oral language. In all cases, after a brief presentation of an assessment system based on some of the above component skills, the problem of comprehension will be discussed.

The Regional Resource Center Reading Inventory

The Regional Resource Center (1971) at the University of Oregon developed a series of materials designed to assess many of the skills identified in the previous discussion. The Reading Inventory is a criterion-referenced device that assesses learner performance in several areas: consonant sounds, vowel sounds, blending 1 (short vowel words), consonant teams, irregular words, blending 2 (long vowel words), and oral passage reading. The blending tasks are composed of nonsense words so that the learner can accurately produce them only on the basis of component skills rather than on the basis of context or memory clues. At least three samples of performance are taken over several days; as discussed under the behaviorally-based approaches, this serves to smooth out the uneven performance that is characteristic of atypical learners. The average performance of these three days is compared to absolute standards of msatery. These minimum proficiency levels were developed by the center personnel on the basis of data from the performance of a number of readers. Figure 9-2 shows the various areas assessed, the purported minimum proficiency levels, and some fictitious scores.

For a teacher concerned with remediation, the fictitious data presented in Figure 9-2 should suggest some direct remedial activities. The learner apparently has weaknesses in vowel sounds and both blending

Name Tina O. Teacher —
Grade 3rd School Lost Road

SUBTEST NAME	TIME	DAY 1 Date ___ Admin. By ___ correct	error	DAY 2 Date ___ Admin. By ___ correct	error	DAY 3 Date ___ Admin. By ___ correct	error	NEEDS HELP IN	RE-TEST Date ___ Admin. By ___ correct	error
1. Consonant Sounds	1 Min. 60/2 60 - 80	40	8	43	9	42	10			
2. Vowel Sounds	30 Sec. 30/2 30 - 40	5	9	7	9	7	10	✓		
3. Blending I	1 Min. 60/2 80 - 100	3	12	3	10	2	9	✓		
4. Consonant Teams	30 Sec. 30/2 45 - 50	20	7	22	10	21	9			
5. Irregular Words	1 Min. 60/2 80 - 100	43	6	45	3	39	9			
6. Blending II	1 Min. 60/2 80 - 100	0	9	2	10	1	13	✓		
7. Oral Reading Van's Cave	1. Min. 100/2 100 - 120	39	12	45	15	46	10			
8. Classroom Reader	1 Min. 100/2 100 - 120	59	5	63	6	65	7			

Title Mothers Go to Work Page 47-48 Grade Level 2.2
Publisher Common (Basal) Regular (circle one)

Fig. 9-2. Reading inventory record sheet.

areas. These difficulties are apparent not only in the named subareas but also in the passage reading section. One might speculate that the learner is more facile with familiar material since performance in the classroom reader is higher than performance in the "Van's Cave" (McCracken & Walcutt, 1963) selection, even though the "Van's Cave" selection is from lower grade-level material than is the classroom reader selection. Apparently, this hypothetical learner has not mastered the component skills to such an extent that she can apply them to novel material.

SUMMARY

The first part of this section has been a discussion of an approach to assessment based on the assumption that decoding is actually a cluster of component skills. These skills can be identified, isolated, shown to be related to the general skill, and to some extent, assessed independently. Although the psychometric characteristics of such an approach remain to be shown, it is apparent that the approach generates assessment data with obvious remedial implications.

A Tentative Comprehending Hierarchy

The definition of reading presented at the beginning of this chapter included a phrase describing comprehending in terms of accessing semantic equivalents for what has been decoded. In the present section comprehending will be treated in much the same manner as decoding was in the previous section: What are the skills the learner must master in order to comprehend print? The following analysis is tenative and, due to the limitations of this chapter, does not cover such higher order concerns as how reading changes one's world view. It is sufficient, however, to imply assessment activities and subsequent remedial steps.

ACCURATE, FLUENT DECODING

As the preceding analysis and the definition of reading implied, the first essential skill for comprehending is accurate, fluent decoding. If learners decode inaccurately, then they are apt to answer questions about what they have read inaccurately. More sophisticated readers may be able to draw a conclusion about what a specific word is from context clues; but for less competent readers—those with whom we are concerned—the number of accurate guesses is likely to be small in comparison to the number of inaccurate guesses. Less competent readers guess from inadequate clues (e.g., pictures) when they should be using all the component decoding skills to accurately identify the word. Similarly, if readers decode dysfluently they are also likely to answer comprehension questions inaccurately. Decoding must become automatic (LaBerge & Samuels, 1974) so that readers can hear what they read just as they hear what is spoken. Poor decoders would hear what they read in such a choppy spread out form, that their memories would be taxed just in retaining one word while moving to the next. Try speaking at about 50 words per minute—less than one word per second—and the value of fluency will be obvious. This provides some support for Starlin's (1971) minimum proficiency decoding rate of 100 words per minute.

SENTENCE STORAGE

For learners to be able to comprehend something that they have read they must be able to store the material in memory for a short period of time. The short-term storage allows learners to consider the meaning and refer back to the material to check whether it is consistent with the material. For these reasons it is important in comprehension to be able to repeat sentences. One of the simplest comprehension tasks (following written directions) illustrates this point. Suppose learners read, "Put an X on the ball." While they examine the various pictures looking for the ball, they must maintain the direction "put an X on." If they cannot maintain the directions, then the answer is more likely to be wrong.

One way to assess sentence storage is to make a statement orally and then ask the learner to repeat it. "Listen: Draw a line under the house that is green. What did I say?" If a learner cannot perform this type of task, then there is little reason to expect adequate performance when the sentence is read rather than heard. If a learner can perform adequately with the oral statement and can decode fluently, then performance on written sentence storage will probably be adequate; however, it still should be checked.

DIRECT COMPREHENSION

Statement storage skill allows learners to answer a raft of questions which require use of all or part of the original material in a statement. For example, suppose learners read the statement "The students read their history text" and are asked the question "What did the students do?" The learners may answer the question with the original statement: "The students read their history text." This type of comprehension has been called literal comprehension by many. Engelmann & Stearns (1974) have called it mechanical comprehension since it requires a simple, mechanical operation to derive the answer. Whatever it is called, the principal characteristic of this type of comprehension is that the answer to a question is available directly from the original statement.

INDIRECT COMPREHENSION

The second general type of comprehension differs from direct comprehension in that the original statement may *not* be used to answer the question. Indirect comprehension requires that learners carry out some additional operation in order to derive the answer. Suppose a learner read, "There were five people in the room." A direct question would be

"How many people were in the room?" An indirect question would be "How many human legs were in the room?" This type of comprehension is required when learners must make inferences based on what they have read. Indirect comprehension includes types of comprehension sometimes referred to as drawing conclusions, using the context, inferential, etc. Again, when learners can accurately and fluently decode, can perform appropriately on the lower levels of comprehending, and can pass orally administered indirect comprehension items, then they are likely to be able to pass written indirect comprehension activities. However, it should not be assumed, but rather, checked.

FOLLOWING DIRECTIONS

When learners can perform adequately in statement storage and in direct and indirect comprehension, they should have most of the skills necessary to be able to perform adequately on even quite complex tasks. Many of the school-related comprehension activities require learners to follow written directions—e.g., "Make a list of the factors which contributed to the defeat of the Confederacy."

To be sure, one could construct an even more elaborate hierarchy of comprehending skills. But the purpose of the present analysis was to identify the essential initial rungs of the ladder. Higher level comprehension skills require mastery of these initial rungs. For example, consider the skill of critical reading. To support the critical reading assertion that an author was inconsistent, a reader must be able to show the passages (sentence storage) which were inconsistent and show the indirect comprehension illustrating the contradiction. Thus, critical reading can be defined in terms of the skills just presented.

Constructing test items which tap the types of comprehension discussed above does not entail laborious work. A teacher must simply ascertain whether a learner can (1) repeat sentences presented orally, (2) repeat sentences which have been read, (3) answer direct comprehension questions based on orally presented material, (4) answer direct comprehension questions based on what has been read, (5) answer direct questions based on orally presented material (6) answer indirect questions based on what has been read, (7) follow both simple and complex oral directions, and (8) follow both simple and complex written directions. When a student cannot pass items in one of these areas then instruction in that area is indicated.

SUMMARY

In this section, a potential system for evaluating reading performance has been proposed. It is based on an analysis of the essential skills in decoding and comprehending. For the diagnostician this analysis would provide an easily administered means of assessment, perhaps a checklist.

The test would be to determine simply whether a learner has mastered each succeeding rung on the ladder. The remedial implications are obvious: If a learner has not mastered a given rung then remediation should begin at that level.

PUBLISHED READING TESTS

Published tests are probably the most commonly used means for ascertaining reading level. Most of these instruments are standardized and, hence, should be considered in terms of the criteria implied in Chapter 3. Standardized reading tests should meet requirements for norming procedures, for reliability and its cousin standard error of measurement, and for administration directions. These topics will not be reiterated here; the reader who does not have a firm understanding of them should review Chapter 3.

There are several general attributes of published reading tests which can be discussed independently of psychometrics. Since they cut across many of the instruments, it is important to examine these characteristics in advance of the more detailed description of tests which follows.

The use of many standardized reading tests must be tempered by the very scores they yield. The information garnered from them is usually in terms of grade levels. This type of information may be useful for (1) crude assignment to curriculum levels, (2) possible assessment of the effects of instructional programs, (3) possible comparisons of different instructional programs (Becker & Engelmann, 1976), and (4) communicating to other professionals (Traxler, 1958). However, grade level information is not particularly useful for diagnostic purposes. Although grade levels may serve as crude information about placement, they do not indicate what skills learners have or do not have and hence what instruction is needed. In order to ascertain the reading skills of atypical learners one needs to gather information about skills rather than general performance. To be sure, some published assessment devices claim to provide diagnostic information. However, there are some questions about these tests; the questions will be discussed when descriptions of some diagnostic tests are presented.

The reading diagnostician who is using standardized instruments with atypical learners faces a problem that is related to the standardizing process. For the most part, standardization is accomplished with an emphasis on normal skill. One purpose of standardizing a test is derivation of norms. These norms are most applicable to the performance of learners who score near the center of the distribution (Cronbach, 1970). However, people concerned with the diagnosis of atypical learner performance deal with students who do not score near the center of the distribution (Hammill, 1971). One way around this problem, of course, is to select a test that is aimed at lower performing learners. The reasoning behind such a decision could be stated as: "I will give these fifth-grade students a primary level test so that their performance will be nearer the center of the test; that will give me a more accurate estimate of their skills." However, such reasoning fails in the face of the standardization process. Primary level reading tests are standardized on children who have primary level skills and are primary aged. Using a primary level test with older children virtually invalidates the test.

Two further problems with the use of standardized tests are particularly associated with the performance of atypical learners. They are related but somewhat separate. First, many reading tests—particularly those that attempt to measure comprehension of silent reading—are made up of multiple choice items. The learner reads a word or passage and then marks one choice from among several. For many items the learner may make the correct choice because he or she read and understood the item. However, for other items the learner may make the correct choice simply on the basis of chance (Robeck & Wilson, 1974; Strang, 1968). Brabner (1969) provided a table that is useful in determining the level of accuracy on a test necessary in order to rule out the possibility that a learner's score reflects chance. For example, on a 50-item test with each item having 4 alternative answers, a learner's score would have to be higher than 19 correct in order to rule out the possibility that a learner was simply guessing.

The related problem is concerned, again, with standardization. Some tests, particularly those that are designed for upper-elementary ages and above, have norms that only extend down to a particular grade level. As a consequence, learners with very low performance levels may fall all the way to the floor of the norms. When this happens, however, the learner is awarded the lowest grade-level score for the instrument. For example, suppose that a sixth-grader is given a test that has, as its floor, a grade-level equivalent of 2.8. If this learner answers zero questions correct on the test—even though he or she may have guessed on many items—then he or she receives the lowest score: 2.8. This score may be entirely spurious; the learner may not even be able to reliably decode the word "cat." But, according to the test results, the learner has second-grade, eighth-month skills. As a consequence, reading achievement tests probably overestimate reading skills (Bradley, 1976; Strang, 1968).

The final point to be made about standardized tests is that they are often tests of silent reading abilities. As such, they do not necessarily indicate a great deal about the learners' decoding skills. As has been argued previously, decoding is the first and essential skill in reading. To be sure, silent reading is probably an important skill. But, for the reading diagnostician, the task is finding out about reader competence at the various skill levels suggested in the previous section. Without knowledge about these competencies the diagnostician has virtually no indication about where to start the remedial process.

These concerns about standardized tests should be kept in mind as the reader proceeds through the following subsections in which some published reading tests are considered. The tests are arranged under four headings: individually administered achievement tests, group administered achievement tests, individually administered diagnostic tests, and group administered diagnostic tests. Admittedly, this organization is somewhat arbitrary; some tests may be given to a group or an individual; some tests yield both achievement and diagnostic scores. However, this organization does lend structure to the vast array of reading assessment instruments. It does not require value judgments about the instruments, yet it provides diagnosticians with entry points to the assessment literature that are likely to correspond to their day-to-day problems.

As Miller pointed out in Chapter 3 of this volume, there are two sources of information about tests and testing with which anyone using tests should be familiar: *Standards for Educational and Psychological Tests* (American Psychological Association, 1974) and the *Mental Measurements Yearbooks* (Buros, 1938–1972). For those interested in reading tests, *Reading: Tests and Reviews II* (Buros, 1975) is probably the most useful source. It contains descriptions of instruments, reviews from the 1972 *Mental Measurements Yearbook,* references to previous *Yearbooks,* and references to other literature sources.

Individual Reading Achievement Tests

Many individually administered reading achievement tests have an advantage not available from group tests: They require the learner to read aloud. (Of course, some other reading tests also require oral reading. Some of them are described in the later subsection on individual diagnostic tests.) One reason this is advantageous is that oral reading provides the tester with the opportunity to test a behavior that is very closely related to the criterion skill. Gilmore & Gilmore's (1968) data indicate that particularly with less capable readers—that is, younger or disabled readers—there are high correlations between oral and silent reading abilities. Zintz (1975) argued that oral reading skills are very important for remedial readers. Another reason oral testing is advantageous is that it provides an opportunity to analyze errors. However, error analysis may be of dubious value (Becker & Engelmann, 1976; Della-Piana & Herlin, 1964; Wells, 1950).

The general form of individually administered reading tests that require oral performance is a series of increasingly difficult passages or words. The following paragraphs describe several such instruments.

The *Gilmore Oral Reading Test* (Gilmore & Gilmore, 1968) is available in two forms and is composed of paragraphs of increasing difficulty, one for each of 10 levels. The first seven paragraphs relate an event and the last three discuss a content area topic. Decoding errors are recorded in a code similar to the one shown in Table 9-2. Each selection is followed by five direct comprehension questions. The test can be administered in about 20 minutes and yields three scores: accuracy, comprehension, and rate. The first two scores are expressed in grade level equivalents; the last score is expressed in a rating. Spache (1976) has criticized the lack of data about the actual reading levels of the passages, suggesting that their readability ought to be determined. Bradley (1976) has indicated that the *Gilmore* overestimates skills in comparison with IRIs, but Silberberg — Silberberg (1977) found that it underestimates skills in the comparisons which they made.

The *Gray Oral Reading Tests* (Gray, 1967) are also oral passage reading tests. The battery is composed of 13 selections ranging from first grade to college level. There are four forms of the *Gray*. Like the *Gilmore,* the *Gray* can be administered in a short period of time. The test yields only a grade equivalent score for accuracy; the percentage of comprehension questions answered correctly is tabulated but not converted to grade equivalents. Errors are recorded in a code similar to the one shown in Table 9-2. However, the *Gray* differentiates between gross and partial mispronunciations, and this has been the subject of some criticism (Hardin & Ames, 1969). Also, testing oral reading at upper grade levels when most classroom reading is done silently was questioned by Spache (1976). Harris (1970) claimed that the *Gray's* use of different norms for girls than for boys was indefensible.

The *Peabody Individual Achievement Test (PIAT)* (Dunn & Markwardt, 1970) includes two subtests focused on reading. The reading recognition subtest requires that the learner match letters in a multiple choice format, name letters, and read words aloud from a list. The reading comprehension subtest requires that the learner read a sentence and then select from four pictures the one that corresponds to the meaning of the sentence. These two subtests require less than 15 minutes to administer. The *PIAT* is designed for use with learners from kindergarten through twelfth grade. Spache (1976) discussed this test at length.

The Wide Range Achievement Test (WRAT) (Jastak, Bijou, & Jastak, 1965) is a general battery that includes a reading section. It covers reading skills from prekindergarten to college, dividing them into two levels depending upon age (learners 12 years or older are tested on level two). The reading test is basically a word list with increasingly more difficult items that the learner reads aloud to the examiner. For learners who make an error within the first 10 words or for those younger than 8 years of age, there are preliminary parts of the test which require the learner to name and match capital letters. The *WRAT* is easy and quick to administer. Although it has been maligned because it appears to be a simple word recognition device, it enjoys a robust reputation and continually produces high coefficients of reliability and validity. Spache (1976) discussed the *WRAT* in some detail, criticizing the face validity of the instrument.

These tests are not, of course, the only individual reading achievement tests. As mentioned before, many of the tests considered under the heading individual diagnostic tests also report grade equivalency scores. Consequently, they may also provide information for the purpose of making placement decisions. Also, several other tests might fit into the above category: the *Individual Reading Placement Inventory* (Smith & Bradtmueller, 1969); the *Slosson Oral Reading Test* (Slosson, 1963), and *Standard Reading Inventory* (McCracken, 1966).

However, the decisions about placement that are made on the basis of any test are decisions that should meet certain requirements. In large part, these requirements concern the reliability of the instruments used. In placing exceptional learners into special programs—one way in which the results of reading tests may be used—a prominent concern should be the reduction of inappropriate placements. Nunnally (1967) has recommended that test devices used for making decisions about people should have at least 0.90 reliability coefficients. As well, attempts to make differential diagnoses on the basis of subtest differences require high levels of reliability. Reliability contributes to the determination of standard errors of measurement. If the difference between subtests is less than two standard errors of measurement, then there is little reasonable basis for saying that the learner is weak in one area and strong in another. For the most part, the tests discussed individually in the above paragraphs have fairly high reliabilities (i.e., $r \geqslant 0.70$). While this level of reliability does not measure up to Nunnally's standard, it is high enough to indicate some dependability.

Group Reading Achievement Tests

Unlike most individually administered tests, group tests usually do not require oral reading performance; it would be difficult to monitor the reading accuracy of a group. Consequently, group tests must depend upon silent reading performance and are not as precise an estimate of reading accuracy. The emphasis in group tests is placed more heavily on comprehension. While this may be an appropriate strategy for assessing the skills of older, competent readers, it may be questionable for assessing the skills of atypical learners who do not read well. More specifically, when learners fail an item that requires comprehension of silently read material, it is possible that the failure may have occurred for at least two reasons: faulty decoding and/or faulty understanding. For the most part, silent reading tests do not provide an opportunity to check the source of errors.

Group administered reading tests are usually used as overall checks on reading progress (i.e., September and June testing). As such, they primarily serve as gross screening instruments. It is often suggested that learners who perform poorly on these tests should be subjected to more detailed assessment via individual diagnostic testing.

The *California Achievement Tests: Reading (CAT)* (Tiegs & Clark, 1970), part of a larger achievement battery, are designed for use with learners in grades 1 through 12. These tests are organized into 5 levels (I: grades 1.5 to 2; II: grades 2 to 4; III: grades 4 to 6; IV: grades 6 to 9; V: grades 9 to 12). Three reading scores—vocabulary, comprehension, and total—result from the *CAT*. The tests take about 65 minutes to administer, depending on the level used.

The *Gates-MacGinitie Reading Tests* (Gates & MacGinitie, 1965) are designed for use with learners in grades 1 through 9. There are 6 levels of the tests (Primary A: grade 1; Primary B; grade 2; Primary C: grade 3; Primary CS: grades 2.5 to 3; Survey D: grades 4 to 6; Survey : grades 7 to 9). Two editions of Surveys D and E are available. Primary A, B, and C yield vocabulary and comprehension scores. Primary CS yields speed and accuracy, vocabulary, and comprehension scores. Each level requires about 45 to 60 minutes to administer and is given in two sessions.

The *Metropolitan Achievement Tests* (Durost, Bixler, Wrightstone, Prescott, & Balow, 1971) include reading sections. The Metropolitan is available in several levels (Primary I: grades 1.5 to 2.4; Primary 2: grades 2.5 to 3.4; Elementary: grades 3.5 to 4.9; Intermediate: grades 5.0 to 6.9; and Advanced: grades 7.0 to 9.5) and has alternate forms. At each level the test yields word knowledge, reading, and total scores. Administration requires about 40 to 60 minutes, depending on the level given.

The *Stanford Reading Tests* (Madden, Gardner, Rudman, Kelly, & Merwin, 1973) are part of a larger achievement battery. There are five levels (Primary 1: grades 1.5 to 2.4; Primary 2: grades 2.5 to 3.9; Intermediate 1: grades 4.0 to .4; Intermediate 2: grades 5.5 to 6.9; and Advanced: grades 7.0 to 9.9). Each level is available in three forms. The Primary 1 level yields scores in word reading, paragraph meaning, vocabulary, and word study skills. The Primary 2 level yields scores in word meaning, paragraph meaning, and word study skills. The Intermediate 1 and 2 levels yield scores in word meaning and paragraph meaning. The Advanced level yields a paragraph meaning score only. The tests require 35 to 95 minutes to administer depending on the level used. Traxler (1958) regarded these tests as the best available series of instruments for annual or semiannual assessment of elementary and junior high school pupils' reading achievement.

For the student of reading tests there are abundant sources of information about the above instruments. In addition to seeking out reviews in the *Mental Measurements Yearbooks* (Buros, 1938–1972), one could consult Farr & Anastasiow (1969), Farr & Roelke (1971), Potts (1968), Robeck & Wilson (1974), Robinson & Hanson (1968), Trela (1967), and myriad other sources for more detailed information. The reliabilities of these instruments, as reported in their manuals, spread from 0.70 to 0.95. Generally, these are in the acceptable range, however, the test user should consult the manuals carefully in order to determine which test might be most useful.

Individual Diagnostic Tests

It is likely that individual diagnostic tests are the most popular reading tests for use in assessing the reading skills of atypical learners. Their popularity probably stems from their similarity to IRIs and the fact that most of them produce scores other than vocabulary and comprehension. Some of them require oral reading and may have an advantage for the reasons discussed previously. Others attempt to produce scores that allow pinpointing of areas of difficulty (e.g., final sound mistakes); whether the areas pinpointed have direct remedial utility is open to question.

In the following paragraphs, several individual diagnostic tests are described. The interested reader would be wise to peruse copies of the instruments and study the outside sources cited in these paragraphs and at the end of the section.

The *Botel Reading Inventory* (Botel, 1970) may not be considered a diagnostic test by some, but others (i.e., Otto, McMenemy, & Smith, 1973; Spache, 1976) have treated it as such. The *Botel* is similar to an IRI in that it yields independent, instructional, and frustration levels over three subtests (word recognition, word opposites reading, and spelling placement) and yields an estimate of phonics mastery on one subtest (phonics mastery test). Different subtests are appropriate for different grade-age learners; in general, the entire battery may be used with students in grades one through four. In all, the battery takes about 30 minutes to administer, but the time may vary depending on learner skills. Spache (1976) discussed the content, construct, and concurrent validity of the *Botel*.

The *Durrell Analysis of Reading Difficulty* (Durrell, 1955) was designed for use with learners in grades one through six. It yields seven subscores: oral reading, silent reading, listening comprehension, flash words, word analysis, spelling, and handwriting. The structure of the *Durrell* is supposed to provide the diagnostician with an opportunity to estimate potential (via listening comprehension) and compare it with performance. The entire battery may take more than an hour to administer and requires considerable practice. Spache (1976), in addition to discussing the psychometric qualities of the Durrell, criticized it for dependence on decoding rate and use of 1937 norms in the 1955 revision.

The *Gates-McKillop Reading Diagnostic Tests* (Gates & McKillop, 1962) have been called the most comprehensive diagnostic reading battery (Otto, McNememey, & Smith, 1973; Spache, 1976). This is understandable since the Gates-McKillop yields 28 scores: omissions, additions, repetitions, mispronunciations (reversals, partial reversals, total reversals, wrong beginnings, wrong middle, wrong ending, wrong in several parts, total), oral reading total, words—flash presentation, words—untimed presentation, phrases—flash presentation, recognizing and blending common word parts, giving letter sounds, naming capital letters, naming lowercase letters, recognizing the visual form of sounds (nonsense words, initial letters, final letters, vowels), auditory blending, spelling, oral vocabulary, syllabication, and auditory discrimination. As discussed below, some of these subtests are of questionable value. Obviously, administering the entire battery would require a great deal of time and considerable expertise. It is designed for use with second through sixth graders and has two forms.

The *Diagnostic Reading Scales* (Spache, 1972) are presented at three levels: kindergarten through fourth grades, fourth through eighth grades, and seventh through thirteenth grades. In his text, Spache (1976) described the scales as being useful for normal readers in the elementary grades and retarded readers in all grades. There are various subscales for each of the three levels. In general, they include word recognition lists, graduated difficulty reading passages, and supplementary tests of phonic knowledge, blending, initial consonant substitution, and auditory discrimination. Harris (1970) criticized the instrument for adopting criteria percentages for determining reading levels (i.e., independent, instructional, and frustration) that are lower than those commonly used. Ramsey (1967) criticized the phonics sections for testing skills that are not directly involved in the act of reading. Spache (1976) defended the test against these criticisms.

The *Woodcock Reading Mastery Tests (WRMT)* (Woodcock, 1973) are a relatively new battery. They are for use with kindergarten through twelfth graders. Six areas are assessed: letter naming, word identification, nonsense word attack, word comprehension, passage comprehension, and total. For each of these areas, several scores may be derived: grade equivalent, percentile rank, age scores, and four levels of criterion scores (easy reading level, reading grade level, failure reading level, and relative mastery of grade level). The battery requires about 30 minutes to administer. Since they are relatively new, the *WRMT* have not been extensively discussed. However, the manual presents reliability data, and Proger (1975) has reviewed the tests.

There are, of course, other individual diagnostic reading instruments such as the *Standard Reading Inventory* (McCracken, 1966) and the *Classroom Reading Inventory* (Silvaroli, 1965). In general, diagnostic reading tests are subject to a number of criticisms in spite of their current popularity. First, a number of subtests attempt to assess skills that are tangentially related to reading problems. Letter naming, for example, may correlate highly with reading skill, but it does not cause reading skill (Samuels, 1970, 1972); ability to indicate what letter begins a spoken word (encoding) does not guarantee ability to reliably produce the speech sound when seeing the symbol (decoding) (Bateman, 1973). Second, there is a question concerning the stability of error scores over time (Becker & Engelmann, 1976). If a learner's scores are highly variable, then any diagnosis based on those scores may be questionable. Presumably, this variability should be revealed in instrument reliability. However, only two of these tests—the *Diagnostic Reading Scales* and the *Woodcock Reading Mastery Tests*—report reliabilities for their subtests in the manuals. For the most part the reported reliabilities are high and acceptable.

Further discussion of these and other instruments may be found in Eller & Altea (1966), Farr (1970), Farr & Anastasiow (1969), Harris (1970), Ramsey (1967), Spache (1976), and Winkley (1971). Buros' (1975) *Reading: Tests and Reviews* is probably the best single source on the subject; in it are descriptions, reviews, and references on innumerable instruments.

Group Diagnostic Tests

Group diagnostic devices are an attempt to provide the type of information that would be available from individual diagnostic tests (e.g., subtest scores of skill in isolated areas) without the cost in terms of time required by the individually administered instruments. As with group achievement tests, group diagnostic devices cannot, by their very nature, sample the critical skills involved in oral reading. They usually have subtests that are designed to tap common problems (e.g., reversals) in reading. They face the same constraints that are faced by all standardized instruments. They must be highly reliable, the subtests must not correlate highly, and decisions based on them must be made with a wary eye on measurement problems. The references within the descriptions and at the end of the section provide the interested reader with sources for further study.

The *Doren Diagnostic Reading Test of Word Recognition Skills* (Doren, 1973) is designed to measure word recognition skills. Subtests focus on the following skills: letter recognition, beginning sounds, ending sounds, vowels, blending, rhyming, whole-word recognition, words-within-words, sight words, speech consonants, and context guessing. The skills involved are assumed to be appropriate for learners in grades one through four. Spache (1976) has criticized the instrument for its lack of subtest norms.

The *McCullough Word Analysis Tests* (McCullough, 1963) include seven subtests: initial blends and diagraphs, phonetic discrimination, matching letters to vowel sounds, sounding whole words, interpreting symbols, dividing words into syllables, and root words in affixed forms. In addition to scores on each of these subtests, an overall score may be derived, and summary scores over the first five (phonetic) and/or the last two (structural) subtests may be determined. Hence, there are ten scores available. The *McCullough* is designed for use with learners in grades four through six and requires about 70 minutes to administer. Harris said that "These are practical, useful tests of reasonable length" (1970, p. 162).

The *Silent Reading Diagnostic Tests* (Bond, Cleymer, & Hoyt, 1955) are designed to yield diagnostic information from silent reading. The battery includes tests named (1) Word Recognition, (2) Recognition of Words in Context, (3) Recognition of Reversable Words in Context, (4) Word-Recognition Techniques: Visual Analysis—Locating Usable Elements, (5) Word-Recognition Techniques: Visual Analysis—Syllabication, (6) Word-Recognition Techniques: Visual Analysis—Locating Root Words, (7) Phonetic Knowledge—General Word Elements, (8) Recognition of Beginning Sounds, (9) Rhyming Words, (10) Letters Sounds, and (11) Word Synthesis. (The tests are not entirely silent, however, areas 7 to 11 require examiner pronunciations.) The *Silent Reading Diagnostic Tests* are designed to be used with third through sixth graders and require about 90 minutes to complete. Provision is made so that an individual's scores on the subtests may be profiled.

The *Standard Diagnostic Reading Test* (Karlsen, Madden, & Gardner, 1968) is made up of several subtests on two levels: mid-2nd through mid-4th and mid-4th through mid-8th grades. Level 1 yields seven scores: comprehension, vocabulary, auditory discrimination, syllabication, beginning and ending sounds, blending, and sound discrimination. Level 2 yields eight scores: literal comprehension, inferential comprehension, total comprehension, vocabulary, syllabication, sound discrimination, blending, and rate. Spache (1976) argued that high correlations among the subtests make it doubtful that the subtest scores reflect independent skills.

As pointed out previously, it is questionable that one can derive any useful information from individually administered, standardized diagnostic tests, because for example, readers make different errors on a second reading of a passage than they made on the first reading. It seems even less likely that a group test would provide useful information. Furthermore, some subtests of the above instruments assess skills that are logically *un*related to reading (e.g., if learners can mark the letter that stands for the first sound heard in a word it is not assured that seeing that letter they make the appropriate sound). For the most part, the four instruments described above are lacking in rigorous psychometric qualities. Some of the subtests have high reliability and validity coefficients, but most do not. Diagnosticians should look closely at the test manuals for documentation of high reliabilities.

SUMMARY

A number of approaches to the assessment of reading skills have been discussed in this chapter. Informal reading inventories which are passages or lists of material that increase in difficulty are one means of deriving an estimated grade level of reading performance. They may reveal diagnostic information from an analysis of errors, but the usefulness of such information is questionable. Widely used, traditional reading tests also provide an estimate of grade level performance. Some of these provide useful diagnostic information about atypical learners' mastery of reading skills, but many tests skills are tangentially related to reading. Behaviorally-based assessment is not designed to identify the grade level performance of readers, but rather to reveal learners' performance in situations that closely resemble actual reading conditions. With behaviorally-based systems it is necessary to establish admittedly arbitrary criterion levels of performance. Essential skills assessment, which is closely allied with behaviorally-based assessment, also does not provide estimates of grade level performance. Instead, the degree of mastery of essential reading skills is considered against criterion levels. Specific information with direct remedial implications is immediately revealed under essential skills assessment.

For teachers and diagnosticians concerned with assessing the reading performance of atypical learners, probably the truest test of an assessment scheme is whether it provides directly applicable remedial information. Does the information derived from the assessment indicate what the learners need to know in order to have improved reading skills? If the learners do poorly in an area tested and the teacher provides remediation so that the learners no longer do poorly in that area, can we be assured that the learners' overall reading ability will improve as a consequence? When questions such as these can be answered positively then the assessment scheme probably provides useful information.

On the basis of the information presented in the present chapter it is possible to outline a general assessment scheme for use with atypical readers. The scheme would incorporate both grade level and diagnostic measures. It would require the learner to read orally, and it would provide a means for continuous monitoring of reading behaviors. In general, this scheme would include one or two individually administered achievement tests such as the *Gilmore,* the *Gray,* or the *WRAT,* an assessment of essential skills in order to pinpoint areas for remediation, and the establishment of an on-going, behaviorally-based monitoring system.

Of course, this assessment scheme would be unwieldly for identifying students with reading problems. For crude screening the common group achievement tests probably are appropriate. However, the assessment scheme presented above is concerned with providing information that leads to remedial planning rather than crude screening.

Atypical learners are usually behind their age peers in mastery of reading skills. Their major task is to learn as much as possible as quickly as possible. Otherwise, there is little opportunity to catch up to their age peers or, at least, to narrow the gap between their performance and the performance of typical learners. To expedite the process of catching up in reading it is important to identify precisely what the learners do not know and, therefore, what they must learn.

REFERENCES

American Psychological Association. *Standards for educational and psychological tests* (Rev. ed.). Washington, D.C.: American Psychological Association, 1974.

Bannatyne, A. Diagnosing learning disabilities and writing remedial prescriptions. *Journal of Learning Disabilities,* 1968, *4,* 28–35.

Baron, J. Phonemic stage ot necessary for reading. *Quarterly Journal of Experimental Psychology,* 1973, *25,* 241–246.

Bateman, B. D. Three approaches to diagnosis and educational planning for children with learning problems. *Academic Therapy,* 1967, *2,* 215-222.

Bateman, B. D. *Essentials of teaching.* Sioux Falls, S.D.: Adapt Press, 1971.

Bateman, B. D. Reading: A non-meaningful process. In B. Bateman (Ed.), *Reading performance and how to achieve it.* Seattle: Bernie Straub and Special Child Publications, 1973.

Bateman, B. D. Teaching reading to learning disabled children. Reading Conference, University of Pittsburgh, April, 1976.

Beck, I. L. & Mitroff, D. D.: *The rationale and design of a primary grades reading system for an individualized classroom*. Pittsburgh: Learning Research and Development Center, University of Pittsburgh, 1972.

Becker, W. C. & Engelmann, S. *Teaching 3: Evaluation of instruction*. Chicago: Science Research Associates, 1976.

Betts, E. A. *Foundations of reading instruction*. New York: American Book, 1946.

Bishop, C. H. Transfer effects of word and letter training. *Journal of Verbal Learning and Verbal Behavior,* 1964, *3,* 215–221.

Bliesmer, E. P. & Yarborough, B. H. A comparison of ten different beginning reading programs in first grade. *Phi Delta Kappa,* 1965, *56,* 500–504.

Bond, G., Cleymer, T., & Hoyt, C. *Silent Reading Diagnostic Tests*. Chicago: Lyons and Carnahan, 1955.

Bormuth, J. R. The cloze readability procedure. *Elementary English,* 1968, *45,* 429–436.

Botel, M. *Botel Reading Inventory*. Chicago: Follett Publishing, 1970.

Brabner, G. Reading skills. In R. M. Smith (Ed.), *Teacher diagnosis of educational difficulties*. Columbus, Ohio: Charles E. Merrill, 1969.

Bradley, J. M. Evaluating reading achievement for placement in special education. *Journal of Special Education,* 1976, *10,* 237–245.

Burmeister, L. Usefulness of phonic generalizations. *Reading Teacher,* 1968a, *21,* 239–356.

Burmeister, L. Vowel pairs. *Reading Teacher,* 1968b, *21,* 445–452.

Buros, O. K. (Ed.) *Mental measurements yearbooks*. (7 vols.) Highland Park, N.J.: Gryphon Press, 1938–1972.

Buros, O. K. (Ed.) *Reading: Tests and reviews II*. Highland Park, N.J.: Gryphon Press, 1975.

Bush, W. J. & Giles, M. T. *Aids to psycholinguistic teaching*. Columbus, Ohio: Charles E. Merrill, 1969.

Carnine, D. W. Phonics versus look-say: Transfer to new words. *Reading Teacher,* 1977, *30,* 636–640.

Cawley, J., Goodstein, H., & Burrow, W. *The slow learner and the reading problem*. Springfield, Ill.: Charles C. Thomas, 1972.

Chall, J. *Learning to read: The great debate*. San Francisco: McGraw-Hill, 1967.

Clay, M. M. Reading errors and self-correction behaviors. *British Journal of Educational Psychology,* 1967, *2,* 11–31.

Cronbach, L. J. *Essentials of psychological testingal (3rd ed.). New York: Harper & Row, 1970.*

Dale, E. & Chall, J. A formula for predicting readability. Columbus, Ohio: Ohio State University, Bureau of Educational Research, 1948.

Della-Piana, G. & Herlin, W. Are normative oral reading errors profiles necessary? In J. Figurel (Ed.), *Improvement of reading through classroom practice*. Newark, Del.: International Reading Association, 1964.

Deverell, A. F. The learnable features of English orthography. In B. Bateman (Ed.), *Learning disorders* (Vol. 4). Seattle: Special Child Publications, 1971.

Doren, M. *Doren Diagnostic Reading Test of Word Recognition Skills* (2nd ed.). Circle Pines, Minn.: American Guidance Service, 1973.

Dunn, L. & Markwardt, F. *Peabody Individual Achievement Test*. Circle Pines, Minn.: American Guidance Service, 1970.

Durost, W. N., Bixler, H. H., Wrightstone, J. W., Prescott, G. A., & Balow, I. H. *Metropolitan Achievement Tests*. New York: Harcourt Brace Jovanovich, 1971.

Durrell, D. D. *Durrell Analysis of Reading Difficulty* (Rev. Ed.). New York: Harcourt, Brace, & World, 1955.

Dykstra, R. The effectiveness of code-and-meaning-emphasis beginning reading program. *Reading Teacher,* 1968, *22,* 17–23.

Ekwall, E. E. Should repetitions be counted as errors? *Reading Teacher,* 1974, *27,* 265–367.

Eller, W. & Altea, M. Three diagnostic reading tests: Some comparisons. In J. A. Figurel (Ed.), *Vistas in reading.* International Reading Association Conference Proceedings, II, Part II, 1966, 562–566.

Engelmann, S. Teaching reading to children with low mental ages. *Education and Training of the Mentally Retarded,* 1967, *2,* 193–201.

Engelmann, S. & Bruner, E. *DISTAR reading I and II.* Chicago: Science Research Associates, 1973.

Engelmann, S. & Stearns, S.: *All about criterion-referenced tests: What they are, how to use them, and how to construct them.* Eugene, Ore.: Engelmann-Becker Learning Center, 1974.

Engelmann, S. & Stearns, S. *DISTAR reading III.* Chicago: Science Research Associations, 1973.

Farr, R. (Ed.), *Measurement and evaluation of reading.* New York: Harcourt Brace Jovanovich, 1970.

Farr, R. & Anastasiow, N. *Tests of reading readiness and achievements.* Newark, Del.: International Reading Association, 1969.

Farr, R. & Roelke, P. Measuring subskills in reading: Intercorrelations among standardized reading tests, teachers' ratings and reading specialists ratings. *Journal of Educational Measurement,* 1971, *8,* 27–32.

Flesch, R. *How to test readability.* New York: Harper & Row, 1949.

Frostig, M., Lefever, D., & Whittlesey, J. *The Marianne Frostig Developmental Test of Visual Perception.* Palo Alto, Ca.: Consulting Psychology Press, 1964.

Fry, E. A readability formula that saves time: Readability graph. *Journal of Reading,* 1968, *11,* 513–516.

Gagné, R. M. *The conditions of learning* (2nd ed.). New York: Holt, 1970.

Gagné, R. M. *Essentials of learning for instruction.* Hinsdale, Ill.: Dryden Press, 1974.

Gates, A. I. & MacGinitie, W. H. *Gates-MacGinitie Reading Tests.* New York: Teachers College Press, 1965.

Gates, A. I. & McKillop, A. S. *Gates-McKillop Reading Diagnostic Tests.* New York: Teachers College Press, 1962.

Gibson, E. & Levin, H. *The psychology of reading.* Cambridge, Mass.: MIT Press, 1975.

Gillespie, D. H. & Johnson, L. *Teaching reading to the mildly retarded child.* Columbus, Ohio: Charles E. Merrill, 1974.

Gilmore, J. V. & Gilmore, E. C. *Gilmore Oral Reading Tests.* Indianapolis: Bobbs-Merrill, 1968.

Glass, G. G. Perceptual conditioning for decoding: Rationale and method. In B. Bateman (Ed.), *Learning disorders* (Vol. 4). Seattle: Special Child Publications, 1971.

Gleitman, L. & Rozin, P. Teaching reading by the use of a syllabary. *Reading Research Quarterly,* 1973, *8,* 448–483.

Goodman, K. Reading: A psycholinguistic guessing game. *Journal of the Reading Specialist,* 1967, *4,* 126–135.

Gough, P. One second of reading. In J. Kavanagh and I. Mattingly (Eds.), *Language by ear and by eye.* Cambridge, Mass.: MIT Press, 1972.

Gray, W. S. *Gray Oral Reading Test.* In H. M. Robinson (Ed.), Indianapolis: Bobbs-Merrill, 1967.

Gurren, L. & Hughes, A. Intensive phonics vs. gradual phoncs in beginning reading: A review. *Journal of Educational Research,* 1965, *58,* 339–346.

Hall, R. V. *Managing behavior,* Part 1. Lawrence, Ks.: H. & H. Enterprises, 1971.

Iallahan, D. P. & Kauffman, J. M. *Introduction to learning disabilities: A psychobehavioral approach.* Englewood Cliffs, N.J.: Prentice-Hall, 1976.

Iammill, D. D. Evaluating children for instructional purposes. *Academic Therapy,* 1971, *6,* 341–353.

Iammill, D. D. Training visual perceptual processes. *Journal of Learning Disabilities,* 1972, *5,* 552–559.

Iammill, D. D. & Larsen, S. The effectiveness of psycholinguistic training. *Exceptional Children,* 1974a, *41,* 5–14.

Iammill, D. D. & Larsen, S. The relationship of selected auditory perceptual skills and reading ability. *Journal of Learning Disabilities,* 1974b, *7,* 429–436.

Iammill, D. D. & Wiederholt, J. L. Review of the Frostig Visual Perception Test and the related training program. In L. Mann & D. Sabatino (Eds.), *First review of special education* (Vol. 1). New York: Grune & Stratton, 1973.

Ianna, P., Hanna, J., Hodges, R., & Rudorf, E., Jr. *Phoneme-grapheme correspondences as cues to spelling improvement.* Washington, D.C.: United States Government Printing Office, 1966.

Iardin, V. & Ames, W. A comparison of the results of two reading tests. *Reading Teacher,* 1969, *22,* 329–334.

Iaring, N. & Bateman, B. *Teaching the learning disabled child.* Englewood Cliffs, N.J.: Prentice-Hall, 1977.

Iarris, A. *How to increase reading ability* (5th ed.). New York: David McKay, 1970.

Iughes, A., Carcus, M., & Trace, A. *The Open Court basic reading program.* LaSalle, Ill.: Open Court Publishing, 1971.

astak, J. F., Bijou, S. W., & Jastak, S. R. *Wide Range Achievement Test.* Wilmington, Del.: Guidance Associates, 1965.

effery, W. E. & Samuels, S. J. Effect of method of reading training on initial learning and transfer. *Journal of Verbal Learning and Verbal Behavior,* 1967, *6,* 354–358.

ohns, J. L., Garton, S., Schoenfelder, P., & Skirba, P. *Assessing reading behavior: Informal reading inventories.* Newark, Del.: International Reading Association, 1977.

ohnson, M. S. Reading inventories for classroom use.. *Reading Teacher,* 1960, *14,* 9–13.

ohnson, M. & Kress, R. *Informal reading inventories.* Newark, Del.: International Reading Association, 1965.

Kaluger, G. & Kolson, C. J. *Reading and learning disabilities.* Columbus, Ohio: Charles E. Merrill, 1969.

Karlsen, B., Madden, R., & Gardner, E. F. *Stanford Diagnostic Reading Test.* New York: Harcourt Brace Jovanovich, 1968.

Karnes, M. *Goal program language development game.* Springfield, Mass.: Milton Bradley, 1972.

Kirk, S. A. In J. M. Kauffman & D. P. Hallahan (Eds.), *Teaching children with learning disabilities: Personal perspectives.* Columbus, Ohio: Charles E. Merrill, 1976.

Kirk, S. A. & Kirk W. *Psycholinguistic learning disabilities: Diagnosis and remediation.* Urbana, Ill.: University of Illinois Press, 1971.

Kirk, S. A., McCarthy, J. J., & Kirk, W. D. *Illinois Test of Psycholinguistic Abilities* (Rev. ed.). Urbana, Ill.: University of Illinois Press, 1968.

Kolers, P. Three stages of reading. In H. Levin and J. P. Williams (Eds.), *Basic studies on reading.* New York: Basic Books, 1970.

Kunzelmann, H. P. (Ed.) *Precision teaching.* Seattle: Special Child Publications, 1970.

LaBerge, D. & Samuels, S. J. Toward a theory of automatic information processing in reading. *Cognitive Psychology,* 1974, *6,* 293–323.

LaPray, M. & Ross, R. The graded word list: A quick list of reading ability. *Journal of Reading,* 1969, *12,* 305–307.

Learner, J. W. *Children with learning disabilities* (Rev. ed.). Boston: Houghton Mifflin, 1976.

Liberman, I. Y., Shankweiler, D., & Orlando, C. Letter confusions and reversals of sequence in the beginning reader: Implications for Orton's theory of developmental dyslexia. *Cortex,* 1971, *7,* 127–142.

Lovitt, T. C. Assessment of children with learning disabilities. *Exceptional Children,* 1967, *34,* 233–239.

Lovitt, T. C. Applied behavior analysis and learning disabilities: Part 1. *Journal of Learning Disabilities,* 1975, *8,* 432–443.

Lovitt, T. C. Applied behavior analysis techniques and curriculum research: Implications for instruction. In N. G. Norris & R. L. Schiefelbusch (Eds.), *Training special children.* New York: McGraw-Hill, 1976.

Lovitt, T. C. & Hansen, C. L. Round one—placing the child in the right reader. *Journal of Learning Disabilities,* 1976a, *9,* 347–353.

Lovitt, T. C. & Hansen, C. L. The use of contingent skipping and drilling to improve oral reading and comprehension. *Journal of Learning Disabilities,* 1976b, *9,* 481–487.

Madden, R., Gardner, E. F., Rudman, H. C., Kelly, T. L., & Merwin, J. *Stanford Achievement Test* (Rev. ed.). New York: Harcourt Brace Jovanovich, 1973.

Mann, L. Psychometric phrenology and the new faculty psychology: The case against ability assessment and training. *Journal of Special Education,* 1971, *5,* 3–14.

Mann, L. & Phillips, W. Fractional practices in special education. *Exceptional Children,* 1967, *33,* 311–317.

Marchbanks, G. & Levin, H. Cues by which children recognize words. *Journal of Educational Psychology,* 1965, *56,* 57–61.

Matthews, M. M. *Teaching to read: Historically considered.* Chicago: University of Chicago Press, 1966.

McCracken, G. & Walcutt, C. *Basic reading.* Philadelphia: J. B. Lippincott, 1963, 1970, and 1976.

McCracken, R. *Standard Reading Inventory.* Klamath Falls, Ore.: Klamath Printing, 1966.

McCullough, C. M. *McCullough Word Analysis Tests.* Princeton, N.J.: Personnal Press, 1963.

Minskoff, E. H., Wiseman, D. E., & Minskoff, J. G. *The MWM Program for Developing Language Abilities.* Ridgefield, N.J.: Educational Performance Associates, 1972.

Money, J. *Reading disability.* Baltimore: John Hopkins Press, 1962.

Monroe, M. *Children who cannot read.* Chicago: University of Chicago Press, 1932a.

Monroe, M. *Diagnostic reading examination.* Chicago: C. H. Stoelting, 1932b.

Newcomer, P. & Hammill, D. ITPA and academic achievement: A survey. *Reading Teacher,* 1975, *28,* 731–741.

Nunnally, J. *Psychometric theory.* New York: McGraw-Hill, 1967.

Orton, S. T. *Reading, writing, and spelling problems in children.* New York: Norton, 1937.

Otto, W., McMenemy, R. A., & Smith, R. J. *Corrective and remedial teaching* (2nd Ed.). Boston: Houghton Mifflin, 1973.

Potts, M. A comparison of vocabulary introduced in several first-grade readers to that of two primary reading tests. *Journal of Educational Research,* 1968, *61,* 285.

Potts, M. & Savino, C. The relative achievement of first graders under three different reading programs. *The Journal of Educational Research,* 1968, *61,* 447–450.

Proger, B. Test review number 18: Woodcock Reading Mastery Tests. *Journal of Special Education,* 1975, *9,* 439–444.

Proger, B. B., Cross, L. H., & Burger, R. M. Construct validation of standardized tests in special education: A framework of reference and application to ITPA research. In L. Mann & D. Sabatino (Eds.), *First review of special education* (Vol. 1). New York: Grune & Stratton, 1973.

Ramsey, W. The values and limitations of diagnostic reading tests for evaluation in the classroom. In T. C. Barrett (Ed.). *The evaluation of children's reading achievement*. Perspectives in Reading, No. 8. Newark, Del.: International Reading Association, 1967, pp. 65–78.

Regional Resource Center. *Reading inventory*. Eugene, Ore.: Regional Resource Center for Handicapped Children Project No. 472917, Contract No. OEC-0-9-472917-4591 (608), University of Oregon, 1971.

Robeck, M. C. & Wilson, J. A. R. *Psychology of reading: Foundations of instruction*. New York: John Wiley, 1974.

Robinson, H. & Hanson, E. Reliability of measures of reading achievement. *Reading Teacher,* 1968, *21,* 307–313; 323.

Rosinski, R. R., Golinkoff, R. M., & Kukish, K. Automatic semantic processing in a picture-word interference task. *Child Development,* 1975, *46,* 247–253.

Roswell, F. & Chall, J. *Roswell-Chall Auditory Blending Test*. New York: Essay Press, 1963.

Rozin, P. & Gleitman, L. The reading process and the acquisition of the alphabetic principle. In A. S. Reber & D. Scarborough (Eds.), *Reading: The CUNY conference*. New York: Lawrence Erlbaum, 1977.

Rugel, R. P. WISC subtest scores of disabled readers: A review with respect to Bannatyne's recategorization. *Journal of Learning Disabilities,* 1974, *7,* 48–54.

Samuels, S. J. Modes of word recognition. In H. Singer & R. B. Ruddell (Eds.), *Theoretical models and processes of reading*. Newark, Del.: International Reading Association, 1970.

Samuels, S. J. The effect of letter-name knowledge on learning to read. *American Educational Research Journal,* 1972, *9,* 74–75.

Sedlak, R. A. & Weener, P. Review of research on the Illinois Test of Psycholinguistic Abilities. In L. Mann & D. Sabatino (Eds.), *First review of special education* (Vol. 1). New York: Grune & Stratton, 1973.

Silberberg, N. E. & Silberberg, M. C. A note on reading tests and their role defining reading difficulties. *Journal of Learning Disabilities,* 1977, *10,* 100–103.

Silvaroli, N. J. *Classroom Reading Inventory*. Dubuque, Iowa: William C. Brown, 1965.

Slosson, R. *Slosson Oral Reading Test*. East Aurora, N.Y.: Slosson Educational Publications, 1963.

Smith, E. & Bradtmueller, W. *Individual Reading Placement Inventory*. Chicago: Follett, 1969.

Smith, F. *Understanding reading: A psycholinguistic analysis of reading and learning to read*. New York: Holt, 1971.

Smith, N. B. *Graded selections for informal reading diagnosis*. New York: New York University Press, 1959.

Spache, G. A new readability formula for primary-grade reading materials. *Elementary School Journal,* 1953, *53,* 410–413.

Spache, G. D. *Diagnostic Reading Scales*. Monterey: California Test Bureau, 1972.

Spache, G. D. *Diagnosing and correcting reading disabilities*. Boston: Allyn & Bacon, 1976.

Starlin, C. Evaluating progress toward reading proficiency. In B. Bateman (Ed.), *Learning disorders* (Vol. 4). Seattle: Special Child Publications, 1971.

Stebbins, L. B. *Education as experimentation: A planned variation model* (Vol. IIIA). Cambridge, Mass.: Abt Associates, 1976.

Strang, R. *Reading diagnosis and remediation*. Newark, Del.: International Reading Association, 1968.

Tiegs, E. W. & Clark, W. W. *California Achievement Tests*. Delmonte Research Park, Monterey, California: McGraw-Hill, 1970.

Traxler, A. E. *Values and limitations of standardized reading tests.* Chicago: University of Chicago Press, 1958.

Trela, T. Comparing achievement on tests of general and critical reading. *Journal of the Reading Specialist,* 1967, *6,* 140–142.

Venezky, R. L.: *Prereading skills: Theoretical foundations and practical applications* (Theoretical Paper No. 54). Madison, Wis.: Wisconsin Research and Development Center for Cognitive Learning, 1975.

Wallach, M. A. & Wallach, L. *Teaching all children to read.* Chicago: University of Chicago Press, 1976.

Waugh, R. P. The ITPA: Ballast or bonanza for the school psychologist? *Journal of School Psychology,* 1975, *13,* 201–208.

Wells, C. The value of oral reading test for diagnosis of reading difficulties of college freshman of low academic performance. *Psychological Monographs,* 1950, *64,* 1–35.

Weschler, D. *Weschler Intelligence Scales for Children* (Rev. Ed.). New York: Psychological Corporation, 1974.

White, O. R. & Liberty, K. A. Behavioral assessment and precise educational measurement. In N. Haring and R. Schiefelbusch (Eds.), *Teaching special children.* New York: McGraw-Hill, 1976.

Winkley, C. K. What do diagnostic tests really diagnose? In R. E. Liebert (Ed.), *Diagnostic viewpoints in reading.* Newark, Del.: International Reading Association, 1971.

Woodcock, R. W. *Woodcock Reading Mastery Tests.* Circle Pines, Minn.: American Guidance Service, 1973.

Ysseldyke, J. Diagnostic-prescriptive teaching: The search for aptitude-treatment interactions. In L. Mann & D. Sabatino (Eds.), *First review of special education.* New York: Grune & Stratton, 1973.

Ysseldyke, J. & Salvia, J. Diagnostic-perspective teaching: Two models. *Exceptional Children,* 1974, *41,* 181–185.

Zintz, M. V. *The reading process, the teacher and the learner* (2nd ed.). Dubuque, Iowa: William C. Brown, 1975.

SUGGESTED READINGS

Buros, O. K. (Ed.) *Reading: Tests and reviews II.* Highland Park, N.J.: Gryphon Press, 1975.

Farr, R. & Anastasiow, N. *Tests of reading readiness and achievements.* Newark, Del.: International Reading Association, 1969.

Salvia, J., & Ysseldyke J. *Assessment in special and remedial education.* Boston: Houghton Mifflin, 1978.

Spache, G. D. *Diagnosing and correcting reading disabilities.* Boston: Allyn & Bacon, 1976.

Starlin, C. Evaluating progress toward reading proficiency. In B. Bateman (Ed.), *Learning disorders* (Vol. 4). Seattle: Special Child Publications, 1971.

James A. Tucker

10
The Assessment of Mathematics, Spelling, and Written Expression

The assessment of academic skill areas for handicapped pupils is difficult even under the most ideal circumstances. To make matters worse, assessment is often completed under appalling conditions, using instruments that scarcely apply, and for purposes that load the results against the child. For example, if a learning disabled child is viewed by his or her school personnel as needing a certain type of placement, the assessment may be unconsciously (or quite consciously) directed at identifying a deficit severe enough to remove the child from one location and place him or her in another. So whether the examiner is assessing mathematics, spelling, or written expression, the first consideration is to determine the purposes for which the assessment data are being collected.

There are only two reasons why academic assessment need be performed. The first is to determine the level of ability in the skill areas being assessed, and the second is to ascertain the best method of remediation once deficits are pinpointed (Mercer & Ysseldyke, 1976; Tucker, 1976). This chapter will assume the frame of reference that tests should provide largely for planning remediation and determining the most appropriate placement in an educational environment. Furthermore, while it is readily recognized that one of the primary reasons for referral of handicapped children to assessment centers concerns their reading ability, the content of this chapter focuses on the more neglected areas of academic ability, namely: mathematics, spelling, and handwriting. This chapter is wholly addressed to these topics while other chapters will supply useful approaches in the psychometric underpinnings of these tests (Chap. 3), behavioral approaches (Chap. 4), and integration into an IEP (Chap. 6).

THE ASSESSMENT OF MATHEMATICS

For the purposes of this discussion, mathematics will be divided into the processes of calculation and reasoning. Mathematics calculation is a rather mechanical process well known to teachers where "practice makes perfect." Mathematics reasoning includes not only the ability to perform the mechanical calculations of addition, subtraction, division, and multiplication, but also employs other skills, some of which are nonmethematical, i.e., reading, as well as conceptual skills, associated with conservation and logic.

In assessing handicapped pupils it is important to establish performance levels in terms of mechanical calculation skills. There is little to be gained by assessing reasoning ability when calculation skills have not been adequately demonstrated. Consequently, this discussion will first focus on the assessment of mathematics in terms of the basic computational skills required to obtain the correct answer to a problem, then proceed to the reasoning necessary to apply the mathematics skills to real life problems.

It is quite easy to evaluate the *product* capability of a child's mathematics ability, but it is more difficult to identify the *process* deficits that may be affecting his or her performance. It is quite simple to determine when a child has the ability to formulate the right answers because his or her answers agree with those on the answer sheet. If he or she provides the correct answers consistently the teacher often assumes that the child knows the process. The child undoubtedly does know the calculation process, but that may be as far as it goes, and while it may be true for the simple process, it may not be true for the more complex processes. When a child fails to come up with the correct answer consistently there is a very good chance that the process that the child uses to derive an answer is faulty—be it the calculation process or the reasoning process. By the term *process,* we mean the systematic method the pupil uses to work through the mathematical problem. The teacher's problem lies in determining which components of that process are at fault. For the problem may lie in basic mathematical skills, mathematical logic, absence of rule learning, or it could be unrelated to mathematics learning, and be related to a deficit in a sensory, motor, perceptual, or language learner characteristic. It is often very difficult to determine which is the case.

Traditionally, mathematics assessment dealt only with the product. Even the presently used standardized mathematics tests are product oriented, probably because the "right or wrong" dichotomy of mathematics lends itself so neatly to standardization. This tradition may be due in part to a misunderstanding concerning the difference between mathematics and arithmetic. Arithmetic implies computational skills, whereas the term mathematics implies a system of logic dealing with measurement, properties, and the temporal and spatial relationships of quantities (Hyatt & Rolnick, 1974). The traditional product orientation has to do with arithmetic, but the more recent trend seems to be toward a process orientation, and is sometimes referred to as *new math*. The so-called new math is now, however, "new" math but rather a new approach to teaching the old logic of math.

Since mathematics is a system of logic, it can be described in its simplest form and developed from there to whatever level of complexity is possible given an individual's capability. One of the primary purposes of assessing the mathematics ability of a child is to make some judgment about the learning limits of the individual's capability. *Testing for limits,* however, should not be confused with testing for current level of performance, and current level of performance should *never* be accepted as a final statement of the child's limit of learning, only his performance on the day of assessment. Limits have often been expanded when the right conditions were discovered. It is simply important to know the present limits that appear, so that remedial programming will present the child with a realistic learning experience thus specifying the curricular adaptation necessary.

Hyatt & Rolnick (1974, p. 272) assert that there is functional similarity between the preschool "normal" child, the mentally retarded, the learning disabled, and the emotionally involved child with respect to learning mathematics:

> If these children are to understand mathematics, they must begin at essentially the same point and travel the same road as any 'normal' child. Their rate and distance of travel may vary, but because mathematics is a logical progression of ideas, all interrelated and dependent upon another, the pedagogical considerations of scope and sequence are largely predetermined.

Given the above rationale, the assessment of mathematics for handicapped pupils is quite similar to that for nonhandicapped pupils. This assumption does not, however, allow for remediating learning process differences for learner characteristic deficits such as arousal, attention span, perceptual-language considerations, or behaviors such as hyperactivity, distractability, or affective involvements. But since these problems are not specifically associated with mathematics, no attempt will be made in this chapter to delineate the assessment problems and solutions associated therewith.

Assessment Tools

Several recent summaries of the literature relative to the assessment of mathematics capability cover nearly all the major methods of assessment, describing specific techniques in great detail. Reisman (1972) presents four chapters dedicated to describing the tools and techniques o mathematics diagnosis. Topics covered include the preparation and use o teacher-made tests, math readiness tests, Piagetian concepts of mathema tics learning, task analysis, Gagne's heirarchy of learning applied to nev math (Gagne, 1970), and standardized mathematics tests. The informatio presented includes a helpful chapter on "How to Prepare an Informa Mathematics Inventory," including the complete *Reisman Inventory o Elementary Mathematics Skills* along with directions for administering it Overall, this publication takes a task analysis approach to mathematic assessment.

Reisman proposes that teachers use the Brownell & Hendrickso (1950) model to determine the learning difficulty of a task. This mode identifies the products of learning along a continuum from zero (0) to some maximum number (N). Four types of learning are discussed: arbit rary associations, concepts, generalizations, and problem solving.

Arbitrary associations are facts that have no meaning, such as the fact that the numeral "2" is equivalent to the word "two," and that both by man-made agreement, stand for an amount of something. *Concepts* are abstractions that must be learned by experience. This is closely as sociated with the ability to classify in that, in arithmetic, the child is re quired to identify the number property of various sets having other prop erties as well. For example, three sets of five buttons might be of differen materials, different colors, and different shapes, but the "fiveness" is recognized by the pupil who grasps the *concept* of "five." *Generaliza tions* are relationships between two or more concepts. An example pro vided by Reisman is that "threeness and fiveness" are "eightness." Hence, 3 + 5 = 8 is a generalization. Generalizations become the means of solving problems. *Problem solving* is learning initiated by a problem and requires an adequate grasp of arbitrary associations, concepts, and generalizations. Using the 3 + 5 example again, if John has 3 apples and 5 oranges, how many pieces of fruit does he have? The typical word prob lems in most math texts are thus reduced to simplest form by determining the arbitrary associations which when understood form the basis for con cept learning, which, in turn, allow for generalizations, and finally the ability to solve the problem.

Mann & Suiter (1974) developed concepts of mathematics assess ment from a learning disabilities approach, and provided a complete de scription of the *Mann-Suiter Grade Level Arithmetic Inventory and Test ing Kit*. This assessment device is intended to assist the teacher in deter mining arithmetic strengths and weaknesses, but is also useful in studying the elements of a mathematics assessment device.

Hyatt & Rolnick (1974) treat mathematics assessment as an evalua tion of the child's abilities in terms of Piagetian theory. Specific directions are provided for teacher-administered tests for conservation of length, number, area, and quantity. In this publication the concept of assessment is inextricably involved with teaching. Examples include the use of Montessori materials and techniques to assess mathematics concepts at the same time that they are being taught. In this way the assessment of mathematics concepts is an ongoing process providing constant feedback at each level of presentation difficulty. This idea is essential to good mathematics assessment and is the basis for most of the better assessment models and techniques. While Hyatt & Rolnick recommend the *Key Math Diagnostic Arithmetic Test* as a commercially available standardized technique that can be used from preschool through the elementary grades, they add that teacher observation of daily performance is the best form of mathematics assessment—especially when the observations are organized by a checklist that relates to behavioral objectives. Hyatt & Rolnick also heavily emphasize the use of readily available, inexpensive materials in the process of mathematics evaluation and instruction.

Mathematics Assessment for Placement

As indicated in the introduction to this chapter, all assessment *should* translate into educational programs to remediate any deficits found. But the realities of life often require that we assess a child's capabilities for the purpose of determining his or her eligibility for special education services. Goodman & Mann (1976) have provided an excellent treatise on the subject. In addition to stressing the importance of directing the assessment toward achievement, they provide information on selecting assessment instruments for screening secondary-level learning disabled students—an area where not much is available.

Selected Commercial Instruments for the Assessment of Mathematics

The following abstracts of selected commercial instruments utilized in assessing mathematics is provided the reader to assist in initial review and serve as a selection of appropriate procedures. It is not meant as a single source guide. The reader is encouraged to read the teacher's guide or test manual for each instrument. Also, if a specific instrument is to be used, the teacher is strongly encouraged to study and practice the use of the test in a standardized manner. The abstracts are presented in accordance with the following descriptors: title, date, author (if known), supplier, brief description, academic level, and other special features of interest. Similar abstracts will be included for spelling and writing assessment instruments.

Basic Education Skills Inventory (BESI)—1972, by Gary Adamson, Morris Shrago, and Glen Van Etten. Available from B. L. Winch and Associates, Box 1185, Santa Monica, Ca. 90405. The BESI is a nonstandardized criterion-referenced inventory intended to diagnose math skill deficits in 30 major activity areas: quantitative concepts, counting skills, basic numbers, number words, number sequence and ordering, basic computational skills, whole numbers, fractional parts and fractions, decimals, percents, transformation skills, and math applications. Grade level is K through six. Scoring is criteiron-referenced, and prescriptive materials are available separately under the title *Prescriptive Materials Retrieval System*.

California Achievement Tests—Mathematics—1970, by Ernest W. Tiegs and Willis W. Clark. Available from CTB/McGraw-Hill, Del Monte Research Park, Monterey, Ca. 93940. The *California Achievement Tests—Mathematics,* is designed for three levels: primary, elementary and intermediate. The tests have a section measuring skill with number facts and operations that provide an adequate survey of skills in fundamentals. At the elementary and intermediate levels the student performs the computation each time and then selects one of five responses. The test at each level also has a "reasoning" section.

The manuals of the California Achievement Tests are well organized and the test is relatively easy to administer. There is adequate presentation of grade, age, and percentile norms.

Comprehensive Tests of Basic Skills: Arithmetic—1970. Available through CTB/McGraw-Hill, Del Monte Research Park, Monterey, Ca. 93940. This test is provided with an extensive and carefully constructed Technical Report, examiners manual, and test coordinator's handbook that tell how the test was constructed and designed. The test is divided into 4 levels covering grades 2.5 to 12. There are three areas covered on the test: computation, concepts, and applications with scores given for each area. A total score can also be derived. The test takes approximately 70 minutes to administer. Scoring can be either manual or computer. The test on computation is more easily geared toward low-ability readers, while these same students may experience difficulty with the tests on concepts and applications.

Design for Math Skill Development—1972, by John Armenia, Lee Von Kuster, Don Kamp, and Dale McDonald. Available from National Computer Systems, Educational Systems, 4401 W. 76th St., Minneapolis, Mn. 55435. This program is a system for management of elementary school mathematics instruction. There are 176 behaviorally stated skill objectives at K through grade six levels, organized in nine strands: numeration and place value, addition and subtraction, multiplication and division, fractions, geometry, measurement, money, time, and graphs. Pupil profiles are kept on key sort cards which are notched when the skill is mastered. Cards are sorted for grouping purposes. There is a *Teacher's Resource File* of materials keyed to the skills.

Diagnosis: An Instructional Aid—Mathematics. Available from Science Research Associates (SRA), Inc., 259 E. Erie St., Chicago, Ill. 60611. This SRA program measures mastery of 142 specific mathematics learning objectives in grades 1 through 4 on Level A, and 421 objectives in grades 3 through 6 on Level B. A screening test identifies broad areas of weakness; criterion-referenced tests called Probes (24 in Level A, 32 in Level B) provide diagnostic information. Areas covered include computation, sets and numeration, operations in problem solving, measurement, geometry, whole number computation, fractional number computation, decimal number computation, and numeration. Tests are correlated to major basal mathematics series and to SRA supplementary math materials in the Prescription Guides. A special feature is student self-scoring of tests.

Diagnostic Mathematics Inventory (DMI)—1975, by John K. Gessel. Available from CTB, McGraw, Hill, Del Monte Research Park, Monterey Park, Monterey, Ca. 93940. DMI measures student mastery of 325 mathematics objectives spanning grade levels 1.5 through 7.5. Norms will be available in 1978. There is one multiple-choice item per objective. Test results are computer printed and include a Premastery Analysis using item distractors derived from common student errors to provide diagnostic information; an Individual Diagnostic Report which is a profile of the student's mastery of objectives; and an Objectives Mastery Report indicating, by class, which objectives each student has mastered or not mastered, class totals of mastery or nonmastery by objectives, and percentage. DMI is the revised version of the Prescriptive Mathematics Inventory.

Diagnostic Tests and Self-Helps in Arithmetic (DTSA)—1955, by Leo J. Brueckner. Available from CTB, McGraw Hill, Del Monte Research Park, Monterey, Ca. 93940. The DTSA is intended to assist in diagnosing specific weaknesses in fundamental arithmetic skills for grades levels 3 through 12 and adults. There are no norms. There are four screening tests and 23 diagnostic tests: basic facts, operations with whole numbers, common fractions, and decimal fractions. Each diagnostic test is accompanied by a self-help exercise which reviews the basic process. It shows how problems should have been thought out, how intermediate steps should have been performed, and how errors could be avoided. This is a relatively old instrument included here mainly because of its relevance to older students, and because of the self-help concept.

Fountain Valley Teacher Support System in Mathematics—1976. Available from Richard L. Zweig Associates, Inc., 20800 Beach Blvd., Huntington Beach, Ca. 92648. Fountain Valley is designed to diagnose student deficiencies in mathematics at grade levels K through 8 and to provide prescriptions for reteaching. It is criterion-referenced, including 785 sequenced behavioral objectives organized in strands: numbers and operations, geometry, measurements, applications, statistics and probability, functions and graphs, logical thinking, and problem solving. The tests are on audio cassettes organized by grade level. Tests can be administered individually or in groups. This is a well-known system.

Kraner Preschool Math Inventory—1976, by Robert S. Kraner. Available from Learning Concepts, 2501 North Lamar, Austin, Tx. 78705. The Kraner Inventory is a criterion-referenced assessment of 70 mathematics skills and concepts in 7 areas: set comparison, counting, cardinal numbers, sequence, position, direction, and geometry/measurement. It is administered individually; the child responds verbally or otherwise through performance. There are three items per skill or concept. Norms are given for ages 3 through 6½ at 6-month intervals. Post-test data can be obtained to evaluate student progress.

Individualized Criterion-referenced Testing: Math (ICRT). Available from Educational Progress Corp., Box 45663, Tulsa, Ok. 74145. The ICRT test items measure mastery or nonmastery of 312 specific, sequentially arranged mathematics skills (objectives) equivalent to grades 1 through 8. There are two test items per objective. Reports are computer printed and include a Student Summary, listing those skills the student has learned, needs to review, and needs yet to learn; an Instructional Grouping Report, listing by objective, students who need instruction on that objective; a Building Summary listing by class and by building the number of students attempting each objective and the number who passed; and a District Summary listing by age the number of students who attempted and those who passed each objective. Objectives have been correlated to more than 50 math programs. The Student Summary includes a prescription listing five resources for each objective. The publishers are reported to attempt to return test reports within five working days.

Key Math Diagnostic Arithmetic Test—1971, by Austin J. Connolly, et al. Available from American Guidance Service, Inc., Publishers Building, Circle Pines, Minn. 55014. Key Math is intended to be a comprehensive assessment of mathematics skills that covers 3 major areas with 14 subtests: content (numeration, fractions, geometry, and symbols); operations (addition, subtraction, multiplication, division, mental computation, numerical reasoning); and applications (word problems, missing elements, money, measurement, time). The test is intended for use at preschool through 6th grade levels and for remedial purposes. There is also an optional Key Math Metric Supplement. The entire instrument can be administered in approximately 30 minutes.

Modern Mathematics Supplement to the Iowa Tests of Basic Skills (MMS)—1968, by E. L. Lindquist, A. N. Hieronymus, and H. D. Hoover. Available from Houghton Mifflin Co., 110 Tremont St., Boston, Ma. 02107. The MMS is considered an updated version of the Arithmetic Concept Test of the Iowa Tests of Basic Skills. By reviewing new text books in math, the authors constructed this test to cover new methods and materials that were developed during the 1960s. This test is appropriate for grades 3 to 9 with 6 overlapping levels. It covers mathematical questions such as content, with placement and emphasis on current objectives. The test takes 30 to 40 minutes to administer and scoring can be done either manually or by computer service. Raw scores may be converted into grade equivalent scores, percentile ranks, or stanines.

Peabody Individual Achievement Test (PIAT)—1970, by Lloyd M. Dunn and Frederick C. Markwardt, Jr. Available from American Guidance Service, Inc., Circle Pines, Minn. 55014. PIAT is a wide-range screening test intended to survey a subject's level of educational attainment in basic skills in five areas: mathematics, reading recognition, reading comprehension, spelling, and general information. Items are sequenced in order of difficulty. The instrument is designed for use with ages K through adult. The test is individually administered and takes about 30 to 40 minutes although the test is not timed. For the five areas tapped, grade equivalents, age equivalents, percentile ranks, and standard scores can be derived.

Project Math, Mathematics Concept Inventory—1976, by J. Cawley, A. Fitzmaurice, H. Goodstein, A. Lepore, R. Sedlak, and V. Althaus. Available through the Educational Development Corp. Project Math is designed to be a program of mathematics for handicapped children. The content of the program reflects mathematical programs usually found in regular grades, preschool through sixth. Project Math is designed to help in the development of skills, concepts, and social growth for slow learners, children with specific learning disabilities, social or emotional adjustment problems and/or economic disadvantages. The total program contains 4 levels. Each task in the program is divided into 3 areas: strand, area, and concept. This division helps the teacher in breaking down each task so that mistakes made by the students can be pinpointed to a very specific problem. Student's responses are recorded on an Individual Learner Profile which can then be used for remediation purposes. Manuals with specific teacher directions are provided.

A Program for Learning in Accordance with Needs (PLAN): *Math*—1973–1975. Available from Westinghouse Learning Corp., 790 Lucerne Dr., Sunnyvale, Ca. 94086. PLAN is a comprehensive system of performance objectives and learning activities keyed to hundreds of optional resources. Criterion-referenced tests and classroom management materials make each course an accountable instructional system at grade levels 1 through 12. Tests are computer scored. When used for placement, the computer generates a suggested list of objectives for the student. When given to measure achievement, the computer prints out the student's score on each objective tested. Teaching-Learning Units have been developed for each objective. This system provides for the possibility of daily printouts for planning teaching activities, facilitates long-range record keeping, reports to parents, and a monthly administrative report detailing students progress in each teacher's class as well as in the school as a whole. The publishers provide teaching workshops on the program.

Sequential Testing and Educational Programming (STEP)—1975, by Sue M. Greenberger and Susan R. Thum. Available from Academic Therapy Publications, 1539 Fourth St., San Rafael, Ca. 94025. STEP is a testing program and resource guide which provides sequenced objectives and assessment procedures in 24 developmental areas which range from sensory input to academic areas such as reading, spelling, and arithmetic. It is based on Osgood's (1957) model and is organized, like the model, by channels and levels and is intended for use from preschool through grade 6. Assessment is criterion-referenced. Each objective has suggested activities and is correlated to commercially available teaching materials. If further assessment is needed, each objective references additional assessment instruments.

Second Step: Sequential Testing and Educational Programming for the Secondary Student—1977, by Sue Madwat Greenberger. Available from Academic Therapy Publications, 1539 Fourth St., San Rafael, Ca.

94025. Second STEP is intended to correlate process functioning and academic functioning with commerically available tests and curriculum materials to permit assessment of developmental skills with content appropriate to the older student. There are 650 developmentally sequenced behavioral objectives. The test can be used with students in grades 7 through 12 whose skills vary from grades 1 through 12, although most of the skills/objectives would ordinarily be attained by age 11. The test items are criterion-referenced. Each objective has suggested activities and is correlated to commercially available teaching materials, and like STEP, provides references to published assessment instruments for further assessment of each objective.

Skiltrac—1976. Available from Center for Educational Innovation (CEI), 750 Brooksedge Blvd., Westerville, Oh. 43081. Skiltrac is a management system which includes curriculum materials and individualized reports for planning and record keeping. The focus is on mathematics skills at K through grade 3. Entry level assessments and specific skill assessments are done by teachers, then an Individual Assessment Plan for additional assessment and an Individual Instruction Plan are prepared by CEI for each student. The Individual Assessment Plans provide suggested assessment patterns for each student based on reported information; suggestions for teaching procedures and post-instructional activities for each skill taught. There is also a Student Grouping Profile available as well as a Student Instructional Record that traces a child's progress through the system. The Individual Instructional Plan is the prescriptive element of the system coupled with PATHS, a book giving specific instructional techniques and activities and a Commercial Reference Book which correlates commercial materials to specific skills. Siltrac is a computer-based system.

Mastery: An Evaluation Tool—1975. Available from Science Research Associates, Inc., 155 North Wacker Drive, Chicago, Ill. 60606. *Mastery* is designed to provide pre- and post-tests of specific skills or objectives in reading and mathematics for grades K-9. The mathematics objectives, developed by the SRA Educational Assessment Laboratory, are divided into two sets; the grades K-2 catalog (1975 objectives) covers numbers and numerals, whole-number computation, measurement, sets, logical thinking, and geometry. The grades 3-9 catalog (352 objectives) covers whole numbers, fractional numbers, integers, rational numbers, real numbers, geometry, measurement, sets, functions, graphing, statistics, probability, logic, and flow charts. Two test forms are available for each grade level K-8. Customized tests are also available for locally specified sets of objectives selected from the *Mastery* catalog.

Stanford Diagnostic Mathematics Test—1976, by Leslie S. Beatty et al. Available from Psychological Corp., 757 Third Ave., New York, N.Y. 10017. This test is designed for use in the early part of an instructional sequence to diagnose specific strengths and weaknesses in understanding the number system and its properties, computation, problem solving, and measurement. The instrument can be used between the grades of 1.6 and 13.0. The test results are computer printed and provide an Instructional Placement Report for each class. This report groups students into three instructional groups according to total scores. A class Summary is also provided. Optionally available are *local norms,* an Individual Diagnostic Report, an Item Analysis for each subtest (a class report), and an Item Analysis with Pupil Responses, which lists each pupil by name with raw and derived scores for the subtests as well as Concept/Skill Domain Progress Indicators.

Stanford Modern Mathematics Concepts Test (MMCT)—1965, by Truman L. Kelley, Richard Madden, Eric F. Gardner, and Herbert C. Rudman. Available from Harcourt, Brace Jovanovich, Inc., 757 Third Avenue, New York, N.Y. 10017. The MMCT aims at providing a measure of achievement for pupils in modern mathematics courses in grades 5 through 9.1. The manual contains an ''Item Content Outline'' that places each test item into one of ten general categories. Some items overlap two or more categories. This test offers many challenging items and information regarding reliability, validity, and norms are presented.

System Fore, by Los Angeles Public Schools. Available from Foreworks, 7112 Teesdale, Ave., North Hollywood, CA 91605. System FORE is an instructional system in language, reading, and mathematics. It consists of developmental sequences, assessment inventories, and a *materials retrieval system*. The learning objectives cover ages 0 to 10. It is a nongraded developmentally sequenced list of objectives. The objectives are correlated to instructional materials and professional texts by page number, record band, lesson number, etc., as well as by mode of sensory input and motor output. Secondary levels are being field tested.

Wide Range Achievement Test (WRAT)—1965, by J. F. Jastak and S. R. Jastak. Available from Guidance Associates of Delaware, Inc., 1526 Gilpin Ave., Wilmington, Del. 19806. The WRAT is a well-known tool for assessment of the basic school subjects. It is probably more often used as a screening tool, however, rather than as a prescriptive or placement instrument. In the math section the subtests are: counting, reading number symbols, solving oral problems, and performing written computations. Grade scores, standard scores, and percentile ranks are provided. The entire instrument takes approximately 20 to 30 minutes to administer.

Wisconsin Contemporary Test of Elementary Mathematics (WCTEM)—1968, by M. V. DeVault, Elizabeth Fennema, K. Allen Neufeld, and Lewis B. Smith. Available from Personnel Press, Inc., 20 Nassau St., Princeton, N.J. 08540. The test is designed to assess modern mathematical concepts that have been developed since 1962. This test is based on contemporary texts and uses modern terminology and symbolism. The WCTEM is designed for grades 3 to 6, with grades 3 and 4 tested together, and grades 5 and 6 tested together. Each test is divided into two parts, facts and concepts, which reveal a separate score. A total score can also be determined. Scoring may be done by computer or manually. The test takes approximately 50 minutes to administer. Suggestions for using test results for instructions are provided as well as explicit directions for administration, scoring, and use of the norm tables.

THE ASSESSMENT OF SPELLING

At one time spelling was a major subject in most public school systems. Today, however, the subject has been reduced to a relatively low priority on the scale of important subjects. We hear much about reading and almost as much about mathematics, but spelling, as a discipline, receives little attention. Unfortunately, this may be a serious error, as spelling has a direct relationship to writing and reading in that they all share common communication requirements and similar learner characteristics. There are schools that believe in teaching reading by teaching children to spell, and there are other programs where a child's handwriting is evaluated via spelling tests, but these programs seem to be decreasing in numbers, or at least not setting any new trends. Evidence suggests that it may be time to bring back the old-fashioned "spell down" as an assessment of spelling proficiency. The element of achievement and public notice involved in such activities tends to create a move toward excellence so as to demonstrate capability under such circumstances.

One of the possible reasons for a decreased emphasis on spelling is the difficulty that theoreticians have had in describing the elements of spelling. Wallace & Larsen (1978) present an extensive review of the nature of English spelling, the factors related to successful spelling, and the processes by which children learn to spell. Wallace & Larsen review 13 commercially available, standardized spelling achievement tests, giving the title, author, date, grade levels, and procedure for use (whether dictated-word, or proofreading). This is followed by a review of three nonstandardized tests of spelling achievement and diagnostics. Their treatise winds up with a discussion of informal spelling assessment techniques and other more specialized techniques and considerations. A review of Wallace & Larsen will introduce the reader to the intricacies of spelling theory as well as to the elements involved in the assessment of spelling problems.

Mann & Suiter (1974) treat spelling assessment in terms of auditory and visual channel problems and provide the *Mann-Suiter Developmental Spelling Inventory*. Spelling errors are listed which are primarily due to visual and auditory channel deficits. For example, if the problem is visual, then auditory instructional and assessment techniques are provided; the same is provided for problems associated with the auditory channel. Following this there is a section providing a multi-sensory approach for problems that are both auditory and visual.

Selected Commercial Instruments for the Assessment of Spelling

Durrell Analysis of Reading Difficulty: Spelling—1955, by Donald Durrell. Available from the Psychological Corp., 757 Third Ave., New York, N.Y. 10017. There are two spelling tests in the Durrell: The phonic spelling of unfamiliar words, and a test using words from a graded list. A brief checklist of difficulties in spelling is used for a broad analysis of errors. The test may be used for grades 1 through 6. Norms are given for grades 2 through 6.

Larsen-Hammill Test of Written Spelling—1976, by S. C. Larsen and D. D. Hammill. Available from Academic Therapy Publications, 1539 Fourth St., Box 899, San Rafael, Ca. 94901. The Test of Written Spelling (TWS) tests ability to spell both phonetically-based and nonphonetic words at grade levels 1 through 8. It is drawn from 10 basal spelling programs and based on a review of 2,000 spelling generalizations. The test can be administered in 20 minutes. Scoring yields spelling age levels, spelling quotients, and grade equivalents for predictable words, unpredictable words, and for the total test. The authors believe the test to be unique in that the dictated-word technique is based upon educational theories that are backed by research findings. This is a standardized instrument based on a sample of more than 4,500 children in 22 states.

Spell Master-Diagnostic Spelling System—1974, by Claire R. Cohen and Rhonda M. Abrams. Available from Learnco, Inc., 156 Front St., Exeter, N.H. 03833. Spell Master is a criterion-referenced test designed to pinpoint the student's specific strengths and areas for progress. The criteria are the basic structural and phonic elements of English spelling. There are 6 levels for grades 1 through 6, and one level for grades 7 and 8. The instrument is scored by recording the number of correct responses and the number of errors. In the misspelled words, specific elements to remediate are identifiable. The elements tested are correlated to seven basal texts. The Supplemental Teaching Guide suggests teaching activities as well. The students can correct their own tests.

THE ASSESSMENT OF HANDWRITING

Handwriting can be viewed as a complex integration of perceptual motor abilities in its simplest form, but to use it as a means of communication requires additional integration of conceptual abilities as well.

Hammill (1973) divides the process of writing into (1) the generation of ideas, (2) syntax, and (3) penmanship. It is quite probable that the child learning to write, does so in reverse order to the listing presented by Hammill. Consequently the assessment of writing should quite probably proceed from the motoric to the conceptual.

This discussion of the assessment of handwriting will center almost exclusively on penmanship since it is viewed as the simplest level of writing in the broadest sense. Problems associated with syntax and cognitive generation are more closely associated with the development of language and should be assessed as such (see Chap. 8). The rationale for this focus is simple: a handicapped pupil is most likely to have problems with the gross motor and fine motor problems in handwriting at a later age level than when these problems are encountered normally. Consequently, with a handicapped child, the handwriting problems that will be noticed first, and therefore need remediation first, are those associated with penmanship.

The most important point for a teacher to remember in teaching or assessing handwriting is that it is quite normal for a young child (under the age of 8 or 9) to reverse letters, to omit strokes or entire letters, and to exhibit uneven letters both in height and spacing. These events are common because the neurological development necessary for proper perceptual integration is not completed until the age of 8 to 10 (Wepman, 1968; Yakoviev, 1962). While some children can become quite proficient at handwriting earlier than this, it is not an indication that a handicapping condition is present unless there is a concert of symptoms supported by apparent lack of development in the ability to perform simple handwriting assignments. Examples of such symptoms include attention span, hyperactivity, anxiety, holding the pencil very tightly, extreme squinting, eyes very close to the paper, etc.

Hammill (1973) provides an excellent overview of the problems associated with writing and addresses in detail a number of informal techniques for assessing not only the quality of penmanship but also readiness for writing.

A forthcoming book by Hammill & Bartel (in process) also treats the subject of handwriting instruction and assessment in detail. They treat the subject of assessment in terms of measuring writing-readiness skills, and review and compare various lists of essential skills. Hammill & Bartel provide an extensive review of the Handwriting subscale of the *Basic School Skills Inventory* by Goodman & Hammill (1975). This scale can be used either as a norm-referenced test or as a criterion-referenced instrument.

Mann & Suiter (1974) provide a summary of handwriting difficulties from the learning disability point of view. They divide their discussion into sections such as, Readiness for Handwriting, Beginning Handwriting, Manuscript Writing, Transitional Writing, and Handwriting for the Older Child. Questions are provided for the teacher to ask the older child in an attempt to ferret out the problems they are encountering with handwriting. Mann & Suiter identify three kinds of writing difficulties: poor overall quality, production that is too slow, and deterioration under press of speed. The discussion is intended to help the reader assess when those problems are present and to help the teacher remediate for the problems found.

Selected Commercial Instruments for Assessing Handwriting

Ayres Scales for Measuring Handwriting—1917, by Leonard P. Ayres. Availabe from Educational Testing Service, Rosedale Rd., Princeton, N.J. 08540. The Ayres Scale was designed as a measuring device rather than a standard. The quality of each writing sample is determined by its degree of legibility. It is intended for use in grades 2 through 8, and the writing is evaluated in terms of quality and speed.

Durrell Analysis of Reading Difficulty: Handwriting—1955, by Donald D. Durrell. Available from the Psychological Corporation, 757 Third Avenue, New York, N.Y. 10017. The Durrell Test of Handwriting is a quick screening instrument indicating speed; letter formation; position of hand, pencil, paper, and body; and height spacing and slant of the letters. The test consists only of copying letters and sentences in one minute samples.

Manuscript Handwriting Analytical Scale; Cursive Handwriting Analytical Scale. Available from Peterson System, 2515 Commerce St., Dallas, Tx. 75201. The two Peterson Grading Scales are designed to help teachers and students evaluate manuscript and cursive handwriting. The scoring can be done by teacher or by self-evaluation. Remedial suggestions are offered for improving and understanding the six qualities of handwriting assessed.

Normal Handwriting Scale—1947, by Albert Grant. Availabe from Zaner-Bloser Co., 612 North Park St., Columbus, Oh. 43215. The Normal Handwriting Scale is a self-diagnostic device providing students with a quick and accessible means of rating the quality of words they frequently write. The scale consists of eight words: *the, and, have, will, are, you, is,* and *of.* The scale is for use in grades 4 through 8. Ratings are made for several samples of each word and then averaged. A total average score may be computed for comparison with tentative midyear norms.

Basic School Skill Inventory (BSSI): *Handwriting Subscale*—1975, byl. Goodman and D. Hammill. Available from Follet, 1010 W. Washington Boulevard, Chicago, Il. 60607. The BSSI assesses a child's handwriting ability on 10 different dimensions: left to right, grasp, printing first name, writing position, drawing geometric figures, copying words, drawing a person, chalk-board to paper copying, staying on the line, and printing last name. The scale is used primarily for screening and readiness purposes. The instrument is norm-referenced to ages 4-0 to 6-11, but can be used as a criterion-referenced test also.

Peek-Thru. Available from Zaner-Bloser, Inc., 612 North Park St., Columbus, Oh. 43215. The Peek-Thru allows the student to check correct letter formation and alignment. For grades 1 through 3 there is a manuscript standard to check against, and for grades 3 through the upper grades there is a cursive standard to check against. There is also an upper grade manuscript standard overlay. The plastic overlay has black letters on red and blue lines similar to writing paper.

Sequential Testing and Educational Programming (STEP)—1975, by Sue M. Greenberger and Susan R. Thum. Available from Academic Therapy Publications, 1539 Fourth St., San Rafael, Ca. 94025. STEP provides several sequenced objectives for several developmental levels of handwriting and related abilities. It is based on Osgood's (1957) model and is organized, like the model, by channels and levels and is intended for use from preschool through grade 6. Assessment is criterion-referenced. Each objective has suggested activities and is correlated to commercially available teaching materials.

SUMMARY

The assessment of mathematics, spelling, and handwriting with the handicapped student should begin with the most simple stage of development and proceed to the more complex. In mathematics this means starting with the calculation skills associated with arithmetic. In spelling it is more difficult to determine what the most simple stage of development is, but it seems to be the memory of rules, such as "i before e, except after c," and the use of mnemonics, if necessary, where memory is faulty. In handwriting, the place to begin assessment is with simple penmanship: Are the letters legible? Is the spacing appropriate? Is the speed adequate?

Once a baseline has been established in such assessment, then remediation follows naturally because the skills mastered can be used to build upon thus increasing the mastery of more complex skills. The maxim that should never be forgotten, however, is that all assessments of academic areas should translate directly into individualized education programs.

REFERENCES

Ayres, L. P. *Ayres measuring scale for handwriting.* Iowa City, Iowa: Bureau of Educational research and Service, University of Iowa, 1917.

Brownell, W. H. & Hendrickson, G. How children learn information, concepts, and generalizations. In M. Corey, (Chairman), *49th yearbook of the national society for the study of education. Part 1: Learning and instruction.* Chicago: University of Chicago Press, 1970.

Gagne, R. M. *The conditions of learning.* (2nd ed.) New York: Holt, 1970.

Goodman, L. & Hammill, D. D. *Basic school skills inventory.* Chicago: Follett, 1975.

Goodman, L. & Mann, L. *Learning disabilities in the secondary school: Issues and practices.* New York: Grune & Stratton, 1976.

Hammill, D. Problems in writing. In D. Hammill & N. Bartel (Eds.), *Teaching children with learning and behavior problems.* Boston: Allyn & Bacon, 1973.

Hammill, D. & Bartel, N. *Teaching children with learning and behavior problems* (2nd ed.). Boston: Allyn & Bacon (in press).

Hammill, D. & Nettie, R. B. *Teaching children with learning and behavior problems.* (2nd ed.) Boston: Allyn & Bacon, 1978.

Hyatt, R., & Rolnick, N. *Teaching the mentally handicapped child.* New York: Behavioral Publications, 1974.

Mann, P. H. & Suiter, P. *Handbook in diagnostic teaching: A learning disabilities approach.* Boston: Allyn & Bacon, 1974.

Mercer, J. R. & Ysseldyke, J. Designing diagnostic intervention programs. In T. Oakland (Ed.), *With bias toward none.* Lexington, Ky.: Coordinating Office for Regional Resource Centers, University of Kentucky, 1976.

Osgood, C. E. A behavioristic analysis. In Colorado University symposium on cognition, contemporary approaches to cognition. Cambridge, Mass.: Harvard University Press, 1957.

Reisman, F. K. *A guide to the diagnostic teaching of arithmetic.* Columbus, Oh.: Charles E. Merrill, 1972.

Tucker, J. A. Operationalizing the diagnostic intervention process. In T. Oakland (Ed.), *With bias toward none.* Lexington, Ky.: Coordinating Office for Regional Resource Centers, University of Kentucky, 1976.

Wallace, G. & Larsen, S. *Educational assessment of handicapped learners.* Boston: Allyn & Bacon, 1978.

Wallace, G. & Larsen, S. Educational assessment of learning problems: Testing for teaching. Boston: Allyn & Bacon, 1978.

Wepman, J. M. The modality concept—including a statement of the perceptual and conceptual levels of learning. In Helen K. Smith (Ed.), *Perception and reading, proceedings of the twelfth annual convention, international reading association*. Newark, Del.: International Reading Assocaition, 1968.

Yakovlev, P. I. Morphological criteria of growth and maturation of the nervous system in man. In L. C. Kalb, R. L. Masland, & R. E. Cook (Eds.), *Mental retardation: Proceedings of the association for research in nervous and mental diseases*. Baltimore: Williams & Wilkins, 1962.

SUGGESTED READINGS

Hammill, D. & Bartel, N. *Teaching children with learning and behavior problems*. Boston: Allyn & Bacon, 1973.

Lambert, N. M., Wilcox, M. R., & Gleason, W. P. *The educationally retarded child: Comprehensive assessment and planning for slow learners and the educable mentally retarded child*. New York: Grune & Stratton, 1974.

Mann, P. H. & Suiter, P. *Handbook in diagnosing teaching: A learning disabilities approach*. Boston: Allyn & Bacon, 1974.

Reisman, F. K. *A guide to the diagnostic teaching of arithmetic*. Columbus, Oh.: Charles E. Merrill, 1972.

SECTION III

Ascertaining and Describing Learner Characteristics in Low-incidence Handicapped Populations

Emphasis in special education has constantly changed due to litigation, legislation, new information from the field itself, and the continuing work of many dedicated lay advocates. One result of this change has been the constant deemphasis of psychoeducational assessment for the purpose of assigning a categorical label to achieve placement for a handicapped child. By the mid-1960s many special educators had declared special classes poorly used "dumping grounds" which contained many misclassified children. It appeared that categorical labels were almost arbitrarily assigned to children. The reaction was a deliberate stance that behavior must be described, not boiled down to noninstructional, meaningless, test scores. Similarly, the demise of the belief that severely handicapped children are diagnostic categorical labels resulted in the widespread practice of deinstitutionalization, normalization, the selection and use of target behaviors, and concern for validating instructional methodology. By the early 1970s the Rehabilitation Act of 1973 (PL 93-516, Section 50A) (1973) and the Education of All Handicapped Children Act (PL 94-142) (1975) required full civil and educational rights for that limited number of persons historically regarded as too unique for serious efforts at rehabilitation. This section provides the reader diagnostic models and implications for those specialized populations which have largely been omitted from discussions of assessment strategies.

Carolyn Scroggs

11

The Assessment of Children with Hearing Handicaps

Vision and hearing are the senses most extensively relied upon by the developing child. Hearing, in particular functions as a continuous warning system to the individual. The major effect of a hearing loss, however, lies in damage to a critical human behavior, the use of language. The seriousness of a hearing loss occurring after speech has developed cannot be minimized, but for the child who is born with a hearing loss, the problem is a critical one.

It is estimated that the human being is exposed to about three million words per year (Van Uden, 1970). From that enormous sample of language, the normal child learns the rules and vocabulary of the language surrounding him (Chapter 8). Moreover the role that language plays in acquiring social, academic, vocational, and everyday living skills is inestimable. It is the responsibility of those providing educational and other services to the hearing impaired population to be cognizant of the effects of communication deprivation in all of these areas and to provide services which will help the hearing impaired individual overcome some of the related deficiencies. In providing these services, accurate assessment of the hearing impaired individual's skills is needed. Unfortunately, a communication disorder makes assessment a complicated task. In many areas the formal and informal assessment tools that have been developed for the hearing population are heavily dependent on language for their accuracy. When the individual to be assessed displays considerable language deficiencies, recognized assessment techniques must often be altered or abandoned. This chapter will discuss the problems that occur because of hearing loss and the types of assessment techniques that can be utilized with children exhibiting these problems.

DEFINITIONS OF HEARING LOSS

The methodology of measuring hearing loss has been developed to the extent that definitions of hearing loss could be based on those measurements alone. However, when the Conference of Executives of American Schools for the Deaf (CEASD) developed definitions of hearing impairment (Report of the Ad Hoc Committee to Define Deaf and Hard of Hearing, 1975), it was recognized that the exact measurement of hearing loss was less critical than how the individual functioned in relation to that loss. The definitions adopted by the CEASD (Report of the Ad Hoc Committee to Define Deaf and Hard of Hearing, 1975) therefore, reflected this functional approach.

Table 11-1
Hearing Loss Impact on Communicating Language and School Placement

Hearing Threshold Levels (ISO)	Probable Impact on Communication and Language	Present Day Implications for Educational Settings	
		*Type**	*Probable Need*
Level I,† 26–54 dB	Mild	Full Integration	Most Frequent
		Partial Integration	Frequent
		Self-Contained	Infrequent
Level II, 55–69 dB	Moderate	Full Integration	Frequent
		Partial Integration	Most Frequent
		Self-Contained	Infrequent
Level III, 70–89 dB	Severe	Full Integration	Frequent
		Partial Integration	Most Frequent
		Self-Contained	Frequent
Level IV, 90 dB and above	Profound	Full Integration	Infrequent
		Partial Integration	Frequent
		Self-Contained	Most Frequent

**Full integration* means total integration into regular classes for hearing students with special services provided under direction of specialists in educational programs for deaf and hard of hearing. *Partial integration* means taking all classes in a regular school, some on an integrated basis and some on a self-contained basis. *Self-contained* means attending classes exclusively with other deaf and/or hard of hearing classmates in regular schools, special day schools or special residential schools.

†It is assumed that these decibel scores were obtained by a qualified audiologist using an average of scores within the frequency range commonly considered necessary to process linguistic information.

From Report of the Ad Hoc Committee to Define Deaf and Hard of Hearing. *American Annals of the Deaf,* 1975, *120,* 509–512. Reprinted with permission.

Hearing impairment was defined as "a generic term indicating a hearing disability which may range in severity from mild to profound. It includes the subsets of *deaf* and *hard of hearing*" (p. 509). A *deaf* person was recognized as "one whose hearing disability precludes successful processing of linguistic information through audition, with or without a hearing aid." (p. 509). A *hard of hearing* person was seen as "one who, generally, with the use of a hearing aid, has residual hearing sufficient to enable successful processing of linguistic information through audition." (p. 509)

It was also recognized that the impact of hearing loss differed depending on the age at which the hearing loss occurred. The CEASD, therefore, developed definitions related to the age at onset, distinguishing between *prelingual deafness* as "deafness present at birth, or occurring early in life at an age prior to the development of speech and language" (p. 510) and *postlingual deafness as* "deafness occurring at an age following the development of speech and language." (p. 510)

The CEASD included in its report Table 11-1, which related the hearing loss of the child to probable impact on communication and school placement.

CAUSES OF HEARING LOSS

The Hearing Mechanism

The ear is divided into three parts, the outer ear, middle ear, and inner ear. The outer ear consists of the pinna or the visible part of the ear and the auditory canal. The outer ear is sealed off from the middle ear by the tympanic membrane. The middle ear is a cavity containing three small bones, the incus, malleus, and stapes. These three bones connect the outer ear to the inner ear, transmitting the vibrations received by the tympanic membrane to the inner ear. The Eustachian tube connects the middle ear to the nasal passages. The inner ear is a bony capsule filled with fluid. The inner ear contains two major parts, the vestibular mechanism which is a balancing mechanism and the cochlea which changes the vibrations received by the ear to nerve impulses. The nerve impulses are sent to the brain via the VIIIth cranial nerve.

Impairment of hearing can occur anywhere along the hearing mechanism—within the ear, along the VIIIth cranial nerve, or within the brain itself. The causes of hearing loss can be broken into two categories, *endogenous* and *exogenous*. Endogenous losses are those which arise from conditions originating within the developing organism, such as genetic anomalies. Exogenous losses are caused by conditions from outside the organism such as disease or trauma.

Conductive Losses

Impairments that occur anywhere in the outer or middle ear are *conductive* losses. Most conductive losses are exogenous in nature, although some conditions are genetic in origin. The most common cause of conductive loss is from middle ear infections or *otitis media*. Infection reaches the middle ear through the Eustachian tube and in such cases, some type of fluid is usually present in the middle ear. The presence of otitis media can cause a reduction of the transmission of the sound waves from the tympanic membrane to the inner ear, resulting in a temporary hearing loss. This condition can become chronic, causing permanent damage to the hearing mechanism. Otitis media is the most frequent cause of hearing loss observed in school-age children (Newby, 1972).

Damage to the eardrum such as perforation can also cause a conductive loss. Perforation can be caused by the insertion of an object in the ear or through ear infections. Hearing can also be effected by excessive wax (cerumen) in the auditory canal. Removal of wax, a procedure done by a physician, is followed by immediate restoration of hearing.

Sensori-neural Losses

Damage to the inner ear or to the auditory pathways leading to the brain is referred to as a *sensori-neural* loss. Most congenital deafness is of the sensori-neural type. It has been estimated that perhaps as many as 50 percent of the sensori-neural losses in children are due to genetic factors (Nance, 1976). Several syndromes are identifiable where other conditions are present, but most genetic hearing losses are detected only because of the presence of other hearing impaired members in the family. Some genetically caused hearing losses do not occur at birth, but appear later in life. Likewise, some may be relatively mild in the young child and become progressively worse over time.

Damage to the sensori-neural mechanism may occur in utero. Rubella or German measles acquired by the mother during the first trimester of her pregnancy can be particularly damaging to the hearing mechanism of the fetus as well as causing other problems. Other diseases such as influenza or those accompanied by high fevers may also be damaging. Certain drugs may also be harmful to the developing fetus. Difficult births and prematurity also appear to be related to hearing loss (Cox & Lloyd, 1976).

Sensori-neural damage can occur after the birth of the infant. Diseases such as meningitis, scarlet fever, measles, and mumps are known to be involved in some hearing losses. Some drugs also lead to hearing loss and, when identified, are prescribed only in life-threatening situations (Newby, 1972).

Generally, the damage from sensori-neural losses is irreversible. One experimental procedure that has been attempted is acupuncture, but it has not been proven successful (Rosen, 1974). Experimental work is also being done with cochlear implants which are designed to stimulate the nerve endings within the inner ear. This procedure has shown some limited success with certain specific types of hearing loss (Glattke, 1976).

TESTS FOR HEARING LOSS

The testing of hearing can be done through the auditory canal (air conduction testing) and through the bones of the skull (bone conduction testing). In air conduction testing, the audiologist explains to the person that he will be wearing earphones and that a tone will be presented in the earphones, one ear at a time. A pure tone is used which sounds like the one produced by a tuning fork. When the patient hears the sound he is to raise his hand. Through a series of steps, the audiologist then can determine the *hearing threshold* of the patient. The hearing threshold is the degree of loudness required for a person to detect a tone at each frequency level tested.

The audiologist may also perform bone conducting testing. Sound can be transmitted directly to the inner ear through the bones of the skull, thereby bypassing the outer and middle ear. As the bony capsule of the inner ear vibrates, the fluid within the cochlea is set into motion allowing the individual to hear the sound being produced.

The Audiogram

The hearing threshold of a client is graphed on an audiogram (Fig. 11-1). Two dimensions of sound are represented on the audiogram. The first, *frequency,* is the pitch of the sound and is measured in *hertz* (Hz) or cycles per second (cps). The second dimension, *intensity* or loudness, is designated by the term *decibel* (dB). Frequency is plotted on the abscissa, the horizontal axis, and intensity on the ordinate or vertical axis. Standardized symbols have been established for air conduction testing. Results of testing the right ear are marked with a circle (O) in red, the left ear with a blue X. A solid line connects the results for each ear. The symbols for bone conduction testing are not standardized so it is necessary to look at the key on each audiogram to interpret the bone conduction testing results correctly. Generally, bone conduction results are recorded using one arrow with the point facing the right for the right ear (>) and the left for the left ear (<). Bone conduction results are not connected with a line (Fig. 11-1).

There also might appear on the audiogram symbols that indicate test-

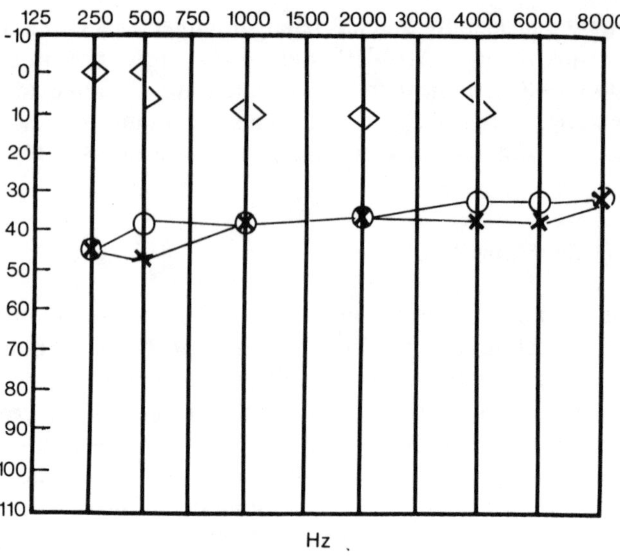

Keys to Audiogram:

	Color	AC	AC (Masked)	BC	BC (Masked)
Right	Red	O	△	>	▷
Left	Blue	X	□	<	◁
Sound Field	Green	W			

Fig. 11-1. Typical audiogram for a conductive hearing loss

ing has been done using masking. Masking is a white noise similar to static which is introduced into one ear through the earphone. Masking is most frequently utilized during bone conduction testing. When the bone conduction vibrator is placed on the skull, the tone sets the bony case of both ears into vibration at the same time, thereby making it difficult to determine if one ear is hearing better than the other. By masking out the sound in one ear, the other ear can be tested.

INTERPRETATION OF THE AUDIOGRAM

A person whose hearing is normal would have the results of testing appear close to zero dB across frequencies. The marking for his hearing threshold would appear near the top of the audiogram. If a person had a hearing loss, however, an audiologist would say that his threshold was *lower* than normal. The term lower is used because the greater the hearing loss, the closer to the bottom of the audiogram the hearing loss is marked. If a person's hearing is improved, it is said that his threshold is *raised;* if his hearing worsens, his threshold has *lowered*. However, if a sound is too quiet for a person to hear, we say that sound is *below* his threshold. If it is loud enough for the person to hear, we say it is *above* his threshold.

Diagnosis as to the type of hearing loss a client has can be made only by an otologist, a physician who is an ear specialist. However, specific types of hearing losses tend to have certain kinds of audiograms associated with them.

A typical audiogram for a conductive hearing loss was shown in Figure 11-1. The results indicate a loss through air conduction testing but none through bone conduction. A person with this type of loss is not able to hear the sound well through the earphones because the middle ear mechanism is not transmitting effectively. However, once the defective middle ear mechanism is bypassed using the bone conduction vibrator, it can be found that the inner ear is functioning normally. Generally, in conductive losses the air conduction scores are relatively the same across all frequencies. This is known as a flat loss or flat curve.

If the bone conduction scores are very close to the air conduction scores as in Figure 11-2, the hearing loss is probably sensori-neural. Bypassing the middle ear made no difference in the scores so there appears to be no damage in the middle ear. As in many sensori-neural losses, the curve is sloping, indicating a greater loss of hearing in the higher frequencies. The arrows pointing downward at 8,000 Hz indicate that the person did not respond at those frequencies.

The results of testing may show that air conduction scores are greater

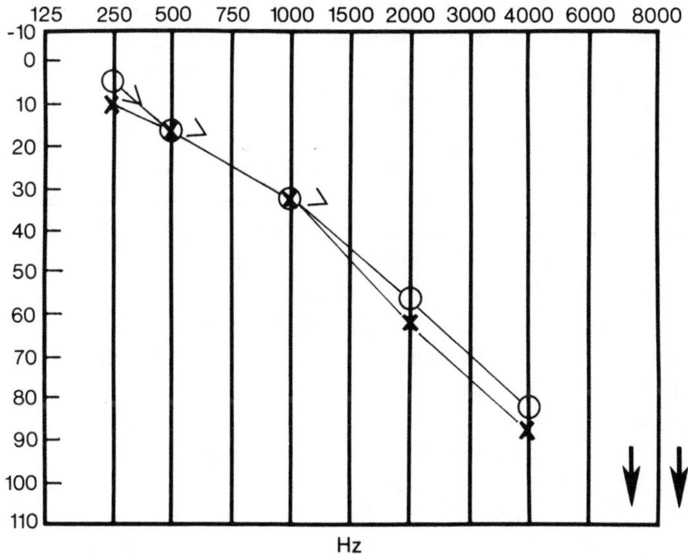

Fig. 11-2. Typical audiogram for a sensori-neural hearing loss.

than the bone conduction scores but the bone conduction scores are also lower than normal. The indication would be that there is a mixed loss. This type of differential diagnosis is important for treatment, as some conductive losses are medically treatable; while most sensori-neural losses are not.

Other Types of Hearing Tests

Information to determine how well a person responds to speech is obtained through a series of procedures called *speech audiometry*. These procedures usually include determining the level at which a person can just detect speech and how well a person can understand what he does hear.

Special procedures have been developed to test the hearing of infants and difficult-to-test groups such as emotionally disturbed and severely mentally retarded children. For the newborn infant *distraction audiometry,* which is dependent on the child responding to sudden loud sounds with certain reflexive movements, is used. For the older infant, and for the difficult-to-test child *operant audiometry* has been developed in which the child is rewarded for responding to the sound. *Play audiometry,* where the child is to respond to sound with an activity such as placing a peg in a hole, is frequently used with the preschooler. Another set of procedures called *respondent audiometry* has also been developed. In respondent audiometry the child is not required to actively respond; rather some type of instrumentation is utilized to determine changes in specific conditions in the body when sound is produced. Brain wave activity, heart beat rate, and respiratory rate are among some of the bodily activities that have been measured.

A new respondent procedure that is now being used extensively is *impedence audiometry*. Impedence audiometry is particularly useful in determining the condition of the middle ear but some information concerning sensori-neural losses can also be obtained. Except for impedence audiometry, operant techniques usually produce more accurate thresholds with difficult-to-test populations and are more easily administered than respondent techniques (Cox & Lloyd, 1976).

It would be ideal if all deaf and hard of hearing children could be identified at birth. Habilitative procedures could then begin immediately including training parents in those skills needed to initiate communication with their children. However, at the present time the technology of testing newborn infants frequently produces inaccurate results (Cox & Lloyd, 1976). It has been recommended that rather than test newborns, those children who are likely to have hearing losses should be placed in a high-risk registry for testing as soon as feasible (American Academy of Ophthalmology and Otolaryngology, American Academy of Pediatrics, and the American Speech and Hearing Association, 1974).

Definition and Placement

Although a child's audiogram may indicate he has a moderate hearing loss, he may be functioning more like a child with a profound loss in terms of communication skills. Therefore, because of the child's functioning, he is likely to be placed in a program for deaf children even though his audiogram might indicate he should be placed in a hard of hearing classroom. Likewise, there are children with profound losses who are so proficient in their communication skills that they are placed in hard of hearing programs or perhaps even in the regular classroom.

Prelingual and postlingual deafness also affect placement in that a child who has acquired language may only need minor assistance with his communication skills, although he is profoundly deaf. Therefore, in terms of placement, the educator will look first toward the child's audiogram but must then assess actual communication skills to determine the most optimal placement for the child.

COMMUNICATION SKILLS

The most direct consequence of a hearing loss is an effect on communication skills. The hearing mechanism no longer is an efficient mechanism for understanding the speech of others. Moreover, persons with a severe enough hearing impairment can no longer monitor their own speech productions which, in turn, effects the quality of speech output. And, if a severe hearing loss occurs early in life, the individual may have considerable difficulty with language acquisition.

A large part of the educational program for hearing impaired students consists of providing them with adequate communication skills. Speechreading (lipreading) is taught to provide the child with a visual system to substitute or supplement the damaged hearing mechanism in speech reception. Auditory training is utilized to help the student interpret distorted auditory input and to improve the monitoring of his own speech productions. Direct training in speech is also an essential component in order that the child be understood by the hearing population. Direct instruction in language acquisition constitutes the most crucial part of training for the prelingually deafened child for nearly all academic, social, and vocational learning is facilitated through language.

Speechreading (Lipreading)

For many persons who have sustained a hearing loss, the normal reception of speech through the auditory channel no longer occurs. The signal has become distorted and may be difficult if not impossible to understand. Speechreading is used to aid the listener to more correctly interpret auditory information in that for most hearing impaired persons, speechreading is used in combination with auditory information for understanding. The profoundly deaf person, however, may receive so little auditory information that he or she may have to rely extensively on speechreading. Although the term lipreading is more commonly known, the term speechreading is more appropriate in that information is obtained not only from the movement of the lips but also from jaw movements, tongue movements, and the facial expression of the speaker.

An early definition of speechreading, developed by Nitchie (1930, p. 341) was "the art of understanding a speaker's thought by watching the movements of his mouth." Both Nitchie and later professionals such as Jeffers & Barley (1971) emphasized that it is important to understand that the speechreader seldom recognizes every single sound that is uttered. Rather, the efficient speechreader gets a general idea of the message being transmitted and fills in the missing information through his knowledge of the structure of the language and his understanding of the concepts being transmitted.

VISIBILITY

Unfortunately, speechreading is an inadequate substitute for audition. The primary reason for the limitation of speechreading is the low visibility of many speech sounds. For the most part, the muscular movements that are required to produce speech sounds occur within the mouth and are, therefore, not visible. It has been estimated that under typical conditions, approximately 60 percent of the sounds are either obscured or invisible (Jeffers & Barley, 1971).

Another serious problem is the visibility of the speaker. Ideally, the speaker should be approximately six feet from the speechreader with his face turned toward the speechreader and the light shining on the face of the speaker rather than coming from behind him. When these conditions are not met, the task of the speechreader can be quite difficult.

It is to be noted that while training can improve the speechreader's skills, some individuals appear to be naturally better speechreaders than others (Coscarelli & Sanders, 1968). It is not well understood what factors contribute to proficient speechreading; for example, intelligence and amount of hearing loss do not appear to correlate significantly with speechreading skills (Simmons, 1959).

Assessing Speechreading Skills

The problems of evaluating the speechreading skills of persons who ave lost their hearing as adults are quite different than the evaluation of hildren who have acquired their losses prelingually. Tests given to hear- ıg impaired adults generally can utilize the total set of English commonly sed. A variety of types of responses can be used including both oral and ritten responses. But for testing children, it is important to take into onsideration the receptive language skills of each child being tested. If ıe testing material contains linguistic structures and vocabulary that the hild does not know, the results of the testing will not give valid informa- on concerning the child's speechreading skills. Moreover, the types of esponses that can be required of children are limited. Young children, for xample, cannot write sentences that they observe.

Formal Tests of Speechreading

Formal tests are available that determine how well an individual peechreads compared to a test group, but formal testing generally does ot provide prescriptive information. Moreover, unlike many types of esting, speechreading tests are not normed on the basis of age, for age oes not appear to directly effect the acquisition of speechreading skills Jeffers & Barley, 1971). Different tests are given to different age groups ot because of an expected difference in speechreading skills, but because f differences in the language skills of the subject and the types of re- ponses that different age groups are able to provide.

Tests for Adults and Hard of Hearing Children

JTLEY FILM TEST

The most commonly used test of speechreading is the *Utley Film Test* Utley, 1945), which can be given to hard of hearing children from age ight to adults. Test materials consist of sentences made up of common olloquial and idiomatic expressions. Each sentence is said once without oice, then the subjects write down what they think has been said. The est can be scored by counting the number of correct words written or by ounting correct sentences. In the latter type of scoring, absolutely cor- ect responses are not required. If the correct thought is understood, the esponse is considered correct, making the scoring of sentences more am- iguous than the scoring of correct words. The Utley test may be given ither "live" or in the film version.

BARLEY SPEECHREADING TEST—CID EVERYDAY SENTENCES

The *Barley Speechreading Test* (Barley, 1964) is similar to the *Utley test* in many respects, with familiar sentences given face-to-face withou voice and with each correct word being given one point. The criterion fo selection of sentences was somewhat different than the *Utley Test,* includ ing specifications such as having the vocabulary appropriate for adults being certain redundancy is high and the level of abstraction low, an using a variety of sentence lengths. As with the *Utley,* caution must b exercised in using this test with prelingually deafened hearing impaire children.

KEASTER FILM TEST OF LIP READING

The *Keaster Film Test of Lip Reading* (Lowell, 1958; Taafe, 1957) i a third test that is commonly used with adults and hard of hearing chil- dren. Two forms, the John Tracy Clinic Form A and Form B are avail- able. This test consists of sentences with each word being individually scored.

Tests for Children

BUTT CHILDREN'S SPEECHREADING TEST

The *Butt Children's Speechreading Test* (Butt & Chreist, 1968) con- sists of two parts: Test A, which is an informal checklist for children under three years of age and Test B, for children three years and older. A mental age of three years is necessary for success on all the items of the complete test. The items are ordered developmentally according to age.

Information for each item in the informal checklist is obtained by observing the child and playing with him. Included are items such as "Does the child attend to face?" (2 mos.), "Does the child inhibit on command?" (18 mos.), and "Can he speechread his own name?" (24 mos.).

Test B is given to the child using toys and other objects and pictures to elicit responses from the child. The child's response is the appropriate motor action. The child is asked to do such things as point to an object from an array of four, point to the picture of a common object, and follow simple directions such as, "Put the baby to bed."

CRAIG LIPREADING INVENTORY

The *Craig Lipreading inventory* (Craig, 1964) is a word and sentence recognition test with the vocabulary having been selected from words generally presented in kindergarten and the first grade. The test is designed for children from the first through the tenth grades. Both parts of the test are multiple choice with four choices. Each choice is presented with both the written response and picture together. The Word Recognition test includes items such as white, corn, thumb, and chair. The Sentence Recognition form consists of sentences such as "A coat is on a chair," "A boy stuck his thumb in the pie," and "Three stars are in the sky." The test can be given to a group of six children at one time, with each child marking his form with the response he perceives. A raw score is obtained from the form with the results differentiating the poor speechreader from the good speechreader.

COSTELLO TEST OF SPEECHREADING

The *Costello Test of Speechreading* (Costello, 1957) differs from the other tests in that an attempt was made to rank the test items from easy to difficult to speechread. The test consists of both word recognition and sentence recognition materials. Vocabulary used in the test was selected from the kindergarten lists. The word test is given by having the subject repeat what he lipreads. Because of speech problems, this section of the test is of limited use with severely and profoundly hearing impaired children. In the sentence section of the test, the child is requested to carry out the action stated in the sentence, an example being "Mother gave the baby a bath." Oral responses are also acceptable.

CAVENDER TEST OF LIPREADING

The *Cavender Test of Lipreading* (Cavender, 1949) was designed for testing hard of hearing children. The test is a multiple choice test with four words listed for each item. The examiner readers a sentence to the subject and the subject underlines one of the four words which he thinks appeared in the sentence. Like most formal tests, this one is designed only to differentiate the poor speechreader from the good one.

Informal Assessment of Speechreading

The formal tests mentioned above are generally adequate for determining whether a hard of hearing child or a postlingually deafened child with adequate language acquisition is a "poor" or "good" speechreader. However, the teacher of the prelingually deafened child or child with language acquisition problems will generally need to construct his or her own tests.

In constructing a teacher-made diagnostic test, it is essential that the items for testing include vocabulary and language structures that are well known to the child. The optimum vocabulary and structures to select would be those that the child uses spontaneously. It may be difficult to obtain adequate diagnostic information concerning preschool children due to the limited vocabulary of hearing impaired children in this age group.

When a child is initially referred for assessment, caution must be taken in interpreting low speechreading scores. If the examiner is unfamiliar with the child, his performance may be poorer than usual (Day, Fusfield, & Pintner, 1928). Likewise speechreading scores can be depressed when the child is tense (Jeffers & Barley, 1971).

AUDITORY SKILLS

Auditory training is the development of listening skills to aid the hearing impaired individual correctly interpret auditory input. The development of these skills is important not only to help the individual better understand what is being said to him, but to help him improve his own speech. The extent to which these skills are acquired is largely dependent on the amount and kind of hearing loss a person has. It is known, however, that given proper auditory training, an individual with even a profound hearing loss can learn to correctly interpret many aspects of speech (Ling, 1976).

Because auditory training can play such an important role in the development of communication skills, it is necessary that adequate assessment procedures be employed. The standardized speech tests utilized by audiologists do not, on the whole, provide prescriptive information which can be used in an auditory training program. Moreover, most of the standardized speech discrimination tests cannot be used with children that have profound hearing losses or who have serious language development problems.

Inventories

One type of assessment procedure is an inventory of the child's skills. Several inventories are available (e.g., Boothroyd, 1971). Inventories on each child are generally taken once or twice a year. They include items such as determining the child's ability to detect his own name, recognize commonly used phrases, and imitate certain rhythm patterns. Although these inventories can provide an ongoing record of the child's auditory skills, a more discriminating analysis may be needed for developing auditory training lessons. One of the more common procedures is assessment through informally constructed tests, a topic we will now examine.

Constructing an Assessment Test

Three different types of evaluation should be included in the assessment test: (1) the evaluation of nonspeech sounds such as those made by musical instruments, (2) the evaluation of specific features of speech such as rhythm and stress, and (3) the evaluation of individual speech sounds. For the speech parts of the test, it is desirable to include both male and female voices since male voices are lower pitched and are easier for many hearing impaired students to hear than the higher pitched female voices.

THE EVALUATION OF NONSPEECH SOUNDS

The first series of sounds to be tested are nonspeech sound for it is desirable to know if the child can detect and respond to sound. A loud, low-pitched drum can be useful for this type of testing. To determine if the child can detect sound the teacher may have the child raise his hand when he hears the drum being struck. The next level of testing is to determine if the child can detect on and off. A drum, xylophone, piano or other noisemaker is used for this item. The child is to raise his hand when he hears the sound and lower it when he no longer hears it. The child is then tested to determine if he can distinguish between high and low sounds. The child can be requested to put his hand up for high sounds and down for low sounds. A piano or xylophone can be used for this test. Loud and soft is a dimension that can be tested in a similar manner. It should be noted that high and low, and loud and soft should not be tested the same day as these two dimensions are easily confused by the child.

A final feature to be examined is the child's ability to imitate differing rhythm patterns. These patterns should vary from a simple one-two even beat pattern to more complex four- and five-beat rhythms. In testing rhythm, caution must be taken in interpreting incorrect responses in that the child may hear the item but not understand how to respond.

THE EVALUATION OF SOME SPECIFIC FEATURES OF SPEECH

Among the features of speech that can be tested are detection of speech, attention to rhythm, and interpretation of stress or accent. Detection of speech should be the first item tested. As in the nonspeech segment, the child is requested to raise his hand when he hears speech and lower his hand when he no longer hears the speech signal. The child's attention to speech rhythm can be tested by having the child lsiten to a paragraph being read. The teacher stops reading somewhere within the paragraph and the student must point to where the teacher stopped. The child who has a severe hearing loss must pay close attention to the number and rhythm of the syllables being produced to perform this task successfully.

Stress can be tested in two ways. The student may be presented with a sheet on which appear identical sentences. Each sentence, however, has a different word underlined (i.e., *He* is here; He *is* here; He is *here*). The teacher then reads one of the three sentences, emphasizing the underlined word. Stresses may also be evaluated by having the child imitate what he hears. The latter method may be necessary for children who cannot read, but may not be very useful for children with severe speech problems.

EVALUATION OF THE IDENTIFICATION OF INDIVIDUAL SPEECH SOUNDS

This section consists of determining which individual speech sounds or phonemes the student can correctly identify. Each vowel and consonant sound is to be tested. A method for testing speech sound identification is to present each sound in a consonant-vowel-consonant combination. The student may be given a multiple choice test sheet with items such as *mog, mag,* and *meg*. The teacher says one of the items while facing the student but covering the lower part of her face so the student cannot lipread her. All vowels can be tested this way where the consonants remain constant and only the vowel is varied. A similar test of consonant sounds can be performed where one consonant is varied and the vowel and other consonant remain the same. The sounds should not be presented in isolation, but rather in combination with other sounds. It is to be noted that with training many profoundly deaf children may learn to hear the differences between vowel sounds but may have considerable difficulty with many of the consonant sounds which are higher pitched (Ling, 1976).

Testing Hard of Hearing Children

For hard of hearing children, a more open-ended evaluation should be utilized (Sanders, 1971). The child may be given a series of familiar questions to answer. Sanders suggests that the questions should be related; testing should be done in both a quiet and noisy setting. It is also suggested that auditory and speechreading skills be assessed together to determine how the student functions as a whole in his receptive communication skills.

Testing Young Children and Multiply Handicapped Children

To test young children, such fine distinctions as suggested above may not be possible due to the child's limited vocabulary. Speech items for the test can be evaluated to some extent, using picture and words with which the child is very familiar. For example, the child may be asked to respond to his own and the names of children in the class and to sentences such as "What is your name?" and "How are you?" (O'Neill, 1975).

SPEECH ASSESSMENT

The purpose of establishing a speech program for children with hearing impairments is to help the child develop speech skills so he can be understood by the public in general. While success in this area has not been attained by all hearing impaired children many have been able to gain a degree of intelligibility which has allowed them a considerable degree of freedom in participating in the hearing world (Ling, 1976). Generally, speech assessment is done by a speech therapist except in programs for hearing impaired children where assessment may be carried out by the teacher (Ling). This section will not attempt to prepare the teacher to do an assessment but rather to understand the procedures that are used for assessment and to interpret reports provided by the speech therapist.

Articulation

The assessment of articulation involves the evaluation of the child's production of the individual speech sounds or phonemes. In most cases, articulation is assessed by having the child recite a series of words. The list may be made up of pictures for younger children and written lists for older children (e.g., Goldman & Fristoe, 1969). Most lists contain each phomeme in the initial, medial, and final position. For example, for the "k" phoneme, the child might be asked to say the words *c*amp, be*c*ause, and ba*ck*. The therapist then notes if the child produces the phoneme correctly, omits the phoneme, or distorts it. If the child distorts the phoneme, notes are made concerning the configuration of the distortion. The teacher may then be provided with the articulation checklist by the speech therapist.

McLean (1976) states that for mentally retarded children and other developmentally disabled children, a sample of spontaneous running speech provides better information for analysis than a test using single words. The articulation errors that children make in running speech may be quite different than the errors in single-word responses. Such a procedure could also be used with hearing impaired children if the speech problems of the child are not too severe. If they are quite severe, however, it can be very difficult to determine just what words the child is using, so analysis of the individual phonemes in the sample may not be possible.

Voice

The speech therapist probably will analyze the voice quality of the child's speech. Usually, this analysis is more subjective than the analysis of articulation with the evaluative statements more general in nature. The evaluator will make statements concerning the overall voice quality, noting whether it is "harsh," "breathy," and so forth, and whether the voice is weak or strong. The therapist will also determine whether the voice is nasal or denasalized.

Overall pitch will also be evaluated because many deaf children experience considerable problems with pitch control. Specific intonation problems are also examined. Intonation is an important linguistic feature of speech as it can lead to an understanding of the intention of the speaker (Takefuta, 1975). For example, the difference between "He is here!" and "He is here?" is largely an intonational difference.

Rhythm

Appropriate speech rhythms can help considerably in the production of intelligible speech (Hood & Dixon, 1969; Heidinger, 1972). Rhythm is evaluated to determine if the child is using correct phrasing and if he is speaking at an appropriate rate.

Intelligibility

Usually, an overall evaluation of intelligibility is made. Although several different procedures are used, the procedure used at Clarke School for the Deaf (1971) is fairly typical. In this approach each child is given a speech intelligibility test semi-annually in which the child is required to read six unrelated sentences into a tape recorder. Six adult listeners who are familiar with the speech of deaf children listen to the tapes and write down what they think the child said. The results are converted to a percentage known as the Speech Intelligibility Score. The child's recordings from each test are spliced together so that cumulative data is kept for each child.

The Speech Report

After the child's speech has been evaluated, the therapist should provide the teacher with a report concerning each of the dimensions discussed. The therapist should then inform the teacher of the speech goals that have been selected for the child and the remediation procedures to be used. The therapist should also inform the teacher specifically what can be done in the classroom to work toward the stated goals.

ASSESSMENT OF LANGUAGE OF HEARING-IMPAIRED CHILDREN

Assessment in language is the core of assessment of hearing impaired children for much learning is very dependent on the progress the child is making in this basic skill. Assessment of language covers three areas. The first is the assessment of syntactic or grammatical development. The second is assessing semantic development or the understanding of meaning. The third area is the assessment of concept attainment.

Assessing Syntactic Development

Language is usually broken into two aspects, expressive and receptive language. The expressive language of the child is the language he or she produces through signing, speaking, writing, and, in some cases, gesturing. The receptive language of the child is the language he understands.

ASSESSING EXPRESSIVE LANGUAGE

Previous to the more widespread use of sign language in the classroom, most syntactic assessment had to be done using written language samples (e.g., Templin, 1950; Simmons, 1962). Spoken utterances were not conducive to analysis as the speech of many hearing impaired children is quite imperfect. While the experienced listener can usually get the drift of what is being said, it is very difficult to know whether a child used a specific feature such as a plural, article, or past tense marker. Developmental schemes were generally not used for analyzing written language. Either adult grammars were used as a basic comparison or the hearing impaired student's written samples were compared with the written samples of normal children. Unfortunately, the analysis of the written language of hearing impaired children is a relatively poor indicator of what the child can do with his expressive language. A more adequate assessment of the child's true expressive language is now possible because of the use of sign language.

Three types of assessment are commonly used, the checklsit, the language sample, and the use of imitation. Published programs frequently include checklists (e.g., Blackwell, 1971). The teacher, over the course of several days, is to note whether the child utilizes certain features and structures that are included in the program. The teacher can either make observations or can attempt to elicit the required structures. No assumption is made that the knowledge of one type of structure implies a knowledge of other types of structures.

The use of a checklist for determing the child's language development has severe limitations. The assumption that the checklist includes the most important features of language is questionable for many inventories are largely based on the intuitions of the writer of the language program. In addition, inventories frequently do not allow for recording or interpreting utterances that do not fit into the patterns included in the program.

Another method for obtaining expressive language information is to take a language sample. The teacher or an observer records the child's utterances over a period of time. The sample is analyzed, generally using some type of developmental scheme such as Lee's Developmental Sentence Types (Lee, 1974) or Brown's Five Stages (Brown, 1973). When this type of analysis uses a development scheme (see Chap. 8), it is assumed that if certain structures appear, then the child can probably produce simpler structures that may not have appeared in the sample. The analysis of the sample should enable the teacher to know what kinds of structures the youngster has under control, usually those features that he uses accurately 90 percent of the time. By using a developmental scheme, the teacher can avoid teaching structures to the child for which he is not prepared developmentally.

Several difficulties are contained in this method of assessment. For one thing, taking a language sample is not an easy procedure. It can be difficult for a teacher to take a language sample while working with several children. Generally, someone else must take the language sample. Second, it is difficult to record exactly what is contained in the utterance. The recorder must be very careful not to unconsciously include those features the child omitted, such as recording a past tense marker the child did not actually use. Moreover, the word order used by hearing impaired children is not necessarily the same order used by normal children so the recorder must be very alert to record precisely the order used. A third problem with the language sample is that hearing impaired children are very likely to use different language structures in different settings. For example, during the language period, a routine may have been established where the youngster is required to say "Today is Wednesday. Yesterday was Tuesday. Tomorrow will be Thursday." He may produce these sentences during the language period every day without error. However, there may be no other appearance of the "to be" verbs at any other time during the day. It should be noted that the language obtained while engaged in academic discourse with the teacher and the language used while involved in conversation with peers can be quite different. A fourth problem lies in the fact that analyzing a language sample may be a difficult task. Usually, a certain amount of knowledge of psycholinguistics is necessary along with a thorough understanding of the theory contained in whatever developmental scheme is being utilized. The fifth and perhaps the most serious objection to the language sample method, however, is that just because a particular feature does not appear, does not mean that the child does not have the feature in his expressive language. It may simply mean that there was no appropriate opportunity for the child to use the feature. It is quite common, for example, to take a sample of 200 utterances and find no instance in which the regular past tense was used simply because there was no occasion in which it was required. However, by having the language sample as a set of information about a student, the teacher can probe for specific features and be alert for the student's use of features not previously observed.

One method that has been developed to overcome some of the problems of obtaining information through a language sample is the use of imitated sentences (Slobin & Welsh, 1973). Research indicates that in most instances a child cannot imitate a feature he cannot produce (Dale, 1976). It would follow then that a suitable method for probing for language features would be to ask the child to imitate specific sentences. The Carrow Elicited Language inventory (Carrow, 1974) is an example of a test based on imitation. However, the use of imitated utterances may have some limitations for hearing impaired children in that many hearing impaired children are specifically trained to imitate sentences, thus distorting the results obtained. There is also some indication that at the early stages of language development, there are some situations in which a child may produce utterances he cannot imitate (Bloom, 1974).

Limitations of Developmental Schemes

A problem with using developmental schemes is that our understanding of language development is rapidly changing. For example, a scheme called pivot-open grammar was recently in common use for analyzing the two-word utterances of children (Braine, 1963). Now pivot-open grammar is usually not considered to be an adequate procedure for analyzing these structures (Brown, 1973).

A second problem in using developmental schemes is the underlying assumption that the order in which language develops in normal children is the necessary order in which language must develop; that is, the proposition that the child cannot produce a structure in Step 2 until he has completed Step 1. It is not known conclusively what sequence is necessary for normal children, much less for hearing impaired children. The possibility that language development is tied to cognitive development is being investigated (Brown, 1973; Edwards, 1973) and there are indications that for the most part hearing impaired children develop normally cognitively (Furth, 1966). If the hearing impaired child is normally progressing, then his cognitive development may be considerably more advanced than his language development. Therefore, developmental sequences that may be necessary for hearing children might have little applicability to hearing impaired children.

Finally, comparatively little is known about the rules of English grammar. Knowledge concerning these structures is more complete at the early stages of development and more superficial in the later stages. Unfortunately, schemes used to evaluate the syntactic growth of hearing impaired children must then deal with a fairly limited set of structures.

ASSESSING RECEPTIVE SYNTACTIC KNOWLEDGE

Tests have been developed which include an assessment scale of receptive language (i.e., Callier-Azusa), but these scales tend to be less complete than the scales for observing expressive language simply because it is so difficult to establish adequate ways of evaluating appropriate responses (see Chap. 8). Usually, these scales provide very general information concerning whether a child's performance is similar to normal children in his age group but they do not provide information concerning the specific language structures the youngster has.

Assessing Syntactic Development in Children Using Sign Language

Most of the information that is available concerning syntactic development deals with the development of grammar of children speaking English; however, many hearing impaired children are exposed to some form of sign language early in life. Some of these children learn Ameslan, a sign language system whose grammar differs considerably from English. If a teacher has a student who has been exposed to Ameslan, she must make every effort to determine if the structures used by the student are Ameslan structures or whether the student is using rules which are based neither in English or Ameslan, but are idiosyncratic to the child.

Vocabulary Assessment of Hearing Impaired Children

While a fairly substantial body of theoretical and research literature exists regarding the syntactic development of normal children, little is known or understood about vocabulary development. Commonly used standardized vocabulary tests include the *Peabody Picture Vocabulary Test* (PPVT) (Dunn, 1965), the *Full Range Picture Vocabulary Test* (Ammons & Ammons, 1948), and part of the *Utah Test of Language Development* (Mecham, Jex, & Jones, 1967). The information that can be obtained from these kinds of tests simply indicates where a student stands in relation to his peers in terms of vocabulary development. They do not provide the teacher with information concerning what specific vocabulary words the child might be expected to have on the basis of his performance. In fact, there is no standardized measure now available which can be of use to the teacher in determining what specific words a child knows. The assessment that a teacher must use with hearing impaired children is one in which the teacher selects the words a child must know to understand a specific topic. She then tests the students to determine which words they know and which they do not. Open-ended assessment for vocabulary is usually the most appropriate. The test can either be a paper-pencil test where the child writes what he knows about a given word, or oral where the student tells the teacher what he knows. Multiple choice or matching tests which are commonly used to assess vocabulary with normal children are inadequate for hearing impaired children as they tell the teacher little about what the student knows concerning a new vocabulary word other than that he may have a vague notion of what the word means.

Concept Assessment

A statement frequently heard in a classroom of hearing impaired children is "He understands the concept but he doesn't have the language to express it." There are no tests available which can provide a teacher with overall information concerning what concepts a child has or does not have. As in vocabulary assessment, teachers must assess the student's knowledge of concepts that are specific to the subject being taught. This can be very challenging when the child does not have the language for discussing the concepts to be evaluated. The teacher must be very ingenious in setting up situations that will test the child's knowledge of specific concepts. For example, if the teacher wishes to test a child's knowledge on safety rules concerning bicycling, the teacher might use a chalkboard on the floor and draw in streets, sidewalks, houses, etc. Then she could use toy bicycles, cars, and people to determine what the child knows about where to ride her bicycle, what to do in intersections, how to ride in traffic, and so forth. The child would be able to demonstrate fairly well what he or she knows about bicycle safety without really having that much language to express the concepts.

INTELLECTUAL ASSESSMENT

Assessing the intelligence of hearing impaired children is no simple matter. All the theoretical and practical problems that apply to testing of normal children also apply to hearing impaired children. Moreover, there are serious additional problems in testing hearing impaired children related to the language problem (Hoemann & Ullman, 1976). Most hearing impaired individuals simply do not have sufficient command of English to respond to the test items; hence, tests that have an extensive verbal component are notoriously unreliable. The literature is replete with examples of hearing impaired children who have been placed in institutions for severely mentally retarded children on the basis of a verbal IQ (Vernon, 1976). Teachers do not usually administer intelligence tests, but may be required to work with the results of these tests. Therefore, it is necessary that they be familiar with the tests being used, the problems with the intelligence testing of hearing impaired children, and the uses that are made of the resulting data.

Tests Used with Hearing Impaired Children

In general, only performance IQ tests are given to hearing impaired subjects. Levine (1974) found that the tests most commonly used for assessing the intelligence of hearing impaired subjects were the Wechsler scales. These tests were used at the preschool (*Wechsler Preschool and Primary Scale of Intelligence,* Wechsler, 1967), intermediate (*Wechsler Intelligence Scale for Children,* Wechsler, 1955), and adult (*Wechsler Adult Intelligence Scale,* Wechsler, 1955) levels (see Chap. 7). Although only the performance scales were used in most cases, parts of the verbal scales were occasionally used. Other frequently used intelligence tests in rank order were the *Leiter International Performance Scales* (Leiter, 1948), *The Grace Arthur Performance Scale* (Arthur, 1947), the *Hiskey-Nebraska Test of Learning Aptitude* (Hiskey, 1966), the *Columbia Mental Maturity Scales* (Burgemeister, Blum, & Lorge, 1959), and the *Merrill-Palmer Scale of Mental Tests* (Sutsman, 1931).

Of the tests commonly used, Vernon (1976) reports that the *Wechsler Intelligence Scale for Children* (1955) is the best test for deaf children ages

9 to 16, while the *Wechsler Preschool and Primary Scale of Intelligence* (Wechsler, 1967) is not as suitable for hearing impaired children. Vernon states that the *Leiter International Performance Scale* (1948 revision) is somewhat lacking in validation but is an excellent test for young hearing impaired children and emotionally disturbed hearing impaired children who could not otherwise be tested. Vernon (1976) suggests that the *Hiskey-Nebraska Test of Learning Aptitude* (Hiskey, 1966) is a useful test for hearing impaired children although it is somewhat weak for three- and four-year-olds. The *Grace Arthur Performance Scale* (Arthur, 1947) was rated as fair at best because timing is heavily emphasized.

For the preschool child Vernon (1976) recommends the *Test for Preschool Deaf Children* (Smith, 1967) but also suggests that the *Merrill-Palmer Scale of Mental Tests* (Sutsman, 1931) is fair for young hearing impaired children.

Problems of Testing Intelligence

With the exception of the *Hiskey-Nebraska,* IQ tests have not been normed on hearing impaired populations. The *Hiskey-Nebraska* is a nonverbal test that provides standard pantomime directions for administration. The 12 nonverbal subtests include measuring such things as bead patterns, memory for color, picture identification, and spatial reasoning. However, the *Hiskey-Nebraska* does not compare favorably with other tests (e.g., the WISC) in areas such as standardization and intercorrelations among subjects (Hoemann & Ullman, 1976).

There does remain some controversy as to whether IQ tests should be normed with hearing impaired populations (Hoemann & Ullman, 1976). It is argued that separate norms for the hearing impaired population are not desirable because this might result in attitudes that are paternalistic and discriminative toward hearing impaired individuals. Also, if IQ tests prove to have good predictive validity in terms of the ability of the individual to function in the larger society, then the general norms might have some usefulness. However, because of the language problem, hearing impaired chidlren are exposed to a different set of experiences than hearing children so norms using deaf populations could provide educators and counselors useful information concerning how a particular youngster is functioning in relation to his hearing impaired peers.

A major problem in administering intelligence tests is that most have a standardized set of verbal instructions for administration. In nearly all cases, these instructions must be modified for hearing impaired children. If the instructions are given verbally, the subject's performance might be quite poor due to his inability to lipread the examiner or understand the language of the instructions. The performance of the client might not then be indicative of his ability to perform the task. The examiner must then resort to signs, pantomiming, gestures, written instructions, or some combination of these. It is not known what effect this change in administration has on the results obtained.

A far more serious problem may be the familiarity of the tester with hearing impaired children. In Levine's survey of psychologists (1974), she found that 65 percent of those who responded had had no experience with the hearing impaired population prior to being involved in psychological practice with this group. Moreover, 83 percent reported that on-the-job training was their only preparation for performing psychological work with hearing impaired individuals. The remaining 17 percent had extremely varied types of training from "instruction from predecessor" to more formal training programs. Furthermore, 50 percent of the examiners reported they had no knowledge of manual language and another 40 percent rated their manual abilities as being poor. Therefore, at least 90 percent of those who are testing hearing impaired students cannot effectively communicate with those who use sign language as their major means of communication.

Testing the Hard of Hearing Child

It can be particularly difficult for the examiner to realize that a hard of hearing child might be more properly administered a performance IQ test than a verbal test. In the one-to-one situation of a quiet testing room, it may appear that the hard of hearing child has few communication problems. However, little of the child's learning takes place in such a setting. Classrooms are generally noisy and the hard of hearing child might not have had the opportunity to acquire the concepts and vocabulary that the normal child has. His performance on the verbal part of an intelligence test can, therefore, be lowered. To prevent the possibility of obtaining an inaccurate score, the psychologist should give the student a test that has both a verbal and performance section. If the child performs much better on the performance section than the verbal section, the results of the verbal section should be considered suspect. If the child is not receiving any special services, the disparate results of the test might indicate that such services would be of benefit to the child.

The Teacher and the Intelligence Test

Most teachers of hearing impaired children are aware of the difficulties of obtaining reliable intelligence test results for hearing impaired children. While many school programs require that the IQ of their students be obtained, teachers only occasionally take interest in the results. The most frequent use of the IQ test is to exclude children who are considered mentally retarded from programs for hearing impaired children (Healey, 1975).

PERSONALITY TESTING

Personality testing has proved to be so difficult that Levine (1976) reports such testing is being done much less frequently now than in the past. If accurate personality testing were possible, the results could be useful to both vocational and guidance counselors. However, personality tests that have been developed are so dependent on adequate communication skills that the results obtained from most personality tests are frequently useless (Bolton, 1976). Many of the written personality tests such as the *Minnesota Multiphasic Personality Inventory* (MMPI) (Hathaway & McKinley, 1967) require at least a sixth-grade reading level. Rosen (1967) found that even hearing impaired clients who had a sixth-grade reading level could not adequately respond to the items on the *MMPI* because of the extensive use of idioms in the test items that were unfamiliar to many hearing impaired individuals. The results of any written test must then be viewed with a considerable amount of suspicion.

Tests that require the client to write extensively also have serious limitations unless the hearing impaired individual has a high level of expressive language. Hearing impaired persons have been diagnosed as schizophrenic on the basis of their written language when, in fact, their bizarre written productions were due to their specific language problems (Vernon, 1976).

The personality tests most commonly used with hearing impaired persons are *Draw-A-Man* (Machover, 1949), *Thematic Apperception Test* (TAT) (Stein, 1955), *Rorschach Ink Blot Test* (Rorschach, 1942), *House-Tree-Person Technique* (HTP) (Buck, 1949), *Rotter Incomplete Sentences Blank* (Rotter & Rafferty, 1942), *Make-A-Picture-Story Tests* (MAPS) (Schneidman, 1952), and the *Bender-Gestalt* (Clawson, 1962).

The *Draw-A-Man Test* is probably the most practical projective test for hearing impaired clients (Vernon, 1976). It is suitable for hearing impaired persons from nine years to adulthood. It is relatively nonverbal and serves as a screening device for detecting very severe emotional problems. The interpretation of the test is very subjective so it is important that the tester be familiar with hearing impaired clients. The *H.T.P.* technique is similar to the *Draw-A-Man* test and requires little verbal communication.

Success using the *Thematic Apperception Test* or the *Children's Apperception Test* is highly dependent on the client possessing a high level of communication either in English or sign language (Vernon, 1976). If the examiner does not have adequate sign language skills then the use of an interpreter is permissible, but this procedure is not as desirable as having the client and the tester communicate directly. The *Rorschach Ink Blot Test* is also subject to the same problems. Vernon states that in theory, a very bright hearing impaired subject might respond to the test through writing, but there is a great possibility this would be unsatisfactory. The *Rotter Incomplete Sentences Blank* can also be used only with subjects who have a high level of vocabulary otherwise the results obtained are questionable.

In administering personality tests it is usually recommended that the examiner begin with the easiest, least verbal tests before proceeding to the more difficult verbal tests. Even so, the results of personality tests must be reviewed with great caution. The highly verbal nature of most tests makes them unsuitable for hearing impaired clients and most personality tests require a high degree of rapport between the examiner and the client. The examiner, in interpreting the results, must always take into account the fact that most hearing impaired clients have generally had a very different set of life experiences than hearing clients.

ACHIEVEMENT TESTING AND ACADEMIC ASSESSMENT

Formal Tests

Until the early 1970s the only achievement tests available to hearing impaired students were those designed to be given to normal students. No norms for these tests were available for hearing impaired students. Moreover, the directions and methods of administering the tests frequently caused the students problems in taking the test. For example, the spelling section of an achievement test sometimes was given by the teacher dictating a list of words to the students. The spelling test thus became a lipreading test with the results giving little indication of the true level of spelling skills of the students.

A second problem with achievement tests was the nature of the content. To some extent success on these parts of the test is dependent on the student being familiar with specific concepts and vocabulary. For example, social studies programs for hearing impaired children are increasingly moving away from the programs offered to normal children. The emphasis is now on developing everyday living skills instead of academic achievement which places hearing impaired children at a distinct disadvantage in handling individual items on the achievement test.

Another serious problem in evaluating the achievement of hearing impaired children is that successful completion of items in many areas is dependent on the student's reading skills. Even if a student does know the concepts being tested, but cannot read the items being presented, he is likely to fail the item.

Recently the Office of Demographic Studies (Academic Achievement Test Performance of Hearing Impaired Children, United States, 1971) conducted extensive nationwide testing of hearing impaired children using the *Stanford Achievement Tests*. There is some indication that profoundly deaf children as a whole make little progress as measured by the achievement tests (Hoeman & Ulman, 1976). For example, 54 percent of these children who were 13 years or older were given either the Primary I or Primary II forms of the battery. This was indicative of the teacher's judgment that the higher level for most tests would be inappropriate for their students.

Probably the most serious complaint concerning achievement tests is that they do not provide useful programming information for the teachers, For example, in the selection of reading material the teacher may look to the results of an achievement test to select a reader at the appropriate reading level. The results of the reading test can keep the teacher from making serious mistakes such as selecting a seventh-grade reader for a student who reads at a third-grade reading level. However, because books that are listed as being at the same level differ considerably in language structure, use of idioms, and vocabulary, a considerable amount of observation of the performance of the student is needed before a selection can be made. Further, most achievement tests do not provide specific information to the teacher concerning the skills and concepts a student has. After achievement testing has been completed many teachers feel that the students have not been fairly evaluated in terms of the general overall advances they have made.

Despite all these difficulties, some formal achievement testing continues. The achievement test being most commonly used today is the *Stanford Achievement Test* (Levine, 1974) utilizing a form which has been designed for administration to hearing impaired students (Trybus & Jenesema, 1976). The *Wide Range Achievement Test* (Jastak, Bijou, & Jastak, 1965) is also widely used, while a few programs are using the *Metropolitan Achievement Test* (Durost, Evans, Leake, Bowman, Cosgrove, & Read, 1962).

Informal Assessment

Because standardized achievement tests yield such a low level of information for academic programming, teachers of hearing impaired children must develop informal tests for academic diagnosis and evaluation.

READING

For hearing impaired children success in reading is in many ways dependent on the level of lanugage acquisition of the student. Because of the language acquisition problems and because of the student's hearing problem, many of the skills normally utilized to help children learn to read cannot be used.

Teaching reading during the first few years for the normal child consists largely of giving the child the skills for identifying printed words that he already has in his expressive and receptive vocabularies. For example, in teaching the normal child phonics the primary task is to have the child match the sounds he produces when "sounding out" a word with a word in his auditory memory. Unfortunately, hearing impaired children frequently do not have the vocabulary presented in the primers in either their receptive or expressive vocabularies. So the process of teaching reading to hearing impaired children becomes one of teaching unfamiliar words to the child, a task very different from teaching the child to identify words he already knows.

For the profoundly deaf child phonics is *not* a usable skill. The principal decoding skill available to these students is, then, the use of contextual information. However, even here hearing impaired children have considerable difficulty. Successful identification of a word is largely dependent on the child having an adequate grasp of grammar. For example, if a child sees the word "jump" in the sentence "The dog jumped over the fence" and the word "jump" is new to him, he can use the rest of the sentence to help him come to a reasonable conclusion as to what the unfamiliar word might be. However, in order for the child to have a reasonable opportunity for identifying the new word he must know that it belongs to the class of verbs. Most children with normal hearing have little difficulty with this task because of their mastery of the rules of grammar. However, hearing impaired children make many errors in selecting even the right grammatical class of words, not to mention the correct word itself, performing at a lower level than even their achievement test results would indicate (Moores, 1970). Nevertheless, in selecting appropriate reading materials the teacher must take into account not only the achievement test scores of the child but also whether the material is constructed in such a way that the child is given an opportunity to develop skills in contextual analysis.

The teacher must also carefully examine the materials for vocabulary load, the use of idioms, and language structures. Most readers at least through the third grade contain a list of the "new" vocabulary words. However, there are likely to be many other words in the reader that are new to the hearing impaired student. In examining the readers for idioms the teacher must keep in mind that for hearing impaired students idioms are as unfamiliar as new vocabulary words and must be taught to the student just as new vocabulary words are. The teacher must also examine the materials for difficult language structures. Readers differ considerably in the language structures they use and the more complex structures are difficult for hearing impaired students to interpret (Quigley, Smith, & Wilbur, 1974).

Given those difficulties, how can teachers initially diagnose their students' reading level and then select appropriate materials? As noted before achievement testing can only give a very rough idea of the level of the reader that can be utilized. One common method used in the regular classroom for selecting an appropriate reader is the placement test where selections from different parts of a reader or from several readers in a series are to be read by the student. The teacher notes the number of errors the student makes and then may ask the student for information concerning what he has read. Some reading series provide placement tests.

This method is usually only partly useful for hearing impaired students. The teacher cannot rely on observing the students' reading aloud. Many hearing impaired students with poor speech will "fake" reading a word. They will attempt to make some sounds which resemble the word using the skills developed in their speech training. Because of the student's poor speech the teacher does not know if the student has made an error in reading or in speech.

If the student is signing, the words for which he used a sign are probably known. If a student fingerspells a word, however, it does not necessarily mean the student does not know the word. It may simply mean he does not know the sign for the word. Moreover, there are many common words for which there are no signs and fingerspelling must be used.

After tentatively selecting material that might be usable, the teacher must then determine its appropriateness by having the student read the material and then questioning the student to determine how much of the material he has understood. Oral questioning is a much more suitable method than using a written test. The teacher can ask open-ended questions and formulate each new question on the basis of the student's responses. Written tests cannot offer this flexibility and are affected by the student's writing skills. Even multiple choice and true-false tests are limited in that a right answer does not tell the teacher whether the student guessed or whether he really knew the right answer. Moreover, all written tests are based on the student's reading skills, which may not be the same skills presented in the text.

ARITHMETIC

In evaluating the arithmetic skills of hearing impaired children it is very important to differentiate between the child's computational skills and skills for solving verbal problems. Hearing impaired children generally perform at a much higher level on computational skills than on verbal problems (Trybus & Karchmer, 1977). For many hearing impaired students it is inappropriate to "place" them in a mathematics series and go through the math series in the sequence presented. Differential diagnosis for each skill is essential to determine which specific skills a student has.

To determine the child's skills the teacher must utilize a diagnostic test that evaluates each skill. Some series provide such tests but often the teacher must develop these tests independently. A good method for developing such diagnostic tests is taking problems from the review tests at the end of units. The teacher can then determine where the child is with regard to each of the many different mathematics skills presented in the text.

SOCIAL STUDIES

Determining what are the skills and concepts to teach a child in the area of social studies is largely dependent on the curriculum adopted by the program. Traditionally, the social studies were designed to help children coming from many diverse backgrounds to become "Americanized." Therefore, the emphasis in social studies was basically factual—learning about the United States, the structure of its government, and its role in world history. Recently, however, this role has become deemphasized and social studies are now trying to teach students the skills used by social scientists to analyze the behavior of groups of people in relation to other groups and to the environment. Social studies are, therefore, more oriented toward a problem-solving approach (Banks & Cleggs, 1977).

The social studies curricula for hearing impaired students are reflecting this change. However, these curricula are also influenced by a deficiency that many hearing impaired students exhibit in the area of everyday living skills (e.g., how to shop effectively, how to use public transportation, and how to fill out application forms). The need of hearing impaired students for acquiring the problem-solving skills presented in the "new" social studies in everyday living is recognized (Grammatico & Miller, 1974). Thus, the ideal social studies curriculum would be the one that utilizes the problem-solving skills developed in the new social studies, which applies these skills to everyday living situations.

Some programs offer a set social studies curriculum but many do not. The teacher is often left with the need to develop a curriculum. The teacher must determine what problem-solving skills and everyday living skills his or her students have. To accomplish this the teacher must pretest every unit that will be presented to make sure that the student has the entry skills needed but does not already know the concepts included in the unit. Testing must be done on a unit by unit basis as there is no "natural" sequence in social studies. An open-ended oral test is probably the most appropriate kind of evaluation tool, for if the test is written the teacher does not know whether the student's reading and writing skills or his social studies concepts are being tested.

SCIENCE

As in social studies the type of placement testing that is done is dependent on the curriculum that is utilized by the program. Testing will be related to both the skills and specific concepts presented in the curriculum. The science curriculum is more likely to follow the regular curriculum than is the social studies due to the problem-solving and experimental basis of most present day science curricula. As in social studies, testing in the sciences should be done orally with open-ended questioning procedures.

PHYSICAL EDUCATION

Hearing impaired studies without any physical problems exhibit the same range of skills as normal students in the area of physical education. However, hearing impaired students frequently do not know the "rules of games" that are often transmitted orally. Therefore, hearing impaired children are frequently excluded from playing games with normal children. It is therefore important that a teacher determine what rules the students know both in terms of formal games taught in physical education and informal games that children play at home. Determination of the student's knowledge of rules can be gained through open-ended questioning and through observing the student playing games.

VOCATIONAL ASSESSMENT

The vocational assessment of hearing impaired students usually takes place during the student's secondary years or during the student's entrance into a postsecondary vocational program. The student may be given a number of tests exploring skills in a variety of areas (Wentling, Butterweck, & Zook, 1976).

Communication Skills

Assessment of the student's speech, speechreading, language, and writing skills will be carried out. The vocational counselor will be particularly concerned to determine what method of communication the student can use on the job. Can the student speechread well enough to understand his employer and fellow workers or will he be dependent on written notes? Can he understand written notes? Is his speech clear enough to be understood or will he have to write notes? If he needs to write notes, can his language structures be understood?

Academic Skills

Reading and mathematics skills are the two academic skills that will likely be assessed. The vocational counselor will want to know if the student can read directions, if he can fill out application forms and other employment forms, and perform other tasks that might be required on the job. The counsellor will test the student's mathematics skills to determine if he can do everyday math such as balancing a checkbook and making change.

Vocational Aptitude

Because of the language problems of many hearing impaired students, a large proportion of the population have jobs involving manual labor (Crammatle, 1962). Vocational aptitude tests that assess manual dexterity and other manually related skills are usually employed.

Vocational Adjustment

Vocational adjustment includes the evaluation of work behavior, including the attitudes, values, and habits of the client (Bolton, 1976). While some vocational programs utilize personality tests to help determine the problems a student might have in vocational adjustment these tests are generally not useful for hearing impaired students. Assessment of the students in this area is, then, usually accomplished in workshops or in on-the-job training sites. From observations it can be determined if the student needs assistance with problems such as getting to work on time, attending to the task and responding appropriately to criticisms (see Chapter 16).

Interest Assessment

Hearing impaired individuals may not be exposed to a wide range of experiences so may have little idea of the variety of jobs available to hearing impaired individuals in the occupational world (Bolton, 1976). Standardized interest inventories assume knowledge about activities which many hearing impaired individuals do not have. It has also been shown that the Geist Picture Interest Inventory (Geist, 1962), which was developed specifically for hearing impaired students, is deficient psychometrically and not useful in guiding clients (Bolton, 1971). Therefore, before the student's interests can be determined a training period is necessary in which the student is exposed to the different kinds of jobs that are available (Lerman & Guilfoyle, 1970).

In general the vocational assessment of hearing impaired students is done partly through the use of tests and partly through observation and training of the student. As in the other areas of assessment, use of many of the traditional tests is limited because of their dependency on a higher level of communication.

THE ASSESSMENT OF HEARING-IMPAIRED MULTIPLY HANDICAPPED CHILDREN

The performance of hearing impaired children that have other handicapping conditions is often much more difficult than the assessment of children who are only hearing impaired. In fact, as Healey (1975) has noted, the performance of the these children worsens as if the handicapping conditions were multiplicative, not additive. The assessment of these children, whose skills may be considerably lower than those of the average three-year-old hearing impaired child, necessitates considerable ingenuity on the part of the examiner who carries through the assessment. In order to assess these children, it is very important that the teacher have a broad knowledge of communication and that he or she be sensitive to any communication attempts on the part of the child. These attempts can be of many different types, including movements of the hand, stiffening of the body, and turning of the head. It is vital that these attempts not be overlooked.

Hearing impaired children with handicapping conditions such as cerebral palsy present a special challenge because it is sometimes difficult to determine if a body movement is part of an effort to communicate or not. With such children training in the use of a language board is sometimes necessary before *any* assessment can be undertaken.

A common problem is that the attention span of the multiply handicapped child is so short that assessment must be conducted over several days. In some cases, this represents a violation of standardized procedures, and perhaps a lower credibility of scores. Timed tests can be detrimental to many of these children, particularly those who have physical problems (Brenner & Thompson, 1967). Caution must be exercised that the cosntruct under investigation is not confounded with a physical inability to respond.

The assessment of hearing impaired, multiply handicapped children demands knowledge of communication skills from birth onward (see

Chap. 8). Overall development may be examined through the use of scales such as the *Callier-Azusa* (Stillman, 1976) and the *Vineland Scales of Social Maturity* (Doll, 1965). However, the results obtained from these scales must be used cautiously in judging the capacity of the child (Vernon, 1976). Academic performance may be measured by the tools and practices associated with the assessment of the severely and profoundly retarded child (see Chap. 13). In many cases and across many problems, the behavioral approach to measurement (see Chap. 4) will provide much useful information.

Because of the communication problems, hearing impaired multiply handicapped children frequently appear to possess far less potential than they really have (Healey, 1975). Therefore, it is essential to establish a thorough program of varied and ongoing assessment to ensure that the goals for the child are not mismatched with what the child is actually able to achieve.

SUMMARY AND CONCLUSIONS

The initial purpose of assessment of hearing impaired children is to determine the type and extent of hearing loss. The most frequent kind of testing is pure tone audiometry which determines the hearing threshold of the child. Reinforcement procedures are utilized with young children or hard to test clients. Respondent audiometry, a type of audiometry that does not require a voluntary response on the part of the child, may be used with young children or difficult to test children, although the use of these procedures is usually no more successful than operant techniques. Impedence audiometry is the most commonly used respondent technique.

Definitions have been developed based on the results of the audiometric testing. However, the definitions used most commonly are usually concerned more with the effects of hearing loss on communication skills than on the hearing threshold of the child.

Communication skills that are assessed include speechreading, auditory skills, speech skills, and language skills. Formal testing in the area of speechreading, auditory training, and speech skills generally provides inadequate information for prescriptive purposes so teachers must devise their own informal tests. Caution must be taken in constructing informal tests to be sure that the language used in the test is within the child's receptive and expressive language capacity.

The tools that are used to assess the language of hearing impaired children vary according to the language program that is being employed. Language features that are assessed are those suggested in the language program. Expressive language is usually easier to assess than receptive language. Vocabulary assessment can be done only on a unit-by-unit asis, in which the vocabulary needed for each instructional unit is as-essed. Caution must be taken in evaluating the language structures of hildren exposed to Ameslan as what may appear to be a grammatical rror may, in fact, simply be the use of an Ameslan structure.

Psychological and personality assessment present serious problems o the psychologist because the vast majority of psychological and per-onality tests are language based. Not only do hearing impaired people requently not have the language to respond appropriately to test items, hey also do not have the same life experiences of the hearing population. Extreme caution must be placed in interpreting the results of psychologi-al and personality tests.

Formal standardized achievement tests generally show very slow cademic growth on the part of hearing impaired students. Because stan-ardized achievement tests do not provide prescriptive information eachers must utilize informal testing measures. In determining the ap-ropriate reader to be used the teacher must pay particular attention to he vocabulary and language structures contained in the test. In mathemat-cs, hearing impaired children generally do much better in computational kills than they do with verbal problems so that assessment for each math kill is essential. In both social studies and the sciences pretesting is ecessary for each unit taught to determine how much of the unit the child nows and in what areas the child needs attention.

Vocational testing generally consists of a battery of assessment in-luding communication skills, academic skills, job potential skills, and vork attitudes. While some of the formalized tests can be used, a consid-rable amount of informal testing and on-the-job evaluation is needed to ully assess the student's needs and skill potential.

In examining all areas of assessment, it can be seen that the problem f the development of adequate communication skills is all pervasive. The esults of formalized tests are greatly contaminated by this factor. Con-truction of informal tests is made more difficult because of communica-ion problems. It does not appear that there is any immediate solution to his problem and it can only be hoped that those who are engaged in as-essing children with hearing impairments are fully aware of the impact of he child's communication problems. Those who are given the results of ssessment must take these problems into consideration when reviewing nd utilizing the results.

REFERENCES

Academic achievement test performance by hearing impaired children, United States: series D (No. 9). Office of Demographic Studies. Washington, D.C.: Gallaudet College, 1971.

American Adademy of Opthalmology and Otolaryngology, American Academy of Pediatrics, and American Speech and Hearing Association. Supplementary statement of join committee on infant hearing screening. *American Speech and Hearing Association* 1974, *16,* 160.

Ammons, R., & Ammons, H. *Full Range Picture Vocabulary Test.* Missoula, Mn Psychological Test Specialists, 1948.

Arthur, G. *A Point Scale of Performance Tests, Revised Form II.* New York: Psychologica Corporation, 1947.

Banks, J. & Cleggs, A. *Teaching strategies for the social studies: Inquiry, valuing, an decision-making.* Reading, Mass.: Addison-Wesley, 1977.

Barley, M. *CID Everyday Sentences Test of Speechreading Ability.* Unpublished material 1964.

Blackwell, P. *Language curriculum.* Rhode Island Schoof for the Deaf, 1971.

Bloom, L. Talking, understanding, and thinking. In R. L. Schiefelbusch & L. L. Lloy (Eds.), *Language perspectives—Acquisition, retardation, and intervention.* Baltimore University Park Press, 1974, pp. 285–311.

Bolton, B. A critical review of the Geist Picture Interest Inventory: Deaf form: Male. *Journal of Rehabilitation of the Deaf,* 1971, *5*(2), 21–29.

Bolton, B. *Psychology of deafness for rehabilitation counselors.* Baltimore: University Park Press, 1976.

Boothroyd, A. *Auditory training handbook.* Northampton, Mass.: Clarke School for the Deaf, 1971.

Braine, M. D. S. The ontogeny of English phrase structure: The first phrase. *Language* 1963, *39,* 1–13.

Brenner, L. O. & Thompson, R. E. The use of projective techniques in the personality evaluation of deaf adults. *Journal of Rehabilitation of the Deaf,* 1967, *1,* 17–30.

Brown, R. *A first language: The early stages.* Cambridge, Mass.: Harvard University Press 1973.

Buck, J. The H.T.P. technique: A qualitative and quantitative scoring manual. *Journal of Clinical Psychology,* 1949, *5,* 37–74.

Burgmeister, B., Blum, L. & Lorge, I. *Columbia Mental Maturity Scale.* New York: Harcourt, Brace, Jovanovich, 1959.

Butt, D. S. & Chreist, F. M. A speechreading test for young children. *The Volta Review* 1968, *70,* 225–244.

Carrow, E. *Carrow Elicited Language Inventory.* Austin, Tx.: Learning Concepts, 1974.

Cavender, B. J. The construction and investigation of a test of lip reading ability and a study of factors assumed to affect the results. Unpublished M.A. thesis, Indiana University 1949.

Clarke School for the Deaf. *Speech development.* Northampton, Mass.: Clarke School for the Deaf, 1971.

Clawson, A. *The Bender Visual Motor Gestalt Test for Children.* Los Angeles: Western Psychological Service, 1962.

Coscarelli, J. E. & Sanders, J. W. The relationship of skill in visual synthesis to lipreading ability. Paper presented at the 44th Annual Convention of the American Speech and Hearing Association, Denver, Colorado, November 16, 1968.

Costello, M. R. A study of speechreading as a developing language process in deaf and in hard of hearing children. Unpublished doctoral dissertation, Northwestern University 1957.

Cox, P. & Lloyd, L. L. Audiologic considerations. In L. L. Lloyd (Ed.), *Communication assessment and intervention strategies.* Baltimore: University Park Press, 1976.

Craig, W. N. Effects of pre-school training on the development of reading and lipreading skills of deaf children. *American Annals of the Deaf,* 1964, *109.*

Crammatte, A. The adult deaf in professions. *American Annals of the Deaf,* 1962, *107,* 574–578.

)ale, P. Language development: Structure and function (2nd ed.). New York: Holt, Rinehart and Winston, 1976.

)ay, H. E., Fusfeld, I. S., & Pintner, R. *A survey of American schools for the deaf: 1924–25*. Washington, D.C.: National Research Council, 1928.

)oll, E. *Vineland Social Maturity Scale*. Circle Pines, Minn.: American Guidance Service, 1965.

)unn, L. M. *Expanded manual for the Peabody Picture Vocabulary Test*. Circle Pines, Minn.: American Guidance Service, 1965.

)urost, W., Evans, W., Leake, J., Bowman, H., Cosgrove, C., & Read, J. *Metropolitan Achievement Test*. New York: Harcourt, Brace & World, 1962.

:dwards, E. Sensory-motor intelligence and semantic relations in early child grammar. *Cognition,* 1973, *2,* 395–434.

'urth, H. G. *Thinking without language*. New York: The Free Press, 1966.

ieist, H. *Manual for the Geist Picture Interest Inventory: Deaf Form: Male (GPII: DM)*. Beverly Hills, Ca.: Western Psychological Services, 1962.

ilattke, T. J. Cochlear implants: Technical and clinical implications. *Laryngoscope,* 1976, *86,* 1351–1358.

ioldman, R. & Fristoe, M. *Test of Articulation*. Circle Pines, Minn.: American Guidance Service, 1969.

irammatico, L. F. & Miller, S. D. Curriculums for the preschool deaf child. *Volta Review,* 1974, *76,* 280–289.

Iathaway, S. R. & McKinley, J. C. *Minnesota Multiphasic Personality Inventory*. New York: The Psychological Corporation, 1967.

Iealey, W. C. *The hearing-impaired mentally retarded: Recommendations for action*. Washington, D.C.: Department of Health, Education, and Welfare, 1975.

Ieidinger, V. A. An exploratory study of procedures for improving temporal features in the speech of deaf children. Unpublished doctoral dissertation, Columbia University, 1972.

Iiskey, M. S. *Hiskey-Nebraska Test of Learning Aptitude*. Lincoln, Neb.: College Press, 1966.

Hoemann, H. W. & Ullman, D. G. Intellectual development. In B. Bolton (Ed.), *Psychology of deafness for rehabilitation counselors*. Baltimore: University Park Press, 1976.

Hood, R. B. & Dixon, R. F. Physical characteristics of speech rhythm of deaf and normal speakers. *Journal of Communication Disorders,* 1969, *2,* 20–28.

Jastak, J., Bijou, S., & Jastak, S. *Wide Range Achievement Test*. Wilmington, Del.: Guidance Associates, 1965.

Jeffers, J. & Barley, M. *Speechreading (lipreading)*. Springfield, Ill.: Charles C Thomas, 1971.

Lee, L. L. *Developmental Sentence Analysis*. Evanston, Ill.: Northwestern University Press, 1974.

Leiter, R. L. *The Leiter International Performance Scale*. Chicago: Stoelting, 1948.

Lerman, A. M. & Guilfoyle, G. R. *The development of prevocational behavior in deaf adolescents*. New York: Teachers College Press, 1970.

Levine, E. Psychological tests and practices with the deaf: A survey of the state of the art. *Volta Review,* 1974, *76,* 298–319.

Levine, E. Psychological contributions. *Volta Review,* 1976, *78,* 23–34 (Monograph).

Ling, D. *Speech and the hearing impaired child: Theory and practice*. Washington, D.C.: The Alexander Graham Bell Association for the Deaf, 1976.

Lowell, E. F. Pilot studies in lip reading. *John Tracy Clinic Research Papers VIII*. Los Angeles: John Tracy Clinic, 1958.

Machover, K. *Personality projection in the drawing of the human figure*. Springfield, Ill.: Charles C Thomas, 1949.

McLean, J. E. Articulation. In L. L. Lloyd (Eds.), *Communication assessment and intervention strategies*. Baltimore: University Park Press, 1976.

Mecham, M., Jex, J., & Jones, J. *Utah Test of Language Development*. Salt Lake City, Ut.: Communication Research Associated, 1967.

Moores, D. An investigation of the psycholinguistic functioning of deaf adolescents. *Exceptional Children,* 1970, *36,* 645–652.

Nance, W. Studies of hereditary deafness: Present, past, and future. *Volta Review,* 1976, *78,* 6–11 (Monograph).

Newby, H. A. *Audiology*. Englewood Cliffs, N.J.: Prentice-Hall, 1972.

Nitchie. E. B. *Lip-reading, principles and practice*. Philadelphia: Lippincott, 1930.

O'Neill, J. J. Measurement of hearing by tests of speech and language. In S. Singh (Ed.), *Measurement procedures in speech, hearing, and language*. Baltimore: University Park Press, 1975.

Quigley, S. P., Smith, N. L., & Wilbur, R. B. Comprehension of relativized sentences by deaf students. *Journal of Speech and Hearing Research,* 1974, *17,* 241–325.

Report of the Ad Hoc Committee to Define Deaf and Hard of Hearing. *American Annals of the Deaf,* 1975, *120,* 509–512.

Rorschach, H. *Psychodiagnostics*. Berne, Switzerland: Hans Huber, 1942.

Rosen, A. Limitations of personality inventories for assessment of deaf children and adults as illustrated by research with the MMPI. *Journal of Rehabilitation of the Deaf,* 1967, *1,* 47–52.

Rosen, S. Acupuncture and Chinese medical practices. *Volta Review,* 1974, *76,* 340–350.

Rotter, J. B. & Rafferty, J. E. *The Rotter Incomplete Sentence Blank*. New York: Psychological Corporation, 1942.

Sanders, D. *Aural rehabilitation*. Englewood Cliffs, N.J.: Prentice-Hall, 1971.

Schneidman, E. S. *Make a Picture Story (MAPS) Manual*. New York: Teachers College (Bur. Publ.), 1952.

Simmons, A. A. Factors related to lipreading. *Journal of Speech and Hearing Research,* 1959, *2,* 340–352.

Simmons, A. A. A comparison of the type-taken ratio of spoken and written language of deaf and hearing children. *Volta Review,* 1962, *64,* 417–421.

Slobin, D. I. & Welsh, C. A. Elicited imitations as a research tool in developmental psycholinguistics. In C. A. Ferguson & D. I. Slobin (Ed.). *Studies of child language development*. New York: Holt, 1973.

Smith, A. J. Psychological testing of the preschool deaf child: A challenge for changing times. Proceedings of International Conference on Oral Education of the Deaf, 1967, *1* . A. G. Bell Association for the Deaf, Washington, D.C.

Stein, M. I. *The Thematic Apperception Test* (2nd ed.). Reading, Mass.: Addison-Wesley, 1955.

Stillman, R. D. *Assessment of deaf-blind children: The Callier Azusa Scale*. Reston, Va.: The Council for Exceptional Children, 1976.

Sutsman, R. *Mental measurement of preschool children. Yonkers on Hudson, N.Y.: World Book Co., 1931.*

Taaffee, G. *A film test of lip reading. John Tracy Clinic Research Papers II*. Los Angeles: John Tracy Clinic, 1957.

Takefuta, Y. Method of acoustic analysis of intonation. In S. Singh (Ed.), *Measurement procedures in speech, hearing, and language*. Baltimore: University Park Press, 1975.

Templin, M. C. *The development of reasoning in children with normal and defective hearing*. Minneapolis: University of Minnesota Press, 1950.

Trybus, R. & Jenesema, C. The development, use, and interpetation of the 1973 Stanford Achievement Test, Special Edition for Hearing Impaired Students. In a Report of the proceedings of the forty-seventh meeting of the Convention of American Instructors of the Deaf. Washington, D.C.: U.S. Government Printing Office, 1976.

Trybus, R. J. & Karchmer, M. A. School achievement scores of hearing impaired children:

National data on achievement status and growth patterns. *American Annals of the Deaf,* 1977, *122,* 62–69.

Utley, J. Development and standardization of a motion picture achievement test of lipreading ability. Unpublished doctoral dissertation, Northwestern University, 1945.

Van Uden, A. *A world of language for deaf children: Part 1 basic principles.* Rotterdam: Rotterdam University Press, 1970.

Vernon, M. Psychologic evaluation of hearing-impaired children. In L. L. Lloyd (Ed.), *Communication assessment and intervention strategies.* Baltimore: University Park Press, 1976.

Wechsler, D. *Wechsler Adult Intelligence Scale.* New York: Psychological Corporation, 1955.

Wechsler, D. *Wechsler Intelligence Scale for Children.* New York: Psychological Corporation, 1955.

Wechsler, D. *Wechsler Preschool and Primary Scale of Intelligence.* New York: Psychological Corporation, 1967.

Wentling, T. L., Butterweck, T. C. & Zook, G. A. Career education and evaluation for hearing impaired adolescents: An example program. *Volta Review,* 1976, *78,* 144–151.

SUGGESTED READINGS

Davis, H. & Silverman, S. *Hearing and deafness.* New York: Holt, 1970.

Frisina, R. (Ed.) Hearing impairment: Trends in the U.S.A. *Volta Reviews,* 1976, *78*(4), 1–147. (Monograph)

Greenberg, J. *In this sign.* New York: Holt, 1970.

Jeffers, J. & Barley, M. *Speechreading (lipreading).* Springfield, Ill.: Charles C Thomas, 1971.

Ling, D. *Speech and the hearing impaired child: Theory and practice.* Washington, D.C.: The Alexander Graham Bell Association for the Deaf, 1976.

Meadow, K. & Schlesinger, H. *Sound and sign; childhood deafness and mental health.* Berkeley: University of California Press, 1972.

Moores, D. *Educating the deaf: Psychology, principles, and practices.* Boston: Houghton Mifflin, 1978.

Russell, W. K., Quigley, S. P., & Power, J. D. *Linguistics and deaf children: Transformation syntax and its applications.* Washington, D.C.: The Alexander Graham Bell Association for the Deaf, 1976.

Gaylen Kapperman

12 Assessment of the Visually Handicapped

This chapter has been written for teachers of exceptional children who are *not* preparing to be specialists with the visually handicapped. Therefore, many technical aspects of assessing visually impaired youngsters such as assessment of braille reading and writing skills, orientation and mobility travel skills, levels of visual functioning in low vision children, and Optacon* reading skills, are not included. The areas that have been included are those which have relevance for the regular educator and most special education teachers. They include vision screening of preschool and school-age children, observation procedures for discovering children with hard-to-find vision problems, the assessment of cognitive and academic functioning in visually handicapped children, and a review of instruments that have been specifically designed for use with the visually handicapped.

DEFINITIONS

An educationally relevant definition of the visually handicapped youngster is not a simple matter to derive. For many years, educators of

*The Optacon is an electronic device recently developed to enable totally blind persons to read print directly without the aid of a human intermediary. With the use of the Optacon, printed symbols are converted to tactually perceivable images on a small screen. The blind user places his left index finger on the screen to feel the symbols move from right to left in the form of vibrating pins.

visually impaired children labored under the definition set for for legal and medical purposes. According to Lowenfeld (1973), a blind person is defined as having "central visual acuity of 20/200 or less in the better eye with correcting glasses; or central vision acuity of more than 20/200 if there is a field defect in which the peripheral field has contracted to such an extent that the widest diameter of visual field subtends an angular distance no greater than 20 degrees" (pp. 29–30). Partially sighted persons have been defined as those whose visual acuity falls within the range of 20/70 down to but not including 20/200. A note of explanation is called for at this point. Distance visual acuity is generally denoted by a fraction in which the denominator indicates the distance at which a person with normal vision can see the object of regard. The numerator indicates the distance at which the visually handicapped person can see that same object of regard with approximately the same degree of clarity. For legal and medical purposes, this measurement is taken in the better eye with the best possible corrective lens being used. That is, the individual who is totally blind in one eye and who has visual acuity of 20/20 (normal vision) with or without corrective lenses in the other eye, is not considered to be visually handicapped under this definition. Visual acuity measures should never be converted to percentages of normal vision because they do not represent fractional portions of normal vision.

The second aspect of the legal definition of blindness, that which deals with the visual field, deserves further clarification. There are several pathological eye conditions that result in constriction of the peripheral field of vision. Individuals who possess these eye diseases frequently have normal or near normal visual acuity in the central portion of their field of vision, but they have greatly diminished visual acuity at the periphery of their visual field. Such eye conditions can drastically limit the ability to travel, read, or perform many other activities. If the visual field is constricted to the point that 20 degrees or less of the field remains, the individual is considered to be legally or medically blind even though he may have visual acuity of 20/20 in the central portion of the field of vision.

Unfortunately, the legal and medical definitions of blindness and partial sight have not served the educator well. Those definitions are of little practical use in specifying educational provisions. In discussing this matter, Barraga (1976, p. 16) has set forth an all-encompassing definition that better fits educational requirements: "a visually handicapped child is one whose visual impairment interferes with his optimal learning and achievement, unless adaptations are made in the methods of presenting learning experiences, the nature of the materials used, and/or in the learning environment." This definition has an advantage in that it is not based upon arbitrarily set limits of visual acuity that have little relevance for the educational program in which a child may become involved.

OBSERVATIONAL IDENTIFICATION OF THE MILDLY VISUALLY HANDICAPPED CHILD

It is not difficult to recognize the totally blind or severely visually limited child. On the other hand, it is much more difficult to identify the child who is mildly visually impaired or who presents eye conditions that do not severely limit his ability to see, but which may deteriorate with the passage of time. There are observable signs of conditions potentially capable of damaging vision of which the professional working with exceptional children should be aware. Many of the more common are listed in Table 12-1. The conditions presented are not necessarily indicative of

Table 12-1
Common Indicators of Visual Problems

1. One eye turns in or out either all the time or intermittently
2. Eyelids are red and/or swollen.
3. Eyes tear excessively
4. Eyelids are encrusted
5. Styes appear frequently on eyelids
6. Child complains of seeing double while engaged in near or far vision tasks
7. Child complains of headaches in forehead or temples
8. Child complains of burning or itching of eyes after close eye work
9. Child complains of nausea or dizziness after close eye work
10. Child complains of blurring of print after reading for short periods
11. Child's head turns as he reads across page
12. Child loses place on page easily while reading
13. Child requires use of finger or marker while reading
14. Child displays short attention span while reading or copying
15. Child omits words while reading
16. Child rereads or skips lines unknowingly
17. Child's comprehension decreases dramatically as reading continues
18. Child mispronounces similar words as reading continues
19. Child repeats letters within words
20. Child cannot write in a straight line across page
21. Child orients drawings poorly on page
22. Child misaligns digits in columns of numbers
23. Child squints, closes, or covers one eye while engaged in close eye work.
24. Child tilts head dramatically while engaged in close eye work.
25. Child shows gross postural deviations while engaged in close eye work.
26. Child blinks excessively while engaged in close eye work.
27. While engaged in close eye work, child brings face too close to object of regard.
28. Child rubs eyes excessively during or after periods of close eye work.
29. Child attempts to avoid all near-centered tasks.
30. Child makes errors in copying from chalkboard.
31. Child squints to see items written on chalkboard or requests to move nearer to chalkboard

pathogenic eye conditions, but they should be viewed as indicators of the possible existence of visual abnormalities. Any child displaying these conditions should be referred for a medical examination of the eyes.

VISION SCREENING

Informal observation by the teacher is important for the detection of eye problems. However, the incidence of eye difficulties is so high that efforts must be made to approach detection in a more systematic manner. Recently, the National Society for the Prevention of Blindness (NSPB) (1969) estimated that 25 percent of all school children suffer from eye defects that require professional care. For example, a very prevalent disorder found among American children is amblyopia ex anopsia (decreased vision through suppression of visual stimuli by the brain). Boyce (1973) estimates that five percent of the preschool population is affected by this condition; Davens (1966) states that each year 100,000 children pass the point beyond which amblyopia can be cured. Since many other eye defects as well as amblyopia can be successfully treated if detected in time and since detection may not occur by unsystematic methods, a well-planned and well-executed vision screening program is a valuable asset in most school programs. However, it must be stressed that vision screening procedures are not designed to diagnose diseases of the visual mechanism. Instead, screening procedures are routinely applied to large populations with the intent of separating those who need medical attention from those who do not require examination by a physician. In order to avoid this confusion in the public's mind, the National Society for the Prevention of Blindness (1969) recommends that vision screening programs *not* be conducted by ophthalmologists or optometrists. In fact, it has been shown that well-trained volunteers, technicians, and teachers can successfully carry out screening procedures.

Lippman (1962) has described the characteristics of a well-designed vision screening test. The instrument must be simple and quick to administer. It should be inexpensive in terms of equipment, materials, and the personnel needed to use it and the results must be valid; that is, they should approximate clinical findings. Finally, the test or procedure should produce a minimum of under- and over-referrals.

It is highly recommended that the person carrying out the vision screening of youngsters be thoroughly familiar with the techniques employed to obtain accurate results. Manuals for the use of specific instruments are available from the manufacturers. Before beginning the screening process, the children should be acquainted with the procedures that will take place. This is especially important for immature youngsters.

In the case of preschool children and developmentally delayed youngsters, practice material can be provided to the parents and/or teachers to train the children to respond correctly to the requests of the vision screening personnel. For best results, the number of adult observers should be kept to a minimum. Children should not be forced to participate; if a child refuses to cooperate, another time can be scheduled to complete the procedures. For those who fail the test, a retest should be scheduled a few days later before referral for medical examination is made. Procedures such as these drastically reduce over-referrals.

The issue of under-referrals (false-negatives) and overreferrals (false positives) is the most difficult problem related to vision screening. It revolves around the fact that stringent standards for passing the test will result in a large number of over-referrals thus undermining the confidence of the public in the screening procedures. However, less stringent standards result in many cases going undetected. Obviously, this second option is not valid for many serious eye conditions may be overlooked, a fact which defeats the purpose of the screening process. Sloan & Rosenthal (1960) contend that cutoffs must be set in order that one will err on the side of too many over-referrals. In this way, one is assured of finding nearly all of the eye defects in the population being surveyed.

The Snellen E Chart is the most commonly used visual acuity instrument. The National Society for the Prevention of Blindness (1969) has recommended pass-fail standards for its use that vary according to the age of the child. In kindergarten through third grade, visual acuity of 20/40 or less should be considered failure. This standard means the inability to identify the majority of letters on the 30-foot line at 20 feet. In the fourth grade and beyond, visual acuity of 20/30 or less should result in a referral. That is, the inability to identify the majority of letters on the 20-foot line at 20 feet constitutes failure. Also, in all grades, a one line difference within the passing criterion between the two eyes should be considered failure. A common Snellen E Chart is shown in Figure 12-1.

Tests for hyperopia (farsightedness) and for muscle imbalance are frequently included in the battery of vision screening procedures. The usual test for hyperopia consists of having the person being screened read the chart through a plus lens.* If the individual can see the letters on the chart better with the lens, he has failed the test and should be referred for medical attention.

There are several tests for muscle imbalance. In general, the objective of these tests is to determine if the two eyes are working together. The *Maddox Rod Test* is the most popular of these procedures. The indi-

*A plus lens is used to correct farsightedness.

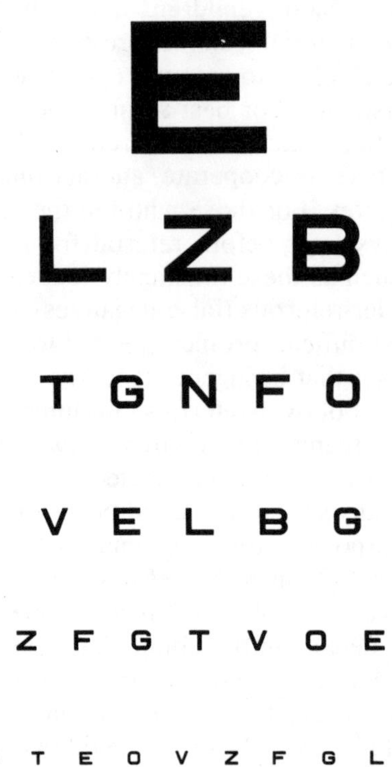

Fig. 12-1. The Snellen E Chart.

vidual being tested looks through a series of glass rods to determine where a red line exists. If the red line appears to be differently situated from one eye to the other, referral should be made. The Maddox Red apparatus is shown in Figure 12-2.

Several companies produce machines for vision screening. They incorporate the Snellen E Chart, the plus lens test, and the tests for muscle imbalance as well as many others. The devices have four major advantages. First, they are portable. Second, they enable the administrator to establish standard testing conditions with respect to illumination. Third, a small area is required to carry out the test. Finally, the confidentiality of results is insured. Two major disadvantages exist with the devices: they are expensive and relatively more complicated to use than the common Snellen wall chart. An example of a machine for testing is pictured in Figure 12-3.

The National Society for the Prevention of Blindness (1969) recommends that preschool children from the age of three years be screened

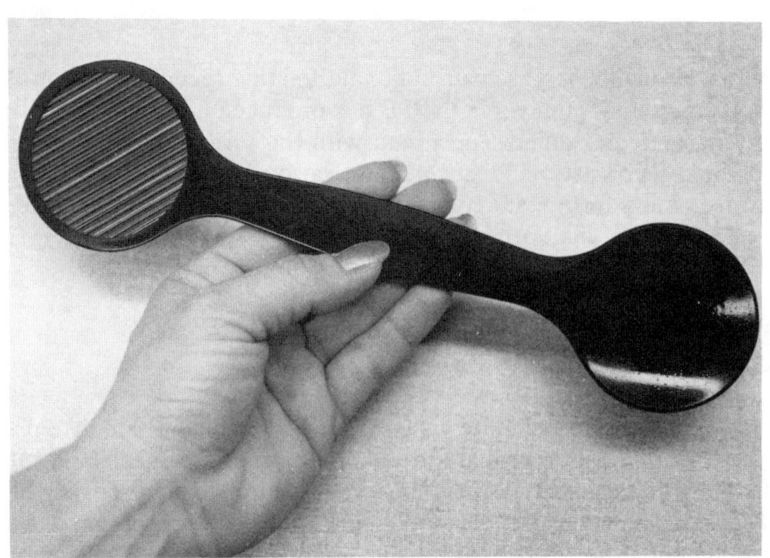

Fig. 12-2. The Maddox Rod Apparatus.

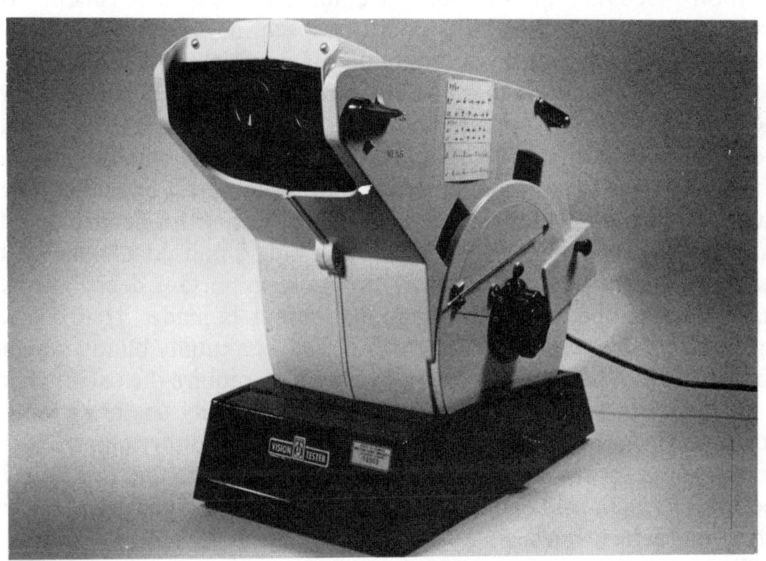

Fig. 12-3. Vision Screening Apparatus.

for visual difficulties. The main rationale for this recommendation is to assure detection of amblyopia. NSPB has produced a Home Eye Test for use by parents and others concerned with the vision of preschool children. The test consists of a test card with variously sized E's, instructions on its use, and a form to be completed and sent to NSPB headquarters if the child fails the test.

ASSESSMENT OF VISUALLY HANDICAPPED CHILDREN

Before an assessment of a visually handicapped child can take place, the youngsters must be brought to the attention of the special education personnel who deal with visually impaired children. The discovery of visually handicapped children generally occurs through one of two avenues depending upon the severity of the disorder. The midly visually impaired are frequently discovered through the process of vision screening and teacher observation. The severely visually impaired children whose handicaps are obvious come to the attention of the special education personnel through referrals by concerned individuals such as parents, medical personnel, social workers, and others in the community.

Upon discovery of the child, a complete visual assessment takes place in order to determine the extent of visual impairment. That is, an opthalmologic or optometric examination is conducted by a qualified individual. Upon receipt of that information, the special education teacher who deals with visually impaired children carries out a visual assessment to determine, beyond mere visual acuity, how well the child sees. Visual acuities obtained from ophthalmologic and optometric examination are frequently of little aid to the special education teacher for determining the appropriate educational program for the child. Upon conclusion of the visual assessment by the educator, the most important decision in the visually handicapped child's educational career is made. That decision revolves around whether to educate the child as a totally blind youngster or to provide educational services for him which require the use of vision. If it is determined that the child has no educationally useful vision, his educational program will center around tactile and auditory approaches to learning. If the results of the visual assessment indicate that the child has some useful vision, his educational program will hinge on visual and auditory approaches to learning.

There are two fundamental purposes for the assessment of visually handicapped children. The first is determination of the appropriate placement and approach for the education of the child. Depending upon many factors which are brought to light in the evaluation process, placement may be made in a residential school for the visually handicapped, a resource room program, or an itinerant teacher plan. These programs provide varying levels of intensity of special educational assistance. For appropriate placement of the child in any one of the programs, accurate assessment of the child's capabilities is required. Many factors in addition to visual capacity must be taken into consideration if appropriate plans are to be formed. In general, the child's level of intellectual, social, and emotional development must be considered in order to insure that he will be provided with the best educational experience appropriate for his level of development.

The second consideration revolves around the most efficacious materials, methods, and techniques to be employed in that program. Usually there are two major approaches to the education of visually handicapped youngsters. In the first decisional step, the teacher must determine whether to use educational procedures that are appropriate for a youngster without useful sight or procedures for a child who possesses useful residual vision. For the blind child (without useful vision), emphasis is placed upon instructional approaches that rely heavily upon the senses of touch and hearing. For visually handicapped youngsters with useful vision, the senses of sight and hearing are emphasized. In the education of visually impaired youngsters, the determination of which one of the two approaches to take is a major decision that must be made with the most accurate information available.

The second fundamental reason for the evaluation of a visually handicapped child is to monitor his progress as he makes his way through the initially chosen educational program. With the continuing development of the child and with changing circumstances, shifts in educational placement and changes in the educational approach are frequently required. As the child grows and develops, a change from a program of concentrated special instruction to a program with less emphasis upon special assistance is often called for. As the child becomes more mature and independent, for example, he may be taken from a resource room program and placed in an itinerant teacher plan. If it is found that the child does not function well in a program offering a lesser degree of special instruction, he may be placed in one which offers greater special assistance. For example, he may be taken from a resource room program and placed in a residential school.

Within a program, the major instructional approach originally thought to be most appropriate for the child may be changed. That is, it may be found that a child who began his educational career with some residual vision has lost most of the use of his sight through a deteriorating visual condition. In such cases, a change from the visual/auditory approach to the tactual/auditory approach is required. This change can take place in any one of the three major program structures (e.g., itinerant teacher plan). Such circumstances can also cause change in the educational program to be implemented. That is, if sight is lost, the child may frequently require greater special assistance for a time. In that event, he may be placed in one of the programs that offers greater assistance than does his present program.

If an accurate visual assessment was performed initially and, upon the basis of that assessment a determination was made concerning the major educational approach to take with the child, he will move from the tactual/auditory approach to the visual/auditory approach very infrequently. Seldom will it occur that a child's vision will improve to the point that he can move from a tactual/auditory approach to a visual/auditory approach. A more frequent occurrence is when the child has been misdiagnosed as having little or no useful sight. Some time later, it is found that, in fact, the child is able to use his vision for educational purposes. In these cases, the shift from the tactual/auditory approach to the visual/auditory approach is mandatory. Any visually handicapped child with usable vision should be encouraged to make use of it to the greatest extent possible. When this is not done, the child has been rendered a great disservice.

In summary, the fundamental purposes for the assessment of a visually handicapped child are twofold. First, accurate evaluation of the child's potential is required to insure the most appropriate educational placement. Second, ongoing assessment should be carried out in order to monitor his progress. Monitoring may reveal that a change in the educational placement or a shift in the educational approach is required.

FACTORS TO BE CONSIDERED IN THE PSYCHOEDUCATIONAL ASSESSMENT OF VISUALLY HANDICAPPED CHILDREN

The existence of a visual impairment in a child has many wide-ranging psychological and social ramifications. Consequently, many factors must be taken into consideration during the assessment of visually handicapped children. Hepfinger (1962, p. 135) has ennumerated many of those factors (Table 12-2). These factors should always be kept in mind when any assessment is conducted.

Bateman (1965) suggests other questions that must be answered by the evaluator of visually handicapped children. Before the investigator begins, he or she must decide upon the fundamental reason for the evaluation. Does he or she wish to compare the blind child to other sighted children? If this is the underlying reason, what behaviors should be as-

Table 12-2
Important Considerations in the Psychoeducational Assessment of the Visually Handicapped Child.

Etiology and degree of blindness
Health history with a hearing test
Attitude of family toward blindness
Home conditions
Opportunities for development
Characteristics of persons closest to child
Child's level in language development, in motor skills, in perception, in comprehension, in reasoning, and learning ability
Relationship of the child to others in his environment
Interest of the child in toys
Methods he employs in discrimination, exploration, and localization
Child's reaction to daily routine
Child's ability to tolerate frustration
Child's ability to postpone satisfaction
Child's ability to independently explore his environment
Child's ability to become part of a group

sessed? If the evaluator is concerned with how well the blind child compares to other visually handicapped youngsters, what weight should be placed upon such factors as the age at onset of blindness, the degree of residual vision present in the child, previous educational experience, and the effects of the home environment? These factors combined with the previous statements of Hepfinger (1962) illustrate the great care and sensitivity that must be exercised in measuring the performance of visually handicapped children.

Emotional reactions to visual impairment on the part of the significant others in the child's life, and thus also on the part of the child, play an important role in development. As Parmelee (1963) states, the evaluator of visually handicapped children must always be on the alert for the effects of emotional factors. A developmental delay caused by the absence of a healthy environment, emotional problems and/or neurological signs are not infrequent. An example is the blind child given to strange movements and peculiar posturing that can mislead the inexperienced examiner into a faulty diagnosis of some type of motor dysfunction. The reader can readily discern that the existence of a visual impairment in a child makes the task of accurate assessment of the child doubly difficult. It is commonly held that the presence of a visual handicap adds one more factor to the myriad of human characteristics upon which a child can vary. For the evaluator of exceptional children, this means that the task is made even more difficult.

ASCERTAINING THE INTELLIGENCE OF THE VISUALLY HANDICAPPED

Estimating the IQ of visually handicapped children is, at best, a dubious undertaking. The major reason is the paucity of appropriately designed instruments for specific use with the visually handicapped. Most of the instruments used for this purpose are adaptations of ones originally designed for use with the sighted population (Stogner, 1970; Tillman, 1973). One major weakness in this method is the assumption that the blind are exposed to the same cultural experiences as are the sighted. As Stogner (1970) points out, this is not a valid assumption. Visually handicapped individuals do not share many of the experiences that are assumed to be common to the general population because many of those experiences depend directly upon vision. For example, because the lack of vision often causes diminished ability to get about, the visually handicapped person is frequently denied access to many of them. This is often compounded by environmental deprivation due to the overprotection of well-meaning adults. These factors, and many others, combine to deny common cultural experiences to the visually handicapped population.

Adapting an instrument for use with the visually handicapped creates a second major difficulty: availability of an appropriate visually disabled population. Historically, test developers have experienced much difficulty in securing large and representative samples upon which to restandardize the adapted instrument (Cundick, Crandell, & Hendrix, 1974). As a result, many test developers have resorted to using only youngsters attending residential schools for the blind, for here large concentrations of visually handicapped children can be found. Thus, children enrolled in day-school programs for the visually handicapped have often been excluded from the standardization sample. Thus, the national population of visually handicapped youngsters is not adequately represented in most standardization samples.

When tests originally designed for use with sighted individuals are used in their unaltered forms with the visually handicapped, a third problem, item appropriateness, arises (Coveny, 1976). Items depending heavily upon visual concepts such as color and movement of objects in the distance are impossible to perceive by touch and therefore place the blind and severely visually limited child at a great disadvantage. It is thus difficult to fairly compare the visually handicapped with their sighted counterparts on items of this type. Unfortunately, such items make up a large proportion of many tests, particularly performance scales of intelligence. As a result, testing of visually handicapped children has resulted in an overemphasis upon verbal scales (Convey, 1976).

Presently there is no well-designed, well-standardized performance test of intelligence for the visually handicapped. Verbal tests are found lacking, too. According to Classen (1954, p. 12), "Differences in home environments which might mold the restricted blind child more than the sighted, and variations in reactions to environment and adjustment to blindness are apt to make purely verbal tests unreliable." These considerations must be kept in mind as the following reviews are examined.

Intelligence Tests Used with the Visually Handicapped

According to Bauman (1972), the most frequently used standardized individual intelligence tests used with the visually handicapped are the verbal scales of the several Wechsler tests (see Chap. 7 for a review of these tests). The Wechsler scales are generally administered in their original forms and studies indicate that a specific subtest score pattern emerges when the verbal scales are used with blind and severely visually limited children. Generally, these groups score high on Digit Span and low on Comprehension and Similarities (Gilbert & Rubin, 1965; Hopkins & McGuire, 1966; Tillman, 1973; Tillman & Osborne, 1969). Lack of interpersonal and cultural experience, visual biases in test content, and difficulty in forming conceptual relationships have been put forth as explanations for poor performance on Comprehension and Similarities (Tillman & Osborne, 1969). High scores on Digit Span are attributed to good short-term memory on the part of visually handicapped children. Despite drawbacks, use of the verbal scales of the Wechsler tests remains popular.

The *Interim Hayes-Binet* (IHB) has long been associated with intelligence testing of the blind. It was originally developed by Samuel Hayes (1943) as an adaptation of the 1937 revision of the *Stanford-Binet*. Unfortunately, the IHB was never properly standardized and is now out of date (Coveny, 1976).

Shurrager & Shurrager (1964) developed the *Haptic Intelligence Scale for the Adult Blind* (HIS). It was intended to be a performance intelligence scale for blind and severely visually limited individuals 15 years of age and older. The HIS was standardized on a national sample of over 700 blind subjects. The instrument consists of six subtests: (1) Digit Symbol, (2) Object Assembly, (3) Block Design, (4) Object Completion, (5) Pattern Board, and (6) Bead Arithmetic. The individual that has had instruction in the use of the Cranmer Abacus is disqualified from taking the Bead Arithmetic subtest. In general, the HIS has not found wide acceptance because it is extremely expensive, cumbersome to administer, and the results are not particularly useful.

Davis (1970) has developed the *Perkins-Binet Intelligence Test for Blind Children* (P-B). It is based upon the 1960 revision of the Stanford-

Binet and includes specific items appropriate for blind and visually handicapped youngsters. The test has two forms: Form U is used with subjects with useful residual vision; Form N is intended for use with totally blind children. Approximately 25 percent of the items in Form U and 30 percent of the items in Form N are performance items. The standardization of the Perkins-Binet has been well-executed. The sample included 2,187 subjects in both residential and day school programs across the country. MA and IQ scores can be determined for subjects aged 5 to 15 years.

The *Non-Language Learning Test* was developed by Bauman (1947). It is designed to measure the ability of a blind subject to learn to properly fit block pieces into recesses in a board. Bauman suggests that the test is useful for blind individuals 10 years of age and older but standardization of this instrument is lacking. Bauman indicates that the test is intended to be used only as a clinical device.

Other Tests Designed for Use with the Visually Handicapped

Several well-known, standardized achievement tests for the normally seeing child are available in large print and Braille for the visually handicapped. These are the *Iowa Test of Basic Skills,* the *Cooperative Sequential Tests of Educational Progress,* the *Cooperative School and College Ability Tests,* and the *Stanford Achievement Test*. Among these, the *Stanford Achievement Test* battery is the only one that has been developed to suit the unique needs of the visually handicapped (Morris, 1974). The remaining three batteries have been transcribed into Braille and large print without regard to item appropriateness for the visually handicapped.

The *Adolescent Emotional Factors Inventory* (Bauman, Platt, & Straus, 1963) is a personality test which was specifically designed for use with visually handicapped adolescents. It was developed and standardized using samples of blind and visually handicapped teenagers from residential schools and public school programs for the visually handicapped. The instrument contains 150 items divided nearly equally among 10 Subscales. The Subscales include: (1) Sensitivity, (2) Somatic Symptoms, (3) Social Competency, (4) Attitudes of Distrust, (5) Family Adjustment, (6) Boy-Girl Adjustment, (7) School Adjustment, (8) Morale, (9) Attitudes about Blindness, and (10) Validation. Nearly all of the interscale correlations are low thereby indicating that the subscales measure different traits. Reliability coefficients for the subscales range from a low of 0.52 for Validation to a high of 0.84 for Sensitivity.

The *Maxfield-Buchholz Scale for Blind Preschool Children* (Maxfield & Buchholz, 1958) is adapted from the *Vineland Social Maturity Scale*. It

Cundick, B. P., Crandell, J. M., & Hendrix, L. A new method for the group testing of blind persons. *The New Outlook for the Blind,* 1974, *68,* 398–402.

Davens, E. The nationwide alert to preschool vision screening. *The Sight-Saving Review,* 1966, *36,* 13–17.

Davis, C. J. New developments in the intelligence testing of blind children. In Proceedings of the Conference on New Approaches to the Education of Blind Persons. New York: American Foundation for the Blind, 1970.

Gilbert, J. G. & Rubin, E. J. Evaluating the intellect of blind children. *The New Outlook for the Blind,* 1965, *59,* 238–240.

Hayes, S. P. A second test scale for the mental measurement of the visually handicapped. *The New Outlook for the Blind,* 1943, *37,* 37–41.

Hepfinger, L. M. Psychological evaluation of blind children. *The New Outlook for the Blind,* 1962, *56,* 309–315.

Hopkins, K. D. & McGuire, L. The validity of the Wechsler Intelligence Scale for Children. *International Journal for the Education of the Blind,* 1966, *15,* 65–73.

Lippman, O. Eye screening. *Archives of Ophthalmology,* 1962, *68,* 148–162.

Lowenfeld, B. (Ed.). The visually handicapped in school. New York: John Day, 1973.

Maxfield, K. E. & Buchholz, S. *A social maturity scale for blind preschool children: A guide to its use.* New York: American Foundation for the Blind, 1958.

Morris, J. The 1973 Stanford achievement test series as adapted for use by the visually handicapped. *Education of the Visually Handicapped,* 1974, *6,* 33–40.

National Society for the Prevention of Blindness. *Vision screening of children.* Publication No. 257. New York: National Society for the Prevention of Blindness, 1969.

Nolan, C. Y. & Morris, J. Development and validation of the Roughness discrimination test. *International Journal for the Education of the Blind,* 1965, *15,* 1–6.

Parmelee, A. H., Jr. The evaluation of the mental development of blind children. *International Ophthalmology Clinics, Diagnostic Procedures in Pediatric Ophthalmology,* 1963, *3,* 885–896.

Shurrager, H. & Shurrager, P. *Manual for the Haptic Intelligence Scale for the Adult Blind.* Chicago: Psychology Research, 1964.

Sloane, A. L. & Rosenthal, P. School vision testing. *Archives of Opthalmology,* 1960, *64,* 143–150.

Stogner, C. P. Evaluation of intelligence, academic aptitude, and achievement of the visually impaired. Selected Papers of the 50th Biennial Conference of the Association for Education of the Visually Handicapped, Philadelphia, 1970.

Tillman, M. H. Intelligence scales for the blind: A review with implications for research. *Journal of School Psychology,* 1973, *11,* 80–87.

Tillman, M. H. & Osborne, R. T. The performance of blind and sighted children on the Wechsler Intelligence Scale for Children. *Education of the Visually Handicapped,* 1969, *1,* 1–4.

SUGGESTED READINGS

Bauman, M. K. Tests and their interpretation. In G. D. Carnes, C. E. Hansen, & R. M. Parker (Eds.), *Readings in rehabilitation of the blind client.* Austin, Tx.: 1971.

Clark, L. L. & Jastrzembska, Z. Z. (Eds.) *Proceedings of the conference on new approaches to the evaluation of blind persons.* New York: American Foundation for the Blind, 1970.

Curtis, W. D., Donlon, E. T., & Wagner, E. (Eds.) *Deaf blind children: Evaluating their multiple handicaps*. New York: American Foundation for the Blind, 1970.

Lowenfeld, B. (Ed.) *The visually handicapped child in school*. New York: John Day, 1973.

Lowenfeld, B. Psychological problems of children with impaired vision. In W. M. Cruickshank (Ed.), *Psychology of exceptional children and youth* (3rd ed.). Englewood Cliffs, N.J.: Prentice-Hall, 1971.

Scholl, G. & Schnur, R. *Measures of psychological, vocational, and educational functioning in the blind and visually handicapped*. New York: American Foundation for the Blind, 1976.

Harvey N. Switzky

13 Assessment of the Severely and Profoundly Handicapped

THE CHANGING ZEITGEIST TOWARD THE EDUCATION AND TRAINING OF THE SEVERELY AND PROFOUNDLY HANDICAPPED

There exists a remarkable parallel between the present period off intense concern with developing the full potential of all severely and profoundly handicapped individuals through early education, training, social, and vocational habilitation, and the period of the late 18th and early 19th century in Western Europe and the United States. Both periods represent a profound change in western society's conceptions, attitudes, and values toward the severely and profoundly handicapped. Traditionally, public schools have excluded severely and profoundly retarded and multihandicapped children (Wolfensberger, 1971; Roos, 1971). The current period represents a rediscovery of some of the aspirations of the Saint-Simonist period in France, when Seguin developed the first systematic educational model and philosophy to teach the mentally retarded to live in society.

Sontag (1976b) argues that the reason these children were rejected was based on the notion that such children really could not learn and that this attitude will have to be changed by providing professionals with information regarding the true characteristics, capabilities, and potential of the severely handicapped. Fortunately, many school administrators, special educators, and teachers are now strongly committed to the education of the severely retarded in public school settings in the community. The rights of the severely and profoundly retarded as full citizens and members of our society are being recognized and expanded (Sontag, 1976a).

Roos (1971) has suggested areas of program emphasis for severely and profoundly retarded individuals (Luckey & Addison, 1974), which may include skill areas such as: (1) sensori-motor training consisting of stimulation of sight, smell, touch, hearing, and muscular responses; (2) physical mobility and coordination training consisting of rolling, crawling, creeping, and walking; (3) activities of daily living such as self-feeding, drying hands, self-toileting, and so on. In the past, such skill areas have usually not been considered to be within the province of a public school education because they were acquired prior to normal school entrance. In fact, such training more closely resembles the components of what has been called adaptive behavior (Balthazar, 1971; Grossman, 1973; Leland, Shellhaas, Nihira, & Foster, 1967; Leland, 1972; Nihira, Foster, Shellhaas, & Leland, 1969). Since assessment should parallel instruction, it is obvious that assessment of the severely handicapped individual is a very unique enterprise.

THE DEVELOPMENT OF AN INDIVIDUAL EDUCATIONAL PLAN

Brown, Nietupski and Hamre-Nietupski (1976, p. 8) suggest that:

> The criterion of ultimate functioning should be the standard by which educational activities as they relate to the severely handicapped student should be judged. The criterion of ultimate functioning refers to the ever changing, expanding, localized, and personalized cluster of factors that each person must possess in order to function as productively and independently as possible in socially, vocationally, and domestically integrated adult community environments.

According to Brown et al. (1976), all educational activities involving the severely handicapped student must relate to the criterion of ultimate functioning or that activity should be terminated. Before engaging in *any* educational activity with severely handicapped students, educators must ask themselves the following questions:

1. Why should we engage in this activity?
2. Is this activity necessary to prepare students to ultimately function in complex heterogeneous community settings?
3. Could students function as adults if they did not acquire the skill?
4. Is there a different activity that will allow students to approximate the criterion of ultimate functioning more quickly and more efficiently?
5. Will this activity impede, restrict, or reduce the probability that students will ultimately function in community settings?
6. Are the skills, materials, tasks, and criteria of concern similar to those encountered in adult life?

As mandated by PL 94-142, the individualized educational program must provide (in writing): (1) the child's current level of educational performance including his current level of adaptive behavior; (2) a date for the initiation of service; (3) the type of services the child is to receive; (4) long-range goals and short-term objectives; and (5) an evaluation schedule to be reviewed at least annually. (See Chap. 6 for a full discussion.) To meet these objectives through the development and implementation of an individualized educational program for a severely retarded child involves the coordination and cooperation of a multitude of services not often found in public school programs. Severely handicapped students manifest a variety of developmental disabilities and defects and require the expertise of physical, occupational, language and speech, and medical and nursing therapists, as well as individuals who can provide visual and auditory assessment and habilitation. In addition, parents, parent surrogates and all family members who "live" with the severely retarded child must be involved in the planning and the implementation of the individualized educational program. It has been fairly well established that the extent and speed of learning for the student depends to a great extent on the educational carry-over and transfer of training from the home environment. Therefore, it is reasonable to assume that the ties between the individual's home and school environments provide great impact on the outcome of the education intervention.

The individualized educational plan must be designed to optimize the match between the learning characteristics of the child and the best learning environment for the child. An individual educational plan designed to achieve this match might be described in the following dimensions: teacher characteristics, curricular characteristics, child characteristics, ecological context of the teaching environment, and instructional methodology. Some progress has been made in defining appropriate characteristics of teachers of the severely handicapped. This group may include paraprofessionals (Blessing, 1967; Horner, 1975; Tucker & Horner, 1977) as well as professionally trained teachers (Bijou & Wilcox-Cole, 1975; Burke & Cohen, 1977; Horner, 1977; Horner, Holvolt, & Rinne, 1976; Sailor, Guess, & Lavis, 1975a; Stainbach, Stainbach, & Mamer, 1976; Stamm, 1975; Wilcox, 1977). Some preliminary attempts to define various models of curriculum for the severely and profoundly handicapped have included use of the functional developmental behavioral approach (Baldwin, 1976; Cohen, Gross, & Haring, 1976; Fredericks, Riggs, Furey, Grove, Moore, McDonnell, Jordon, Hanson, Baldwin, & Wadlow, 1976; Lent & McLean, 1976; Somerton & Meyers, 1976; Williams & Gotts, 1977), the social learning developmental approach (Bepko, Alter, & Goldstein, 1976; Reiss, 1974) and the Piagetian approach (Bricker, 1976; Bricker & Bricker, 1976; Robinson, 1976;

Stephens, 1977). Balthazar and his colleagues (Balthazar & English, 1969; Balthazar & Phillips, 1976a, 1976b; Noar & Balthazar, 1975; Phillips & Baltohazar, 1976) have begun to outline a taxonomy of behavioral characteristics of severely handicapped individuals that may have great relevance for educators in terms of aptitude by treatment interactions. Ecological considerations concerning teaching environments have been analyzed by a variety of investigators (Blackard, 1976; Bronfenbrenner, 1976; Bronfenbrenner, 1977; McGurk, 1977; Miller & Switzky, 1978; Switzky & Sedlak, 1977). Characteristics of instructional methodologies have been discussed by many educators (Bricker & Iacino, 1977; Bricker, Bricker, Iacino, & Dennison, 1976; Brown & York, 1974; DeSpain, Williams, & York, 1975; Smith, Smith, & Edgar, 1976; Williams, 1975; Williams, Brown, & Certo, 1975), and will be fully explored in the following sections. It will be a challenge for future educational researchers to untangle the complex interactions among these dimensions. For now it must be assumed that these dimensions do underlay effective learning structures for the severely retarded and any effective assessment strategy must be attuned to collecting data on such cases.

ASSESSMENT AND INSTRUCTIONAL MODELS

Direct and Individualized Instructional Procedures

The dominant instructional model for the education of the severely handicapped is based on the behavioral approach. The behavioral model is concerned with teaching specific skill building activities to students as derived from direct assessment of ongoing student behavior (see A. Repp. Chap. 4). According to Haring & Gentry (1976) the instructional management dimensions of individualizing instruction include: (1) precisely identifying the general goals which one wishes to achieve; (2) specifying those goals in terms of enabling objectives which lead to the achievement of the goal; (3) identifying the activities and resources necessary to achieve the specified goals; and (4) systematically inspecting progress toward these goals. Dimensions of direct instruction include: (1) assessing pupil performance; (2) setting goals, objectives, and aims; (3) systematic planning of instructional/management programs; (4) selecting suitable instructional materials; (5) specifying instructional procedures; (6) arranging motivational facors; and (7) evaluaing pupil progress.

In this model the teacher is viewed as the "manager" of all classroom activity and one who works with a team of professionals and paraprofessionals to accomplish the various goals involved in providing educational activities to severely handicapped children. In order for a severely handicapped child to learn a skill it must be defined precisely in objective measurable operations. The exact responses that the child must make in order to acquire the specified skill and the sequences that these responses must be made have to be defined exactly. Techniques based on task analysis (Bigge & O'Donnell, 1976; Mager, 1962; Mager & Pipe, 1970) may be especially useful. The task analytic approach to instruction precisely delineates starting points and terminal objectives. It also assures that subskill and subcomponent responses that the child has to make in order to acquire the terminal skill take place. Also teacher activities will be carefully delineated and precisely specified in order to guarantee that the child will make the required responses. Instruction is tailored to each child's individual level of functioning, with each child proceeding through a chain of behavioral sequences at his or her own rate under optimal motivational and reinforcement control. Longer periods of time will be spent on behavioral sequences involving high error rates, and behavioral sequences on which the child demonstrates mastery will be skipped. In order to be of any value however, the teacher must continually and reliably measure the child's progress toward skill acquisition. That is, assessment is an essential, ongoing feature of such a model.

The Development Model and Its Implications for Assessment and Instruction

Educational assessment of the severely handicapped child is undertaken in order to formulate a set of precise educational goals and instructional objectives. Therefore, models of curriculum and models of educational assessment are ultimately tied together. One of the primary weaknesses in the field of special education is the lack of comprehensive systems that provide structure and guidance for determining what to teach and criteria for subsequent evaluation of those materials (Hobbs, 1975).

The model which many special education professionals (Haring & Bricker, 1976) believe holds the greatest promise for building and implementing a comprehensive approach is one derived from the (normative) developmental model. In this regard, Haring & Bricker (1976) emphasize three tenets derived from the (normative) developmental model which may provide the needed structure and guidance: (1) growth or changes in behavior follow a developmental hierarchy, e.g., children generally learn to vocalize before uttering words; (2) behavior acquisition moves from simple to more complex responses, e.g., children learn to focus their eyes before they learn to read; and (3) more complex behavior is the result of coordinating or modifying simpler component response forms, e.g., according to the Piagetian point of view (Piaget, 1963), the hand-eye coordination scheme is the result of coordination of two primary circular reactions, visual tracking and grasping.

Hogg (1975) raises two questions concerning the relevance of normative development for educational planning and the relationship between normative development and educational program objectives: (1) Can information on normative development provide educational objectives in a *direct* fashion so as to provide the contents of curricula in the form of developmental sequences as training guides? (2) Must adequate educational theory first establish the content of curricula prior to implementing developmental information in educational procedures? Hogg (1975) argues strongly that information on normative developmental sequences *cannot* provide educational program contents in a direct fashion.

Bijou (1966), Bricker (1970), Haring & Bricker (1976), and many other professional workers using the techniques of behavior modification have felt that behaviors that are normative developmentally can serve as educational objectives for severely handicapped children. Indeed Bricker (1970) has said that the primary objective of special education for the mentally retarded is to develop a process to teach "normal" behavior. However, does normative-developmental information embedded within the techniques and procedures of behavior modification form an educational theory for the mentally retarded? Should normative development be an educational aim? For that matter are all behaviors developed during childhood equally significant or even desirable?

One cannot assume that behaviors that are clearly adaptive for a "normal" child will be similarly adaptive for a severely handicapped child. Ultimately the choice of what is to be taught must be considered in terms of the future roles and cultural expectations. The contents of a curriculum must possess "ecological validity" (Brooks & Baumeister, 1977), and reflect whatever the ultimate functioning level of the person is assumed to be (Brown et al., 1976).

The course of development for individual children may vary considerably from the ideal as a function of those children's particular interaction with their culture and environment. Thus, in terms of educational aims, schedules of normative development may provide an unstable norm. Rather than base curriculum on idealizations of developmental behavioral sequences that are only significant to child development theorists, educational objectives should be based on "ecological validity" and the long-term goals related to the level of ultimate functioning for the severely handicapped.

Despite this it does not necessarily follow that knowledge of normal development is irrelevant to developing educational objectives. As a result, knowledge of the normative developmental sequences and integration of behaviors may be useful in drawing attention to some of the essential components of a skill. However additional non-normative behavioral sequences may have to be added to allow severely and profoundly multi-handicapped children to acquire a skill.

Since not all the stages and sequences of normative development must be absolutely followed, two of the more important questions an educator must ask are: (1) which developmental behaviors, and (2) what sequences of mastery are essential for the development of more advanced skills in the severely handicapped? For any skill that one wishes to teach a severely handicapped child, it would be immensely helpful if one knew which "preskills" or "enabling objectives" one must teach the child first. We might in this way save the child and the teacher considerable time teaching things which are not essential. At the same time, the teacher must be aware that sequences of behavior may be taught to severley handicapped children that are not important to the normal child in the achievement of a particular goal. At this stage of our knowledge much of the information that is needed to effectively teach severely handicapped children is unknown and remains a difficult empirical question because of the extreme variability among severely handicapped children and their small numbers. Mira (1977) and Yurk and Williams (1977) also came to very similar conclusions.

The Constructive-Interaction Adaptation Approach of Bricker and Bricker

Bricker and Bricker and their students (Bricker, 1970; Bricker & Bricker, 1971; Bricker & Bricker, 1972; Bricker & Bricker, 1973; Bricker & Bricker, 1974; Bricker, 1976; Bricker & Bricker, 1976; Bricker, Dennison & Bricker, 1976; Bricker, Bricker, Iacino & Dennison, 1976; Bricker & Iacino, 1977; Filler, Robinson, Smith, Vincent-Smith, Bricker & Bricker, 1975; Robinson, 1976) have proposed a model which combines information on normative developmental sequences embedded within an adequate educational theory. The model could provide a comprehensive approach to the education of severely handicapped children and does yield a partial answer to some of the problems that Hogg (1975) discussed.

The constructive-interaction adaptation approach represents an amalgam and integration of operant behavioral approaches and those based on developmental sequences. The model emphasizes mechanisms for changing behavior and altering patterns of behavioral control within Piaget's cognitive model of development. The constructive-interaction adaptation approach relies heavily on the idea that the development of an organism depends on both biological and environmental influences. These lead to the development of a set of (cognitive) structures progressively constructed by continuous interaction between the organism and the external world. Following the ideas of Piaget, the constructive-interaction adaptation approach suggests that the exercise of inborn reflexes in the infant such as sucking, grasping, and looking form the basis of all subsequent development. The infant, through subsequent interaction with the environment, modifies his basic reflexive behavior into successively more complex levels of development during what Piaget has called the sensori-motor stage. In essence, the environment impinges on the infant and the behavior of the infant (schemata) acts on the environment in a stream of interactions that result in progressively more sophisticated adaptations. These produce more complex responses (schemes) to progressively more complex environments. Even undifferentiated random movements exhibited by a young infant or a severely handicapped older child can have an effect on the environment, which in turn changes the probabilities for alterations of the rates, the intensities, or the topographies of these responses.

The sensori-motor phase of development which is probably most important for young infants and severely retarded children, consists of six distinct stages of development or successive stages of organization: (1) the stage of reflex exercises; (2) the stage of primary circular reactions (formation of habits and motor perceptions); (3) the stage of secondary circular reactions (formation of intentional acts and the development of comprehension); (4) the stage of coordination of secondary schemata and their application to new situations (ends and means and constancy of objects); (5) stage of tertiary circular reactions (invention of new means, sensorimotor intelligence); and (6) the stage of the beginning of thought (the invention of new means through mental combinations, internalization of the sensorimotor schemata). (For details, see Flavell, 1963; Hunt, 1961; Piaget, 1963.) The task for those using the constructive-interactive adaptation approach becomes one of translating Piaget's developmental sequences which form the sensorimotor phase into an operational curriculum that is appropriate for either infants or severely retarded children.

The first step in generating an operational curriculum is to construct a "map" of the "developmental milestones," i.e., an "overview" of the behaviors representing the curricular domains that occur during the sensori-motor period. This "map" and "overview" can be represented as a developmental program lattice, which presents the order and interdependence of behaviors that emerge within and across skill sequences during the sensori-motor period. This begins with reflexive responding and extends to the emergence of symbolic processes and intentional behavior. William Bricker and Ghisela Chatelanant (Filler et al., 1975, p. 219) have developed a developmental program lattice for the sensorimotor period which is presented in Figure 13-2. This map or lattice provides not only a theoretical framework for development within the

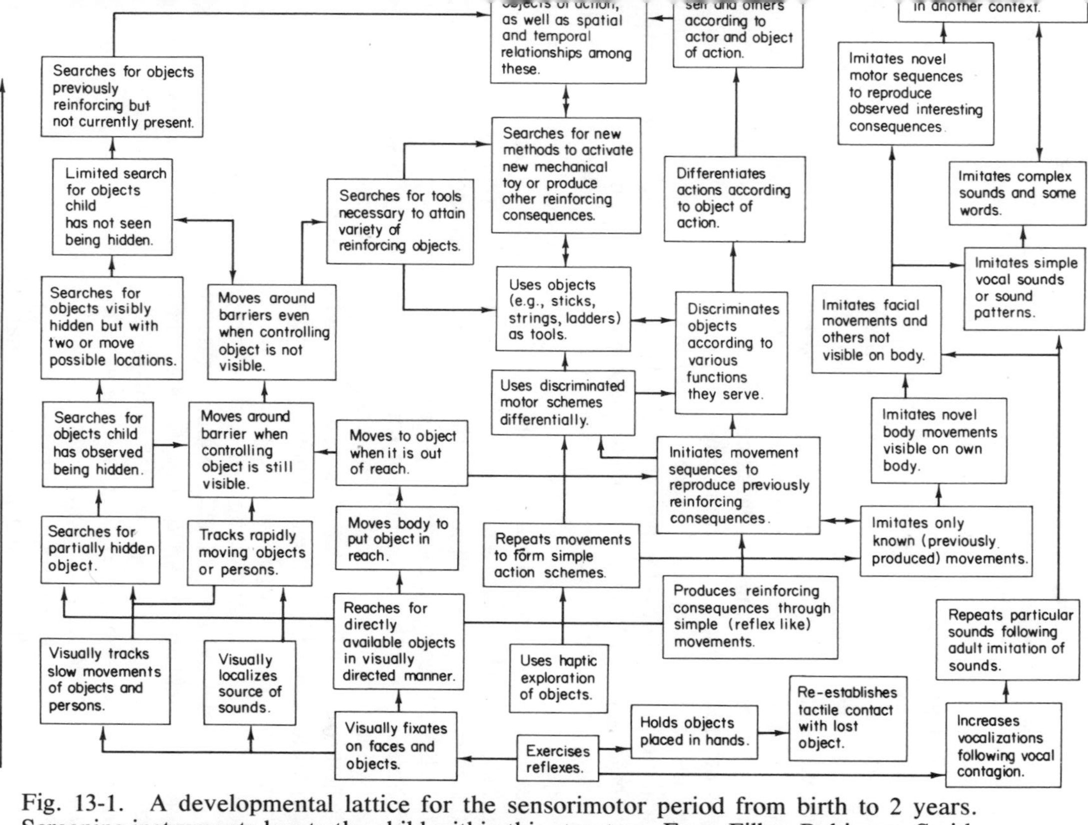

Fig. 13-1. A developmental lattice for the sensorimotor period from birth to 2 years. Screening instruments locate the child within this structure. From Filler, Robinson, Smith et al. in N. Hobbs (Ed.), *Issues in the classification of children* (vol. 1), 1975. Reprinted by permission.

sensori-motor period, but also the key content areas and organizational framework to direct training activities. Represented along the vertical dimension of the lattice are increasingly complex forms of developmentally sequenced behavioral schemes which are constructed as a function of more and more sophisticated interactions between the child and the environment. Schemes of equal distance from the bottom of the lattice are believed to come into existence at about the same time. The left-right dimension of the lattice is arbitrary and represents various schemes. The uppermost boxes in the lattice represent the terminal behavioral states of the sensori-motor period which includes the preverbal cognitive prerequisites for syntactic, phonological, and semenatic processes; the prerequisites for understanding physical causality, space, time, seriation, and number; and a primitive classification for understanding environmental events, including social relationships. Continuing upward on any vertical pathway (beginning with "exercising of the reflexes") provides a theoretical hierarchy of developmental behaviors in which an infant or a severely handicapped child might adapt to his environment. Thus, the developmental program lattice provides the developmental order and relationships among the various schemes. Assessment procedures consist of techniques to locate the child within the lattice's developmental space; programming becomes a matter of "creatively engineering" environmental interactions that will provide the stimulating mechanisms for moving the child to the next, more complex form of behavior by expanding each program box into a sequence of training targets and to suggest possible activities which would allow the child to reach and maintain the established goals. Using the lattice as a guide, the teacher's responsibility is to generate a set of activities to allow the child to learn each specific target behavior. These targets and the relevant activities necessary to accomplish them compose the daily school program for each child.

In order to locate the child within the developmental space, the Brickers and their students (Robinson, 1972) have constructed a screening device constructed from several available scales including the *Uzgiris-Hunt Scales,* the *Albert Einstein Scales,* the *Bayley Scales,* the *Gesell Developmental Schedule* and Piaget's own descriptions of the sensorimotor period. The screening device requires repeated testings with the child, perhaps in different settings, so that reliabile, ecologically valid data can be acquired. Assessment testing of a scheme is performed sequentially until the response of the child is no longer appropriate. Here the assessment phase ends and the instruction phase begins. The initial forms of instruction are used to explore the parameters of the child's behavioral repertoire for that scheme in order to determine the reasons for the child's failure and what specific alterations of the task might stimulate further development. Assessment and instruction are closely linked so that the assessment phase leads directly into the training phase. Locating a child's skill level in the sensori-motor domain provides an immediate answer to the ever present teacher's question, "What do I teach?" Since every child can be located somewhere in the developmental lattice, the next step in the lattice sequence is the most logical training target.

As the child learns, it becomes increasingly possible to plan instructional programs involving more complex targeted skills since each succeeding objective is constructed on the previously demonstrated scheme. The structure of the developmental lattice requires that with each succeeding step upward on the progressive path of the lattice, training becomes more complex and interrelated and requires a subtle elaboration of existing skills. The constructive-interactive adaptation approach has provided developmental lattices and subsequent training routines in the areas of language development (Bricker, Dennison, & Bricker, 1976), motor behavior (Bricker, Davis, Wahlin, & Evans, 1976), as well as in object constancy (Robinson, 1972).

The constructive-interactive approach relies heavily upon careful delineation of the sequences of developing behavioral schemes which are largely unknown (even in nonhandicapped population), and verifying their presence and order in severely handicapped populations. The validation of this approach will require years of research with many handicapped populations and in many environmental settings. Nevertheless, the research may pay off by providing the knowledge base for efficient and effective teaching. For now, we may concentrate upon the best practice procedures for delineating behavioral characteristics.

FUNCTIONAL DEVELOPMENTAL ASSESSMENT SYSTEMS

Sailor & Haring (1977), in extending the analysis of educational assessment strategies have defined three types of functional developmental assessment systems falling along a continuum of comprehensiveness. These systems both detail the analysis of learner characteristics and the time needed for administration. The system scale ranges from position 1 systems (screening instruments) to position 3 systems (full-detailed and comprehensive instruments). Position 1 assessment systems are basically screening systems which are completed quickly and present an overview of the child's current level of skill over various behavioral skill domains. These screening instruments include items such as the *Camelot Behavioral Checklist* (Foster, 1974), the *Developmental Record* (Hutton & Talkington, 1974), the *Denver Developmental Screening Test* (Frankenburg & Dodds, 1975), the *Progress Assessment Chart of Social and Per-*

sonal Development (Gunzburg, 1974), the *TARC Assessment System* (Sailor & Mix, 1975), the *Fairview Developmental Scale* (Giampiccalo & Boroskin, 1974), the *Portage Project Guide to Early Education: Instructions and Checklist* (Shearer, Billingsley, & Frohman, 1970), the *Caine-Levine Social Competency Scale* (Caine, Levine, & Elzey, 1963), and the *Vineland Social Maturity Scale* (Doll, 1947). These systems are useful to the teacher to establish the educational process. The *Camelot Behavioral Checklist,* the *TARC Assessment System,* and the *Vineland Social Maturity Scale* will be presented in greater detail in the following section as examples of Position 1 assessment systems.

Position One Instruments

THE CAMELOT BEHAVIORAL CHECKLIST

The Camelot Behavioral Checklist (Foster, 1974) has three distinctive features: (1) a large sampling of items (399) from the behavioral domain of very early childhood to adulthood, (2) items which can be stated as behavioral objectives, and (3) an arrangement of the items following an empirically derived increasing order of difficulty.

The items consist of two-to-seven-word behavioral descriptions in order of difficulty of the items within domains. The checklist is grouped into the following 10 behavioral domains and 40 subdomains: (1) Self-help, including eating behaviors, dressing-undressing, toileting, cares for own health, knowledge of self, bathing, hair care, and grooming; (2) Physical Development, including balance and ambulation, body movements, and sensory development; (3) Home Duties, including house cleaning, care of clothing, food preparation, car maintenance, and operation of appliances; (4) Vocational Behavior, including work and job skills; (5) Economic Behavior, including shopping, handling of money, and the use of credit cards; (6) Independent Travel, including travel and transportation skills; (7) Numerical Skills, including arithmetic and time-telling skills; (8) Communication Skills, including receptive and expressive language, reading and writing, and telephone skills; (9) Social Behavior, including spectator and participatory skills; (10) Responsibility, including social responsibility, response to emergencies and security.

The checklist is scored by judging whether the individual "can do" (+) or "needs training" (−) on each of the 399 behavioral descriptions. Behaviors scored as "can do" refer to those that the individual can now do and further training is not required. Behaviors scored as "needs training" mean that the individual cannot presently perform the behavior or performs it in less than normal manner and that further training should be planned.

The Camelot Behavioral Checklist can be administered in three different ways: (1) by one person from memory, i.e., a parent, teacher, teacher's aide; (2) by a "team of individuals" completing different items from memory; and (3) by one or two persons completing the items by directly observing the behavior of the individual being assessed. The checklist is seven pages long. Foster (1974) recommends the use of one of the first two methods as a basis for preliminary selecting of target behaviors and then using direct observation of the behaviors selected for training during pretest or baseline periods.

The items on the scale scored "can do" are transferred to the Camelot Behavioral Checklist Profile which consists of 40 columns of numbers, one column for each subdomain. The numbers in each column correspond to the numbers of the items. Only items scored "can do" are circled. The numbers in each column represent the items in a descending order of difficulty. The level of difficulty is based on the percentage of individuals in the original sample of 624 mentally retarded persons (characteristics unknown) who needed training on that item. Therefore, the selection of "targets" for training should start with the lowest uncircled item number in any subdomain and precede upward. When all gaps have been filled, targets can be selected which will expand an individual's behavioral repretoire beyond the highest circled item on the item profile. For example, in the behavioral domain Self-Help, the subdomains of eating, dressing and undressing, and toilet use are presumably arranged in increasing order of difficulty. Items of the eating subdomain should be trained before items on the dressing and undressing subdomain and before items on the toilet use subdomains are trained, and so on.

The number of "can do" items in each domain is totaled and entered in the appropriate box on the item profile sheet. The totals for each domain and the total of all domains are transferred to the Camelot Behavioral Checklist Score Profile which consists of 11 columns, one column for the checklist total. The score profile provides a quick representation of the numbers of behaviors within each domain which the individual has acquired or not acquired. The score profile also shows the individual's performance percentile rank relative to the original standardization group, in terms of the percentage of the standardization group who had also acquired that level of behavior within each of the behavioral domains and for the total score. Thus an individual's score can be examined in terms of his performances relative to his own profile and his percentile rank relative to the standardization sample. Once the target or terminal behaviors have been determined, a *Skill Acquisition Program Bibliography* (Tucker, 1974) or similar curriculum reference can be used to identify any programs that have been developed for these behaviors.

THE TARC ASSESSMENT SYSTEM

The *TARC Assessment System* (Sailor & Mix, 1975) was developed with the cooperation of the Topeka (Kansas) Association for Retarded Citizens in order to provide a short-form behavioral assessment instrument to formulate instructional objectives and subsequent curriculum selection. The System provides a quick assessment of observable behavioral characteristics thus allowing a ''snapshot'' of the current functioning level of severely handicapped youngsters on four behavioral domains: (1) Self-Help Skills; (2) Motor Skills; (3) Communication; and (4) Social Skills.

The TARC System is predicated on the fact that there currently exists a wide spectrum of applied technology which is immediately available to meet the educational goals of severely handicapped children. The TARC System is a means of getting this curriculum technology out to educators to help them get started in an educational setting (i.e., classroom, day-center, institution, or whatever). The TARC System is designed to provide a means for meeting these needs by relating curriculum selection directly to assessment and the derivation of instructional objectives. The System utilizes a four-stage procedure to arrive at curriculum selection which consists of: (1) assessment, (2) profiling, (3) derivation of instructional objections, and (4) curriculum selection (Sailor, 1975; Sailor & Mix, 1975; Sailor & Horner, 1976). The TARC Inventory may be used to: (1) demonstrate accountability for education or rehabilitation by repeated testings over time, (2) provide an educational assessment on which to base precise instructional objectives for individual children, (3) provide for an educational assessment on which to base general instructional goals for a class, and (4) assess the effects of a particular instructional strategy or curriculum (e.g., language development program) or behaviors within a programmed skill domain (i.e., communication) as well as on the child's progress in other skills.

Assessing the child requires the rater to make a series of judgments (e.g., choose one of five or six scaled items which best describe the child on a particular skill) and categorical judgments (e.g., choose any number of a series of items which best describes the child's current performance) based on careful observation of the child in a group or class setting during a two-week interval prior to making the assessment. The rater should observe the child during the various ''skill-tapping'' activities presented in the inventory in order to determine if the various behaviors are or are not present in the child's current repertoire of behavior (Sailor, 1975).

The TARC Inventory is intended to selectively tap a few skill areas and produce scores within each of the following domains and subdomains: (1) Self-Help, including Toileting (urination and bowel functions), Eating (utensil use, neatness, drinking and behavior at mealtime) and Clothing (dressing and undressing); (2) Motor, including Small muscle (fine motor), Large muscle (gross motor) and Pre-academic motor skills relevant for classroom education; (3) Communication, including Expressive and Receptive language skills, and Pre-academic communication skills relevant for classroom education, and (4) Social, including Behavior (direction following, group behavior, individual behavior, interaction with peers and adults, cooperation, emotional control) and Pre-academic social skills relevant for classroom education.

The TARC inventory was standardized on 283 severely handicapped children of both sexes ranging in age from 3 to 16, from institutions and day centers. Sailor & Mix (1975) claim that the TARC Inventory is most discriminative at the lower ranges and that interrater reliability is good.

Scores on the assessment summary sheet from the various domains and subdomains can be plotted on a profile sheet and direct comparisons can be made between individual scores and the averaged scores of the standardization sample. The standardization sample scores have been transformed into standard scores with a mean of 50 and a standard deviation of 20. In formulating instructional objectives, the TARC System employs the logic that the child should first receive educational instruction and training on those areas in which he is most deficient relative to his peers. A child's score may also be examined in terms of his performance relative to his own profile. The profile sheet can be considered an analysis of the child's relative strengths and weaknesses from the standpoint of his own overall level of functioning. A given child may have a profile superior to the standardization group (i.e., no single score falls below the midpoint on the scale) but show peaks and valleys indicating relative areas of strengths and weaknesses. Educational programs can be established to remediate these relative areas of impairment.

The teacher using the TARC System has two options: (1) producing the graphic profile of the child's performance, deriving instructional objectives and then obtaining curricula to meet the specific objectives, or (2) mailing the score sheet to Sailor to allow a computer to provide instructional objectives and appropriate curricula.

Under the computer programmed option, the teacher receives a print-out of the profile plotted by the computer and a series of tables identifying the specific behaviors that the child was and was not able to perform as identified from the raw data of the inventory. The chief advantage of the computer program in the TARC System is the facility of matching existing curricula to logically derived instructional objectives.

Formulating instructional objectives either by the teacher or by the computer according to the TARC System (Sailor, 1975; Sailor & Horner, 1975) should be based on the following premises: (1) a severely handicapped child should be trained first and most intensively in those educational areas in which he is most deficient relative to his own overall level of functioning, and (2) the specific behavioral components of those skills should be trained in an order which corresponds to the frequency of those behaviors in the TARC standardization program. The computer or the educator will scan the Profile and Pre-academic Skills table and select those performances that are the most obvious skill deficits relative to the standardization sample and to the child's own performance average. The computer or educator will derive a list of instructional objectives ranked from top to bottom on the basis of the scored severity of deficit. The process of curriculum selection, the final stage of the TARC System, may best be accomplished by the computer option for those individuals who are new to the field and not very familiar with existing educational technology. The final stage of the TARC System is designed to put the educator in touch with the curricula most likely to succeed in fulfilling the instructional objectives derived from the computer programs.

The Kansas Neurological Institute has compiled a comprehensive bibliography (Sailor, Guess, & Lavis, 1975b) of educational technology for the severely handicapped. This bibliography, which is constantly updated, forms the basis of the computer programmed library retrieval system which is a component of the TARC System. Each of the entries in this component consists of an existing, available "canned" program to meet a particular instructional objective or educational need. The computer library system includes a reference for the program under its domain and subdomain (e.g., Motor; small muscle), together with its cost, where it can be purchased, how much training is required to administer it, where the training can be obtained, what research supports it, to what population it is useful. Also, an abstract describing the program is included.

The TARC System, having derived instructional objectives from the Assessment Inventory, activates the retrieval system to print out a list of available programs to meet each instructional objective. The print-out appears in ranked order in terms of which programs are most likely to succeed in fulfilling each instructional objective from present information.

In summary, the TARC System is intended to provide beginning educators a procedure which allows them to get started educating the severely handicapped children and a reference tool to help them with the curriculum selection process.

THE VINELAND SOCIAL MATURITY SCALE

The Vineland Social Maturity Scale (Doll, 1965) provides an outline of detailed performances in respect to which children show a progressive capacity for looking after themselves and for participating in activities that lead toward ultimate independence as adults. The items of the scale are arranged in order of increasing average difficulty (i.e., normal average life age, LA), and represent progressive maturation in six behavioral domains: self-help, self-direction, locomotion, occupation, communication, and social relations. The self-help domain is divided into three subdomains of self-help: general; eating; and dressing. This maturation in social independence is taken as a measure of progressive development in social competence. Standardization data was collected on nonhandicapped individuals, 10 males and 10 females from birth to 30 years of age for a total of 620 subjects to determine the normal average life age (LA) of the items. The *Vineland* is not a rating scale but requires sophisticated skill in interview technique. The items of the scale are to be scored on the basis of information obtained from an informant intimately familiar with the person scored, such as the mother, the father, a close relative, guardian, attendant, teacher, teacher's aide, or professional person. A major value of the scale for those working with the profoundly handicapped is in interviewing the parents and other family members in order to incorporate them into the assessment process and eventually into the process of education.

According to Doll (1965), the scale affords: (1) a standard schedule of normal development that can be used repeatedly for the measurement of growth or change, (2) a measure of individual differences and consequently of extreme deviation, (3) a qualitative index of variation in development in abnormal subjects, (4) a measure of improvement following special treatment, therapy, or training, and (5) a schedule for reviewing developmental histories in the clinical study of retardation, deterioration, and rates or stages of growth and decline.

The 117 items on the scale are brief, two- to five-word phrases further elaborated by short sentences in the manual of directions. The items are grouped into 17 age ranges, birth to 25 years and older. The number of items in some of the 17 age categories useful to educators of severely handicapped children are as follows: (1) Birth to 1 year, 17 items (taping mostly self-help skills); (2) 1 to 2 years, 17 items (taping most self-help skills); (3) 2 to 3 years, 10 items (taping mostly self-help skills); (4) 3 to 4 years, 6 items (split among locomotion, socialization, and self-help); (5) 4 to 5 years, 6 items (taping self-help); (6) 5 to 6 years, 5 items (split among all domains); (7) 6 to 7 years, 4 items (mostly self-help); and (8) 7 to 8 years, 5 items (mostly self-help skills). Over the age range birth to 8 years, 39 items sample the self-help domain, 7 items sample the locomotion domain, 11 items sample the occupation domain, and 9 items sample the communication domain.

The score for each item is subjectively determined. An examiner interviews an informant who is required to judge and describe how much, to what extent, and in what ways the individual usually or habitually behaves. The examiner has to make a number of judgments in order to determine a score. Doll (1965) claims that the *Vineland Social Maturity Scale* is not a rating scale and scores are not to be based on mere opinions. The informant does not make the scoring judgment. This is done by the examiner after obtaining from the informants as much detail as practical regarding the behavioristic facts which reveal the manner and extent of the subject's actual performance on each item. How does the recorder make these judgments?

To score an item (+), the judgments required are: (1) the behavior described by the informant conforms to the item description in the manual, (2) the behavior is performed without need of undue prodding or artificial incentives, (3) the behavior is habitually performed, and (4) the behavior is performed only with occasional assistance in case of special circumstances.

To score an item "+F," the judgments required are: (1) the behavior described by the informant did conform to the item description in the manual but was not performed by the subject at the time of examination because of special restraint or lack of opportunity, and (2) the subject formerly did perform the item successfully when no restraints were imposed or where the opportunity was present.

To score an item "+N.O." (No Opportunity), the following judgments are required: (1) the subject has not performed the behavior yet, due to special restraint or lack of opportunity; and (2) the subject would usually or habitually perform the behavior or quickly learn to do so if the restraints were removed or opportunities were provided.

To score an item plus-minus (±), the examiner has to judge: (1) if the behavior is occasionally performed but not ordinarily performed with full success, and (2) performance is more than cursory or fitful.

To score an item minus (−), the examiner has to judge: (1) if performance has not yet been successful; and (2) if successful performance has been only rarely so, or accomplished under extreme pressure or unusual incentive.

The total score (the social age, SA) is obtained by adding to the basal score (the highest of all the continuous pluses), the additional scattered credits beyond the basal score until two consecutive minus scores are encountered. Each additional (+) counts as one point, (+F) counts as one point, (+N.O.) counts as one point, (±) counts as 0.5 points. The Age Scores can be converted to ratios or social quotients (SQ) by dividing the subject's social age score by his life age and multiplying by 100. The extent to which an individual's social age is below his life age is the extent to which the individual is considered socially immature. The Social Age is reported to be highly related to mental age on the *Stanford-Binet Intelligence Test* ($r = 0.86$). Information on the *Vineland Social Maturity Scale* can provide a very gross index of social functioning and provide the beginnings of a rapport-building system with the parents and with the "significant others" of the severely handicapped. Information cannot easily be used for programmatic or administrative purposes.

Position Two Instruments

Position 2 assessment systems are recommended by Sailor & Haring (1977) for less systematic educational assessments and for the formulation of the Individual Education Plan as mandated by PL 94-142. These assessment devices fall between the quick overviews of learner characteristics provided by Position 1 assessment systems and the elaborate assessment models represented by Position 3 assessment systems. Position 2 assessment instruments include the *Pennsylvania Training Model, Individual Assessment Guide* (Somerton & Turner, 1975; *APT; A Training Program for Citizens with Severely or Profoundly Retarded Behavior* (Brady & Smiloritz, 1974), and the *Uniform Performance Assessment System* (Bendersky, Edgar, & White, 1976). The *Pennsylvania Training Model, Individual Assessment Guide* and the *Uniform Performance Assessment System* will be presented in greater detail as examples of Position 2 assessment systems.

THE PENNSYLVANIA TRAINING MODEL—INDIVIDUAL ASSESSMENT GUIDE

The Pennsylvania Training Model (Somerton & Turner, 1975) is designed to help teachers develop specific programs for severely and multiply handicapped children. There are four major steps in the model: (1) obtaining an overview (global assessment) of the child's skill development from the Curriculum Assessment Guide to identify skill areas of strength and weakness; (2) intensively assessing those areas of deficit from the Competency Checklists in order to more precisely pinpoint those skills that are present, and those skill areas that are absent from the child's behavioral repertoire; (3) developing a detailed analysis to ameliorate a deficient skill by the use of task analysis, in order to formulate an individualized plan of instruction through the use of the Individual Prescriptive Planning Sheet; and (4) implementing this educational plan of instruction and continually assessing the child's progress so that modifications in the program can be made.

The Curriculum Assessment Guide provides gross screening of competence in six behavioral domains: (1) Sensory Development, (2) Motor Development, (3) Activities of Daily Living, (4) Communication, (5) Perceptual-Cognitive Development, and (6) Social and Emotional Development. The assessment items and criteria for successful performance are clearly presented in simple phrases. Sensory Development is divided into Tactile, Auditory, and Visual subdomains, each consisting of five assessment items. Motor Development is divided into two subdomains, Gross and Fine Motor each consisting of five assessment items. Activities of Daily Living is divided into six subdomains, each consisting of five assessment items, Feeding and Toileting, Toilet Training, Dressing and Undressing, Washing and Bathing, Nasal Hygiene and Oral Hygiene. Communication and Perceptual/Cognitive Development are divided into subdomains, and consist of five assessment items each. Social and Emotional Development is divided into two subcategories, Social Interaction, consisting of five assessment items, and Behavioral Compliance, whose assessment items are undefined by the authors, Somerton & Turner (presumably leaving it up to the raters to make up their own assessment items). All items are roughly arranged in order of developmental level and complexity of behavior. Scoring the individual's performance is done by putting an "X" on those items already achieved by the child and writing the date of administration. Those items assessed, but not resulting in any response or an incorrect response, should also have the date written in so that it is evident that the individual has not acquired these skills. It is not necessary to assess all 70 items presented or to attempt to complete a total assessment in a specified period of time. The performance of the individual in the assessment items is to be obtained by means of a continuous data recording system that would present in graphic or tabular form the length of time it took the individual to achieve a particular assessment objective. This information can be expressed depending on the task in terms of: (1) the total number of days the task was presented, (2) the number of trials to successfully reach criterion, (3) the total time spent on the task, and (4) the total number of correct responses. The intent of the Curriculum Assessment Guide is to provide an overview as to the amount of time required to achieve skills in the different behavioral domains. This specific information is useful in deciding which skill areas are in most need of development as well as measuring the individual's rate of skill acquisition in a given area.

The 14 Competency Checklists (one for each subdomain of behavior) are used diagnostically and prescriptively to specifically and precisely assess the child within a particular skill area following global assessment on the Curriculum Assessment Guide. The assessment items on the Checklists are also organized in order of developmental level and complexity of behavior. However, the authors note that each child will not necessarily perform each of the competencies in order and may even skip items. The competencies can be utilized to determine several components of a particular behavior. The purpose of the Competency Checklist is to help the rater (teacher) understand how and where individual behaviors fit into the child's overall developmental progress. The child's competency in a particular subdomain is rated on a four-point scale: (1) "0"—No competency (0 percent correct responses); (2) "1"—moderate competency (25 percent correct responses); (3) "2"—adequate competency (75 percent correct responses); and (4) "3"—complete competency (100 percent correct responses). An overall score of competance on each Competency Checklist can be obtained by adding the score for the items on the checklist.

As might be expected, the Competency Checklists have the greatest number of assessment items in the domain of Activities of Daily Living (219), followed by Motor Development (75), Communication (66), Sensory Development (61), Perceptual/Cognitive Development (35), and Social/Emotional Development (19). There is some ambiguity in determining what scale score a child had reached on the Competency Checklists. The authors do not define precisely how many trials per day, or how many days each assessment item should be presented, nor do they precisely define in behavioral terms the criterion response. This type of ambiguity in scoring is less in the Curriculum Assessment Guide. The criterion responses are much better defined here. However, the authors still do not provide any indication of precisely how many trials per day, or how many days each assessment item should be presented.

The Competency Checklists permit the teacher to analyze the specific educational needs of each student, and provides the teacher with a curriculum plan, i.e., a series of behavioral expectancies and activities to facilitate behavioral change (Somerton & Myers, 1976). The authors do not make explicit how to determine which deficit skills should be taught to the child. This would probably depend upon the child's most deficient areas (as based on scores from the various subdomains), and the personal views, needs, and expectations of the "school" and the parents. Nevertheless, the Pennsylvania Training Model Educational Planning System uses an Individual Prescriptive Planning Sheet (IPPS) to develop the educational program for the child.

The components of the IPPS consist of: (1) Antecedents (the preparation for instructional activity and the procedures), (2) Behavior (the correct and incorrect behavior), (3) Consequences (the behavioral consequences to the child when the correct behavior is performed and (4) Criteria (the behavioral criterion for learning, as well as the required number of trials over a given number of sessions). See Somerton & Myers (1976) and Somerton & Turner (1975) for further details.

The Pennsylvania Training Model Educational Planning System encourages continuous program monitoring via graphs or charts in order to determine if an individual child is progressing educationally or if that child's educational plan needs to be modified. (See Somerton & Turner, 1975.)

The Uniform Performance Assessment System

The *Uniform Performance Assessment System* (UPAS) is an experimental behavioral checklist listing educational objectives in the form of behavioral descriptors with accompanying criterion tests. UPAS is designed to monitor the performance of severely handicapped children in order to determine how many of the total number of desired skills a child has at any given time or how many new skills a child has learned since the last assessment. UPAS is currently being developed by the Center for the Severely Handicapped at the Experimental Education Unit, Child Development and Mental Retardation Center, College of Education, University of Washington, at Seattle (Bendersky, Edgar, & White, 1976).

The ultimate goals of the authors of UPAS are to develop an information system to monitor and measure growth (i.e., to pinpoint the skill level on the continuum of development) in severely handicapped children from birth until these children possess marketable vocational skills. This information system should also be capable of summarizing, analyzing, and reporting information in a manner that facilitates program planning, evaluation, and reporting. The UPAS will be designed to: (1) optimize a direct relationship between assessment items and those skill areas which are thought to be necessary for the success of the pupil, (2) insure that measurement procedures will be clear and simple so that accurate (reliable) measures are readily obtained, (3) require a short period of time to administer, (4) produce results that can be easily interpreted, especially with respect to the precise identification of a student's standing relative to the desired sequence of development from birth to vocational placement in order to develop, monitor, and change educational programs, and (5) to be administered no less than every three months, i.e., four times a year.

The basic format of UPAS (Bendersky, 1976) is a behavioral checklist of educational objectives in the form of behavioral descriptions (the record sheet), with accompanying criterion tests. The list of behavioral objectives are ordered in terms of developmental level according to the general sequence in which there is agreement that those behaviors would normally be achieved. The criterion test, one for each educational objective, consists of: (1) a description of the skill (to be assessed), (2) the equipment and materials needed to carry out the assessment, (3) the test/observation procedure, (4) the criteria for "yes" (what criterion of behavior the child has to perform), (5) the criteria for "no" (an example of behavior that is not the criterion), and (6) criteria for scoring. (The tester records "yes" on the record sheet if the child's performance meets the criterion for yes, and "no" if the child's performance meets the criteria for no.) The number of checked behaviors at any given point in time indicates the position of the child in the sequence, or how many behaviors in the overall sequence the pupil has acquired and how many remain to be acquired.

There are three kinds of UPAS assessments planned, each tapping four skill categories in each of the major developmental levels (Bendersky, Edgar, & White, 1976). They are grouped as follows: (1) Level A assessment, consisting of skills that are normally achieved by children between the ages of birth and 6 years; (2) Level B assessment, consisting of skills that are normally achieved by children between the ages of 6 and 12 years; and (3) Level C assessment, consisting of skills that are related to vocational placement. Level A taps: (1) preacademic skills consisting of behavior involved in the development of basic auditory and visual discriminations, fine motor development, rudimentary counting, and those behavioral prerequisites to higher level "cognitive" development; (2) motor skills such as basic body movement, locomotion, and perceptual motor skills; (3) social/self-help skills such as responding to others, dressing, eating, toileting, and play behavior; and (4) communication skills involving receptive and expressive language, communication of basic needs, basic vocabulary and language development. Level B taps: (1) academic skills including traditional reading, writing, and arithmetic; (2) physical fitness/motor skills involving basic physical fitness and gross motor muscle games; (3) social skills consisting of play and game-playing behavior and more advanced self-help skills; and (4) communication skills involving "creative" speech, writing, and reading skills. Level C taps: (1) applied academic skills such as reading, writing, and arithmetic specific to practical situations; (2) physical fitness skills involving basic physical fitness activities and group games; (3) vocational skills specific to job placement such as promptness and independent work behavior; and (4) independent living skills involving those basic survival behaviors necessary for independent living in the community such as cooking and washing clothes. Level A of UPAS is currently available; Level B and Level C are still in the experimental stages.

Level A UPAS (Bendersky, 1976) consists of 64 items of preacademic skills, 62 items of motor skills, 53 items of social/self-help skills, and 68 items of communication skills. The rater reads each sequence of skills, marking the yes column beside those skills the rater knows the child possesses, and marking the no column beside those skills the rater knows the child does not possess. Those skills which the rater is uncertain of are assessed to see if the child makes the criterion response. The rater marks the "ins" column if the child has received instruction in that skill within the three month period prior to testing. Provision is made for the recording of a quantitative measure of some skills. The rater need not complete each evaluation in one long session. The intent is for the evaluation to be done at a more relaxed pace during the first month (of the three-month evaluation period). Interobserver reliability is reported to be very high.

The UPAS checklist is a guideline for program planning and curriculum sequencing. The checklist is not viewed as replacing other forms of assessment but as an aid in placing a child's individual progress pattern into a common perspective with apicture of overall development. Computer programs to analyze UPAS data and plan intervention strategies are currently under development at the University of Washington.

Position Three Instruments

Position 3 assessment systems are the most complex and time consuming devices. Sailor & Haring (1977) recommend Position 3 assessment devices be used following initial screening to further formulate instructional objectives. These assessment devices include such instruments as the *Balthazar Scales of Adaptive Behavior* (Balthazar, 1971, 1973, 1976); the *AAMD Adaptive Behavior Scale* (Nihira, Foster, Shellhaas, & Leland, 1975); the *AAMA Adaptive Behavior Scale-Public School Version* (Lambert, Windmiller, Cole, & Figueroa, 1975); the *Uzgiris-Hunt Scale* (Uzgiris & Hunt, 1975); the *Bayley Scales* (Bayley, 1969); the *Cattell Infant Intelligence Scale* (Cattell, 1940); the *Gesell Developmental Schedules* (Gesell, 1949); the *Developmental Resource* (Cohen, Gross, & Haring, 1976); the *Wabash Guide to Early Developmental Training* (Wabash Center for the Mentally Retarded, 1977); the *Behavioral Characteristics Program; The Santa Cruz Special Education Management System* (Office of the Santa Cruz County Superintendent of Schools, 1973); the *Language Intervention Program for Developmentally Young Children* (Bricker, Dennison, & Bricker, 1976); the *Motor Training Program for the Developmentally Young* (Bricker, Davis, Wahlin, & Evans, 1976); the *Callier-Azusa Scale-F Edition* (Stillman, 1977); and *A Manual for the Assessment of a "Deaf-Blind" Multiply-Handicapped Child-Revision Edition* (Collins & Rudolph, 1975). A most promising assessment device appears to be *The Behavior Rating Inventory for the Retarded* (Sparrow & Cicchetti, 1978). The *Behavioral Characteristics Progression, The Santa Cruz Special Education Management System* (Office of the Santa Cruz County Superintendent of Schools, 1973); the *Uzgiris-Hunt Scale* (Uzgiris & Hunt, 1975); the *Balthazar Scales of Adaptive Behavior* (Balthazar, 1971, 1973, 1976); and the *AAMD Adaptive Behavior Scale* (1975) will be presented in greater detail in the following section as examples of Position 3 assessment systems.

THE BEHAVIORAL CHARACTERISTICS PROGRESSION, THE SANTA CRUZ SPECIAL EDUCATION MANAGEMENT SYSTEM

The Behavioral Characteristics Progression (BCP), *The Santa Cruz Special Education Management System* (Office of Santa Cruz County Superintendent of Schools, 1973) has assessment, instructional, and communication functions. The assessment information provided by the BCP can provide the teacher with an extensive and comprehensive chart of pupil behaviors to identify which behavioral characteristics are part of that repertoire and which are not so that the teacher can develop individualized and appropriate learner objectives for each student. As a communication tool, the BCP functions as an historical recording device which can be used throughout the school years of the child to display progress and to help communicate this information to the educational team.

The BCP is a nonstandardized, criterion-referenced continuum of behaviors in chart form. It contains 2,400 observable traits which are referred to as "behavioral characteristics" (BC). These "behavioral characteristics" are organized into 59 categories of behavior, "the behavioral strands." "Behavioral strands" can have up to 50 "behavioral characteristics" ordered in terms of increasing developmental level and complexity of behavior. Each "behavioral strand" has "identifying behaviors" describing behavioral deficits that children might display in each of the "behavioral strands." The "identifying behaviors" assist the teacher in identifying the basic areas of need for each child and in determining priorities of learner objectives.

The behavioral strands, the number of behavioral characteristics, and summaries of the behavioral characteristics within each strand are as follows:

1. Health (severity of problem health behaviors)—11BC
2. Attendance and promptness (degree of presence in school and time-telling behaviors)—25BC
3. Feeding/eating (degree of competency in eating skills)—50BC
4. Drinking (degree of competence in drinking skills)—34BC
5. Toileting (degree of competency in toilet skills)—19BC
6. Grooming (degree of competency in washing, showering, and personal hygiene skills)—50BC
7. Dressing (degree of competency in independent dressing skills)—50BC
8. Undressing (degree of competency in independent undressing skills)—42BC

9. Nasal hygiene (degree of competency in maintaining hygienic and socially acceptable conditions of the nose)—18BC
10. Oral hygiene (degree of competency in toothbrushing behavior)—24BC
11. Self-identification (degree of competency in pointing to body parts, knowing family members, and information about self)—50BC
12. Sensory Perception (degree of competency in discriminating among stimuli on the basis of touch, taste, smell)—47BC
13. Auditory perception (degree of competency in discriminating among stimuli on the basis of auditory cues)—47BC
14. Visual Motor I (degree of competency in interpreting simple fine-visual motor skills)—50BC
15. Visual Motor II (degree of competency in integrating complex visual motor skills)—50BC
16. Gross Motor I (degree of competency in demonstrating simple mobility, eye-hand coordination and gross motor skills)—50BC
17. Gross Motor II (degree of competency in demonstrating complex gross motor skills, motor sports)—50BC
18. Prearticulation (degree of competency in controlling mouth parts)—50BC
19. Articulation (degree of competency in making vowel and consonant sounds)—48BC
20. Language comprehension (degree of competency of competency in understanding communication)—29BC
21. Language development (degree of competency in using gestures, sounds, and words to communicate)—50BC
22. Listening (degree of competency in attending and reacting to verbal communication)—39BC
23. Adaptive behaviors (degree of competency involving exploratory play and problem solving skills)—40BC
24. Impulse control (degree of competency in controlling disruptive behaviors and accepting criticism)—40BC
25. Interpersonal relations (degree of competency in cooperating and interacting with others in social situations)—50BC
26. Responsible behaviors (degree of competency in accepting rules, obeying authorities and demonstrating socially approved behaviors)—32BC
27. Personal welfare (degree of competency in demonstrating safe behaviors in hazardous conditions)—50BC
28. Self-confidence (degree of competency in expressing oneself in situations requiring opinions)—27BC
29. Honesty (degree of competency in demonstrating socially ap-

proved behavior in regard to property, accepting blame, and producing own work)—18BC

30. Social speech (degree of competency in using socially appropriate language with respect to time, places, persons and situations)—43BC
31. Social eating (degree of competency in demonstrating table manners and eating appropriately)—36BC
32. Attention span (degree of competency in attending to easy or difficult tasks for various amounts of time)—38BC
33. Task completion (degree of competency in completing assigned tasks and evaluating the product)—34BC
34. Reading (degree of competency in decoding written symbols into spoken ones through visual discrimination)—50BC
35. Math (degree of competency in using arithmetic operations to solve problems)—50BC
36. Practical math (degree of competency in using arithmetic operations to use money, to tell time, to weigh and measure objects)—50BC
37. Writing (degree of competency in producing written symbols to communicate)—50BC
38. Spelling (degree of competency in translating sounds and words into written symbols using auditory discrimination)—50BC
39. Reasoning (degree of competency in demonstrating cognitive processes by classifying and judging pictures and words)—50BC
40. Music and rhythms (degree of competency in demonstrating rhythmic, singing and instrument-playing behavior)—34BC
41. Arts and crafts (degree of competency in painting, drawing, and designing art objects)—33BC
42. Prevocational skills (degree of competency in developing work-related skills)—50BC
43. Kitchen skills (degree of competency in demonstrating skills required to shop for, prepare, cook, and serve a meal as well as cleaning kitchen)—50BC
44. Homemaking skills (degree of competency in demonstrating skills required to clean a house, to do laundry, and operate related appliances)—50BC
45. Outdoor skills (degree of competency in demonstrating skills required to maintain lawn and garden and exterior of house)—49BC
46. Sign language (degree of competency in using signs to communicate)—50BC

47. Finger spelling (degree of competency in using fingers to spell words)—50BC
48. Speech reading (degree of competency in reading lips to understand verbal communication)—50BC
49. Orientation I (degree of competency in locating self, traveling, and locating one's position in relationship to the environment)—46BC
50. Orientation II (degree of competency in traveling, and being aware of environment)—44BC
51. Mobility I (degree of competency in locomoting)—50BC
52. Mobility II (degree of competency in locomoting and traveling)—50BC
53. Wheelchair use (degree of competency in using wheelchair to move safely and efficiently in the environment)—49BC
54. Ambulation (degree of competency in sitting and walking around the environment)—50BC
55. Posture (degree of competency in maintaining erect and socially appropriate posture and correct walking form)—0BC
56. Swimming (degree of competency in performing swim-related skills, floating and kicking)—50BC
57. Articulation I (degree of competency in pronouncing all vowel and consonant sound combinations—45BC
58. Articulation II (degree of competency in pronouncing all vowel and consonant sound combinations)—42BC
59. Health (degree of competency in being free of symptoms of ear, nose, throat, mouth, eyes, skin, and hair)—0BC

The BCP provides a very fine-grained set of behavioral objectives for all degrees of handicap, ranging from mildly handicapped to profoundly handicapped.

The BCP consists of three components: the BCP Binder, the BCP Observation Booklet, and the BCP Charts. All of these components present the behavioral strands, the behavioral characteristics, and the identifying behaviors, but in different formats. The BCP Binder is a loose-leaf binder that presents a behavioral strand on the top of the page, the behavioral characteristics in boxes running horizontally across the page, and the identifying behaviors on the bottom of the page for a single student. The BCP Binder is used with students who require only assessment and instruction on a few of the BCP behavioral strands. The BCP Observation Booklet is also a loose-leaf book that presents on a page the behavioral strand and the date of observation and the identifying behaviors. The behavioral characteristics are listed horizontally down the page and columns six boxes long, run across the page, next to each behavioral characteristic. The teacher then can assess up to six students on the behavioral characteristics making up each behavioral strand on each page. The BCP Charts are large (18 in. by 49 in.) sheets that presents the student's name and identifying behaviors on the top of the sheet. The behavioral strands are listed in boxes horizontally, and next to each behavioral strand are boxes listing the behavioral characteristics associated with each behavioral strand. There are three BCP Charts: (1) BCP 1-22, which presents the behavioral strands containing the self-help, perceptual motor, and language behaviors, (2) BCP 23-45, which presents the behavioral strands containing social, academic, recreational, and vocational behaviors, and (3) 46-59, which presents the behavioral strands containing sign language, finger spelling, wheelchair use, and other behaviors particularly appropriate for the deaf, blind, and orthopedically handicapped. The charts are meant to be placed on the classroom walls to show each pupil's progress.

The teacher initially studies the identifying behaviors on the BCP charts to determine which problem behaviors the student shows. In terms of the number and severity of the identifying behaviors the teacher decides which behavioral strands are most important for each pupil's assessment which will be recorded in the BCP Observation Booklet. Depending on the behavioral strands chosen, the teacher may do the assessment alone or use other professionals such as the school nurse, the occupational and physical therapists, or the school psychologist. Observation and assessment requires that the teacher set up an observation schedule that includes: (1) who will observe; (2) days, times, and situations that observation will take place; (3) pupils who will be observed; (4) what behavioral strands will be observed; and (5) materials that will be needed in assessment. The teacher need not observe and assess behavioral characteristics in the order that they are organized in the BCP Observation Booklet. The BCP is meant to be used as an observational tool and not as a standardized formal testing instrument. Many of the behavioral characteristics on the BCP usually are performed by students over the school year, without the teacher having to actively elicit them. However, many behaviors may have to be elicited if they were not previously a part of the daily school routine. In order that a characteristic be considered part of a pupil's behavioral repertoire, the pupil must perform the behavior at least 75 percent of the time he is given the opportunity to do so in varied environments, with different observers and at different times of the day. The BCP Observation manual provides for guidelines on how many trails per day or for how many days each assessment item should be presented, that is, how many opportunities a pupil should have to make the criterion response to make sure that the pupil does, indeed, possess the behavior.

The criterion responses for the more complex behavioral characteristics are somewhat ambiguous as well, but for the most part, criterion responses are well defined.

Four types of responses are recorded in the BCP Observation Booklet: (1) blank—if the behavioral characteristic was not displayed because the pupil had no opportunity to make the response; (2) minus ("–")—if the behavioral characteristic was not displayed and the pupil had the opportunity to make the response; (3) one-half ("½")—if the behavioral characteristic was displayed less than 75 percent of the time and the pupil had the opportunity to make the response; (4) check "√")—if the behavioral characteristic was displayed at least 75 percent of the time and the pupil had the opportunity to make the response; (5) "H"—if the pupil's physical handicaps preclude demonstration of the behavioral characteristic; and (6) "E"—if the equipment or materials necessary to display the behavioral characteristics are unavailable. The teacher must be sure that all observations concerning the pupils are verified by other observers, although the BCP Observation Booklet states no formal method to accomplish this or what degree of interobserver agreement would be sufficient.

Following observation using the BCP Observation Booklets, all information should be dated and transferred to the large BCP Charts and the BCP Binder in the following way: (1) Leave behavioral characteristics box blank—if the pupil did not perform the behavioral characteristic; (2) Fill in half the box—if the behavior is performed with aid, or in certain situations only, or less than 75 percent of the time; (3) Fill in box completely—if the pupil performed the behavioral characteristic unassisted at the criterion level; (4) Put an "H" in the box—if the pupil's physical handicaps precluded demonstration of the behavioral characteristic; and (5) Put an "E" in the box—if the equipment of materials necessary to display the behavioral characteristic were unavailable.

From an analysis of each pupil's BCP Chart, which presents the identifying behaviors and patterns of behavioral characteristics, areas of strength and weakness can be determined. Priority areas for remediation involve the identifying behaviors for the Health and Posture Behavioral Strands (strands 56 and 59). Learner objectives are determined from behavioral strands which indicate the greatest pupil needs as well as an estimated date of attainment and the methods and procedures used to implement these objectives. This information is also recorded on the BCP Chart and the BCP Binder by marking a vertical line around the behavioral characteristic box and the estimated date. When the objective is attained the box is filled in and dated.

A BCP learner's objective worksheet is constructed for each pupil, which contains the strand name, its number, the objective, the estimated attainment date, the actual attainment data, and the methods and procedures to implement the objectives. This worksheet can be given to parents and shown to other professionals to inform them of the pupil's progress. The pupil is observed on a continuum basis to determine his progress and the appropriate information is recorded in the binder, the worksheets and on the chart. Thus the child's program is constantly being revised.

The Behavioral Characteristics Progression, The Santa Cruz Special Education Management System is a fine-grained guide for program planning and curriculum construction. It allows the teacher to finely observe the pupil's behavior characteristics over a wide range of behaviors for a wide spectrum of exceptional children, ranging from mildly to profoundly handicapped.

THE UZGIRIS-HUNT SCALES

The *Uzgiris-Hunt Scales* (Uzgiris & Hunt, 1975) consist of six scales which measure various schemes developed during Piaget's sensori-method period: (1) the development of visual pursuit and the permanence of objects (including the visual pursuit of slow-moving objects, searching for simply hidden objects and searching for complexity hidden objects); (2) the development of means for obtaining desired environmental events (including the development of eye-hand coordination, repeating actions that produce an interesting result and foresightful problem solving); (3) the development of imitation: vocal and gestural (including differentiation in vocal productions, development in imitation of sound patterns, and the imitation of familiar and unfamiliar gestures); (4) the development of operational causality (including efforts to prolong interesting inputs and actions to reinstate interesting spectacles); (5) the construction of object relations in space (including the development of localizing objects in space and the development of appreciating spatial relationships between objects); and (6) the development of schemes for relating to objects (including exploration and play behavior with objects, showing and naming objects).

The purpose of using the Uzgiris-Hunt Scales is to determine what schemes the child possesses so that adequate planning can be done for the child. An example of this approach was presented in the discussion of Brickers' constructive-interaction adaptation approach, which uses a developmental program lattice for the sensori-motor period to direct training activities for the child. By the use of the Uzgiris-Hunt Scales one can locate the child within the lattice's development space and plan educational objectives to help the child move on to more complex forms of behavior.

The *Uzgiris-Hunt Scales* have very explicit directions for arranging the eliciting situations appropriate for each of the scales. These directions precisely specify: (1) the position of the child and the nature of the physical space around the child helpful in presenting the situation; (2) the objects to be used in the situation; (3) the instructions for actions to be carried out by the tested; (4) the number of times the situation should be repeated to insure that reliable information is obtained; and (5) the various activities that a child might perform in the situation as well as the critical criterion response that indicates that the child has achieved a step in the scale. The scales are arranged hierarchically in terms of increasingly complex and developmentally more advanced schemes, ranging between 7 and 14 scale steps depending on the scale. The number of scale steps passed on each scale can be derived for each child. Films are available which demonstrate the administration and scoring procedures (Uzgiris & Hunt, 1966a, 1966b).

Although the *Uzgiris-Hunt Scales* were originally standardized on young infants, ranging in age from birth to 24 months, they have been recently standardized on 63 severely retarded children, ranging in age from 42 to 126 months (Kahn, 1976). Interexaminer reliability for the younger children on the scales ranged between 0.95 to 0.78, Test-retest reliability ranged from 0.96 to 0.90 and Scalogram Analysis, as assessed by Green's Index of Consistency, ranged from 1.00 to 0.81, which indicated that for these younger chidlren, the test has high reliability and high item stability.

THE BALTHAZAR SCALES OF ADAPTIVE BEHAVIOR

Balthazar has developed three scales to be used exclusively with severely and profoundly handicapped children: *Balthazar Scales of Adaptive Behavior I: The Scales of Functional Independence—BSAB-1* (Balthazar, 1971); *Balthazar Scales of Adaptive Behavior II: The Scales of Social Adaptation—BSAB II* (Balthazar, 1973); and *Training the Retarded at Home or in School: A Manual for Parents, Teachers and Home Trainers* (Balthazar, 1976).

BSAB-I (Balthazar, 1971) is designed to provide objective and standardized measures of adaptive, functionally independent behaviors of ambulatory, severely or profoundly retarded or younger moderately retarded individuals, based on direct observations of the individual in his own environment. The Scale measures rank order, and classifies a broad range of self-care behaviors. The BSAB-I is designed to measure the representative behavior of the individual and does not claim to evaluate "aptitude" or "intelligence" in terms of any external standards or norms. BSAB-I is arranged in three scales. First, eating scales are designed to measure the representative behavior of the subject as demonstrated by specific skills observed during the course of one or more meals. The skills are grouped into five major classes with up to 13 items each, including dependent feeding, finger foods, spoon usage, fork usage, and drinking. A supplementary eating checklist is provided as well, which provides information on degree of self-service, use of assistive devices, type of food ingested, position in which individual is fed, rate of eating, use of advanced utensils, and degree of supervision while fed; Second, dressing (and undressing) scales are designed to elicit optimal performance in the individual being assessed. The rater observes the individual putting on and taking off shoes, socks, pants, briefs, undershirt, regular shirt, skirt, or dress. Third, a toileting scale which obtains information by interview format regarding the individual's day-time and night-time bladder and bowel control.

BSAB-II (Balthazar, 1973) is designed to provide objective measures of social coping behaviors in ambulatory severely and profoundly mentally retarded individuals, and in younger retarded children based on direct observations of the individual in his own environment. Like the BSAB-I, the BSAB-II is designed to measure the representative or typical behavior of the individual and does not presume to measure an individual's general intelligence or aptitudes. Specifically, the BSAB-II comprises eight social scale categories: (1) Unadaptive Self-directed Behaviors, including failure to respond, stereotypic behaviors, nondirected repetitive verbalizations, inappropriate self-directed behavior and disorderly, nonsocial behavior; (2) Unadaptive Interpersonal Behaviors, including inappropriate contact with others and aggression-withdrawal (3) Adaptive Self-directed Behaviors, including generalized, exploratory recreational activiites; (4) Adaptive Interpersonal Behaviors, including fundamental social behaviors: noncommunication and social vocalization and gestures, and appropriate response to negative peer contract; (5) Verbal Communication, including nonfunctional, repetitious or inarticulate verbalization and (functional) verbalization;(6) Play Activities, including objective relations, playful contact and play activities; (7) Response to Instruction, including response to simple complex-instructions, response to firmly given instructions and cooperative contact; and (8) Checklist items of assisted or unassisted personal care skills.

The BSAB-I and BSAB-II provide more comprehensive measures of functional self-help skills and social/coping behaviors, whereas *Training the Retarded at Home or in School: A Manual for Parents, Teachers and Home Trainers* (Balthazar, 1976) utilizes many of the same subscale items and a simpler scoring system appropriate for less formal use in the home and school by parents, teachers, and training practitioners who are directly involved with a child, adult, or with small groups of children. *Training the Retarded* is a direct observational tool arranged into: (1) an eating schedule record grouped into six major classes, with up to 13 items each, including dependent feeding, finger foods, napkin usage, drinking, spoon or fork usage, and knife usage (A supplementary eating checklist in included which provides information on degree of self-service and manner of eating.); (2) a dressing schedule record very similar to the dressing and undressing scales of BSAB-I; (3) a toileting schedule record that directly assesses daytime toileting behaviors, as well as daytime and night-time bladder/bowel control; (4) a grooming schedule that assesses bathing, washing, brushing teeth and similar self-help skills; and (5) a social schedule record, including communication skills (basic communication, vocalization, and gestures and use of words), response to instructions (firmly repeated instructions and simple/complex instructions), and play (exploratory and recreational activity, object relations, playful contact, and play activities). The items on *Training the Retarded* seem to be tapping slightly more complex behaviors than the items on BSAB-I or BSAB-II. All of the items on BSAB-I, BSAB-II, and in *Training the Retarded* are brief phrases more fully elaborated in the manuals. Thus items are very explicitly defined.

The BSAB Scales can be used to: (1) provide precise objectives for the design and development of behavioral programs to be used in interdisciplinary programs in institutions, day-care settings, rehabilitative settings and, in slightly different format (Balthazar, 1976), in home and school settings; (2) provide a formalized structured method for measuring change in behaviors, both quantitative and qualitative, resulting from a given program or treatment so that one can evaluate and measure the effectiveness of that program or treatment; (3) provide a means of grouping subjects for classification purposes (Balthazar & Phillips, 1976a); (4) provide a means of evaluating manpower staffing patterns and inservice training programs; and (5) provide a research tool to measure and determine developmental trends, the meaningfulness of certain adaptive (or maladaptive) behaviors, as well as the effects of environmental changes upon the behavior of severely and profoundly mentally retarded individuals.

No special background is needed to administer the scales or the manual. Parents, paraprofessionals, high school graduates, or university undergraduates can easily learn to administer the scales. The scales and the manuals include very explicit self-instruction procedures for administration and scoring. A major prerequisite for using the scale is the desire for accuracy and a conscientious plan for aiding and helping children.

The basic paradigm employed in the use of the Balthazar Scales involves: (1) a *prebaseline study* in which the rater acquaints himself with the child and his environment, including the interpersonal factors in the environment, selects the baseline subscale items for evaluation and handles and problem areas that occur to obstruct objective evaluation; (2)

baseline study where the rater, after having selected the behaviors to be measured, initiates his observations; (3) *program intervention,* which involves implementation of the strategies to cause behavior change; and (4) *retest,* during which measures are taken of specific behaviors in terms of the stated program objectives in order to test the efficacy of an individual program.

Schedules for administration of the Balthazar Scales have been standardized so that no rating occurs in less than three days or more than seven days. Ratings are distributed so that no one rating will occur at the same time of day. Retest ratings are distributed in periods of three-month intervals to provide feedback for program adjustment.

The procedures for scoring the BSAB-I are as follows:

1. In administering the eating scales, the rater should be situated so as to be able to clearly observe the subject without interfering with the serving of the meal or interacting with the subject.
2. Observation should occur during one or more meal periods. (The instructions are not clear as to how many meals should be observed so that data can be considered to be valid.)
3. All subscale items are scored individually on a 0 to 10 point scale proportionately so that if an item occurred 10 percent of the time it receives a point score of "1"; 30 percent of the time, a point score of "3"; 0 percent of the time, a point score of "0"; and 100 percent of the time, a point score of "10."

Some of the subscale items are indented while others are not. The indented subscale items represent skills of greater complexity. Consequently, a subscale item can never receive a higher score than the item from which it is indented. For each class of eating skills on the eating scales, a subtotal score is obtained. The five classes of eating skills are added to yield a total scale score. The supplementary eating checklist is scored by placing a checkmark by those that apply, leaving blank those that do not apply, and printing N.O. (no opportunity) if opportunities to perform the behavior are not provided.

The Dressing Scales are administered in such a manner as to elicit *optimal* performance of the individual, i.e., the highest level of dressing skills of which the individual is capable. Each item is scored on a 7-point scale (0 to 6) as follows: (1) Six—independent, perfect performance; (2) Five—independent, imperfect performance; (3) Four—supervised; (4) Three—assisted, partially; (5) Two—assisted, primarily; (6) One—cooperative, and (7) Zero—no particiaption. The individual assessed is encouraged by verbal and/or material reinforcement by the rater, and is given the opportunity to peform all stages of dressing and undressing on the standard clothing items to the best of his or her ability. A total score is derived from adding the individual's point score on each of the clothing items.

The procedure for scoring the BSAB-II are as follows: The subjects are observed when engaged in typical activities in familiar settings by raters who try to maintain "low visibility" by making themselves as inconspicuous as possible. In order to obtain a representative record of an individual's behavior, it is necessary to observe and rate the individual during different periods in the day and on different days of the week. To achieve measures of typical behavior, no more than one-third of them should be obtained on any one day. Observations should extend over a period of at least three days in a given rating week. The measurement system used is frequency counts per unit of time. The score for each item is based on six 10-minute observation sessions per individual. Scoring is done by occurrence (a simple frequency count (tally) of each subscale behavior each time it occurs) or by scoring by 1-minute intervals (a tally made in each minute containing at least one instance of the behavior). Multiple behaviors occurring together are each tallied beside the appropriate item on the tally sheet. These tallies are then transcribed to the scoring summary sheet, and the cumulative frequency, mean or median becomes the score for the item.

The procedures for scoring *Training the Retarded* are as follows: In administering the eating schedule record, at least three meals should be observed. The parent or teacher may use a point system to rate the proportion of the time a behavioral item occurs. An item receives a "10" if it occurs all the time, an "8" if it occurs more than one-half of the time, a "5" if it occurs one-half the time, a "2" if it occurs less than one-half the time, and a "0" if it never occurs. A pass-fail system may be used also. The parent or teacher notes if the child succeeds (passes) or does not succeed (fails) a given behavior.

The dressing schedule is administered as in BSAB-I except that each item is scored on a 5-point scale (0 to 10) as follows: (1) "10"—independent, perfect performance; (2) "8"—supervised; (3) "5"—assisted, partially; (4) "2"—assisted, primarily; and (5) "0"—no participation or partially cooperative. The pass-fail system may also be used.

In administering the toilet schedule record, the child should be observed for at least one month and no less than five times per week. Each behavioral item is scored "10," "8," "5," "2," or "0" depending on the proportion of time the item occurs, as in assessing the items on the eating schedule record or the pass-fail system may be used. The scoring of the items on the grooming schedule record is similar.

The items on the social schedules record are assessed during a 10-minute session. Each behavioral item is scored "10"; "8"; "5"; "2"; or

"0" depending on the proportion of time the items occur as stated previously, or the pass-fail system is used.

A profile of each of the scales in BSAB-I can be plotted, as raw scores or percentile scores. Performance tables showing percentile ranks for the various scores are provided for the standardization population consisting of institutionalized retarded individuals ranging in age from 5 to 57 years (median = 17.3 years, semi-interquartile range = 8.4) classified as severely to profoundly retarded in terms of AAMD classification. These tables are based on 122 subjects for the Eating Scales, 200 subjects for the Dressing Scales and 129 subjects for the Toileting Scales. High and low scores can be studied and deficient skills can be identified for intensive programmatic intervention. The inter-rater reliability for the scales are as follows: (1) eating scales = 0.97, (2) dressing scales = 0.97, (3) toileting scales = 0.94. Concurrent validity was established by relating total BSAB-I scores with total *Vineland Social Maturity Scale* and *r* ranged between 0.59 to 0.67.

A profile of each of the scores in BSAB-II can be plotted in terms of mean or median (cumulative frequency over the six 10-minute sessions). The Appendix (Balthazar, 1973) presents mean cumulative frequencies for the scale items on BSAB-II for a population consisting of 288 ambulatory, institutionalized individuals ranging in age from 5 to 57 years (median age = 17.3 years, semi-interquartile range = 8.4 years) all classified as severely to profoundly retarded in terms of AAMD classification. Interobserver agreement is considered to be relatively high. The standardization samples can only be used cautiously, since more extensive standardization needs to be done on both BSAB-I and BSAB-II. BSAB-II profiles can provide information on social coping skills. Programs can be developed to improve skills or to increase the frequency of desirable behaviors and reduce the frequency of undesirable behaviors. The repeated administration of the BSAB Scales can determine the progress that has been made, and provide a basis for the selection of new targets and a criterion for moving individuals into new training environments.

Training the Retarded (Balthazar, 1976) outlines a strategy by which the parent/teacher: (1) observes the child, (2) specifies a target behavior from the particular point in the Schedules where the child fails, (3) suggests programs of intervention, and (4) allows the parent/teacher to retest and see if training progress has been sufficiently established. When the target behavior has been accomplished three sessions without error, a new target behavior is selected.

THE AAMD ADAPTIVE BEHAVIOR SCALE

The AAMD Adaptive Behavior Sale (Nihira, Foster, Shellhaas, & Leland, 1975) is a behavior rating scale for mentally retarded, emotionally disturbed, and other developmentally disabled individuals used to assess the effectiveness of the individual in coping with the natural and social demands of his or her environment. Adaptive behavior is operationally defined by 110 behavioral items that reflect environmental demands placed upon developmentally disabled individuals in personal and social functioning operating at AAMD's moderate and severe levels of retardation.

The Scale is divided into two parts. Part I is designed to assess 10 behavior domains organized along developmental lines and considered important in the development of independence in daily living. The items on this scale are brief, one-to-four word title phrases that are often followed by four to seven phrases describing independent behavioral functioning. The behavioral domains in Part I consist of the following: (1) independent functioning, (2) physical development, (3) economic activity, (4) language and development, (5) numbers and time, (6) domestic activity, (7) vocational activity, (8) self-direction, (9) responsibility, and (10) socialization. Many of the behavioral domains are divided into subdomains. The independent functioning domain is divided into eight subdomains of eating, toileting, cleanliness, appearance, care of clothing, dressing and undressing, travel, and general independent functioning. The physical development domain is divided into two subdomains of sensory development and motor development. The economic activity domain is divided into four subdomains of money handling and budgeting and shopping skills. The domain of language development is divided into three subdomains of expression, comprehension, and social language development. The domain of domestic activity is divided into three subdomains, cleaning, kitchen duties, and other domestic activities. The domain of self-direction is divided into three subdomains, initiative, perseverance, and leisure time.

Part II is designed to assess the frequency of maladaptive behaviors related to personality and behavior disorders in the individual and is divided into 14 behavior domains. The items on these domains are one-to-four word title phrases, followed by phrases describing 4 to 12 behaviors that are examples of members of the class of behavior identified by the following: (1) violent and destructive behavior, (2) antisocial behavior, (3) rebellious behavior, (4) untrustworthy behavior, (5) withdrawal, (6) stereotyped behavior and odd mannerisms, (7) inappropriate interpersonal manners, (8) unacceptable vocal habits, (9) unacceptable or eccentric habits, (10 self-abusive behavior, (11) hyperactive tendencies, (12) sexually aberrant behavior, (13) psychological disturbances, and (14) use of medications.

Part I and Part II are scored as norm-referenced tests, based upon a standardization sample of 4,000 mentally retarded institutionalized residents of 68 facilities in the United States, ranging in age from 3 to 69 years. The scores in each of the 10 domains of Part I and the 14 domains of

Part II were converted to percentile ranks for II different age groups (3, 4, 5, 6 to 7, 8 to 9, 10 to 12, 13 to 15, 16 to 18, 19 to 29, 30 to 49, and 50 to 69 years). The use of percentile ranks allows one to determine an individual's relative standing in relation to the standardization sample on each of the 24 domains.

Nihira et al. (1975) suggests that the Adaptive Behavior Scale be used: (1) to identify areas of deficiency that individuals or groups have in order to facilitate proper and useful assignment of curricula and placement in training programs; (2) to provide an objective basis for the comparison of an individual's ratings over a period of time in order to evaluate the suitability of his/her current curricular training program; (3) to compare ratings of the same individual under different situations, e.g., home, school, ward, in order to study how different environmental factors influence his or her behavior; (4) to compare ratings by different raters in order to gain additional understanding of the relationship between certain raters and persons being rated, e.g., mother and child, father and child; (5) to provide a common medium of information exchange within as well as between organizations through a standardized reporting system; (6) to stimulate the development of new training programs and research; and (7) to provide descriptions of groups of individuals which will facilitate making useful and realistic administrative decisions concerning programming and staff needs.

AAMD Adaptive Behavior Scale data are based on behaviors that can usually be observed. There is a certain degree of subjectivity in making some of the ratings, because the rater is forced to make decisons about items that the individual may have no opportunity to perform. Nihira et al. (1975) suggest three different types of administrative procedure for obtaining information about an individual upon which to base the score for each item, the first person assessment procedure, the third party assessment procedure, and the interview method. The first person assessment procedure is used when the rater is thoroughly familiar with both the individual being assessed and the scale items. The third party assessment procedure is used when multiple administrations are required, when varied sources of information are used or when the rater thoroughly knows the individual being assessed but is unfamiliar with the use of the scales. In this case, a third party who is familiar with the scales asks the raters about each of the items on the scale. The interview method is used to obtain less detailed information than the third party assessment procedure. The interview method is a quick means of obtaining information from raters (parents, teachers, aides) who are highly familiar with the person being evaluated by an interviewer, who asks general questions and is highly knowledgeable about the scales.

There are three types of items in the Scale that require different scoring procedures. Each procedure requires that the rater judge which of the descriptions best conforms to the description provided by the informant (or best conforms to the behavior of the individual being rated if the rater and informant are the same person). The rater enters the total score for each item in the circle to the right of each item, the subdomain totals in triangles, and domain totals in rectangles. The first type of item requires the rater to select and circle the number of the description that represents the level of independent performance of the individual and enter this number as a score. The second type of item requires the rater to make multiple responses. The rater places a check beside each description judged to conform to the behavior of the individual being evaluated. The descriptions checked are summed and entered as the item score or, in the case of descriptions of negative behaviors, subtracted from the total number of descriptions and entered as the item score. The third type of item appears only in Part II and requires that the rater judge not only whether a description conforms to the behavior of the individual, but whether it occurs frequently or occasionally. Each description scored as "frequently" receives two points and each description scored as "occasionally" receives one point. The total number of points is entered as the score for the item. The item scores within each domain are added and a profile of all the domains can be plotted. This profile shows not only the relative standing on each domain in relation to the institutionalized standardization sample, but also the relative position of the domains to each other. It is difficult to interpret the scores obtained in relation to the institutionalized standard sample group. It would have been more appropriate, especially in these days of deinstitutionalization and community living opportunities, if a standardization sample consisting of noninstitutionalized handicapped persons had been used. (This has been done for higher functioning mildly and moderately retarded public school children by Lambert, Windmiller, Cole, & Finueroa, 1975.)

It is suggested by Nihira et al. (1975) that profiles on Part I be considered separately from Part II. It is easier to understand and predict general lines of developmental continuity and growth expectations as measured by Part I; whereas, the measures of conduct and personality disturbances as assessed by Part II do not easily fit into any developmental sequence. However, if the main areas of deficiency seem to be in Part II (maladaptive behaviors), consideration should be given to reducing the individual's maladaptive behaviors to see if the Part I profiles will improve.

Individuals with domain scores at or near the top of the percentile ranks probably perform well enough in these domains that the teacher can concentrate educational intervention on the remaining domains, preferably in the relatively strong domains ("hills") rather than around the relatively weak domains ("valleys"). It is believed that an individual who is able to do some things in one domain is more likely to be trained to do more things in that domain than in a domain where the individual shows lesser proficiency. An exception to this procedure would be if the lower scores were a result of environmental or institutional restriction. Experience has taught the authors that if an individual achieves further success in "hill" domains, the individual may become more motivated generally and achieve gains in the domains which were initially "valleys." When there are many low scores in the profile, it is suggested that the higher ones be the basis of educational intervention. The authors suggest that the domains themselves follow a developmental sequence, with behaviors in the domain of physical development being acquired first and those of economic activity later (Nihira, 1976). If both these domains are low, programs for physical development should take priority.

Considerations for interpreting Part II profiles are based primarily on the impact the maladaptive behaviors is having on the individual, his environment, the age of the individual in relation to the behavior, as well as the attitudes of the community and staff. High priority areas should be those that are particualrly repulsive to members of the community, where the retarded person must eventually reside.

Interobserver reliabilities are relatively high for domains on Part I (r ranged from 0.93 to 0.71, r = .86). Inter-observer reliabilities are much lower for domains on Part II because of marked skewedness in score distribution. Scores were dichotomized and the ϕ Coefficient was used to estimate the reliability (ϕ ranged from 0.77 to 0.37, mean $\phi = .57$). The use of the AAMD ABS Part I and Part II Scores should be done with caution. Nihira, et al. (1975) and McDevitt & McDevitt (1977) particularly caution users on the interpretation of Part II Scores.

Validity studies on the Scales are increasing and show them to be of great potential usefulness (Foster & Nihira, 1969; Guarnaccia, 1976; Nihira, 1969a, 1969b, 1976).

Programming should be developed from the profile information on both parts of the scale as follows: (1) determination of individual needs as they relate to community and agency needs, (2) establishment of priority rankings of sets of behaviors which require work, (3) establishment of individualized educational programs based on both (1) and (2), and (4) reassessing the individual to see if the program should be changed and progress has been made.

A FINAL NOTE

The guidelines and review sources provided in Chapter 3 can be used to complement the references provided in this section of the chapter. Taken together, these resources should enable the reader to critically evaluate any measurement or assessment instrument. In conducting that activity for the instruments cited in this chapter it is wise to bear in mind Sailor & Haring's (1977) position—purpose distinction for tests for the severely and profoundly handicapped. In this way measurement instruments can be better selected not only for their technical adequacy but also for the "type" and "scope" of the hypothesis that they may conceivably shed some light on.

SUMMARY

The teacher cannot undertake the education of the severely and profoundly handicapped mechanically and unthinkingly without any consideration for the future roles and expectations about the ultimate level of functioning of their students and without an adequate educational theory. One should only use assessment systems based on the normative developmental model for only these systems are totally embedded within an adequate educational theory that can provide the contents of a valid curriculum. The constructive-interactive-adaptive approach of the Brickers and the developmental lattices that were developed (involving the test-teach system) were presented as examples of this educational point of view. Sailor & Haring's notions of the three types of functional developmental assessment systems are important practical considerations for classroom teachers of the severely and profoundly handicapped.

The optimal sequence of assessment and instruction within each skill domain remains an elusive empirical question that will lead researchers on a merry chase for years to come. It remains true that the responsibility at this stage of our history for the development of educational programs resides primarily on the expertise, clinical sensitivity, and art of the teacher. These individuals will have to integrate the bits and pieces of methodology and knowledge that are known in order to fulfill the challenge of Itard.

REFERENCES

Baldwin, V. I. Curriculum concerns. In M. A. Thomas (Ed.), Hey don't forget about me. Reston, Va.: Council for Exceptional Children, 1976.

Balthazar, E. E. *Balthazar Scales of Adaptive Behavior, Section I: The scales of functional independence* (BSAB-I). Champaign, Ill.: Research Press, 1971.

Balthazar, E. E. *Balthazar Scales of Adaptive Behavior II: Scales of social adaptation* (BSAG-II). Palo Alto, Ca.: Consulting Psychologist Pres, 1973.

Balthazar, E. E. *Training the retarded at home or in school.* Palo Alto, Ca.: Consulting Psychologist Press, 1976.

Balthazar, E. E. & English, G. E. A system for the social classification of the more severely mentally retarded. *American Journal of Mental Deficiency,* 1969, *74,* 361–368.

Balthazar, E. E. & Phillips, J. L. *Categorical versus categorical-dimensional judgements of behavior: The purpose of a label.* Unpublished manuscript. Madison: Central Colony and Training School Research Department, 1976a.

Balthazar, D. E. & Phillips, J. L. Social adjustment in more severely retarded, institutionalized individuals: The sum of adjusted behavior. *American Journal of Mental Deficiency,* 1976b, *80,* 454–459.

Bayley, N. *Infant Scales of Psychomotor and Mental Development.* New York: Psychological Corporation, 1969.

Bendersky, M. (Ed.) *The Uniform Performance Assessment System, manual and assessment materials, 0–6 year Scale, 1st revision.* (Experimental Education Unit, Child Development and Mental Retardation Center), Seattle: University of Washington, 1976.

Bendersky, M., Edgar, E., & White, O. *Uniform performance assessment system* (UPAS). (Experimental Education Unit, Child Development and Mental Retardation Center, Working Paper 65.) Seattle: University of Washington, 1976.

Bepko, R. A., Alter, A., & Goldstein, M. The readiness level of the Social Learning Curriculum. Personal communication, 1976.

Bigge, J. L. & O'Donnell, P. A. *Teaching individuals with physical and multiple disabilities.* Columbis, Oh.: Charles E. Merrill, 1976.

Bijou, S. W. A functional analysis of retarded development. In N. R. Ellis (Ed.), *International review of research in mental retardation* (Vol. 1). New York: Academic Press, 1966.

Bijou, S. W. & Wilcox-Cole, B. The feasibility of providing effective educational programs for the severely and profoundly retarded. In *Educating the 24-hour retarded child.* Arlington, Tx: National Association for Retarded Citizens, 1975, pp. 9–25.

Blackard, K. *A systematic process of training parents in management and instruction of their severely/profoundly handicapped children.* Seattle: University of Washington, 1976.

Blessing, K. R. Use of teacher aides in special education: A review and possible implications. *Exceptional Children,* 1967, *34,* 107–113.

Brady, J. F. & Smilovitz, R. (Eds.), *APT: A training program for citizens with severely or profoundly retarded behavior.* Spring City, Pa.: Pennhurst State School, 1974.

Bricker, D. D. & Bricker, W. A. *Toddler research and intervention project report: Year I.* Behavioral Science Monograph No. 20, Institute on Mental Retardation and Intellectual Development. Nashville: George Peabody College, 1971.

Bricker, D. D. & Bricker, W. A. *Toddler research and intervention project report: Year II.* IMRID Behavioral Science monograph No. 21, 1972.

Bricker, D. D. & Bricker, W. A. *Toddler research and intervention project report: Year III.* IMRID Behavioral Science Monograph No. 22, 1973.

Bricker, D. D. & Iacino, R. Early intervention with severely/profoundly handicapped children. In E. Sontag (Ed.), *Educational programming for the severely and profoundly handicapped.* Boston: Council for Exceptional Children, 1977.

Bricker, D., Bricker, B., Iacino, R., & Dennison, L. Intervention strategies for the severely and profoundly handicapped child. In N. G. Haring & L. J. Brown (Eds.), *Teaching the severely handicapped.* New York: Grune & Stratton, 1976.

Bricker, D. D., Davis, J., Wahlin, L. & Evans, J. *A motor training program for the developmentally young.* Mailman Center for Child Development Monograph Series, No. 2, 1976.

Bricker, D. D., Dennison, L., & Bricker, W. A. *A language intervention program for developmentally young children.* Mailman Center for Child Development Monograph Series, No. 1, 1976.

Bricker, W. A. Identifying and modifying behavioral deficits. *American Journal of Mental Deficiency*, 1970, *75*, 16–21.

Bricker, W. A. Service of research. In M. A. Thomas (Ed.), *Hey don't forget about me.* Reston, Va.: Council for Exceptional Children, 1976.

Bricker, W. A. & Bricker, D. D. An early language training strategy. In R. L. Schiefelbusch & L. L. Lloyd (Eds.), *Language perspectives: Acquisition, retardation, and intervention.* Baltimore: University Park Press, 1974.

Bricker, W. A. & Bricker, D. D. The infant, toddler and preschool research and intervention project. In T. D. Tjossem (Ed.), *Intervention strategies for high risk infants and young children.* Baltimore: University Park Press, 1976.

Bronfenbrenner, U. The experimental ecology of education. *Educational Researcher*, 1976, *5*, 5–15.

Bronfenbrenner, U. Toward an experimental ecology of human development. *American Psychologist*, 1977, *32*, 513–531.

Brooks, P. E., Baumeister, A. A plea for consideration of ecological validity in the experimental psychology of mental retardation: A guest editorial. *American Journal of Mental Deficiency*, 1977, *81*, 407–416.

Brown, L., Nietupski, J. & Hamre-Nietupski, S. Criterion of ultimate functioning. In M. A. Thomas (Ed.), *Hey don't forget about me.* Reston, Va.: Council for Experimental Children, 1976.

Brown, L. & York, R. Developing programs for severely handicapped students: Teacher training and classroom instruction. *Focus on Exceptional Children*, 1974, *6*(2), 1–11.

Burke, P. J. & Cohen, M. The quest for competence in serving the severely/profoundly handicapped: A critical analysis of personnel preparation programs. In E. Sontag (Ed.), *Educational programming for the severely and profoundly handicapped.* Reston, Va.: Council for Exceptional Children, 1977.

Caine, L. F., Levine, S., & Elzey, F. F. *Caine-Levine Social Competency Scale.* Palo Alto, Ca.: Consulting Psychologist Press, 1963.

Cattell, P. *The measurement of intelligence of infants and young children.* New York: The Psychological Corporation, 1940.

Cohen, M. A., Gross, P. J., & Haring, N. G. Developmental pinpoints. In N. G. Haring & L. J. Brown (Eds.), *Teaching the severely handicapped.* New York: Grune & Stratton, 1976.

Collins, M. T. & Rudolph, J. M. *A manual for the assessment of a deaf-blind multiply-handicapped child.* Lansing, Michigan: Midwest Regional Center for Services to Deaf-Blind Children, 1975.

DeSpain, C., Williams, W., & York, R. Evaluation of the severely retarded and multiply handicapped. In L. Brown, T. Crowren, W. Williams, & R. York (Eds.), *Madison's alternative for zero exclusion: A book of readings.* Madison: Madison Public Schools, 1975.

Doll, E. A. *Vineland Social Maturity Scale.* Minneapolis: American Guidance Service, 1947.

Doll, E. A. *Vineland Social Maturity Scale: Condensed Manual of Instructions.* Circle Pines, Minn.: American Guidance Service, 1965.

Filler, J. W., Robinson, L. L., Smith, R. A., Vincent-Smith, L. J., Bricker, D. D., & Bricker, W. A. Mental retardation. In N. Hobbs (Ed.). *Issues in the classification of children* (Vol. 1). San Francisco: Jossey-Bass, 1975.

Flavell, J. H. *The developmental psychology of Jean Piaget.* Princeton: Van Nostrand, 1963.

Foster, R. W. *Camelot behavioral checklist.* Parsons, Kn.: Camelot Behavioral Systems. 1974.

Foster, R. W., & Nihira, K. Adaptive behavior as a measure of psychiatric impairment. *American Journal of Mental Deficiency,* 1969, *74,* 401–404.

Frankenburg, W. & Dodds, J. *The Denver Developmental Screening Test*—Revised. Denver: Ladola, 1975.

Fredericks, H. D., Riggs, C., Furey, T., Grove, D., Moore, W., McDonnell, J., Jordon E., Hanson, W., Baldwin, V., & Wadlow, M. *The teaching research curriculum for moderately and severely handicapped.* Springfield, Ill.: Charles C Thomas, 1976.

Gesell, A. *Gesell Developmental Schedules, Form IJ.* New York: The Psychological Corporation, 1949.

Giampiccalo, J. & Boroskin, A. *Fairview Developmental Scale.* Costa Mesa, Ca.: Fairview Hospital, 1974.

Grossman, H. (Ed.), *Manual on terminology and classification in mental retardation, 1973 revision.* Washington, D.C.: American Association on Mental Deficiency, 1973.

Guarnaccia, V. J. Factor structure and correlates of adaptive behavior in noninstitutionalized retarded adults. *American Journal of Mental Deficiency,* 1976, *80,* 543–547.

Gunzburg, H. C. *Progress assessment chart of social and personal development.* Birmington, England: SEFA, Ltd., 1974.

Haring, N. G. & Bricker, D. Overview of comprehensive services for the severely/profoundly handicapped. In N. G. Haring & L. J. Brown (Eds.), *Teaching the severely handicapped.* New York: Grune & Stratton, 1976.

Haring, N. G. & Gentry, N. D. Direct and individualized instructional procedures. In N. G. Haring and R. L. Schiefelbusch (Eds.), *Teaching special children.* New York: McGraw-Hill, 1976.

Hobbs, N. *The futures of children: Categories, labels and their consequences.* San Francisco: Jossey-Bass, 1975.

Hogg, J. Normative development and educational programme planning for severely educationally subnormal children. In C. C. Kiernan & F. P. Woodford (Eds.). *Behavioral modification with the severely retarded.* Amsterdam: Associated Scientific Publishers, 1975.

Horner, R. D. Teacher proficiency checklist. Unpublished manuscript. Personnel Preparation Program, Department of Special Education, University of Kansas,1975.

Horner, R. D. A competency-based approach to preparing teachers of the severely and profoundly handicapped: Prospective II. In E. Sontag (Ed.), *Educational programming for the severely and profoundly handicapped.* Reston, Va.: Council for Exceptional Children, 1977.

Horner, R. D., Holvoet, J., & Rinne T. Competency specifications for teachers of the severely and profoundly handicapped. Unpublished manuscript. Personnel Preparation Program, Department of Special Education, University of Kansas, 1976.

Hunt, J. McV. *Intelligence and experience.* New York: Ronald Press, 1961.

Hutton, W. D. & Talkington, L. W. *The development record.* Corvallis, Ore.: Continuing Education Publications, 1974.

Kahn, J. V. Utility of the Uzgiris-Hunt Scales of sensorimotor development in the severely and profoundly retarded children. *American Journal of Mental Deficiency,* 1976, *80,* 663–665.

Lambert, N., Windmiller, M., Cole, L., & Figueroa, R. *AAMD Adaptive Behavior Scale-Public School Version: Manual.* Washington, D.C.: American Association on Mental Deficiency, 1975.

Leland, H. Mental retardation and adaptive behavior. *Journal of Special Education,* 1972, *6,* 71–80.

Leland, H., Shelhaas, M., Nihira, K., & Foster, R. Adaptive behavior: A new dimension in the classification of the mentally retarded. *Mental Retardation Abstracts,* 1967, *4,* 359–387.

Lent, J. R. & McLean, B. M. The trainable retarded: The technology of teaching. In N. G. Haring & R. L. Schiefelbusch (Eds.), *Teaching special children.* New York: McGraw-Hill, 1976.

Luckey, R. E. & Addison, M. R. The profoundly retarded: A new challenge for public education. *Education and Training of the Mentally Retarded, 1974, 9,* 122–130.

Mager, R. F. *Preparing instructional objectives.* Belmont, Ca.: Fearon, 1962.

Mager, R. F. & Pipe, P. *Analyzing performance problems or: You really oughta wanna.* Belmont, Ca.: Fearon, 1970.

McDevitt, S. C. & McDevitt, S. C. Adaptive behavior scale, part II: A cautionary note and suggestions for revisions. *American Journal of Mental Deficiency,* 1977, *82,* 210–212.

McGurk, H. (Ed.), *Ecological factors in human development.* New York: Elservier North-Holland, 1977.

Miller, T. L. & Switzsky, H. N. The least restrictive alternative: Implications for service providers. *The Journal of Special Education,* 1978, *12,* 123–131.

Mira, M. Tracking the motor behavior development. *Mental Retardation,* 1977, *15,* 32–37.

Nihira, K. Factorial dimensions of adaptive behavior in adult retardates. *American Journal of Mental Deficiency,* 1969a, *73,* 866–878.

Nihira, K. Functional dimensions of adaptive behavior in mentally retarded children and adolescents. *American Journal of Mental Deficiency,* 1969b, *74,* 130–141.

Nihira, K. Dimensions of adaptive behavior in institutionalized mentally retarded children and adults: Developmental perspective. *American Journal of Mental Deficiency,* 1976, *81,* 215–226.

Nihira, K., Foster, R., Shellhaas, M., & Leland, H. *Adaptive Behavior Scale: Manual.* Washington, D.C.: American Association on Mental Deficiency, 1975.

Noar, E. M. & Balthazar, E. E. Provision of a language index for severely and profoundly retarded individuals. *American Journal of Mental Deficiency,* 1975, *79,* 717–725.

Phillips, J. L. & Balthazar, E. E. Social compatability in more severely retarded institutionalized individuals: An index of socially ambivalent behavior. *Mental Retardation,* 1976, *14,* 46–47.

Piaget, J. *The origins of intelligence in children.* New York: Norton, 1963.

Reiss, P. The development of a social learning curriculum for moderately retarded children. Unpublished manuscript. Curriculum Research and Development Center, Yeshiva University, 1974.

Robinson, C. C. Analysis of stage four and five object permanence concepts as a discriminated operant. Unpublished doctorial dissertation. George Peabody College, Nashville, 1972.

Robinson, C. C. Application of Piagetian sensorimotor concepts to assessment and curriculum for severely handicapped children. *AAESPH Review,* 1976, *8,* 5–10.

Roos, P. Current issues in the education of mentally retarded persons. In W. J. Cegelka (Ed.), *Proceedings: Conference on the Education of Mentally Retarded Persons.* Arlington, Tx.: National Association for Retarded Citizens, 1971.

Sailor, W. The TARC System: Instructional objective for the severely handicapped. *AAESPH Review,* 1975, *1,* 1–13.

Sailor, W., Guess, D., & Lavis, L. W. Educational technology for the severely handicapped: A comprehensive bibliography, unpublished syllabus. Kansas Neurological Institute: Personal Preparation Program for the Education of the Severely Handicapped. 1975a.

Sailor, W., Guess, D., & Lavis, L. W. Preparing teachers for the education of the severely handicapped. *Education and Training of the Mentally Retarded,* 1975, *10,* 201–203.

Sailor, W. & Haring, N. G. Some current directions in education of the severely/multiply impaired. *AAESPH Review,* 1977, *2,* 3–23.

Sailor, W & Horner, D. R. Educational and assessment strategies for the severely handicapped. In N. G. Haring & L. J. Brown (Eds.), *Teaching the severely handicapped* (Vol. 1). New York: Grune & Stratton, 1976.

Sailor, W. W. & Mix, B. J. *The TARC assessment system.* Lawrence: H & H Enterprises, 1975.

Santa Cruz County Superintendent of Schools. Behavior characteristics progression. The Santa Cruz special education management system. Santa Cruz, Ca., 1973.

Shearer, D., Billingsley, J., & Frohman, A. *A portage guide to early education: Instructions and checklist.* Portage, Wis.: Cooperative Educational Service Agency, N. 12, 1970.

Somerton, E. & Meyers, D. G. Educational programming for the severely/profoundly mentally retarded. In N. G. Haring & L. J. Brown (Eds.), *Teaching the severely handicapped.* New York: Grune & Stratton, 1976.

Somerton, M. E. & Turner, K. D. *Pennsylvania training model, individual assessment guide.* Harrisburg, Pa.: Pennsylvania Department of Education, 1975.

Sontag, E. W. Federal leadership. In M. A. Thomas (Ed.), *Hey don't forget about me.* Reston, Va.: Council for Exceptional Children, 1976a.

Sontag, E. W. Zero exclusion: Rehtoric no longer. *AAESPH Review,* 1976b, *1*(3), 105–114.

Smith, D. D., Smith, J. D. & Edgar, E. B. Protypic model for the development of instructional materials. In N. G. Haring & L. J. Brown (Eds.), *Teaching the severely handicapped.* New York: Grune & Stratoon, 1976.

Sparrow, S. S. & Cicchetti, D. V. Behavior rating inventory for moderately, severely, and profoundly retarded persons. *American Journal of Mental Deficiency,* 1978, *82,* 365–374.

Stainbach, S., Stainbach, W., & Mamer, S. Training teachers for the severely and profoundly handicapped: A new frontier. *Exceptional Children,* 1976, *42,* 203–210.

Stamm, J. M. A general model for the design of a competency-based special education professional preparation program. *Education and Training of the Mentally Retarded,* 1975, *10,* 196–200.

Stephens, B. A Piagetian approach to curriculum development for the severely, profoundly and multiply handicapped. In E. Sontag, (Ed.), *Educational programming for the severely and profoundly handicapped.* Reston, Va.: Council for Exceptional Children, 1977.

Stillman, R. *the Callier-Azusa Scale.* Dallas: Callier Center for Communication Disorders, 1977.

Switzky, H. N. & Miller, T. L. Service delivery systems for the mentally retarded and the least restrictive environment. *Mental Retardation,* 1978, *16*, 52–54.

Switzky, H. N. & Sedlak, R. Considerations toward an ecological assessment in the "home" for severely/profoundly handicapped and educational programmings. Unpublished manuscript. Northern Illinois University, 1977a.

Switzky, H. N. & Sedlak, R. The instructional process for severely/profoundly retarded children and youth. Unpublished manuscript. Northern Illinois University, 1977b.

Tucker, D. J. & Horner, R. D. Competency-based training of paraprofessional teaching associates for education of the severely and profoundly handicapped. In E. Sontag, (Ed.), *Educational programming for the severely and profoundly handicapped.* Reston, Va.: Council for Exceptional Children, 1977.

Tucker, D. J. *Skill Acquisition Program Bibliography.* Parsons, Kan.: Camelot Behavioral Systems, 1974.

Uzgiris, I. C. & Hunt, J. McV. *Assessment in infancy: Ordinal scales of psychological development.* Urbana: University of Illinois Press, 1975.

Uzgiris, I. C., & Hunt, J. McV. (Producers). *Object permanence*. Champaign: University of Illinois, Motion Picture Service, 1966a (Film).

Uzgiris, I. C., & Hunt, J. McV. (Producers). *Object relations in space*. Champaign: University of Illinois, Motion Picture Services, 1966b (Film).

Wabash Center for the Mentally Retarded. *Wabash Center for the Mentally Retarded guide to early developmental training*. Boston: Allyn & Bacon, 1977.

Wilcox, B. A competency-based approach to preparing teachers of the severely and profoundly handicapped: Perspective I. In E. Sontag (Ed.), *Educational programming for the severely and profoundly handicapped*. Reston, Va.: Council for Exceptional Children, 1977.

Williams. W. Procedures of task analysis as related to developing instructional programs for the severely handicapped. In L. Brown, T. Cranner, W. Williams & R. York (Eds.), *Madison's alternative for zero exclusion: A book of readings*. Madison: Madison Public Schools, 1975.

Williams, W., Brown, L., & Certo, N. Basic components of instructional programs. *Theory in practice,* 1975, *14,* 123–136.

Williams, W. & Gotts, E. A. Selected considerations on developing curriculum for severely handicapped students. In E. Sontag (Ed.), *Educational programming for the severely and profoundly handicapped*. Reston, Va.: Council for Exceptional Children, 1977.

Wolfensberger, W. *The Principle of normalization in human services*. Toronto: Leonard Crainford, 1972.

York, R., & Williams, W. Curricula and ongoing assessment for individualized programming in the classroom. In R. York, P. Thorpe, & R. Minisi (Eds.), *Education of the severely and profoundly handicapped people*. Hightstown, N.J.: Northeast Regional Resource Center, 1977.

SUGGESTED READINGS

Bathazar, E. E. & English, G. E. A system for the social classification of the more severely mentally retarded. *American Journal of Mental Proficiency,* 1969, *74,* 361–368.

Banus, B. S. *The developmental therapist*. Thorofare, N.J.: Charles B. Slack, 1971.

Bobath, K. & Bobath, R. An assessment of the motor handicaps of children with cerebral palsey and of their responses to treatment. *American Journal of Occupational Therapy,* 1958, *21,* 10–29.

Bricker, D., Bricker, B., Iacino, R., & Dennison, L. Intervention strategies for the severely and profoundly handicapped child. In N. G. Haring and L. J. Brown (Eds.), *Teaching the severely handicapped*. New York: Grune & Stratton, 1976.

Bronfenbrenner, G. Toward an experimental ecology of human development. *American Psychologist,* 1977, *32,* 513–531.

Brown, L., Nietupski, J. & Hamre-Nietupski, S. Criterion of ultimate functioning. In M. A. Thomas (Ed.), *Hey, Don't forget about me*. Reston, Va.: Council for Exceptional Children, 1976.

Cohen, M. A., Gross, P. J., & Haring, N. G. Developmental pinpoints. In N. G. Haring and L. J. Brown (Eds.), *Training the severely handicapped*. New York: Grune & Stratton, 1976.

Filler, J. W., Robinson, L. L., Smith, R. A., Vincent-Smith, L. J., Bricker, D. D., & Bricker, W. A. Mental retardation. In N. Hobbs (Ed.), *Issues in the classification of children* (Vol. 1). San Francisco: Joseey-Bass, 1975.

Haring, N. G. Measurement and evaluation procedures for programming with the severely and profoundly handicapped. In E. Sontag (Ed.), *Educational programming for the severely and professionally handicapped.* Reston, Va.: Council for Exceptional Children, 1977.

Luckey, R. E. & Addison, M. R. The profoundly retarded: A new challenge for public education. *Education and Training of the Mentally Retarded,* 1974, *9,* 122–130.

Robinson, C. C. Application of Piagetian sensorimotor concepts to assessment and curriculum for severely handicapped children. *AAESPH Review,* 1976, *8,* 5–10.

Sailor, W. & Horner, P. R. Educational and assessment strategies for the severely handicapped. In N. G. Haring & L. J. Brown (Eds.), *Teaching the severely handicapped* (Vol. 1). New York: Grune & Stratton, 1976.

Stephens, B. A Piagetian approach to curriculum development for the severely, profoundly, and multiply handicapped. In E. Sontag (Ed.), *Educational programming for the severely and profoundly handicapped.* Reston, Va.: Council for Exceptional Children, 1977.

Appendix. Review of the Characteristics of Assessment Instruments for the Severely and Profoundly Retarded Population

Assessment Tool and Author	Denver Developmental Screening Test—Frankenburg, Dodds & Fandal	AAMD Adaptive Behavior Scale—Nihira, Foster, Shellhaas, & Leland	APT: A Resource Book for use with citizens who show severely/profoundly retarded behavior.	The Developmental Resources Cohen & Gross,
Publisher and Approximate Cost	University of Colorado Medical Center—1970	AAMD, 5201 Connecticut Ave., N.W., Washington, D.C. 20015 1975	Pennhurst State School—1973	Grune & Stratton, New York, N.Y.—1978
Purpose	Designed & standardized to meet the need of having a simple, useful tool to aid in the early discovery of children with developmental problems.	A behavior rating scale used to assess effectiveness of individual in coping with the natural & social demands of his/her environment. The Scale is divided into 2 parts. Part I is designed to assess behavioral domains important in the development of independence in daily living. Part II is designed to assess frequency of maladaptive behavior related to personality & behavior disorders in the individual.	Developed primarily as an evaluation & training program for individuals who exhibit severely or profoundly retarded behavior.	To define in precise measureable terms the behavioral pinpoint, i.e., the essential first step in program development which is derived from normative sequences of development.
Areas of Assessment:				
Skill Domains				
Fine Motor	X	X	X	X
Gross Motor	X	X	X	X
Visual Perceptual		X		X
Auditory Perceptual		X		X
Tactile Perceptual				
Gustatory Perceptual				
Olfactory Perceptual				
Kinesthetic Perceptual		X	X	X
Orientation and Mobility		X	X	
Dressing and Undressing	X	X	X	X
Personal Hygiene		X	X	X
Eating	X	X	X	X
Toileting		X	X	X
Cognitive Development		X	X	X
Social-emotional	X	X	X	X
Environmental Awareness	X	X	X	X
Receptive Language	X	X	X	X
Expressive Language	X	X	X	X
Pre-vocational		X	X	
Vocational		X	X	
Leisure Time		X		X
Pre-reading		X		X
Pre-writing		X		X
Pre-math		X	X	X

Test Background				
Population		Severely retarded ambulatory school-age children.	Individuals who exhibit severely or profoundly retarded behavior.	Severely handicapped school-age children.
Age Range	1 mo. – 6 yrs.	3 yrs. to 21 yrs.	birth to adult	
Reliability	test-retest = 95.8% inter-examiner = 90%	inter-observer reliability in Part I. $r = .93 - .71$ ($f = .86$); for Part II r lower due to marked skewedness in score distribution.	not given	
Criterion Reference	yes	yes	yes	
Validity	√	Validity of scales being explored.	not given	
Criterion Reference	yes	yes	yes	
Normative Reference	yes	yes	no	
Standardization Population	1,036 normal children 2 wks. to 6.4 yrs. old.	4,000 institutionalized M.R. at all levels of functioning from 3 – 69 yrs.	not given	non-standardized
Administration				
Group/Individual	individual	individual	individual	individual
Verbal/Non-verbal Response Required	both required	both required	both required	both required
Direct Observation/Third Party	both	both	both	direct observation
Time Required to Administer	not given	not timed	not timed	
Ease of Administration and Scoring	Easy to administer; scoring is complicated.	Relatively complex procedures fully explained in manual.	both very explicit	
Interpretation				
Raw Score				
Developmental level	X			X
Norm Range	X			
Chronological Age				X
Grade Level				
Criterion Level	X		X	
Skill Rate				
Ease of Interpretation		ABS yields a Profile Summary in which functioning of the individual may be compared with the normative behavior of institutionalized individuals.		
Percentile Rank		X		
Additional Comments		ABS scale is a major instrument used To assess the adaptive behavior of the higher level severely retarded, ambulatory individuals. AAMD		

Assessment Tool and Author	Guide to Early Developmental Training Wabash Center for the Mentally Retarded, Inc.	Caine-Levine Social Competency Scale Caine, Levine, & Freeman	Cattell Infant Intelligence Scale Psyche Cattell	Gesell Developmental Schedules Arnold Gesell
Publisher and Approximate Cost	Allyn & Bacon, Inc., Boston 1977	1963	1940	1940
PURPOSE	To provide teacher with a resource which will assist in developing a curriculum for a group of children by first determining the most appropriate goals & training procedures for the individual child.	Evaluation of the extent of skill development which permits the child to achieve self-sufficiency.	To determine the "intelligence" of the child through measurement of sequential abilities.	
Areas of Assessment: **Skill Domains**				
Fine Motor	X	X	X	X
Gross Motor	X		X	X
Visual Perceptual				
Auditory Perceptual	X			
Tactile Perceptual	X			
Gustatory Perceptual				
Olfactory Perceptual				
Kinesthetic Perceptual	X			X
Orientation and Mobility				
Dressing and Undressing	X			
Personal Hygiene	X			
Eating	X			
Toileting	X			
Cognitive Development	X			
Social-emotional		X	X	X
Environmental Awareness	X			
Receptive Language	X	X	X	X
Expressive Language	X	X		X
Pre-vocational				
Vocational				
Leisure Time				
Pre-reading	X			
Pre-writing	X			
Pre-math	X			

Test Background				
Population	Infants, pre-schoolers, & early school-age children who are developmentally disabled or TMH or SMR/PMR.	Severely retarded & trained handicapped.	Young mentally and/or physically handicapped children.	
Age Range	infant through school-age	ages 5–13	3 mos. to 30 mos.	
Reliability	not given	test/retest on sample of 35 subjects = .88–.97		tester/observer for a small sample = .90 to .99
Validity	not given			
Criterion Reference				
Normative Reference				
Standardization Population		716 TMH; IQ range-25–59, MA range—2–7 yrs.; CA range 5–13 yrs.	274 normal children at 3, 6, 9, 12, 18, 24, 30, & 36 mo.	
Administration				
Group/Individual	both	individual		
Verbal/Non-verbal	both	both required		
Response Required				
Direct Observation/Third Party	direct observation	direct observation		
Time Required to Administer		30–40 minutes		
Ease of Administration and Scoring	Activities explicitly stated.	Criterion behavior not clearly defined.	Should be used by an experienced diagnostician.	Probably requires an experienced diagnostician.
Interpretation				
Raw Score				
Developmental Level	X		Provides an IQ score.	Provides a developmental quotient (DQ)
Norm Range				
Chronological Age				
Grade Level				
Criterion Level				
Skill Rate				
Ease of Interpretation				
Percentile Rank		X		
Additional Comments	none	none	none	none

Assessment Tool and Author	The Developmental Record Hutton & Talkington	Callier–Azusa F Scale Robert Stillman (Ed.)	A Manual for the Assessment of a "Deaf-Blind" Multi-handicapped child Michael T. Collins, James H. Rudolph	Camelot I Behavior Checklist Ray W. Foster
Publisher and Approximate Cost	1974	University of Texas at Dallas, Callier Center for Communication Disorders, 1966 Inwood Rd., Dallas, Tx. 75235 1977 No cost from SWRD-B Center	Midwest Regional Center for Services to Deaf-Blind Children, P.O. Box 420, Lansing, Mi. 48902 No cost 1975	Camelot Behavioral Systems, P.O. Box 60T, Parsons, Ka. 67357
Purpose	To obtain a rapid descriptive picture of individual functioning & progress along a developmental continuum.	To assess the developmental level of deaf-blind & other severely & profoundly handicapped children & to measure child's progress in response to the educational program.	To assess a deaf-blind child's progress in individual skill areas.	To identify specific training objective for severely handicapped persons & to provide a summary or classification score directly based on these objectives.
Areas of Assessment: **Skill Domains**				
Fine Motor	X	X	X	X
Gross Motor	X	X	X	X
Visual Perceptual		X	X	X
Auditory Perceptual		X	X	X
Tactile Perceptual		X	X	X
Gustatory Perceptual				X
Olfactory Perceptual				X
Kinesthetic Perceptual	X	X	X	X
Orientation and Mobility		X		X
Dressing and Undressing	X	X	X	X
Personal Hygiene	X	X	X	X
Eating	X	X	X	X
Toileting	X	X	X	X
Cognitive Development		X	X	
Social-emotional	X	X	X	X
Environmental Awareness		X	X	X
Receptive Language	X	X	X	X
Expressive Language	X	X	X	X
Pre-vocational				
Vocational				X
Leisure Time		X		
Pre-reading		X		
Pre-writing		X		
Pre-math				

Test Background				
Population	Mentally & physically handicapped, sensory impaired & those with language deficits.	SMR/PMR, deaf/blind, multi-handicapped.	Deaf/blind.	Suitable for moderately & severaly retarded adults & children. Adapted for handicapped.
Age Range	birth to adult	birth to 108 mos.	not stated	not given
Reliability	test/retest = .97	not given	not given	not given
Validity		not given	not given	not given
Criterion Reference		Criterion responses are well defined.	yes	Criterion behaviors not specific.
Normative Reference		no	no	Percentile ranks of domain score. Totals of standardization are provided.
Standardization Population	not given	not given	not given	624 MR persons; characteristics not given
Administration				
Group/Individual	both	individual	individual	individual
Verbal/Non-verbal Response Required		both	both	both required of tester
Direct Observation/Third **Party**		both	both	both
Time Required to Administer		2 wk. minimum period of observation required	not timed	not timed
Ease of Administration and Scoring	Straightforward & clearly defined.	Easy to score and graph.	Simple checklist.	Simple checklist.
Interpretation				
Raw Score		X		X
Developmental Level		X		
Norm Range				
Chronological Age				
Grade Level				
Criterion Level				
Skill Rate				
Ease of Interpretation		Score & graph provide ease of interpretation.		Child's score interpreted in terms of percentile rank relative to standardization sample or in terms of his performances (cont.) relative to his own profile; are extremely difficult to interpret.
Percentile Rank				
Additional Comments		Very systematic assessment of low functioning individuals. Scale is particularly comprehensive at the lower developmental levels.		Gross screener to define very coarsely the behavioral strengths & weaknesses of the individual criterion behaviors not well defined. Raw scores are provided which can be graphed. Skill-acquisition programmed bibliography available to identify programs to ameliorate target behavior.

Assessment Tool and Author	A Language Intervention Program for Developmentally Young Children Diane Bricker, Laura Dennison, William Bricker	A Motor Training Program for the Developmentally Young Diane Bricker, Jacque Davis, Linda Wahlin, James Evans	Behavior Characteristics Progression	Uzgiris–Hunt Ordinal Scales of Psychological Development
Publisher and Approximate Cost	Mailman Center for Child Development 1976	Mailman Center for Child Development	VORT Corp., P.O. Box 11132, Palo Alto, Calif. 94306 Bklet - 6.95; Charts - 3.95; Binder - 8.95 1973	Univ. of Illinois Press, Urbana, Il. 1975
Purpose	Development "generative" linguistic system as developed in Piaget's sensorimotor period for all children who have limited language repertoires.	To map out in detail the necessary adaptive motor responses & the sequences in which these responses can most effectively be trained.	To provide assessment/instruction information so teacher can form individualized & appropriate learner objectives for each student. Provides complete information to show progress throughout school life of child.	To determine which schemes: (1) development of visual pursuit & permanence of object (2) development of means for obtaining desired environments (3) development of vocal & gestural imitation (4) development of operational casusality (5) construction of obj. relations in space (6) development of schemes for relating to objects the child possesses so that adequate educational planning can be developed for child.
Area of Assessment:				
Skill Domains				
Fine Motor		X	X	X
Gross Motor	X	X	X	X
Visual Perceptual	X	X	X	X
Auditory Perceptual		X	X	X
Tactile Perceptual		X	X	
Gustatory Perceptual			X	
Olfactory Perceptual			X	
Kinesthetic Perceptual		X	X	X
Orientation and Mobility		X	X	X
Dressing and Undressing			X	
Personal Hygiene			X	
Eating			X	
Toileting			X	
Cognitive Development	X		X	X
Social-emotional			X	X
Environmental Awareness		X	X	X
Receptive Language	X		X	X
Expressive Language	X		X	X
Pre-vocational			X	
Vocational			X	
Leisure Time			X	
Pre-reading			X	
Pre-writing			X	
Pre-math			X	

	infants & toddlers—expanded to include all children who have a limited language repertoire.	0toddlers 0–24 mo. & severely/profoundly handicapped children.	mildly to severely handicapping conditions, including deaf-blind & orthopedically handicapped.	
Age Range	birth to 21 yrs.	birth to 21 yrs.	birth to 21 yrs.	birth to 21 yrs.
Reliability	not given	not given		interexaminer—95.–.78 test/retest—.96–.90
Validity	Lattice structure of program implies face validity.	Motor training lattice implies face validity.		
Criterion Reference	Criterion behaviors very specific.	Criterion behaviors very specific.	Criterion for some items highly explicit & for others ambiguous.	Criterion behavior very specific.
Normative Reference	not norm referenced	not norm referenced		
Standardization Population	Developmentally delayed infants & toddlers.	Developmentally delayed infants & toddlers.	non-standardized	Normal infants, birth to 24 mos.
Administration				
Group/Individual	individual	individual	group	individual
Verbal/Non-verbal Response Required	both required of tester	non-verbal	both required	both required
Direct Observation/Third Party	direct observation	direct observation	both	observation
Time Required to Administer	not timed	not timed	not timed	not timed
Ease of Administration and Scoring	fairly complicated procedure	fairly complicated procedure	fairly complex	fairly complex but directions are explicity.
Interpretation				
Raw Score				
Developmental Level	X	X		
Norm Range				
Chronological Age				
Grade Level				
Criterion Level	X	X	X	X
Skill Rate				
Ease of Interpretation	Sequence of language training & assessment very explicit.	Sequence of motor training & assessment very explicit.	Some criterion levels ambiguously defined so that interpretation may be difficult.	Very explicit.
Percentile Rank				
Comments	Language intervention program arranged in terms of a lattice of language training which represents the developmental map& necessary training components for the development of a generative linguistic system. Program is of the test-teach variety which provides very complete & explicity assessment items & training components. Program is complex & will require training to be used effectively.	Motor training program arranged in terms of a lattice of motor training components for the development of adaptive behavior responses. Program is of the test-teach variety which provides very complete & explicit assessment items & training components program is complex & will require training to be used effectively.	The BCP is a non-standardized criterion referenced observation instrument which lists 2,400 observable traits referred to as behavioral characteristics & provides a system by which a teacher may observe patterns of behavior characteristics from which areas of strength & weakness can be determined. It is a fine-grained guide for program planning & curriculum construction which allows teacher to finely observe a pupil's behavior characteristics over a wide range of behavior for a wide spectrum of exceptional children, ranging from mildly to profoundly handicapped.	The Uzgiris-Hunt Scales can be used by curricular models using a Piagetian approach, e.g., Bricker's Constructive Interaction Adaptation Approach which uses a developmental lattice for the sensorimotor period to direct training activities for the child. By use of the U-H scales, one can locate the child within the model's developmental space & plan educational objectives to help the child move on to more complex behavior.

Assessment Tool and Author	Fairview Language Scale Alan Boroskin	Fairview Developmental Scale James Fiam Piccalo, Alan Boroskin	Bayley Scales of Infant Development Nancy Bayley	Pennsylvania Training Model Individual Assessment Guide Somerton & Turner
Publisher and Approximate Cost	Research Dept. Fairview 2501 Harbor Blvd., Costa Mesa, Ca. 92626 Manual–.50; 100 Scales–$10.00 1971	Research Dept., Fairview 2501 Harbor Blvd., Costa Mesa, Ca. 92626 Manual–.50; 100 Scales–$10.00 1974	The Psychological Corporation 1969	Pennsylvania Department of Education 1975
Purpose	Provide a scale that can be completed by para-professionals and provide a score for evaluation of progress.	Provide a scale that can be completed by paraprofessionals and provide a score for evaluation of progress.	To provide adequate measurement of the current developmental progress of infants	To assist teachers in developing specific educational programs for severely & profoundly and multiply handicapped children by providing a gross screening of child's skill development & more intensive screening of areas of deficit.
Areas of Assessment:				
Skill Domains				
Fine Motor		X	X	X
Gross Motor		X	X	X
Visual Perceptual			X	X
Auditory Perceptual			X	X
Tactile Perceptual			X	X
Gustatory Perceptual				
Olfactory Perceptual				
Kinesthetic Perceptual			X	
Orientation and Mobility			X	
Dressing and Undressing				X
Personal Hygiene		X		X
Eating				X
Toileting				X
Cognitive Development			X	X
Social-emotional	X	X	X	X
Environmental Awareness		X	X	
Receptive Language	X	X	X	X
Expressive Language	X	X	X	X
Pre-vocational				
Vocational				
Leisure Time				
Pre-reading				
Pre-writing				
Pre-math				
Test Background				
Population	SMR/PMR institutionalized	SMR/PMR institutionalized	Infants and/or young mentally or physically handicapped children.	Severely & profoundly multiply handicapped children, birth to 21 yrs.
Age Range	birth to 12 mos.	birth to 2 yrs.	2 mo. to 30 mo.	birth to 21 yrs.
Reliability	X	.71–.94	split half on normal child 2–30 mos. mental—.81–.93 (.88 Md); motor—.68–.92 (.84 Md);	not given
Validity	X	X	mental scale scores correlated .57 with Stanford-Binet IQ test scores for	not given

Normative Reference			yes	no
Standardization Population		163 M.R. residents	1262 normal child. 2–30 mo.	not standardized
Administration				
Group/Individual			individual	individual
Verbal/Non-verbal Response Required			both required	both required
Direct Observation/Third Party			direct observation	direct observation
Time Required to Administer			45 to 75 min.	not timed
Ease of Administration and Scoring			Difficult to administer & score. Requires an experienced tester.	Ambiguity in determining scale scores and criterion responses.
Interpretation				
Raw Score	X	X	X	Obtained on competency checklist which gives fine-grained measure of child's skills
Developmental Level	X	X	X	
Normal Range	X	X		
Chronological Age				
Grade Level				
Criterion Level				
Skill Rate		Obtained from curriculum assessment guide which provides gross screening of child's skills		
Ease of Interpretation	Raw scores from mental scale are transformed into Mental Development. Indexes ranging from 50 to 150. Raw scores from motor scale are transformed into Psychomotor Development. Indexes ranging from 50 to 150. These indexes cover more than 3 S.D. on either side of the average MD1 or DD1 for each age.	Ambiguity in determining what a scale score is on competency checklists due to lack of precision in defining the criterion response. Criterion responses better defined in curriculum assessment guide; however, no indication is given of how many trials per day or for how many days each assesment item should be presented.		
Percentile Rank				
Additional Comments	Quick & easy to administer if evaluator knows child well.	Quick & easy to administer if evaluator knows child well.	This test measures: (1) mental ability in terms of child's responses to visual & auditory stimuli, manipulation and play with others, responses involving social interaction, memory and abstract reasoning; (2) motor ability, as assessed through child's gross & fine motor behaviors. The MDI & the PDI may be useful in early identification and diagnosis of sensory and central nervous system dysfunctions and other developmental disabilities. The scores obtained are difficult to convert directly into any plan of educational intervention.	There are 4 major steps Educational Planning System: (1) obtaining global assess of child's skill development using curriculum assessment guide, (2) intensively assessing areas of deficit using the competency checklists, (3) developing a detailed analysis to ameliorate a deficient skill through the use of Individual Prescriptive Planning Sheets, ad () continually assessing the child's progress.

Assessment Tool and Author	(UPAS) Uniform Performance Assessment System, Level A, 1st Revision Bendersky (Ed.)	The TARC Assessment SMYSTEM Wayne Sailor, & Bonnie Jean Mix	Progress Assessment Chart of Social and Personal Development (PAC) H. C. Grenjburg	Portage Guide to Early Education
Publisher and Approximate Cost	Experimental Education Unit, Child Development & M.R. Center $6.50	H & H Enterprises,	SEFA Publications Ltd. England 1974	Cooperative Educational Service Agency 12, Portage, Wisc. 1976
Purpose	To monitor the performance of severely & profoundly handicapped children to determine how many skills a child has.	To provide a short-form behavioral asessment instrument to formulate instructional objectives & subsequent curriculum selection.	To give a tentative overall picture of social functioning and dysfunctioning.	An assessment, curricular instrument which allows parents and teachers to increase the child's adaptive behavior, as a parent training model.
Areas of Assessment:				
Skill Domains				
Fine Motor	X	X	X	X
Gross motor	X	X	X	X
Visual perceptual	X			X
Auditory perceptual	X			X
Tactile perceptual				X
Gustatory perceptual				
Olfactory perceptual				
Kinesthetic perceptual	X			X
Orientation and Mobility	X		X	X
Dressing and undressing	X	X	X	X
Personal hygiene	X	X	X	X
Eating	X	X	X	X
Toileting	X	X	X	X
Cognitive Development	X	X	X	X
Social-emotional		X	X	X
Environmental Awareness		X	X	X
Receptive Language	X	X	X	X
Expressive Language	X	X	X	X
Pre-vocational			X	
Vocational			X	
Leisure time			X	
Pre-reading	X	X	X	
Pre-writing	X		X	
Pre-math	X		X	
Test Background				
Population	Severely/profoundly handicapped children 0–6 yrs.	Severely handicapped children.		Can be used with all exceptional children functioning at level of development associated with normal children from birth to 6 yrs.
Age range	0–6 yrs.	3–16 yrs.		birth to 6 yrs.

Test Background, continued

Reliability	not given	inter-rater — .85 – .59 test/retest — .80 & greater		not given
Validity	not given	not given		not given
Criterion reference	yes	yes		Criterion behaviors not precisely specified.
Normative reference	no	yes		Items & activities provided derived from developmental milestones of normal children.
Standardization population	non-standardized	283 severely handicapped children, 3 – 16 yrs.	several populations of M.R. children	Normal child ranging in age from birth to 6 yrs.
Administration				
Group/Individual	individual	individual		individual
Verbal/non-verbal response required	both required	both		both required
Direct Observation/Third Party	direct observation	direct observation		direct observation
Time Require to Administer	not timed	20 – 25 minutes		not timed
Ease of Administration and Scoring	All criteria for each object explicitly defined.	fairly easy		Relatively easy to administer; scoring criteria ambiguous.
Interpretation				
Raw Score		X		
Developmental Level			X	X
Norm Range		X	X	X
Chronological Age				X
Grade Level				
Criterion Level	X			X
Skill Rate				
Ease of Interpretation	Very easy to administer, score, & interpret.	Interpretation of scores is very simple.		Criterion responses not well defined.
Percentile Rank				
Additional Comments	UPAS is an experimental behavioral checklist, listing educational objectives in the form of behavioral descriptors with accompanying criterion tests. The ultimate goal of the UPAS is to develop an informational system to monitor and measure growth (i.e. to pinpoint the skill level on the continuum of development) of the severely/profoundly handicapped child from birth until the child possesses marketable vocational skills.	The TARC system is based on the idea of providing a quick assessment of observable behavioral characteristics to obtain a "snapshot" of current functioning levels of severely handicapped children. It is designed to meet the needs of educators in providing educational programs for severely handicapped children by relating curriculum selection directly to assessment & the derivation of instructional objectives.		Provides a simple assessment instructional model to be used by relatively inexperienced people in both home and school settings.

Assessment Tool and Author	Vineland Social Maturity Scale Edgar A. Doll	Balthazar Scales of Adaptive Behavior I: The Scales of Functional Independence (BSAB-I) Earl Balthazar	Balthazar Scales of Adaptive Behavior II: The Scales of Social Adaptation (BSAB-II) Earl Balthazar	Training the Retarded at Home or in School: A Manual for Parents, Teachers, and Home Trainers Earl Balthazar
Publisher and Approximate Cost	American Guidance Service, Inc. Publishers Bldg, Circle Pines, Minn. 55014 $4.80 1965	Research Press Co., 2612 N. Mattis Ave. Champaign, Ill., 6180 1971	The Consulting Psychologist Press, Inc., 577 College Ave., Palo Alto, CA. 94306 1973	The Consulting Psychologist Press, Inc., 577 College Ave., Palo Alto, CA. 94306 1976
Purpose	Provides an outline of detailed performances in respect to which children show a progressive ability for looking after themselves & for participating in activities which lead toward ultimate independence as adults.	To provide objective and standardized measures of functionally adaptive independent behaviors of ambulatory, severely or profoundly retarded, or young moderately retarded individuals, based on direct observation of the individual in his own environment.	To provide objective measures of social coping behaviors in ambulatory severely and profoundly mentally retarded individuals, and in younger retarded children, based on direct observations of the individual in his environment.	To assess functional self-help skills and social coping behaviors in home and school settings.
Areas of Assessment:				
Skill Domains				
Fine Motor	X			
Gross Motor	X			
Visual Perceptual	X			
Auditory Perceptual	X			
Tactile Perceptual				
Gustatory Perceptual				
Olfactory Perceptual				
Kinesthetic Perceptual	X			
Orientation and Mobility	X			
Dressing and Undressing	X	X		X
Personal Hygiene	X			X
Eating	X	X		X
Toileting	X	X		X
Cognitive Development	X			
Social-emotional	X		X	X
Environmental Awareness	X		X	X
Receptive Language	X		X	X
Expressive Language	X		X	X
Pre-vocational	X			
Vocational	X			
Leisure Time	X		X	X
Pre-reading				
Pre-writing				
Pre-math				
Test Background				
Population	All exceptional individuals ranging from mildly to profoundly retarded.	Severely/profoundly retarded or younger moderately retarded children.	Severely and profoundly retarded ambulatory individuals & younger retarded children.	Severely & profoundly retarded age, ambulatory, & younger moderately retarded children.
Age Range	birth to adult	school-age yrs for SMR/PMR preschool yrs. for moderately retarded	5 yrs. to 21 yrs.	school-age for SMR/PMR; pre-school age for moderately retarded
		inter rater = .97-.94	not in manual	not given

Validity	Social Age reported to correlate highly with mental age, validity co-efficient = .86.	Concurrent Validity Coefficient ranged from .59–.67 when total BSAB/I scores related to total Vineland Social Maturity scores.	not in manual	not given
Criterion Reference		yes	yes	yes
Normative reference	X	Can plot scores in terms of percentile ranks.	Can plot scores in terms of percentile ranks.	no
Standardization Population	620 normal subjects of each sex at each yr. from birth to 25 yrs.	institutionalized SMR/PMR from 5–7 yrs. (median = 17 yrs.)	institutionalizes SMR/PMR ambulatory 5–57 yrs. (median = 17 yrs.)	non-standardized
Administration				
Group/Individual	Informants may be interviewed as a group or individually.	individual	individual	individual
Verbal/non-verbal Response Required	Verbal response required of informant	non-verbal	both required	both required
Direct Observation/Third Party	third party Obs.: Toileting is in interview format	Eating and Dressing scales are direct Obs.: Toileting interview format.	direct observation	direct observation
Time Required to Administer	30 min.	not timed	6–10 min. sessions	Eating—Must observe at least 3 meals; Toileting—must observe for 1 mo. 5 times a wk.; Social—10 min. observation session.
Ease of Administration and Scoring	Administration requires sophisticated interviewing; scoring is relatively complex.	fairly complex	fairly complex	Relatively easy to administer and score.
Interpretation				
Raw Score	X	X		
Developmental Level	X (life age)			
Norm Range	X			
Chronological Age				
Grade Level	X			
Criterion Level				Interpreted in terms of percent of time behavior occurs, or pass/fail system can be used; i.e. child succeeds or does not succeed.
Skill Rate			Measurement system used frequency counts per unit of time; the score for each item based on 6–10 minute observation sessions per individual.	
Ease of Interpretation	Evaluations are far less objective than implied by the final scoring methods utilized.	Plotted scores relatively easy to interpret.	Requires sophisticated examiner to interpret scores.	Easiest of the BSAB tests to score & interpret.
Percentile Rank		X		
Additional Comments	Information in VSMS can provide a very gross index of social functioning & provide the beginning of rapport in building system with parents and "significant others" of severely/profoundly handicapped. Information cannot easily be used for programatic or administrative purposes.	The BSAB-I is designed to measure representative behaviors of the individual in the areas of eating, dressing, & toileting and does not claim to measure "aptitude" or "intelligence" in terms of any external standards or norms.	The BSAB-II provides extremely comprehensive measures of social coping behavior. Like BSAB-I, it is designed to measure representative behaviors and does not presume to measure "aptitude" or "general intelligence."	This test utilizes many of the same skill items as in the BSAB-I & BSAB-II, but uses a simpler scoring system appropriate for less formal use in the home & school by parent & teachers. The items assessed seem to be tapping slightly more complex behaviors than BSAB-I & BSAB-II.

William C. Morse

14 The Teacher and Assessment of Socioemotional Deviance

THE PARTICULAR ROLE OF THE TEACHER

This chapter is directed to teachers as diagnostic agents for socioemotional problems of pupils. This position is taken because teachers have always functioned as the first line of defense for the mental health of children and adolescents. They observe behavior and they attempt remediation. No other trained profession sees all of the children and youth as they function in many diverse school settings in the normal course of school life.

If anything, the role of the teacher has become more critical since the days of Wickman's (1928) early studies. Wickman's data reveal that teachers had a different set of sensitivities than the holy trinity of mental health—psychiatry, social work, and psychology. Overall, teachers were more concerned about symptoms of defiance toward authority and group disruption while mental hygienists were more concerned about withdrawal and isolation. These differences reflected the reality of the professional roles as well as theory: mental health workers had difficulty with the noncommunicative child while teachers could not conduct their classes with disrupting youngsters. Moreover, the gap between educators and the mental health professions has been reduced. For example, it is now clear that aggressive behavior is one of the more critical signs of social emotional deviance (Kohlberg, LaCrosse, & Ricks, 1972) and teachers continue to be particularly good in noting such deviant behaviors. Once teachers have the help to get the disruptive children assimilated, they are aware and concerned over the withdrawn, sad youngster.

They have profited from more formal training and sensitivity from the mental health fields and are now aware of cues to covert conditions and underlying motivation.

There are many reasons for moving toward a common awareness of people with problems and the current inclusion of teachers as team partners. Mental health is a first order societal problem in the broadest sense and has become an obligation for all of us. Previously, teachers were to spot and refer, and not work directly in the remediation of the problem. They screened, so to speak, and then referred to the expert (who, incidentally, was often not available). But concepts have changed. The emphasis on community and ecological psychology has made both diagnosis and remediation programs attuned to the actual life setting (which occupies 24 hours each day) rather than putting all the emphasis on the clinical settings (which may occupy one hour each week). The behavior we are concerned about happens in a life setting (the school). Thus, it has become common to study behavior under normal conditions and attempt to provide remedial experiences in the normal setting. A notable change is that the child no longer goes to the clinic but rather the special diagnosticians now often come to observe in the classroom. A case in point occurred when a teacher referred a wildly acting out youngster to a psychologist, who found him meek and pleasant in the one-to-one interview with a stranger. While both saw the same child differently, they were both right in their observations. Ecological differences produced the behaviors, but failing to recognize this, the resulting contrast in views did little to build rapport.

However, it should be recognized that not every essential condition is revealed in the school setting. We see *what* more than we know *why* it occurred, and are left dealing only with symptoms unless we understand the *why*. Also, the child with internalized conflicts who keeps his worries to himself is less easy to comprehend. We need observations and the understanding of both the action personnel and the clinicians when we are trying to study another person's behavior.

Not only are teachers group workers and managers of a social arena that gives them a unique "slant," but they also have the many roles of what Bronfenbrenner (1970) has called the "upbringers." Teachers, like parents and responsible adults, are obligated to enhance socialization, a very difficult task these days. They also must require conformity and "work," some of the latter not seen as either relevant or enjoyable by certain pupils who are legally forced to be in school regardless. Teachers can be sued for negligence if the pupils have not learned all of which they are capable. This is not to say there is no place for amusement and personal satisfaction in school; it is just that even the reasonable demands of the school may not be enjoyable for some children. School is to facilitate the cognitive, affective, and motor domains and this embodies a wide gamut of interests, attitudes, values, self-feelings, academic knowledge, and skills as well as motor competencies. Some of these events will be less than fun for even normally adjusted children.

Bringing up the new generation has never been easy, even in rigid authoritarian cultures. The history of punishments and deprivation applied to "shape" youth is evidence enough of that fact. But the important point at the moment is this: the judgments of the teacher about social and emotional adjustment are in a culture which is diverse and variant. There is no longer a simple answer to, "what behavior is normal?" Instead, we just ask "normal in what context, and for what values?" The arbitrary simplicity applied in the past is no longer acceptable, and this condition must be incorporated in the teachers' competencies to observe behavior for deviant potential. It is further complicated by the fact that behavioral limits differ in various classrooms, schools, and communities. Some of the variance may be responsible to reasonable differences and others due to idiosyncratic adult attitudes. Certainly cultural differences which do not harm the self or others (e.g., such as the punishment meted out for speaking Spanish on the playground) are no longer to be considered deviant. In fact, the goal now is to encourage all reasonable diversity and individuality. This goal has become the norm rather than a uniformity of behavior. Discussions among teachers reveals differences. Certain teachers are too easy and others unfairly demanding.

The certainty about limits has become vague in family, school, and community life in the times in which we are living. The open multi-value culture has produced such diversity that symptoms which used to be seen as serious are no longer so judged. But there are also certain conditions which have increased the problems and are recognized as adding hazard to normal adjustment for the new generation of children and youth. The widespread aggression in wars, crime, and confrontation is evidence as acceptable behavior. The images of success depicted in mass media are largely those of material wealth, being the best at what you do, independence regardless. Popular singers and cult figures are built-up systematically as the picture of success, especially if there is a rags to riches immediacy without work. Freedom, aggression, and sex have become passwords. "You can't make me!" "I won't do it because I don't feel like it." Confrontation is the common style. Why work if you do not have to? The mixture of children's figures for identification today contain the admirable and the antisocial. Since so many of the life styles depicted in the mass media are alien to the expectations of the school and teachers it is no wonder there is more "misbehavior." Many children come to school without the basic learning which can only come from intimate family experience where one's identity, socialization, and capacity to trust are generated. The school is expected to replace what the family primary group should have provided, but this is not the function of the school. It is a secondary group organization, a peer society, with very few adults. Many children are not yet ready to function at this level, since they have not developed identity, trust, and basic socialization. Such a youngster behaves in an inappropriate way in the school setting because he or she is not yet emotionally mature enough to utilize it. In short, he or she attempts to "act out," and becomes a problem.

The accentuation of the negative in our society is, of course, only one side—the side which fosters problem symptoms for teachers. There is also the current antimaterialism emphasis (sometimes combined with antiscientific and antiestablishment emphasis), there are new ecological concerns, more sensitivity to fairness and justice for all. These are positive and counteractive qualities in the current society, though sometimes even the positive values are difficult for schools with a conservative rigidity. All of these conditions make the task of interpreting and judging normal and deviant behavior more complex since the value base itself is vastly more complex. The conflict and confusion of values in our society enters into all of the subsequent sections of this chapter.

ASSETS AND LIMITATIONS OF THE TEACHER IN BEHAVIORAL ASSESSMENT

Able or biased, teachers have a critical function in the observation of behavior. In addition to helping with other team members in the final understanding of the pupil's problem, they are very likely to be the ones who alert others to problematic possibilities. It is important that they not miss significant symptoms and thus delay getting help to a youngster. It is also important not to start complicated diagnostic processes without good reason; teachers, therefore, are the mental health gatekeepers.

Assets of the Teacher

There are many reasons why the teacher can function as an expert screener indicating a child who should be considered for detailed study by various mental health experts. This begins with raising questions, not immediately answering them. Here the teacher's qualifications are unique.

1. Teachers are generally trained in at least the rudiments of mental health; it is part of their accountability that they do become so informed. Many teachers are long-time students of the field and can match the other professions in making a contribution to child study.

2. Teachers see many children, the vast number of which are normal

youngsters. This gives them a comparative sense of the significance of given behavior. They know that the use of the term "normal" describes a considerable behavioral range. Thus, the teacher is in an excellent position to point out symptoms that are extreme, relative to the typical youngster's performance. A symptom cannot be separated from the age relevancy. An adolescent with a mild preoccupation with sexual innuendo is not atypical, but the preadolescent who is immersed in sexualizing the world is atypical; this is the same symptom but different meaning. Every age has its typical developmental tasks and frustrations, as Erickson (1964) indicates. Adolescent temper tantrums are of significance; a preschooler who explodes once in a while would not be considered disturbed unless the intensity were much greater and the return to balance delayed much beyond the normal child.

3. Teachers usually see the children in many settings: at work, play, relating to peers, dealing with authority, at free times, creative periods, under stress, and so on. This prevents the very possible sampling error when a person is only with a child for a brief time in a forced setting such as giving psychological tests. The teacher is thus able to provide information on the *depth* and *spread* of deviant behavior and specific relationships to various external conditions. Some children have trouble everyplace and we can see that they carry their symptoms within. Others respond deviantly only to certain specifics in the environment. Whether the deviance has a tripping mechanism in the environment is very important information in diagnosing and planning.

4. The teacher sees the youngster over a time period which serves to iron out the inevitable ups and downs in normal growth. The extensive time span allows for information on the *persistence* of a condition. Progressive changes up or down over a year can suggest important qualifications to a set of behaviors sampled at a given point. A youngster can have a period of disruptive behavior which disappears as he learns to cope.

5. The teacher does not live only with limitations and problem behavior. Teachers also see assets. A pupil may not do his teacher's bidding but may be an excellent peer leader on the playground. This view of many functions provides a needed balance; behavior problem youngsters often become stereotyped as complete failures. In fact, unless we find and capitalize on the pupil's assets, we will waste a great deal of effort in trying to help. Thus, a teacher can list both negative and positive symptoms due to the widespread opportunity for observations.

6. Teachers of the elementary and middle school (and to a lesser degree those of high school in some instances) come to know something about the child's total life. Outside of school, life events are inevitably brought in to school at various times. Parents are sometimes even too well known. Siblings may be in the school and provide cues. The home support

that the youngster gets is usually apparent to teachers. Home crises and catastrophies are often shared with a trusting teacher. This prevents "case" myopia where everything gets blamed on the pupil. One of the essential distinctions which must be made later is the genesis of the variant behavior. Does it *come from outside* (family, neighborhood, etc.) with the school as that place where the pressure is acted out? Is there difficulty *both* at home and at school? Is it a school problem alone or a school problem which has *spread* to the outside world? Later on, the source of the trouble (in contrast to where the acting out takes place) will be critical for planning. As teachers come to be aware of the total life of the child, they can put some evaluative stricture on the symptoms they observe.

7. Teachers worthy of their professional assignment do not refer children who demonstrate problem behavior without first trying to rectify the behavior. They search out motivations. They try alternative methods of helping. They intervene. Thus considerable data can be gathered at the beginning of the maladapted behavior. By careful examination of the efforts made by teachers on their own as well as with consultation, we need not start at zero in planning. In fact, a great deal is known or can be gleaned by careful examination of what has been tried and how well it worked or failed in altering behavior.

Just as teachers have particular assets in screening and observation *there are professional pitfalls which must be guarded against* if the mental health effort is to take full advantage of their potential.

8. All of us have what is called countertransference, that is, a certain behavior will bother us unduly because of our own particualr life experience. A child who does not follow set routines becomes a critical concern to one teacher regardless of the reasons. Defiance may stir up one's insecurity about control. Sexual behavior which is normal for an age may set off sensitivities. We all have the residue of unfinished business. It is easy to ignore some symptoms we should not and to overreact to others which may not be that important. Teachers need to monitor such natural countertransference in three ways. First comes self understanding and awareness so that we can consciously control such reactions. The second is to consult with colleagues and in frank discussion verify our judgments. Third, is to recognize the four levels of judgment concerning variant behavior, which will be elaborated later.

9. Many teachers find a schedule, checksheet, or pattern for observing behavior and collecting information useful. There are such materials and procedures that increase the comprehensiveness and accuracy of the teacher's contribution (Long, Morse, & Newman, 1976). Several of these can be found within the materials cited in the Suggested Readings section at the end of the chapter.

BASES FOR EVALUATING SYMPTOMATIC BEHAVIOR

The problem many on-the-line workers have in evaluating the significance of behaviors is to clarify the judgmental source. Otherwise, casual signs get confused with essential socioemotional deviance. The balance between the individual's rights and social obligations requires continual attention.

There are five reference points which a teacher uses in evaluating behavior which merits attention. The first is recognizing *growth pains*. The second already alluded to, is *eliminating bias from personalized irritations*. The third is being aware of *time and place misbehavior*. *Interference* with routines is the fourth. The fifth is recognition of *truly deviant symptoms*.

PAINS OF GROWTH

Teachers generally recognize that any growing youngster with an intact ego and even a minimum of spunk will behave independently at times, even willing to pay the price for misbehavior. Always operating at the cutting edge of capability, there are new situations to be faced as one matures. Sometimes a pupil just does not know yet what is proper to do. In fact, they may be chagrined when they are asked to consider an action. To grow is to venture into possible error; to teach is to recognize that a quota of misbehavior should be allowed. Knowing the developmental issues of a particular age, a teacher is able to recognize what one can expect from four year olds, the typical fourth grader, or the fourteen-year-old adolescent, and does not confuse going through a developmental period with deviance.

TEACHER-PERSONALIZED BIAS

As was suggested in a prior section, one must eliminate personal sensitivities when judging pupil behavior. A child may not be hurting or bothering anyone but, if they are not doing what the teachers feel they should, they may be seen as deviant. Teachers' casual conversations reveals many differences in what bothers the adult when determining what behavior of children is significant for their future. Certain teachers have reputations of being unfairly tough, while others let children get away with a great deal. A problem student to one teacher may be seen as a pleasant student by another. Sometimes the child is different due to the interaction with various adults or because of different classroom conditions. But it may also be the child is running the gamut of adult variance—what bothers one may not bother another. We have to ask the question, "What will be the import of this behavior (which concerns me) on the destiny of the pupil.'' While we cannot expect every teacher to interpret the blips on the radar screen exactly the same way, there should be some general rationality across the profession.

TIME AND PLACE MISALIGNMENT

Many call it misbehavior when a pupil is doing nothing really wrong, but just in an improper place or the wrong time. Exuberance takes over, talk increases, and excitement peaks. The teacher's designated task is forgotten. Yet social exchange is in fact a sign of normality, and excitement is a reasonable emotion. The loudest of the group may become the target for judgment of misbehavior. The pupil may feel, ''Gee, you can't even laugh in here. She doesn't want us to have any fun. Can't even talk to your friends.'' Or an adolescent pair may be demonstrating their intense involvement with one another rather than paying attention to Shakespear's Romeo and Juliet. The pair picked the wrong time and place for their remonstrances.

There are so many times when teachers become concerned about behavior when it is not illegitimate at all but occurs at the wrong time or place. Take that behavior to the gym, playground, lunch hour, or after school—not here, now, many teachers will say. If this is fact, then we are dealing with minor symptoms and not basic deviance. Rather than seeing such reaction as evidence of pathology, we should be empathic with the legitimate motivation.

INTERFERENCE WITH ROUTINES

This is really a special case of time and place but is a significant source of overweighing symptomatic behavior. We have these rules, one teacher said we have a rule for everything. Hidden or forgotten rules get activated. Ad hoc rules fixate misbehavior: Walk, don't run in the halls; fit in, there are traffic patterns for up and down stairs. Bells ring and decide what behavior is legitimate; ready or not, this is reading period. Of course, certain rules are useful for mass group institutions like schools. But many of the rules are for the convenience of the administrating adults. Some, which even may appear trivial, are legal rules based upon school law and teacher responsibility. Children are often provoked into ''testing the law'' as part of their environmental exploration to see what they can get away with. The point is, walking the wrong way in the hall is hardly equivalent to driving the wrong way on a major highway, though such comparisons are sometimes made.

One way to separate this deviance from really serious behavior is to recognize the more ephemeral and arbitrary the rule, the more exorcised we adults become about its violation. Lectures are given and pseudoserious implications are invented. As the base for judgment is recognized as superficial, adult agitation seems to increase. But we should know when we are dealing with less than a federal offense. As we recognize the condition to be one of convenience, we can try to work out a solution with the youngster. Silly or unneeded rules can be changed. Maintained reasons should be examined.

Of course even these minor violations may be symptomatic of real problems. We can try various procedures and may still see no sign of mitigation. Persistence and inflexibility around minor violations need to be recorded. There are many career testers and constant opposers where the symptoms, though remaining at the annoyance level, are the tip of the dangerous iceberg—John kept coming late: the matter is discussed and he is able to beat the bell most of the time from then on. Ralph protests he is sorry for being late. It won't happen again. But it does, repeatedly. There seems to be a tinge of covert hostility, and an underlying rejection of school which he denies. The iceberg is there. The behavior observed is not of itself a big issue: what it represents is. A scrap on the playground is "settled," just a piece of normal behavior. A blood feud which never stops and shows up in new places even though we try to deal with it, certainly is of a serious order. A preadolescent girl, Ginger, is ready to "beat anyone's butt off, even two at a time." But it is all talk and she gets along quite well most of the time. The aggressive talk is part of her neighborhood survival course, and we talk about how we should talk in school as a "time and place" matter. If the symptom can be altered by reasonable teacher handling, we certainly should not consider it as a talisman of pathology.

THE VERY SERIOUSLY DEVIANT

When all is said and done, there are some children and youth who present significant social and emotional deviance. Either they started out with biological limitations and/or were taught by life experience unsatisfactory patterns of coping.

The question of what is normal and what should be judged seriously deviant has become a cause celebre. On one hand, institutions in their fear of collapse and disintegration engendered by anyone different or not compliant often become critical of any variance. At the other extreme are those who see the traditional "normal" person as the real sick one, since the society as a whole is seen as neurotic and distorted.

We have already discussed certain personal and situational aspects of making judgments about behavior. Granting that we must avoid these pitfalls, there is still the concern for children with deviant behavior which is not ephemeral. In a democratic society, the struggle between individual rights and societal rights is a never ending struggle which vacillates back and forth from time to time. In the evolution of new standards, legally and by common consent, the definition of deviancy changes. The democratic social contract implies certain types of behavior and thus defines legal deviance but even here with children, running away from school can make one a delinquent even if no one is threatened by the act. The special case of children and youth, not of legal age, constitutes a particularly difficult area for judging by symptoms. In delinquent and mental health decisions it is only now that the rights of minors have received attention. The basic issues first center around the protection of person and property. Persons who prevent others from being safe (physically and psychologically) are seriously deviant. Still the line is hard to draw, and sometimes it is not until an overt act is seen that the danger is appraised as real. We expect that our possessions will be inviolate—a pencil is safe, a bike will not be taken, one's private space will not be invaded, or a house will not be vandalized. In mental health symptomology, a person who is self-destructive or who is a danger to others is seriously disturbed. Not only does society need protection, the individual needs protection from his own inclinations. One of the implied individual rights is for help and all the assistance we can provide.

When it comes to children nothing is so simple. Violating deep and abiding social sanctions is one thing; prognosis about the future is another. Neurotic behavior can be considered self-defeating. Suicide is complete self-destruction. Low self-esteem is painful. Inner feelings of despair are certainly poor omens for the future. It is neither right or practical to "wait until he does something big" when it may be too late, though there are cases where this seems the only course when the legal decision makers refuse to accept judgments. A parent may listen to the recital of symptoms and choose to ignore the significance, for example. But we are obligated to prevent serious disturbances when possible, and to prevent the serious from becoming more fixed and devastating. The only way we can operate is to observe the behavior of the youngster which is a critical role of every teacher. The behaviors and particular symptoms which are recorded give the basis for referral and case study. Augmented by information from the home, psychological tests, and astute interviews, these symptoms gradually become woven into a pattern which suggests the general overall nature of the deviation. One does not imply from symptoms alone, but the teacher's role is only to help with the diagnosis, not to decide the overall pattern.

All symptoms are related to the light they shed on the self concept and self-esteem of the pupil. The self concept consists of the constructs one associates with the "what and who I am." This summation of personality is accompanied by a state of self-esteem which is the judgment of how much of a success or failure the self concept represents. Of course the individual in some serious disturbances has no real self concept, and some of the self perceived "selves" of children are defensive and not in keeping with the observations of teachers or peers. The most delicate and determinant aspect of any of us is the self concept. As teachers observe the pupil in action over time and many settings, they are often in an excellent position to give useful information concerning the self concept.

William James (cited in Felher, 1974) has said when two people meet there are actually six: the self each thinks he is, the self of each as seen by the other, the self each really is! In dealing with self concept, the teacher develops a perception of what the pupil really is, adding up all the cues available. But even more important is to understand how the pupil, both consciously and unconsciously, perceives himself. The main goal is to learn how the individual sees inner and outer life for, from his point of view, all of his behavior is logical and reasonable. It is the pupil's self-perception which determines his behavior. As we observe the evidence of the cognitive, affective, and motor self-perceptions we are in a position to see how these aspects set the style of behavior. If I am bright but think I am dull, cognitive experiences will be filtered by my perceptions and I will behave "dull." If my motor skill is self-presumed to be high and very important as a way to deal with others, being "pushy" comes naturally and I rationalize the times I lose. If I feel unworthy of being liked, I suspect those who offer relationship and my affective disposition is projected into behavior. One's behavior does not violate his self construct, though there may be inconsistencies, inadequacies, and confusions in the integration of the self. All behavioral cues lead us to an awareness of the self concept.

While we never really know another human being, this is the closest we will get. If it makes sense of the behavior we know we are in the right direction.

Also, in considering various symptoms, adults are inclined to underestimate the intensity of feeling which underlies much symptomatic behavior. There is nothing superficial or casual (though it may alternate rapidly) about the emotions and motivations of children and youth. Every moment is for real. Anger, frustration, fear, hate, and boredom are real. Times of attachment, love, joy, success, and personal preoccupations are real. The needs for a sense of independence, for being cared about and for being protected are for real. What this means is, behind the symptoms we record are well-springs of emotion, woven in a unique pattern for each individual.

There are four basic self adjustment patterns which will be delineated to conclude this section. The reason for presenting these four is to help one organize the symptoms which are overt into a dynamic design. But no two youngsters of the same pattern will look exactly alike, and mistakes and individual nuances are the rule. We do not deal with types, we deal with individuals and the individuality overrules the self type. But without thinking of the integrating style of self-development represented by the symptomatic behavior, the symptoms themselves have little integrity.

ACUTE REACTIVE

It is difficult to imagine a self living under severe stress, continually unable to cope with the given reality but not able to get out from under. What we mean is that it is not the individual alone but the situation which is pathological. The child *reacts* to the situation sometimes with inadequacy, failure, and despair. At other times there is a dominance of fight and the struggle goes on as the child tries to protect himself. He may live in a home which is rejecting, ambivalent, scapegoating, or even brutal. It may be that school demands are impossible. Some of these youngsters respond reasonably at times or some days or places. They generally test people or situations that are reasonable in contrast to the high stress ones they face. The testing is to see if trust can be given to what is often a reasonable segment of the environment. The importance of this pattern is to alert us to the fact that the child *may be giving normal reactions to an abnormal condition*. It is the external, not internal, which is deviant. Of course, if it persists too long the effects merge into the self concepts of internalized problem styles to be noted later.

Mary began to rule, demand inordinate attention, disrupt the groups in the classroom, and pay little attention to the tasks. After talks with the teacher, she would be her old self for a brief time. There also were her good days when she came smiling and happy to school. In the parent conference it was revealed that there was a serious break in the family, and a separation period had been planned with the high probability of a divorce. The mother said that Mary took it very hard when the father was away; she cried and was upset. The fact that she was reacting to a current situation beyond her ability to cope does not mean it was unimportant, only that she was not characterlogically disturbed. For most children, at least a year of professional help is necessary to enable them to learn to cope with such a family breakup and such situational stress can easily lead to chronic maladjustment.

George found himself in a dilemma. His adolescent behavior alienated his father with whom he had been close. It seemed he could no longer ever please or satisfy his father. His churlish behavior in school got him in trouble with teachers and exacerbated the difficulties. He responded "What do I care." The father, facing disappointments in his business, was unable to deal with his son's new behavior and alienation increased. George was reacting to stress. He was labeled a serious problem case. This fit with his father's produced self-reflection and became a career line for George, much to the dismay of his "good family" and all who knew him.

It is important to make an ecological examination to discover if there are legitimate reasons for new life traumas that are presenting dilemmas to children. When one cannot cope, it is "normal" to react in ways that are symptomatic of difficulty. Sometimes conditions can be rectified; sometimes a child learns to live with the situation; sometimes the reaction pattern persists and becomes chronic. As a matter of fact, the way children become chronically disturbed is through what they learn in trying to survive in crisis situations. And many children have lived in continual crisis, with their problem behavior being reinforced by a constant press of an unfortunate nature.

The fascinating thing is how many children, growing up in what we would agree are disasterous conditions, do make it. They often respond well to a positive "life splinter," a teacher, or a friend, or they work out some ability and develop a strong self concept in spite of the odds.

It has been estimated that as many as one-third of the children who are referred for help as seriously deviant because of their symptomatic behavior are really intact children and youth doing better than most of us might in very trying conditions.

NEUROTIC, CONFLICT-RIDDEN YOUNGSTERS

The balanced support and freedom needed by children as they grow up is very difficult to provide. When this is lacking, a conflict develops in the child over not doing or being able to do what the child thinks he should. Guilt and anxiety result, usually starting with relationships in the family but often generated by the school environment as well. There is a poor self concept and low self-esteem. These children may act out their frustration with aggression to others and hostile behavior. They may endlessly test others in order to provoke reactions and punishment. Often they show signs of contriteness after a discussion but they seem unable to follow through with self-control. Some are defensive and project the blame on others.

Not all neurotic children act out: some "act in" and consequently demonstrate a very low self concept and continually feel they are a failure regardless of contrary evidence. They do not grow secure on praise and support. There is a despair and lack of hope with withdrawal and depression.

Jane was like this—never a problem in school except that she was distracted, day-dreamy, and a loner with no friends. She was lost in the junior high. There was seldom even a rare smile on her sad face. She usually did not know the answers when called on but managed to pass her courses. Her teachers said "she really isn't here. She is in a shell." The truth was, as an unwanted child she had been tolerated but unloved by her parents and she was given the role of family scapegoat. The older siblings joined in on "poor Mary," whose failures were contrasted with their successes. Left alone much of the time as a baby, neglected as a child, and now treated as a failure going into adolescence, she was depressed and unhappy, feeling worthless. It was no longer a simple reactive condition. She had incorporated a self image which went with her all the time. Her self-esteem was very low. She projected her own inner reality and expected to be neglected and rejected. And, in keeping with her own self-fulfilling prophesy, most of the time she was.

William was a wild one—starting with kindergarten and still as a junior high pupil. He was excluded more times than the record shows. The parents used severe punishment techniques but nothing helped. After a blowup he calmed down, apologized, and was okay for a while. He brought things for his teacher and his peers and loved sports where he was a sometime leader. There was no question that he was a warm youngster. After a blowup, he finally told his teacher it was becasue of his red hair and temper. He thinks he is adopted because they don't care about him. He wants to grow up to be a teacher and help people but he thinks he is too dumb. He began to make some progress near the end of the school year to only begin his disruptions all over again. The kids were frightened when he threw things and swore or fought. In junior high his reputation is of a troublemaker. As one examines the self concept, it is anything but a satisfied, integrated early adolescent.

The neurotic child may combine some of the acting out with the acting in. We speak of passive-aggressive alternations. But basic is internal conflict and anxiety which underlies the symptomatic behavior a teacher sees.

VALUE DEFICIENCY DEVIATIONS

The society is producing and increasing a number of inadequately socialized individuals. The essential problem is not caring for the rights of others and emphasizing ones own impulsive demands. The attitude is "do your own thing regardless." They are not conflicted, not guilty, and not anxious internally—only anxious about being caught or stopped. Often they are defiant and sometimes even good con artists. They know how to get material things rather than develop human relationships where they are superficial in giving as well as utilizing human concern. The social codes we try to live by are not incorporated, the main problem being an amoral self concept. Fortunately, there are not many complete psychopaths with no caring or empathy at all. We do read, too often, of even preadolescents who murder without any feeling of guilt. They seem to be attuned to the excitement of the event. But there are more and more sociopathic persons in society; some take what they want whenever they think they can get away with it. Lying comes easy and many adults cannot deal with an easy "liar to your face." Since they operate from a lack of values system, they cannot lose. What they do not like to do they avoid if at all possible. After all, life is to be enjoyed; pleading or trying to activate guilt which does not exist are useless. Their loyalties are very limited and transitory. While it is not their fault, we have learned that one needs to understand their nature to be able to help them. Rather than become angry, we must appraise their symptoms for what they represent and respond with a consistent, honest thoroughness that makes it unprofitable for them when they do not conform. However, demands must be reasonable and balanced with significant gratifications.

There are several special problems related to the behavioral cues in this pathology. A complete absence of any social values is probably very rare, fortuantely. When this happens the condition of primary narcissism exists when only the self counts. Everything leads to personal gratification regardless of the effect on others. The self is an octopus taking in all that is possible. In the place of the satisfactions of relationships are the pleasures in things and excitement, daring, and taking chances and demonstrating one's superiority. Some delinquency is of this nature but all pathologies can produce delinquent behavior. They really cannot appreciate how another person feels, or if they do, they do not care. There are subcultures where a pupil can be "socialized" to believe certain taking advantage of others is the real way life is. Others are semisocialized and have deep concern for their family or ethnic group but not for outsiders. Other "look alikes" are children who pretend they do not care when they do at some level. They can mislead us to believe there is no empathy until we recognize indirect signs of guilt along with the defensive behavior. It has been pointed out how fear or anger can make us act indifferently. If a person feels maligned, then looting becomes legitimate but does not mean you have no social values. In war, the mechanism of making the enemy "gooks" or subhumans is one way we submerge their humanity; afterwards we often show signs of contriteness to atone for what we have done.

If there is any one area of self-development that we must learn to understand better it is the development of the social, human characteristics. We must study the capacity for love, caring, empathy, and submergence of superficial values for more fundamental ones. It is what society is all about and the challenge of our time.

PSYCHOTIC AND AUTISTIC PATTERNS

These are the most severe socioemotional disturbances. Time was when a regular or even special public school teacher of the disturbed never saw a psychotic youngster. With mainstreaming (having special education children stay in the regular class) this has been changed, although the dire problem of these youngsters require special, early, and parent-related life programming. The term psychotic is so foreboding that it should not be used. Also, since again the specific nature and promise of the individual child is the important thing, we should talk, instead, of children with profound problems. They are frequently limited in final prognosis but each has the potential to learn much more than was previously recognized. Some are able to function within the normal range.

Also, because these children's observed behavior in and of itself does not reveal the why, there are cases of pseudo-psychosis. Their behavior looks like a manifestation of psychosis, but may be imitative or the product of a different genesis.

The evidence of psychosis is tenuous to define but the deviant behavior is bound to be observed. Only after exhaustive study can the seriousness be ascertained because there are pseudo-psychotic and bizarre behaving children who do not have the essential personality pattern.

Basically the disturbance pervades all of the self, or even prevents the development of an intact self. Some children have a history of severe deviance from birth or at least from three years and on. They are called autistic if they do not relate to adults or peers, have no or very limited language, cannot function in a reasonable environment, do not communicate, and are presumed to lack any sense of identity. Achievement is arrested or nonexistent and simple tasks are not learned without intensive systematic effort. They are usually given a certain repetitive, unusual behavior; preoccupation with a gadget; fearfulness; gestures; unusual gait; etc. Some are hyperactive and destructive. Their developmental lag is so severe that they are usually excluded from school or placed in a special day school design. Often poor handling produces fearful and tearful responses added to what is believed to be the biological condition. They do not attend to the caretakers unless made to and thus are very hard to teach.

There are other children who do not start out different, but have a gradual remission of growth or a precipitous break in their progress. (The severely depressed and schizophrenic categories are the labels often attached.) The self-identity becomes confused; withdrawal is characteristic; severe phobic and paranoid reactions may appear. Preoccupation with a given object may dominate behavior. Outer reality is converted to fit the inner state. There is often a great deal of fear and uncertainty, reasking of the same questions. Fantasy may become the basis for a presumed real self.

All people compensate and have methods of coping for pressures and feelings, real or contrived. But, as we assess the symptoms and try to fit them together, we can use our own life experience to appreciate the meaning of the pupil's behavior. It is important to remember that the teacher is the only trained professional who is in a position to watch over the development of all children with a keen sensitivity for important symptoms of deviation.

SUMMARY

We emphasize that one cannot reduce any human being to a category or type. We cannot even do justice in a set of statements, a precis or even a case study. To imply doing so is to dehumanize. As a teacher knows, the nuances are always there and the individuality stands out in bold relief. The patterns are the gestalt or integrating factor that makes for basic understanding and planning ability but a teacher finds that the specifics of giving help are often surprising and experimental. The teacher is still a professional making many moment by moment clinical judgments to expedite the understandings of the student.

Disturbed and disturbing children should not be thought of as a class by themselves.. They are human beings with problems and handicaps. Often the socioemotional state is a fellow traveler with other special education conditions—the learning disability or retarded for example. Because we all share the human experience, the symptoms are not foreign to our own "normal" experience. Who has *not* had a period of depression, or been angry, or had a temporary lapse of values? Escaped into our own world for a while? The difference is that we do not live with this as our chronic self state.

REFERENCES

Bronfenbrenner, U. *Two worlds of childhood*. New York: Russell Sage Foundation, 1970.

Erickson, E. H. *Childhood and society*. (Rev. ed.) New York: Norton, 1964.

Felher, D. W. *Building positive self concepts*. Minneapolis: Burgess Publishing, 1974.

Kohlberg, L., LaCrosse, J., & Ricks, D. The predictability of adult mental health from childhood behavior. In B. B. Wolman (Ed.), *Manual on child psychopathology*. New York: McGraw-Hill, 1972.

Long, N. J., Morse, W. C., & Newman, R. G. *Conflict in the classroom*. (3rd ed.) Belmont, Ca.: Wadsworth, 1976.

Wickman, E. K. *Children's behavior and teachers' attitudes*. New York: Commonwealth Fund, 1928.

SUGGESTED READINGS

French, A. P. *Disturbed children and their families*. New York: Human Sciences Press, 1977.

Friedman, R. *Family roots of school learning and behavior disorders*. Springfield, Ill.: Charles C Thomas, 1973.

Hobbs, N. (Ed.) *Issues in the classification of children* (Vols. 1 and 2). San Francisco: Jossey-Bass, 1975.

Johnson, O. G. *Tests and measurements in child development*. Handbook II: Vol. 1 and 2. San Francisco: Jossey-Bass, 1976.

Kessler, J. W. *Psychopathology of childhood*. Englewood Cliffs, N.J.: Prentice-Hall, 1966.

Newman, R. *Groups in schools*. New York: Simon & Schuster, 1974.

Rutter, M. *Helping troubled children*. New York: Plenum Press, 1975.

Rhodes, W. C. & Tracy, M. L. *A study of child variance* (Vols. 1 and 2). Ann Arbor, Mich.: University of Michigan Press, 1972–75.

Walker, D. K. *Socioemotional measures for preschool and kindergarten children*. San Francisco: Jossey-Bass, 1973.

Wing, L. *Autistic children: A guide for parents and professionals*. New York: Brunner/Mazel, 1972.

David A. Sabatino

15
The Seriously Handicapped

Throughout the history of the education of the handicapped, two phenomena are clearly evident. There has been very little concentrated effort directed at measuring behaviors, traits, or characteristics of the seriously handicapped. Generally speaking, the seriously handicapped have been regarded as untestable. Second, until quite recently, there was a prominent view maintained that since "they" were untestable, "they were," therefore, untreatable. Concerted efforts by public school officials to concentrate on program development for severely handicapped are now just occurring. There are at least three reasons for the educational neglect of the seriously handicapped.

First, this group was generally not viewed as capable of profiting from public education (Sontag, 1976). Those that held this stance usually included the seriously mentally retarded (severe and profound), those individuals multiply handicapped by primary and concomitant sensory, physical, and mental disability, or those persons with serious emotional disturbance.

The National Center for Educational Statistics (1976) estimates the number of severely handicapped children and youth in the United States to be about 1.5 million. Of these, 460,000 are severely or profoundly retarded, 41,000 severely multiply handicapped, and approximately 900,000 are seriously emotionally disturbed. The magnitude of the educational needs of this population and the zero-reject concept (the belief that all handicapped chidlren should be provided full educational opportunities in the public schools) will necessitate a major revision in the traditional definition of what constitutes a program of education.

It has been believed that few seriously handicapped children or youth evidenced progress in even the most rudimental activities of daily living and were always dependent to some degree in relationships with another person in the functional performance required to maintain life. It was assumed that state or private agencies should offer maintenance programs designed to provide life-long care. It failed to dawn on those providing maintenance programs that they were denying children independence, and reinforcing dependence (Brown, Nietupski, & Hamre-Nietupski, 1976).

Second, the reader should be aware that a long-standing relationship exists between the degree of development of clinical observation and measurement devices used to operationalize a specific collegial definitions for a group of handicapped and the extent to which programs are also developed for that group of handicapped children. Table 15-1 representing the percentage of served and unserved handicapped by specific categorial groups in 1975–76, emphasizes that point.

For example, when diagnostic clarity in definition and the operational procedures defined in daily practice are well stabilized, there is general professional agreement and that group of handicapped will be receiving broad-scale services. As the table indicates, services are well-developed for the speech impaired, mentally retarded, crippled (orthopedic) and other health impaired, deaf, and visually handicapped. Obviously, when speech production interferes in communication, when a person's function of an operationally defined intelligence test places their performance in the mentally retarded range, or where obvious sensory-physical impairments, e.g., deafness, blindness, or orthopedic disabilities occur, a high degree of diagnostic stability results. Conversely, when definitions of handicapping conditions are played against the backdrop of a given cultural or subcultural value, as in the case of behavioral disorders, professional agreement is difficult to obtain. In practice, conditions that are more difficult to diagnose generate a related inability to produce programs, which in turn places additional requirements on the absence of diagnostic sophistication—a cycle most difficult to stop.

Finally, the multiply handicapped present a difficult assessment problem that has generated a serious professional preparation backlash. In the absence of required diagnostic sophistication, there has been little reason to prepare diagnosticians to work with almost any group of low-incidence handicapped. Levine (1974) surveyed 151 education facilities and 11 agencies to determine the utilization of psychological services for the deaf. The highest percentage of returns came from schools exclusively for the deaf—102 responded of the 134 listed in the 1971 American Annals Directory. Of the 102 who responded, 28 reported having no psychologist in their schools at the time of the survey. Of the 154 psychologists who

Table 15-1
Estimated Number of Handicapped Children Served and Unserved by Type of Handicap

	1975–76 Served	1975–76 Unserved	Total: Child Served and Unserved	Total: Percent Served	Total: Percent Unserved
Speech impaired	2,020,000	273,000	2,293,000	88	12
Mentally retarded	1,350,000	157,000	1,507,000	90	10
Learning disabilities	260,000	1,706,000	1,966,000	13	87
Emotionally disturbed	255,000	1,055,000	1,310,000	19	81
Crippled and other health impaired	255,000	73,000	328,000	78	22
Deaf	45,000	4,000	49,000	92	8
Hard of Hearing	66,000	262,000	328,000	20	80
Visually Handicapped	43,000	23,000	66,000	65	35
Deaf, blind, and other	(not readable)		40,000	40	60

responded, 28 percent reported on psychological testing experience prior to testing the deaf. Sixty-five percent reported no experience with deafness prior to their current work. Although 65 percent of the institutions surveyed were using sign language in combination with words, only 50 percent of the psychologists could use (or read back) sign language. Eighty-three percent of respondents report on-the-job learning as their only preparation for psychological work with the deaf. The 156 respondents listed five areas of difficulty in assessing the deaf. One of those was the difficulty in assessing the multiply handicapped.

The contents of this chapter will focus on two major unserved and, therefore, difficult to assess populations: the multiply handicapped and the seriously emotionally disturbed. Operationally, there are not many standardized measurement instruments or observational techniques developed for use with the multiply handicapped or emotionally disturbed. Therefore, until the 11 categories of handicaps were specified by PL 94-142 (1975), little attention was paid to those children with multiple handicaps or those seriously behaviorally disturbed. The chapters on sensory development specified the difficulties and recommended some of the procedures for ascertaining descriptively those handicaps related to vision and hearing. But, when vision, hearing, communication, and motoric problems exist in combination, it becomes extremely difficult to know if the person is receiving meaningful sensory information and how to measure the persons' response, particularly when both the manual motor and motor speech response modes are impaired. Two focal points will be described, one representative of multiple handicaps (cerebral palsied). The second serious handicapping condition to be reviewed frequently appears with concomitant disabilities, but it is devastating to person and family when it is the sole disability. The focal group for that discussion are children with serious behavior (emotional disturbance) disorders. The chapter will conclude wth brief descriptions of other difficult to assess subpopulations of handicapped and highlight a few of the available diagnostic procedures that can be used in the schools.

MULTIPLE HANDICAPPING CONDITIONS

The National Advisory Committee's 1973 Special Study Institute for Leadership Preparation for Educators of Crippled and Other Health Impaired Multiply Handicapped Populations, Task Force VI, provides a working definition of the multiply handicapped (Connor and Cohen, 1973).

> Crippled and other health impaired-multiply handicapped populations are composed of those individuals with physiological impairment and concomitant educationally related problems, requiring some modification of programs to meet their educational needs.
>
> These are developmental tasks ordinarily and commonly mastered in infancy, early childhood, adolescence, early adulthood, middle age, and later maturity. When the normal learning of these tasks is affected by a physical or health impairment or related disability, the individual regardless of age becomes part of (a multiply handicapped) population. . . . Limitations of physical dexterity, locomotion, and vitality produce a multiplicity of secondary functional deficits. Taken together, they in turn affect psychological as well as intellectual growth and performance. Lack of early social and educational experience and exposure, often accompanied by recurrent periods of hospitalization, combine to form possible perceptual and conceptual deficits. Personal rejection by peers, owing to the inability of the handicapped person to keep physical pace in the activities of daily living and also because of certain "embarrassing" physical problems associated with their condition, such as drooling or disfigurement, or the need for special prophylactic equipment, like catheters, affect social adjustment as well as self-acceptance.

The Committee (Task Force II, p. 38) felt that multiple handicapped children and adults function at the full range of levels. They described four levels.

> 1. At a mainstream level, handicapped persons, with opportunity for support and monitoring by trained COHI-MH specialists, nurses, and other personnel, are capable of responding to either usual or modified methods and materials;
> 2. At a second level, the population can function in educational or vocationally oriented settings if provision is made for alternate strategies and periodic reevaluation;

3. At a third level, it is necessary to vary not only the teaching strategies but also the content and focus of the educational program;
4. There is also a fourth level at which the population needs opportunities for the development of alternate strategies and a curriculum for the acquisition of knowledge and skills directed toward self-help, survival, and self-enhancement.

Rubella is an example of a disease that presents a multiple sequelae with the child. The frequent occurrence of deafness as a sequel of maternal rubella in pregnancy has been well documented (Sheridan, 1964). Following the 1963–64 rubella epidemic in the eastern section of the United States, Hardy, Monif, & Sever (1967) found indications of severe hearing loss in 10 of 17 infants whose mothers had contracted the disease during pregnancy. Interestingly, these investigators noted that although the auditory defects were most frequent among those children whose mothers had contracted rubella in the first trimester of pregnancy, they also occurred in infants whose mothers suffered rubella as late as the fourth month of pregnancy. Bordley, Hardy, & Hardy (1962) found that 31 of 49 subjects from the 1963–64 epidemic failed a preliminary auditory screening test and 24 of these failed a hearing retest.

In addition to the hearing impairment, a general retardation in the physical development of rubella-affected children has been observed. Barr, Anderson, & Wedenberg (1973) reported that in comparing rubella children with other deaf children, the rubella groups showed arrested development that could not be attributed to their hearing losses. Lundstrom (1952) in a follow-up study of Swedish rubella children, showed that first-trimester rubella children were shorter and weighed less than did control group children and that this underdevelopment continued to be more evident at three years of age. Desmond & Rudolph (1970) noted that 81 percent had a head circumference below the third percentile, and 66 percent had a length and body weight below the third percentile at 18 months of age.

In considering the intellectual capacities of rubella children, Vernon (1969) comments that a low intelligence quotient is characteristic of rubella children. Myklebust (1958), in a study of deaf multiply handicapped children noted substantially reduced performance on the Hiskey Test. Miller (1967, p. 89) concludes that "there is little doubt that among rubella children of the 1963–64 epidemic a substantial portion may have severe brain damage and mental retardation." Lawson & Myklebust (1970) found the incidence of eye defects was twice that for hearing impaired as normal hearing subjects. Hartung (1970) found that deaf children do not retain visual perceptual imagery nearly as well as normal children under short-term memory conditions.

It is obvious that the number of multiply handicapped children is raising in the general population (Douglas and Henderson, 1961). The reasons are many, but a major one is that advanced medical practices are now saving lives. Although many infants now live through the catastrophic events of the perinatal stage, the prevalence of severe multiple handicaps among them has increased. One example is the premature infant. As the birth weight of the premature child decreases, the probability of multiple handicaps rises sharply. This is particularly true of the more disabling conditions—mental retardation, cerebral palsy, and behavioral disorders from brain injury. In the period from 1933 to 1955 alone, the mortality rate was reduced 55 percent (Hardy & Pauls, 1959).

The full significance of prematurity and its possible ramifications are illustrated by the fact that the condition takes a higher toll on infant life than any other single factor. It also ranks as one of the leading causes of death among the general population, accounting for 10 percent of the total mortality (Knoblock, Rider, Harper, & Pasamanick, 1956). A condition of this type and of this pathological magnitude, often involving the central nervous system, could logically be expected to result in multiple sensory motor disabilities.

Vernon (1969) studied 1,468 deaf or profoundly hard-of-hearing children. He found the deaf and hard-of-hearing premature infant to have lower intelligence, obtain poorer school achievement, and have a number of multiple handicapping conditions, many of them associated with central nervous system pathologies. The most striking finding here is that slightly over two-thirds of premature deaf children are multiply handicapped. The disabilities other than deafness include cerebral palsy, mental retardation, aphasia, visual pathology, and emotional disturbance. Thirty-three percent have one disability other than hearing loss, 27 percent have two additional handicaps, and 7.9 percent have three disabilities in addition to deafness. The syndromes most frequently found were aphasia with emotional disturbance and aphasia with cerebral palsy. In cases where four or more major handicaps were present (7.9 percent) cerebral palsy and/or mental retardation were almost always involved.

Most cases of severe multiple handicaps have a common etiology (Vernon, 1969). Brain damage, or trauma to the central nervous system, tends to produce multiple pathologies, which manifest themselves by impairing the sensory receiving, motoric response, and neural organizational capability of the person (Holt, 1965). When certain areas of the brain receive damage, they may confuse the ability to receive and express meaningful language, associate the meaning of words and concepts, or use symbols in reading, writing, and numerical relationships. The language function may remain intact, and damage can occur to the motor speech production, or to the use of the extremities, which is particularly evident in manual motor control. In Chapter 13, an intense review of diagnostic procedures with the severe and profoundly mentally retarded was provided, and a general discussion of cerebral palsy was also reviewed in Chapter 2. The reader may wish to review these chapters and the two chapters on sensory handicaps (Chaps. 11 and 12).

For our purposes, let us examine cerebral palsy in light of its potential multiply handicapping effects. The two fundamental processes which are critical in any assessment procedure are: (1) the manner by which the learner processes incoming sensory, motor, and aurally received information, and (2) the degree to which responses are impaired by manual motor disability, involvement of the upper and lower extremities, or motor speech impairment.

In short, it is the examiner's responsibility to be aware of how much information and what type of information is being received by the client's central nervous system, and the limitations being imposed on responses by disabling conditions.

Illingworth (1958) reported that 50 percent of the children with cerebral palsy have one or more visual sensory problems. Subsequent work by Holt (1964) indicated that 40 to 45 percent of the visual problems reported were strabismus, 10 to 13 percent were nystagmus, 7 to 10 percent optic atrophy, and 6 percent were defects of the retina and choroid. To summarize these two reports, about 17 percent of the cerebral palsied children had mildly impaired vision, while 13 to 15 percent had moderate visual problems or were totally blind.

As is the case of visual sensory function, visual perceptual development is also a very common manifestation of the cerebral palsied child. The tests commonly administered are the *Bender Visual Motor Gestalt Test* (Koppitz, 1969), the *Developmental Test of Visual Perception* (Frostig, Lefever, & Whittlesey, 1961), the *Visual Retention Test* (Benton, 1955), the *Visual Design Test* (Wood and Shulman, 1940), and the *Draw-A-Person Test* (Harris, 1963). It is rare to see a diagnostician note the variance in functional performance on visual perceptual tests resulting from the perceptual as opposed to the motoric response. Equally true, there are few studies available that report on the specific type of perceptual problem, be it discriminatory or memory. The more common report indicates those significances between the cerebral palsy population and non-cerebral palsy groups on some assumed characteristic or trait (Cruickshank, 1953). There is, of course, always the interesting relationship between brain damage and behaviors such as hyperactivity, hypoactivity, catastrophic reaction (an emotional outbreak for no known reason) and arousal and attention patterns which contribute greatly to the differences of establishing and mastering attention. It is always assumed these phenomena are not only related (Denhoff, 1967) but driven by that common causative factor—*brain damage*.

Hearing and perceptual interpretation of sound are much more difficult to ascertain than visual sensory and visual perceptual function. Generally speaking, most cerebral palsied children, or other children with severe or profound mental retardation, have a great deal of difficulty focusing on and discriminating sound. While most sources describing hearing impairment among brain damaged populations agree, the incidence of handicaps is much higher than for normal children, they disagree on the exact incidence.

Fisch (1957) and Mowatt (1961) report that as many as one in four or roughly 25 percent of the known cerebral palsy population do have audiometrically measured hearing loss. There is not any conclusive evidence to suggest the incidence or type of auditory perceptual impairment. The reason is the difficulty in distinguishing sensory hearing impairment, and especially deafness, from severe perceptual disorders such as agnosia, or the subtle receptive language disorders, which are all symptomatic of disinterest in meaningful sound and an inability to understand meaningful language symbols (agnosia). The necessity for painstaking differential diagnosis (Myklebust, 1957), to rule out what is or is not a contribution to a handicapping condition is a dilemma requiring the services of at least an audiologist, language specialist, and psychologist.

The distinction between sensory hearing, perception, and language becomes even more critical when examining speech and language production. Irwin (1972) has made intensive studies of the speech difficulties experienced by cerebral palsied children. The incidence of speech (articulation error) difficulties ranges from 50 to 85 percent (Cruickshank & Raus, 1955) in cerebral palsied populations. Irwin (1972) worked with seven important special production variables: articulation, sound discrimination, abstraction, vocabulary, sentence structure, syntax, and manifest anxiety. The relationship between articulation and sound discrimination was 0.21 (the coefficient of determination, $r^2 = .04$). That means the coefficient of nondetermination is 0.96 or that there is an absence of relationship in the amount of 96 percent. It can be assumed, therefore, that many cerebral palsied children have speech (articulation deficits) which are motor related and not perceptually related to the high incidence of sound discrimination problems. That finding should wave the red flag for the examiner. It strongly suggests that motor output or response measures may cause a great deal of the speech error seen in this population. What, then, of the manual motor response for those whose visual perception is disturbed? The point is that most tests measure several characteristics and therefore are not free of traits. The examiner's difficulty in accounting for functionally impaired traits as being described by a test is an intensely difficult one when more than one disability exists.

Most experienced examiners agree that there are two pronounced difficulties in assessing multiply handicapped children. The first is working around the combined response deficits caused by manual-motor and motor speech problems. If children's ability to communicate what they are asked or shown is interfered, and their manual motor or motor speech ability to show what they recognize as distinctions is impaired, how does the examiner ascertain what the child knows?

The second problem is that of detecting unsuspected disability-producing conditions. One example is regular or irregular *petit mal* seizure patterns that interfere with stimulus input. To the experienced examiner, there is always the fear that the child is not receiving information during assessment or in the classroom because of subtle seizure activity. All seizures are not earmarked by convulsive disorders. Hopkins, Bice, & Colton (1954) reported that the percent of children with seizures from a population of 1,265 was 29.2 percent. Perlstein & Barnett (1952) found in 1,000 cerebral palsied persons that 50 percent of all spastic cases and 15 percent of all athetoid cases had convulsive disorders while Denhoff & Robinault (1960) note that when 50 randomly sampled cerebral palsied children were studied, 30 had clinical seizures, while 18 others had convulsive tendencies. Differential diagnosis must be made between non-seizure related aberrant behaviors, emotionally related disturbances, and nonconvulsive seizural symptoms.

The problem increases when the diagnostician recognizes that 35 to 60 percent of cerebral palsied populations who have seizures are on some type of medical (pharmacological) control. While they may not be having active seizures, they may well withdraw, become sleepy, show sleep disturbances, become irritable, complain of headaches, show some tremor activities, or epigastric distress. A drug may merely mask the convulsive disorder, or produce behaviors which may be in reaction to the drug.

Reynell (1973) describes those factors involved in different types of physical handicaps. From the data presented in Table 15-2, it can be seen that under *Extent of Handicap* for cerebral palsies and spina bifida that chances for multiple handicaps is extremely high. On the other hand, there are several purely motor problems that do not generate concomitant handicaps.

Educationally, the four specific concerns that should become focal elements in the assessment of the serious handicapped are: (1) the degree of sensory or motor disability and extent to which it interferes with information processing; (2) the capability of organizing meaningful perceptual information, filtering unwanted perceived data, and integrating it into meaningful units for transmission in the nervous system; (3) the receptive, associational (concept formation abilities) and expressive language (free from motor speech); and (4) the capability of the nervous system to achieve self-arousal, focus attention, and avoid catastrophic reaction, suggesting emotional liability. Obviously, distractability, hyper- and

Table 15-2
Factors Involved in Different Types of Physical Handicap

Handicap	Brain Involvement	Type	Unimpaired Learning Experience	Intellectual Learning Disorder	Extent of Handicap
Cerebral palsies	Yes	Congenital	Usually none	Primary	Multiple
Spina bifida with associated hydrocephalus	Yes	Congenital	Usually none	Primary	Multiple
Limb deficiency	No	Congenital	Usually none	None or secondary	Usually confined to physical disability
Poliomyelitis	No	Acquired	Usually some, often much	None or secondary	Usually confined to physical disability
Muscular dystrophy	No	Acquired	Usually some, often much	None or secondary	Usually confined to physical disability

From Reynell, in Mittler (Ed.), The psychological assessment of mental and physical handicaps, 1973, p. 444.

hypoactivity, untriggered emotional outbreaks, all disrupt peer-adult and self-relationship. The most difficult assessment task is to describe those learner characteristics meaningful to management of the child suspected of brain injury, who displays multiple handicaps in the presence of a serious primary disability.

SERIOUS EMOTIONAL DISTURBANCE (OR BEHAVIORAL DISORDERS)

Serious emotional disturbance carries with it all of the relative social value relatedness characterizing behavioral disorders. But, in addition, it can be distinguished through Quay & Werry's (1972) organization of the four major behavioral disorder diagnostic classifications in children and by the fact that the behavior is driven by nondirected, disoriented inner-feelings. Quay & Werry (1972) defined personality disorders (serious emotional disturbance) as: social withdrawal, hypersensitivity, and heightened anxiety. In contrast to conduct disorders, immature personality development, and socialized delinquency, the behaviors of serious emotional disturbance are less socially aggressive, rarely directed at a specific agency or person, and less under the control of the person. Generally, the intelligence or capability for school achievement and selected peer adjustment are not major factors for children with mild emotional instability (Gravick, 1955; Rutter, 1964).

Rhodes & Tracy (1974) describe psychotic children as a very small group so severely disturbed that they fail to judge reality, live in a fantasy world, and do not relate well to other people. There is a maturational lag in motor, intellectual, and social functioning. Deep underlying anxiety is pervasive. Interests are narrowed and often repetitive. Identity is confused or lacking. Language is almost always affected. Behavior ranges from self-destructive, screaming, and temper tantrum responses to passive haunted isolation (Stoecher, 1972; Wing, 1972). There are also children where the diagnostic condition is never certain, and the possibility always exists of severe retardation, brain injury, and autism, even in various combinations. In short, disruptiveness that can be described in terms of a mix of inappropriate behaviors against a structure of normal affect is a rough description of mild emotional disturbance, character disorder, and behavioral disorders, in general. When the emotional structure or inner feelings of the child or youth are not integrated or form a recognizable emotional substructure, a serious emotional disorder may exist. Historically, childhood schizophrenia was considered a form of psychopathology related to autism. In the mid-1940s, the two (autism and childhood schizophrenia) were distinguished. Based on Goldfarb's (1944) work, childhood schizophrenia was considered to be a regression in the overall state of development achieved by the child or youth in terms of an emotional level obtained and then lost. Childhood autism as described by Kanner (1949) is a condition associated with limited affect, characterized by children who have never gained an advanced behavioral state, and are, in fact, "different" from the time of birth. Kanner (1954) reports five identifying factors of autism. They are:

1. The parents were never comfortable with other people.
2. Their marriage and family life was cold and formal.
3. The mother showed little affection toward the child.
4. Fathers were not emotionally involved with the children.
5. Rules were provided the child mechanically.

Rimland (1964), after a careful review of the autistic literature, noted that the population was mostly males, who were first born or only children. Vaillant (1962) reports that cases of infantile autism have been reported since 1809. Kanner is credited with establishing the condition in 1943. Keeler (1958) specified the following characteristics from a review of the literature:

1. Children were beautiful, healthy, and precocious, if not extremely alert.
2. Normal development occurred for the first few months.
3. About the fourth month, the child failed to make the usual visual anticipatory movements.
4. Head-banging rocking, and general apathy for surroundings also begins about that time.
5. Repetitive, ritualistic play, with obsessive interest in specified toys begins.
6. Unusual language behavior, with "I" or "yes," is usually absent from the child's speech with only about one-half of all autistic children able to express motor speech until the sixth or seventh year. Speech is characterized as a literal use of language, dependent upon metamorphosis, with a part-whole confusion, and delayed echolalia.

Obviously, there has been much controversy over the true etiology of autism. Kanner (1954) advanced a belief in "emotional starvation." Rimland suggested the possibility of brain damage to the subcortical (mid-brain stem) areas of the central nervous system.

Schain & Yannet (1960) specify that the diagnostic criteria of autism must include evidence of:

1. severe personality disorders with extreme self-preoccupation,
2. the onset must occur before two years, and
3. overall, the motor development is generally intently well-developed, while the language development is generally intently delayed.

The controversy, which resulted among authorities over the etiologies and diagnostic characteristics, has been confusing at best, providing the practitioner with little more than clinical insights or intuition, not hard symptoms, through which to sort. To bring the problem into the 1970s, an interpretation of serious emotionally disturbed has been provided by federal regulations (Federal Register, August 22, 1977), a part of the 11 groups of handicapped children served by PL 94-142.

> (8) "Seriously emotionally disturbed" is defined as follows:
>
> (i) The term means a condition exhibiting one or more of the following characteristics over a long period of time and to a marked degree, which adversely affects educational performance:
>
> (A) An inability to learn which cannot be explained by intellectual, sensory, or health factors;

(B) An inability to build or maintain satisfactory interpersonal relationships with peers and teachers;

(C) Inappropriate types of behavior or feelings under normal circumstances;

(D) A general pervasive mood of unhappiness or depression; or

(E) A tendency to develop physical symptoms or fears associated with personal or school problems.

(ii) The term includes children who are schizophrenic or autistic. The term does not include children who are socially maladjusted, unless it is determined that they are seriously emotionally disturbed.

Diagnostically, this definition is yet incomplete. Perhaps Morse's (1974, pp. 126–140) outline of seven common myths surrounding the diagnosis of the seriously emotionally disturbed will provide a useful discussion.

1. *The myth that the diagnostic dilemma is simply a semantic one.* The theoretical differences would still be with us, and are more basic than semantics. Diagnosis cannot take place apart from a theoretical base, acknowledge, or implied.
2. *The myth that "diagnosis" is accomplished by a given set of instruments and techniques* administered by the diagnostician's guild. Part of this myth is that diagnosis is a sacred rite and the information can be understood only by the high priests of mental health. What is necessary in a diagnostic study is what is needed to help a youngster. There are times when we already know enough to make decisions and the simple difficulty of doing it is holding us up, yet a battery of tests is often given anyway.
3. *The myth that naming, labeling, or cataloging is diagnosis.* The issue is *differential diagnosis,* which is the sorting out of specific behaviors, and it has meaning in a more complete sense. For example, if one finds that a child is aggressive, the questions are: aggressive to what targets, under what conditions, and with what frequency? Certain "organic" children are high on impulse and low on control and are called aggressive. A boy may be aggressive in modeling after a male image as some boys do in relationship to their fathers. Some children feel very anxious and guilty about their aggression and others not at all. The point here is that aggressive behavior is a symptom needing further exploration, and does not signify a diagnostic syndrome merely constituting one symptom.
4. *The myth that history or etiology stipulates the pattern or form deviation may take.* The search for one-to-one relationships between given life experience and a consequent behavior is supported by two false premises: first that we can determine the psychological forces which

cause a behavior, and second, that all youngsters will react with the same behavior to identical forces or environments.

5. *The myth that symptoms by themselves signify a given intervention.* There is often a desire to short circuit understanding and apply a remedy based upon an isolated symptom. Another common practice, is to apply one style of remediation irregardless of the condition.
6. *The Janus myth that deviation is either in the child or in the setting.* Behavior is always interactive and even the most deeply rooted behavior is mitigated or increased by external conditions.
7. *The myth that socioemotional deviance is a thing apart from normal experience rather than part of an emotional continuum.* Anxiety, hostility, sexual arousal, alienation, depression, and periods of nonfeeling, autisticlike fugues and times of intense preoccupation are but a few human conditions occurring in all of us.

As we pursue assessment of the severely emotionally disturbed, it is well to remember: "As we develop our diagnostic schema we must be certain that these myths are not made a part of the processes" (Morse, 1974, p. 141).

To counteract these myths, Morse (1974, pp. 140–144) provides nine criteria for a viable diagnostic process.

1. The central purpose of the diagnostic process is to provide understanding of the child's current condition.
2. The goal of diagnosis is to discover what interventions are indicated.
3. Etiological conditions may be studied, but only if they contribute to understanding the present condition.
4. An area of diagnosis that must be considered is the value structure of the youth and feelings he maintains about those values.
5. Screening should be an essential first step in the diagnostic process, permitting a group of students to be viewed against the class and school setting.
6. Differential diagnosis should not become an end in itself, but conducted to insure that the intervention is based upon the best understanding of the "self" possible.
7. In the interest of humanistic concern for the youngster, every effort should be made to collate pertinent information from all spheres of the individual's being, his physical-neurological, physical-perceptual and his reactive-behavioral.
8. Labels and categories have little common meaning to those working with the socioemotionally disturbed children in the educational setting.

9. A profile or a listing alone is not a proper diagnosis; a diagnosis provides a pattern of the self unique to that person.

Morse has put the nine criteria into place with an *Open Process for Diagnosing Socio-emotional Impairment in the Educational Setting.*

The schematic outline for diagnosis is presented in Table 15-3. The basic diagnostic study concentrates on four basic concerns: (1) the status of the self, (2) biological conditions, (3) social relationships, and (4) academic achievement in the school environment. Attention in each area is centered around the current state of the youth's affect, the case history can help elucidate the present condition to some degree. But the purpose of the diagnosis is to prepare output treatment measures reflecting the person's current status.

In some instances, the chart serves as a profile, illuminating the dimensions to be examined. This is particularly true of the self-status material where a dimension from high to low self-esteem is predicated. A summary of the findings can be considered on a profile basis. For example, high self-esteem in a psychopathic configuration does not have the same significance as high self-esteem in a child with a mild anxiety situation. A profile nonetheless escapes the deadend of categorical classification. In the final analysis, the examiner working with the seriously handicapped must provide a schema of personological characteristics capable of generating interventions. There has been a diagnostic propensity to draw heavily on interpersonal comparisons, which are simply interesting but rarely helpful for program planning. Profiles do emphasize intrapersonal comparisons. A series of "principles" for assessing the seriously handicapped are necessary to safeguard the reliability/validity, if not usability, of a profile. Table 15-4 provides ten principles for determining characteristics of learning for the seriously handicapped.

In short, the one rule of assessment applicable to all evaluation is that the data collected and manner in which it is reported is only as good as the examiner. The general rule in assessing the seriously handicapped is that there simply is not a statistical basis that can consider the range and complexity of disabilities influencing the response. But, in Meehl's (1954) classical book, *Clinical versus Statistical Prediction,* the clinical process was not more accurate than the statistical and as the complexities of human disability increased, so did the problems in actual decision making. Professional judgment is required, and in the words of Meehl, it is frequently necessary to ". . . use our heads instead of a formula." There simply is not any formula available for assessing the seriously handicapped, and there is no substitute for deriving a educational and behavioral management plan short of a team assessment. The minimum membership of such a team is a special educator with diagnostic skills,

Table 15-3
A Paradigm for Open System of Diagnosis

Areas of Concern	Assessment of Current Condition (see Table 15-2)	Relevant Etiological Factors	Goals Long/Short Term	Intervention Processes Tried Proposed	Evaluation Long/Short Term
A. Self status Self concept Self-esteem Emotional state Values—character Empathic potential Reality testing B. Biological Aspects Growth patterns Traumas Neurological conditions Nature and impact of special disabilities C. Social Relationship Peer Group role Authority Family role D. Academic Attitudes toward school, learning, etc. Cognitive processes Achievement	Specific behavior in these areas with which the teacher, school, home, etc, must cope.	Selective historical information that illuminates and clarifies the current state: developmental age norms, life stress, disabilities, early experiences, relation of growth to, etc.	Immediate and long-term goals for school and elsewhere in child's life.	What has already been tried? How well did it work? Why? What new psychological approaches are needed? Who will be responsible? Specifically what will be done?	Regular reevaluation of status related to long and short term goals.

Table 15-4
Ten Principles for Ascertaining Learner Characteristics with the Seriously Handicapped

1. All diagnosis depends upon a:
   a. common specific etiology
   b. common set of observable signs and symptoms
   c. known cause
   d. known outcome that, through specific interventions, can be altered (Clarizio & McCoy, 1976).
2. The examiner must be aware of the inhibition or blockage of stimuli received by the handicapped child, and the effect the disability has on the response. The general principle is particularly true in measuring the receptive and expressive language of children and youth who have difficulty in meaningful sounds (speech stimuli) and in communicating verbally.
3. Rarely will one assessment session be sufficient with the multiply or seriously handicapped. Usually, the examiner will need to build a relationship, reduce the anxiety of the child or youth in a strange environment, and initiate a rigorous systematic effort of determining how the child or youth processes information utilizing a systematic assessment procedure (see Chap. 6).
4. Test scores with young, brain-damaged, and emotionally disturbed children tend to show extreme unreliability. Formal test results should be viewed as temporal, at best, becoming outdated quickly. Test scores should be viewed as the extreme lower limit of the function which the child is capable (Smith, 1969).
5. Children or youth who present the limited function associated with serious handicapping conditions should be seen by examiners experienced in braille or manual sign language, and who are capable of understanding unusual (eye motion or head motor) response mechanisms.
6. The examiner must report, to the limit possible, the degree of interference of specified disabilities. Far too frequently, children with motor speech deficits have been subjugated by a disability that was never considered a reason, or taken into consideration, for the low performance demonstrated.
7. Generally speaking, group and time tests should not be used with the seriously handicapped (Hiskey, 1955).
8. Components to be reviewed during the evaluation process are:
   a. A measure of intelligence
   b. an evaluation of personality structure
   c. a test for behavioral symptoms associated with brain damage
   d. a measure of educational achievement
   e. an appraisal of communication skills
   f. aptitude and interest testing
   g. case history data
   h. reports of a physical examination.
9. A common source of assessment bias centers around the individual characteristics of the examiner. Different examiners have differing expectations and experiences, and therefore, elicit different responses from the child, parent, and teacher (Stuart, 1970).

(continued on next page)

Table 15-4 (continued)

10. Another source of assessment bias centers around individual characteristics of the child. Because clinical judgment is an interpersonal process, it is only natural that characteristics of the child contribute to this outcome (Stuart, 1970). The child's attitude, comfort, and feeling of well-being are instrumental in the type of response elicited, especially with the more seriously handicapped.

speech and language therapist, audiologist, pediatric neurologist, a psychiatrist or psychologist sensitive to the schools, and occupational and physical therapist when needed.

DIFFERENTIAL DIAGNOSIS—TEAM ASSESSMENT

By 1960 the state of the diagnostic art has assumed a new focus. The history of assessment from Galton and then Binet had unintentionally but unequivocably established a model for child assessment. That model was one examiner face to face with one child or youth. That model used in the schools, but commonly referred to as the "clinical" model, gained a time-honored place in the training processes for new clinicians. Thus, it was advisedly taught as "the" process.

There are two additional modes by which the traditional clinical model of one adult with one child in a specified assessment setting (generally a small room, with a "don't disturb sign") should be viewed. First, the sterile clinical setting, may not be ideal for determining school-related behaviors. A child may perform differently in a neutral environment with an unfamiliar examiner. One of the major arenas for determining school-related assessment is the classroom. How that assessment is accomplished will vary widely, depending upon the age of the student, type of class, teacher's training, and attitudinal flexibility, but, more important, is the skill of the examiner.

One of the other agenda's accomplishments was a set of unstructured (naturalistic) observations taken outside the classroom demonstrating that the communication process with teachers is greatly aided. A classroom teacher can now become an active participant in the child study process, with the interpretive help of the examiner. The change in communication pattern which is so vital is that the "one foot in the door" hall conference followed two weeks later by a "written psychological report" may give way to active management to correct unwanted behaviors and implement instruction immediately, treating students as something more than names on waiting lists. Mittler's (1973) statement that "Even the best conducted test administered under ideal circumstances can be a waste of time and effort unless the findings are communicated in such a way that they can be understood and acted on by those who read the report'' is true. In Chapter six, we have recommended that a graphic profile replace the verbally written report. It must also be clearly understood that a school record is a public record, and therefore open to public scrutiny. Said another way, a teacher securing a report from an examiner is placed squarely in an interpretive setting of explaining what that report means, as implemented by an IEP. There are numerous studies which indicate that the communication process quickly falters, losing much and gaining much in translation, as information goes from one person to another.

Parents are now very important receivers as well as time-honored transmitters of information. Unfortunately, for years (they have only played a transmission of information role) they were essentially providers of the childs' history, which did not aid them in their work with children or youth. Now, it is simply the law that they receive information that is meaningful for a management plan that may be implemented at home. In short PL 94-142, actively involves the parents into the instructional and behavioral management process. They are no longer passive components of the diagnostic process, *parents are now members of the diagnostic team.*

That brings us to the second aspect: What is a Diagnostic Team? And, how can the change in diagnostic setting facilitate the team. Once again, neither requirements for team assessment nor the implications for where the team is to work, can be taken for granted. The mandatory federal law (PL94-142) requires that (1) all teachers in contact with the child be team members, regular and special education alike, and (2) that supportive services be provided by other professions as needed. The two principles that appear to be most confusing are: What constitutes support services and which members of the support team prepare IEPs. Support team members are not direct providers of instruction. They are generally: school psychologists, speech and language therapists, adaptive physical education staff, occupational therapists, audiologists, physical therapists, physicians, and the other professionals who would constitute either diagnostic or management procedures for the handicapped. The team focus must be one of generating instructional or behavioral management. The contributing team at staffing conferences will prepare supplemental or recommended IEPs. The teacher has the final judgment as to which IEPs constitute initial utilization and the sequential arrangement of those to follow. In short, the team may generate what should be considered in writing, the teacher will, by necessity, develop a balanced program of what will result for the child. All of the action and reaction is of course dependent upon the professional judgment of the teacher. Therefore, the interplay between teacher and team is critical from several standpoints.

First, that a common language exists, second that goals to be obtained be derived, and most advisedly, the teachers have continuing access to a formal review process with the team, which means the support staff serves the instructional staff on a quick call basis (same day notice).

An outstanding difference between team assessment and the old clinical model is that team assessment represents a multidisciplinary group collected to focus on a child, boiling down information collected across disciplines into interdisciplinary institutional and behavioral management plans appropriate to the school setting, which means those plans must be within the comfort level and skill level of the teacher. Team assessment means continuing staff development of one member with another. The captain of the team, if there need be one, is a neutral administrator in support of the teacher asking the questions related to the resources needed to bear on the problem in question, i.e., to find a solution. That solution is not an IEP completed to compliance, it is a workable management plan. One fact that must be recognized is that physicians, and in particular, school psychologists, are no longer the "main" team members, they are contributing members only. The teacher is the implementer in the educational setting, and therefore the central person, whose judgment must:

1. convey a willingness to learn from all disciplines;
2. include the ability to communicate to those in other disciplines;
3. represent a balance between what is reality in the educational setting, protecting and advocating the two extremes of overzealous team members, and those who have no confidence in either the system of education, or the process of instruction.

REFERENCES

Abeson, A. A continuing summary of pending and completed litigation regarding the education of handicapped children. *Council for Exceptional Children,* 1973, *6.*

Barr, B., Anderson, J., & Wedenberg, E. Epidermology of hearing loss in childhood. *Audiology,* 1973, *12,* 426–437.

Benton, A. L. *The revised visual retention test, clinical and experimental applications.* New York: The Psychological Corporation, 1955.

Bordley, J. E., Hardy, W. G., & Hardy, M. P. Pediatric audiology. *Pediatric Clinics of North America,* 1962, *9,* 1147–1158.

Brown, L., Nietupski, J., & Hamre-Nietupski, S. Criterion of ultimate function. In M. A. Thomas (Ed.), *Hey don't forget about me.* Reston, Va.: Council for Exceptional Children, 1976.

Clarizio, H. F. & McCoy, G. F. *Behavior disorders in children* (2nd ed.). New York: Thomas Y. Crowell, 1976.

Connor, F. P. & Cohen, M. *Leadership preparation.* New York: Teachers College Press, 1973.
Cruickshank, W. M. The multiply handicapped cerebral palsied child. *Exceptional Children,* 1953, *20,* 16–22.
Cruickshank, W. M. & Raus, G. M. (Eds.). *Cerebral Palsy, its individual and community problems.* Syracuse: Syracuse University Press, 1955.
Denhoff, E. *Cerebral palsy—the preschool years.* Springfield, Ill.: Charles C Thomas Publisher, 1967.
Denhoff, E. & Robinault, J. P. *Cerebral palsy and related disorders.* New York: McGraw-Hill, 1960.
Desmond, M. M. & Rudolph, A. The clinical evaluation of low birth-weight infants with regards to head trauma. In C. R. Angle and E. A. Berring (Eds.), *Physical trauma and an etiological-agent in mental retardation.* Bethesda, Md.: Hail Institute of Neurological Disease and Stroke, 1970.
Dolphin, J. E. & Cruickshank, W. M. Visual-motor perception in children with cerebral palsy. *The Quarterly Journal of Child Behavior,* 1953, *3,* 198–209.
Douglas, A. A. & Henderson, J. L. (Eds.). *Cerebral palsy in childhood and adolescence.* Edinburgh: E. & S. Livingston, 1961.
Federal Register, Public Law 94-142, 1977, *42*(163), 197.
Fisch, L. Hearing impairment and cerebral palsy. *Speech,* 1957, *21,* 43.
Frostig, M. Lefever, D. W., & Whittlesey, J. R. B. A developmental test of visual perception for evaluating normal and neurologically handicapped children. *Perceptual and Motor Skills,* 1961, *12,* 383–392.
Goldfarb, W. Effects of early institutional care on adolescent personality: Rorschach data. *American Journal of Orthopsychiatry,* 1944, *14,* 441–447.
Goodenough, F. L. *Measurement of intelligence by drawing.* New York: Harcourt Brace & World, 1926.
Gravick, S. Intellectual performance as related to emotional instability in children. *Journal of Abnormal and Social Psychology,* 1955, *51,* 653–656.
Hardy, J. H., Monif, G. R., & Sever, J. L. The lack of association between the appearance of complement fixing antibodies and the recovery of virus in a child with congenital rubella. *Pediatrics,* 1967, *39,* 289–290.
Hardy, W. G. & Pauls, M. D. Atypical children with communication disorders. *Children,* 1959, *6,* 13–16.
Harris, D. B. *Children's drawings as measures of intellectual maturity.* New York: Harcourt, Brace, & World, 1963.
Hartung, J. E. Visual perceptual skill, reading ability, and the young deaf child. *Exceptional Children,* 1970, *36,* 603–608.
Hishey, M. S. *Nebraska test of learning aptitude* (revised). Lincoln: University of Nebraska, 1955.
Holt, K. S. *Assessment of cerebral palsy* (Vol. 1). London: Lloyd Burke, 1965.
Holt, L. B. *Pediatric ophthalmology.* London: Hy. Kimpton, 1964.
Hopkins, T. W., Bice, H. V., & Colton, K. C. *Evalaution and education of the cerebral palsy child.* Washington, D.C.: International Council of Exceptional Children, 1954.
Illingworth, R. S. *Recent advances in cerebral palsy.* London: J & A Churchill, 1958.
Irwin, O. C. *Communication variables of cerebral palsied and mentally retarded children.* Springfield, Ill.: Charles C Thomas, 1972.
Kanner, L. Austistic disturbances of affective contact. *Nemous Child,* 1943, *2,* 217–240.
Kanner, L. General concept of schizophrenia at different ages. *Proceedings from the Association of Research of Neurological and Mental Disorders,* 1954, *33,* 451–453.
Keeler, W. R. *Psychopathology of communication.* New York: Grune & Stratton, 1958.

Knoblock, H., Rider, R. J., Harper, P. A., & Pasamanick, B. Nueropsychiatric sequelae of prematurity: A longitudinal study. *Journal of the American Medical Association,* 1956, *161,* 581–585.

Koppitz, E. M. *The Bender Gestalt Test for young children.* New York: Grune & Stratton, 1964.

Lawson, L. J. & Myklebust, H. Opthalmological deficiencies in deaf children. *Exceptional Children,* 1970, *37,* 17–20.

Levine, E. Psychological tests and practices with the deaf: A survey of the state of the art. *The Volta Review,* 1974, *76,* 298–314.

Lundstrom, P. Rubella during pregnancy: Its effects upon prenatal mortality, the incidence of congenital abnormalities, and immaturity: A preliminary report. *Acta Paediatr,* 1952, *41,* 583–594.

Meehl, P. E. *Clinical versus statistical prediction.* Minneapolis: University of Minnesota Press, 1954.

Miller, H. C. Scope and incidence of congenital abnormalities. *Pediatrics,* 1967, *5,* 320–324.

Morse, William C. Concepts related to diagnosis of emotional impairment, in *State of the art: Diagnosis and treatment.* Des Moines, Iowa: Midwest Regional Resource Center, 1974.

Mowatt, J. Ear, nose and throat disorders: Deafness. In J. L. Henderson (Ed.), *Cerebral palsy in childhood and adolescence.* Edinburgh: E & S Livingstone, 1961.

Myklebust, H. H. *Auditory disorders in children.* New York: Grune & Stratton, 1954.

Myklebust, H. H. The deaf child with other handicaps. *American Annals for the Deaf,* 1958, *103, 487*–509.

National Center for Education Statistics (NCES). Washington, D.C.: Government Printing Office, 1976.

Perlstein, M. A. & Barnett, H. E. Nature and recognition of cerebral palsy in infancy. *Journal of the American Medical Association,* 1952, *148,* 1389–1397.

Quay, H. C. & Werry, J. S. (Eds.) *Psychopathological disorders of childhood.* New York: John Wiley, 1972.

Reynell, J. Children with physical handicaps. In P. Mittler (Ed.), *The psychological assessment of mental and physical handicaps.* Norwich, Great Britain: Tavistock Publications, 1973.

Rhodes, W. C. & Tracy, M. L. *A study of child variance* (Vol. 1). Ann Arbor: University of Michigan, Institute for the Study of Mental Retardation and Related Disabilities, 1972.

Rimland, B. *Infantile autism.* New York: Appleton, 1964.

Rutter, M. A tri-axial classification of mental disorders in childhood. *Journal of Child Psychology and Psychiatry,* 1969, *10,* 41–61.

Schain, R. J. & Yarnet, A. Infantile autism: An analysis of 50 cases and a consideration of certain neurophysiologic concepts. *Journal of Pediatrics,* 1960, *57,* 560–567.

Sheridan, T. B. Final report of a prospective study of children whose mothers had rubella in early pregnancy. *British Medical Journal,* 1964, *2,* 536–539.

Smith, R. M. (Ed.). *Teacher diagnosis of educational difficulties.* Columbus, Ohio: Charles E. Merrill, 1969.

Sontag, E. W. Zero exclusion: Rhetaic no longer. *AAESPH Review,* 1976, *1,* 105–114.

Stoecher, U. T. *A treatment study of an autistic child.* Arlington, Va.: Council for Exceptional Children, 1972.

Stuart, R. *Tuck or treatment—how and when psychotherapy fails.* Urbana, Ill.: Research Press, 1970.

Vernon, M. Characteristics associated with post-rubella deaf children: Psychological, educational, physical. *Volta Review,* 1969, *3,* 176–188.

Wing. L. *Autistic children: A guide for parents and professionals.* New York: Brunner-Mazel, 1972.

Wood, L. & Shulman, E. The Ellis visual design test. *Journal of Educational Psychology*, 1940, *31*, 591–598.

SUGGESTED READINGS

Jones, H. G. Principles of psychological assessment. In P. Mittler (Ed.), *The psychological assessment of mental and physical handicaps*. London: Tavistock Publications, 1973.

Mittler, P. F. Assessment of handicapped children: Some common factors. In P. Mittler (Ed.), *The psychological assessment of mental and physical handicaps*. London: Tavistock Publications, 1973.

Reynell, J. Children with physical handicaps. In P. Mittler (Ed.), *The psychological assessment of mental and physical handicaps*. London: Tavistock Publications, 1973.

Appendix. A Review of Diagnostic Devices Used with the Seriously Handicapped

To conclude, let us examine a few devices that are used to describe the seriously handicapped, and were not described in other chapters. In the absence of an endorsement of these descriptive instruments, the reader should recognize that an absence of tests or diagnostic procedures is evident. Probably related to the recent history of diagnostic involvement with the multiply and seriously handicapped.

ADAPTIVE BEHAVIOR SCALES

Authors: K. Nihira, R. Foster, M. Shellhaas, H. Leland
Age: 3–12 and 13–over
Variable: Mentally retarded and emotionally maladjusted
Type of measure: Rating scale
Description of Measure: A two-part measure with ratings in 24 areas of social and personal behavior for use in evaluating effectiveness in coping with environmental demands. Designed to facilitate classification of mental retardation and emotionally disturbed persons. Administration of measure takes 25 to 30 minutes by anyone familiar with the subject. 111 items in measure.
Reliability and Validity: Interreliability, for adult only, 0.40 to 0.86. No internal consistency measures. Mean scores by sex and levels of intelligence are provided. No correlations are provided for the relationship between IQ and scale scores.
Obtaining Measure: American Association on Mental Deficiency
5201 Connecticut Avenue, N.W.
Washington, D.C. 20015

AUTISM PERFORMANCE SCALE

Author: D. T. Saposnek
Age: 2½ years to adulthood
Variable: Degree of autistic withdrawal
Type of Measure: Rating scale
Description: Eleven behavioral categories, broken down into 18 behavioral items. Behavior is rated before and after a treatment procedure.

Reliability and Validity: Two raters observed 22 children equaling 42 percent agreement on 55 percent of the rating judges differed by on rating. For all ratings on which the two raters differed by one category, the ratings were the same direction from the pre- to the post-treatment rating. On 3 percent of the ratings there was a difference of two rating categories in opposite directions from the pre- to the post-treatment rating.

Obtaining Measure: Donald T. Saposnek
Pediatric Treatment Center
County of Santa Cruz
290 Pioneer Street
Santa Cruz, CA 95060

THE AYRES SPACE TEST

Author: A. J. Ayres

Age; 3 years and up (11)

Variable: Brain damaged children

Type of Measure: Formboard-spatial discrimination

Description of Measure: Includes 60 formboard items requiring relatively simple spatial discrimination. Intended primarily for a diagnostic tool for the detection of brain damage in children. 3 scores: accuracy, time and accuracy less adjustment for time. An individual test requiring 20 to 30 minutes for administration.

Reliability and Validity: Norms derived on 15 males and 15 females for children 3 years to 10 years of age.

Obtaining Measure: Western Psychological Services
Box 775
Beverly Hills, CA 90213

BEHAVIOR PROBLEMS CHECKLIST

Authors: John F. Feldhusen and John R. Thurston

Age: Elementary through high school

Variable: Socially approved and aggressive-disruptive classroom behavior

Type of Measure: Checklist

Description of Measure: Designed to help teachers designate children whose behaviors would be considered socially disapproved. Eighteen behavior traits on this 3-point rating scale. 15 minutes to complete.

Reliability and Validity: Reliability satisfactory through interteacher and intrateacher renominations: 0.77 interteacher; 0.75 intrateacher.

Obtaining Measure: John F. Feldhusen
Educational Psychology Section
Purdue University SCC-G
West Lafayette,IND 47906

BEHAVIOR-RATING CHECKLIST FOR AUTISTIC CHILDREN

Author: Victor Lotter

Age: Prepubertal children

Variable: Autistic children

Type of Measurement: Checklist

Description of Measure: 24 items in 5 areas of behavior (speech, social behavior, movement peculiarities, response to sound and repetitive/ritualistic behavior). Ratings based upon contemporary behavior at 8 to 10 year old handicapped children. 3 point rating scale.

Reliability and Validity: From a group of 54 cases, 32 who were classified as autistic by one rater, an independent rater agreed on 28 of hte 32.

Obtaining Measure: Victor Lotter, Epidemiology of austistic conditions in young children. I: "Prevalence." *Social Psychiatry,* 1966, *1,* 124–137.

BURKS' BEHAVIOR RATING SCALE (BBRS)

Author: Harold Burks

Age: Preschool through Grade 8

Variable: Behavioral Disordered

Type of Measure: Rating scale

Description of Measure: Designed to identify patterns of pathological behavior shown by children. 116 items utilized in 20 areas. Scales attempt to gauge the severity of certain symptoms as seen by an outsider. Measures overt behaviors. 10-minute administration.

Reliability and Validity: No reliability data.

Obtaining Measure: Arden Press
P.O. Box 804
El Monte, CA 91734

BURKS' BEHAVIOR RATING SCALE FOR ORGANIC BRAIN DYSFUNCTION

Author: Harold F. Burks

Age: Preschool, K-6

Variable: Behavior of organic brain dysfunction

Type of Measure: Rating scale

Description of Measure: A one-page test with rating done by teacher. Four scores are vegetative-autonomic, perceptual-discriminative, social-emotional, and total. Administration is 5 minutes.

Reliability and Validity: No reliability data.

Obtaining Measure: Arden Press
P.O. Box 804
El Monte, CA 91734

Cost: \$5.50 per set of manual and 25 tests.

THE CHILD BEHAVIOR RATING SCALE

Author: Russell N. Cassel
Age: Grades K-3
Variable: Child adjustment of normal and handicapped children
Type of Measure: Rating Scale
Description of Measure: A rating scale to be completed by teacher or parents regarding child adjustment in six areas: self, home, social, school, physical and total. 5 to 10 minutes administration. 78 items. Designed for preschool children, primary grade children and "children unable to read or handicapped in completing conventional pencil-paper tests."
Reliability and Validity: Correlation between mother and father ratings, 0.66. Presumed to have high face validity. No reliability coefficients present.
Obtaining Measure: Western Psychological Service
12031 Wilshire Blvd.
Los Angeles, CA 90025
Cost: $6.50 per 25 tests, $2.00 per manual

DEVEREAUX CHILD BEHAVIOR RATING SCALE

Authors: George Spivack and Jules Spotts
Age: 8–12
Variable: Emotionally disturbed, mentally retarded children
Type of Measure: Rating scale
Description of Measure: An instrument used in the assessment of atypical children. Designed for use by raters familiar with child's behavior. 17 scores (47 items) in the form of "Compared to normal children, how often does the child . . ." 10 to 20 minutes for administration.
Reliability and Validity: Reliability data with median correlation of .83; one week stability rating; test-retest reliability .83; factor score reliability .93. No validity data.
Obtaining Measure: Devereaux Foundation Press
Devon, PA 19333

DIAGNOSTIC CHECKLIST FOR BEHAVIOR
DISTURBED CHILDREN, FORM E2

Author: Bernard Rimland
Age: 3 years and up
Variable: Autism in Children (classification of childhood psychoses)
Type of Measurement: Checklist
Description of Measure: Designed to identify classical autism (Kanner's syndrome) from undifferentiated psychotic children loosely classified

as autistic. Designed to be administered by child's parent with questions concerning pregnancy, delivery, early postnatal life, speech, behavior and behavior patterns through age five. 80 items.

Reliability and Validity: Effective in differentiating children with classical autism from remainder of children classified as autistic. Construct validity conducted through item-analysis; biochemical studies performed on a double-blind basis. Children scoring high. Biochemical abnormalities in blood platelets were not found in psychotic children who scored low.

Obtaining Measure: Institute for Child Behavior Research
4758 Edgeware Road
San Diego, CA 92116
Cost: Less than 5 copies—no charge, 10 copies —$1.00, 50 copies—$3.00

GLENWOOD AWARENESS, MANIPULATION AND POSTURE INDEX (GAMP I)

Author: Ruth C. Webb

Age: All ages of profoundly retarded

Variable: Sensori-motor integration

Type of Measurement: Rating scale

Description of Measure: Comprised of 3 parts of 25 items each. Awareness scale evaluates functioning of sensory receptors through approach-avoidance stimuli as well as basic memory processes. Manipulation scale evaluates fine motor ability, intentionality and responses to body and verbal language. Posture index evaluates subject's progress toward independent ambulation. Each item presented three times and rated by number of times it is performed. Two persons need to administer the GAMP I.

Reliability and Validity: Awareness and manipulation subjected to a split-half reliability study with 40 PMR subjects. Results awareness, r = 0.69; manipulation, r = 0.83. Validity study made by correlating the results on the awareness and manipulation sections with scores on Binet short form intelligence with the following correlations, awareness, r = 0.37; manipulation, r = 0.72.

Obtaining Measure: Ruth C. Webb
Glenwood State Hospital
Glenwood, IA 51534

PORTEUS MAZE—ARNOLD ADAPTATION

Author: S. D. Porteus, adaptation by G. F. Arnold

Age: 3–12 years

Variable: Foresight and planning capacity in cerebral palsied children

Type of Measure: Maze

Description of Measure: Consists of a paper-pencil maze. Materials are manipulated by examiner while the subject responds with appropriate head movements either right, left, up or down indicating direction. Valuable in predicting the success in meeting the practical and social demands of life.

Reliability: Results obtained for a small group of cerebral palsied and normal children. When computed in terms of IQs, the correlation with the Stanford-Binet are low and statistically insignificant values; however, the Porteus measures different abilities than those covered in the Stanford-Binet.

Obtaining Measure: Arnold, Gwen, F. A technique for measuring the mental abilities of the Cerebral Palsied. *Psychological Service Center Journal,* 1951, *3,* 171–180.

HARTFORD SCALE OF CLINICAL INDICATORS OF CEREBRAL DYSFUNCTION IN CHILD PSYCHIATRIC PATIENTS

Authors: P. N. Graffagnino, F. G. Bucknam, & M. H. January

Age: 2–17 years

Variable: Cerebral dysfunction

Type of Measure: Rating scale

Description of Measure: A rating scale of 30 clinical items to be rated as "present" or "absent." Data acquired during first four to six interviews with parents and child. The higher the score the more likely cerebral dysfunction. Scale divided into three sections: (1) symptoms and signs related to impulsivity of direct aggression, (2) symptoms and signs related to compensatory adjustment against impulsivity or aggression, and (3) items from early history.

Reliability and Validity: Objectivity of rater scoring was checked by two independent raters with scoring agreements of 92 percent and 93 percent. Rating scale scores and EEG findings were checked by analysis of variance and t-test procedures.

Obtaining Measure: Graffagnino, P. N., Boehouwer, C., and Reznikoff, M. An organic factor in patients of a child psychiatric clinic. *Journal of the American Academy of Child Psychiatry,* 1968, *7,* 618–638.

PUPIL BEHAVIOR INVENTORY (PBI), EARLY EDUCATION VERSION

Authors: Rosemary Sarri and Norma Radin

Age: 3–8 years

Variable: Behavior in class setting

Type of Measurement: Rating Scale

Description of Measure: Contains 54 behaviors rated on a 5-point scale. Used to evaluate intervention programs when administered by the same teachers before and after the intervention. Also used to assess school performance in studies related to parent socialization practices to child's school performance.

Reliability and Validity: Reliability has not been assessed but there is evidence of concurrent and construct validity. Example: Factor Academic Motivation correlated significantly with independent measure of this predisposition assess by trained psychologists.

Obtaining Measure: Norma Radin
School of Social Work
University of Michigan
Ann Arbor, MI 48104

SEIKEN CHECKLIST FOR AUTISTIC CHILDREN
(CLAC)

Authors: Kosaku Umetsu, K. Matita, I. Takamura, et al.

Age: 1–10 years

Variable: Behavioral characteristics of autistic children

Type of Measure: Checklist

Description of Measure: Aims at (1) determining individual characteristics of autistic child, (2) helping establish therapeutic programs, (3) providing material for parental interviews, (4) evaluating therapeutic effectiveness. Composed of five point rating scale covering child's behavior such as eating, expression, human relationships. Measure to be utilized by professional observers. Results transcribed on rating psychogram, thereby illustrating each individual feature visually while still present a Gestalt.

Reliability and Validity: Statistical analysis not yet complete regarding validity and reliability. Comparison thus far was made on the basis of studies with control groups of 254 normal (ages 1–6), 42 mentally retarded (ages 4–6), and 44 deaf (ages 3–6) children. Results clarify the characteristic profile of developmental arrest in each autistic child and contribute to differential diagnosis of other disturbances.

Obtaining Measure: Makita, K., Umetsu, K. An objective evaluation technique for autistic children: An introduction of CLAC scheme. *Acta Paedopsychiatrica,* 1972, *39,* 237–253.

SELECTED DESIGN

Author: George Siskind

Age: 13 years to adult

Variable: Screening device for cerebral dysfunction

Type of Measure: Design-copying test

Description of Measure: The evaluation for possible cerebral dysfunction depends on the quality of performance in copying 3 geometric designs. Scoring for adequate performance is done by comparison with a scoring guide with particular attention to angles on the right side of the design. Administration and scoring required. 8–10 minutes.

Reliability and Validity: A group of 80 protocols—35 adult psychiatric patients diagnosed with cerebral dysfucntion, 35 adult psychaitric patients with no cerebral dysfunction and 10 normal college students. Unsophisticated judges correctly identified 31 of 35 protocols. False positives were 4, 4, and 2 for an average error of 8 percent. A group of 55 adolescents (13–18 years) tested on Selected Design were judged by 2 unsophisticated judges. 32 of the 50 were previously identified as having cerebral dysfunctions. The judges correctly identified 77 percent and 79 percent of the protocols, with 4 and 5 false positives.

Obtaining Measure: George Siskind
Psychology Department
Larue D. Carter Hospital
1315 West Tenth Street
Indianapolis, IN 46202

SOUTHERN CALIFORNIA MOTOR ACCURACY TEST

Author: A. Jean Ayres

Age: 4–7 years

Variable: Manual motor development and visual perception

Type of Measure: Tracing a line

Description of Measure: An indiviudal test where subjects must trace a line design. 2 scores: accuracy adjusted (accuracy and speed). Skill tested develops rapidly during fourth year then shows decreasing acceleration until the seventh year.

Reliability and Validity: Split-half reliabilities range from 0.67 to 0.93. Test-retest reliabilities from 0.91 to 0.92. Validity established through comparison of 100 six and seven-year-olds with suspected perceptual deficits and 50 of those had no known deficit. Standardization 280 children.

Obtaining Measure: Western Psychological Services
12031 Wilshire Blvd.
Los Angeles, CA 90025

TEACHING RESEARCH MOTOR-DEVELOPMENT SCALE

Authors: H. D. Bud Fredericks, V. L. Baldwin, P. Doughty, & L. J. Walter

Age: Moderately and severely retarded children, preschool to high school

Variable: Motor development

Type of Measure: Motor-proficiency test

Description of Measure: A downward extension of the Lincoln-Oseretsky Motor Development Scale. Material for administering tests are standard materials found in classroom. Measure most useful for charting the motor development progress of retarded children. Measure has 51 items. Examples are: standing on tiptoe with eyes closed, touching fingertips, placing match sticks in box, tracing mazes, etc. Each item is described with following format: equipment, number of trials, directions, scoring criteria, and points.

Reliability and Validity: None reported.

Obtaining Measure: Fredericks, H. D., Baldwin, V. L., Doughty, P., & Walter, L. J. *The teaching research motor-development scale for moderately and severely retarded children.* Springfield, Ill.: Charles C Thomas, 1972.

SECTION IV

Learning and Behaviorally Descriptive Models Extended into New Service and Program Delivery Systems

Early childhood and career education are not new; programs do exist in the schools and each year their numbers increase. However, the problem is that the vast majority of educational assessment procedures were developed for elementary school children, and therefore current assessment practices are often inefficient or erroneous when used with the preschool and secondary school-age youth.

The contents of the two chapters of this section, one on assessment in early childhood and one on career assessment for adolescents, are devoted to describing the state of the art in these undeveloped and critically important areas. Each contains the outline of a model, a rationale for the information that is to be gleaned, and specific procedures for acquisition of necessary assessment information. Close scrutiny of this section is advised because these areas are now truly incorporated into the special education network of services.

Edward Earl Gotts

16
Early Childhood Assessment

This chapter considers early childhood assessment from both developmental and physical perspectives. It concentrates on the period from birth to about six years of age, or the beginning age of required school attendance. Because all areas of early child behavior and development are the concern of special educators, this chapter aims to be comprehensive. Adaptations of assessment procedures for children having particular handicaps are treated in other chapters.

Before examining the assessment process, this chapter first reviews a variety of issues which influence the why, how, where, what, and who of early childhood assessment. These issues in the first half of the chapter are basic to the special educator wishing to study and participate in child development. The second half of the chapter considers specific assessment procedures as these relate to programming for exceptional young children.

ISSUES IN EARLY ASSESSMENT

Need for Programs

Early childhood education began to achieve a new and wider prominence in the mid-1960s as a result of several developments. Professors Susan Gray and James Miller, together with many other workers at the George Peabody College's Demonstration and Research Center in Early Education (DARCEE), Nashville, Tennessee, studied the effectiveness of home interventions with pre-school-age children who were at a developmental level that indicated possible mental subnormality. Investigators in several other centers began to explore aspects of early intervention. Notable contributions have come from the High/Scope Educational Research Foundtion, Ypsilanti, Michigan (David Weikert, Dolores Lambie, and others); the Rehabilitation Research and Training Center in Mental Retardation, University of Wisconsin, Madison (Rick Heber and others); the Diagnostically-Based Curriculum Program for psychosocially disadvantaged, mentally retarded preschool children, Indiana University, Bloomington (Boyd McCandless, Howard Spicker, and Walter Hodges); the Parent Education Project, University of Florida, Gainesville (Ira Gordon and others); the Home-Oriented Preschool Education (HOPE) Project, Appalachia Educational Laboratory, Charleston, West Virginia (Roy Alford, Benjamin Carmichael, and others); and additional contributors too numerous to list. All of these workers have succeeded in showing that young children at risk for mental retardation could be helped.

Nearly all the mid-1960s investigators of early invention began with a concern for high-risk populations. Nearly all believed that mild retardation is often a result of one's early experiences; mild degrees of retardation could, therefore, be reversed by providing different kinds of early experience. Head Start was spawned in this climate of opinion, and consequently focused initially on psychosocial aspects of the "disadvantaged." Early education for all handicapped children, however, had not yet arrived. Even efforts such as Project Memphis (Quick, Little, & Campbell, 1974), and the PEECH Project, University of Illinois (Merle Karnes and others), which were started from this period up through the later 1960s and early 1970s to serve children identified as handicapped (i.e., in contrast to children "at risk"), were designed to assist primarily the mildly handicapped. Furthermore, mildly handicapped often meant *mildly delayed* or mentally handicapped, in the beginning years of these projects. The programs, as a result, did not encompass services for children with specific handicapping conditions.

During the later years of this period, however, a shift began to occur toward broadening the work to include handicapped children. The previously mentioned investigators of programs for young handicapped children (e.g., Karnes) were suddenly joined by many workers in the field. For example, the University Affiliated Facilities Network, members and affiliates of the United Cerebral Palsy Associations, the Council for Exceptional Children, and the Association for Retarded Citizens began to think in terms of providing early preventive, ameliorative, and remedial services for all children who might require them. Practitioners pioneered and tested new approaches to working with all types of young handicapped children.

It was in this general climate of ideas and results that the Bureau of Education for the Handicapped (BEH), (USOE-DHEW), received Congressional authorization in 1968 to create the Handicapped Children's Early Education Programs (HCEEP). These are referred to collectively as the First Chance Network. A Technical Assistance Development System (TADS) was established at the Frank Porter Graham Child Development Center, University of North Carolina, Chapel Hill, to provide special support services for the First Chance Network.

Despite all these new developments, most of the individual states continued to provide custodial and other care to severely and profoundly handicapped young children through the traditional live-in institutions such as state hospitals and schools. This is not surprising, because at this time many states still did not have even universally provided kindergartens. By the mid-1970s state legislation on kindergartens and other early education programs remained a tangled patchwork. State legislation lagged far behind the forward movement and potential inherent in early intervention for the handicapped.

PL 94-142

The response of the U.S. Congress to this state of affairs was Public Law (PL) 94-142. This law requires development of an individualized education program (IEP) for each handicapped child, and free, appropriate education for all handicapped children ages 3 to 18 by September 1, 1978, in some states. This IEP must further be translated into the child's own primary language.

Thus, as can be seen from the foregoing brief overview, educational programs are coming for all young handicapped children. An amazing transition has occurred in only a little over a decade. Children, who were so recently thought of as able to benefit only from custodial care, are now to participate to the fullest extent possible in the benefits of a free and individualized public education. Implementation of PL 94-142 will in the future require even greater efforts to identify and assess the possible needs of individual infants and preschool children for special needs.

Who Should Be Tested?

Formal testing is a particular kind of data collection. It involves sampling children's responses in a standardized situation and manner; that is, children are placed in a standard situation where either the examiner's request or the physical attributes of the situation or materials otherwise invite a response. The children's responses are then evaluated according to specific scoring criteria.

Formal testing can, therefore, be thought of as placing particular task demands upon a child under observation. This fact emphasizes a particular shortcoming of formal testing, when viewed in relation to one of the most prominent characteristics of young children, namely, their tendency to continue doing what interests them instead of adapting to the task demands required by adults. Although this tendency grows weaker from birth through five years of age, it is still readily evident in five-year-olds (Butler, Gotts, & Quisenberry, 1975, chap. 6). Evidence further suggests that children of lower socioeconomic background, including some from minority groups, adapt even less to testing demands made during the preschool years than do children of middle socioeconomic background (Hertzig, Birch, Thomas, & Mendez, 1968).

In short, formal testing is a data collection method that conflicts with a prominent behavioral tendency of young children. Therefore, it may generally be desirable to collect data on young children by methods other than formal testing. This chapter will focus on some of these alternatives to testing. Testing may be the method of choice when the question is, How well does the child adapt to the demands of a specific task? Who, then, should be tested in early childhood? The best answer is that most young children should not, unless the test is necessary to establish their eligibility to participate in a preschool program or for other compelling reasons. However, if the adult administering the testing is familiar to the children, is well-liked by them, and is skillful in securing their cooperation, then this argument against testing young children loses much of its force. If the examiner succeeds in getting young children to adapt willingly and comfortably, then the testing may be justified on the grounds of the information which it provides. An additional point is discussed later in this chapter under the heading, Parent Involvement.

Early Identification

Early identification is widely practiced today, but its purpose and methods are not always well understood. The purpose of early identification is to determine whether a child will be designated by a procedure to require special services, and to specify the kinds of special service needed. The ultimate purpose of both screening and assessment is to identify children needing special services and to indicate the services which they need. Therefore, screening has no purpose unless it leads to services. Thus, screening for early identification is not an inherently virtuous activity for special educators; it takes on meaning only as it produces programmatic or special service results for children.

To some readers, the preceding may seem to be obvious and hardly worth emphasizing. But the fact is that in some communities early identification campaigns have been conducted with little regard or planning for how the identified children will be served. When this happens, special educators have an extra responsibility to clarify for others the purpose of early identification within a total process of meeting the special needs of young children. They can also point out that early identification generates its own risks when children are labeled as possibly handicapped. These added risks can only be tolerated if the children will receive the benefits of services.

The methods of early identification are a source of considerable confusion. Ideally, *screening* is any inexpensive yet accurate method of identifying those children who, as subsequent assessment will often show, need special services. This definition explicitly avoids specifying the method by which screening is conducted. Yet some persons will claim that screening is not formal testing, while others insist that it requires formal testing. Early identification can be performed by testing, observation, completion of a checklist by someone who knows the child well, interview with the parent or others, from records, and from various combinations of these. No matter how it is conducted, quality early identification results in inexpensive and accurate identification of children needing assessment.

Examiner Qualifications

Examiner qualifications is an issue that is partly legal, partly professional, and partly personal. Although state certification laws vary, assessment work is generally performed by persons having titles such as school psychologist, psychometrist, or director of special services. Whatever the title may be, this is a person who has completed a prescribed course of study at a recognized institution and who has been certified to perform assessment. Usually this person has the responsibility to consider and integrate data from many sources on children, including those from the classroom or other early childhood setting. This person's legal responsibility also usually includes (1) stating that a child is or is not eligible for special placement or services, and (2) recommending that a placement be or not be made. Screening, on the other hand, may be performed by almost anyone who is working under supervision, and following training of the person responsible to the program for utilizing its results.

The specific educational background and experience needed for early childhood assessment is not usually required of, or demonstrated by, persons who are primarily certified to perform assessment of school-age children. For this reason, early childhood special educators will often find that assessment of young children is performed by someone other than the school psychologist, psychometrist, or director of special services. The assessment may, for example, be carried out by a psychologist in a private practice or in a community clinic. The legal basis of the examiner's qualifications in such instances is derived from (1) state licensing or certification by a board of psychological examiners, or (2) supervision by a board-recognized person, or (3) employment within a public institutional setting (e.g., child guidance clinic or community mental health clinic).

The professional qualifications for performing assessment of young children often coincide with the legal ones in terms of professional identity as a psychologist or director of special services. Professional qualifications, however, imply something more. They imply that no matter what one's legal status may be, the professional will not engage in assessment activities that are beyond his or her own competencies. It is unfortunate to note that early childhood assessment is too often carried out by persons who are in some sense legally eligible to assess children but who are not professionally qualified. Often these persons either use an expanded form of screening and call it assessment or administer assessment procedures to young children that are more appropriate for older children. This problem of formally testing young children has already been discussed. Special educators in early childhood are, therefore, well advised to inquire as to how their program selects persons to assess infants and preschoolers.

Beyond legal and general professional qualifications, the personal qualifications of the examiner should be considered. To assess young children, the examiner must know about early physical development, about sequences of behavioral development, and about how perinatal and other factors may be significant to the overall assessment. In addition, the examiner must be able to interact and play with the children. Someone who feels qualified to evaluate only with a test kit at a work table or desk will necessarily miss much of the significant interaction in the young child's life. It is advantageous if the examiner enjoys young children, as they are aware of relationships at their own emotional level, and respond to the examiner accordingly.

The ability to establish rapport and work with parents is important for all childhood assessment, and it is a necessity for early childhood assessment. The younger the child, the more personally resourceful the examiner must be at shifting frame of reference and assessment techniques to accommodate the child's rapidly changing interest and orientation. Some helpful suggestions to the examiner are given by Terman & Merrill (1960, pp. 50–54, however, observe their bias regarding parents on p. 57). See also Wechsler (1967, chap. 8) and Bayley (1969, chap. 8) in this connection. The foregoing are some of the hallmarks of a successful examiner, which if present, should inspire an added degree of confidence in the examiner's findings and recommendations.

Yet the examiner can possess these qualifications and still be ineffective in communicating the assessment to others in written form. As a result, the special educator should communicate to the examiner some reasonable expectations regarding the report. A helpful set of criteria for evaluating assessment reports has been developed by Meyers, Sundstrom, & Yoshida (1974). Reports should (1) be clear and concise when explaining unfamiliar terms, (2) be responsive to the reasons for referral, (3) review essential background briefly, (4) report on other needs or issues that emerge during assessment, (5) make pointed recommendations that apply to the child's learning situation, and (6) interpret clearly the essentail test results. (See also chap. 6 this volume.)

Alternatives to Formal Testing

Whether the question is screening or assessment, there are alternatives to formal testing. These are described below.

INFORMAL ASSESSMENT

First, developmental measures can be collected within the context of an ongoing early childhood program, with data collection occurring over several days. This process eliminates much of the structured quality such testing possesses when administered in a formal clinic situation. However, this procedure can affect the age-normative frame of reference of standardized developmental tests, such as Gesell, making children appear to perform slightly beyond their age levels. If the teacher's concern is with developmental description and planning, the loss of exact age norms will prove to be of minor concern or consequence. A variation on this alternative is to conduct developmental assessment primarily through observation. Much more will be said about these two possibilities in the second part of the present chapter.

ASSESSMENT CLASS

Another alternative that may be developed is analogous to the *assessment classroom* as it is used in assessing older children. This approach might appropriately be called the *assessment program setting* to distinguish it from the more typical early childhood program setting. The assessment program setting would be staffed by one or more special educators who have a specialty in diagnostic programming for young children, coupled with strengths in early development. Children would spend a variable amount of time in this assessment setting and would then be placed in an ongoing program group. Some precedents exist for an assessment program setting model, especially in remedial or therapeutic day-care and nursery school programs. A similar assessment can be conducted in less time in a play interview. This technique is most often used by child psychologists and psychiatrists. Despert (1964) describes one approach to using the play interview in assessment.

INVOLVING A THIRD PARTY

A third general alternative is to collect information from parents, teachers, day-care workers, and others who know the young child well. This can be accomplished by interview or by having them complete standard checklists or child-rating forms. Although these approaches usually draw upon the informant's past observations and knowledge of the child, these persons can be requested to supplement their knowledge by further observing the child, and then to answer specific questions that remain unclear. From this brief presentation of alternatives, it is clear that assessment and screening are not wholly reliant on formal clinical methods.

Description Versus Diagnosis

Handicapped legislation has traditionally established child eligibility by diagnostic category. Diagnosis is of course an outgrowth of the medical model or disease orientation. Recently the behavioral and psychoeducational models have replaced the medical model in the thinking of special educators. The newer models have only recently begun to affect the formulation of legislation for the handicapped by improving the limitations of the old traditional diagnostic categories with young children. Nevertheless, categorical programs (e.g., for mentally retarded, visually impaired, etc.) continue to dominate special education, including programs for preschool handicapped. Infant programs, on the other hand, seem to be moving away from assignment of children by category.

The focus of both behavioral and psychoeducational specialists has been a movement away from diagnosis and toward description. Description of children's learning abilities, needs, and difficulties generally lends itself well to educational planning and programming. For this reason, it may be expected that descriptive assessment will continue to increase in popularity over diagnostically oriented assessment. But because categorical identification of children for services has been a politically effective strategy in the special education movement, it can also be predicted that diagnosis will be around for a considerable time as a means of establishing eligibility.

Environment Specific Behaviors

A common error of assessment is to imagine that children have a repertoire of generalized ability and personality traits that are exhibited in nearly all situations. The ecological frame of reference suggests that different environmental settings are associated with different behavior repertoires from an early age (Wright, 1967). This fact leads to the concept that young children display behaviors directly related to the environmental circumstance.

For example, infants behave very differently when parents are present than when they are absent. A two-year-old behaves differently when a favorite toy is in hand than when it cannot be found. Thus, from an adult perspective, the qualities of the environment that influence infants and young children are fairly specific rather than global.

One way of understanding why young children display these kinds of environment specific behaviors is to consider the degree to which behavior is *stimulus-bound* at different ages. *Stimulus-bound* refers to behavior that is directly predictable from the presence of a stimulus. For instance, the reaction of an infant to a flashing light is highly predictable, that is, the behavior is stimulus-bound. But a child of preschool age may display a variety of reactions to the same flashing light. In consequence, the preschool child is said to be less stimulus-bound than the infant. Thus, in response to natural stimuli, children become less stimuli-bound with increasing age. In other words, children's environment specific behaviors decline in relation to specific physical aspects of the environment throughout early childhood, but these still occur at a high level through five years of age.

On the other hand, in relation to socially defined or conventionally defined environmental qualities (i.e., the more abstract qualities of environment such as "places to be quiet") children show an increase of these learned environment specific behaviors with increasing age, although five-year-olds admittedly ignore many such social definitions either when their wishes conflcit with custom, or when they "forget."

The high prevalence of the former or natural type of environment specific behaviors and the low prevalence of the latter or learned type provide further perspectives on why testing is not an especially appropriate assessment technique in early childhood. Because young children are low in learned environment specific behaviors, they are less responsive than older chidlren to the learned behaviors required in adapting to a testing situation. Further, because they are still high in natural environment specific behaviors, the testing situation, which is atypical of the child's natural environment, is less likely to elicit typical behavior or even representative behavior than it is with older children.

Parent Involvement

Parents should be actively involved in the assessment of young children, not just to provide consent for the process or even to furnish data, although these are both important (see chap. 5). The younger the child, the more essential it is for parents to participate actively in the assessment. This requirement becomes apparent when one examines the manuals for several infant appraisal instruments (e.g., Bayley, 1969). Some of these treat parents as a primary data source and some permit the examiner to have parents assist in test administration. This approach directly relates to the earlier discussion of a circumstance under which the testing of young children may be appropriate, i.e., by a familiar person who is liked by the child and is skillful at eliciting the child's cooperation. Many parents fit this description or comes much closer to it than does an unfamiliar examiner.

Comprehensive Screening and Testing

Screening programs can be conducted with varying degrees of effort. Surprisingly, the effectiveness of a screening program may not show a clear relationship to the total effort or expense involved. The British, for example, have developed a national program of keeping "high risk" registers (Meier, 1973) of children who may develop problems or have special needs. Despite the considerable effort and expense involved in keeping such registers, there are many problems with them and they are generally no more effective than other simpler methods.

One problem, for example, is that the registers may define risk in several ways, leading to the inclusion of the same children in several lists of the register. Further, many more children are exposed to various risks than actually develop later problems. The register is, therefore, kept on many children who will never develop problems; consequently, the register is not particularly discriminating. In fact, so many children who never develop problems get entered into the register that little practical advantage comes from the effort. The underlying conceptual problem of the register is that it assumes a general agreement regarding important risk factors. Such agreement does not exist. And even if the register offered some practical advantages to selecting children for services, there would remain an enormous and inaccurate listing of "at risk" children who are thereby labelled in some sense as being different or as problems, but who will never develop significant problems.

In contrast, one-time screening/testing efforts have proven successful to the extent that they (1) succeeded in reaching the entire community, and (2) examined the children's physical and behavioral functions comprehensively. To be considered comprehensive, screening/testing should include vision, hearing, motor functions, speech and language, social and emotional development, general health history, and intellectual processes. It is distressing to observe that some early childhood programs conduct screening programs that ignore several of these areas.

An example of an important omission can be considered. Suppose that vision screening is not conducted, but rather that a screening program relies on results of less direct behavioral measures of visual perception. Some possible consequences are: First, preschoolers with visual-motor problems may show normal visual perceptual functioning, because they have not yet encountered tasks (e.g., reading) that will overtax their limited visual-motor control. The problem, thus, remains undetected until later. Second, other preschoolers with undetected visual-motor problems may be compensating successfully at present by relying on other skills, but simple behavioral measures of visual perception do not distinguish between performances based on purely visual-motor functions and compensatory functions.

A similar difficulty can be anticipated for each of the other recommended areas if a screening program is not comprehensive: errors of inference will be made. Sometimes these will be errors of the sort already cited for vision screening, resulting in a failure to detect a problem. At other times a problem may be identified but incorrectly attributed to some other source. For instance, suppose that screening reveals a child whose overall language is delayed. Imagine further that hearing was not tested. Under these circumstances, a child who may appear to be mentally retarded, in fact has a mild hearing loss. Some brighter children can compensate enough for a mild hearing loss to make them difficult to distinguish from a mentally retarded child, if only gross behavioral functions are assessed. These possible outcomes illustrate the dangers of ignoring any of the areas that belong in a comprehensive screening effort.

Cultural Fairness and the Young Child

Preschool children, even more so than primary level children, are not yet fully socialized. Thus, it is meaningless to refer to a testing procecure as culturally fair. Because the young child has not integrated all aspects of culture, the criterion of cultural fairness seems inapplicable in the more general sense which applies to elementary and secondary level testing.

There is a more specific sense in which this general notion applies. Because young children are stimulus-bound, if they are to be tested, they should be assessed under stimulus conditions that are as familiar and comfortable as possible. As guidelines, testing should be performed by a familiar adult, of the same general background as the children's parents if possible. Children should be examined in the language or dialect which they experience at home. Assessment should occur in a familiar setting such as the home or a day-care room or other location in which the children have spent considerable time. The examination should focus on experiences and materials which the children are known to encounter everyday at home or in outside settings. If these guidelines are followed, then there is some basis for claiming that the examination is culturally relevant to the child's experience. The prior discussion of how young children respond to task demands serves, nevertheless, to introduce a final note of caution, especially regarding children of lower socioeconomic and/or minority background.

Relevance to Programming

Screening or assessment may be performed in the most elegant or skillful manner, but it is virtually useless unless it relates to anticipated programming. If a community can provide or obtain only the barest medical services, for instance, it is difficult to justify elaborate medical screening.

Even the availability of appropriate services cannot assure a match to individual children's needs. What is required here is that the assessment process accurately identify the child's learning needs and then address these in terms of the available services. This matching process needs to be quite specific and should lead to an initial plan that clearly guides those who will work with a particular child.

Another issue of considerable importance is that PL 94-142 requires that all handicapped children shall have an IEP. The new handicapped legislation is making the IEP more than a concept, but a reality. Special educators must now look forward to preparing an IEP for all children. When that day comes, the necessary conditions for mainstreaming will also have been achieved. For the present, there is a new criterion against which to test the relevance of assessment to programming: Does the assessment support development of an IEP? This may be added to the six criteria which were mentioned earlier as being applicable to assessment reports.

Uses of Assessment

Assessment can serve several purposes. It is useful for initial placement, for periodic reevaluation of children in special placements, to determine readiness to reenter a regular preschool placement, and for evaluation of progress in special placements. These last two uses of assessment are discussed later under their own subheadings.

REEVALUATION

In addition to its use in initial placement, assessment should be used for periodic reevaluation of children who have been placed in a special preschool program. Periodic reevaluation is even more important in the preschool years than later. This is so because children develop rapidly at this time, and prior assessment results soon become outdated. Reevaluation is accomplished to determine whether individual children still require special placement or might be as well served by a different placement. Reevaluation can also highlight children's changing needs and suggest adjustments required within a special program. Reevaluation serves to document progress within the special placement, so that parents will be informed of their children's (1) development and long-range prospects, and (2) needs for special services that may be available from other sources in the community. Finally, reevaluations can be used administratively to improve the assessment process itself by identifying oversights in prior evaluations and determining how they might be averted in the future.

Determining Readiness

Readiness is most often used in a specialized sense to refer to children's preparation for first-grade level learning experiences (Ilg and Ames, 1964). Readiness, in this sense, has a place in early childhood screening, but is not especially germane to the present consideration of most early childhood handicaps. However, it is noteworthy that many moderate and some mild learning disabilities may first appear on a kindergarten or first-grade readiness test.

Readiness is also used in a more general sense to indicate that a child will benefit from particular educational experience, i.e., is ready for the experiences provided at a particular or prescribed level. Children who are currently in a special preschool placement may be assessed to answer the question of whether they could be returned to a regular placement. These kinds of assessment are frequently initiated at the request of the special class teacher, unlike the periodic reevaluation or review of all exceptional children in special placements.

Determining Progress

So far, the purposes of assessment have been discussed in regard to meeting the needs of individual children. Assessment can also be used to evaluate special programs and the effectiveness of the placement process. A question that might be raised, for example, is whether children in special placements develop more rapidly than similar children in regular placements. Or, do children in special placements develop more rapidly than would be predicted from their rate of development prior to placement?

A system-wide plan might be developed whereby results would be combined for all or a representative sample of children who were undergoing periodic reevaluation of their special placements. The composition of the sample (e.g., in terms of types of handicaps) and the particular measures selected would be designed to answer broader questions about how well special education is performing and how children have progressed in their special placements. The same findings, on the other hand, would serve the additional purpose of periodic reevaluation of individual children. In addition, assessment may serve a variety of special research purposes connected with program evaluation of children's progress.

ASSESSING THE YOUNG CHILD

Developmental Perspectives

Many of these ideas on early childhood development and assessment have been presented elsewhere by the author in different forms and contexts (Butler, Botts, Quisenberry, & Thompson, 1971; Butler, Gotts, & Quisenberry, 1975; Gotts, 1975; Butler, Gotts, & Quisenberry, 1978). From these writings, an essential group of foundations for assessment can be summarized as a set of propositions or statements.

1. Nearly all early development occurs in a recognizable sequence, at least within its own particular area of development (e.g., within the social, emotional, or language area). Assessment implications of this proposition are considered later in the present section.
2. Specific marker behaviors or developmental milestones (i.e., specific observable behaviors) can be identified as relating to larger developmental areas.
3. Behaviors can be classified into categories representing different levels of specificity (e.g., at general, intermediate, and specific levels).
4. Physical developments can be classified similarly into categories of different specificity.
5. Measures based on more specific categories of development are more useful for instructional applications. This proposition is developed in the next three sections of this chapter.
6. Developmental tests at present have practical advantages over more general trait-focused measures (e.g., they are more useful to teachers than are measures of intelligence).
7. Developmental tests may be thought of as a special kind of criterion-referenced measures (see Gotts, 1975 for a discussion of this viewpoint).
8. Screening and assessment should encompass both the physical and behavioral characteristics of children.
9. Assessment is an ongoing process that uses children's progress within a planned program as one source of data.
10. Assessment results are nearly always tentative. An open-ended perspective of their meaning is, therefore, appropriate.
11. Assessment has a practical role in early childhood program planning.
12. Assessment measures should be selected judiciously, based upon the practical and administrative concerns which occasion the assessment.

Proposition number one calls for assessors and users of assessment to take a developmental perspective. Taking a developmental perspective in assessment entails two procedures: (1) looking directly at specific developmental behavior, and (2) interpreting children's overall performance in terms of particular developmental sequences or theories. This section examines the second of these procedures in terms of some of the most prominent and potentially useful theories; the first procedure of taking a developmental perspective in assessment unfolds in the following three sections.

Erikson's Theory

Erik Erikson's (1963) view of development is one that is widely used in early childhood programs. It readily applies to early assessment. Erikson is a life-span developmental psychologist, i.e., his theory encompasses development from infancy through old age. This chapter briefly examines those portions of his theory that apply to early childhood.

Erikson sees major developments as occurring in stages. Each stage of life presents a new challenge or developmental crisis to the individual child. Children pass through three of these stages in their early years. The challenge of each stage is either resolved or not resolved—partial resolutions are not possible. The overall outcome and implications of each stage are positive if the crisis is resolved and negative if the crisis is not resolved. Erikson recognizes that children's resolution of developmental challenges results from both their own efforts and from their surrounding social environments. The social environments of children make it either easier or more difficult for them to resolve the developmental crises of childhood.

TRUST

The first developmental crisis is experienced in infancy. Children learn to perceive their social environment as supportive and nurturing or as hostile and threatening. Children who perceive their interpersonal environment as supportive and nurturing develop trust, the positive outcome of the first stage. Alternatively they may develop mistrust to the extent that they perceive their environment as hostile and threatening.

In assessing young children, some appraisal should be made of their interpersonal relationships to determine the extent to which they exhibit trust or mistrust. Interviewing parents and observing children and their parents together provide two sources of data on this stage of development. There is also a pair of simple scales that can be completed by teachers (Schaefer & Aaronson, 1967a) or parents (Schaefer & Aaronson, 1967b), which measure the extent to which children display love versus hostility. The love-hostility dimension is one of the three global areas covered by each of these scales. *Love-hostility* is an overall designation that summarizes adult ratings for four trait descriptions of children on considerateness, kindness, resentfulness, and irritability. The love-hostility scale is not specifically designed to measure trust or mistrust, but it comes as near to doing so as is possible with any simple measure. A more complicated measure of love-hostility can be derived from use of the "Assessment Outline of Early Child Development" (Flapan & Neubauer, 1975).

It is evident that interview of the parents can be helpful in establishing what kinds of early factors have contributed to the child's development of trust. Assessment should focus on factors in the social environment that have furthered or hindered the development of trust, as well as on whether the child manifests trust or mistrust.

What may not be as apparent is that some children, because of their own temperaments, will have a more difficult time than others in establishing a trusting relationship with parents. The pioneering work by Thomas, Chess, & Birch (1968) in this field suggests that some children are more vulnerable to developing behavior disorders. Those children of an initially "slow to warm up" type and a "difficult" type are surely more likely to have problems developing trust. It must not, therefore, be assumed that parents in any sense directly cause children to develop mistrust, nor should such assumptions be pursued in parental interviews. What should be sought is an understanding of the kind of environmental match that is suited to the child's own temperament-related needs, and then, an understanding of how the parents' management techniques might be reoriented to improve this match. Whatever perspectives and advice would apply to management at home would probably apply to classroom management as well. Because temperament is so relevant to a proper understanding of the dynamics of children's functioning, temperament assessment should be conducted. This has been facilitated by recently developed instruments (Thomas & Chess, 1977). One of these is specifically designed for use by teachers (Thomas & Chess, 1977, Appendix B).

AUTONOMY

The second major crisis of development, in Erikson's view, leads either to autonomy or to shame and doubt as its outcomes. This crisis occurs during the toddler period. A sense of autonomy results from children learning to control their speech, bodies, and bodily fucntions, i.e., they learn that they, not others or chance, are in control of what they do with their bodies.

Information about the child's development of autonomy or shame is best determined by interview and observation. The absence of autonomy or conflict over it will often show up in such ways as: (1) a struggle with others over possession of what is "mine"; (2) clinging to toys or hoarding them rather than playing with them; (3) repeated refusal to cooperate, accompanied by determined resistance and "no" response; (4) negative, pouting mood, or excessive shyness; (5) a love-hate relationship with parents; (6) temper tantrums; and (7) defiance at times. There are no easy-to-use measures of autonomy or shame, although the Flapan & Neubauer (1975) assessment outline can be learned for this purpose. Although it does not measure autonomy directly, any satisfactory measure of self-help skills gives some indication of progress toward autonomy. Self-help skills either far behind or in advance of motor skills may suggest an autonomy problem.

Temperament will again play a vital role in many children's mastery of the autonomy-shame crisis. Children who are highly active and also reactive to stimulation, for example, often find it more difficult to tolerate parents' restraints and other normal expressions of concern for their safety. Therefore, temperament should be evaluated and its relationship to this developmental crisis appraised. Motor handicapped children may have exceptional problems in achieving autonomy, as may blind children.

INITIATIVE

In typically developing children, the third crisis of development emerges during the third through sixth years of life. Its outcome is initiative or guilt. The sense of initiative is expressed as wanting to know, to make suggestions, to take a turn at something or to try it out, to be invited, to win, to be seen, to figure out simple riddles, to try out new roles, and above all, to be an active rather than a reactive person. This active stance displays itself in imagination as well as overt behavior, Distortions will be seen in the foregoing areas among children who do not master the crisis of initiative. Either excessive display of initiative or its absence indicates an unfavorable outcome of the crisis. For example, curiosity may be distorted into a driven kind of exploratory activity and need to know, or the stiffled stagnation of curiosity may appear as disinterest and even inability to become interested.

Initiative is not directly measured by the *Behavior Inventories* (Schaefer & Aaronson, 1967a; 1967b) but it can be roughly estimated from two of their dimensions: introversion–extroversion, and positive task orientation–negative task orientation. The former of these summarizes the traits: verbal expressiveness, gregariousness, social withdrawal, and self-consciousness; the latter, perseverance, concentration, hyperactivity, and distractibility. Once more Flapan & Neubauer's (1975) assessment outline can be used if a more in-depth and conceptually precise procedure is needed.

Temperament is influential at this stage in identifiable ways. Children of active disposition will more strongly experience a drive to master this crisis, although parents may be put off when the children seem to intrude into areas usually reserved for adults. Temperamentally inactive children may begin to lag behind others especially in the development of outgoing social skills.

Piaget's Theory

Simultaneously with the personal and social developments conceptualized by Erikson, equally fundamental conceptual skills are also being mastered by young children. Piaget has concentrated his efforts on understanding the order in which conceptual development occurs through adolescence. The present chapter, however, looks only at the early childhood Piagetian stages.

STAGE I

During infancy, the form of conceptual activity that occurs has a sensory and motor orientation. The stage of sensory-motor intelligence progresses through six substages (Piaget & Inhelder, 1969). The first substage last for about the first month of life and marked by reflexive activities. The second substage lasts from one to four or five months. During this time, infants repeat the same movements over and over, using parts of their body only, without involving objects in their actions. These bodily-centered and repeated actions are called *primary circular reactions*. From 4 or 5 up to 8 or 9 months, substage three, secondary circular actions occur. These are movements which are repeated for their effects in the immediate environment. Now infants succeed in interacting repeatedly with selected parts of the environment. During substage four (from 8 or 9 through 11 or 12 months), two or more secondary circular reactions (movements) become coordinated in the itnerest of attaining some goal, with one of the movements serving only as a means of facilitating the accomplishment of the other movement. The infant's orientation now seems to be toward the result (goal) with the means (movements) being instrumental to accomplishing the goal. From about 12 to 15 months (substage five) infants begin to perceive relations between incidentally discovered means and the result or goals which they desire. A familiar example occurs when an infant chances to discover that the pull string on an inaccessible toy causes it to move; the string then is pulled to draw the toy toward the infant. Manipulations now are investigative (tertiary circular reactions) with the infant closely regarding the effects of the manipulations. During the sixth substage (from 15 to 18 months, to perhaps 2 years), infants first demonstrate a capacity to accomplish their intended goals without using physical trial and error; instead they begin to manipulate symbolically. Thus, after carefully scrutinizing a situation, children will suddenly act to accomplish some result as if by insight. This fact demonstrates that memory proper or mental representation is present, that is, the child has attained a general symbolic function. A major transition has occurred; the child is free to solve some problems without having the materials at hand to manipulate.

Woodward (1963) has applied Piaget's conceptions to assessment of exceptional children. To move from her work to direct assessment activities requires, however, a thorough grasp of Piaget's theory. Uzgiris & Hunt (1975) have made the process of Piagetian assessment more accessible by developing ordinal scales of sensory-motor development. These are not easy enough to use that a nonspecialist would want to undertake their mastery. But for programs serving infants or extremely slow developing children who manifest infant level behaviors over several years, this system of infant behavior analysis is worth serious consideration.

STAGE II

The second major stage conceptualized by Piaget extends from about 2 to 6 or 7 years of age and is divided into sub substages: the preconceptual (1½ to 4 years) and inutitive (4 to 6 or 7 years).

Language begins to be used extensively in the first or preconceptual substage, but children use nouns as if they represent something in between totally private or individual meaning and a more general or socially consensual meaning. Children now rely on how things appear in direct experience, that is, they engage in perceptual thinking. This is why they label objects and discuss them as if their nature were changeable from time to time, just as perceptions change with each new perspective. From these facts it is clear that preconceptual children lack a general frame of reference from which to judge that variations in appearance of an object do not alter the fundamental nature of the object. The preconceptual substage is also notable for the amount of imaginative play that occurs. *Imaginative play* is play in which children invent symbols for their needs because they still lack sufficient language for this purpose. An invented symbol is a need oriented, mental representation that has the character of being an imagined action. Piaget believed the child's mental images at this stage are mental imitations of what once were external actions.

Further, this is a period of "productive play" (Butler, Gotts & Quisenberry, 1978) in contrast to the "sensory-motor play" of the preceding six substages. Sensory-motor play centers around the exercise and mastery of sensory and motor functions that enable the child to produce effects upon the physical environment. Productive play aims to produce products. However the products of this stage are what the child means them to be, i.e., they are not intended to match a conception of external reality.

There are at present no classroom usable measurement scales for looking at development from a Piagetian perspective during this substage. But the teacher or examiner who wishes to perform Piagetian assessment will find it useful to concentrate on children's conceptual attainments relative to objects, classes, number, space, time, causality, and other nature concepts. This approach is illustrated by Butler, Gotts, & Quisenberry (1975, pp. 88–89). These authors discuss for each of these conceptual areas the typical behaviors of children of differing developmental ages, e.g., the child's concept of *object* or thing is traced from about 24 to 72 months of age. Alternatively, the characteristics of preconceptual children can be observed by the nature of their play (Butler, Gotts, & Quisenberry, 1958, chap. 2). That is to say, systematic observation of the content, objects used, and formal character or style of children's play tells much about the child's level of development. Another useful reference on play has been prepared by the National Assocaition for the Education of Young Children (1971).

The final substage of the preschool period is the intuitive substage. Its most advanced achievements occur past the end of the preschool period, usually in the early primary level years among typical American children. Children now become capable of using their perceptions to guide trial-and-error attempts to solve simple problems of quantity. However, these guiding perceptions are quite limited, because the intuitive level child attends at any single moment to only one perceptible stimulus attribute (e.g., attends to the length of a row of objects while overlooking their density or spacing; attends to the height of a cylinder of fluid, simultaneously forgetting its diameter or perceived width). Furthermore, during the earlier or preschool portion of the intuitive substage, children do not easily "decenter" or shift their attention from one stimulus attribute to another. Trial-and-error performance begins to improve once they can shift attention and, hence, perspective more easily. Decentering occurs more readily in the later part of the intuitive period, and intuitive problem solving ability increases correspondingly.

Besides failing to decenter relative to static stimulus attributes, intuitive level children are inclined to focus on only those changes that they intend (and, hence, to which they attend) to make. For example, while they rearrange the objects in two sets to make the sets equal, they may attend primarily to the areas over which the two object sets are dispersed. By attending to area, their actions are thereby directed (intended) to alter area. In turn, they perceive the areas to be equal, because of the intent behind their actions, even though the sets may remain unequal in number. Or, intuitive children will confuse effects of their own actions with the physical processes which they are observing. For example, a child who is holding a balance beam level on a balance scale, as a method of equalizing the weight (i.e., instead of altering the weights themselves), will believe that the balance will remain level after the hand is removed (Woodward, 1963, p. 308), Furthermore, children express surprise when, upon removing their hands, the balance does not remain level as intended! Some of them will repeatedly place their hands back on the balance and then remove them again as if expecting the action to alter the reality. Like the preconceptual child, the intuitive child thus shows that ''intended results'' powerfully affect perception.

Unlike the preconceptual child, however, the intuitive level child attempts repeatedly to alter a set of materials to make them conform in some way to physical reality—albeit a reality which is seen only one part (or attribute) at a time. The preconceptual child in contrast is usually content to assimilate or distort external reality to match the intended outcome, that is, the preconceptual child attends more to intentions, whereas the intuitive child attends more to the intended results of actions in terms of the multiple attributes of reality which are affected by those actions, one attribute at a time.

The play of intuitive level children is better described as ''reproductive play'' (Butler, Gotts, & Quisenberry, 1978) because of its concern with reproducing reality, i.e., its concern with ther match between intentions and external reality. Play thus reflects the overall movement of children during this substage toward increased attention to physical reality. But the reality of the intuitive child is a limited reality based on perceptions rather than concepts.

Procedures have been developed for measuring at least one characteristic of four- through 5-year-olds in Piagetian terms, i.e., the ability to conserve quantity (Goldschmidt & Bentler, 1968). The measure does require direct testing of children. Results from the Goldschmidt & Bentler (1968) approach approximate, but do not correspond exactly to those results obtained by a Piagetian clinical testing procedure. Piagetian conceptual development in children can be studied observationally using the concept categories mentioned earlier. It is further possible, by making sequential observations across time and in varied play settings, to analyze children's problem-solving skills and their movement toward logical thought (Butler, Gotts, & Quisenberry, 1975, pp. 115–117). Observation can also be used to determine the developmental level of children's play in terms of the essentially Piagetian distinctions: sensory-motor, productive, and reproductive play (Butler, Gotts, & Quisenberry, 1978).

The next section of this chapter examines the most general level at which areas of development are usually considered. The reader will soon recognize parallels between the present section and the so-called domains of the next section. Erikson's theory deals with one of the three most general behavioral development categories, the affective domain; Piaget's deals with a second of these, the cognitive domain; but no highly developed theory deals with the third, the domain of perceptual-motor development. Kirk, McCarthy, & Kirk (1968) have adapted mediational theory to cover selected aspects of perceptual-motor development, and Gesell (1949) created a theory of motor development. Neither of these attempts, however, has created a framework for perceptual-motor development having a generality like Erikson's or Piaget's, in their respective domains. Perceptual-motor assessment cannot, therefore, be guided by a validated general theory.

Areas of Development

GENERAL DEVELOPMENT

Broad, general areas of development are often referred to as behavioral domains. Traditionally, behavior is divided into three behavioral domains: (1) the affective or social-emotional, (2) the language-cognitive, and (3) the psychomotor or perceptual-motor. Curriculum planning and educational evaluation may be organized in terms of these three domains. In general, the three-domains framework is too abstract and nonspecific to be useful for descriptive assessment. However, if the domains are further divided into more specific developmental areas (e.g., see Butler, Gotts, & Quisenberry, 1975), the domains become usable as a way of looking at assessment. For example, an assessment battery can readily be evaluated to see how well it samples from each of the domains.

One of the few behavioral measurement traditions which seems to have developed out of a domains orientation is the intelligence test. Individual intelligence tests, such as the *Stanford-Binet* measures (Terman & Merrill, 1960) and *Wechlser* (e.g., 1967), sample widely from the language-conceptual domain. A more recent development has been batteries concentrating on perceptual-motor functioning, e.g., the Ayres (1972) *Southern California* tests.

In addition to the behavioral domains, there is the overall physical domain. It can be reasoned that "physical domain" also provides too nonspecific an orientation to be useful for assessment, although it serves as a reminder that a comprehensive assessment should include appraisal of children's physical status. Therefore, these general, domain orientations are mainly useful to assessment of global aspects of development such as intelligence. Domain-oriented measures may, nevertheless, via use of subtest scores (e.g., Wechsler's and Ayres' tests), serve to appraise more specific behavioral areas.

INTERMEDIATE DEVELOPMENT

A more intermediate level of specificity characterizes the conceptual organization underlying several widely used developmental tests. Instruments of this type generally follow or diverge only slightly from Gesell's four category conception. Gesell (1949) divided early behavior into four developmental areas: personal-social, adaptive behavior (fine motor), (gross) motor, and language, Several developmental scales identify self-help as another area. Instruments which have generally adopted this conceptual orientation are the *Developmental Profile* (Alpern & Boll, 1972), the *Denver Developmental Screening Test* (Frankenburg, Dodds & Fandal, 1970), Sheridan's (1968) test, the *Protage Project Checklist* (Shearer, Billingsley, Frohman, Hilliard, Johnson & Shearer, n.d.), the *Project Memphis Scale* (Quick, Little, & Campbell, 1974), the *Learning Accomplishment Profile* (LAP) (Sanford, n.d.), and literally scores of locally devised scales used in programs of screening and assessment. These instruments are selectively described later in this chapter in the section "Measures and Uses" (see Table 16-3, p. 560).

Some measures that fit conceptually into this intermediate specificity group do not attempt to deal with as many categories. The *Vineland Social Maturity Scale* (Doll, 1965), for instance, samples from the self-help area primarily. The Vineland is also an example of an attempt to subdivide the self-help area into further separate skill areas.

Thus, much more specifically than the domains orientation, this intermediate level of description has demonstrated its conceptual value for organizing developmental behaviors into measurable categories. General, domains-oriented measures have tended to focus on trait-like qualities that communicate less about actual development in a descriptive sense. Conceptually intermediate measures, exemplified by developmental tests, communicate more directly about developmental processes. Further, these types of scales are now widely used in early childhood programs for high-risk and handicapped children.

Physical development can also be thought of at an intermediately specific level. For example, physical development can be divided into somatic and physiologic development; can be measured and such measurement can be used descriptively.

Overall, then, intermediately specific notions of development lead readily to measurement. Compared to general or domain conceptions, measures derived from intermediate conceptions can be adapted to a more descriptive approach, and, consequently, they better communicate the process of development than do general or trait-focused measures.

It may be reasoned, however, that intermediately specific measurement systems are not entirely ideal for developmental assessment. They are still too abstract, tending as a result to group into a single category, areas of development that might better be examined separately. For example, whereas "social development" is a more specific and satisfactory category than is "affective domain," social development, nevertheless, is still a fairly gross category for practical early assessment. Instructional planning for social development could be better implemented if the measurement indicated the areas of social development in which the child had particular needs. A teacher can formulate a social IEP in only the most general way from a knowledge of a child's tested social developmental level. What would be more practical for instructional planning are measures based on a set of more specific developmental categories from which a teacher could infer actual skills that need to be developed.

Current developmental tests have another shortcoming. They do not provide measures of several important categories which they might reasonably be expected to include. For instance, developmental tests provide almost no useful information on either emotional development or perceptual development—and *emotional* and *perceptual* are certainly as important as are the *social* and *motor* categories which developmental tests do measure. But even after considering the shortcomings of existing developmental tests, it should be remembered how much more useful they are to early childhood programs than are traditional domain-oriented tests of development.

SPECIFIC DEVELOPMENT

Physical development can be thought of at a more specific level by focusing on anatomic-physiologic systems as the organizing principle. Examples of specific areas are neurosensory, alimentary or gastrointestinal, musculoskeletal, circulatory, immunologic, respiratory, endocrine, and so on. These conceptual categories lend themselves well to data collection and study. Moreover, they are extremely useful for looking at physical development descriptively during the early years of life. To illustrate this, the musculoskeletal system undergoes many changes throughout early development. "Skeletal age" can be determined by X-ray exam, the relative body proportions represented by legs, torso, and head change throughout early development, and so on.

A similar gain can be seen in potential descriptive power when conceptually specific measures of behavioral development are used. For example, the developmental conceptions underlying such tests as the *Illinois Test of Psycholinguistic Abilities* (ITPA) (Kirk, McCarthy, & Kirk, 1968) and the *McCarthy Scales of Children's Abilities* (McCarthy, 1972) are more specific than those of the five-category developmental tests. Ayres' (1972) tests, mentioned earlier, not only cover a specific domain, but at the subtest level have this same conceptual advantage of specificity over typical developmental tests. While the ITPA, McCarthy, and Southern California tests are more developmentally specific in conception, they are less satisfactory for direct developmental description than are developmental tests. That is, they result in scores that can be equated with ages in a normative sense, but what they do not provide is any description of how a typical child of a specific age might behave.

What seems to be needed is a battery of measures which relate to "areas of development-specific" but which do not lose touch with the direct, descriptive quality of developmental tests. In 1974 the need for such a battery was established and a program for development was undertaken by the Division of Early Development, Appalachia Educational Laboratory (AEL). Prior work at AEL had resulted in a competency base for early childhood education (Troutt, 1974) around which the battery was to be developed. Revisions of the competency base eventually led to recognition of 59 developmental competencies in early childhood (Table 16-1).

Creating direct measures of 59 competencies would have been an enormous task and, in the long run, would have proved impractical for use in programs. Therefore, a conceptual clustering procedure was developed and administered to determine how the 59 competencies might best be combined to reflect the interrelationships among competencies during the preschool years. This procedure was also designed to reduce the number from 59 competencies down to a more manageable size.

Procedures were then used to determine which competencies belonged together, in the sense that experts in early development agreed that the competencies belong together, and that they develop our of similar types of learning experience. A satisfactory degree of agreement was attained among the experts, resulting in identification of 14 competency clusters that included all of the 59 original competencies. These competency clusters appear in Table 16-2. The table shows the manner in which these clusters relate conceptually to the five scales of one widely used instrument, the *Developmental Profile* (Alpern & Boll, 1972).

Developmental items were, at the same time, selected from nearly all existing instruments and assigned to the competencies that they most closely matched. After competency clusters were formed, the developmental items were combined for each of the 14 clusters. From these, a smaller number of items was selected for inclusion in a series of 14 experimental scales, one for each cluster (Gotts, Dankert, & Lawhon, 1977). A priority was given to including items that could be scored from observation of children only, i.e., without requiring formal testing.

The procedures for constructing the 14 *Appraisal of Individual De-*

Table 16-1
Child Competencies: Appalachia Preschool Curriculum

Competency Name
Ability to:
1. form concepts (example: concept of "same," "different")
2. discriminate by sound
3. discriminate by sight (example: 3-D and 2-D, shapes, colors)
4. discriminate by touch
5. sort (to group and label, to categorize)
6. ordinate (by size, by number, by numerals)
7. conserve (to understand equality and inequality of sets through changes)
8. measure (to estimate weight, distance, for example)
9. denote spatial relationships
10. judge physical and personal causation
11. recognize the passage of time
12. recognize familiar geographic and natural phenomena (e.g., lakes, clouds, thunder)
13. use imagination to play; to pretend
14. operate on quantity (to add, to subtract)
15. perceive from partial information
16. remember, recall
17. recognize the social functions of language (i.e., that it permits people to relate)
18. label (to attach names to objects, feelings, events)
19. explain (for example, to explain the function of something)
20. describe (for example, from a picture)
21. articulate (to be understood)
22. express feelings.
23. use nonverbal cues (including facial, vocal, gestural)
24. comprehend statements and questions
25. use typical sentence constructions
26. use language to seek new information (to ask questions)
27. further own play by talking aloud
28. recognize others' expressed emotions
29. construct (i.e., with materials requiring hand-eye coordination)
30. copy
31. draw
32. use body to express feelings
33. control large muscles (balance, coordination)
34. control small muscles (actions not covered in 29–31)
35. initiate action (to explore, be curious, to start things)
36. plan action (to anticipate, to assess resources)
37. persist in action (in face of distractions, to complete)
38. be self-reliant (examples: independent dressing, washing, grooming; to show confidence)

Table 16-1 (continued)

Competency Name
Ability to:
39. sustain health and safety standards (to avoid dangers)
40. accept or try new things (such as new foods or routines)
41. wait a short time for something
42. accept some rules
43. prefer particular activities (likes, dislikes)
44. release tensions (motorically and verbally)
45. show courtesy
46. follow willingly the directions of a favored adult (such as a parent or teacher)
47. respond as much to social as to concrete reinforcement
48. assume appropriate social behaviors (shares, cooperates, makes positive social contacts)
49. get attention (to arouse interest or concern)
50. maintain attention of others
51. adopt the perspective of another (to role play, to interact with another's role)
52. respect the individuality of others
53. imitate the actions of a favored adult
54. prefer the company of a "friend"
55. feel secure with adults, while acting independently
56. understand own place within the family
57. understand who he or she is
58. assert own rights (especially against an intrusive "invader")
59. pay attention (to sounds, sights and interpersonal stimuli)

velopment Scales (AIDS), (Gotts, Dankert, & Lawhorn, in press) have been described in some detail to demonstrate for the reader the sense in which the resulting scales are: (1) comprehensive (i.e., they cover the range of development identified in the 59 competencies, and include areas omitted from typical developmental tests (see Table 16-2); (2) specific (i.e., inspection of Table 16-2 reveals how specific the scales are in relation to the Developmental Profile); (3) descriptively developmental (i.e., items come from existing developmental tests, and results are directly interpretable in terms of the items themselves, as well as from the developmental age levels which the individual items reflect); and, therefore, (4) useful for instructional purposes (i.e., the scales reveal in a direct and readily understood manner how the child is developing in each area, they are easily administered and interpreted, and they provide information for differential planning of instruction relative to 14 areas of early development).

In this section and the two preceding sections of the chapter, general, intermediate, and specific areas of development have been considered.

Table 16-2
Competencies Clusters Resulting From Combining of 59 Competencies

Cluster	Name of Cluster (Competency #)*	Developmental Profile Match
1	Gross Motor (33)	Physical
2	Hand-eye Coordination (29,30,31,34)	Academic
3	Perception (2,3,4,9,15)	Not represented
4	Independence (38,39)	Self Help
5	Social Maturity (28,41,42,45,47,48,52,54)	Social
6	Relating to Adults (46,53,55)	Social
7	Attention Getting (49,50)	Social
8	Self Concept (56,57,58)	Not represented
9	Emotional Expression (22,32,44)	Not represented
10	Fantasy or Imagination (13,51)	Not represented
11	Responding to Environment (35,36,37,40,43,59)	Not represented
12	Language (17,19,20,21,23,24,25,26,27)	Communication
13	Conceptual Development (1,5,10,11,12,16,18)	Academic
14	Number Concepts (6,7,8,14)	Academic

*See Table 16-1 for competency names.

General, intermediate, and *specific* have referred to the degree of conceptual specificity with which developmental behaviors are classified. The purpose of this threefold analysis has been to demonstrate that special educators can benefit from using a more specific or differentiated framework for areas of development. Many texts today emphasize specific behavioral analysis; this, too, is useful. This emphasis on specific categories of development complements specific behavioral analysis by (1) providing a conceptual framework for tracing developmental change, and (2) moderating the risk resulting from specific behavioral analysis, i.e., that one item of behavior after another will be modified in desired directions, while somehow the overall developmental needs of the child escape systematic attention. The 14 categories of Table 16-2 cry out in warning: Every IEP should seek to promote young children's development in as many specific areas as possible.

Measures and Uses

In the course of the chapter so far, several measures and their applications have been mentioned. The four parts of this section make specific recommendations for measures which may be used for: screening, observing/describing, formal testing or appraisal, and classifying.

SCREENING

Zehrbach (1975) provides useful perspectives on all screening (although he has focused on three through five year olds) by comparing the actual success of various methods of locating and screening. He recommends beginning with a media campaign, then conducting a door-to-door or telephone survey using volunteers, then using roundup screening followed by rescreening as needed. For other general perspectives screening, one should consult Meier (1973). If resources are needed for screening, Frankenburg & North (1974) should be studied, and the applicable resources sought through Medicaid and its emerging modifications, Another general assist in screening is available from CEC-ERIC (n.d.).

Very early screening efforts should consider a parent rating scale reported by Hoopes (1967). Screening of handicapped children throughout the period of infancy is well served by the work of Haynes (1976).

For more general early childhood screening the "Early Warning Signs" brochure is a model of simplicity (Bertram & Clay, 1976). It is completed directly by parents, who are referred by it to a local address for additional assistance if needed for their child. The DDST (Frankenburg, Dodds, & Fandal, 1970) and the *Developmental Profile* (Alpern & Boll, 1972), as well as many local developmental evaluation procedures, are also suited to screening. All of the preceding procedures are somewhat more subject to measurement error than is desirable, but this limitation can be offset if a brief history is taken during screening and if careful and periodic followup is possible. The Schaefer & Aaronson (1967a; 1967b) inventories fit into this general screening category also. Behar & Stringfield (1974) have developed a device that is similar conceptually to the two preceding inventories, and can screen three through six year olds. The Flapan & Neubauer (1975) outline was intended for screening, but in this writer's opinion it is better suited for inclusion in an assessment. Zehrbach's (1975) approach to screening has been incorporated into a commercially available program for identifying two and one-half through five and one-half year olds requiring services. The program is called CIP or *Comprehensive Identification Process* (Zehrbach, 1976). Pamphlets dealing with special areas of screening such as vision and hearing are best obtained from a local professional who provides these services. An overall indicator of satisfactory physical development is the rate of a child's growth in height, weight, and head circumference (Butler, Gotts & Quisenberry, 1975, pp. 65–68). A summary appears in Table 16-3 of characteristics of the measures mentioned throughout the *Measures and Uses* portion of the chapter. Other measures from earlier portions of the chapter are included as well.

Table 16-3
Summary of Characteristics of Measures

Instrument & Source	How Completed*	Ages Covered	Areas Covered†	Time‡ (mins.)	Validity Tested	Reliability Tested	Norms Available
CIP (Zehrbach, 1976)	a & b	2½–5½ yrs.	a,b,c,d,f,g,i	0:30	Yes	0.92	No
Infant Scale (Hoopes, 1967)	b/d	Infancy	a,i	N/A	Yes	76%–90%	No
Early Warning Signs (Bertram & Clay, 1976)	d or b	1–5 yrs.	b,c,d,f,g,h	0:05 – 0:10	No	No	No
Denver-DDST (Frankenburg et al., 1970)	a	1 mo.–6 yrs.	a,b,c,d	0:10 – 0:20	Yes	80%–95%	Yes
Developmental Profile (Alpern & Boll, 1972)	b or a	2 mos.– 12 yrs.	a,b,c,d,e	0:30 – 0:40	Yes	Yes	Yes
Infant Behavior Inventory (Schaefer & Aaronson, 1967a)	d	1–3 yrs.	a	N/A	Yes	Yes	No
Classroom Behavior Inventory (Schaefer & Aaronson, 1967b)	d	3 yrs.– primary level	a	N/A	Yes	Yes	No
Preschool Behav. Invent. (Behar & Stringfield, 1974)	d	3–6 yrs.	a	N/A	Yes	Yes	No
REEL (Bzoch & League, 1970)	b or d	0–36 mos.	c	0:10	In progress	0.71	Yes
Bayley (1969) Scales	a,c	2–30 mos.	d, b/c, a	0:45 – 0:75	Yes	High	Yes
Gesell (1949) Scales	a,c	1–72 mos.	a,b,c,d	0:45 – 0:75	Yes	Yes	Yes
Slosson (1963) Intelligence§	a	4 yrs.–adult	b/c	0:10 – 0:20	Yes	High	Yes
Wechsler (1967) WPSSI	a	4–6½ yrs.	b,c	0:50 – 0:75	Yes	High	Yes

Table 16-3 (continued)

Stanford-Binet (Terman & Merrill, 1960)	a	2 yrs.–adult	b,c	0:60 – 0:90	Yes	High	Yes
Ordinal Scales (Uzgiris & Hunt, 1975)	a,c,	0–2 yrs.	b	N/A	Yes	Yes	No
Sheridan (1968)	a,c,b	1 mo.–5 yrs.	a/h, b/f, c/g, d	N/A	No	No	No
Portage Checklist (Shearer et al., no date)	d,c	Birth–5 yrs.	a,b,c,d,e	N/A	No	No	No
Memphis Scale (Quick et al., 1974)	d,c	Birth–5 yrs.	a,b,c,d	N/A	No	No	No
LAP (Sanford, no date)	a/c,d	Birth–6 yrs.	a,b,c,d,e	N/A	No	No	No
Vineland (Doll, 1965)	b	Birth–Adult	e,c,a	N/A	Yes	Yes	Yes
Social Competency (Levine et al., 1969)	c	2½–5½ yrs.	a,c	N/A	Yes	Yes	Yes
ITPA (Kirk et al., 1968)	a	28 mos.–10 yrs./varies by subtest	c	0:45 – 0:60	Yes	Yes	Yes
Southern California Tests (Ayres, 1972)	a	4–10 yrs.	b,d	0:75 – 0:90	Yes	Yes	Yes
McCarthy (1972) Scales	a	28 mos.– 8 yrs./7 mos.	b,c,d	0:45 – 0:60	Yes	Yes	Yes
Flapan & Neubauer (1975)	c	Birth– 6½ yrs.	a,h	0:10 – 0:20	Yes	Yes	No

**a*—direct administration, *b*—interview of parent/teacher, *c*—observation, *d*—respondent's recall and judgments. Methods separated by a slash (/) are used together.

†*a*—personal-social, *b*—fine motor—adaptive or academic, *c*—language, *d*—gross-motor-posture, *e*—self-help, *f*—sight, *g*—hearing, *h*—play, *i*—medical. Areas shown separated by a comma (,) are measured by separate scales; areas shown separated by a slash (/) are measured by the same scale.

‡*N/A*—not available.

§The *Slosson* (1963) is a screening measure only for infancy up to 4 years of age.

OBSERVING/DESCRIBING

Developmental appraisal instruments rely heavily on observing and describing behavior. Those already discussed in this chapter can be used to provide guidance to systematic observation and description. A listing of specialized observational measures is available in Butler, Gotts, Quisenberry, and Thompson (1971, see ED 059 783, pp. 227–231). Certainly the REEL (Bzoch & League, 1970) is worthy of mention as a guide to observing language development from birth up through 3 years. Temperament observationis worth learning (Thomas & Chess, 1977) and the various social competency scales fit in this category as well (Doll, 1965; Levine, Elzey, & Lewis, 1969).

FORMAL TESTING OR APPRAISAL

All of the usual standardized tests belong in this classification as do developmental instruments that are administered by direct testing. The cautions mentioned earlier in the chapter suggest that methods other than testing are to be preferred except under a particular set of favorable conditions. An exception can be made for developmental tests, when they are administered as previously discussed. For infant testing, the Bayley (1969) is a standard, yielding separate motor and mental scores, and providing an Infant Behavior Record for describing general aspects of the infant's behavior. For children beyond infancy, the Gesell (1949), despite its outdated and unsatisfactory norms, is the recommended developmental test. In view of the considerable interest shown in developmental evaluation, it is surprising that no one has yet undertaken to replace the Gesell with a newer, more satisfactorily normed test.

CLASSIFYING

Classification is not a goal of special education. It is only a means of providing services. No standard, educationally oriented guide to classification has been developed and adopted; individual states have considerably different approaches to educational classification, making widespread agreement unlikely. Psychiatric diagnosis and classification of children offers no useful alternative either. For a better perspective of the issues underlying child classification, the reader should consult Hobbs (1975) thoroughly and often, although most of the needed answers still remain to be discovered.

THE HOLISTIC VIEW OF THE CHILD

Serving the whole child or the entire child is a truism in education, but it is seldom practiced as vigorously as needed. Seeing the entire child in total context is the goal of assessment, and it too is often dishonored in practice. There may be a relationship between these two notable failures of aspiration in education. Perhaps serving the whole child remains only a truism because assessment has failed to see and communicate the entire child. It is true that assessment creeps along in many places because examiners are inadequately prepared and rely on inferior measurement tools. But these are only a part of the problem. Examiners become assessors not through acquiring better tests and testing skills; these only make them better examiners. To function as assessors of young children, professionals need to take account regularly of the many assessment issues and conceptual perspectives that are alluded to in this chapter. Then they need to synthesize, in a creative—even artistic—fashion all of their perceptions, thoughts, and written evaluations about an individual child.

SUMMARY

This chapter initially addressed itself to many of the vital issues that must be viewed prior to the assessment of young children. The requirement for programs that legitimize the purpose of assessment and the topic of who should be assessed were given attention. Alternatives to formal assessment procedures were related and the multiple purposes that assessment can address were discussed. In the second section of the chapter, a review of two immensely important theories of development was offered. This review was followed by a discussion of meausrement techniques schematized across the examiner's purpose of the assessment and the particular developmental area of interest. A caution to consistently view the child in a holistic manner completed the chapter.

Yet, after all of the foregoing display of assessment artistry, no one has time to sit back and admire the result. Instead, the perspectives and recommendations must result in a program for the child. Moreover, assessors only partially know how to assess an individual. Each young child has the potential for surprising and confounding the assessor. Assessment is, therefore, an open-ended art form; it is a chapter rather than an entire biography. The assessor and teacher should, consequently, be eager to discover from the child new material that will help to write a more promising next chapter. These discoveries and their communication can provide some of the peak moments in any educator's life.

These thoughts bring to mind incidents from the writer's own experience. For one, there was a mildly retarded boy who turned out to be a nearly deaf, but gifted child who had compensated sufficiently well, so that his deficiency was not discovered for some time. Or, there was an emotionally disturbed girl who was in reality a temperamentally active child whose pattern of reactivity was compounded by low blood sugar. Then there was the autistic (diagnosed) preschool boy who actually suffered from a rare apraxia. All of these surprise children had once been classified but refused to stay there—and fortunately someone was listening when each child presented new material.

REFERENCES

Alpern, G. D. & Boll, T. J. *Developmental profile manual.* Aspen, Col.: Psychological Development Publications, 1972.

Ayres, A. J. *Southern California sensory integration tests.* Los Angeles: Western Psychological Services, 1972.

Bayley, N. *Manual for the Bayley scales of infant development.* New York: Psychological Corporation, 1969.

Behar, L. & Stringfield, S. *The preschool behavior questionnaire.* Durham, N.C.: LINC Press, 1974.

Bertram, C. L. & Clay, B. L. *Evaluation of early warning signs brochure.* Charleston, W. Va.: Appalachia Educational Laboratory, 1976.

Butler, A. L., Gotts, E. E., & Quisenberry, N. L. *Early childhood programs: Developmental objectives and their use.* Columbus, Oh.: Charles E. Merrill, 1975.

Butler, A. L., Gotts, E. E., & Quisenberry, N. L. *Play as development.* Columbus, Oh.: Charles E. Merrill, 1978.

Butler, A. L., Gotts, E. E., Quisenberry, N., & Thompson, R. P. *Literature search and development of an evaluation system in early childhood education.* (5 Vols.) ED 059 780–ED 059 784. Urbana, Ill.: ERIC-ECE, 1971.

Bzoch, R. L. & League, R. *The Bzoch-League receptive-expressive emergent language scale.* Gainesville, Fla.: Anhinga Press, 1970.

CEC-ERIC. *Early childhood identification: A selective bibliography.* Exceptional Child Bibliography Series No .606. Reston, Va.: The Council for Exceptional Children (n.d.).

Despert, J. L. Using the first interview as a basis for therapeutic planning. In M. R. Haworth (Ed.), *Child psychotherapy: Practice and theory.* New York: Basic Books, 1964.

Doll, E. A. *Vineland social maturity scale.* Circle Pines, Minn.: American Guidance Service, 1965.

Erikson, E. H. *Childhood and society* (2nd ed.). New York: Norton, 1963.

Flapan, D. & Neubauer, P. B. *The assessment of child development.* New York: Aronson, 1975.

Frankenburg, W. K., Dodds, J. B., & Fandal, A. W. *Denver developmental screening test: Manual* (rev. ed.). Denver, Col.: Ladoca Project & Publishing Foundation, 1970.

Frankenburg, W. K. & North, A. F., Jr. *A guide to screening for the early and periodic screening, diagnosis and treatment program (EPSDT) under MEDICAID.* Washington, D.C.: HEW, 1974, (SRS) 74-24516.

Gesell, A. *Gesell developmental schedules.* New York: Psychological Corporation, 1949.

Goldschmid, M. L. & Bentler, P. M. *Manual: Concept assessment kit—conservation.* San Diego, Ca.: Educational and Industrial Testing Service, 1968.

Gotts, E. E. Use of developmental testing in early childhood programs. *Viewpoints,* 1975, *51*(1), 75–82.

Gotts, E. E., Dankert, E., & Lawhon, D. *Appraisal of individual development scales (AIDS): Experimental edition.* Miami, Fla.: Educational Communications, Inc., in press.

Haynes, U. *Infant appraisal.* Columbus, Oh.: NCEMMH, Ohio State University, 1976 (Reissue).

Hertzig, M. E., Birch, H. G., Thomas, A., & Mendez, O. A. Class and ethnic differences in responsiveness of preschool children to cognitive demands. *Monographs of the Society for Research in Child Development,* 1968, *33* (1, Serial No. 117).

Hobbs, N. (Ed.) *Issues in the classification of children.* 2 Vols. San Francisco: Jossey-Bass, 1975.

Hoopes, J. L. *An infant rating scale: Its validation and usefulness.* New York: Child Welfare League of America, 1967.

Ilg, F. L. & Ames, L. B. *School readiness.* New York: Harper & Row, 1964.

Kirk, S. A., McCarthy, J. J., & Kirk, W. D. *Illinois test of psycholinguistic abilities* (rev. ed.). Urbana, Ill.: University of Illinois Press, 1968.

Levine, S., Elzey, F. F., & Lewis, M. *California preschool social competency scale.* Palo Alto, Ca.: Consulting Psychologists Press, 1969.

McCarthy, D. *McCarthy scales of children's abilities.* New York: Psychological Corporation, 1972.

Meier, J. *Screening and assessment of young children at developmental risk.* HEW Publication No. (OS) 73-90. Washington, D.C.: U. S. Government Printing Office, 1973.

Meyers, C. E., Sundstrom, P. E., & Yoshida, R. K. The school psychologist and assessment in special education. Report of an ad hoc committee of Division 16. *School Psychology Monogrpah,* 1974, *2*(1).

National Association for the Education of Young Children. *Play: The child strives toward self-realization.* Washington, D.C.: NAEYC, 1971.

Piaget, J. & Inhelder, B. *The psychology of the child.* New York: Basic Books, 1969.

Quick, A. D., Little, T. L., & Campbell, A. A. *Memphis model of individual program planning and evaluation.* Memphis: Memphis State University, 1973. (Available from: Belmont, Ca.: Lear Siegler/Fearon, 1974.)

Sanford, A. R. *Learning accomplishment profile (LAP).* Chapel Hill, North Carolina: Student Stores, no date.

Schaefer, E. S. & Aaronson, M. *Classroom behavior inventory: Preschool to primary.* Washington, D.C.: National Institute of Mental Health, 1967a.

Schaefer, E. S. & Aaronson, M. *Infant behavior inventory.* Washington, D.C.: National Institute of Mental Health, 1967b.

Shearer, D., Billingsley, J., Frohman, A., Hilliard, J., Johnson, F., & Shearer, M. *The Portage guide to early education: Instructions and checklist.* Portage, Wisc.: Cooperative Educational Service Agency, no date.

Sheridan, M. D. *The developmental progress of infants and young children.* London: Her Majesty's Stationery Office, 1968.

Terman, L. M. & Merrill, M. A. *Stanford-Binet intelligence scale, Form L-M.* (3rd rev.) Boston: Houghton Mifflin, 1960.

Thomas, A. & Chess, S. *Temperament and development.* New York: Brunner/Mazel, 1977.

Thomas, A., Chess, S., & Birch, H. G. *Temperament and behavior disorders in children.* New York: NYU Press, 1968.

Troutt, G., Jr. *A competency base for curriculum development in preschool education.* (4 Vols.) Charleston, West Va.: Appalachia Educational Laboratory, 1974. ED 104 057–ED 104 060.

Uzgiris, I. E. & Hunt, J. McV. *Assessment in infancy: Ordinal scales of psychological development.* Urbana, Ill.: University of Illinois Press, 1975.

Wechsler, D. *The Wechsler preschool and primary scale of intelligence.* New York: Psychological Corporation, 1967.

Woodward, M. The application of Piaget's theory to research in mental deficiency. In N. R. Ellis (ed.). *Handbook of mental deficiency: Psychological theory and research.* New York: McGraw-Hill, 1963, pp. 297–324.

Wright, H. F. *Recording and analyzing child behavior with ecological data from an American town*. New York: Harper & Row, 1967.

Zehrbach, R. R. Determining a preschool handicapped population. *Exceptional Children*, 1975, *41*, 76–83.

Zehrbach, R. R. *CIP. Comprehensive Identification Process. Screening kit*. Bensenville, Ill.: Scholastic Testing Service, 1976.

SUGGESTED READINGS

Friedlander, B. Z., Sterritt, G. M., & Kirk, G. E. (Eds.) *Exceptional infant (Vol. 3). Assessment and intervention*. New York: Brunner/Mazel, 1975.

Lichtenberg, P. & Norton, D. G. *Cognitive and mental development in the first five years of life: A review of recent research*. Rockville, Md.: National Institute of Mental Health, 1970.

Mayer, C. A. *The understanding young children series*. 5 Booklets. Urbana, Ill.: ERIC-ECE, 1974, (Catalog # 114–118).

Meier, J. *Screening and assessment of young children at developmental risk*. DHEW Publication No. (OS) 73-90. Washington. D.C.: U.S. Government Printing Office, 1973.

NAEYC. Play: *The child strives toward self-realization*. Washington, D.C.: National Association for the Education of Young Children, 1971.

Prince, D. (Ed.) *Tool kit 76: Head Start services to handicapped children*. Washington, D.C.: Project Head Start, OCD-DHEW, 1976.

Roedell, W. C., Slaby, R. G., & Robinson, H. B. *Social development in young children: A report for teachers*. Washington, D.C.: National Institute of Education, 1976.

Spicker, H. H., Anastasiow, N. H., & Hodges, W. L. (Eds.). *Children with special needs: Early development and education*. Minneapolis: Leadership Training Institute, University of Minnesota, 1976.

Stephens, B. (Ed.) *Training the developmentally young*. New York: John Day, 1971.

TADS. *A catalogue of instructional and evaluative materials: First chance products*. TADSCRIPT #3. Chapel Hill, N.C.: Technical Development Assistance Program, 1974.

Thomas, A. & Chess, S. *Temperament and development*. New York: Brunner/Mazel, 1977.

Sidney R. Miller

17
Career Education: Lifelong Planning for the Handicapped

Previous chapters have largely addressed the traditional assessment areas associated with handicapped students in the schools. This chapter will focus on the nontraditional—the assessment and preparation of handicapped youth for a career and a contributing role in society.

The handicapped youth is experiencing a precarious life period. Unlike the preteenager, the adolescent has developed cognitive aptitudes that are more difficult to measure and perhaps more resistant to change. For this age group cognitive and social changes require different test instrumentation and educational programming than is provided children only a few years younger. This reality is magnified when the adolescent is handicapped and perhaps thwarted from normal career developmental paths. For example, Martin (1972) found that only 20 percent of the youth leaving high school were prepared for jobs or college, 40 percent were underemployed, and 26 percent unemployed.

Until recently special and mainstream educators have unanimously sought to apply rules of assessment and instruction to the education of handicapped youth which often do not fit. Several investigators (Goodman & Mann, 1976; Heiss, 1977; Tarver & Hallahan, 1976) have advocated traditional academic and intelligence criteria for the assessment and instruction of the educationally handicapped youth. In truth, traditional educational assessment is being continued despite the passages of federal PL 94:482 (1973) which provides for the education of educationally handicapped youth in vocational settings, and PL 94:142 (1975), which specifies that students ages three to 21 years shall be entitled to a free appropriate education. These laws have given impetus, first, to a reconsideration of programs offered youth, second, to the assessment instruments used with students 3 to 21 years old, and third, to the development of the integrated career education program: the marriage of the academic and vocational. It is in this context that we will describe assessment in career education.

The student who reaches the seventh or eighth grade and who is significantly academically or behaviorally retarded is a prime candidate for an education based on academic and vocational preparation (Miller, 1975). To adequately serve educationally handicapped youth, the special educator, the vocational educator, and the school counselor must adapt and adopt procedures and assessment instruments that determine: (1) the student's needs and interests, (2) attitudes toward life preparation and work, (3) vocational and academic aptitudes, (4) social attitudes and values, (5) competencies to function in a job simulation station, and (6) competency to interface school-related information and skills to the requirements of work.

The difficulty confronting special educators in designing an assessment and instructional mechanism for secondary handicapped students is best articulated by Brolin (1976). Brolin noted that the major difficulty with the area of career/vocational education is that the field lacks a systematic body of knowledge. The reasons for this deficit are multiple. First, little attention has been lavished on the field. A review of 38 vocational programs (Miller, 1975) indicates that only three employed a program efficacy design, and none sought to integrate the academic with the vocational. Second, in the years previous to 1971, the traditional academic areas received the greatest attention and funds, while career and vocational education areas received little attention and support. Third, the educational community has considered the training of youth in career education, unrelated to college and university preparation, as something less than academically and socially elevating. For the regular educator the elite students were the college-bound; for the career and vocational educator the desired candidates were those with academic skills and who presented no behavioral deviance.

CAREER EDUCATION FOCUS

The tendency of the late 1950s and 1960s to prepare the secondary school population for higher education has retarded the public educator's willingness to become involved in career oriented programs that do not focus entirely on academics. The rigidity of educational personnel and the institutions they represent, however, is only one side of the equation. The other side is that the advocates of integrated career education have failed to define clearly their focus and articulate their educational goals. A review of the literature demonstrates that the career education movement has not yet clearly defined its mission (Goldhammer & Taylor, 1972; Jepsen & Retish, 1974; Hoyt, 1976). Career educators vary their definitions, scope, and purpose, and usually advocate a mixture of activities and practices from more established disciplines. Accepting this background, career education might be defined as the process of students preparing themselves to assume . . . or continue development . . . in various occupational areas through the acquisition of basic academic or vocational performance skills and competencies as they are related to specified areas of interest in either industry, the crafts, the arts, or professions. The process of career preparation is multifaceted, inclusive of academic achievement, work attitudes, vocational aptitudes, and work experience (Jones, Blaney, & Sabatino, 1975). It is thus necessary to operationalize a career education program for educational handicapped youth and to assess and train the students in many of the following areas:

1. Psychomotor skills (both gross and fine motor)
2. Language skills (including reading and verbal fluency)
3. Numerical skills (mathematics)
4. Self-image
5. Attitude toward others, school, and work
6. Career interests
7. Work experience
8. Physiological factors, including handicaps and general appearance

The development of the assessment process begins with counseling and tests, then moves to the experience-based job and work stations, and concludes at the end of a timed sequential path with appropriate placement and career education opportunities. The following is a semester long, step-by-step, assessment pattern, recommended by Alpern & Sabatino (1975).

First day: Consultation: The initial contact determines the compatibility of the adult and student; establishes the student's general career interests, interpersonal attitudes, and physical appearance.

First week: Assessment. Formal and informal assessment is conducted to determine the student's academic competencies, personal characteristics, and vocational aptitudes and interests.

Second week: Consultation and staffing. Student and teacher discuss interests and identified academic competencies, career goals, and personality variables. The student and teacher establish the types of academic program and job simulation stations available and determine the student's choices.

Third, fourth, and fifth week: Job station assessment. The academic and job station teacher informally pre- and post-tests the student's aptitude, interest, and competencies in each of the simulated stations. The data from the tests will be used to guide the decision concerning work station placement and concurrent academic experiences.

Sixth week to the end of school semester: Work station placement and assessment. The student's on-site ability to function appropriately at the work station and in the classroom is assessed to determine whether competencies, work habits, and effective personal interaction with others is demonstrated.

Last week of semester: Evaluation and consultation. The student and teacher discuss the student's experiences, learned skills, and future educational and work plans. It is during this period that the student's academic and work goals for the coming semester are established.

In order to effectively develop an assessment and programming mechanism for secondary educationally handicapped youth, as recommended by Jones, Blaney, & Sabatino (1975), there is a need to establish and operationalize a best practice procedure. Anadam & Williams (1971), Ariel (1971), and Wagner (1972) noted that traditional models of assessment were no longer viable, and Ariel (1971) called for a look at alternative models. The following is an attempt to provide an synthesis of approaches into a useful model.

Froehlich & Hoyt (1959) noted that the first step in working with youth is fact-finding, and this must be accomplished through a consultative process in which the student and educator are acknowledging the intent of the process. To effectively interact with youth the educational counselor needs to clearly delineate the intent of the interaction. He or she must: (1) determine the type of data that is needed for effective career/vocational program, (2) establish an interpersonal interaction that will enable the educator to obtain the information in an informal manner, (3) organize the collected data so that it can be used effectively in outlining alternatives, (4) reach general and/or specific conclusions regarding the educational and experiential base, (5) encourage the youth to participate in the process of data collection and decision making, and (6) establish a procedure that enables all the participants in the decision to evaluate its efficacy.

With the general consultative format determined, the educator needs to determine some basic student characteristics. Though a list of these characteristics could be extensive, below are 11 major factors that the educator should consider:

1. *Physical Appearance.* The student's physical appearance tacitly expresses the importance he or she places on the experience. Appearance is often a major factor to an individual meeting a student for the first time for the appearance provides information from which to make a judgment about employment desirability.

2. *Punctuality.* An individual's early or late arrival to a meeting may reflect their attitude toward and the importance they place on an experience.
3. *Oral Communication.* The ability an individual possesses in communicating effectively with others is an essential component in human interaction. Those handicapped by poor fluency, inappropriate vocabulary, and improper syntax frequently experience severe difficulties in working with others and maintaining open channels of communication.
4. *Following Directions.* The individual who can listen and follow work instructions will regularly achieve higher approval than the student who either cannot or will not.
5. *Reliability.* Individuals who assume responsibility for completing tasks in the agreed manner and who can thus be trusted by an employer are not only more employable, but they are more likely to retain the work position.
6. *Cooperation.* In working with individuals it is important that youth not only understand how to work with others, but how to interact with them in a mutually productive manner.
7. *Initiative.* The individual able to identify work needs and assume initiative in accomplishing them is highly prized by most organizations. Those able to assume initiative are self-starters, who, not only make a contribution to themselves but also to the employer.
8. *Leadership.* The leader is someone who can determine long- and short-term needs and initiate action that leads to the realization of these needs. The youth who can lead without offending or threatening the employer is an individual who can grow in a work station.
9. *Innovation.* Youth possessing the competency to view alternative strategies and select modes different from those presently being practiced may find him- or herself either applauded or criticized. Such youth must be carefully placed to avoid conflicts.
10. *Flexibility.* Individuals unable to adapt old behavior or adopt new behaviors to meet and resolve new problems frequently come into conflcit with those committed to solving the problem.
11. *Social Perceptions.* The youth's perception of his or her community and the values practiced by the individuals who live and work in it will influence the youth's response to specific work and behavioral expectations. Those youth with inaccurate perceptions will face equivalent difficulties in work stations as the individual with rejecting values.

Awareness and determination of the student's behavior relative to the above factors will assist the educator to informally determine the level of the major job-related behaviors. This information, combined with data from formal assessment, will aid in identifying appropriate training and career goals with the student.

Frequently, decisions on career direction are based on too few factors. Erickson & Wentling (1976) and Sawin (1969) noted the need to use a variety of measures and procedures to effectively assess youth. Many authors also emphasize that the informal consultation process is not intended as a therapeutic period, but an information collection sharing time during which the educator and student can learn more about each other and share insights concerning career opportunities and potential training opportunities.

INFORMATION GATHERING

A number of professionals have recommended procedures to elicit information in a friendly information gathering format (Burton, 1962; Cannel & Kahn, 1953).

1. General information questions should be asked at the beginning so that the student is put at ease.
2. The questions asked should be within the student's experience and knowledge.
3. The vocabulary should be easily understood by the student and should not place the individual in an uncomfortable position.
4. The discussion must follow a logical pattern that makes sense to the student and does not require radical shifts in thought.
5. The educator's statements should be clear and definitive.
6. The questions should be phrased so that the student feels comfortable with the direction and intent of the discussion.
7. The questions should not be phrased in a way that expresses the educator's bias and values.

The information obtained from the student–teacher interaction can be used to assist the educator in determining formal assessment procedures that need to be pursued along with some general conclusions concerning the types of social environments that would be most receptive to the youth.

Formal Interest Tests

Besides the use of the informal interest and personality procedures just discussed, the career counselor should consider formal interest and personality measures to affirm or clarify estimates or guesses reached by the counselor. There are some factors that make pursuing the information of formal assessment devices attractive. For example, Brolin (1976), Goodman & Mann (1976), and Sawin (1969) each noted that the assessment needs to focus on a variety of variables—something formal tests can accomplish well. Further, Erikson & Wentling (1976) noted that a variety of methodologies can be combined to assess the student's skills and readiness for specific career/vocational experiences. Formal tests, with their varied formats and approaches, accomplish this with comparative ease. But, despite this, Jones, Blaney, & Sabatino (1975) have warned that there is no magic in formal test instruments; tests can merely help substantiate or reject the conclusions of the educator, student, parent, and psychologist drawn from other observational procedures.

The interest inventory presents a paradox since discrepancies often exist between what an individual contends are his or her interests and what formal tests claim are the student's interests. Froehlich & Hoyt (1959) noted that the formal interest test, like other formal tests, must be dealt with as though it were only a single piece of data and not the only valid data. The interest test, when compared with intelligence and achievement tests, is a newcomer to the area. It is by most estimates about four decades old, and has grown in popularity among educators who have sought to assess the interests of youth who are seeking to identify career pathways. These pathways may range from a physicist to an automobile mechanic, from the university instructor to the crafts person. Among the factors identified by Super (1956), as being covered by the interest inventories, are the areas of science, people, literature, clerical, mechanical, arts, music, outdoors, and social concerns. Each of the areas represent interest groups and offer a referrent for determining career direction. The two following interest tests may yield data that will enable the educator and student to achieve clear career goals and preparation direction.

The *Kuder Occupational Interest Survey (KOIS),* is published by Science Research Associates, Inc., for ages 11 through adulthood. It provides the educator and student general data on the student's occupational interests. The KOIS is a 100-triad inventory in which the respondent indicates his most and least preferred activity from three choices. An individual's score represents the correlation between his or her responses and those of individual's involved in 37 occupations and 19 college majors (normed on female populations), and 20 additional occupations and 8 college major scales (normed on men). The highest KOIS scores in each occupation and college major is reported separately for each sex. Walsh (1972) noted that only concurrent validity information is provided in the test manual. This data indicates that the KOIS adequately discriminates between various existing occupational groups, but no information on predictive validity is provided. With regard to reliability, Walsh (1972) reported that test-retest coefficients for a two-week interval were quite adequate for 25 twelfth graders and 25 college students. A three year test-retest study involving three groups of college students majoring in engineering (n=93) produced a median group reliability coefficient of 0.89. Walsh found these results encouraging, but called for studies utilizing larger populations.

Dolliver (1972) outlined the following advantages of the KOIS over the *Strong Vocational Interest Blank:*

1. Scoring of college major interests
2. The covering of a broader range of occupations (specifically more technical and trade level occupations)
3. Using the same form for males and females
4. Provision of scores for female examinees on certain male occupations and college major scales
5. Recently tested norm groups

The *Vocational Agriculture Interest Inventory,* published by Interstate Printers and Publishers, Inc., is for boys age eight. This inventory is composed of 75 items dealing with agricultural concepts. The examinee rates each item on a 5-point scale ranging from "strongly like" to "strongly dislike." According to Campbell (1972), scoring weights were developed by comparing a criterion group of "Successful Vocational-Agriculture Students" to a group of eighth grade boys from 20 schools. The normative data provided in the manual is generally inadequate, and no data on validity or reliability is cited. Campbell (1972) criticized the test for its poor psychometric foundations, but did point to its development by three professional agriculture educators as a strong point in its favor.

The *California Occupational Preference Survey (COPS)* is published by Educational and Industrial Testing Service for ages 14 to adulthood. The test measures: science professional, science skilled; technical professional, technical skilled; outdoor; business professional, business skilled; clerical; linguistic professional, linguistic skilled; aesthetic professional, aesthetic skilled; and service professional, service skilled. The COPS utilizes a free response format to identify individual occupational preferences. Interests are divided into 14 occupational clusters, 6 of which are further divided into professional versus skilled classifications. Bauernfeind (1972) maintained that this procedure is useful in determining whether a student's vocational interests require postsecondary education. Bodden (1972) also commented on several of the survey's noteworthy features. First, it is useful with a variety of populations—college students, college-bound high school students, and non-college-bound secondary pupils. Also, the test items almost exclusively involve descriptions of activities rather than a conglomerate of activities and occupational titles. Bodden maintained that this may help eliminate response bias resulting from occupational ignorance and status considerations. Third, student interests are keyed to Dictionary of Occupational Title job references. Bauernfeind (1972) pointed out that the survey items are clearly and concisely written and that the self-scoring booklet encourages student/counselor discussion and vocational planning. French (1972) praised the construction of the survey's scales, its consideration of both professions and skills, and the instructive nature of the test and manual. The COPS free-response format has been both applauded and criticized. Bodden (1972) maintained that this procedure may be more comfortable and less restricting for the respondents. However, French (1972) pointed out this format facilitates faking of desired scores, and leads to spuriously high or low scores from students who too strictly interpret the descriptors "like" or "dislike."

The psychometric properties of this instrument are such that French (1972) reported that the instrument's construct validity appears to be quite high, but criticized the lack of data on predictive validity. Bodden (1972) also noted a dearth of validity information, and, in addition, criticized the lack of data on norm groups and the failure to provide correlations between the COPS and other established interest inventories. With regard to reliability, Bodden considered coefficients obtained with high school groups satisfactory, but questioned the absence of reliability data on college populations. Long-term reliability figures are less adequate: the median (test-retest) coefficient for one year is 0.66, and for two years equals 0.63. A final point advanced by Bodden involved the homogeneous keying of the test, and the possibility that high scores may, therefore, not always match the interests of persons actually engaged in the expected occupation.

Formal Aptitude Tests

Beyond the interest measures, educators must identify the basic academic skills and aptitude competencies of the students. Since academic measures are widely known and have already been discussed in preceeding chapters (See Lloyd, chap. 9 and Tucker, chap. 10), this section will focus on aptitude measures.

For the early childhood and primary level teacher aptitude is the assessment of basic sensory-motor and perceptual (auditory and visual) functions. For the career/vocational educator, aptitude assessment includes perception and sensory-motor skills, but these skills are integrated into a composite, multifactor, mental ability test. As Froehlich & Hoyt

(1959) note, the simple scholastic aptitude test that yields a single score has definite limitations if it is to be used to assess a student's readiness for specific career preparation. The work of Thurstone (1938) enabled the designers of tests to identify seven basic factors related to mental ability. They are verbal meaning, space, reasoning, number, word-fluency, memory, and perception. It was not Thurston's contention that these factors were the only ones related to mental ability, and subsequent researchers have sought to further delineate mental ability and achievement-related factors (Guilford, 1967; Guilford, Kettner, & Christensen, 1956; Bloom et al. 1956), but many test designs still rely upon Thurston's findings and postulates.

Super (1956) and Vernon (1960) note that multifactor constructs or clusters are part of specified behaviors directed at performing identified tasks and jobs. Similar factors are also present for a variety of careers such as health and industrial occupations. It is for this reason that aptitude tests cover similar factors associated with the interest inventory, and some are designed to identify the aptitude level as they relate to occupational preparation.

The *General Aptitude Test Battery* (GATB), published by the Bureau of Employment Security, U.S. Department of Labor for ages 16 and over, is useful in determining career directions that youth and adults should pursue. It produces measures in 10 areas: intelligence, verbal, numerical, spatial, form perception, clerical perception, aiming, motor speed, finger dexterity, and manual dexterity. The B-1001 edition of this battery includes eight pen-and-paper tests plus four performance tests: Book I (1966) contains three tests—tool matching, name comparison, and computation; Book II (1966) includes four tests—three-dimensional space, arithmetic reasoning, vocabulary, and form matching; Part K (1965) contains a mark-marking test; a fourth component (pegboard) is comprised of two tests, place and turn; and the final section (Finger Dexterity Board) is composed of two tests, assemble and disassemble. The manual states that the battery "is designed to measure capacities to learn various jobs," but its developers have failed to provide evidence indicating that high scorers on a specific test learn to perform a job more competently than low scorers.

It is maintained that the GATB subtests should be viewed as indices of current learning status (concurrent validity) not projected potential (predictive validity). Data reported from a GATB longitudinal follow-up study support this assumption. In addition he advanced several other criticisms of the GATB. First, the battery utilizes a multiple cut-off method to ascertain if the individual passed or failed the minimum qualifying scores for a job or job cluster. This approach has been criticized as greatly limiting the utility of the battery. Second, the GATB has also been charged with being too highly speeded. Weiss (1972) noted that the average score on the most highly speeded subtests declined most rapidly as a function of age and since it is unfair to assume that learning potential declines with age, and more likely that response speed, test-taking skills, and motivation contribute to this interaction, the GATB may be biased against the older examinee. Unless the test undergoes some major revisions, its future utility is questionable. But, despite these criticisms, the GATB remains the best researched of the multiple aptitude batteries. Its validity data is strong, and with the necessary revisions, it should remain a useful tool in vocational planning.

The *Differential Aptitude Test* is published by the Psychological Corporation for ages 13 and over. It measures six areas: verbal reasoning, numerical reasoning, space relations, mechanical reasoning, clerical speed and accuracy, and language usage. The tests are easily administered, scored, and interpreted. An extensive sample of 50,512 U.S. public school children in grades 8 through 12 in 43 states comprised the norm population. However, the test is considerably overrepresented and, in addition, information concerning the ethnic and socioeconomic characteristics of the sample is lacking. Separate norms for boys and girls are provided. The manual provides extensive evidence of the test's validity. Quereski (1972) noted that correlations of DAT scores with high school educational and vocational careers are high. According to this author, DAT performance can adequately differentiate various occupational groups.

The *Nonreading Aptitude Test Battery* is published by the United States Training and Employment Services for ages 14 to adults. This measures nine areas: intelligence, verbal, numerical, spatial, form perception, clerical perception, motor coordination, finger dexterity, and manual dexterity. The Non-reading Aptitude Test Battery is a nonreading version of the General Aptitude Test Battery. It is composed of 10 pen-and-paper tests, and four performance tests. Book 1 (1969) includes two tests, Picture-Word Matching, and Oral Vocabulary; Book 2 (1969) contains a Coin Matching exercise; Book 3 (1969) includes a Matrices test; Book 4 (1969) is the Tool Matching exam; Book 5 (1969) concerns Three-Dimensional Space; Book 6 (1969) is the Form Matching test; Book 7 (1969) is Coin Series; and Book 8 (1969) contains the Name Comparison test. The battery also includes Part 8 of the General Aptitude Test Battery, Mark Making (1965); the two tests of the Pegboard section of the GATB, Place and Turn; and the two tests of the GATB Finger Dexterity Board, Assemble and Disassemble.

The above tests are general tests of aptitude but more specific measures for selected areas have been developed, such as the *Bennett Mechanical Comprehension Test,* published by the Psychological Corporation for ages 14 to adulthood. The purpose of the test, according to the manual, is "to measure the ability to perceive and understand the relationship of physical forces and mechanical elements in practical situations." The new forms of the test, S and T (1969), contain 68 items. The test format consists of large drawings of various mechanisms followed by questions designed to measure the respondent's understanding of their purpose and function.

Bechtoldt (1972) rated the 1969 forms high for simplicity of instruction and response, legibility, picture adequacy, and face validity. Hambleton (1971), however, found some of the drawings to be rather outdated, but praised the areas of knowledge they propose to tap, and the conciseness of the test instructions. Bechtoldt (1972) criticized the test manual for failing to detail the process of item selection and test construction. Only the mean values and ranges of discrimination and difficulty indices are reported, thus, the criteria for item selection remains unclear. The test is normed on six industrial groups and four groups of eleventh and twelfth grade students drawn from one city's technical and academic schools (Roberts, 1972). In summary, both Bechtoldt (1972) and Hambleton (1971) recommended the use of the *Bennett Mechanical Comprehension Test* in conjunction with a battery of other aptitude tests until its reliability and validity are more soundly established.

Other aptitude measures directed at specific populations are *Mechanical Handyman Test for Maintenance Workers,* published by International Personnel Management Association; *Short Occupational Knowledge Test for Carpenters,* published by Science Research Associates; the *Short Occupational Knowledge Test for Draftsmen,* published by Science Research Associates, Inc.

In general, research has indicated that currently two of the more stable general aptitude measures are the *General Aptitude Test Battery* (GATB) and the *Differential Aptitude Tests*. The suggestion of predictive stability in aptitude tests should be welcome news for educators who have been saddled until recently with instruments for dubious validity and reliability. The predictive significance of many general and specific aptitude tests were and are suspect, for two reasons. First, the vocational related aptitudes and values, according to research, are poorly defined in youth until 14 to 15 years old. And, second, the cost of establishing the predictive validity of an individual's vocational aptitude must, of necessity, be based on longitudinal data, collected over several years. Longitudinal studies are expensive, requiring close and continuous monitoring of a large number of subjects who are likely to be living and moving over a wide geographic area.

In using aptitude tests, the educator should also be aware that these instruments are often more valuable as a measure of what aptitudes a student does *not* possess. Froehlich & Benson (1948) noted that an individual must possess certain minimum aptitudes to succeed in any specified area. Lack of the aptitude or aptitudes will frequently argue for alternative vocational training. But, possession of the aptitudes will not conversely argue that the individual will succeed in specific vocations, since success is based also on interest, social and personal motivation, family expectations, peer pressures, and numerous other factors.

CONSULTATIVE PROGRAMMING

Following the completion of all phases of formal and informal testing on areas of achievement, personality, interest, and aptitudes, the educator and the student need to discuss the results to determine the future training direction and placement alternatives that are available. It should be evident that the flow of information based on the testing will be most advantageously used when controlled by the educator. The educator can most effectively guide the student by explaining the results and noting that aptitude and interest measures by design have scoring peaks and valleys. The programming phase should focus on several variables:

Student academic and aptitudinal strengths and weaknesses. This discussion will enable the student to determine his or her readiness for specific vocational opportunities. Failure to do this may leave the student believing that the school and the educator are unwilling to offer opportunities he or she is qualified to pursue.

Discrepancy of belief and measurement. Discuss the agreement or discrepancy between the student's stated interests and what the interest inventory measured. Collectively, the student and educator must resolve any discrepancies and agree on what the information indicates.

Matching student traits with school capability and community vocations. The need to realistically discuss the interface of the student's background with training and vocational opportunities must proceed on four fronts. First, many educationally handicapped and academic retarded youth must become familiar with their career opportunities and the related jobs that are available in industry, commerce, and government. Without this information youth tend to perceive narrow employment opportunities (i.e., pipe fitting, plumber) and are unable to relate their skills in other career fields (i.e., tool and dye makers, air conditioning installation, metal working). Second, consideration must be given to the changing configuration of the United States' economy and the resulting employment opportunities. Third, youth, once out of formal training, are often unaware of the employment agencies and training centers that can better prepare them or upgrade their skills so that they can obtain and retain employment. Efforts must be made to create an awareness of these helping agencies. Fourth, in career planning, youth must become acquainted with the many union and guild restrictions on membership and employment.

Student needs. The student needs to be made aware of the type of further training he or she will be required to pursue if he or she is to achieve vocational goals. The unrealistic expectation of proficiency achievement in a vocational area may lead to educational disenchantment and social alienation, thus, the negation of the educational systems and societies longitudinal commitment.

The design of a program which responds to the student's needs, interests, and competency. The program that fails to integrate the essential personal, educational, and social variables will not promote the youth to better prepare him or herself. Therefore, the program must of necessity address: (1) academic goals, (2) vocational goals, (3) performance objectives, and (4) the strategies that will be used.

ORGANIZING THE FORMAL BACKGROUND DATA

Integrating all sources of data is an initial task that must be accomplished if career planning is to be effective. A myriad number of possibilities exist, but Figure 17-1 provides a convenient and useful procedure.

Once the information from the counseling, tests, and other sources are collapsed, as in Figure 17-1, the data evaluation procedures must be formated in order that educational personnel can extract information that will enable them to understand the youth's overall skills, interests, needs, attitudes, and behavior. This can be achieved by establishing a program sheet similar to the following (Fig. 17-2).

Aptitude

GATB:	10 (High)	9	8	7	6	5	4	3	2	1 (Low)
1. Intelligence										
2. Verbal										
3. Numerical										
4. Form Perception										
5. Clerical Perception										
6. Aiming										
7. Motor Speed										
8. Finger Dexterity										
9. Manual Dexterity										

Academics

Durrell Listening/Reading Skills:	10	9	8	7	6	5	4	3	2	1
1. Listening Skills										
2. Reading Skills										
Peabody Individual Achievement Test:										
1. Mathematics Subtest										

Fig. 17-1. Test and data profile.

Interest

California Occupational Preference Survey:

	(High) 10	9	8	7	6	5	4	3	2	(Low) 1
1. Science Professional										
2. Technical Skilled										
3. Outdoor										
4. Business Professional										
5. Business Skilled										
6. Service Professional										
7. Service Skilled										

Personality

California Test of Personality:

	(High) 10	9	8	7	6	5	4	3	2	(Low) 1
1. Self-reliance										
2. Personal Worth										
3. Personal Freedom										
4. Feeling of Belonging										
5. Withdrawn Tendencies										
6. Nervous Symptoms										

Observation Classroom and Interview Data

(High) 10 9 8 7 6 5 4 3 2 1 (Low)

1. Physical Appearance
2. Punctuality
3. Oral Communications
4. Follow Directions
5. Reliability
6. Cooperation
7. Initiative
8. Leadership
9. Innovative
10. Flexibility
11. Social Perception

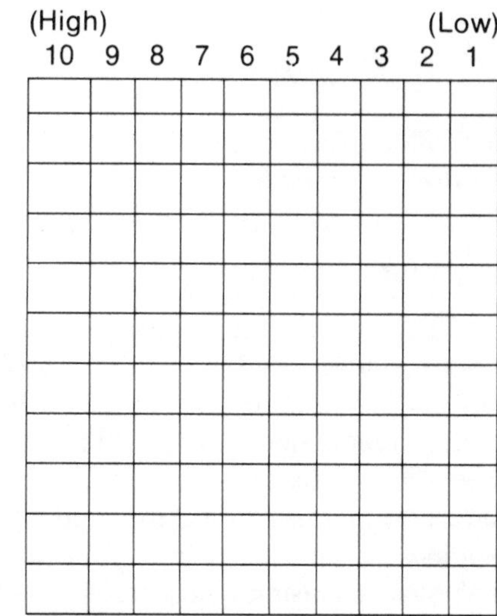

Fig. 17-1 *(continued).*

Perceptual-Motor Skills	Goals and Objectives:
Strengths	Responsible Personnel:
Weaknesses	Outcome:
	Placement:
Social Skills, Interests, and Attitudes	Goals and Objectives:
Strengths	Responsible Personnel:
Weaknesses	Outcome:
Conceptual Level	Goals and Objectives:
Strengths	Responsible Personnel:
Weaknesses	Outcome:
Language Skills	Goals and Objectives
Strengths	Responsible Personnel:
Weaknesses	Outcome:
Mathematic Skills	Goals and Objectives:
Strengths	Responsible Personnel:
Weaknesses	Outcome:

Overall Expectations:
Career Education-Academic Integration
Job Status
Work Statia Status

Fig. 17-2. Career programming format.

INFORMAL ASSESSMENT OF WORK-RELATED ACADEMIC SKILLS

Work Samples

Brolin (1976) suggested the work sample as a criterion-based procedure for assessing the student's performance as it relates to the specific process or product associated with the job. Alpern & Sabatino (1975) further recommend that youth be assessed on their ability to interact with peers and colleagues at the work station. However, unlike the student's interests and aptitudes, the student's performance at the job and work station can be best assessed informally. The informal procedures can be achieved by using commercial or self-made instruments and checklists that identify and assess target behavior demonstrated to be essential variables to job and work success. One of the best procedures is the job and work sample. Job and work samples enable the student to perform and the educator to assess in a condition that approximates reality and avoids placing the youth in an actual work situation for which he or she may be unprepared. The sampling process enables the youth and the educator to assess the appropriateness of job and work and the student's attitudes associated with the experiences. The station should be viewed by the student as a preview rather than a test. Many field-based educators contend that employers view with greater favor the results of work and job sample rather than test results. As with any procedure, there is criticism. Among the criticisms are that such judgments are too subjective, the samples do not satisfactorily approximate real situations, and that personality variables are often the factors that lead to employment problems, not performance competencies. Recently, some school districts have been seeking to have personnel develop informal work and job samples. To achieve this, and develop packages that are useful, personnel have been carrying through a step-by-step process similar to the following:

Using local departments of employment, newspaper's classified employment advertisements, and contracting major employers, the schools have sought to determine: (1) what jobs are most suitable, (2) what jobs are likely to be developing within the next 5 to 10 years, and (3) what personal and professional competencies are the potential employers evaluating when they hire an individual and when they decide whether the person will be retained. The data collected can be categorized into various job cluster groupings (industrial, business, marketing, applied biological and agricultural occupations) to make identification of sampling packages earlier and more able to be generalized.

Once personological data is collected, school personnel determine whether: (1) the job is one the students can perform, (2) the student can be trained to perform, (3) the job opportunities are short- or long-term, and (4) the job lends itself to the sampling procedure.

When specific samples are identified as appropriate to the school's needs, *task analysis* is undertaken to determine the specific steps a job requires and the independent and overlapping skills that are necessary. This step is critical in the design and development of the sample package, since failure to identify critical steps and skills can lead to poor sampling and student failure. The most effecttve way of analyzing a job is through on-site observation and the questioning of those who perform the job. Dependency by the school personnel on recollections and job descriptions in books frequently results in poor job work samples.

The design of the sample must be carefully carried out by the educator. Before the sample is constructed the school must determine whether any specialized equipment is necessary, and, if so, whether it either has or can gain access to the equipment. Berelson (1954) and George (1956) have noted that the content analysis needs to be sequentially analyzed and this recommendation must be applied to the development of the content material. Among the other factors that must be considered in the development of the sample are:

1. Steps required to perform the task
2. Time required to complete the task
3. Visual format of material presentation
4. Procedures to be employed in assessing the student's readiness and performance of the sample
5. The prerequisite and overlapping skills that are required to perform satisfactorily on the sample
6. The temperament variables associated with success work on the job
7. Procedures to be employed in presenting the material to the youth.

Among the variables to be considered in presentation are:

1. A review of job samples
2. Sampling procedures
3. Expected time the sample will require
4. Procedures to follow when difficulties are encountered
5. The educator's role in the process.

Once the prototype sample is complete the school personnel must administer it to students to assess its effectiveness. It is essential that all factors associated with the design of the package are met and that the students demonstrate interest in the process and can achieve success with the sample. Professional test designers accept the fact that any task or test is imperfect and requires modification even after the final package is completed.

Work Station Assessment

The work station placement is located on an actual work site under close employee and educational supervision. It generally has a two-fold purpose. First, it gives the student an opportunity to discover and assess the factors associated with the specific job (Alpern & Sabatino, 1975). Second, it moves the school personnel into the field where they are called upon to evaluate the student, their preparation efforts, and the conceptual framework of school's educational model (Miller, 1975).

The evaluation of the student should reflect the input of the three primary parties, the student, the employer, and the on-site educator. Again, it is important that the youth be provided data on how others evaluate his or her performance. Evaluation tools must reflect the student's positive behaviors and be a guide for the behaviors that require more training and/or attitudinal changes. Among the variables that require assessment are the following:

JOB APTITUDE

Does the student possess the cognitive and psychomotor aptitudes that are required by the job. If the student lacks aptitude, what specific skills and overlapping skills are required for improved performance.

WORK JUDGMENT

Does the student possess the knowledge to determine when specific operations are to be undertaken and when they are to be delayed? The student should also be assessed on his or her ability to make judgments concerning the appropriate use of equipment and materials associated with the work.

INITIATIVE

The quality and quantity of job performance is often influenced by the individual initiative demonstrated in the work situation. The student who will obtain clarification on work schedule and job responsibilities, or begin new activities, is more likely to succeed than the individual who is unwilling to question and inquire, and try something new.

ADAPTABILITY

Can the student alter or change his or her behavior, task direction, or job responsibilities without either disrupting others or becoming disorganized by the changes? The individual capable of adaptive behavior will be able to cope in the changing world better than one who questions why it cannot be like it used to be.

PERSONALITY CHARACTERISTICS

As noted earlier, qualities of appearance, social skills, and quality of voice and mannerism can influence the prospective employer's decision in hiring as well as influence the attitude of colleagues at a particular work site. Often the personality characteristic is more influential in employer decision than competency.

TEMPERAMENT AND INTERESTS

The student's ability to cope with the frustrations, disappointments, patience and/or impatience required by the work situation will affect the student performance. Students' technical competence to perform a job may fail because either their temperament was inappropriate or they lack the interest to learn more about the people and the job.

ATTITUDE

The student's attitude toward work and those individuals he or she will work with is a significant variable in the determination of job appropriateness. Attitude is one of the more significant variables to measure in developing accurate performance criteria.

GENERAL

Besides the variables above, the employer, student, and educator must become aware of general factors such as communication skills, acceptance by others, and personal reliability. Awareness of these general factors will assist all parties to assess the student's progress and other's reactions.

SUMMARY AND CONCLUSION

Brolin (1976) noted the area of career education is handicapped by the lack of knowledge concerning the area, and Halpein, Raffeld, Irvin, & Link (1975) have stated that many questions are yet unanswered. Yet, Hoyt (1972) observed that despite the area's newness, career education offered educators a broader, more flexible model to serve students having varying interests and goals. The career education model and the realities facing contemporary education articulate the need to significantly alter the now traditional secondary programs that focus on preparing youth for higher education. Contemporary educators, responding to the new demands of students, parents, the courts, and the legislative need to recognize that preparation of youth for careers requires different processes of counseling and assessment than have been previously used.

Counseling requires that the school personnel not only know what resources exist inside the institution's walls, but also what resources exist in the community and region. In addition, the school personnel need to be aware of the career patterns within the United States in order that appropriate training recommendations and services can be provided.

Career education assessment processes must transcend the purely academic study that represents existing diagnostic models (Jones, Blaney, & Sabatino, 1975). Career education must contain the assessment of achievement, along with career aptitudes, interests, needs, values, and personality variables. All the preceeding factors, obtained through formal and informal procedures, will enable the educators to determine with the student, the integrated program that matches student skills and needs with existing career opportunities and available training job and work stations.

Until educators implement diagnostic systems that effectively measure student performance levels, the efficacy of career/vocational education will be open to question. The historical look of appropriate diagnostic systems has impaired the educator's ability, first, to design appropriate educational models, and, second to measure the effectiveness of the program on specified youth. When the model is in place and the professional educators seek to evaluate its validity, then the goal of providing free and appropriate education can be pursued.

REFERENCES

Alpern, S. & Sabatino, D. A. *Establishing a meaningful career education plan* (Manual on Integrated Career Education). Springfield, Ill.: Department of Corrections, 1975.

Anadam, K. & Williams, R. A model for consultation with the classroom teacher and behavior management. *The School Counselor,* 1971, *18,* 253–259.

Ariel, A. Behavior therapy for self-direction (doctoral dissertation, University of Southern California, 1971). *Dissertation Abstracts International,* 1971, *32,* 4408-A.

Bauernfeind, R. H. Review of the California Occupational Test Survey. In O. K. Buros (Ed.), *The seventh mental measurements yearbook* (Vol. 2). Highland Park, N.J.:The Gryphon Press, 1972.

Bechtoldt, H. P. Review of the Bennett Mechanical Comprehension Test. In O. K. Buros (Ed), *The seventh mental measurements yearbook* (Vol. 2). Highland Park, N.J.: The Gryphon Press, 1972.

Bennett Mechanical Comprehension Test. New York: Psychological Corporation, 1972.

Berelson, B. Content analysis. In G. Lindzey (Ed.), *Handbook of social psychology, I, Theory and method.* Reading, Mass.: Addison-Wesley Publishing Co., 1954.

Bloom, B. S., Engelhart, M. D., Furst, E. J., Hill, W. H., & Krathwohl, D. R. *Taxonomy of educational objectives, handbook I: Cognitive domain.* New York: McKay, 1956.

Bodden, J. L. Review of the California Occupational Preference Survey. In O. K. Buros (Ed.). *The seventh mental measurements yearbook.* (Vol. 2). Highland Park, N.J.: The Gryphon Press, 1972.

Brolin, D. E. *Vocational preparation of retarded citizens.* Columbus, Oh.: Charles E. Merrill Publishing Co., 1976.

Burton, W. H. *The guidance of learning activities* (3rd ed.). New York: Appleton, 1962.

California Occupational Preference Survey (COPS). Knapp, R. R., Grant, B., & Demos, G. D. Educational and Industrial Testing Service, 1966–1970.

Campbell, D. P. Review of the vocational Agricultural Interest Inventory. In O. K. Buros (Ed.), *The seventh mental measurements yearbook* (Vol. 2). Highland Park, N.J.: The Gryphon Press, 1972.

Cannel, C. F. & Kahn, R. L. The collection of data by interviewing. In L. Festinger & D. Katz (Eds.), *Research methods in the behavioral sciences.* New York: Dryden Press, 1953.

Differential Aptitude Tests. Bennett, G. K., Seashore, H. G., & Wesman, A. G. New York, Psychological Corporation, 1947–1969.

Dolliver, R. H. Review of the Kuder Occupational Interest Survey. In O. K. Buros (Ed.), *The seventh mental measurements yearbook* (Vol. 2). Highland Park, N.J.: The Gryphon Press, 1972.

Erickson, R. C. & Wentling, T. L. *Measuring student growth.* Boston: Allyn & Bacon, 1976.

French, J. W. Review of the California Occupational Preference Survey. In O. K. Buros (Ed.), *The seventh mental measurements yearbook* (Vol. 2). Highland Park, N.J.: The Gryphon Press, 1972.

Froehlich, C. P. & Benson, A. L. *Guidance testing*. Chicago: Science Research Associates, 1948.

Froehlich, C. P. & Hoyt, K. B. *Guidance testing*. Chicago: Science Research Associates, 1959.

General Aptitude Test Battery (GATB). Bureau of Employment Security, U.S. Department of Labor, 1946–1970.

George, A. L. Prediction of political action by means of propaganda analysis. *Public Opinion Quarterly*, 1956, *20*, 334–335.

Goldhammer, K. & Taylor, R. E. *Career education: Perspective and promise*. Columbus, Oh.: Charles E. Merrill, 1972.

Guilford, J. P. *The nature of human intelligence*. New York: McGraw-Hill, 1967.

Guilford, J. P., Kettner, M. W., & Christensen, P. R. A factor analytic study across the domains of reasoning, creativity and evaluation: II. Administration of tests and analyses of results (Report No. 16, Psychological Laboratory, University of Southern California, 1956).

Goodman, L. & Mann, L. *Learning disabilities in the secondary schools*. New York: Grune & Stratton, 1976.

Halpein, A. S., Raffeld, P., Irvin, L., & Link, R. Measuring social and prevocational awareness in mildly retarded adolescents. *American Journal of Mental Deficiency*, 1975, *80*(1), 80–89.

Hambleton, R. K. Review of the Bennett Mechanical Comprehension Test. In O. K. Buros (Ed.), *The seventh mental measurements yearbook* (Vol. 2). Highland Park, N.J.: The Gryphon Press, 1971.

Heiss, W. Relating educational assessment to instructional planning. *Focus on Exceptional Children*. Denver, Col.: Love Publishing, 1977, *9*(1).

Hoyt, K. B. Career education and career choice. *American Vocational Journal*, 1972, *47*, 84–88.

Hoyt, K. B. Career education for special populations. *Monographs on Career Education*. Washington, D.C.: U.S. Department of Health, Education, and Welfare, 1976.

Jepsen, D. A. & Retish, P. M. Cross-disciplinary approach to teaching career guidance. *Exceptional Children*, 1974, *40*, 514–516.

Jones, R. W., Blaney, R. L., & Sabatino, D. A. *Ascertaining vocationally retarded behaviors* (Manual on integrated career education). Springfield, Ill.: Department of Corrections, 1975.

Kuder Occupational Interest Survey (KOIS). Kuder, G., Chicago: Science Research Associates, Inc., 1956–1970.

Martin, E. Individualism and behaviorism as future trends in educating handicapped children. *Exceptional Children*, 1972, *38*, 517–525.

Mechanical Handyman Test. Chicago: International Personnel Management Association, 1957–1965.

Miller, S. R. Secondary assessment and programming. Unpublished paper, 1975.

Non-reading Aptitude Test Battery. United States Training and Employment Services. Washington, D.C.: U.S. Government Printing Office, 1969.

Quereshi, M. Y. Review of the Differential Aptitude Tests. In O. K. Buros (Ed.), *The seventh mental measurements yearbook*. Highland Park, N.J.: The Gryphon Press, 1972.

Roberts, A. O. H. Review of the Bennett Mechanical Comprehension Test. In O. K. Buros (Ed.), *The seventh mental measurements yearbook* (Vol. 2). Highland Park, N.J.: The Gryphon Press, 1972.

Sawin, E. I. *Evaluation and the work of the teacher.* Belmont, Ca.: Wadsworth Publishing Co., 1969.

Short Occupational Knowledge Test for Carpenters. Campbell, B. A. & Johnson, S. O. Chicago: Science Research Associates, 1969–1970.

Short Occupational Knowledge Test for Draftsmen. Campbell, B. A. & Johnson, S. O. Chicago: Science Research Associates, 1969–1970.

Super, D. E. (Ed.) The use of multi-factor tests in guidance. Washington, D.C.: *American Personnel and Guidance Journal,* 1956.

Tarver, S. & Hallahan, D. P. Children with learning disabilities. In D. P. Hallahan & J. M. Kaufman (Eds.), *Teaching children with learning disabilities personal perspective.* Columbus, Ohio: Merrill, 1976.

Thurstone, L. L. *Primary mental abilities.* Chicago: University of Chicago Press, 1938.

Vernon, P. E. *The structure of human abilities* (rev. ed.). London: Methuen, 1960.

Vocational Agriculture Interest Inventory. Walker, R. W., Stevens, G. Z., & N. K. Hoover, Danville, Ill.: Interstate Printers and Publishers, Inc., 1965.

Wagner, H. Attitudes of and toward disadvantaged students. *Adolescence,* 1972, *7*(28), 435–446.

Walsh, T. P. *Blueprint for the possible: A citizen's program for better schools.* Washington, D.C.: Chamber of Commerce of the United States, 1972.

SUGGESTED READINGS

Bailey, L. J. & Stadt, R. *Career education: New approaches to human development.* Bloomington, Ill.: University of Illinois Press, 1973.

Brolin, D. F. *Vocational preparation of retarded citizens.* Columbus, Oh.: Charles E. Merrill, 1976.

Erikson, R. C. & Wentling, T. L. *Measuring student growth.* Boston: Allyn & Bacon, 1976.

Goldhammer, K. & Taylor, R. E. *Career education: Prospective and promise.* Columbus, Oh.: Charles E. Merrill, 1972.

Index

a
b
c
d
e
8 f
9 g
0 h
1 i
8 2 j